THE WORLD WAR II
DESK REFERENCE

THE WORLD WAR II DESK REFERENCE

GRAND CENTRAL PRESS

Paul Fargis, Publisher
Judy Pray, Executive Editor

EISENHOWER CENTER FOR AMERICAN STUDIES

Douglas Brinkley, Director
Kevin Willey, Assistant Director
Michael Edwards, Research Associate

EDITORS

Michael E. Haskew
Douglas Brinkley

ASSISTANT EDITOR

Richard Steins

MAP EDITOR

Philip Schwartzberg, Meridian Mapping

CONTRIBUTORS

Bill Anderson
Alan Bisbort
Hannah Borgeson
Michele Camardella
Paul Hatcher
Michael Hull
Polly Kummel
Chris McGowan
Sam McGowan
Robert Smith
Flint Whitlock
John Wukovits

THE WORLD WAR II
DESK REFERENCE

WITH THE EISENHOWER CENTER FOR AMERICAN STUDIES

DIRECTOR DOUGLAS BRINKLEY
EDITOR MICHAEL E. HASKEW

CASTLE BOOKS

This edition published in 2008 by
CASTLE BOOKS ®
A division of Book Sales, Inc.
114 Northfield Avenue
Edison, NJ 08837

This edition published by arrangement with and permission of
HarperCollins Publishers Inc
10 East 53rd Street
New York, NY 10022

A NOTE FROM THE EDITORS

Every attempt has been made to ensure the publication is as accurate as possible and as comprehensive as space would allow. If errors are discovered, we would appreciate hearing from you. Please address suggestions and comments to Grand Central Press, 27 West 24th Street, Suite 510 New York, NY 10010.

Designed by Fritz Metsch

ISBN-13: 978-0-7858-2427-5
ISBN-10: 0-7858-2427-8

Printed in the United States of America

Contents

A sailor and a nurse, locked in a celebratory kiss in New York's Times Square, have come to symbolize V-J Day—August 15, 1945.

Map Index

Photo Credits

Foreword

A few years ago, when writing *The American Heritage History of the United States,* I went looking for a first-rate reference work to help me fact-check my chapters on World War II; it didn't exist. To be sure, there had been published various encyclopedias and specialized studies of the seminal event, but nothing to my liking. This seemed odd. After all, books about the "greatest generation" had become mainstays on bestseller lists, critically acclaimed movies such as *Saving Private Ryan* and *The Thin Red Line* had done well at the box office, and our country, on the whole, seemed ready to learn exacting details about the war. The History Channel, in fact, was running so many documentaries on the Second World War that it became known as "The Hitler Channel." Every town in America paid homage to their own "citizen soldier" who lost a leg in Sicily or an arm at Iwo Jima or a life in North Africa. Given such widespread interest on the subject, it only made sense that a handy reference book be available so that the public can look up the number of soldiers killed at the Battle of the Bulge or the code names of military operations. The wait is over. This book—*The World War II Desk Reference*—more than fills the bill. It explains in clear, unadorned prose, backed by rosters of statistics, time lines, and thumbnail sketches, the global cataclysm that was World War II.

More than 12 million American men and women entered the U.S. armed forces in World War II. Millions more worked and sacrificed at home to help the Allied cause to defeat hatred and tyranny. When the war was over, those young Americans came home—a generation of Americans that came of age during the Great Depression, that became a generation of warriors and finally a generation of creators: building an interstate highway system, taking on segregation in the South, conquering disease, and putting men on the moon. This volume embraces the totality of the war years in all its brutal destruction and ragged glory.

But this volume is not a typical almanac. Throughout this book, the reader will find touching oral histories from the people who witnessed the war firsthand. Many of the excerpts come from the University of New Orleans's Eisenhower Center for American Studies and the Peter Kalikow Oral History Project, which has become the largest repository of D-Day and Battle of the Bulge oral histories in the world. Taken from people on both sides of the war and from all parts of the world, they offer a glimpse into what was for many a very personal war. They collectively add a human dimension to the sea of facts presented here.

But World War II, of course, is the story of high command. This book has reminded me anew of what an extraordinary job President Franklin D. Roosevelt did leading our nation. I've long maintained that America became *the* leader of the world on January 1, 1941, when Roosevelt toiled late in his small study on the second floor of the White House. Accompanied by his adviser Harry Hopkins, speechwriter and playwright Robert Sherwood, and his speechwriter Samuel Rosenman, he was putting the final touches on his State of the Union address, which he would deliver before a joint session of Congress on January 6. There remained only the question of how to close the speech. After a long silence, the president began dictating what became his famous declaration

of hope for "a world founded upon four essential human freedoms"—freedom of speech and expression; freedom of religion; freedom from want; and freedom from fear. These were, he said, not a vision for "a distant millennium" but "a definite basis for a kind of world attainable in our own time and generation." (You can read a longer excerpt of this speech in Chapter 15, "Documents, Organizations, and Monuments.")

Such was the power of Franklin Roosevelt's personality that he managed to turn America from a nation of provincial isolationists into one of forward-thinking globalists. As newspaper editor William Allen White declared with remarkable foresight, the president had given the world "a new Magna Carta for democracy." According to White, the Four Freedoms, which became the moral cornerstone of the United Nations, marked "the opening of a new era for the world." The tables had been turned: isolationist voices such as aviator Charles Lindbergh, Senator Burton Wheeler, and *Chicago Tribune* publisher Robert McCormick were becoming obsolete.

Of course, Roosevelt had noteworthy allies, such as Winston Churchill, and you'll read about them here (see Chapter 5, "Politicians and Demagogues"). In August 1941, Roosevelt and Churchill had a series of secret meetings on warships off the Newfoundland coast. The two leaders released the Atlantic Charter, which set forth a list of common war aims in broad terms, including "the final destruction of the Nazi tyranny" as well as Roosevelt's Four Freedoms. Probably the most compelling statement of the war, the charter enunciated "certain common principles" on which the Anglo-American democracies "base their hopes for a better future for the world." Perhaps more important, the two leaders established, as Robert Sherwood would later write, "an easy intimacy, a joking informality, and a moratorium on pomposity and cant and also a degree of frankness in intercourse which if not quite complete, was remarkably close to it." Despite its cozy relations with Churchill's Britain, the United States was still officially neutral.

It would not remain so for long. The Germans increased their military activities in the North Atlantic in September 1941, and the next month a U-boat sank the U.S. ship *Kearny,* killing 11 U.S. sailors. On October 27, Roosevelt declared to the nation that "the shooting has started," and he announced that he had ordered the U.S. Navy to sink upon sight any German ship found in American waters. The president proved right three days later when the U.S. destroyer *Reuben James* was sunk, claiming the lives of more than 100 American servicemen. A formal declaration of war seemed inevitable, and by November the public was prepared for a call to arms.

The deciding aggression came not from Germany, however, but from Japan, with which U.S. relations had deteriorated throughout the Hoover and Roosevelt administrations as a result of Japanese expansion in Manchuria and China and American opposition to it. The surprise attack on the U.S. military installations at Pearl Harbor commenced on the morning of Sunday, December 7, 1941, and World War II finally engulfed America.

The U.S. garrison on the island of Oahu, ill-prepared and disorganized, was astonished by the wave of Japanese attack planes that sank or damaged 19 U.S. ships and claimed some 2,400 American lives. Read the oral histories in this book and learn how our soldiers reacted to such a surprise attack. Indeed, had the Japanese pressed on, they probably could have captured the islands without much of a struggle. Surprised themselves at the extent of their success, the attackers instead withdrew. In fact, the assault on Pearl Harbor was a strategic blunder, because none of the U.S. Pacific Fleet's three aircraft carriers was present at Pearl Harbor, and all the sneak attack accomplished was uniting the American soldiers and the American people in a crusading zeal that sustained them throughout the war. Soon millions of Americans wore enameled pins proclaiming they would "Remember Pearl Harbor." In any event, Japan's attack on the Hawaiian bases established in minutes a U.S. commitment to a foreign-born war.

After a stirring address by the ever-persuasive President Roosevelt, the Senate unanimously approved a war resolution against Japan, which only one member of the House—Republican Congresswoman Jeannette Rankin of Montana—voted against. On December 11, Germany and Italy also declared war on the United States, making things easier for Congress: that same day both houses voted unanimously to recognize a state of war with those Axis nations as well. The attack on Pearl Harbor had permanently shattered America's sense of security, and the United States entered World War II unified as never before. Whereas sizable minorities had opposed every previous U.S. war, after December 7, 1941—which Roosevelt called "a date which will live in infamy"—virtually every American agreed that it was time to go all out for victory. As George Orwell accurately noted on BBC radio upon hearing FDR's January 6, 1942, State of the Union address, America had made a "complete and uncompromising break . . . with isolationism."

Under FDR's leadership, America broke the shackles of isolationism. We became the robust "Arsenal of Democracy." Our industrial mobilization effort was astounding. General Motors became America's largest defense contractor, with output worth $12 billion, while Curtiss-Wright ($7.09 billion) and Ford Motor Company ($5.26 billion) followed closely behind in wartime production. In this volume the reader will find detailed information on how war materiel helped us in various campaigns and battles of the Pacific theater, such as Leyte Gulf, Corregidor, and Guadalcanal. Death counts followed, but so did stories of victory. Better than any volume I know, this book tells how Americans pulled together on the front lines and on the home front to win the war. The fact that FDR organized his forces and managed the nation without chaos and with such optimistic forbearance boggles the mind.

But the war was still long for the fighting. It took until November 1943 for the shaky, often bickering alliance of Great Britain, the United States, and the Soviets to agree on military strategy. After some heated discussions, the British and Americans committed to the cross-channel attack and designated the overlord—the supreme commander would be Dwight D. Eisenhower. Stating the plan was simple: find a suitable beach, gather a landing force, isolate the battlefield, and land the men. Once a beachhead was established, pour in the logistical follow-up, and then break into the countryside. Executing the plan was not so simple. Crossing the treacherous English Channel, with its unexpected storms, enormous tides, and tricky currents, would be just the first step of the amphibious assault.

The date for D-Day was originally set for May 1, 1944, to allow for a dawn invasion at low tide, when beach obstacles that could impede the landing craft would be visible. But it soon became apparent that the May 1 date would find the Allies still short of the landing craft necessary to mount the great invasion. Reluctantly, Eisenhower reset D-Day to the next suitable date—June 5, 1944. The force continued to assemble as British, Canadian, and American youth in uniform flooded into southern England.

Read Chapter 7 ("Campaigns and Battles: Europe and the Atlantic") and you'll learn that a great storm forced the postponement of D-Day to June 6. On that day, shortly after 6 A.M., the invasion rolled ashore. The assault beaches were named, from right to left, Utah, Omaha, Gold, Juno, and Sword. The Americans attacked Omaha and Utah, the Canadians Juno, and the British Gold and Sword. At Sword, Gold, and Utah, enemy resistance was light and the Allied forces had considerable success.

At Juno, meanwhile, the invading Canadians faced a beach littered with partially submerged obstacles. When engineers were unable to clear paths, landing crafts were forced to feel their way in. The troops waded ashore and zigzagged through the obstacles, but German mines took a heavy toll. In the first hour of the invasion at Juno, assault team members faced a 50-50 chance of becoming casualties.

At Omaha Beach itself everything went wrong. The tanks launched to support the infantry sank. With few exceptions, units did not land where planned because strong winds and total currents had scattered the boats in all directions. Throughout the landing, the formidable German defensive positions showered deadly fire upon the ranks of the invading Americans. Bodies and damaged craft littered the sand. Omaha was designed to be a killing zone.

At 8:30 A.M. all Allied landings ceased at Omaha: the force on the beach was on its own. Slowly, in small groups, the troops scaled the cliffs. Navy destroyers sailed in, scraping bottom in the shallow water and blasting away point-blank at the German fortifications. By noon enemy fire had decreased noticeably as the German defensive positions were taken from the rear and exits opened. By nightfall the Americans—who had suffered 2,500 casualties—held positions nowhere near the planned objectives, but they did have a toehold. In 18 harrowing hours, the walls of Hitler's Fortress Europe had been breached.

D-Day was the high-water mark of the Allied effort in World War II. From that moment onward victory in both Europe and Asia seemed inevitable. But how long would it take to win? How many more soldiers would have to die in flyspeck Pacific Islands and frozen forests in Belgium and France? Just think of the words that permanently entered world history in the 14 months between D-Day and Hiroshima/Nagasaki—Auschwitz, Yalta, kamikaze, Potsdam, atomic bomb, the Bulge, Hitler's bunker—the list could go on. Through all the death marches and urban incinerations and sniper attacks, the principles of the Four Freedoms held forth. Now, almost 60 years since

D-Day and the Japanese surrender to General Douglas MacArthur on the deck of the U.S.S. *Missouri,* we are still fighting for the Four Freedoms to prevail in a world rife with terrorism, dictators, and weapons of mass destruction. This volume reminds us that a democracy aroused can conquer any evil. We must, therefore, make sure that when writing or speaking about World War II, we get our facts straight. Every statistic in this volume, every kernel of information, played a role in the war, which still dominates our lives. The book I couldn't find has arrived.

Douglas Brinkley
Director of the Eisenhower Center
for American Studies
at the University of New Orleans

An angry mushroom cloud boils above the city of Nagasaki, Japan, on August 9, 1945. More than 70,000 people died in the blast of the second atomic bomb. Nagasaki had been the secondary target that day. A thick cover of clouds had saved Kokura from destruction.

Preface

The magnitude of a truly global war such as World War II is virtually impossible to comprehend, much less condense into a single volume.

More than 50 million people died and virtually every ocean and continent was touched by the conflict, and its geopolitical impact remains with us. From the depths of the Atlantic to the steppes of Russia, from the frozen arctic to the swelter of Pacific islands and the deserts of North Africa, places that might otherwise have remained obscure for all time became the stages where the drama of history unfolded.

The dark vision of Adolf Hitler and Nazi Germany, Benito Mussolini's dream of a new Roman Empire for Fascist Italy, and the territorial ambitions of Imperial Japan gave rise to a struggle so widespread and so costly that it is unrivaled in human history. Uneasy allies, the great democracies of the United States and Britain and the Communist regime of the Soviet Union emerged victorious.

Considering the vast array of images from the war, which have been burned into our collective consciousness, the most compelling and at the same time the most chilling is probably that of the fiery mushroom cloud rising toward the heavens from the apocalyptic ground zero of a nuclear blast. The war began with many of the world's armies still relying on the horse for transportation and ended at the dawn of the nuclear age. Its battlefields were a proving ground for advancing technology. Computers, radar, and the jet and rocket engines were just a few of the wonders to emerge. The V-1 and V-2 rockets, weapons that the Germans used to terrorize British cities, were, ironically, developed from the same technological innovation that carried men to the surface of the moon.

Perhaps in no other conflict has man's potential for cruelty to his fellow man been so dramatically and horrifically realized. Decades after the end of World War II, we are haunted by the memory of the Holocaust. The voices of survivors join with the mute testimony of the photographic record of Axis atrocities. The genocide of Auschwitz, Dachau, and the Rape of Nanking resonate across the years. Retribution came with the war crimes trials in Nuremberg and Tokyo, exposing to the world the depth of totalitarian evil.

In the wake of World War II, the map of Europe was redrawn. The fracturing of relations among former allies and the burgeoning competition between democratic and communist philosophies led to a Germany that was divided for more than 50 years. And with the polarization of the European nations into the North Atlantic Treaty Organization (NATO) and the Warsaw Pact the continent was transformed into two armed camps, each poised to annihilate the other during the restlessness of the cold war. Each side probed its adversary for weakened resolve, battling on a smaller scale through proxies and surrogates around the globe. While in China, the world's most populous country, after years of civil war, a Communist regime emerged.

During World War II, civilian populations were not spared in the conflagration of total war. Cities were bombed. Millions were killed. Still more became homeless refugees. Everywhere, the home front saw lasting change. The new participatory role of women in the United States during the war foreshadowed an unprecedented period of independence for them following the war and gave rise to the two-income household. As a result of their work experience in the factory and office, the way had been paved for women to continue to advance professionally and politically.

The desegregation of the U.S. armed forces hastened the Civil Rights movement which can, in part, be attributed to the minority experience in World War II. And the return of tens of thousands of GIs from the battlefields of Europe and Asia resulted in the postwar phenomenon known as the baby boom.

The combination of pent-up demand for consumer goods, a return to peacetime production, and rising disposable income fueled a postwar economic boom in the United States. And with the assistance of the Marshall Plan for Western Europe, war-ravaged nations began to rebuild. From the ashes of defeat, West Germany grew to prosperity, and a phoenixlike Japan developed into an economic colossus.

While the end of the cold war may have eased tensions between the world's two superpowers, the United States and the USSR, conflict among nations and peoples is a seemingly inevitable condition. With the demise of colonialism, new sovereign nations of the Third World have emerged, while the advent of the United Nations continues to hold some hope for a peaceful future.

The tragedy of World War II, its horror and its hope, captivate us and continue to shape our lives. Lessons can be learned, hopefully preventing such a cataclysmic chapter in human history from occurring again. But continued unrest in the Middle East, the Balkans, and elsewhere; the events of September 11, 2001; and the growing specter of terrorism remind us that peace and stability are at best fragile and at worst elusive. Given the growing level of interest in the war and the demand for concise, accurate information concerning this watershed event, the Eisenhower Center for American Studies presents this product of extensive research, thorough analysis, and comprehensive scope.

Using This Book

In preparing *The World War II Desk Reference*, the Eisenhower Center for American Studies assembled a group of experts on World War II who share a passion for history and a perspective on the significance of the war. Each has written widely on the subject in the past, developing a great understanding of the course of events and the political and social developments that they engendered.

The World War II Desk Reference is designed as a resource for both the novice and the experienced student of the War. The center chose the desk reference format in order to provide the greatest amount of information in the most readable and user-friendly style. Charts, graphs, and tables complement the brief, factual descriptions of people, politics, battles, conferences, and military equipment. Selected oral histories, photographs, illustrations, and maps provide insights into the complexities of a global war and convey an immediate sense of the emotions generated more than 50 years ago. While there are many perspectives from which to view the conflict, the availability of resources contributed to a primary focus on U.S. involvement (while striving for balance in coverage.)

This book is arranged by theme. It is not intended to serve as a chronological narrative of World War II but rather as a source of basic information and as a companion to further, in-depth study of this great conflict. Chapters and subsections have clear titles to guide the reader, and each contains a short introduction. A time line of the two decades from 1931 to 1950 assists the reader in seeing the global nature of the war and arranging significant events in historical context, and a comprehensive glossary places definitions of unfamiliar words at the user's fingertips. The text is cross-referenced and provides sources of additional information throughout; a complete index appears at the back of the book.

Because the World War II generation is aging, the conflict is drifting that much further from the realm of current events and into that of history. Although we regularly read or hear stories involving some aspect of the war, be it about reparations, memorials, stolen art, or movies, the conflict carries a much greater sense of history than ever before. The study and scholarly interpretation of the war will continue, and the Eisenhower Center for American Studies offers this book as an indispensable asset in the continuing quest for greater knowledge and understanding of World War II.

The 20th century was one of the most violent in history, and World War II was by far the most violent of its events. The true value in the remembrance of the war lies in a commitment to peace. In this new millennium, remembering the lessons of the previous one will serve us and our children well.

Michael E. Haskew
Chattanooga, Tennessee

CHAPTER 1

Time Line of World War II

This time line provides an overall perspective on World War II, including the years immediately preceding and following the conflict. It was a global war, fought in Europe, on the Atlantic, across the islands of the central and western Pacific, and in the countries of eastern and central Asia. Time lines covering specific subject areas can be found in each particular chapter; this main time line is useful as a linear, year-by-year measure of the war on all fronts, providing a brief overview of the scope of the conflict as well as the staggering human costs of a worldwide conflagration that took some 50 million lives.

1918

NOVEMBER 11: World War I (1914–18) ends with the surrender of Germany and Austria-Hungary to the Allied powers (the United States, France, and Great Britain).

1919

JUNE 28: The Treaty of Versailles formalizes the surrender of Germany and creates the League of Nations, a multination international organization created to preserve the peace. The treaty also imposes harsh reparation terms on Germany.

1920

MARCH 19: The U.S. Senate fails to ratify the Treaty of Versailles. U.S. failure to join the League of Nations weakens that organization.

1923

Germany is devastated by inflation, which leads to increasing political instability and to the weakening of its democratic government; the Nazi Party under Adolf Hitler begins to grow.

1929

OCTOBER 29: The stock market crash in the United States sets off a worldwide economic depression, which weakens democratic governments all over the world and strengthens the appeal of dictators and militarists in Europe and Asia.

1931

SEPTEMBER 19: Japan invades Manchuria, China; its forces occupy Changchun, Kirin, and Mukden; the first Japanese aggression on Asian mainland occurs.

SEPTEMBER 21: The Chinese government appeals to the League of Nations for assistance against the Japanese invasion.

DECEMBER 12: French troops leave the Saarland, an area inhabited by a large number of ethnic Germans and occupied by France in accordance with the Treaty of Versailles.

1932

JANUARY 9: Its economy in shambles, Germany defaults on World War I reparation payments to Allied nations that were mandated in the Treaty of Versailles.

FEBRUARY 28: The Japanese proclaim the puppet state of Manchukuo in the occupied Chinese territory of Manchuria.

MARCH 13: Nazi leader Adolf Hitler runs a close second to World War I hero and incumbent President Paul von Hindenburg in the German presidential election.

MAY 15: The assassination of Japanese Prime Minister Tsuyoshi Inukai leaves the nation's government dominated by the military.

JULY 31: Nazis win 230 seats in the German Reichstag (legislature) and become the largest party in that body.

NOVEMBER 8: Franklin D. Roosevelt is elected president of the United States.

DECEMBER 2: General Kurt von Schleicher becomes chancellor of Germany but is unable to form an effective government in the face of mounting Nazi opposition.

1933

JANUARY 30: Adolf Hitler becomes chancellor of Germany through appointment by President Paul von Hindenburg. He gains office with the assistance of politicians who believe they can keep him in check.

FEBRUARY 27: The Reichstag building burns in Berlin; in order to secure unlimited powers for Hitler, the Nazis falsely accuse the Communists of setting the blaze.

MARCH 23: The Reichstag gives Hitler dictatorial powers.

MARCH 27: Japan withdraws from the League of Nations after the League criticizes its policies in China.

JULY 14: Germany outlaws all political parties except the Nazi Party.

SEPTEMBER 2: Nazi Germany and Fascist Italy sign a friendship accord. They agree to support each other politically and not to go to war with each other.

OCTOBER 14: Germany formally withdraws from the League of Nations.

The Reichstag, home of the German parliament, burns furiously on the night of February 27, 1933, as firemen rush to fight the flames. The Nazis blamed the fire on the Communists and used the event as a pretext to crack down on political opponents.

1934

JUNE 30: Hitler orders the purge and murder of top leaders in the SA (Sturmabteilung), his paramilitary storm troopers, as a way of appeasing the regular German army, which is threatened by the SA.

JULY 25: Nazi sympathizers in Austria assassinate Chancellor Engelbert Dollfuss during an attempted coup. Mussolini protests German meddling in Austrian affairs, and the Nazis back down from further violence.

AUGUST 2: German President Hindenburg dies; Hitler assumes office of president and total dictatorial power.

DECEMBER 29: Japan repudiates the Washington and London treaties of 1921 limiting the naval tonnage of the signatories in order to expand its navy.

1935

JANUARY 13: A plebiscite in the Saarland favors union with Germany over France.

APRIL 1: President Franklin D. Roosevelt signs the first U.S. Neutrality Act.

AUGUST 15: The Nazis ban marriages between Germans and Jews.

SEPTEMBER 15: The Nuremberg Laws strip Jews of most of their rights as German citizens.

OCTOBER 3: Italy invades the East African nation of Ethiopia.

OCTOBER 19: The League of Nations approves partial sanctions against Italy in response to the invasion of Ethiopia.

1936

MARCH 7: German troops occupy the Rhineland region of Germany, which had been demilitarized by the Treaty of Versailles.

MAY 5: The Italians capture the city of Addis Ababa; organized resistance in Ethiopia ends.

JULY 17: The Spanish Civil War begins.

AUGUST 1: The German government hosts the games of the 11th Olympiad in Berlin.

OCTOBER 25: Hitler and Mussolini form the Rome-Berlin Axis declaring common foreign policies in Europe.

NOVEMBER 25: Germany and Japan agree to Anti-Comintern Pact (see Chapter 2, "Causes of War"), pledging mutual support against the Soviet Union.

DECEMBER 10: King Edward VIII of England abdicates and is succeeded by his younger brother, who is crowned King George VI.

1937

APRIL 27: The Condor Legion, consisting of German airmen supporting the Spanish Nationalists of Generalissimo Francisco Franco, bombs the Spanish city of Guernica during the Spanish Civil War.

MAY 28: Neville Chamberlain becomes prime minister of Great Britain.

JUNE 11: Soviet dictator Josef Stalin begins a purge of Red Army generals and other members of the officer corps.

JULY 7: Small Japanese and Chinese forces skirmish at the Marco Polo Bridge in China, marking the beginning of the Sino-Japanese War as Japanese troops advance toward Peking.

JULY 28: Peking falls to Japanese troops.

NOVEMBER 12: Japanese troops capture Shanghai.

NOVEMBER 20: Chiang Kai-shek establishes a new Chinese capital at Chungking.

DECEMBER 11: Italy quits the League of Nations.

DECEMBER 12: Japanese aircraft attack and sink the U.S. gunboat *Panay* on the Yangtze River in China. Japan apologizes for the incident.

DECEMBER 13: Japanese troops capture the Chinese city of Nanking and begin the infamous Rape of Nanking in which thousands of Chinese civilians are massacred.

1938

FEBRUARY 20: British Foreign Secretary Anthony Eden resigns in protest of the appeasement policy of Prime Minister Neville Chamberlain toward Germany (giving in to German demands rather than risk war).

MARCH 13: German troops occupy Austria; Hitler proclaims the union, or Anschluss, of Germany and Austria.

APRIL 10: Edouard Daladier, a supporter of appeasement, becomes French prime minister.

JULY 28: Japanese and Soviet forces clash in Manchuria.

SEPTEMBER 12: Hitler demands the right of self-determination for ethnic Germans in the Sudetenland region of Czechoslovakia.

SEPTEMBER 29: Munich Conference; Britain and France appease Hitler by forcing Czechoslovakia to cede Sudetenland to Germany (see Chapter 2, "Causes of War").

OCTOBER 5: Czech president Eduard Beneš resigns in protest against dismemberment of Czechoslovakia.

NOVEMBER 3: The Japanese proclaim a "New Order" in Asia, i.e., their domination of the western Pacific and Southeast Asia.

NOVEMBER 9: Kristallnacht, the Night of Broken Glass. Nazis destroy synagogues and arrest Jews across Germany in a state-sponsored pogrom.

1939

MARCH 10: German forces occupy the remainder of Czechoslovakia, which ceases to exist as a nation; Germany annexes Bohemia and Moravia, and Slovakia becomes a Nazi protectorate (see Chapter 2, "Causes of War").

MARCH 21: Hitler demands that Poland cede the free city of Danzig to Germany and grant access to it.

MARCH 28: Madrid falls to Franco, ending the Spanish Civil War.

MARCH 31: Britain and France pledge to defend Poland in the event of aggression.

APRIL 7: Italian troops invade Albania.

AUGUST 23: Germany and the Soviet Union stun the world with the announcement of their nonaggression pact. A secret protocol plans the partition of Poland and provides for Soviet occupation of the Baltic States of Estonia, Latvia, and Lithuania.

SEPTEMBER 1: German forces invade Poland, igniting World War II in Europe.

SEPTEMBER 3: Great Britain and France declare war on Germany; the German submarine *U-30* sinks the British liner *Athenia,* killing 112, in the first action on the Atlantic.

SEPTEMBER 5: The United States announces its neutrality in the European conflict.

SEPTEMBER 17: Soviet forces cross the Polish frontier.

SEPTEMBER 27: Warsaw, the Polish capital, falls to the Germans.

NOVEMBER 8: Hitler escapes an assassination attempt at a beer hall in Munich—the last serious attempt on his life until 1944.

NOVEMBER 30: The Soviet Union invades neighboring Finland.

DECEMBER 17: Believing (incorrectly) that he would have to face a superior British force, the commander scuttles the German pocket battleship *Admiral Graf Spee* outside the harbor of Montevideo, Uruguay, following the Battle of the River Plate.

1940

MARCH 12: Finland and the Soviet Union sign a peace treaty ending their conflict.

MARCH 20: Edouard Daladier resigns as French prime minister and is replaced by Paul Reynaud, who has opposed a policy of appeasement in the past.

JOSEPH W. GRIGG, WAR CORRESPONDENT FOR UNITED PRESS

Germans Invade Poland

I was a member of the first group of foreign newspapermen to reach Warsaw. We arrived there on October 5th, the day on which Hitler held his victory parade amid the ruins of the former Polish capital. . . . The whole center of the city had been laid in ruins by the two-day fury of the German bombardment and air bombing. Dead horses still lay rotting in the parks, their carcasses half hacked up by starving Polish troops during the siege. New graves bulged the grass alongside streetcar tracks. Bomb craters made it difficult to drive along some of the main streets. The brand new central railway station was scarcely recognizable. The Polish population looked bewildered and stunned. . . .

For an hour we stood alongside Hitler as tank after tank, motorized infantry, guns and more tanks, thundered past along the tree-lined avenue where most of the foreign embassies and legations are situated. No Pole saw that victory parade. The street where Hitler stood and those along which the gray German columns rolled had been cordoned off and no Pole was allowed nearer than a block distant.

—From *Poland: Inside Fallen Warsaw* (United Press, 1939), as published in *A Mammoth Book of Eyewitness World War II*, ed. Jon. E. Lewis (New York: Carroll & Graf, 2002), 39–40.

APRIL 9: German troops invade Norway and Denmark.

MAY 2: British forces evacuate Norway.

MAY 10: German forces invade France, the Netherlands, Belgium, and Luxembourg; Winston Churchill becomes British prime minister upon the resignation of Neville Chamberlain; Belgium's Fort Eben Emael, long considered impregnable, falls quickly to German glider troops.

MAY 17: The Germans capture Brussels, Belgium.

MAY 20: German soldiers reach the English Channel, cutting off the Low Countries from France.

MAY 26: Hundreds of boats, including many small private vessels from Britain, help in the evacuation of more than 300,000 British and French soldiers from the beleaguered beach at Dunkirk, France.

JUNE 4: Hitler orders preparations for Operation Sea Lion, the invasion of Great Britain.

JUNE 10: Italy declares war on Britain and France.

JUNE 14: The German army triumphantly enters Paris.

JUNE 16: World War I hero Marshal Philippe Pétain, an advocate of appeasement and collaboration, succeeds Paul Reynaud as prime minister of France.

JUNE 22: France and Germany conclude an armistice, in which France is humiliated; France is forced to sign in Hitler's presence in the same railroad car in which Germany surrendered in 1918.

JULY 1: Marshal Pétain organizes new French government at Vichy. Germany occupies all of northern and northwestern France.

JULY 10: The Battle of Britain, the massive German bombardment of the British Isles, begins.

DEMAREE BESS, AMERICAN WAR CORRESPONDENT

As Paris Is Evacuated

By dawn on Monday, the streets were thick with people. They had been packing their belongings all through that frightening night, and by four o'clock in the morning they were in full flight. Every vehicle with wheels was pressed into service. Some of the automobiles which passed our windows must have come from museums. Long queues stood at the taxi garages; there were two thousand people waiting at the depot nearest our hotel. But most Parisians had no motor vehicles, nor hope of hiring any. They left their homes on foot, pushing baby carriages and laden bicycles, carrying packs on their backs, leading a child by one hand, and clutching a dog or a gas mask with the other.

At twilight on Monday, Paris was blotted out by a blanket of black smoke. Was the wind blowing the cannon fumes from the adjacent battlefields? Was this smoke screen a clever device to protect our city? Or was the French army destroying its oil supply before it fell into German hands? No one knew. The French government itself had evacuated during the day, and no one remained behind to answer the anxious questions of the people.

—From *The Story of World War II*, ed. Curt Reiss, 1944, as published in *A Mammoth Book of Eyewitness World War II*, ed. Jon. E. Lewis (New York: Carroll & Graf, 2002), 73–4.

Initial attacks focus on military airfields, not civilian targets.

JULY 16: Prince Fumimaro Konoye becomes Japanese prime minister; Hideki Tojo, an army general, becomes minister of war.

AUGUST 23: The Luftwaffe (German air force) Blitz of London and other British cities begins. By switching their attacks away from airfields to cities, the Germans unwittingly save the Royal Air Force and fail in their effort to bomb Britain into submission.

SEPTEMBER 3: The United States and Great Britain conclude the "Destroyers for Bases" deal.

SEPTEMBER 17: Believing Britain is essentially defeated, Hitler postpones Operation Sea Lion in order to prepare for the invasion of the Soviet Union.

SEPTEMBER 27: Germany, Italy, and Japan sign the Tripartite Pact, by which the three nations agree to come to the aid of one another if attacked by a country not already participating in a war in Asia or Europe.

OCTOBER 28: Italy invades Greece, as part of its campaign to dominate southeastern Europe.

NOVEMBER 11: British naval aircraft attack the Italian naval base at Taranto and inflict heavy damage.

Written in both French and German, a Nazi placard warns of potential reprisals for acts of violence against German armed forces personnel in occupied France.

DECEMBER 9: British troops begin an offensive against Italian forces in the Western Desert in Egypt.

DECEMBER 29: President Franklin D. Roosevelt declares that the United States is an "arsenal of democracy," meaning the United States will rearm to protect itself.

1941

JANUARY 22: The British capture the Libyan port of Tobruk.

FEBRUARY 7: British forces capture 20,000 Italians at Beda Fomm, Libya.

FEBRUARY 12: German General Erwin Rommel, "the Desert Fox," arrives in Tripoli to head the German Afrika Korps.

MARCH 11: The U.S. Congress approves the Lend-Lease Act, under which the United States "lends" arms and materiel to the British while technically remaining neutral (see Chapter 2, "Causes of War").

MARCH 28: The British Royal Navy pummels the Italian fleet in the Battle of Cape Matapan.

APRIL 6: Germany invades Yugoslavia and Greece to help rescue the bumbling Italian campaigns in Albania and Greece.

APRIL 13: The Soviet Union and Japan sign a neutrality agreement.

MAY 10: Deputy Führer Rudolf Hess flies to Scotland and parachutes to earth on a self-appointed peace mission. Hitler denounces Hess as a lunatic.

MAY 20: German airborne troops assault the island of Crete and drive out the British.

MAY 24: The German battleship *Bismarck* and cruiser *Prinz Eugen* sink the British battle cruiser *Hood*.

MAY 27: After an epic sea chase British naval forces, led by the battleships *King George V* and *Rodney,* sink the *Bismarck*.

JUNE 22: Hitler launches Operation Barbarossa, the invasion of the Soviet Union, in direct violation of Germany's nonaggression pact with the Soviet government.

JUNE 27: Japan announces its formulation of the Greater East Asia Co-Prosperity Sphere, a polite term for the Japanese domination of East and Southeast Asia.

AUGUST 11: Roosevelt and Churchill issue the Atlantic Charter, which later serves as a basis for the formation of the United Nations.

AUGUST 20: German forces begin the 900-day siege of the Soviet city of Leningrad.

SEPTEMBER 28: The Germans massacre 33,000 Jews at Babi Yar in Kiev, Ukraine.

OCTOBER 16: General Hideki Tojo is elevated to prime minister of Japan.

OCTOBER 31: A German submarine torpedoes the U.S. destroyer *Reuben James*. Roosevelt believes the United States will go to war against Germany first.

DECEMBER 7: Japanese forces attack the U.S. Pacific Fleet at Pearl Harbor, plunging the United States into World War II. Japan attacks the Philippines as well.

DECEMBER 8: The United States and Great Britain declare war on Japan.

DECEMBER 10: Japanese aircraft sink the British battleship *Prince of Wales* and the battle cruiser *Repulse* near Malaya.

DECEMBER 11: Germany and Italy declare war on the United States; the United States reciprocates.

DECEMBER 23: The Japanese capture Wake Island, a Pacific outpost previously fortified by the United States.

DECEMBER 25: Hong Kong, the British crown colony, falls to the Japanese.

1942
JANUARY 13: German U-boats begin an intensive campaign attacking Allied shipping along the U.S. coast.

FEBRUARY 15: The Japanese capture 130,000 British troops with the fall of Singapore, on the tip of the Malay Peninsula.

FEBRUARY 27: The Japanese rout U.S. naval forces in the Battle of the Java Sea.

MARCH 11: U.S. General Douglas MacArthur leaves the fortress island of Corregidor in the Philippines, in Manila Bay, as the Japanese close in.

APRIL 10: The infamous Bataan Death March begins, following the surrender of U.S. forces on Bataan, Philippines.

APRIL 18: Led by Colonel Jimmy Doolittle, American bombers attack Tokyo, the Japanese capital.

MAY 1: The Japanese capture Mandalay, Burma, as their forces push through Southeast Asia toward the border of British-controlled India.

MAY 7–8: The U.S. and Japanese fleets clash in the Battle of the Coral Sea.

JUNE 4: The Battle of Midway, a devastating defeat for the Japanese, begins. The sinking of four of their carriers marks the end of their offensive in the central Pacific.

JUNE 21: Rommel's Afrika Korps captures the Libyan port of Tobruk.

JULY 1: The monthlong first Battle of El Alamein begins, and the British stop Rommel in Egypt short of Alexandria.

JULY 31: German forces cross the Don River in Russia on the Eastern front as they attempt to resume their offensive in Russia, which was stalled in December 1941.

AUGUST 7: In their first island offensive in the western Pacific, U.S. troops land on Guadalcanal in the Solomon Islands.

AUGUST 8: Field Marshal Bernard Law Montgomery takes command of the British Eighth Army in Egypt.

AUGUST 19: The British-Canadian raid on the English Channel town of Dieppe in occupied France is a disaster.

OCTOBER 23: British attacks open the decisive second Battle of El Alamein in Egypt.

NOVEMBER 4: Rommel and the Afrika Korps begin a long, fighting retreat to Tunisia.

NOVEMBER 8: In Operation Torch, Allied troops land in North Africa, the first major Allied offensive in the western theaters of war; their commander is U.S. General Dwight D. Eisenhower.

NOVEMBER 12: U.S. and Japanese forces fight the first naval Battle of Guadalcanal, followed by a second that concludes three days later.

NOVEMBER 23: A Soviet counteroffensive begins at Stalingrad against the German Sixth Army; the battle ends in February 1943.

1943
JANUARY 14: The Casablanca Conference begins, ending 10 days later with a resolution for the unconditional surrender of the Axis powers.

JANUARY 23: The British Eighth Army captures Tripoli, Libya.

JANUARY 27: The U.S. Army Air Forces bomb Germany for the first time, joining the British Royal Air Force, which has been bombing Germany since 1940.

FEBRUARY 1: The Japanese begin an eight-day evacuation of Guadalcanal.

FEBRUARY 2: German Sixth Army surrenders to the Soviet forces at Stalingrad, the major turning point in the war on the Eastern Front.

FEBRUARY 14: Rommel batters inexperienced American troops at the Kasserine Pass in Tunisia.

APRIL 7: Converging Allied forces (the British from the east and the Americans from the west) link up in Tunisia.

APRIL 18: U.S. fighters shoot down the airplane carrying the Japanese naval commander Isoroku Yamamoto, architect of the attack on Pearl Harbor.

APRIL 19: The uprising of the Warsaw Ghetto begins; it is brutally crushed by the Germans.

MAY 13: German troops in North Africa surrender. A conference between U.S. President Franklin D. Roosevelt and British Prime Minister Winston Churchill begins in Washington, D.C., setting a tentative date of May 1944 for the invasion of France.

JUNE 21: Allied forces begin their successful effort to recapture the island of New Georgia in the Solomons.

JULY 5: The Battle of Kursk (Soviet Union), which includes the largest tank engagement in history, begins on the Eastern Front.

JULY 9: Operation Husky, the Allied invasion of Sicily, begins.

During the uprising of the Warsaw Ghetto in the spring of 1943, a group of Jewish civilians is herded together by German troops. Although the resistance in Warsaw was brutally suppressed, it inspired armed resistance to the Nazis in other cities of Eastern Europe.

JULY 22: The Sicilian city of Palermo falls to the U.S. Seventh Army.

JULY 25: Mussolini is ousted by the Fascist Council and replaced by Marshal Pietro Badoglio as head of the Italian government.

JULY 27: Combined British and American bombing creates a devastating firestorm in the German city of Hamburg.

AUGUST 1: U.S. bombers raid the oil refineries in Ploeşti, Romania, and lose 54 aircraft.

AUGUST 17: Messina, Italy, falls to the Allies, and Sicily is secured.

SEPTEMBER 8: General Eisenhower announces the unconditional surrender of Italy.

SEPTEMBER 9: Allied forces land on the Italian mainland at the coastal town of Salerno.

SEPTEMBER 16: The Allies take Lae, New Guinea, in the western Pacific.

SEPTEMBER 30: The U.S. Fifth Army captures Naples, Italy.

OCTOBER 13: New Italian government declares war on Germany. German forces occupy northern and central Italy.

NOVEMBER 1: U.S. Marines land on Bougainville in the Solomon Islands.

NOVEMBER 6: Soviet troops capture Kiev from the Germans.

NOVEMBER 18: The British Royal Air Force begins a concentrated bombing effort against the German capital of Berlin.

NOVEMBER 20: U.S. Marines capture Tarawa in the Gilbert Islands, while army troops take neighboring Makin.

NOVEMBER 22: Churchill, Roosevelt, and Chiang Kai-shek meet at Cairo to discuss military operations in China.

NOVEMBER 28: The Big Three—Roosevelt, Churchill, and Stalin—meet for the first time, at Teheran, Iran, and formally promise Stalin to open a second front in Europe in 1944.

DECEMBER 24: Eisenhower is named Supreme Commander, Allied Expeditionary Force, in preparation for the invasion of Western Europe.

DECEMBER 28: Canadian forces break the Germans' Gustav Line in Italy, which had barred entrance to the road to Rome.

1944

JANUARY 22: American landings at Anzio, Italy, attempt to flank German defensive positions.

FEBRUARY 1: U.S. Marines land on Kwajalein in the Marshall Islands.

FEBRUARY 15: U.S. bombers destroy the abbey of Monte Cassino in central Italy, a mountaintop fortress used by the Germans to block Allied forces from moving northward.

FEBRUARY 17: U.S. carrier-based aircraft begin two days of attacks that destroy the Japanese naval base at Truk in the Caroline Islands.

MARCH 29: British troops begin a three-month stand against the Japanese at Imphal, India.

APRIL 5: The British withstand two months of fighting against the Japanese at Kohima, India.

MAY 12: German forces in the Crimea surrender to the Red Army.

JUNE 4: Rome is the first Axis capital to fall to the Allies.

JUNE 6: Operation Overlord: the Allies storm the beaches in Normandy, France, on D-Day.

JUNE 15: U.S. troops land on Saipan in the Marianas, completing the island's capture on July 9.

JUNE 19: The U.S. Navy wins a decisive victory in the Battle of the Philippine Sea, and the Japanese lose approximately 400 planes in two days during the "Great Marianas Turkey Shoot," a huge naval battle fought exclusively by carrier-based aircraft.

JUNE 29: The French port of Cherbourg falls to U.S. troops.

JULY 10: British and Canadian troops finally take Caen, France, after a devastating aerial bombardment.

BRIGADIER GENERAL DAVID E. THOMAS, 82ND AIRBORNE

Countdown to D-Day

As part of our preparation in the medics for the D-Day invasion, we gave each medic a canteen of alcohol, which we thought we would use for sterilization purposes when we got to Normandy. I doubt that a drop of it ever got out of England. That's a fact. And while we were in this enclave, we were briefed and re-briefed on sand tables. I didn't pay all that much attention. I had been in the airborne long enough to know that night jumps never went off as planned. And I'll guarantee you that this was the way it was in Normandy. It certainly did not go off as planned.

While we were locked up I wasn't doing very well in the poker game so I thought I better go and listen to the Chaplain, not wishing to miss touching all the bases. About the time I was sitting down on a cot in the last row and the only seat left in the house, Chaplain Elder says, "Now, the Lord is not particularly interested in those who only turn to him in times of need." I thought, "Gee, he must have seen me come in." So I got up and left again. I still didn't do very well in the poker game, which didn't do my morale any good for what was coming up for us.

As you know, the 1st jump on the 5th was canceled and we jumped on the 6th. We took off, oh, I don't know, 11:00 something. Something like that. We headed out over the channel and as far as you could look all you could see was C47 aircraft and fighters escorting them. It looked like we had the whole damn Army coming in airborne.

—Eisenhower Center for American Studies Archives

JOHN D. BOONE, 82ND AIRBORNE

Pilots Prepare for D-Day

Faces blackened and bodies loaded to the hilt, our company formation was called before our departure to the planes to leave around 22 or 2300 hours. Our company commander, Captain Gerard A. Ruddy, talked to us and presented a well thought out speech. We were prepared, he said, and it was up to us to use that preparation and ingenuity to take care of the Germans. In his talk, he said among other things, he would rather die than have to bury one of his men.

Fortunately, or unfortunately, he did not have to face the sadness of a burial since he, himself, was killed on D-Day. In conclusion, he said "Sergeant Boone, come up here and sing us a song." I went up there as commanded and sang *Stout Hearted Men*. After that, it was "Give them hell, men!" And we were dismissed to go to our planes.

—Eisenhower Center for American Studies Archives

JULY 20: Hitler escapes assassination as a bomb, planted by plotters from the German army, detonates at his headquarters in East Prussia.

JULY 21: U.S. Marines land on Guam in the Marianas.

JULY 25: U.S. air and ground units begin Operation Cobra, the breakout from France's hedgerow country in Normandy.

AUGUST 1: As Red Army troops near the Polish capital, the Warsaw Uprising begins. Soviet forces allow Germans to crush the Poles.

AUGUST 3: U.S. and Chinese troops capture Myitkyina in Burma.

AUGUST 15: During Operation Dragoon, the Allies land in southern France.

AUGUST 19: Resistance fighters rise up in Paris as Allied troops approach the city.

AUGUST 25: Free French troops lead the Allies into Paris.

AUGUST 31: The Red Army captures the Romanian capital of Bucharest.

SEPTEMBER 3: British troops liberate Brussels, Belgium.

SEPTEMBER 15: American forces land on Peleliu in the western Pacific, securing it a month later.

SEPTEMBER 27: The 10-day Allied airborne offensive known as Operation Market-Garden ends in failure with heavy losses in Holland.

OCTOBER 10: The Red Army reaches the Baltic Sea.

A young woman waves to French soldiers manning American-built Sherman tanks during the victorious summer of 1944. The Free French Second Armored Division, commanded by General Philippe LeClerc, was given the honor of liberating Paris.

OCTOBER 14: Implicated unjustly in the July 20 plot to kill Hitler, Rommel is forced to commit suicide.

OCTOBER 20: U.S. troops under General Douglas MacArthur return to the Philippines at Leyte; partisans under Tito liberate the Yugoslav capital of Belgrade.

OCTOBER 21: Aachen, the capital of Charlemagne's Holy Roman Empire, is the first major city in Germany to fall to the Allies.

OCTOBER 25: The U.S. Seventh Fleet virtually destroys Japanese naval power with the end of the Battle of Leyte Gulf, the largest and most complex naval engagement in history.

NOVEMBER 24: Massive B-29 bombers raid Tokyo for the first time from bases in the Marianas.

DECEMBER 16: The Battle of the Bulge begins; the last desperate German offensive in the West opens with a massive German assault in Belgium and Luxembourg.

DECEMBER 26: General George Patton's Third Army relieves troopers of the U.S. 101st Airborne Division, who had been encircled at the Belgian crossroads town of Bastogne.

1945

JANUARY 1: Operation Bodenplatte: German fighter aircraft launch attacks on Allied installations in the West and lose nearly 300 planes.

JANUARY 12: The Red Army unleashes a major offensive across the Vistula River in Poland.

JANUARY 17: Soviet forces capture Warsaw.

JANUARY 26: The Red Army liberates the Auschwitz (Poland) concentration camp.

FEBRUARY 4: The Yalta Conference begins. Roosevelt, Churchill, and Stalin discuss postwar Europe.

FEBRUARY 13: Soviet troops capture the Hungarian capital of Budapest; Allied air raids set off a firestorm in the German city of Dresden.

FEBRUARY 19: U.S. Marines land on Iwo Jima and secure the island as a haven for crippled bombers after 36 days of bloody fighting.

FEBRUARY 23: U.S. forces drive into the Ruhr Valley, the industrial heart of Germany.

MARCH 3: U.S. troops liberate the Philippine capital of Manila.

MARCH 7: U.S. forces capture the German city of Cologne and secure an intact railroad bridge over the Rhine River at Remagen.

MARCH 9: An incendiary raid on Tokyo by U.S. bombers kills more than 80,000 Japanese.

MARCH 20: The Allies capture Mandalay as the Japanese continue to retreat on all fronts.

MARCH 28: U.S. troops capture Frankfurt and drive eastward toward the Elbe River in Germany.

MARCH 30: Soviet troops capture the city of Danzig and drive deeper into the German heartland.

APRIL 1: On Easter Sunday, U.S. troops land on Okinawa, only 300 miles from the Japanese main islands. The Allies trap more than 300,000 German soldiers in the Ruhr Valley.

APRIL 6: Japanese kamikaze attacks begin in earnest against U.S. vessels off Okinawa.

APRIL 11: U.S. troops halt their advance eastward at the Elbe River.

APRIL 12: President Franklin D. Roosevelt dies of a cerebral hemorrhage early in his fourth term and is succeeded by Vice President Harry S. Truman.

APRIL 13: Vienna falls to the Red Army.

APRIL 15: British troops liberate Germany's Belsen concentration camp.

APRIL 16: The Red Army, in its final thrust to capture the German capital, launches a massive offensive against Berlin.

APRIL 17: U.S. troops land on Mindanao in the southern Philippines.

APRIL 18: American troops enter Czechoslovakia.

APRIL 23: U.S. and British armies arrive at Italy's Po River.

APRIL 25: During a two-month conference in San Francisco, delegates from 50 countries agree to the United Nations charter. U.S. and Soviet troops meet at Torgau on the Elbe.

APRIL 28: Italian partisans execute Mussolini.

APRIL 29: U.S. troops liberate Germany's Dachau concentration camp.

APRIL 30: Hitler and his wife, Eva Braun, commit suicide in his bunker in Berlin; Admiral Karl Dönitz becomes head of the German government.

MAY 3: German resistance in Berlin ends; British troops capture Hamburg; Indian soldiers liberate Rangoon, Burma.

MAY 7: All German forces surrender unconditionally to the Allies.

MAY 8: VE (Victory in Europe) Day.

MAY 9: Soviet troops march into Prague.

MAY 11: Australian troops capture Wewak, the last Japanese bastion in New Guinea.

MAY 23: SS chief Heinrich Himmler commits suicide in British custody.

JUNE 22: The U.S. 10th Army secures Okinawa after nearly three months of fighting and more than 50,000 casualties.

JULY 5: Churchill loses bid for reelection.

JULY 16: The United States successfully tests the atomic bomb at Alamogordo, New Mexico. The

DOROTHEA VON SCHWANENFLÜGEL

Living in Berlin as the Soviets Approach, April 1945
The radio announced that Hitler had come out of his safe bomb-proof bunker to talk with the fourteen to sixteen year old boys who had "volunteered" for the "honor" to be accepted into the SS and to die for their Führer in the defense of Berlin. What a cruel lie! These boys did not volunteer, but had no choice, because boys who were found hiding were hanged as traitors by the SS as a warning that, "he who was not brave enough to fight had to die." When trees were not available, people were strung up on lampposts. They were hanging everywhere, military and civilian, men and women, ordinary citizens who had been executed by a small group of fanatics. It appeared that the Nazis did not want the people to survive because a lost war, by their rationale, was obviously the fault of all of us.

—From _Laughter Wasn't Rationed: A Personal Journey Through Germany's World Wars and Postwar Years_ (Alexandria, VA: Tricor Press, 2000).

face of the postwar world comes into focus during the Potsdam Conference, which ends on August 2.

JULY 26: The results of the British election, held three weeks earlier, are announced, Churchill is defeated and is replaced as prime minister by Labour Party leader Clement Attlee.

JULY 30: A Japanese submarine torpedoes the U.S. heavy cruiser *Indianapolis,* which delivered parts for the atomic bomb to the island of Tinian in the Marianas.

AUGUST 6: The United States drops the first atomic bomb on the Japanese city of Hiroshima.

AUGUST 8: The Soviet Union declares war on Japan.

AUGUST 9: The United States drops the second atomic bomb on the Japanese city of Nagasaki.

AUGUST 14: Japan surrenders to the Allies; Emperor Hirohito announces in a broadcast to the nation that Japan is giving up.

AUGUST 15: VJ (Victory in Japan) Day.

AUGUST 23: The first American troops land in Japan.

SEPTEMBER 2: Japanese diplomats sign the instrument of surrender aboard the battleship *Missouri* in Tokyo Bay.

NOVEMBER 20: Nuremberg war crimes trials begin; major Nazi leaders are tried before an international tribunal in a trial that lasts 11 months.

1946

JANUARY 1: Emperor Hirohito renounces his divinity.

MARCH 5: In a speech in Fulton, Missouri, Churchill says that an "Iron Curtain" has fallen down the middle of Europe, dividing the free nations of the West from Soviet-dominated dictatorships in Eastern Europe.

MARCH 6: War begins in Indochina as France, seeking to regain former colonial possessions,

Japanese military commanders and diplomats stand solemnly at attention on the deck of the battleship USS *Missouri* in Tokyo Bay, September 2, 1945. The delegation represented the defeated nation of Japan during the surrender ceremonies, which ended World War II.

fights against communist-nationalist insurgencies.

APRIL 10: War crimes trials of major Japanese leaders begin in Tokyo.

OCTOBER 16: The Allies execute convicted German war criminals in Berlin's Spandau Prison; Luftwaffe chief Hermann Göring commits suicide and escapes the noose.

1947
MAY 23: The British government agrees to the partition of India, creating separate nations of India and Pakistan.

JUNE 5: U.S. Secretary of State George C. Marshall proposes a massive aid plan for the economic recovery of Europe—the so-called Marshall Plan.

JULY 4: The United States grants independence to the Philippines.

AUGUST 15: India and Pakistan, formerly under British rule, become independent nations.

NOVEMBER 29: The United Nations discloses a plan for the partition of Palestine.

1948
FEBRUARY 25: Communists seize power in Czechoslovakia.

MARCH 31: Congress passes the bill funding the Marshall Plan.

MAY 14: The nation of Israel is born following the partition of Palestine and is immediately recognized by the United States. Neighboring Arab states launch a war to destroy Israel but are defeated.

JUNE 24: The Soviet Union blockades West Berlin; a massive airlift follows, keeping the divided city supplied.

NOVEMBER 2: Harry S Truman is elected president of the United States.

DECEMBER 23: The Allies execute major Japanese war criminals.

1949
APRIL 4: The North Atlantic Treaty Organization (NATO) is formed.

JULY 14: The Soviets complete their first atomic test.

OCTOBER 1: The Communist victors in a long civil war declare the creation of the People's Republic of China; Chiang Kai-shek's Nationalist forces flee to the island of Taiwan and set up the Republic of China.

DECEMBER 27: Indonesia gains independence from the Netherlands.

1950
JANUARY 31: President Truman authorizes the building of the hydrogen bomb.

MARCH 8: The Soviet Union announces that it possesses the atomic bomb.

JUNE 25: North Korean forces cross the 38th parallel and invade South Korea, triggering the Korean War, which lasts until 1953.

CHAPTER 2

Causes of War

The roots of World War II (1939–45) lay in the previous global conflagration—World War I (1914–18)—a conflict that shattered the old Europe and left unresolved the many international tensions, rivalries, hatreds, humiliations, and centuries-old grievances. The Treaty of Versailles essentially redrew the map of Europe. The accord was signed in the glorious Hall of Mirrors of the Versailles palace in June 1919, and was supposed to end the war and guarantee a peaceful future by setting up the League of Nations, an international organization devoted to resolving world disputes. But the United States failed to ratify the treaty and never joined the League, thus weakening it from the very beginning. And, equally important, the treaty imposed harsh reparation payments on Germany. Not only did the payments cause an economic disaster for Germany, whose economy was staggered by inflation in the early 1920s, but they became a political rallying cry for Adolf Hitler and the Nazi Party. Hitler did not come to power in Germany until 1933, but he and his party were a hugely destabilizing force on the German political scene throughout the 1920s. Hitler trumpeted that the Versailles Treaty was foisted on the German people by traitors and, more ominously as a warning for the future, the Jews.

The political instability of the post–World War I period affected not only Germany, but other nations in Europe as well. By the early 1920s, Benito Mussolini and his Fascist followers had seized power in Italy.

STATUS OF EUROPE BEFORE WORLD WAR I

Mussolini and Hitler believed that military means to achieve their goals for expansion and domination were justified. They glorified war, believing it made their people stronger and more heroic. The same philosophy of force found root also in Japan, although under different circumstances. In that country, an ambitious military became dedicated to the expansion of Japanese power into China and all of eastern Asia. These regimes were greatly influenced by the harsh realities of the economic depression that ravaged the world in the 1930s, causing widespread social and political upheaval. But these men and their governments alone could not have brought about World War II. Their schemes for national expansion and domination were aided by complacency and fear of war that infected the Western democracies, including the United States. In Europe, for example, Hitler repeatedly challenged the terms of the Versailles Treaty, and he was allowed to get away with his many transgressions, including the militarization of the Rhineland, the seizure of the Czech Sudetenland, and the annexa-

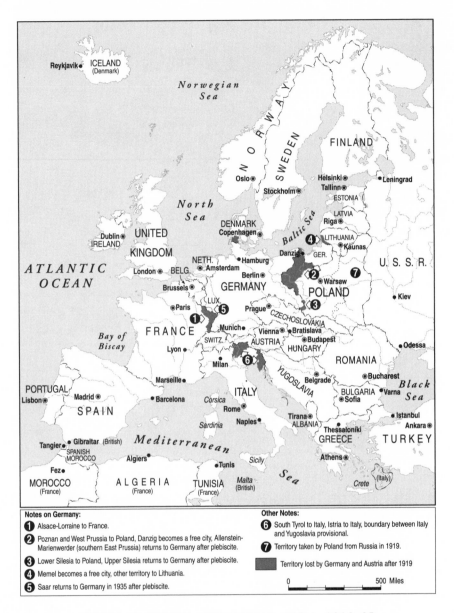

Notes on Germany:

1 Alsace-Lorraine to France.

2 Poznan and West Prussia to Poland, Danzig becomes a free city, Allenstein-Marienwerder (southern East Prussia) returns to Germany after plebiscite.

3 Lower Silesia to Poland, Upper Silesia returns to Germany after plebiscite.

4 Memel becomes a free city, other territory to Lithuania.

5 Saar returns to Germany in 1935 after plebiscite.

Other Notes:

6 South Tyrol to Italy, Istria to Italy, boundary between Italy and Yugoslavia provisional.

7 Territory taken by Poland from Russia in 1919.

Territory lost by Germany and Austria after 1919

0   500 Miles

STATUS OF EUROPE AFTER WORLD WAR I, 1918–35

tion of Austria. He had little reason to believe that his invasion of Poland in 1939 would be opposed by the democratic West. When it was, war was the only means left to challenge the dictator.

Historians continue to argue about the causes of World War II. Perhaps a war might have been averted, some say, had the victors of World War I not imposed such crushing conditions on Germany in the hope of establishing a permanent peace; or if the League of Nations had actually worked the way it was envisioned to; or the United States had not isolated itself from global problems after World

War I; or the world's economy had not collapsed and thereby led the Germans, Italians, and Japanese to turn to dictators and militarists to lift them out of their misery. These and other factors came to a head in 1939, and the result was a deadly six-year conflict that would redefine global power.

What follows is an alphabetical list of the topics that are essential for an understanding of the background and causes of World War II; unless otherwise noted, cross-references refer to entries within this chapter.

ANSCHLUSS A German word meaning "annexation." After becoming chancellor of Germany in 1933, Adolf Hitler was determined to unite Austria with Germany. Gambling that the British and French would not intervene in objection, Hitler simply sent his army into Austria and annexed it to the "Greater German Reich" on March 13, 1938. As they crossed the border, German troops were met by cheering crowds throwing flowers. (See Germany's Expansionist Policies.)

ANTI-COMINTERN PACT On November 25, 1936, Germany signed the Anti-Comintern Pact with Japan, the first formal agreement between the two future allies; it declared that both countries were united against communism (meaning the Soviet Union). It was basically a mutual defense pact in which each agreed to come to the other's aid in the event of attack by the USSR. Italy joined the agreement the following year. See also Chapter 4, "Allies, Enemies, and Bystanders."

ANTI-SEMITISM Broadly speaking, anti-Semitism is the hatred of, or animosity toward, people of a Semitic heritage, most commonly Jews and Arabs. In modern usage, however it refers exclusively to the hatred of Jews. Anti-Semitism had been a part of European culture for centuries, and several nations had periodically carried out pogroms against the Jews. Hitler developed his hatred of Jews while living as a struggling artist in Vienna before World War I and made one goal of his regime the elimination of Jewry from Germany and, eventually, all of Europe. After World War II was over, nearly 6 million European Jews were dead. (See Nuremberg Laws.)

APPEASEMENT Granting concessions to an aggressor in order to preserve peace. The word has become associated with British Prime Minister

A brown-shirted member of the Nazi SA stands beside a sign hung at the door of a Jewish-owned store in Berlin. It reads, "Germans, defend yourselves, do not buy from Jews." A Nazi-sponsored boycott of Jewish businesses throughout Germany was begun on April 1, 1933.

Neville Chamberlain and his September 29, 1938, meeting with Hitler in Munich, where he and French Premier Edouard Daladier attempted to buy peace by agreeing not to oppose Germany's plan to take possession of the German-speaking portions of Czechoslovakia. (See Munich Pact.)

AXIS POWERS The alliance of Germany, Italy, and Japan in World War II. Although Hitler and Mussolini initially were antagonistic toward each other, in 1936 they formed the Rome-Berlin Axis. After Italy signed the Anti-Comintern Pact (see above), the three powers then became known as the Rome-Berlin-Tokyo Axis.

BLITZ Term (from the German word meaning "lightning") used to describe the intense German air raids against British cities and military installations from July 1940 through January 1941, and then during the spring of 1941, until Germany invaded the Soviet Union.

BLITZKRIEG Literally, "lightning war." Using a combination of dive-bombers, paratroops, and infantry riding on tanks and other armored vehicles, the Germans were able, in the early stages of the war, to overwhelm their enemies. The Germans used the technique effectively in the invasions of Poland, Denmark and Norway, France, the Low Countries, the Balkan States, Crete, and the Soviet Union.

BOLSHEVISM/COMMUNISM A political system advocated by Vladimir Lenin in Russia between 1903 and 1917 and based on the writings of Karl Marx. The two terms are generally interchangeable. The word *bolshevism* comes from the Russian word *bolshinstovo,* meaning majority. Hitler and Mussolini both claimed that Bolshevik agitators were trying to overthrow the governments of Germany and Italy, and both leaders used the general public's fear and hatred of bolshevism/communism to their own ends. Hitler also equated bolshevism with "world Jewry."

BRITAIN, PREWAR Despite emerging victorious from World War I, Britain was economically and spiritually devastated. The country had lost almost one million men, its treasury was exhausted, and its empire was coming apart. The economic depression of the 1930s further eroded the British economy and Britons' fighting spirit, making them vulnerable to an aggressive dictator like Hitler.

EMILY

Life as a Jewish Girl in Hitler's Country

Hitler came to power in 1933, an event which had very little effect on the 10-year old, happy and carefree little girl I was then. We lived in Nuremberg, my life was warm and comfortable. . . . Gradually various problems arose. A difference was made between Aryan and non-Aryan children. The non-Aryan–Jewish children were told one day to sit at the back of the class; from then on Jewish children were not allowed to join Latin lessons. We could not understand the reason and our small group of Jewish girls cheered each other by assuming that we would probably have done better than the others! The non-Jewish girls had to join the Hitler Youth.

In the Hitler Youth, apart from singing and parading, they were taught all kinds of anti-Semitic things and started to hate their old friends. I was hurt and puzzled. I had not changed, so why were they not my friends any more? Gradually, only the Jewish girls were my friends. "Jew stinker" was often shouted at us. Whenever possible, I would shout back "I am the Jew and you are the stinker," and then I had to run away fast—if there were more of "them."

—http://atschool.eduweb.co.uk/chatback/english/memories/~emily.html

COMMUNISM See Bolshevism/Communism.

CZECH CRISIS Before World War I, the states of Bohemia, Moravia, and Slovakia were part of Austria-Hungary; after the war, the Czechs and Slovaks formed a single nation, Czechoslovakia, which quickly became the most prosperous, progressive, and democratic country in Central Europe. But, by the 1930s, unrest had begun to brew. Although the Czechs comprised only about half the population, they controlled the economy and government, which angered the Slovaks as well as the German-speaking minority that occupied the Sudetenland region in the west that borders Germany (see Chapter 4, "Allies, Enemies, and Bystanders").

In the 1935 elections, the Sudetenland Nazi Party won 62 percent of the vote of Germans in Czechoslovakia; the party then encouraged the German-speaking populace to clamor for unification with Germany, claiming they were being oppressed by the Czechs; the Nazis' aim was to provoke a crisis that would allow Hitler to destroy Czechoslovakia and incorporate the Sudetenland into the German Reich.

In late summer 1938, Hitler demanded that Czechoslovakia turn over the Sudetenland to Germany by October 1 or face invasion. Czechoslovakia refused, and the Czechs began mobilizing for war behind border fortifications that rivaled those of the Maginot Line. Britain readied its fleet for action, and France began calling up its reserves. Hitler responded by putting his armed forces on a high state of alert, despite the objections of his generals, who worried that Germany was not ready for war.

That September, as the crisis deepened, British Prime Minister Neville Chamberlain, along with French Premier Eduoard Daladier, rushed to Germany to meet with Hitler in an attempt to make peace and avert war. Telling the Czechs that they would not stand behind them over the Sudetenland, Chamberlain and Daladier essentially gave in to Hitler and sealed Czechoslovakia's fate. (See Appeasement; Munich Pact.)

DANZIG/POLISH CORRIDOR When the Treaty of Versailles dismembered Germany and created an independent Poland, the Baltic seaport city of Danzig, historically German, was cut off from the rest of the country by a narrow corridor of Polish land and declared a free city. (See Chapter 4, "Allies, Enemies, and Bystanders"). In the 1920s, German anger about the situation grew. After the Sudetenland annexation of 1938, (see Czech Crisis), Poland was justifiably wary of German intentions. In October 1938, Germany had already hinted that Danzig should be returned to the Reich; Poland rejected the suggestion. Further, in March 1939, British Prime Minister Neville Chamberlain, shocked at Germany's invasion of the remainder of Czechoslovakia that month, announced that Britain would defend Poland's sovereignty in the event of attack. In response, a furious Hitler ordered his

With the caption "Take me to Czechoslovakia, driver," this political cartoon originally appeared in the September 8, 1938, edition of the *Chicago Daily News*. The commentary refers to Hitler's demand for self-determination for ethnic Germans living in the Czech Sudetenland.

reluctant generals to draw up secret plans for an invasion of Poland, code-named "Case White." Although the German generals insisted that their armed forces were not ready for war, Hitler felt that his potential adversaries—France, Britain, and the Soviet Union—were too weak and distracted by their internal problems to do anything except protest loudly if he invaded Poland. (See Polish Crisis.)

DICTATORSHIPS, RISE OF In times of national strife, people sometimes look for a strong leader who seems to have the answer to their problems—often at the cost of their personal liberties. The period between the two world wars saw a rise in the number of dictators, all of whom promised that they could end the chaos if they were given extraordinary power: these included Vladimir Lenin and, later, Josef Stalin in the Soviet Union; Benito Mussolini in Italy; Adolf Hitler in Germany; and Francisco Franco in Spain. In Asia, the Japanese military intimidated and eventually controlled the government. A czar or king had recently ruled in Russia, Germany, and Spain, so the people were used to a strong figurehead; Italy and Japan retained their monarchs, who did little to prevent the dictators from embroiling their nations in war.

DIPLOMATIC FAILURES France and Britain had lost millions of men and were in a weakened economic condition after World War I. They did little to thwart Hitler's aggressive designs on the rest of Europe until 1939. The League of Nations did not have the power to do much other than declare sanctions against Germany, Italy, and Japan when they overstepped the bounds of international propriety (see Chapter 4, "Allies, Enemies, and Bystanders"). Russia had disengaged from Europe's squabbles, and the United States had likewise withdrawn from international affairs. As a consequence, Hitler, Mussolini, and Japan felt they had free rein to pursue their respective policies of hegemony.

ECONOMIC COLLAPSE AND SOCIAL UNREST Economic collapse and the resulting social unrest were leading causes of World War II. After World War I, U.S. investors plowed money into postwar Europe, hoping to reap huge profits as the continent rebuilt and retooled. Lured by high-flying U.S. stocks, however, speculators soon switched their investments from the rebuilding of Europe to risky ventures. On October 24, 1929, the bubble burst as the New York stock market crashed. Soon banks and financial institutions all over the world were failing: thousands of companies went out of business, millions of workers found themselves jobless, currencies plummeted in value, and fear and chaos reigned everywhere. Unemployed workers the world over began pushing their respective governments to do something about the crisis. Few governments did or could, but men who would exploit the situation for their own gain were more than eager to step in.

FASCISM From the Latin *fasces,* meaning a bundle of rods carried in ancient Rome as a symbol of authority. *Webster's Collegiate Dictionary (Tenth Edition)* defines fascism as "a political philosophy, movement, or regime that exalts nation and race above the individual and that stands for a central autocratic government headed by a dictatorial leader, severe economic and social regimentation, and forcible repression of opposition."

As a wounded veteran returning to Milan after World War I, Benito Mussolini observed the chaos tearing Italy apart: War debts had bankrupted the country, inflation was rampant, famine was widespread, strikes disrupted industry, and millions of ex-soldiers were unemployed and angry. In March 1919, Mussolini gathered the disaffected veterans and formed a new political group, the Fascio di Combattimento. Adolf Hitler was so impressed with Mussolini's style of leadership that he modeled his Nazi Party after the Fascists. (See Nazism.)

FRANCE, PREWAR Like Britain, victory in World War I had bled France white. The country had lost more than 1.3 million soldiers, and its economy, not to mention large portions of its northeastern provinces, was ruined. During the worldwide Great Depression, the unstable governments of France fell with alarming regularity; in 1933 alone, the country had five premiers. To partly offset its loss of military power, France began construction of the Maginot Line in 1929. Although its army was still large, the leadership was old and weak, the weapons and tactics were outmoded, and a deep sense of defeatism pervaded the country, leaving it vulnerable to Hitler's aggressions.

GERMANY'S EXPANSIONIST POLICIES After Hitler was appointed chancellor of Germany in 1933, one of his first acts was to flout the restrictions of the Treaty of Versailles, which had reduced the size and composition of Germany's armed forces. Hitler greatly expanded Germany's military capabilities and helped revive Depression-ravaged German industry by placing huge orders for new weapons and munitions. Germany's rearmament destabilized the balance of power in Europe and contributed to the growing tensions of the 1930s.

On March 7, 1936, to test the resolve of France and Great Britain, both of which were beset with internal problems, Hitler ordered three battalions into the Rhineland, an area that the Treaty of Versailles had expressly forbidden Germany to remilitarize (see Versailles, Treaty of, and Rhineland, Remilitarization of). When France and Britain failed to confront him, Hitler became emboldened. Later that year, he sent troops and planes to assist Francisco Franco in his bid to topple the elected government of Spain (see Chapter 4, "Allies, Enemies, and Bystanders," and Chapter 5, "Politicians and Demagogues"). Again, no one confronted Hitler.

Hitler's next move was union with a country that he believed was rightfully Germany's: his

birthplace, Austria. After Hitler had threatened the reluctant Austrian government, German troops crossed the border on March 12, 1938, and received an enthusiastic reception from the population; Hitler's first conquest was a bloodless coup. (See Anschluss; also Chapter 11, "The Home Front," and Chapter 12, "Man's Inhumanity.")

Hitler's Germany continued to expand: Nazi agitators in the German-speaking Sudetenland region of Czechoslovakia were clamoring for self-rule, claiming that the Czechs were repressing the more than three million Sudeten Germans. Trying to prevent war, the leaders of Britain and France told the Czech government that they would not assist the Czechs if Hitler invaded and urged the Czechs to meet his demands; on September 29, 1938, Britain and France signed the Munich Pact, which "gave" (even though it wasn't theirs to give) the Sudeten territory to Germany (see Munich Pact;

Strutting SA storm troopers parade past their Führer (leader), Adolf Hitler, on the streets of Nuremberg in November 1935.

Czech Crisis; also Chapter 5, "Politicians and Demagogues.")

But Hitler wanted more than the Sudetenland, and in early 1939 he bullied Czechoslovak President Emil Hacha into "inviting" German troops to cross the border (under threat of Prague's being leveled); the Czech provinces of Bohemia and Moravia—the remainder of Czechoslovakia—became German "protectorates," and Czechoslovakia ceased to exist as a nation.

Then it was time to dispose of Poland, which Hitler hated with a passion. He soon fomented a phony crisis over the port city of Danzig, which was separated from Germany proper by the Polish corridor—a strip of land that was part of the reestablishment of Poland under the Versailles Treaty. Determined to wipe Poland off the map, Hitler entered into a secret agreement with the Soviet Union: If the USSR did not interfere with Germany's invasion of Poland, Hitler would agree to partition the country, giving the Soviets the eastern third of the nation. Germany attacked Poland by air and land on September 1, 1939. (See Danzig/Polish Corridor; Polish Crisis; also Chapters 3–7, 9, and 11–13.)

Although France and Great Britain declared war on Germany two days later, Hitler refrained from attacking them immediately. Instead, in order to secure access to iron ore deposits via trade with neutral Sweden, Germany invaded Denmark and Norway on April 9, 1940. Then, on May 10, Germany violated the neutrality of the Netherlands, Belgium, and Luxembourg; on May 12, German armies outflanked the Maginot Line, invaded France through the supposedly impregnable Ardennes Forest, and drove a wedge between the French forces and a British army that had reinforced northern France. The British were forced to evacuate more than 300,000 men at Dunkirk (see Chapter 7, "Campaigns and Battles: Europe and the Atlantic"), and France formally surrendered on June 22, 1940. Germany partitioned France into a German-controlled zone in the north and west and a French-controlled zone (actually a Nazi puppet government in Vichy) in the southeast.

> Hitler knows that he will have to break us in this island or lose the war. If we can stand up to him, all Europe may be free, and the life of the world may move forward into broad, sunlit uplands; but if we fail, then the whole world, including the United States, and all that we have known and cared for, will sink into the abyss of a new dark age. . . . Let us therefore brace ourselves for our duty and so bear ourselves that if the British Commonwealth and Empire lasts for a thousand years, men will say, "This was their finest hour."
>
> —Winston Churchill,
> speech to the House of Commons,
> June 18, 1940

Hitler then concentrated on defeating Great Britain by bombing its cities and military installations, while increasing efforts to sink U.S. ships that were supplying Britain with food, ammunition, and other essential war materiel. But unable to gain the mastery of the skies that would enable him to mount an invasion, Hitler set aside his attempts to crush Britain and focused on the East. Long a proponent of Germany obtaining "living space" in Eastern Europe, he invaded the Balkans, crushing Yugoslavia in April 1941. Then, before dawn on June 22, 1941, he sent three million men crashing into the Soviet Union on a 1,000-mile front, with the mission of taking the major cities, destroying the Soviet army, and capturing the vital Caucasus oil fields. For the first six weeks, the campaign went well for the Germans. As the advance neared Moscow, however, Soviet resistance began to stiffen, the brutal Russian winter closed in, and the German offensive, code-named "Barbarossa," literally froze in its tracks (see Chapter 5, "Politicians and Demagogues," and Chapter 12, "Man's Inhumanity").

GREAT DEPRESSION See Economic Collapse and Social Unrest.

GREATER EAST ASIA CO-PROSPERITY SPHERE The name the Japanese gave to the "Southern Resources Area"—Malaya, the Philippines, Indochina, and the Dutch East Indies—which the Japanese believed they were divinely ordained to rule. To many, this term is simply a euphemism for the Japanese empire. (See also Chapter 10, "Intelligence, Espionage, and Propaganda.")

HATREDS AND GRIEVANCES In Europe and to some degree in Asia, nationalism and ethnic rivalries were causes of World War I and World War II. For example, Serbia's hatred of its domination by the Austro-Hungarian Empire led to the assassination in 1914 of Archduke Franz Ferdinand, heir to the Hapsburg throne—and touched off World War I. Hitler's racial hatred of Jews and Slavs underlay his decision to expand eastward and invade Poland and the Soviet Union. The Japanese believed they were racially superior to the Chinese and, especially, the Americans. Politically, their fury at the United States for trade embargoes and for interfering with their plans to take over Southeast Asia led to the attack on Pearl Harbor.

HEGEMONY The preponderant influence or authority of one nation over others. Examples of such relationships between nations are those of Germany, which dominated politics in neighboring Austria during the 1930s and ultimately annexed the country, and Japanese dominion over Korea, which the Japanese formally annexed in 1910. After World War I, Japan also ruled other Pacific territory under a League of Nations mandate. The quest for hegemony—Germany's drive to conquer all of Europe, and the Japanese belief in their divine right to rule all of the western Pacific and East Asia—was a contributing factor in the outbreak of war.

IMPERIALISM The advocacy, policy, or practice, of a nation of building an empire, that is, of having power and control over another nation or nations. In the context of World War II, imperialism relates most directly to aggression against sovereign states for the purpose of gaining territory or other resources.

> Italy wants peace and quiet, work and calm. I will give these things with love if possible—by force if necessary.
> —Benito Mussolini, 1922

ITALY'S EXPANSIONIST POLICIES After World War I, Italy was beset by civil unrest and a failing economy. In this atmosphere, Benito Mussolini and his party, the Fascists, set out to achieve power. In October 1922, fearing a coup, Italian King Victor Emmanuel sacked his weak prime minister and invited Mussolini to form a new government. At first, Mussolini focused on restoring stability to the country's economy and social order, but he had bigger ambitions.

Mussolini envisioned the restoration of the glory of ancient Rome through military conquest. Italy had three colonies in Africa: Libya, Eritrea, and Italian Somaliland. Three decades earlier, Abyssinia (today Ethiopia; see Chapter 7, "Politicians and Demagogues") had humiliated Italy by routing an Italian army; Mussolini decided it was time to pay back the Abyssinians. On October 2, 1935, Italy declared war on Abyssinia, and Italian divisions drove deeply into the nearly defenseless country. Despite sanctions imposed by the League of Nations, Italy's offensive continued. On May 5, 1936, Addis Ababa, the capital, fell. However, the effort had stretched Italy's resources to the maximum, and Mussolini was about to plunge into another costly adventure, this time in Spain. In the summer of 1936 he committed nearly 70,000 troops in support of Franco's revolution.

More foreign entanglements followed. On April 7, 1939, Mussolini invaded Albania, which he saw as a perfect base for future operations against Greece and Yugoslavia. On June 10, 1940, once he saw France and Britain in retreat,

Mussolini followed Hitler's lead and declared war on those two nations and, on August 4, invaded British Somaliland. In September, Italian troops based in Libya invaded British-controlled Egypt. In October, Mussolini invaded Greece—a botched operation that would go badly and require Germany's assistance.

JAPAN'S EXPANSIONIST POLICIES Japan naturally expected to be treated as an equal by the Western powers. After all, it had helped the British oust the Germans from the Chinese port city of Tsingtao in 1914 and had fought the Kaiser's troops in the German Pacific islands of the Marshalls, Ladrones, Pelews, and Carolines; after the war, the Allies mandated these islands to Japan.

> Should hostilities break out between Japan and the United States, it is not enough that we take Guam and the Philippines or even Hawaii or San Francisco. We would have to march into Washington and sign the treaty in the White House. I wonder if our politicians who speak so lightly of a Japanese-American war have confidence as to the outcome and are prepared to make the necessary sacrifices?
>
> —Admiral Isoroku Yamamoto,
> letter to Ryoichi Sasakawa,
> January 24, 1941

Japan was clearly the most powerful and prosperous nation in East Asia after World War I. International trade was booming, its factories were turning out a variety of consumer goods, its army and navy were both large and strong, and the Japanese citizen was enjoying the fruits of democracy. Japan's small landmass was insufficient to support its population, and its home islands lacked the natural resources that it required. Its ultraconservative military leaders eyed Southeast Asia, but their plans for military adventurism were scuttled in 1922 when Japan joined a disarmament treaty proposed at the Washington Naval Conference that restricted the number of warships that Japan (and the other signatories) could build and prohibited them from establishing bases in the Pacific. Matters were not helped when the U.S. Immigration Act of 1924 halted all Japanese immigration.

Rebuffed by the West, Japan again looked toward the Asian mainland and China where the Nationalists (Kuomintang) and Communists had joined forces to overthrow the warlords in the northern provinces in 1926; by 1928, the Nationalists, under Chiang Kai-shek, and Communists, under Mao Tse-tung, were battling each other across the country—an opportunity that Japan decided to exploit. Throughout the 1930s, the U.S. denounced Japanese incursions into China. The Roosevelt administration also took measures restricting trade with Japan.

At Mukden (today Shen-yang), the capital of Liaoning Province, a group of Japanese officers manufactured an incident on September 18, 1931. Claiming that an explosion on the South Manchuria Railway was the work of Chiang's guerrillas, Japan's Kwangtung Army used the event as a pretext for occupying Mukden and much of northern Manchuria.

While internecine warfare continued to rip China apart, the Japanese expanded their campaign in 1933 by invading Jehol Province. Under pressure from the League of Nations to withdraw its army, Japan instead withdrew from the League. Despite demands by Japan's civilian leaders to end the war, the military, influenced by the ambitious Colonel Hideki Tojo, among others, ignored them.

In July 1937, a skirmish between Chiang's forces and Japanese troops at the Marco Polo Bridge near Peking (today Beijing) was the excuse that Japan needed to widen the war; in mid-August, Japanese troops landed near Shanghai, and the air force bombed the city. Nanking was overrun in December, and the Japanese army brutally raped, pillaged, and burned its way through the city, murdering an estimated 300,000 men, women, and children. (See Chapter 12, "Man's Inhumanity.")

By the end of 1937, Japan controlled a large

赤魔不死大亂不止

容共抗日是滅亡中國，望速猛醒建設樂土。

A Japanese poster warns citizens of occupied China that tolerating the Communists while fighting the Japanese will lead to their ruin.

Thus emboldened, and thinking that the Soviets had the same ineffectual army that Japan had defeated in 1904, the Japanese attacked the USSR in August 1939, but the assault was decisively repulsed.

When Britain and France declared war on Germany the following month, Japan declared its neutrality. With the British and French focused on Europe, and the Netherlands occupied by the Germans, Japan saw the opportunity to invade their Southeast Asian colonies and gain control of the region's resources.

Japan's military leaders knew that such an offensive might bring them into confrontation with the United States, but they felt that they had no choice. Without the resources, Japan would be seen as a second-rate military power and would grow weaker as its potential enemies—especially the United States—grew stronger. On September 22, 1940, Japan moved to complete its occupation of Indochina, then set its sights on conquering the other nations of the region, all the while expecting the United States to intervene. (See Pearl Harbor.)

JINGOISM (INTENSE NATIONALISM) Jingoism is a condition of extreme chauvinism or nationalism marked by a belligerent foreign policy. Certainly, this definition applies to Germany, Italy, and Japan during World War II. Hitler believed that Germans were the "master race" and were destined to rule over those he considered "subhuman" which led the Nazis to attempt to eliminate Jews, Gypsies, Poles, Slavs, Russians, and other "undesirables" from the world. Mussolini and the Japanese militarists also saw themselves as leaders of a race of superior beings, which gave them the "right" to brutally subjugate any who stood in their way.

LEAGUE OF NATIONS Even before World War I, President Woodrow Wilson believed that the establishment of an international body to settle disputes and prevent future wars was essential.

portion of eastern China—from the border of Outer Mongolia to the Great Wall—and was determined to capture even more. In February 1939, Japan invaded China's Hainan Island and, the next month, took the Spratly Islands, which would make excellent air and naval bases for a thrust into Southeast Asia. Here were the riches that Japan lacked and that it needed to fulfill its plans for conquest: rubber and tin from Malaya; iron ore from the Philippines; rice from Indochina and Burma; and, from the Dutch East Indies, coal, bauxite, iron, lead, nickel, potash, phosphates, and that most precious commodity—oil. The major powers uttered a few protests when the Japanese sank British and U.S. ships in the region but did nothing to curtail Japan's aggression.

While at the Paris Peace Conference of 1919, he convinced the other Allies to adopt his vision, and they established the League in January 1920 in Geneva, Switzerland. In the end, the League proved to be little more than an international debating society. Aggressor nations routinely ignored sanctions by the League, and in the 1930s, Italy, Japan, and Germany withdrew from the organization. The United States had never joined in the first place because Congress, reflecting the public's feelings of deep isolationism, would not ratify the Versailles Treaty or accept membership in the League of Nations. The League was dissolved in 1946 after the formation of the United Nations.

I object in the strongest possible way to having the United States agree, directly or indirectly, to be controlled by a league which may at any time . . . be drawn in to deal with internal conflicts in other countries, no matter what those conflicts may be.
—Massachusetts Senator Henry Cabot Lodge, Republican majority leader, in address to the Senate, opposing President Wilson's proposal that the United States join the League of Nations, August 1919

LEBENSRAUM Literally, "living space." Hitler's excuse for invading neighboring nations, especially in the East, was that Germany needed more space for its expanding population. (See Germany's Expansionist Policies.)

LEND-LEASE Although Britain had survived the Blitz of 1940, a German invasion was still expected, and U.S. President Franklin D. Roosevelt devised a program that would help the beleaguered British; he called it "Lend-Lease," whereby the United States would "lend" ships and materiel to the British, presumably to be "returned" after the war. It was clearly a way of getting around the U.S. neutrality laws (acts that restricted trade to belligerents), but Roosevelt knew that if the United States did nothing to help Britain, Hitler might win the war. Congress had passed the first three neutrality acts between 1935 and 1937. Among other things, the 1935 act mandated that if a state of war existed anywhere in the world, the United States would cease arms shipments to any combatant. In 1936, Congress added another provision, prohibiting U.S. banks from lending money to belligerents. The 1937 act allowed warring nations to purchase nonmilitary goods from the United States but only on a cash-and-carry basis. It further forbade U.S. citizens from traveling aboard ships flying the flag of a belligerent. How could the president rally the American people—who were against yet another bloody war—to his side? Roosevelt made his case in one of his famous "fireside chats," in December 1940—equating helping the British fend off Hitler with lending a garden hose to a neighbor whose house is on fire. The American people understood the gravity of the situation, and on March 11, 1941, Congress passed the Lend-Lease Act and billions of dollars' worth of armaments were on their way to Britain and, later, to China and the Soviet Union.

The people of Europe who are defending themselves do not ask us to do their fighting—they ask us for the implements of war. . . . We must be the great arsenal of democracy.
—U.S. President Franklin D. Roosevelt, radio address, December 1940

MAGINOT LINE By the time World War I ended, the French lost approximately 70 percent of the more than eight million who had been mobilized for war. To block any future German invasion route through the provinces of Alsace and Lorraine, the French embarked on an ambitious program to build the greatest defensive fortification since the Great Wall of China. The Maginot Line (named for André Maginot, the former war minister) was to run from the Swiss border to the English Channel. In 1929, construction began on a series of interconnected, well-armed, underground fortifications that stretched for hundreds of miles and ultimately cost six billion francs. By building the Maginot Line where they did, in Alsace-Lorraine, and leaving their border with Belgium unfortified (to avoid offending the Belgians), the French practically guaranteed that the next invasion would come through Belgium.

MEIN KAMPF Adolf Hitler was sentenced to five years in prison for his part in the attempt to overthrow the Bavarian government in 1923, in the infamous Beer Hall Putsch, and he spent nine months living in relative luxury in Landsberg fortress prison. The incarceration gave him the time to compose his thoughts and put them down in a rambling, venom-filled treatise titled *Mein Kampf* ("My Struggle" or "My Battle"). In the book, which later every member of the Nazi Party was expected to own, Hitler laid down his political viewpoints and expounded on his theories of racial purity and Aryan supremacy, Germany's destiny to rule the world, and the elimination of the Jews.

> Wherever I went, I began to see Jews, and the more I saw, the more sharply they became distinguished in my eyes from the rest of humanity. . . . Gradually, I began to hate them. For me, this was the time of the greatest spiritual upheaval I have ever had to go through. I had ceased to be a weak-kneed cosmopolitan and became an anti-Semite.   —Adolf Hitler, *Mein Kampf*, 1923

MUNICH PACT In September 1938, in an attempt to prevent a war, British Prime Minister Neville Chamberlain and French Premier Edouard Daladier flew to Germany—first to Bad Godesberg and then on a second trip to Munich. By allowing Hitler to occupy the Sudetenland in exchange for a promise of no wider conflict, Chamberlain and Daladier believed they could avert war. Thoroughly browbeaten by Hitler, Chamberlain returned to England with Hitler's signed pledge that Germany and Britain would never again go to war with each other. "It is peace for our time," Chamberlain proclaimed, and the free world cheered with relief. The pledge, as events would soon disclose, was literally not worth the paper on which it was printed. (See Appeasement; Czech Crisis.)

MUNICH BEER HALL PUTSCH In September 1923, the German Republic was in a state of crisis. Inflation had virtually destroyed the economy, monarchists were attempting to bring down the elected government of German President Friedrich Ebert, and Chancellor Gustav Stresemann had announced a resumption of reparations payments and the end of passive resistance against the French who were occupying the Ruhr (see War Reparations). The German nationalists and Communists were outraged, and they both denounced the government at Weimar. To head off the expected violent protests and to restore order, Ebert declared a state of emergency, and the Reichstag passed an act that gave the army near dictatorial powers in running the country.

The government of the state of Bavaria, however, refused to accept this decree and declared its own state of emergency, named right-wing monarchist Gustav von Kahr as Bavarian state commissioner, and granted him widespread power. Worried that Bavaria might secede, restore the monarchy, and form an independent state with Austria, Berlin tried to impose its will on the Bavarian government; Kahr refused to yield.

Hitler, who had been waiting for an opportunity to seize power, took the offensive. By enlisting the support of the Bavarian police and army units, Hitler, backed by his SA (Sturmabteilungen or storm troopers), decided to kidnap the leaders of the Bavarian government and take control of the state. On November 8, while Kahr and other government leaders were addressing a large crowd at a beer hall in Munich, an armed Hitler and his SA thugs broke in, arrested the leaders, and proclaimed a Nazi takeover of

Bavaria. While much of Hitler's act was a bluff, he was convincing enough—with a pistol in his hand—to persuade Kahr and the others to join his revolution. He planned to march on Berlin and overthrow the national government.

Once Berlin learned of the coup, or *Putsch* in German, Ebert's government began assembling troops to suppress it. The next day, Hitler, accompanied by the World War I hero General Erich Ludendorff and several hundred armed Nazis, marched toward the center of Munich but soon were halted by a line of police. Gunfire broke out, and by the end of the confrontation 16 Nazis and three police lay dead or dying in the street; Hitler fled but was later arrested and sentenced to a light prison term. While in prison, he wrote *Mein Kampf* (see above). Hitler's "brav-ery" and fierce nationalism during the Munich Beer Hall Putsch made him a national figure in Germany.

NAZISM   The political, social, and economic doctrines of the National Socialist German Workers' Party, or Nazis, for short. Within this totalitarian form of government, the leader (or *Führer*) was all-powerful; the state controlled all aspects of the economy, information, and individual lives and promulgated the idea that the pure Aryan or Nordic race was superior to all others.

NUREMBERG LAWS   Once Hitler was the supreme authority in Germany, he instituted a series of repressive reforms, known as the

---

FRED C. PATHEIGER, 101ST AIRBORNE DIVISION

A German Fighting for the Allies

I was born on December 22, 1919, in Rastatt, Germany. When Hitler got into power, my mother, grandmother, and aunt had to join the [Nazi] party. I had to join the Hitler Youth or I couldn't have gone to school, and so forth and so on, and I discovered one day, while [still] a youngster crawling into the living room and listening to them speak, that, much to my amazement, my grandfather on my mother's side was Jewish, which I had no idea of, and which really did not matter to me, although the anti-Semitic feeling existed in Germany. . . .

My aunt went with a fellow. They were going to get married, and she owned up to him about her background. And when he found out that her father had been Jewish, well, that was it. He reported it, and we were all in trouble. We had to get out of the party, I had to get out of the Hitler Youth. Now this was in about the mid-thirties, and, of course, I continued to go to school, and my mother made overtures to distant relatives over here in Chicago to get me out of the country. Of course, I would have been nothing but cannon fodder.

The others remained over there. We tried to get them over here, but the Nazis kept bringing one obstacle after another. Then . . . we finally had everything set well, just before Pearl Harbor, and made arrangements to bring them over here via Japan, but then Pearl Harbor happened, and that did not work out. . . . They succumbed in the concentration camps later on. I did not learn this until after the war from other remote relatives.

Anyway . . . I wanted to get into the service, so I went to my draft board and registered, classified 1-A. No, first of all, I was classified as an enemy alien. . . . At that time, it took ten years to become a citizen. I came over here in '38. So I wrote to J. Edgar Hoover of the FBI and told him why I wanted to get into the service. I felt I wasn't fighting the German people but Nazism, and [I told him about] what had happened to me over there. So he wrote me a very nice letter stating that it was out of his hands, unfortunately; however, I should go to my draft board and fill out an alien's acceptability form.

—**Eisenhower Center for American Studies Archives**

Nuremberg Laws (1935), whose purpose was to strip Germany's Jews of their rights and citizenship; eliminate them from the military, civil service jobs, and teaching positions; and prohibit marriage between Jews and Aryans. As the years went by, the Nuremberg Laws left the Jews defenseless against Nazi thuggery.

PARIS PEACE CONFERENCE OF 1919
The representatives of World War I's four major victors—France, Great Britain, Italy, and the United States—gathered at the Palace of Versailles outside Paris to decide the fate of Germany, which the Allies blamed for starting the war. President Woodrow Wilson led the U.S. delegation toward what he hoped would be a just and lasting peace.

Wilson proposed a list of "Fourteen Points"—including setting up of the League of Nations that would prevent future wars by settling international disputes through peaceful means. But the other nations, bitter from the bloody toll of the war, were out to punish Germany, and to them the Fourteen Points were not severe enough. To make certain that Germany could never again threaten the peace of Europe, the Great Powers developed and adopted the Treaty of Versailles (see Versailles, Treaty of), which was designed to reduce Germany to a minor power.

PEARL HARBOR By early 1941, Japan's military leaders believed that a preemptive strike against U.S. military facilities in the Pacific would be necessary to gain a quick victory and prevent the United States from interfering with Japan's plans for the domination of Asia. The main target was the huge U.S. naval base at Pearl Harbor, Oahu, Hawaii. Admiral Isoroku Yamamoto was chosen to formulate the attack, and training for the operation soon began.

In May 1941, Yamamoto presented his plan to the Naval General Staff, most of whom were unenthusiastic about a mission that they regarded as too risky. Few thought that the bulk of the Japanese fleet could sail 4,000 miles undetected and launch a successful surprise attack against the mightiest base of the United States. But Yamamoto's plan gained a major supporter in October when Premier Fumimaro Konoye was forced to resign and was replaced by the hard-liner General Hideki Tojo, who also named himself minister of war.

Plans for the Pearl Harbor strike plunged ahead. The planners decided that the naval task force of six carriers and other escort vessels would take a northern route. U.S. reconnaissance flights from Hawaii rarely patrolled north of the islands because the U.S. military considered those sea lanes too rough to ever be used as an attack route. The task force sailed from Tankan Bay in the Kuriles on November 26. The plan to cripple the U.S. fleet—called Operation Z—was under way.

In the meantime, Japanese Ambassador Kichisaburo Nomura was in Washington, D.C., along with special envoy Saburo Kurusu, hoping to negotiate a settlement of the differences between his country and the United States. On December 1, the United States intercepted a message from Tokyo directing all diplomatic and consular posts to destroy their codes, ciphers, and classified documents—an obvious sign an attack was imminent. However, the United States did not know exactly when or where it would take place, since decoded Japanese messages referred to multiple targets, such as messages asked Pearl Harbor, Manila, Panama, and even Seattle. The United States mistakenly thought the U.S. interests, including Pearl Harbor, were too strong to be attacked.

At dawn on Sunday, December 7, 1941, the first wave of fighters, torpedo planes, dive-bombers, and high-altitude bombers, launched from aircraft carriers 200 miles to the north, began streaming over Oahu and heading for Pearl Harbor. At 7:40 A.M., with no U.S. planes challenging him, the mission leader issued the code "Tora! Tora! Tora!" ("Tiger! Tiger! Tiger!") informing the fleet that the attack indeed was a surprise. Some planes peeled off to strafe airfields and army installations, while others dove straight for the battleships and smaller warships sitting in the shallow harbor. The first bombs fell shortly before 8:00 A.M. Once the Americans realized that this was not a surprise training maneuver, they sprang to their guns and fought back. A few U.S. planes even managed to scramble and engage the enemy in the air.

At about 8:05, an armor-piercing bomb dropped onto the battleship *Arizona*'s forecastle, penetrated its decks, and detonated in its forward magazine, instantly killing 1,177 of the *Arizona*'s crew and marine detachment.

The message went out: "Air raid Pearl Harbor. This is no drill." The raid continued unabated for two hours. By the time the final wave of Japanese planes had flown off to the north, they had sunk or badly damaged 20 American ships, including 8 battleships, and had destroyed most U.S. aircraft on the ground. Fortunately for the United States, the precious aircraft carriers that Yamamoto had hoped to catch at Pearl Harbor were far out at sea, untouched. The Japanese also attacked U.S. installations at Midway on December 7; the following day, Guam and Wake Island also felt Japan's fury. On December 8, Congress declared war on Japan.

The United States had suffered a devastating blow but one from which it would recover: even many ships thought to be damaged beyond

---

LOUIS MATHIESON, USS *OKLAHOMA*

As Pearl Harbor Is Attacked

Saturday, December 6, 1941, I had duty. My watches were from four p.m. to eight p.m., and four a.m. to eight a.m., December 7, 1941, in the ice machines. As I was looking forward to making the eight a.m. liberty boat ashore, my relief, Mike Galajdik, relieved me fifteen minutes early. I took my clothes off and placed them in my locker (my locker was located in the ice machine room). Wrapped a towel around me and with my shoes on, a bar of soap in my hand, I headed for the engineers' showers on the main deck, starboard side of the ship. That meant going up three decks to the main deck.

My brother Harry arrived at the same time, coming from the evaporators. We were just about to enter the shower when the general alarm went off. Our first reaction was consternation. Why would the officers call general quarters on a Sunday morning? Suddenly, the officer of the deck came on the intercom: "All hands, man your battle stations! Goddamn it, get going! This is it!" Just then, "BOOM!" The ship seemed to dip forward a little. Actually, the bow came up. I grabbed my shoes and towel and ran for my battle station, Repair Number Five in the machine shop. It was located just aft of the ice machines and just over the port and starboard engine rooms. Arriving there, my job was to close the armor hatch to the main deck when the station was fully manned.

Then we were hit by another torpedo. It must have hit us, as the ship seemed to leap up about a foot and a half, or maybe just the deck under me. The noise was horrendous. There were two explosions. I can recall seven torpedo hits in all. Years later, I learned we were hit by nine torpedoes. Some of these hits were simultaneous. With the second hit, my feet were knocked out from under me, and I landed on the deck. At this time I was really getting excited, my mind seemed to be whizzing so bad I thought it was going to explode. I wanted to cry, but I had to control it.

The lights went out, [then] they seemed to come back on again. Then another torpedo hit, and they went out for good. All of this was taking place at once. I thought I was going to die at any moment.

—Eisenhower Center for American Studies Archives

repair would sail again to inflict punishment on the Japanese and Germans in the months and years ahead.

AMERICAN CASUALTIES AT PEARL HARBOR, OAHU, HAWAII, DECEMBER 7, 1941

	Killed, Missing, and Died of Wounds	Wounded
Navy	2,008	710
Marine Corps	109	69
Army	218	364
Civilians	68	35
Totals	2,403	1,178

Source: Gordon William Prange, *At Dawn We Slept* (New York: Penguin, reprint ed. 1991), p. 539.

POLISH CORRIDOR See Danzig/Polish Corridor.

POLISH CRISIS Of all the states created at Versailles, Poland generated the least enthusiasm among the Western powers. Besides having few friends in the West, anti-Bolshevik Poland was despised by Stalin, and war between Poland and the Soviet Union seemed a genuine possibility. In April 1939, Hitler renounced the nonaggression pact that Germany had signed with Poland (see Chapter 4, "Allies, Enemies, and Bystanders"), and Polish leaders, convinced that Hitler would back down once confronted with a show of force, vowed to resist if German troops attempted to take Danzig (Gdansk). For its part, Poland agreed to a mutual assistance pact with Britain and France. Although Britain and France had no great love for Poland, they knew that German expansion had to be stopped.

By August 1939, tensions had become unbearable. The Vatican was urging Poland to avoid war by giving Danzig and the Polish Corridor to Germany; the German training ship *Schleswig-Holstein* entered the harbor at Danzig in a show of gunboat diplomacy; and the United States was asking all parties to step back from the brink. Hitler's generals continued to remind their Führer that Germany was not yet ready for war. Final calls for a negotiated settlement mediated by Britain were made; Hitler countered with a demand that the Poles send a plenipotentiary to Berlin to take part in direct talks.

With tensions high and uncertainty in the air, Britain and France began mobilizing. Geographically situated between two adversaries, Poland (and the rest of the world) was stunned when, on August 22, Germany and the Soviet Union concluded a nonaggression pact (formally, the Molotov-Ribbentrop Pact, or Nazi-Soviet Nonaggression Pact; see Chapter 4, "Allies, Enemies, and Bystanders"). What the Poles did not know was that Stalin had agreed to look the other way if Hitler chose to attack and bring down the Polish state in return for substantial amounts of Polish territory once the country was carved up. The Soviets agreed to actually invade Poland from the east.

Hitler decided to manufacture a scenario that would "justify" his invasion. In his script, the Poles would attack the German radio station at Gleiwitz on the evening of August 31. Playing the part of the Poles were SS troops costumed in Polish army uniforms. They fired a few bullets, made some noise, and killed a few "Germans"—in this case, drugged concentration camp inmates in German uniforms—and delivered an anti-German speech in Polish over the radio before the transmitter went dead. At 4:45 the next morning, September 1, 1939, the *Schleswig-Holstein* opened up on Polish military installations in Danzig, and at dawn German divisions poured across the borders.

Polish resistance was brave but futile; the Poles were outnumbered in tanks six to one; in planes four to one; in artillery three to one. Colorful ranks of lancers on horseback were no match for machine guns, Polish cities crumbled under Luftwaffe bombs, and German armored columns moved swiftly toward Warsaw. Within three weeks, the Germans had defeated the Polish army—about 40 divisions strong; on September 27, after weeks of furious combat and bombardment, Warsaw fell.

Britain and France demanded that Germany withdraw. When Hitler failed to respond, both nations declared war on Germany on September 3. The Anglo-French response took Hitler by surprise, for he had completely miscalculated the two nations' resolve. Another full-scale war in Western Europe had begun.

REICHSTAG FIRE On February 27, 1933, the Reichstag (German parliament) building in Berlin burned under suspicious circumstances. For propaganda purposes, Hitler blamed the fire on a mentally deficient Dutch Communist (whom the Nazis undoubtedly hired to do the job), declared a state of emergency, and gave the storm troopers the police power to arrest anyone and imprison them. Hitler used the arson to make a case that the Communists were a threat to peace and stability in Germany and to convince the middle and lower classes that, unless they voted for the Nazis at the upcoming parliamentary elections, the Communists would take over Germany. Despite the intimidation, the voters in March 1933 still refused to give the Nazis a clear majority. Hitler then asked parliament to give him absolute power to run the government. After the Nazis arrested the Communists and other members of parliament whom they suspected would oppose Hitler, the pro-Nazi members passed the Enabling Act that essentially ceded unlimited "emergency" powers to Hitler for five years. Every five years, for the remainder of Hitler's regime, the puppet Reichstag dutifully renewed the Enabling Act and extended the emergency powers.

THE RHINELAND, REMILITARIZATION OF In the winter of 1935–36, angered by France's treaty with the Soviets, Hitler declared invalid the 1925 Locarno Pact, an agreement by which the nations of Europe guaranteed their respective borders. With France and Britain preoccupied with Italy's invasion of Abyssinia, Hitler persuaded his nervous general who feared massive military retaliation by France, to reintroduce troops into the Rhineland, in direct contravention of the Treaty of Versailles. On March 2, 1936, three German battalions marched in to the cheers of the citizens. France asked Britain for help in countering this move but was rebuffed. The West's failure to act was a signal for even greater German aggression in the future.

RUSSO-FINNISH WAR Using the world's fixation with the Polish crisis as a cover, the Soviet Union demanded territorial concessions from neighboring Finland; the Finns refused. On November 30, 1939, Russian planes bombed Helsinki, and 600,000 Soviet troops crossed the border. Although greatly outnumbered, the Finns inflicted heavy casualties on the Soviets until the Finns were forced to surrender in March 1940 (see Chapter 4, "Allies, Enemies, and Bystanders"). In 1941, part of the German invasion of the Soviet Union came through Finland, and Finland joined the Germans in the assault; the Soviets replied by bombing Finnish cities.

SIEGFRIED LINE (WEST WALL) Germany's answer to France's Maginot Line (see above), the Siegfried Line was a line of fortresses, pillboxes, minefields, and antitank obstacles designed to stop (or at least slow) any invasion of Germany from occupied France.

SITZKRIEG ("PHONY WAR") Sitzkrieg literally means "sitting war" and describes the period between the time France and Great Britain declared war on Germany (September 1939) and the actual outbreak of the fighting (the German invasion of Denmark and Norway in April 1940). The three nations mobilized their armies and put their factories into full wartime production, but except for some artillery shelling along the Maginot Line, no real combat took place at this time.

SOCIAL UNREST See Economic Collapse and Social Unrest.

SOVIET UNION, PREWAR After the Bolshevik Revolution of 1917, the new Soviet Union withdrew from World War I. Under Lenin's direction, the new nation signed an armistice with Germany on March 3, 1918, at Brest-Litovsk. One of Germany's major foes was out of action.

After Lenin died in 1924, he was succeeded by his party secretary, Josef Stalin. Stalin, a master manipulator and schemer, destroyed anyone who dared challenge him. Eventually, he ruled with absolute power. To overcome any real or imagined opposition to his rule, in 1935 he initiated a purge of Communist Party members and military officers; about 700,000 met their deaths. He sent millions more whom he suspected of disloyalty to concentration camps or had them executed.

Although Germany and the Soviet Union were bitter rivals, in August 1939 Stalin and Hitler signed a nonaggression pact for the purpose of carving up Poland between them (see Chapter 4, "Allies, Enemies, and Bystanders"). For Hitler, this was a ruse that lulled the Soviet Union into lowering its guard; on June 22, 1941, three million German troops invaded the Soviet Union. The defenders were sent reeling and the German forces plunged deeply into that vast country.

An unexpected result of Germany's assault on the Soviet Union was that the British, fiercely anti-Communist, had now gained an unlikely ally, the Soviets, early in the war with Germany. Also, the United States extended the Lend-Lease program to the Soviets. The Germans were practically at Moscow's gates in December 1941 when the brutal winter weather halted the German advance, just as it had stopped Napoleon's more than a century earlier.

SPANISH CIVIL WAR Like many other European nations after World War I, Spain was a country in crisis. Agricultural laborers and urban workers were in revolt, and economic depression was pervasive. With armed insurrection a distinct possibility, King Alfonso XIII agreed to general elections in 1931, with the consequence that the newly elected republican government forced his abdication. Acts of violence swiftly followed; riots raged in the major cities as agricultural workers burned churches and lynched their landlords, army officers joined right-wing organizations to oppose the republican government, and movements to restore the monarchy sprang up. General elections in 1936 brought more chaos, as left-wing candidates came to power. Political assassinations multiplied, and the country appeared to be headed for catastrophe.

It was during this upheaval that Generalissimo Francisco Franco appeared as a savior—or at least as someone with enough power to overthrow the republic and restore order. Taking advantage of the turmoil in July 1936, two other officers joined Franco, the former commander of the Spanish Foreign Legion, in a coup attempt. Franco gave the signal for his followers to reclaim Spain for the monarchists, and Spain exploded into a savage civil war. Franco asked Mussolini and Hitler for military aid, and both men responded with troops, planes, and other armaments. Eventually, 6,000 Germans and 60,000 Italians fought in Spain.

The Loyalists—those factions, generally on the political Left, who were dedicated to the preservation of the republic—appealed to the West for help. France sent weapons and 200 planes; Britain and the United States sent only food and clothing. Volunteers from several nations, including the United States, Canada, and France, arrived to bolster the left-wing Loyalist forces. The Soviet Union also sent men and materiel in the battle between bolshevism and fascism.

Franco asked the German Condor Legion to help him bomb into submission his foes in the northern provinces. One of the worst incidents occurred in the Basque town of Guernica when, on April 26, 1937, German bombers flattened the town and killed or wounded about 2,500 inhabitants. The world was appalled but did nothing.

The civil war, which claimed more than 600,000 lives, ended on March 30, 1939, when the last of the Loyalist holdouts gave up. A new dictatorship in Europe was born, and Franco rewarded Hitler's help by granting Germany access to Spain's deposits of iron ore and magnesium. The Spanish Civil War gave Hitler and Mussolini the opportunity to flex their military muscle in preparation for a later war. And, presumably, it gave them an ally in Western Europe. Franco, however, unlike Mussolini, kept his distance from Hitler's aggressive ventures, and as a result, he and his regime survived into the 1970s.

TRADE EMBARGOES AGAINST JAPAN A major flashpoint between the United States and Japan was the trade embargoes that the United States had imposed as punishment for Japanese aggression in Asia, especially its rampage thoughout China and Southeast Asia. After Japan occupied Indochina in 1940, Congress enacted a law that forbade the export to Japan of vital minerals and chemicals, aircraft parts, and equipment; additionally, the government froze Japanese assets in the United States. On August 1, the United States and Great Britain also punished Japan with a total ban on the importation of oil.

In exchange for lifting the embargoes, the United States demanded that Japan pull its troops out of China and Indochina. Such conditions were unacceptable to Japan. Giving in to U.S. demands would involve a tremendous loss of face—not to mention a waste of all the blood and money that Japan had expended in those operations. President Franklin D. Roosevelt suspected that Japan might attempt to seize the oil that it needed and vainly sought to convene a conference at which peaceful negotiations might replace war.

The Americans had broken the secret Japanese diplomatic code and were reading messages passing back and forth between Tokyo and the Japanese diplomatic service. On July 31, 1941, Japan's Foreign Ministry sent an ominous message to Ambassadors Hiroshi Oshima in Berlin and Nomura in Washington that read, in part: "Commercial and economic relations between Japan and third countries, led by England and the United States, are gradually becoming so horribly strained that we cannot endure it much longer. Consequently, our Empire, to save its very life, must take measures to secure the raw materials of the South Seas. Our Empire must immediately take steps to break asunder this ever-strengthening chain of encirclement which is being woven under the guidance and with the participation of England and the United States, acting like a cunning dragon seemingly asleep." It was an ominous message, one that the United States failed to comprehend fully. Pearl Harbor was attacked three months later.

U.S. ISOLATION After World War I, a large majority of Americans believed that the country had been dragged into a foreign conflict that was none of its business. Although President Woodrow Wilson had advocated continued U.S. participation in world affairs, he was unable to convince the Republican-controlled Congress and they refused his call to join the League of Nations in 1919. For the next two decades, the United States was not officially involved in politics beyond its borders. This policy of isolation was not in itself a cause of World War II, but the U.S. absence from the League of Nations made that body weaker than it might otherwise have been.

Moreover, the United States, because of its postwar isolationism, was supremely unprepared for the coming war. In 1940, the U.S. Army was only the 18th largest in the world. The industrial sector was still trying to emerge from the morass of the Depression and produced few tanks or warplanes—and those it did produce were far inferior to German and Japanese armaments. Except for President Franklin D. Roosevelt and Army Chief of Staff George C. Marshall, few

Americans seemed terribly concerned; even the secretary of war, Henry Woodring, was an isolationist, and well-known personalities such as the aviator Charles Lindbergh and John L. Lewis, head of the Congress of Industrial Organizations, argued against U.S. involvement in the world's troubles.

The United States had been reluctant to prepare for war. Isolationist sentiment lingered, and Britain and eventually the Soviet Union would receive massive amounts of aid through lend-lease.

But once France fell in June 1940 and Britain was forced to retreat at Dunkirk, the United States realized that war with Germany or Japan—or both—was not far off, and the country began inexorably to move itself onto a war footing. On September 16, 1940, Roosevelt authorized measures that placed four national guard divisions on full-time status for a year. Factories and shipyards that had been building tanks, trucks, and warships stepped up production. In October, the United States drafted the first of 10 million men into the military in preparation for the coming ordeal.

VERSAILLES, TREATY OF In June 1919, representatives of the four major victorious nations (France, Great Britain, Italy, and the United States) met at Versailles, outside Paris, to develop a treaty that would end the war and determine Germany's future role in the world. U.S. President Woodrow Wilson, fearful that too onerous a treaty would only embitter Germany and lead to a new war, advocated less harsh terms, but his efforts were unsuccessful. The other victors were hell-bent on having Germany pay for the staggering number of human lives lost and the devastation of much of northeastern France. The war had wiped whole cities, towns, and villages from the map, destroyed industries, and left roads, bridges, and railroads unusable, while Germany was physically untouched. The total material cost of the war was estimated at $337 billion.

As Wilson feared, the 230-page treaty humbled and humiliated Germany. The Allies stripped Germany of its African colonies and mandated its Pacific colonies—the Marshalls, Marianas, and Carolines—to Japan's control; New Zealand and Australia received German Samoa and German New Guinea, respectively. The treaty also required Germany to return the provinces of Alsace and Lorraine to France. To rebuild France, and to compensate the victorious nations for their expenditure of lives and treasure, Versailles required the Germans to pay huge reparations for the reconstruction of Belgium and northern France. But the victors could not agree on a total sum, a task they left to a Reparations Committee.

Versailles also demilitarized the Rhineland and placed it and the Saar regions under Allied occupation for as long as 15 years, and it imposed serious restrictions on Germany's military capabilities by limiting it to a 100,000-man army with no warplanes or tanks and a navy with no more than six battleships. Finally, the treaty resurrected the nation of Poland and specified that the former East Prussian port city of Danzig would be cut off from the rest of Germany by a strip of land that was mandated to Poland, thus giving Poland access to the Baltic Sea. (See Danzig/Polish Corridor; League of Nations; Paris Peace Conference of 1919; War Reparations. See also Chapter 4, "Allies, Enemies, and Bystanders.")

WAR REPARATIONS As an advance on the later-to-be-determined reparations resulting from the Treaty of Versailles, the Allies billed the Germans 20 billion gold marks ($5 billion). Eventually, the victors determined that Germany owed a total of $35 billion, which was to be paid at a rate of $500 million per year. The Germans were stunned and outraged, but as the vanquished they had nothing to say in the matter. Britain and the United States were eager to see the German economy resuscitated in order to have another international trading partner; the

French, on the other hand, were more concerned about security and preferred that their neighbor be economically incapable of ever rearming.

For a few months, Germany did pay, but then stopped. By the end of 1921, it had defaulted, and the Allies granted one deferment and moratorium after another. In 1923, runaway inflation on a scale never before seen was ravaging the German economy, and the German mark became worthless almost overnight. Suddenly, German consumers needed millions of marks to buy even the most basic staples, such as milk and bread, and inflation instantly wiped out the savings of the normally frugal German middle class.

In 1923, the French, pressured by the Americans and British, agreed to grant Germany a two-year moratorium on reparations to allow it to accumulate enough capital to resume paying its debt. French Premier Raymond Poincaré proposed to his Anglo-American counterparts that nearly two-thirds of the total be floated as bonds to pay France's war debt to the United States and Great Britain, with the other third, 50 billion gold marks, paid directly as reparations, much of it to France. The British vetoed this idea, so Poincaré ordered French troops into the Ruhr, Germany's industrial heartland, to seize coal mines and steel mills. Although the Versailles Treaty gave France every right to do this, Britain and the United States—along with Germany—denounced French "aggression."

More relief for Germany was on the way. In 1924, the Dawes Plan reduced Germany's annual payments; the Young Plan in 1929 cut them even more. The United States then began pressing its allies—Britain and France—to repay their war debts. Britain had borrowed $4 billion from the United States and France $3.5 billion. Both countries had asked the United States to cancel their debts, as the loans had gone toward the common victory, and both nations were stunned when President Woodrow Wilson and his successors in the 1920s rejected the idea. Britain reluctantly agreed to pay its debt (whose interest

had swelled to $11 billion) over 62 years, while the French agreed to pay nearly $7 billion. Ironically, Germany borrowed billions from U.S. bankers and investors to pay its debts and never paid a pfennig from it own resources.

The issue of war reparations—or rather, the way they were portrayed in Germany by the Nazis—was one of the elements that destabilized the Weimar Republic and led to Hitler's rise to power.

WEIMAR REPUBLIC In November 1918, German workers and soldiers in Kiel revolted against the continuation of World War I. The rebellion quickly spread to other cities, and Kaiser Wilhelm II fled to exile in Holland on November 9; two days later, the armistice went into effect, but street fighting between factions of the extreme Left and Right threatened to tear Germany apart. To save the nation, a republic was declared in January 1919, and the Germans elected a national assembly that met in Weimar, near Berlin. Thus, the moderate government, headed by Friedrich Ebert, became known as the Weimar Republic. But a staunch monarchist sentiment remained within Germany, undermining the new government's authority.

The challenges for a fledgling democracy were numerous. At the heart of German discontent was the widespread belief that the army, undefeated on the battlefield, had been undone by internal enemies—primarily Bolsheviks and Jews. Furthermore, the crushing weight of the Treaty of Versailles had created a deep resentment within the German people against their conquerors, especially the French. In 1923, runaway inflation ravaged the German economy, and the government appeared ready to fall. In 1923, however, Gustav Stresemann, a Reichstag deputy and founder of the right-liberal German People's Party, became chancellor and restored some degree of order. The next year, the Great Powers reduced their demands for reparations, and at the Locarno Conference of 1925 Stresemann signed treaties with France and Great Britain that improved Germany's relations with them. The Weimar government might have succeeded in bringing about permanent stability in Germany had the worldwide economic depression not unraveled everything and allowed Hitler and his Nazi Party to come to power.

> The world must be made safe for democracy.
> —U.S. President Woodrow Wilson, 1917

WORLD WAR I AND ITS STAGGERING COST On June 28, 1914, in the Bosnian capital of Sarajevo, the fanatical Serbian nationalist Gavrilo Princip assassinated Archduke Francis Ferdinand, heir to the throne of the Austro-Hungarian Empire. Princip's act triggered a chain reaction: A belligerent Germany encouraged Austria-Hungary to declare war on Serbia, which in turn brought Russia in on Serbia's side. This alliance angered Germany, which then declared war on Russia; France allied itself with Russia, causing Germany to declare war on France. After Germany violated neutral Belgium to invade northeastern France, Great Britain declared war on both Germany and Austria-Hungary. A localized Balkan dispute suddenly exploded into a massive conflict that led to billions of dollars of property damage, a nearly inconceivable death toll, and an even more terrible future war. World War I bled Europe dry, leaving both the victors and vanquished economically ravaged, demoralized, and politically unstable. In this atmosphere, another war became more likely.

WORLD WAR I CASUALTIES

The Allies	Killed	Wounded	Missing
Belgium	45,500	78,600	74,000
France (and colonies)	1,368,000	3,600,000	557,000
Great Britain (including Canada, Ireland, and colonies)	942,000	2,111,000	198,000
Greece	23,000	14,150	1,000
Italy	680,000	947,000	600,000
Japan	1,350	11,900	x
Montenegro	3,000	10,000	7,000
Portugal	8,150	14,780	x
Romania	300,000	105,000	80,000
Russia	1,700,000	4,950,000	2,500,000
x = Unavailable			

Source: *World Book Encyclopedia*

The Allies	Killed	Wounded	Missing
Serbia	45,000	133,000	153,000
United States	116,500	204,000	4,500
Subtotals	**5,229,500**	**12,179,430**	**4,174,500**
The Central Powers			
Austria-Hungary	1,200,000	3,620,000	2,200,000
Bulgaria	87,500	155,000	13,700
Germany	1,935,000	4,216,000	990,000
Ottoman Empire	725,000	1,565,000	x
Subtotals	**3,947,500**	**9,556,000**	**3,203,700**
Totals	**9,177,000**	**21,735,430**	**7,378,200**
x = Unavailable			

Source: *World Book Encyclopedia*

CHAPTER 3

The Economics of World War II

BUY WAR BONDS

How did nations in the depths of economic crisis create vast supplies of modern weaponry? And how did they finance total war? How did Germany, in particular, manage to keep military production at relatively high levels throughout the war, even though Allied bombers regularly destroyed factories and advancing Allied troops cut supply lines? The economic catastrophe of the 1930s was one of the root causes of war—the social and political unrest created by a worldwide depression gave birth to political extremists like Hitler and Mussolini. And ironically, it was war that ended the Great Depression as nations geared up their manufacturing industries and provided full employment to their underworked citizens.

The Depression had savaged the world's economies beginning in the early 1930s. By 1932, about three million people in Great Britain were unemployed. By February 1933, the U.S. unemployment rate was an astounding 28 percent. But no nation at that time was suffering as much as Germany. The export-oriented economy found its foreign markets disappearing. Banks failed, businesses went bankrupt, and unemployment in 1933 soared to 30 percent, making the German people turn toward radical political leadership. Enter Adolf Hitler.

In many ways the economic history of World War II comes down to an economic battle: the United States versus Germany—and the United States versus Japan. Flouting the restrictions of the Treaty of

Versailles, Hitler helped revive German industry by placing massive orders for weapons and munitions beginning in 1933. Although Germans soon had jobs, shortages continued—war production had shoved aside the production of consumer goods. To finance its war machine, the Reich printed money that was used only internally and off budget, causing other European nations to fail to detect the secretly financed military buildup. Germany also raised sales and income taxes (as well as other taxes), and pushed its corporate tax rate as high as 30 percent of earnings.

In 1939 the economic hardships faced by Japan, which had been run by a military government since 1932, stemmed not from the Depression but from a trade embargo established by the United States in reaction to Japan's expansionism in China. Japan had a fairly elementary solution for getting what it needed to run its war: invasion. But invasion is expensive. By 1943, the Japanese economy had mostly collapsed, and Japanese civilians, who had never been enthusiastic about the war, bore shortages that included their dietary staple of rice.

In the United States, when Franklin D. Roosevelt took the oath of office in March 1933, the nation's economy was reeling from the ham-handed efforts of Herbert Hoover and Congress to deal with the economic disaster in which 10,000 banks had failed. Roosevelt's New Deal programs attempted to restructure the economy and put people back to work, but by 1940, when the government began to quietly put the United States on a war footing, unemployment was still nearly 15 percent.

The United States ran huge deficits during the war years, borrowing from private banks and the Federal Reserve Bank to fund the war. The U.S. government raised income taxes—and for the first time levied them from ordinary Americans, not only the wealthiest. But also fueling the wartime economy—and war production itself—was the American can-do spirit. The productive engines of U.S. capitalism created war goods at fantastic rates. The Americans kept themselves and their armed forces of 15 million men and women fed and equipped and created $48 billion worth of food and other goods (approximately $480 billion in today's dollars) that were shipped to Allied nations during the conflict. As in World War I, the United States made the difference for the victorious Allies.

Prewar Economic Conditions

World War II began at the end of the Great Depression, which meant that poverty and unemployment still affected the populations of the belligerent nations. However, the industrial bases of these nations were relatively intact and once war began they committed large portions of their economies to making war goods. The capsule national profiles that follow describe conditions leading up to the war through its conclusion. The nations are listed alphabetically.

GERMANY

Of all the major powers in World War II, Germany should have been least prepared for war. First, Germany suffered more than any industrialized nation from the ravages of the Depression. Second, Germany went into the Depression with a less productive economy than its European neighbors did, and the German people had been vulnerable to economic hardships brought on, for example, by rampant inflation in the 1920s.

Nevertheless, by the time Germany invaded Poland on September 1, 1939, the Wehrmacht was a disciplined, well-equipped army that first overwhelmed the Poles, then French and British troops. For much of the 1930s, Germany concentrated much of its productive power on making war goods. German industries reached full capacity making state-of-the art guns, cannons, tanks, airplanes, and other war materiel.

GREAT BRITAIN

Unlike the United States, Great Britain had pulled out of the Depression by the mid-1930s, although high tariffs and a sluggish U.S. economy limited how much the businesses of the British Isles could export abroad. Yet Britain was not as well prepared for war as its economy would have allowed.

Although its geography as a relatively small island nation made Britain vulnerable to disruption of its shipping through German submarine warfare, in World War II it never faced the food crises it had in World War I, when German submarines sank a dangerously high number of supply ships. However, even though the Royal Air Force had by late 1940 secured a lasting respite from invasion by German troops, Great Britain was exhausted both financially and militarily. The United States stepped in with its Lend-Lease program, which would ultimately send $31.3 billion worth of war goods to cash-strapped England. Like the United States, the British were forced to resort to deficit financing and borrowing to pay for the war, and by 1945, they were economically drained. The postwar years were, in many ways, as difficult as the war years and some kinds of food rationing continued into the early 1950s.

JAPAN

Whereas the United States was rich in natural resources and had a solid business base, the economic position of Japan was much more tenuous. Japan is a collection of mountainous islands poor in natural resources such as oil and not suitable for large-scale farming. These conditions no doubt fueled the passion of the military government for invading Japan's Asian neighbors in order to secure needed arable land and raw materials.

In 1939, Japan had a modern industrialized economy, which had developed quickly starting in the late 19th century after Japan's first contacts with the United States. But its economy was always dependent on the ability to import sources of energy (coal and fuel) and even basic foodstuffs such as rice. By the early 1940s, Japan had faced additional and severe economic hardships because of the trade embargo imposed by the United States in the late 1930s in retaliation for Japanese aggression in China and Southeast Asia.

Although Japanese manufacturing quality in the 1930s was not at the level it would reach in the late 20th century, the Japanese were still able to turn out well-made war goods such as battleships, aircraft carriers, and the highly regarded Mitsubishi Zero fighter plane.

Japan's invasions of numerous Asian nations created a kind of Japanese empire in Asia, but one of the major motivations was the Japanese desire for the rice and other raw materials of their Asian neighbors. These were the goods that Japan needed to continue the war.

UNION OF SOVIET SOCIALIST REPUBLICS

The Soviet Union entered the war less prepared than any nation, Axis or Allied. At the time of the Russian Revolution of 1917, the country was an impoverished agricultural land with a small industrial base. Soviet economic policy had also damaged the country, and Josef Stalin's purges of the high ranks of government and the armed forces of the mid-1930s had almost destroyed the country's military capacity, which became painfully clear when the Soviets invaded Finland in 1939. Although the Soviets "won" that war by overwhelming the Finns with superior numbers,

The Great Depression was a unique economic calamity that began in the United States and spread to the industrialized nations of the world. National economies shrank, unemployment rose, and governments fell. From the end of 1930 to the end of 1941, unemployment in the United States *averaged* more than 10 percent of the workforce.

At its lowest point, the Great Depression left 40 percent of U.S. production idle, and from 1930 to 1933, about 10,000 banks failed, fueling the economic collapse and the near demise of the Republican Party. However, the Great Depression did not lead to dictatorship or violent revolution in the United States.

Economists have different theories about what caused the Great Depression. One theory, espoused by the economist Benjamin Anderson in his book *Economics and the Public Welfare,* is that the stock market crash on October 29, 1929, occurred because "fundamentally wrong policies had been pursued" by the U.S. government and especially the Federal Reserve System. Specifically, the Fed throughout most of the 1920s stuck to a policy of rapid expansion of the nation's money supply, creating inflation and a disproportionate relation between the amount of money in circulation and the real value of goods and services.

Another explanation for the Great Depression comes from the Nobel Prize–winning economist Milton Friedman, who also blames the Federal Reserve System but for different mistakes from those outlined by Anderson. According to Friedman, the central *bank* reversed its expansionary activities of the 1920s by standing by and permitting thousands of bank failures when it had tools to stop bank runs by providing emergency cash.

After the 1929 stock market crash, the subsequent liquidity crisis and U.S. government policies soon combined to throw the nation—and the world along with it—into depression. Although the economic downturn in the United States would have been severe, in the absence of government bungling it would not have continued for a decade.

President Herbert Hoover and Congress made into law the politically popular but economically disastrous Smoot-Hawley Tariff in 1930, setting U.S. tariff rates at record highs and thereby severely disrupting trading relations with the rest of the world. More than 1,000 economists signed a letter begging Hoover to veto this bill, but he ignored their advice. Hoover demanded that businesses hold wages and prices stable, but doing so in the face of a falling money supply created unsold inventories and massive layoffs.

Congress and Hoover made even more errors. In 1932, Congress doubled income tax rates and levied a large number of other new taxes in the hope that a balanced federal budget would calm jittery financial markets. Like the Smoot-Hawley Tariff, the tax increase failed to raise revenues and created even more obstacles to recovery. By February 1933, unemployment in the United States stood at 28.3 percent.

During the 1932 presidential campaign, Democratic candidate Franklin D. Roosevelt promised tax relief and smaller government, but as president he continued many of Hoover's policies. For example, the National Industrial Recovery Act of 1933 was basically a resurrection of the Hoover administration plan to organize the entire U.S. economy into a European-style series of cartels.

Hungry New Yorkers queue up in a breadline in 1932 as the Great Depression ravages the world economy. No nation was immune to the effects of the economic calamity, which facilitated Hitler's rise to power in post–World War I Germany.

Nevertheless, Roosevelt fashioned a revolution of sorts in the United States because his programs greatly increased both the scope and scale of central government involvement in the economy. The times were desperate, Roosevelt called for desperate measures, and the voting public was willing to support him. Unlike Hoover, Roosevelt was also a charismatic leader and his personality as much as his policies helped hold the country together during the crisis years. Other nations—Germany and Italy, for example—turned to dictators whom they hoped would lead them out of the Depression.

the better-armed and better-led Finnish soldiers had savaged the Red Army.

Although Stalin had already implemented near-complete communism by the beginning of the war, much of the Soviet Union's economy was also bolstered by investment from the United States and other Western nations in the 1930s, as private European and U.S. firms, along with thousands of unemployed workers, regarded the "Russian experiment" optimistically.

At the beginning of World War II, the Soviet Union was by all measures an extremely backward country economically. Its bureaucracy hampered war production, and the terrible disruptions to the farm economy that had begun with Stalin's forced collectivization a decade earlier meant that food production was still lagging behind its prerevolutionary levels. Despite all these economic deficits, the Soviet people heroically rose to the challenge, and through great suffering and the deaths of more than 17 million people, were able to throw back the German invaders. By the end of the war, the Soviet Union had become a major power.

UNITED STATES

When war broke out in Europe in 1939, the United States still suffered from double-digit unemployment. Although President Franklin D. Roosevelt's New Deal had expanded the central government, it had not ended the Great Depression.

A majority of business executives told a 1939 *Fortune* magazine poll that they lacked confidence in the Roosevelt administration and generally were pessimistic about the future. When the government began to quietly mobilize the nation in preparation for war in 1940, many business owners were reluctant to pursue War Department contracts, despite the promise of more revenues, sales, and profits. Only in late 1940 and 1941, after Roosevelt began to install business leaders on war production boards, did the business climate begin to change. The New Deal, in fact, was over. Once on a wartime footing, the United States realized its almost unending capacity to produce the soldiers and war materiel necessary to fight a two-front war. Its business activity had been down for more than a decade, but when the nation went to war, those once-idle factories became engines of "the arsenal of democracy." The United States, unlike any other nation in the war, had an incredible depth of economic capacity that allowed it to overwhelm its enemies.

Reestablishment of the World Monetary System

In the fall of 1944, Allied financial ministers, politicians, and bankers met at Bretton Woods, New Hampshire, to hammer out a new international financial system. From those meetings at the Hotel Mount Washington came a series of agreements that the conferees expected would at least provide international stability and foster trading relations that had been lost since 1914.

THE NEW DEAL

When President Roosevelt took office in 1933, the United States was suffering from the Great Depression. He enacted programs called The New Deal to create jobs, bring relief, and end the Depression. The New Deal, fostered by FDR to end the Depression, consisted of two different sets of policies. The "first" New Deal, which lasted from 1933 to 1935, created a series of business and agricultural cartels in order to prop up prices, which had fallen by about 33 percent since 1930; the best-known programs were created by the National Industrial Recovery Act (NIRA, which created the National Recovery Administration, the NRA) and the Agricultural Adjustment Act.

The NRA, which used a blue eagle as its symbol, organized much of the U.S. economy into cartels governed by codes that regulated wages, prices, and working conditions.

From oil to steel to dog food, the NRA tried to end competition among firms and to take the volatility out of the stock market. However, in the end, the measures became increasingly unpopular with many business owners and the general public. From its implementation in June 1933 until December of that year, industrial production *fell* by about 25 percent. Furthermore, the stock market turned out to be even more volatile during the NRA period than before or after, according to one economic study.

The other mainstay of the first New Deal was the Agricultural Adjustment Act (AAA), which attempted to stimulate an increase in crop and livestock prices. The law taxed agricultural processors, then used the proceeds to destroy crops and farm animals in order to shrink the supply of farm commodities and thus cause prices to rise.

The U.S. Supreme Court struck down the NIRA and the AAA as unconstitutional in 1935, stating Congress had delegated some of its own powers to the executive under the original legislation, which was unconstitutional. This angered Roosevelt and his followers, but it also led to a surge in private business investment.

This first New Deal had two lasting legacies. The first was the establishment in 1933 of the Tennessee Valley Authority (TVA), still the nation's largest electricity producer. The TVA first concentrated upon building dams on the Tennessee River and its tributaries, producing electricity first through hydroelectric power and later with coal-fired and nuclear plants. The second was the Civilian Conservation Corps (CCC), which employed young men to do various public works projects in the nation's parks and forests. A number of those projects, including the construction of roads, bridges, and trails are still in use today.

The second New Deal was showcased by the 1935 Fair Labor Standards Act, better known as the Wagner Act (after its sponsor, Senator Robert Wagner of New York). This law took union elections and labor disputes out of the courts and into the jurisdiction of the National Labor Relations Board, which consisted mostly of union sympathizers. Not surprisingly, the percentage of unionized firms grew quickly, especially in the iron, steel, and automobile industries. The other piece of landmark legislation was the creation of Social Security, which established a benefit system for older people and injured workers and is now the largest government pension system in the world.

In 1938 the nation suffered a depression within the Depression. In the aftermath of the Wagner Act and the raising of interest rates by the Federal Reserve System, whatever progress the economy had made because of growing employment suffered a setback; the unemployment rate moved from a low of 12.5 percent in September 1937 to 20.2 percent a year later.

Because the unemployment rate in 1939 averaged about what it had been in 1931, some economists argue that the New Deal had failed both to put people back to work and to enhance private investment. However, others argue forcefully that the appeal and success of the New Deal had less to do with economics than with the expansion of political power by the central government. Still others argue that the New Deal was really about hope, and that Roosevelt and his programs helped stabilize the nation.

What, then, is the legacy of the New Deal and Franklin Delano Roosevelt? Although the New Deal did not end double-digit unemployment, it did increase the power of the presidency and the central government. Moreover, it changed the focus of the national political debate. The New Deal and Franklin Roosevelt changed the ways that people view the role of the state in American life. The Great Depression forced Americans to wonder whether a system of free market capitalism was capable of bringing both economic growth *and* economic stability. Whether the Depression was a failure of capitalism or a failure of government policies, the U.S. economy ever since has felt, for better or worse, the guiding hand of government far more than before the nation's economy collapsed in the early 1930s.

The New Deal as a focus of public life ended abruptly when the United States entered World War II in 1941. From that date on, the American industrial machine was unleashed, and with factories all over the land producing war materiel—and with millions of American men in uniform replaced by women in the workforce—the U.S. economy bounded out of depression.

The conferees, in effect, set the world on a U.S. dollar standard. They fixed the dollar at $35 an ounce of gold, with other currencies then set against the dollar. Because the Roosevelt administration in 1933 made it illegal for Americans to own gold in forms other than jewelry, coins (in coin collections), or other consumer products (such as watches or candlesticks), the $35 an ounce applied only to non-U.S. citizens or foreign governments.

The fixed exchange rates lasted for almost 30 years, until 1971, when President Richard Nixon abandoned the gold standard for a "floating" exchange system which meant that the value of currencies were determined by the financial markets. This system is still in place today.

Other Bretton Woods institutions still survive, however. The International Monetary Fund and its World Bank subsidiary came from those 1944 meetings, and the General Agreement on Trade and Tariffs, the forerunner of today's World Trade Organization, was formed in order to bring down destructive trade barriers that had sprung up during the 1930s.

That the U.S. government was able to finance both its own war efforts and much of the war effort of the Allied nations is testament to the underlying strength of the U.S. economy. The productive might of the United States ultimately turned the tide of war, as the early defeats of the conflict soon gave way to victory after victory. A new international financial system was designed to be one more pillar of postwar economic stability.

Milestones in the Financing of World War II

By the beginning of World War II, governments worldwide were sophisticated in financing large wars. World War I had proved that nations could finance and fight near-total warfare by raising taxes, selling war bonds, and printing money—lots of it. Monetary creation by central banks in France and Germany permitted almost endless expansion of credit, which the governments then used to pay for armies and equipment.

The Great Depression ravaged much of the world during the 1930s, bringing poverty and unemployment to nations that had mostly recovered from World War I and creating an atmosphere in which political demagogues thrived. Adolf Hitler came to power in 1933—although German voters had rejected him only a few years earlier—because his political party, the National Socialists, promised to restore prosperity. How Hitler ended the Depression in Germany is no secret. He did it by rearming the country.

Germany was not the only country that helped end its economic depression through rearmament. Japan, where a ruling military clique had parlayed depression into political power, was furiously rearming throughout the 1930s. As the war clouds threatened Europe, the United States also began to rearm, although it would take the nation's entrance into World War II in 1941 to realize the full extent of the depression-ending effects of defense spending.

But how did nations pay for the war? Each country had a different set of policies, but World War I had taught the simple and basic lesson that wars are paid for by increasing taxes, borrowing, or just printing money—and usually in some combination of all three. Countries like Great Britain and the Soviet Union also relied heavily on U.S. aid during the war to keep their economies afloat. The war, in short, placed a tremendous strain on the economies of all nations involved, whether Axis or Allied.

The story of how the Germans managed to produce and pay for their war effort is fascinating. Moreover, much of the German war buildup went somewhat undetected by France, Great Britain, and the United States. The war financing methods of the United States are also a lesson in the finances and economics of the 1930s and 1940s, a time when depression had savaged the major industrial nations.

GERMAN WAR FINANCING

Although Germany quickly geared its ailing economy toward making war goods in the 1930s, the immediate burst of government spending did not end the massive unemployment crisis or bring prosperity to the Third Reich. On the contrary, the German people were almost as economically deprived during Hitler's "peaceful" years as they had been during the Depression. During the 1930s, the Germans had jobs, but the consumer goods that they wanted were less available, because feeding the war machine took precedence.

The German worker was a servant of the state and did not engage in strikes or other acts of independence or defiance. In real terms (adjusting for inflation), wages in the 1930s were down from Depression-era levels and the shortages of consumer goods were vast. Two years before Germany invaded Poland, Germans were already seeing their goods rationed as the government touted the slogan "Cannons instead of butter."

During the peace years, Hjalmar H. G. Schacht, who had headed the Reichsbank (Germany's central bank), also took on the duties of minister of economics. Economics and finance bored Hitler, but Schacht proved quite effective in that position, enabling Germany to both finance its military buildup and hide those expenditures from Great Britain, France, and the United States.

One casualty of the post–World War I era was the German mark. Its hyperinflation of 1923 was the most famous bout of inflation in history (see table on p.51). To make do in international trade, Germans often had to resort to barter.

Here is how Germany financed its war efforts:

• The Reichsbank issued *Metallforschung* bills, or "Mefos," which Germany used only for internal trades. These expenditures did not appear in the government's budget and therefore escaped detection by other European nations, which would have been concerned with the Reich's military buildup.

• The Reich increased taxes on purchases or services used by individuals, including health insurance, "voluntary contributions" to the Nazi Party, income taxes (top rate set at 65 percent), and a one-time tax on property owners in 1942.

• Germany taxed its corporations, at 20 percent of earnings (passed in 1934), then 25 percent of earnings (passed in 1936), and later 30 percent of earnings (passed in 1937).

• The Nazi government borrowed from banks and individuals. Banks were the largest holders of war bonds, which also served as collateral for bank loans to German industries that were making war goods. In 1941, the Nazi government created the "Iron Savings Account," which gave tax breaks to Germans who "contributed" at least 20 Reichsmarks each month. The increase in individual deposits created more money for the government to borrow.

• Germany looted the nations that it conquered and even looted people murdered in concentration camps, reclaiming gold from tooth fillings and selling hair. Denmark provided dairy products for the Reich, whereas Eastern Europe provided "guest workers" for what was actually slave labor.

When the Germans invaded Poland in September 1939, the nation's economy was already effectively a wartime economy, giving Germany a distinct advantage over the Allies, which had yet to convert their economies to large-scale war goods production. That same year, Hitler nationalized the Reichsbank.

Although the full collapse of the German mark in 1923 had reintroduced more primitive forms of barter to the once productive German economy, during the war Germans continued to use the Reichsmark, despite the continuing battlefield losses that decreased its value. It also may have something to do with the severe punishment that came to those who refused to accept money for normal business transactions, and because, simply, there was no alternative.

In the end, it was not the lack of internal financing, hard currency, or even foodstuffs that brought down the Third Reich. Germany lost the war because it could not vanquish its greatest foe, the United States, a nation that financed and produced not only a staggering amount of war goods and personnel but also served as the financial and manufacturing engine that helped keep other Allied nations afloat.

HYPERINFLATION IN GERMANY, 1923

Although it was not the largest hyperinflation in world history, the 1923 collapse of the German mark is certainly the most famous. A currency that was stronger than the French franc at the end of World War I in 1918 fell five years later to one-trillionth of its 1914 prewar gold value.

The table below shows the sudden and absolute deterioration of the mark, which accelerated rapidly after the end of World War I.

Year	Consumer Price Index* (1929 = 100)
1914	67
1915	84
1916	110
1917	164
1918	196
1919	269
1920	661
1921	870
1922	9.766
1923	10.324
1924	83
1925	91

*The consumer price index (CPI) measures the rate of inflation by comparing price changes within a designated "basket" of goods. Statisticians each month check prices, then "weight" the goods in the "basket" according to their relative use in the economy.

Although the mark was weak after the German defeat in 1918 and subsequent political turmoil, it did not collapse until a 1923 strike in the Rhineland protesting French occupation. The German government tried to support the strikers by paying them with newly printed money.

As the table above makes clear, the hyperinflation quickly ended in 1924. The German

Ministry of Finance and the Reichsbank issued a new currency, the Reichsmark, to replace the old mark. This currency remained in use until 1948, when Finance Minister Ludwig Erhardt introduced the Deutschmark, which in turn was replaced by the Euro in 2001.

U.S. WAR FINANCING

That the United States was able to move from the Great Depression to "the arsenal of democracy" in several years is testament to the productive power of U.S. enterprise. However, "war prosperity" in the United States was something less than what one would typically call prosperity. Americans had no problem finding work during the war because the economy was geared almost totally to making war goods, but, like their German counterparts, American workers could not easily spend much of that newly earned cash, because few consumer goods were available and nearly everything else was rationed.

In addition to making war goods, the United States also provided approximately $48 billion in credits (about $486 billion in today's currency) to the Allies so they could buy U.S. goods. That sum did not include U.S. war expenditures. Like

the Third Reich, the United States resorted to taxation, borrowing, money creation, and other methods to finance its efforts.

U.S. war financing also continued New Deal goals, including one of redistributing wealth. For example, Roosevelt used the war to seek confiscation of all net incomes greater than $25,000. In 1942, after Congress refused to enact legislation that would have set tax rates at such levels, Roosevelt issued an executive order that would have accomplished the same objective, but Congress quickly repealed it in a bill authorizing an increase in government debt.

Roosevelt managed to retain the 40-hour workweek, although many in Congress wanted to replace it with a 48-hour week. Even the chairman of the Federal Reserve Board testified that having to pay overtime would greatly increase the cost of war goods—and thus create a drain on war financing—but the White House stood firm, and workers earned large sums for overtime—even if they had nowhere to spend it.

Roosevelt also expanded the New Deal by encouraging unions to organize at companies making war goods. Because government contracts were often the only business to be had,

---

BERNARD BERNSTEIN, ASSISTANT GENERAL COUNSEL, U.S. TREASURY

Paying for War

In October 1942, Under Secretary of the Treasury Dan Bell called me. . . . We began to work on the financial plans in connection with the invasion—projected invasion—of North Africa. . . .

We were interested especially in two things, what was the currency to be used by the invading forces—our forces and the British—and what was to be the rate of exchange between that currency and the North African currencies which were based on the French franc. . . .

We took the identical currency, regular U.S. currency, just put a yellow seal there instead of the green seal. . . . We wanted on the one hand to have a currency of strength, that would get us the supplies and whatever else we would have needed when we invaded. Yet if the unfortunate should happen, and we should be defeated in the invasion and thrown out, we didn't want a usable large stock of U.S. currency to fall into German hands. We wanted to be in a position to repudiate the yellow seal dollar without damaging the circulation of regular U.S. currency.

—http://www.trumanlibrary.org/oralhist/bernsten.htm

employers faced strong pressures from the government not to resist union organizing attempts.

The government also put wage and price controls in place in 1942 to combat the inevitable inflation caused by huge increases in the money supply. The Office of Price Administration tightly controlled prices and wages at all levels. The government also instituted a strict rationing system that required individuals to use ration stamps to buy goods. Not surprisingly, a thriving underground market arose to skirt the price and allocation restrictions.

This is how the U.S. government raised the money to pay for the war effort:

- Direct taxation: Although the Roosevelt administration first wanted to increase taxes on those in the highest income brackets, Congress in 1942 began to tax those in lower income brackets. This was the first time that many Americans would actually pay income taxes. The government also developed the withholding system, in which individuals paid income taxes with each paycheck instead of paying a lump sum once a year. Top earners paid more than 90 percent on annual incomes greater than $100,000. Also, corporations were subject to "excess profits" taxes, and consumers of alcohol and tobacco paid high excise taxes for those products.
- U.S. government borrowing: Unlike during World War I, when individuals and corporations held the bulk of government war bonds, in World War II the government borrowed mostly from private banks and the Federal Reserve Bank, funding much of the war through methods similar to those used by Hitler to fund Nazi operations. Most debt was short-term and paid by more borrowing. Budget deficits were at record levels during that period.
- Creating new money: The Federal Reserve System was the engine behind providing U.S. banks with enough liquidity to purchase large amounts of government bonds.

The banks then used bank notes as assets to provide new reserves that enabled them to make loans to firms making war goods.

The U.S. government's policies were similar to policies that other countries followed during World War I when they made liberal use of their central banks to finance the war. Because those policies greatly expanded bank reserves, the result was heavy inflation in France and Germany in the years immediately after World War I. U.S. economists were so mindful of that inflation that many signed a memorandum in 1945 protesting the government's policies.

Indeed, on average from 1946 to 1948, the United States suffered from double-digit inflation, which would not occur again for nearly 30 years. However, overall adjustment to the postwar economy went much more smoothly than what

BUY WAR BONDS

A colorful poster features Uncle Sam exhorting Americans to buy war bonds. Hollywood luminaries and heroes of the conflict joined in the effort to finance the great military undertaking. In the wake of the war, the coffers of many countries were empty.

Germany and France experienced after World War I because of the pent-up demand for consumer goods by people with the money to buy them.

Mobilization for the War and the Home Front

No nation can fight for long without supplying its armed forces with the equipment that they need, and the provision of food, clothing, and weapons is the responsibility of those managing the home front.

Total war requires the large-scale transformation of production from consumer goods to military equipment. To accomplish such a feat manufacturers must retool their factories and build new ones. For example, an automobile factory that is to produce tanks must undergo a total transformation of its assembly lines, not to mention changes in specifications for precision machinery that makes components. The process is difficult, uneven, and time consuming.

Because the Axis nations had long before switched their large productive capacities from civilian to military goods, Germany and Japan were better prepared for war in 1939 than the Allied nations of Great Britain, France, and the United States. Furthermore, citizens of Axis nations already were accustomed to being deprived of food and consumer goods, unlike the people in Britain, the United States, and Western Europe. Although the Allies had increased their military-goods production by 1939, they had not made the transitions at the levels of their enemies, which meant that they were unable to throw war materiel into the field as quickly as the Axis forces did.

As the war dragged on, however, the productive capacity of the United States, Great Britain, and the Soviet Union continued to grow even as U.S. bombers pounded German and Japanese factories and transportation arteries and slowly wore down Axis production capabilities. For much of World War II, German soldiers were well armed and well fed. However, their U.S. and British opponents generally were better armed and better fed after 1943.

Changing an economy from production of civilian to military goods—along with the innovations in production of war materiel that occur during the war itself—not only requires changes in machinery and assembly lines but also stretches labor capacity. The mix of skilled and unskilled labor is different for war goods than for civilian products. This problem is exacerbated by labor shortages that are inevitable during a full-scale war because of the high level of skill involved in producing several war products.

GERMAN AND JAPANESE HOME FRONTS

Almost all participants in the war, Allies and Axis nations alike, had to resort to some form of conscription and coercion to ensure that they would have soldiers in the field and workers in the factories. Germany and Japan, in addition to the normal sources of labor, also used slave laborers from conquered lands.

During World War II, Germany's economy suffered more from labor shortages than shortfalls in war materiel. With the Wehrmacht taking more and more able-bodied German men, Albert Speer, Hitler's armaments minister, turned to German women and to slave labor. Despite Hitler's strong belief that women "should remain in the home," German industries actually employed a higher percentage of women than did those in Great Britain. Germany forced about seven million *Ausländer* (foreigners), about one-fifth of the entire German workforce, to work in German factories and businesses. Most workers came from conquered Eastern European nations. The Germans also used Soviet prisoners of war, in stark violation of the Geneva Accords, which Germany had signed. The working conditions were often appalling, especially for Jews, Russians, and other Eastern Europeans, and thousands died in the factories and mines of the Reich.

Unlike Germany, Japan had never signed the

Geneva Accords. Furthermore, the Bushido code of the Japanese soldiers—fight to the death and never surrender—led them to disdain captured enemy troops. As a result, the Japanese beat, tortured, and often killed prisoners of war and forced thousands to work as slave laborers in Japan and elsewhere in the newly conquered nations of the Japanese empire. Prisoners worked—and died—by the thousands building railroads and bridges in the steamy jungles of Southeast Asia. Those shipped to Japan toiled in factories, suffering from ill treatment at the hands of both government officials and company employees. The Japanese enslaved not only prisoners of war. The military-dominated government forced thousands of Koreans to work in Japan, including approximately 15,000 "comfort women" from Korea who were forced into prostitution to serve Japanese soldiers.

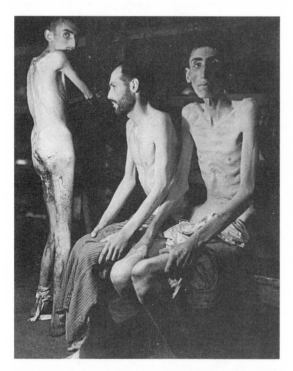

When they were liberated in the spring of 1945, inmates of the Buchenwald concentration camp weighed as little as 70 pounds. Forced to work as slave laborers for the Nazis, their ranks were thinned by starvation and rampant disease.

The suffering of civilians in wartime Germany and Japan was considerable. Civilians bore the brunt of the bombing by the Allies and were deprived of food and other basic goods. In Germany, for example, the diet standards were considerably higher for soldiers than for civilians. The German government began food rationing in 1939, before the invasion of Poland, making some exceptions for holidays. Civilian deprivation went even further, however. Also strictly rationed for civilians in those early years were basic items like soap and hot water.

Every new wave of Allied bombing destroyed homes and belongings, and by 1943 German civilians found even fewer consumer goods available. Unlike in peacetime, when residents of large cities enjoyed higher standards of living than their rural counterparts, residents of places like Berlin and Frankfurt suffered more than country dwellers, who were less frequent targets of Allied bombers and at least had more access to food.

By the end of the war, German civilians were simply surviving—but kept their sense of humor. As bombers leveled their cities and towns, Germans facetiously reminded each other of Hitler's promise to architecturally re-create Germany, saying, "Give me four years and I promise you won't recognize your towns."

Japanese civilians lived at near subsistence levels even before the Allied bombing began, because the Japanese government started to ration rice in 1940. Fresh vegetables were few, and as Allied forces began to take back Japanese military gains of the late 1930s and early 1940s, the situation became even worse. At the same time, the need for iron and steel led the government to strip schools and other public buildings of stoves and radiators.

By 1943, the Japanese economy had mostly collapsed, and shortages burdened the Japanese civilian population, which had never been enthusiastic about the war. From the beginning, the military government recognized the lack of civilian "war fever" and appealed to the

German industrial might certainly contributed to the success of the Nazi war effort, especially in the early years when the Wehrmacht rolled inexorably across Western and Eastern Europe. The relationship of businesses and business leaders to the Nazi government, however, is much more complicated than is often presented.

In the early 1930s, the German people faced difficult political choices. The nation was reeling from the worldwide depression, and all Germans had lost confidence in the existing political order. Nazism was primarily a populist movement that did not ordinarily appeal to wealthy business elites—the average Nazi Party member or supporter was as likely to despise capitalists as much as he hated communists. On the other hand, German industrialists had political pull of their own and had given some financial support to the Nazis—perhaps sensing that the party might well come to power one day. Germany during the Hitler years was not a bastion of free enterprise, but neither was it truly socialist, at least not in the conventional sense. The Nazis permitted private ownership of property and business—unlike the Soviet Union—but closely regulated the activities of businesses by setting prices and directing production. The number and scope of state-owned enterprises also grew rapidly during the 1930s.

The typical view of Germany from 1933 to 1945 is that business leaders enthusiastically supported Hitler, rearmament, and the war. This school holds that Hitler was a pawn of business owners who wanted to pacify workers and increase profits. However, Hitler hated classic liberalism and free markets. He showed little interest in economics itself and viewed the economy, more like the mercantilists of the 17th and 18th centuries, not as a mechanism for generating wealth but as an instrument for creating military power. As he became more powerful, industrialists came to understand that Hitler expected them to do *his* bidding, not the other way around.

In the mid-1930s, the Hitler regime moved the economy further in the direction of autarky, economic controls, and the manufacture of war goods. Hitler's goal was war, and he would never have permitted German business owners to establish a free economy. German businessmen responded to the orders from Berlin and the Führer and were quite productive in making war goods. Like most other Germans, who were not necessarily enthusiastic about starting war with their neighbors but proved to be formidable fighters, German industrialists against many odds produced enough war materiel to make the Wehrmacht one of the best-equipped armies in history—albeit temporarily.

After the war, some German industrialists were tried as war criminals for their role in rearming Germany and also for the manufacture of all the implements of the concentration camp system that killed millions of Jews, including the design and construction of the death chambers and the invention of the gas used to put people to death.

Japanese people's traditional values of national unity, loyalty, and patriotism. By 1945, the Japanese home front was suffering acute shortages and the ravages of increased bombing in its cities, which were firebombed by waves of U.S. B-29 bombers; in March 1945, more than 80,000 Japanese died in an incendiary raid on the center of Tokyo. The atomic bombings of Hiroshima and Nagasaki all but eradicated the two cities and killed hundreds of thousands of civilians.

THE BRITISH HOME FRONT

During World War II, the British people faced dangers and endured hardships unlike any they had experienced in the past. Although the first year of the war was unexpectedly quiet, by the summer of 1940 the German Luftwaffe began attacking British airfields. Then, on the afternoon of September 7, 1940, German bombers switched the attacks to London and other large cities. The government began a program of massive evacuation of children from the cities to safe areas in rural parts of the country, where they were temporarily boarded in the homes of local citizens. The majority of children were evacuated with their classmates, but their parents remained behind in the cities. It was difficult for the children, who grew homesick, and for the parents, who were left behind.

Air raids became a routine part of British life after 1940. The most intense period of the "Blitz" occurred between September 1940 and the spring of 1941, during which time London and other major cities were heavily bombed. In the latter years of the war, the Germans sent destructive V-1 rockets, which fell indiscriminately on cities across the British Isles. In all, more than 1.4 million people were made homeless by the German bombing, and more than 40,000 civilians died.

Daily life on the British home front was characterized by shortages and rationing (especially of meat, eggs, and fat). But the British people, rallied by the eloquence of Prime Minister Winston Churchill, faced these challenges with legendary bravery. The British economy, however, was in a shambles by war's end. British industry did not have the capacity to produce enough weapons and non-war-related goods necessary to win the conflict. Britain was sustained by Lend-Lease and other forms of U.S. aid during the war, which placed unprecedented strains on the economy. Even with this assistance, however, the British industry, in decline before the war, never fully recovered in the postwar years.

THE U.S. HOME FRONT

After the Japanese attacked Pearl Harbor, whatever reluctance Americans had to fight was gone. The U.S. effort would need all the patriotism generated by Pearl Harbor, for while American citizens would not bear the hardships of their enemies, World War II would stretch their levels of endurance.

In late 1941, U.S. firms were already producing war goods, but the U.S. economy was not yet in total war mode. The transition did not take long, and when it came, Americans discovered that their lives would change in many ways.

U.S. entry into the war did not create immediate prosperity. U.S. unemployment did fall from more than 14 percent in early 1940 to less than 2 percent by 1944, but this was due to a huge portion of the male labor force serving in the armed forces. Although these men were technically employed, military "jobs" often involved dangerous, even life-threatening, conditions and did not pay well. Even in the civilian sector, having a job and money did not necessarily translate into living well. Rations, the need to relocate to

Stop this monster that stops at nothing... PRODUCE to the limit!

This is YOUR war!

A poster depicting the Axis enemy as a monster urges American workers to produce war materiel for the ultimate victory.

U.S. BUSINESSES GO TO WAR

Simply put, the war could not have been won by the Allies without the war materiel that was produced by privately owned factories. Few people doubted the capacity of U.S. businesses to turn out war goods. U.S. industrial might had helped turn the tide in World War I, and when war came again, manufacturers were more than willing to accept government payment for goods—along with the slew of regulations and policies that accompanied war contracts. War production meant that workers could find jobs, and businesses could again make profits.

In the Great Depression, the social policies of the Roosevelt administration had led many big business owners to wonder about the future of private enterprise. But their questions were answered when the U.S. government began to mobilize for war and President Franklin D. Roosevelt turned to the business community for help. He asked business leaders to lend their expertise on his war mobilization board and as patriots, business leaders answered the call and, wherever possible, converted their business to wartime production.

The U.S. War Production Board, which oversaw the manufacture of war goods, permitted producers to operate on a cost-plus basis. The government would finance the building of a manufacturing plant and would then agree to pay the costs of production for businesses, with a small percentage (about 5 percent) for profits. Unfortunately, cost-plus reimbursement contained an underlying moral hazard. Businesses did not have an incentive to control their costs, because Uncle Sam was picking up the tab. Therefore, the government responded not only with some management of production but also with controls on wages and the price of producers' goods, the latter in order to keep down costs.

The suppression of wages was an important part of the government's command system of production, because it kept employers from using higher wages to recruit employees from rival firms. This led to what is now considered to be a staple of employment: tax-free benefits. The growth of benefits—from health insurance to paid vacation—exploded because of U.S. wartime price and wage controls.

U.S. firms did not make huge war profits because of the price controls and heavy corporation taxes. However, because government contracts were the only ones available, firms cooperated with the authorities. U.S. companies were astoundingly productive in their efforts, as business executives, workers, bureaucrats, and politicians generally worked together toward a common aim: defeating Germany and Japan.

centers of war production, and transportation difficulties—whether the result of rationing, high prices, or lack of availability—all took their toll. But Americans found that they could spend their rapidly accumulating dollars at movie theaters, so people flocked to see the latest pictures—and the newsreels that gave updates on the war.

With men in the service, women took to the new civilian jobs in droves. "Rosie the Riveter" became the new symbol of the workforce and clearly was an integral part in making war goods—from small arms ammunition to the Boeing B-29 Superfortresses that dropped atomic bombs on Hiroshima and Nagasaki. The changing roles of women in the workplace would also help trigger many social changes in the United States. Although women were dismissed from the jobs after the war, which were then given over to the returning soldiers, the American woman would never fully return to the role of a housewife. By the time of the feminist revolution in the 1970s, women had claimed their right and obligation for positions in the labor force (see Chapter 11, "The Home Front").

THE CONTROVERSIAL WILLOW RUN PLANT

Among the most controversial manufacturing plants built during World War II was Ford Motor Company's Willow Run facility in Ypsilanti, Michigan, then a rural college town 30 miles from Detroit. Constructed in 1941 to build B-24 bombers, the factory exemplified both the virtues and the pitfalls of the U.S. mobilization for war.

Ford broke ground on Willow Run months before Pearl Harbor; company executives had convinced government officials that the firm could mass-produce bombers on an assembly line, much as Ford produced automobiles. The plan was grandiose and so was the price tag: $65 million, all underwritten by taxpayers. It was also controversial because no one was certain the plan would work.

The L-shaped building was a mile long and a quarter mile wide. Optimistic Ford and government officials hoped the giant facility would turn out 1,000 bombers a day and employ 100,000 workers. However, after a year of war, the plant was producing far fewer bombers than anticipated, personnel problems abounded, and people began to jokingly call the facility "Willit Run?"

Ford's plant was the victim of overly aggressive planning and a failure to foresee how the war would limit the available workforce. Furthermore, Henry Ford's antilabor stance also hindered production. For one thing, because the factory was located 30 miles from Detroit—home to most of the available workers—gasoline rationing and a shortage of tires meant a more difficult commute for employees. For another, the company successfully torpedoed a federal housing plan designed for 30,000 people, going so far as to personally rip up surveying stakes set out by the government for the project, which was to house workers near the plant. In the end, the government built 10,000 units of temporary housing. This meant that most of Willow Run's workers had an hour-long commute from Detroit each way, and either had to carpool or take a bus that cost 70 cents a day, about 10 percent of a day's wage.

These hardships led to high employee turnover—about 50 percent a month—and extremely high absentee rates. Henry Ford's autocratic nature did not endear him to employees, many of whom decided that they could find better work closer to home. At the end of 1943, Willow Run had 35,000 workers, about 20,000 fewer than the company needed to run the plant close to capacity. The goal of 1,000 planes daily became the awful reality of 1 per day.

However, Ford management finally recognized its failures, scaled back the plant, moved more than 500 machines to other locations, and reduced the plant's labor requirements. After the downsizing, production increased and the huge facility became more manageable.

At the same time, the workforce stabilized, morale improved, and by war's end, the plant had produced more than 8,700 bombers and employed some 42,000 people. While the number was not close to the grandiose figures that Ford first envisioned, the plant made a significant contribution to the war effort. After the war, Willow Run became a commercial airport that served the Detroit metropolitan area.

Workers at Ford Motor Company's mammoth Willow Run plant rivet a section of the wing to a B-24 Liberator bomber in 1943.

Economic Performance by Nation, 1929–45

The tables that follow track the economic performances of some key belligerents and neutral nations from 1929 through World War II. The categories and figures are self-explanatory; however, some figures are suspect, because they were produced by totalitarian governments. Second, because of wartime price controls the indexes of inflation do not accurately reflect the actual depreciation of the currencies listed. The countries are listed alphabetically.

AUSTRALIA

Australia served as a vital supply and logistics base for the Allied prosecution of the Pacific war. The Japanese threatened to invade Australia early in the conflict, and the fall of Australia could have forced the United States to withdraw to its own West Coast, conceding the entire South Pacific to Japan.

AUSTRALIA (MILLIONS OF AUSTRALIAN POUNDS)

Year	Inflation	Unemployment Percentage	GDP	Per Capita Income	Imports (billions of Australian pounds)	Exports (billions of Australian pounds)	Farm Production (thousands of metric tons)
1929	1	6.7	1,712	2,677.51	130	139	4,472
1930	0	9.8	1,566	2,423.02	119	98	6,868
1931	–8	16.4	1,287	1,972.11	62	90	6,216
1932	–4	19.7	1,210	1,839.74	51	96	6,867
1933	–4	18.9	1,264	1,906.48	65	98	5,878
1934	0	16	1,356	2,030.85	68	114	4,651
1935	0	14	1,432	2,129.05	83	104	5,042
1936	1.1	11	1,574	2,322.21	95	124	5,284
1937	3.2	8.8	1,717	2,511.70	103	148	6,258
1938	2	7.5	1,857	2,691.69	127	142	5,264
1939	2.8	8.8	1,819	2,610.50	113	123	7,073
1940	4.2	9	1,980	2,812.89	132	150	3,329
1941	5.2	4.9	2,145	3,016.87	124	135	5,919
1942	7.8	1.9	2,497	3,477.23	170	160	5,542
1943	3.6	0.9	2,858	3,950.24	244	126	4,354
1944	0	1	2,905	3,974.00	243	147	2,787
1945	0	1.2	2,842	3,844.69	214	155	5,450

Source: *International Historical Statistics: Asia and Oceania 1750–1993*, ed. B.R. Mitchell (London: MacMillan, 1998).

FRANCE

Much of France spent four years under German occupation, causing the nation to lose a degree of its own economic identity. Extremely high inflation characterized the years of occupation.

FRANCE (FRENCH FRANCS)

Year	Inflation	Unemployment (Thousands of Workers)	GDP	Per Capita Income	Imports (millions of French francs)	Exports (millions of French francs)	Farm Production (thousands of metric tons)
1929	6.4	10	63,912	1,550.13	58,221	50,139	41,690
1930	1	13	62,079	1,491.92	52,511	42,835	37,670
1931	−4	64	58,372	1,394.45	42,206	30,436	38,100
1932	−9.3	301	54,584	1,303.96	29,808	19,705	41,960
1933	−3.4	305	58,453	1,395.39	28,431	18,474	41,840
1934	−3.5	368	57,883	1,379.80	23,097	17,850	34,050
1935	−8.5	464	56,417	1,345.18	20,974	15,496	37,450
1936	6.7	470	58,535	1,396.01	25,414	15,492	37,650
1937	26.3	380	61,956	1,476.54	42,391	23,939	38,420
1938	13.9	402	61,671	1,489.63	46,065	30,590	43,470
1939	6.1	418	N.A.	N.A.	43,785	31,590	41,560
1940	18.9	961	N.A.	N.A.	45,770	17,511	25,670
1941	17.2	395	N.A.	N.A.	24,936	15,777	22,440
1942	20.6	124	N.A.	N.A.	25,952	29,664	24,005
1943	23.9	42	N.A.	N.A.	13,960	35,407	23,175
1944	22.4	23	N.A.	N.A.	9,769	25,557	22,864
1945	N.A.	68	N.A.	N.A.	57,027	11,399	18,515

Source: *International Historical Statistics: Europe 1750–1993*, ed. B.R. Mitchell (London: MacMillan, 1998).

GERMANY

Some detail concerning economic conditions in Germany is vague because of the nature of the country's totalitarian regime. The production of war materiel, growth of the nation's armed forces, and the implementation of large public works projects helped to prop up employment figures after the rise of the Nazi Party.

GERMANY (REICHSMARKS)

Year	Inflation	Unemployment Percentage	GDP	Per Capita Income	Imports (millions of Reichsmarks)	Exports (millions of Reichsmarks)	Farm Production (thousands of metric tons)
1929	1	13.1	51,694	798.48	13,359	13,486	79,760
1930	–4	15.3	49,289	757.36	10,349	12,036	93,827
1931	–8.3	23.3	43,913	671.24	6,713	9,592	80,464
1932	–11.4	30.1	41,760	635.42	4,653	5,741	73,433
1933	–1.3	26.3	47,375	717.47	4,199	4,872	82,066
1934	2.6	14.9	52,102	784.55	4,448	4,178	81,846
1935	1.3	11.6	60,352	902.52	4,156	4,270	79,873
1936	1.3	8.3	66,226	983.31	4,228	4,778	87,104
1937	0	4.6	73,167	1,078.68	5,495	5,919	101,084
1938	1.2	2.1	81,335	1,199.10	5,449	5,264	100,509
1939	0	N.A.	N.A.	N.A.	5,207	5,653	93,263
1940	3.7	N.A.	N.A.	N.A.	5,012	4,868	92,490
1941	2.4	N.A.	N.A.	N.A.	6,925	6,840	82,552
1942	2.3	N.A.	N.A.	N.A.	8,691	7,560	90,048
1943	1.1	N.A.	N.A.	N.A.	8,258	8,588	75,280
1944	2.2	N.A.	N.A.	N.A.	N.A.	N.A.	74,243
1945	–2.6	N.A.	N.A.	N.A.	N.A.	N.A.	N.A.

Source: *International Historical Statistics: Europe 1750–1993*, ed. B.R. Mitchell (London: MacMillan, 1998).

GREAT BRITAIN

The British economy was devastated by the cost of World War I and hit hard by the Great Depression, although by the mid-1930s its effects had begun to wane. Interestingly, during the war years unemployment became virtually nonexistent as both men and women contributed to the effort to win the conflict, either in uniform, on the factory floor, or on the farm.

GREAT BRITAIN (MILLIONS OF POUNDS)

Year	Inflation	Unemployment Percentage	GDP	Per Capita Income	Imports (millions of pounds)	Exports (millions of pounds)	Farm Production (thousands of metric tons)
1929	–1	7.3	7.3	94.892	1,221	729	11,636
1930	–4	11.2	11.2	94.33	1,044	571	10,780
1931	–6.3	15.1	15.1	88.77	861	391	8,677
1932	–2.2	15.6	15.6	83.98	702	365	10,848
1933	–3.4	14.1	14.1	89.39	675	368	12,322
1934	1.2	11.9	11.9	95.46	731	396	13,195
1935	1.2	11	11	98.61	756	426	11,647
1936	3.5	9.4	9.4	101.13	848	441	11,356
1937	4.4	7.8	7.8	105.06	1,028	521	10,562
1938	1.1	9.3	9.3	107.90	920	471	11,335
1939	1.1	5.8	5.8	111.68	886	440	12,342
1940	1.7	3.3	3.3	128.64	1,152	441	14,002
1941	8	1.2	1.2	136.72	1,145	365	16,207
1942	0.8	0.5	0.5	137.81	1,206	391	19,506
1943	–0.8	0.4	0.4	139.34	1,885	337	20,335
1944	1.7	0.4	0.4	131.85	2,360	327	19,038
1945	0.8	0.5	0.5	122.09	1,517	436	20,037

Source: *International Historical Statistics: Europe 1750–1993*, ed. B.R. Mitchell (London: MacMillan, 1998).

ITALY

With the end of Fascist rule in Italy in 1943, Benito Mussolini had governed his nation longer than any other dictator of the period. Because Italy had been a battleground for several years and its government was unstable, details on the Italian economy are murky.

ITALY (MILLIONS OF LIRA)

Year	Inflation	Unemployment (thousands of workers)	GDP	Per Capita Income	Imports (millions of lira)	Exports (millions of lira)	Farm Production (thousands of metric tons)
1929	32.7	301	136	3.35	21,303	14,767	117.1
1930	−25.4	425	128	3.13	17,347	12,119	140
1931	−10.3	734	127	3.07	11,643	10,210	120.3
1932	−2.3	1,006	132	3.17	8,268	6,812	111.6
1933	−5.9	1,019	131	3.12	7,432	5,991	138.3
1934	−5	964	131	3.09	7,675	5,224	142.4
1935	1.3	N.A.	144	3.37	7,790	5,238	167.4
1936	7.8	N.A.	142	3.30	6,039	5,542	143.8
1937	9.6	874	143	3.30	13,943	10,444	200.2
1938	7.7	810	153	3.50	11,273	10,497	148.3
1939	2	706	162	3.68	10,309	10,823	N.A.
1940	19	N.A.	154	3.46	13,220	11,519	181
1941	16	N.A.	151	3.36	11,467	14,514	N.A.
1942	15.2	N.A.	144	3.19	14,038	16,047	N.A.
1943	68	N.A.	129	2.87	N.A.	N.A.	N.A.
1944	344.6	N.A.	95.3	2.12	N.A.	N.A.	N.A.
1945	97	N.A.	76.6	1.69	N.A.	N.A.	N.A.

Source: *International Historical Statistics: Europe 1750–1993*, ed. B.R. Mitchell (London: MacMillan, 1998).

JAPAN

In the 86 years between the opening of Japan to trade with the West by a U.S. naval delegation and the bombing of Pearl Harbor, the Japanese people transformed their society from one that was feudal to one that was industrialized and heavily influenced by the West. Aided by the United States in its postwar recovery, Japan became an economic colossus by the end of the 20th century.

JAPAN (MILLIONS OF YEN)

Year	Inflation	Unemployment Percentage	GDP	Per Capita Income	Imports (billions of yen)	Exports (billions of yen)	Farm Production (thousands of metric tons)
1929	−1.1	N.A.	13,735	216.43	2,765	2,604	15,531
1930	−14.3	5.3	13,882	215.39	2,005	1,871	16,924
1931	−12.8	6.1	13,942	212.96	1,686	1,480	15,169
1932	1.5	6.8	14,071	211.80	1,936	1,802	16,157
1933	5.8	5.6	14,660	217.40	2,464	2,351	18,289
1934	2.7	5	16,239	237.72	2,970	2,789	14,971
1935	1.3	4.6	16,631	240.14	3,272	3,276	16,485
1936	5.3	4.3	17,157	244.70	3,641	3,585	18,253
1937	8.8	3.7	21,220	300.43	4,765	4,188	18,821
1938	14.9	3	21,935	308.88	3,794	3,939	18,136
1939	12	N.A.	22,117	309.84	4,165	5,163	19,163
1940	16.1	N.A.	20,796	289.10	4,653	5,418	17,790
1941	1.5	N.A.	21,130	295.11	4,088	4,384	17,350
1942	3	N.A.	21,405	296.05	2,924	3,506	18,791
1943	5.9	N.A.	21,351	291.281	2,939	3,055	18,439
1944	11.8	N.A.	20,634	279.59	N.A.	N.A.	17,813
1945	47.2	N.A.	N.A.	N.A.	N.A.	N.A.	13,739

Source: *International Historical Statistics: Asia and Oceania 1750–1993*, ed. B.R. Mitchell (London: MacMillan, 1998).

SWEDEN

Sweden managed to remain a noncombatant throughout World War II, trading with combatants sometimes under the threat of invasion. Swedish iron ore exports were critical to the expansion of the German war machine.

SWEDEN (MILLIONS OF KRONOR)

Year	Inflation	Unemployment Percentage	GDP	Per Capita Income	Imports (millions of kronor)	Exports (millions of kronor)	Farm Production (thousands of metric tons)
1929	–1	11.2	5,711	934.69	1,783	1,812	5,588
1930	–3	12.2	6,038	984.99	1,662	1,550	5,867
1931	–3	17.2	5,614	912.84	1,428	1,122	4,816
1932	–2.1	22.8	5,482	887.05	1,155	947	6,757
1933	–1.1	23.7	5,609	904.67	1,096	1,079	6,822
1934	0	18.9	5,957	957.71	1,305	1,302	7,100
1935	1.1	16.1	6,301	1,009.77	1,476	1,297	6,721
1936	1.1	13.6	6,704	1,070.92	1,633	1,514	6,475
1937	3.2	10.8	6,810	1,084.39	2,123	2,000	6,947
1938	2.1	10.9	7,033	1,116.34	2,082	1,843	7,113
1939	3.1	9.2	7,277	1,151.42	2,499	1,889	7,018
1940	12.9	11.8	6,958	1,094.02	2,004	1,328	6,444
1941	13.2	11.3	6,954	1,088.26	1,674	1,345	5,880
1942	8.5	7.5	7,173	1,115.55	1,780	1,319	6,168
1943	0.7	5.7	7,294	1,123.88	1,814	1,172	6,546
1944	1.4	4.9	7,561	1,152.59	1,677	853	5,513
1945	0	4.5	8,100	1,219.87	1,084	1,758	5,724

Source: *International Historical Statistics: Europe 1750–1993*, ed. B.R. Mitchell (London: MacMillan, 1998).

Switzerland had the highest profile of the neutral nations, providing financial and banking services to Hitler's Third Reich. Much information about the relationship between the two nations during the war has only recently come to light.

SWITZERLAND (MILLIONS OF SWISS FRANCS)

Year	Inflation	Unemployment Percentage	GDP	Per Capita Income	Imports (millions of Swiss francs)	Exports (millions of Swiss francs)	Farm Production (thousands of metric tons)
1929	0	1.8	8,470	2,106.96	2,731	2,098	1,054
1930	–2	3.4	8,560	2,113.58	2,564	1,762	837
1931	–5.1	5.9	7,900	1,936.27	2,251	1,349	1,008
1932	–7.5	9.1	8,140	1,985.36	1,763	801	927
1933	–5.8	10.8	8,510	2,065.53	1,594	853	1,047
1934	–1.2	9.8	8,560	2,067.63	1,435	844	1,112
1935	0	11.8	8,560	2,062.65	1,283	822	975
1936	1.3	13.2	8,580	2,057.55	1,266	882	945
1937	4.9	10	8,780	2,100.47	1,807	1,286	1,200
1938	0	8.6	8,870	2,116.94	1,607	1,317	1,160
1939	1.2	6.5	8,950	2,125.89	1,889	1,298	997
1940	9.3	3.1	8,780	2,075.65	1,854	1,316	1,298
1941	14.9	2	8,400	1,976.47	2,024	1,463	1,601
1942	11.1	1.9	8,170	1,904.42	2,049	1,572	1,689
1943	5	1.4	8,410	1,946.75	1,727	1,629	2,342
1944	2.4	1.6	8,560	1,963.30	1,186	1,132	2,394
1945	0.8	1.6	9,100	2,063.49	1,225	1,474	2,298

Source: *International Historical Statistics: Europe 1750–1993*, ed. B.R. Mitchell (London: MacMillan, 1998).

UNION OF SOVIET SOCIALIST REPUBLICS

The virtually closed society of the Communist Soviet Union allowed little information to be published about the nation's economic condition before or during the war. The assumption is that the arming and equipping of the nation's fighting forces necessitated dramatic increases in production and employment.

UNION OF SOVIET SOCIALIST REPUBLICS (MILLIONS OF RUBLES)

Year	Inflation	Unemployment	GDP	Per Capita Income	Imports	Exports	Farm Production (millions of metric tons)
1929	N.A.	N.A.	127	N.A.	N.A.	N.A.	117.1
1930	N.A.	N.A.	134.5	N.A.	N.A.	N.A.	140
1931	N.A.	N.A.	137.2	N.A.	N.A.	N.A.	120.3
1932	N.A.	N.A.	135.7	N.A.	N.A.	N.A.	111.6
1933	N.A.	N.A.	141.3	N.A.	N.A.	N.A.	138.3
1934	N.A.	N.A.	155.2	N.A.	N.A.	N.A.	142.4
1935	N.A.	N.A.	178.6	N.A.	N.A.	N.A.	167.4
1936	N.A.	N.A.	192.8	N.A.	N.A.	N.A.	143.8
1937	N.A.	N.A.	212.3	N.A.	N.A.	N.A.	200.2
1938	N.A.	N.A.	216.1	N.A.	N.A.	N.A.	148.3
1939	N.A.	N.A.	229.5	N.A.	N.A.	N.A.	N.A.
1940	N.A.	N.A.	250.5	N.A.	N.A.	N.A.	181
1941	N.A.	N.A.	N.A.	N.A.	N.A	N.A.	N.A.
1942	N.A.	N.A.	N.A.	N.A.	N.A	N.A.	N.A.
1943	N.A.	N.A.	N.A.	N.A.	N.A	N.A.	N.A.
1944	N.A.	N.A.	N.A.	N.A.	N.A	N.A.	N.A.
1945	N.A.	N.A.	N.A.	N.A.	N.A	N.A.	N.A.

Source: *International Historical Statistics: Europe 1750–1993*, B.R. Mitchell (London: MacMillan, 1998).

UNITED STATES

As was the case with World War I, it was U.S. wartime production that helped to win World War II. War production soared during the years 1940 to 1944 in the United States. Imports and exports more than doubled or tripled during the war years as well.

UNITED STATES (DOLLARS)

Year	Inflation	Unemployment Percentage	GDP	Per Capita Income	Imports (millions of dollars)	Exports (millions of dollars)	Farm Production (billions of metric tons)
1929	0	3.2	203.6	1,671	5,886	7,034	23.8
1930	−2.3	8.7	183.5	1,490	4,416	5,448	22.5
1931	−9	15.9	169.3	1,364	3,125	3,641	24.4
1932	−9.9	23.6	144.2	1,154	2,067	2,474	23.5
1933	−5.1	24.9	141.5	1,126	2,044	2,402	23.4
1934	3.1	21.7	154.3	1,220	2,374	2,975	20.2
1935	2.2	20.1	169.5	1,331	3,137	3,265	22.5
1936	1.5	16.9	193	1,506	3,424	3,539	21.5
1937	3.6	14.3	203.2	1,576	4,256	4,553	24.7
1938	−2.1	19	192.9	1,484	3,045	4,336	24.9
1939	−1.4	17.2	209.4	1,598	3,366	4,432	26
1940	0.7	14.6	227.2	1,720	3,636	5,355	26.2
1941	5	9.9	263.7	1,977	4,486	6,896	28.1
1942	10.9	4.7	297.8	2,203	5,356	11,769	30.9
1943	6.1	1.9	337.1	2,465	8,096	19,134	30.2
1944	1.7	1.2	361.3	2,611	8,986	21,438	30.2
1945	2.3	1.9	355.2	2,538	10,232	16,273	29.8

Source: B. R. Mitchell, *Historical Statistics of the United States, 1750–1970* (London: MacMillan, 1998).

CHAPTER 4

Allies, Enemies, and Bystanders

Location, not alliances, determined the fate of many nations in World War II. Poland, France, and other countries bordering Germany were invaded and suffered through years of occupation. Many countries not in the line of fire, however, were faced with a difficult decision: Should they side with the Axis or the Allies or remain neutral? The United States, for example, tried to remain neutral for years while still supporting the Allies with money and war materiel under the Lend-Lease Act. The United States did not stay neutral for long and was soon a full partner of the Allies.

When Germany invaded Poland in 1939, Britain and France could no longer ignore Germany's aggression, and they declared war. The Soviet Union was bound by its recent nonaggression pact with Germany and became a huge benefactor of the partitioning of Poland. But within two years, Germany violated that 1939 pact by attacking the Soviet Union on a 1,000-mile front, thus forcing the USSR into an unsteady alliance with Great Britain and the United States.

Although the Soviet Union fought Germany alongside its Allies, it honored its nonaggression pact with Japan; Japan fought the British and the Americans, while it honored its nonaggression pact with the Soviets. The Soviet Union and Japan did not become enemies until after Germany fell and just before Japan surrendered.

Legend:
- German territory in 1936
- Territory occupied by Germany in 1939
- Territory occupied by Germany in 1938
- Czechoslovakian territory occupied by either Hungary or Poland

Notes on German Expansion (and other Territorial Changes):

❶ Saarland votes to rejoin Germany in plebiscite, 1935.
❷ Germany reoccupies Rhineland, 1936.
❸ Germany annexes Austria, March 1938.
❹ Sudetenland given to Germany by Munich agreement, March 1938.
❺ Hungary annexes Slovak territory, November 1938.
❻ Germany occupies Czechoslovakia, March 1939.
❼ Ruthenia occupied by Hungary, March 1939.
❽ Poland occupies Teschen, March 1939.
❾ Memel annexed by Germany, March 1939.

GERMAN EXPANSIONISM: EUROPE AT THE OUTBREAK OF WORLD WAR II

Countries that seemed to have been on the fringes of the world community before the war, such as Portugal and Turkey, found themselves at the center of activity and courted by all sides. Others, such as Spain, began the war as a neutral, but as Germany showed its strength throughout Europe, Spain became a "nonbelligerent" with strong ties to Germany and the Axis powers (and for a time supplied troops to the Russian front). As Axis fortunes declined, however, Spain cut those ties and later declared its neutrality again—and war never came to the Iberian Peninsula. Still others, principally the

Americas, found that location was insulation from the devastation that ravaged Europe, North Africa, the Middle East, China, Southeast Asia, Indonesia, and the islands of the Pacific.

Axis, Allied, and Neutral Countries

The following list includes the principal Allied, Axis, and neutral nations of the war. Even though a nation may have changed sides, it will be listed here on one side only—the side to which it gave its primary allegiance. For example, even though Italy, after beginning the war as a member of the Axis, changed sides following the overthrow of Mussolini, Italy is considered a member of the Axis and not the Allies because of its long identification with the Axis cause. Some other Axis nations also turned against Germany in the final days of the war, but as with Italy, their primary identification is as Axis partners. No Allied nation switched to the Axis side in the waning days of the war.

Axis Nations

Austria*	Japan*
Croatia	Romania*
Germany*	Slovakia
Hungary*	Thailand
Italy*	USSR

Allied Nations

Abyssinia	Costa Rica
Albania	Cuba
Argentina*	Czechoslovakia*
Australia*	Denmark*
Belgium*	Dominican Republic
Bolivia	Egypt
Brazil*	El Salvador
Bulgaria*	Equador
Canada*	Finland*
Chile	France*
China*	Greece*
Colombia	Guatemala

Haiti	Paraguay
Honduras	Peru
Iceland*	Poland*
India	Saudi Arabia
Iran*	South Africa*
Iraq*	Syria
Lebanon	Turkey*
Luxembourg*	United Kingdom*
Mexico	United States of
Netherlands*	America*
New Zealand*	Uruguay
Nicaragua	USSR*
Norway*	Yugoslavia*
Panama	

Neutral Nations

Republic of Ireland*
Portugal*
Spain*
Sweden*
Switzerland*

*Asterisks designate countries highlighted in the following section.

Nations Involved

World War II consisted of many separate wars; each nation had its separate alliances and enemies, and, as has been noted, some nations changed alliances during the war. Civil war (in China, Spain, and Yugoslavia, for example), largely influenced or dominated the participation of some nations in the world war, whereas others saw the war as a time to take a clear patriotic stand against foreign aggression (for example, Greece, Finland, and, ironically, the Soviet Union). For explanations of many of the treaties involved, see the Treaties section of this chapter.

What follows is an alphabetical survey of the leading players—Axis, Allied, and neutral—involved in World War II.

AXIS NATIONS

Austria

The defeat of imperial Germany after World War I caused the dissolution of its ally, the Austro-Hungarian Empire. In 1920 a new constitution created the first Austrian Republic, but defeated Austria remained economically depressed and politically unstable throughout the 1920s and 1930s. In the 1930s, the rise of Austrian Nazism became a new destabilizing factor. In reaction, Engelbert Dollfuss, chancellor and leader of the Christian Social Party, dissolved the parliament in 1933 and ruled by decree. Dollfuss was assassinated in July 1934 during an unsuccessful Nazi takeover attempt instigated by Hitler and was succeeded by his minister of education, Kurt von Schuschnigg.

Despite the setback in 1934, Hitler continued to plan for the eventual absorption of Austria into the German Reich. On February 12, 1938, Hitler met with Schuschnigg and issued a series of demands. These included the appointment of the Austrian Nazi Artur Seyss-Inquart as minister of security in the Austrian cabinet, a general amnesty for all Austrian Nazis under detention, and the official incorporation of the Austrian Nazi Party in the government-sponsored Fatherland Front, a conservative political party. Hitler knew that Schuschnigg could never accept such demands, thus setting up an excuse for the use of force.

On March 9, Schuschnigg announced that a general election would be held throughout Austria on the following Sunday, March 13. On March 11, Reichstag president Hermann Göring demanded that the vote be canceled, that Schuschnigg

resign, and that Seyss-Inquart become chancellor. He warned, "If nothing is done within this period, the German invasion of Austria will follow." When Hitler's demands were not met, German forces entered Vienna on March 12, and on March 13, Hitler declared the dissolution of the Austrian Republic and the annexation, or *Anschluss,* of Austria into the German Reich.

In October 1943, the United States, Britain, and the Soviet Union signed the Moscow Declaration, which proclaimed the reestablishment of an independent Austria as an Allied war aim.

Soviet troops entered Vienna in April 1945. In October, the Western powers recognized the provisional government of the Socialist leader Karl Renner, and Austria held national elections in November.

Much as they had done in Germany, the United States, France, Britain, and the Soviet Union divided Austria into four occupation zones. Vienna, like Berlin, also had four zones. Austrian civilian and military deaths in the war have been estimated at 334,000.

Germany

Germany had been a loose confederation of states before the country's unification under Otto von Bismarck (chancellor, 1871–90). After Bismarck, Kaiser Wilhelm II envisioned a Germany that would have a leading role in world affairs and a "place in the sun." By the early 20th century a militarist Germany and a militarist Europe were heavily armed, and the continent's intricate system of alliances and secret agreements eventually led to war in 1914. Appalling casualties and social disillusionment in World War I led Germany to capitulate in 1918. Kaiser Wilhelm II abdicated, and Germany became a republic.

The Treaty of Versailles (1919), which ended the war, imposed harsh terms on Germany. It gave Alsace-Lorraine to France and West Prussia to Poland; it created a Polish corridor between Germany and East Prussia, and Germany lost its colonies (see Chapter 2, "Causes of War"). The treaty also limited the size of the German army and navy; placed Allied troops in the Rhineland; and charged the Germans with full responsibility for the war, which included payment of reparations for the total cost of the war. Because the new German government (the Weimar Republic) accepted the Treaty of Versailles, the German people saw it as weak and placed on it the blame for Germany's defeat.

In 1923, Germany defaulted on its reparations payments, and France occupied the Ruhr (see Chapter 2, "Causes of War"). A collapsing economy led Germany to print large amounts of paper money to pay reparations to France. The resulting inflation wiped out the German middle class and was responsible for the destruction of much of Germany's personal and business wealth (see Chapter 3, "The Economics of World War II"). Although Germany recovered and instituted a more responsible monetary policy, the stock market crash of 1929 once again plunged Germany into economic crisis.

From this chaos arose Adolf Hitler's Nazi Party, which by 1932 was the largest party in the Reichstag, the German parliament. In 1933, President Paul von Hindenburg appointed Hitler chancellor. In 1934, upon the death of Hindenburg, Hitler consolidated the offices of president and chancellor and became the sole leader, or Führer, of the German state. Hitler demanded complete loyalty and obedience from the German people, and in return he promised to restore German strength, honor, power, and prestige.

Between 1933 and 1939, Hitler rearmed Germany, annexed Austria, seized the Sudetenland region of Czechoslovakia with the acquiescence of France and Britain, and then seized the remaining Czech territories. He also forged an alliance with Italy and Japan (which became known as the Axis). On September 1, 1939, Germany invaded neighboring Poland. France and Britain declared war two days later. In 1941, Hitler invaded the Soviet Union, initiating a titanic battle that went on for almost four more years. The entrance of the United States into the war in 1941 tipped the balance in favor of the Allies, and by 1944, following the successful D-Day invasion of France, Allied troops were closing in on Germany from the east and the west. Hitler committed suicide on April 30, 1945, and seven days later, Germany formally surrendered to the Allies.

In the wake of World War II, Germany was a ruined nation, its cities bombed to rubble, more than 7 million soldiers and millions of civilians dead, and the country divided into four zones of occupation. Its most egregious legacy, however, was the systematic mass murder of almost 6 million Jews (the Holocaust), a policy that was carried out with a special vengeance in the war years 1941 to 1945.

Hungary

On November 11, 1918, the Austro-Hungarian Empire was officially dissolved, and on June 4, 1920, the Hungarian government accepted the Treaty of Trianon, which stripped Hungary of much of its prewar territory and separated it from Austria. During the 1930s, the Hungarian government established close relations with Italy and Germany. In 1938, pursuant to the Munich Pact and the partition of Czechoslovakia, Hitler gave part of Slovakia and all of Ruthenia to Hungary. Afterward, Hungary withdrew from the League of Nations and in January 1939 became a signatory to the Anti-Comintern Pact, the mutual defense pact against the Soviet Union (see Chapter 2, "Causes of War").

Hungary officially declared neutrality at the outbreak of World War II in 1939, but its government was really pro-German and, as a result, benefited greatly from Hitler's aggression. The Axis gave Hungary northern Transylvania (which was taken from Romania) in 1940, and when Germany attacked Yugoslavia in 1941, Hungary invaded Croatia. Hungary declared war against the Soviet Union on June 27, 1941, and against the other Allies on December 13, 1941. The Hungarian fascist militia, called the Aerocross, which fashioned itself after the Waf-

A column of German supply wagons rolls past a road sign during the invasion of Poland in September 1939. The German conquest of western Poland was completed in about a month. Partners in the aggression, elements of the Soviet Red Army invaded Poland from the East.

fen (Armed) SS, ruthlessly assisted Hitler in the "final solution" (the murder of European Jews). The Hungarians established two ghettos for Jews in Budapest, although one was protected through the auspices of Swedish diplomacy and the intervention of Raoul Wallenberg, a charismatic Swedish diplomat. Nonetheless, of the 500,000 Jews in Hungary (including 100,000 Christians of Jewish descent) at the beginning of the war, 203,000 died at the hands of their countrymen or the Germans.

Total Hungarian casualties included 136,000 military killed or missing, approximately 250,000 wounded, and approximately 300,000 civilian casualties. Many were soldiers in either Hungarian or German uniform fighting on the Russian front.

Italy

Italy was allied with France and Great Britain during World War I and suffered half a million dead and a million wounded. After the war, poverty was rampant, and Italy was on the verge of revolution. Taking advantage of the instability under the socialist government, Benito Mussolini and his Fascists staged a theatrical "march on Rome" in 1922 and so intimidated the establishment that King Victor Emanuel III called on Mussolini to form a new government. In time, Mussolini became known as Il Duce (the Leader), and all political power was vested in him personally. Mussolini's regime had the effect of halting the growth of communism in Italy and ended unemployment (largely by putting most unemployed men in the army).

STATUS OF OCCUPIED EUROPE, JUNE 1941

Map legend:
- Germany (Third Reich), June 1941
- Axis controlled countries, allied or occupied
- Neutral

0   500 Miles

Between 1933 and 1935, Mussolini was wary of the rise of Hitler's Germany, a more powerful neighbor to the north. Italy pledged protection to Austria and protested Germany's violations of the Treaty of Versailles (see Chapter 2, "Causes of War"). But Mussolini had his own agenda of aggression. The Italian invasion of Ethiopia (which was bound to Italy by various trade agreements and which Italy wanted to integrate into its empire) began on October 3, 1935. The League of Nations censured Italy, but by mid-1936 Italy had annexed Ethiopia into the Italian empire and incorporated it, along with Eritrea and Italian Somaliland, into a colony called Italian East Africa (see Chapter 2, "Causes of War").

> On this 10th day of June, 1940, the hand that held the dagger has struck it into the back of its neighbor.
> —U.S. President Franklin D. Roosevelt after Italy's last-minute involvement before France's surrender

When the Spanish Civil War broke out in 1936, both Italy and Germany provided substantial men

Dates of Italian Acquisition:
1. Italians in control of Eritrean port of Assab by 1885.
2. Italians gain control over Eritrea, and establish protectorate over Abyssinia from 1889–96, when Abyssinia gains independence.
3. Italians lease Somali ports from Sultan of Zanzibar, and purchase them in 1905.
4. Libya annexed by Italy from the Ottoman Empire in 1911.
5. Italy annexes Dodecanese from Ottoman Empire in 1911.
6. 1939–40 Italy conquers Abyssinia.
7. 1939 Italy annexes Albania.

ITALIAN EXPANSIONISM, 1885–1940

and materiel to Franco's Nationalist forces, and Italy's foreign policy became increasingly tied to that of Germany. Mussolini had come increasingly under Hitler's sway, and he believed that Italian glory could be restored through an alliance with Germany. In addition, he admired and envied Hitler and was willing to follow him in international affairs. In 1937, Italy joined the Anti-Comintern Pact with Germany and Japan and withdrew from the League of Nations. When Germany annexed Austria, Italy ignored its previous pledge to aid Austria. In 1938, Mussolini gave firm support to Hitler's position against Czecho-

slovakia. Additionally, under pressure from Germany, Fascist Italy began to oppress its Jews in a series of laws that, among other things, excluded Jews from employment in civil and military administrations.

When World War II began, Italy did not immediately join in the conflict. Instead, it waited for Germany to attack France, and when that nation was close to surrender, it declared war and invaded across the French-Italian border.

Italy had occupied nearby Albania in April 1939, and after Hitler's successes in France and in the Balkans, Mussolini used Albania as a springboard into Greece. The Greek invasion, however, was a fiasco, and German forces were sent in to rescue the Italian army. In August 1940, Italian forces occupied British Somaliland, and forces from Italian Libya and Italian East Africa attempted to overwhelm the British army in Egypt. After all these attempts failed, Italian troops in North Africa came increasingly under German control.

The Allied invasion of Sicily began on July 9, 1943, and the battle for Italy followed. The Sicilian invasion led to the fall of Mussolini's government and his arrest. The Allies and the new prime minister, Pietro Badoglio, signed an armistice on September 3, 1943. Meanwhile, German paratroopers rescued Mussolini from prison, and the Germans set him up in a puppet state in northern Italy. Central and northern Italy fell under German control in 1943 after Mussolini's ouster, and brutal warfare ensued from 1943 to 1945, as the Allies battled their war northward along the Italian peninsula. By war's end, Italy lay in ruins. Total Italian casualties included 226,900 military and approximately 60,000 civilians killed or missing. In April 1945, Mussolini was captured by Communist partisans and shot.

Japan

Japan's awakening to the outside world might be traced to 1720, when the Shogun Yoshimune repealed a ban on European books. In Western tradition, the opening of Japan began in 1853 with the U.S. government's formal mission, led by Commodore Matthew Perry, to the emperor; it resulted in a treaty establishing trade relations between the United States and Japan.

At this time the Japanese warlords had medieval weapons and were in awe of the sophistication of Western military materiel. So in less than 90 years, Japan developed a sophisticated manufacturing society and a powerful army and navy capable of challenging other world powers.

HAROLD HART, 91ST BOMB SQUADRON, U.S. ARMY AIR FORCES

Held Prisoner in Japan

The Japanese tried to reconstruct the Nichols Field runways near Manila. Details of men were sent there to dig rock and dirt from one end of the runway and dump it into a swamp at the other end. Filipino prisoners were also used but kept separate from the Americans. We at Cabanatuan [a Japanese prison camp for U.S. and Filipino soldiers captured at Bataan and Corregidor in January 1945] had always heard stories about the Nichols Field detail. The head Jap was referred to as the "White Angel." He was very mean and worked the prisoners long hours and hard. These stories were told to us by returning POWs who were too ill to work and were replaced by others from the main camp at Cabanatuan. This is how I was sent to Nichols on detail . . . as a replacement.

I was scared, for I only weighed a little over a hundred pounds. And I didn't think I could survive. Regardless, I had to go and sometime later found myself in an area of Manila near Nichols Field. We were encamped in an old school. Practically no facilities were provided. Straddle trenches were the only means. Each morning we were counted and marched along the streets to the field. Saddened Filipinos lined the street, trying to give us something or to wave the V for victory sign to us. We were forbidden to turn our heads or look sideways at them. However, we did see these people. Many sugar cakes, cigarettes, and articles were smuggled to the prisoners as they marched along. The Filipinos did this knowing [that] if they were caught, it meant death.

—Eisenhower Center for American Studies Archives

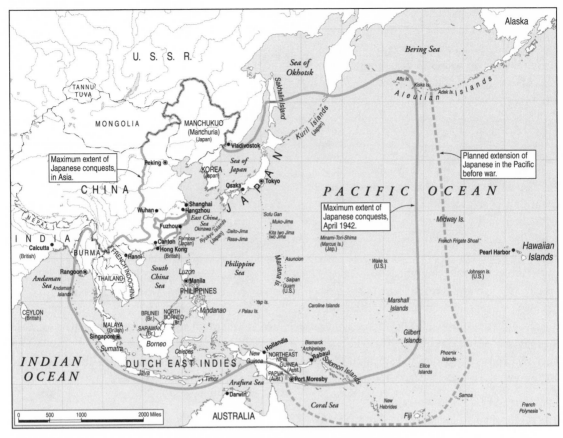

JAPANESE EXPANSIONISM, 1910–45

In the 1890s, Japanese foreign policy became more aggressive and resulted in the Sino-Japanese War, which ultimately gave control over Korea, Formosa (today Taiwan), and the P'eng-hu Islands to the Japanese.

In 1904, war broke out between Japan and Russia (the Russo-Japanese War), which Japan won in less than 18 months. From this conflict the Japanese gained territorial interests in the Liaodong Peninsula, and Russia ceded the southern half of Sakhalin Island and acknowledged Japanese interests in Korea, which was formally annexed to Japan in 1910.

Japan fought on the side of the Allies during World War I, which resulted in Japanese occupation of German Far Eastern territories and also in the expansion of Japanese interests in China

(see Chapter 2, "Causes of War"). In the 1920s, Japan turned its attention to China, pursuing a policy aimed at domination of that vast country. On September 19, 1931, Japanese troops seized arsenals in Manchuria and forced the withdrawal of the Chinese troops in the area. Occupying the entire region, Japan established Manchuria as a separate puppet state called Manchukuo and crowned Henry Pu Yi (the last emperor of China) as Emperor K'ang Te. When the League of Nations called upon Japan to cease hostilities in China, Japan simply withdrew from the League. Japan and China signed an armistice in May 1933, but after an incident between Japanese troops and a Chinese patrol on July 7, 1937, Japan recommenced hostilities against China and overran northern China.

After the fall of France in 1940, the Japanese occupied parts of French Indochina with the consent of Vichy France. At that same time, with the Netherlands occupied by Germany, Japan began making inroads into the Dutch East Indies. In September 1940, Japan entered into the Tripartite Pact with Germany and Italy, pledging mutual aid for a period of 10 years, but in September 1941 Japan signed a neutrality pact with the Soviet Union.

The German successes increased Japanese ambitions in Asia, but the Japanese realized their objectives in the western Pacific and East Asia faced the opposition of the United States. U.S. President Franklin D. Roosevelt replied by imposing embargoes on scrap iron shipments to Japan, which the Japanese were using to make war materiel. He also froze Japanese assets in the United States and cut off shipments of oil. In effect, this was an economic blockade of Japan—an act of war. By the summer of 1941, Japan was considering a preemptive strike against the United States to neutralize it militarily (see Chapter 2, "Causes of War").

The resulting Japanese attack on Pearl Harbor on December 7, 1941, was an extreme miscalculation by the Japanese government. With one blow Japan aroused and united a nation, which up to that day was still debating isolationism and pacifism, and that ultimately led to Japan's demise. When Japan followed up the attack on Pearl Harbor with the immediate conquest of British possessions in the Far East, including Hong Kong and Singapore, the Allied response against Japan would be complete. By 1942, Japan was already on the defensive in the Pacific, and gradually, island by island, the U.S. navy moved closer and closer to the Japanese mainland. In 1945, the United States used its ultimate weapon—the atomic bomb—on the cities of Hiroshima and Nagasaki to bring an end to the war, and within days, the exhausted Japanese surrendered.

Total Japanese military killed or missing have been estimated at 1,740,000, with 94,000 military wounded and 41,000 prisoners of war; 393,400 civilians were killed and 275,000 are estimated wounded or missing.

Romania

At the outset of World War II, Romania was economically dependent upon Germany, largely because of German reliance on Romanian oil that was vital for the German war machine. In June 1940, after France fell and at the height of German power, Germany coerced Romania into submitting to the Soviet demand for Bessarabia and northern Bukovina, and that same year Germany demanded and Romania allowed the cession of northern Transylvania to Hungary. In September 1940, Romania ceded southern Dobruja to Bulgaria. These losses represented one-third of Romania's territory and population (including 3 million ethnic Romanians) and led King Carol II to abdicate in favor of his son,

A cartoon by artist Arthur Szyk responds to the disastrous attack launched by the Japanese against Pearl Harbor on December 7, 1941.

Michael. The de facto leader of the country, however, was General Ion Antonescu, who created a military dictatorship and aligned the country with Germany.

Romania assisted Germany in its June 1941 invasion of the Soviet Union. Although a desire to regain Bessarabia and northern Bukovina motivated many Romanians, Antonescu regarded the invasion of the Soviet Union as a "great holy war" against godless communism. Because Romania had invaded Britain's new ally, Britain delivered an ultimatum to Romania in November 1941 and officially declared war on Romania on December 7, 1941. After Germany's declaration of war against the United States on December 11, Romania declared war against the United States on December 12.

By January 1943, the Allies defeated the Axis at Stalingrad and decimated two German armies, two Romanian armies, and one Italian army. With the war turning against them and the Red Army approaching, King Michael had Antonescu arrested in August 1944, and all Romanian forces then surrendered to the Soviets. The loss to Hitler was tremendous: an ally that had contributed 20 divisions to the Eastern Front and had 30 more divisions in Romania itself.

On August 24, 1944, Romania entered the war on the Allied side against Germany and Hungary, helping to drive the Germans from Romania, Hungary, and Czechoslovakia and contributing what became at that time the fourth-largest Allied army in the European theater (behind the Soviet Union, the United States, and Great Britain).

Military casualties (killed and wounded) have been estimated at 794,000 (624,000 fighting with the Axis, 170,000 against), and 340,000 civilians were killed.

ALLIED NATIONS

Argentina

When World War II began, Argentina had a German population of about 60,000, as well as 110,000 people of German descent. Argentina's Italian population included 780,000 people of Italian birth and 2.2 million citizens of Italian descent. Argentina's Nazi Party in Buenos Aires alone had about 60,000 members. Fearful of antagonizing its German and Italian citizens, Argentina did not join the Allies but remained neutral in the early years of the conflict.

In 1942, the United States publicly accused Argentina and Chile of serving as espionage centers for the Axis powers. After the Federal Bureau of Investigation provided Argentina with the evidence behind these accusations, the Argentine government arrested 38 people.

When it became obvious that the Axis had lost the war, Argentina finally declared war on Germany and Japan on March 27, 1945. It ratified the UN Charter on September 8, 1945.

Because of its large German population and right-wing government, after the war, Argentina became a refuge for Nazi war criminals. It has been estimated that as many as 40 high-ranking German Nazi refugees were given sanctuary in Argentina, including Nazi leader Adolf Eichmann.

Australia

The Balfour Report of 1926, which was codified in the Statute of Westminster in 1931, confirmed that the Dominions of the British Commonwealth, including Australia, were independent sovereign states that shared a common monarch with Great Britain. Therefore, when Britain declared war on Germany on September 3, 1939, Australia was free to declare itself a belligerent or not. Although Australia had suffered severely during World War I, it declared itself a cobelligerent with Britain and sent its armed forces to assist in Europe.

When the Pacific war broke out, the Japanese quickly captured U.S. and British possessions and bombed and threatened to invade Australia. On February 19, 1942, 188 Japanese aircraft bombed the northern port of Darwin, sinking 17 ships, shooting down 22 defending fighters, and killing 240 sailors and civilians. Japanese raids continued on Darwin, Wyndham, Broome, Katherine, and Dailywaters. The Australian military fought with distinction in all major theaters of the war. Australia's contribution of more than one million uniformed personnel was disproportionate to its small population (less than eight million in 1939). The war resulted in approximately 69,200 Australian military casualties (29,400 killed and missing, 39,800 wounded), and 26,400 prisoners of war.

Belgium

In 1914, at the beginning of World War I, German troops had invaded Belgium to get to France, ignoring Belgium's status as a neutral nation. The country suffered terribly during four years of war, and in 1919 the Treaty of Versailles required Germany to cede Eupen-et-Malmédy and Moresnet to Belgium. In the next year, Belgium signed a military alliance with France. In 1925, Britain, France, Germany, and Italy entered into the Pact of Locarno with Belgium in which they mutually affirmed Belgium's territorial inviolability.

As Germany began to rearm in the mid-1930s, Belgium reaffirmed its neutrality, although it agreed to accept aid from France and Britain in the event of a German invasion. As the French fortified the defensive Maginot Line along the French-German border, the Belgians, struggling to maintain a neutral stance, refused to extend it to include the border between Germany and Belgium.

On May 10, 1940, without warning or declaration of war, Germany invaded Belgium. Within a few short weeks, the Belgian government fled to Paris, then moving to London after the fall of France. In the German attack of 1940, Belgian casualties amounted to approximately 7,500 soldiers killed, 15,900 wounded, and 200,000 taken prisoner. The total number of Belgian casualties wearing either Allied or German uniform is unknown. Civilian casualties for the war are estimated at 12,000. The Belgian government returned to Brussels in September 1944 in the wake of the advance of the Allied armies.

Brazil

When World War II began, Brazil was ruled by a dictator, Getúlio Dornelles Vargas, who had come to power in the early 1930s following a bloody coup and civil war. Although Vargas's government more closely resembled Fascism and Nazism than it did a democracy, Vargas was hostile to Germany, partly because of the antigovernment activities toward his regime from the Brazilian Nazi party, the Integralistas.

After the United States became involved in the war in late 1941, Brazil became a principal supplier of rubber and other vital war materiel. Consequently, Brazilian shipping became a target of German submarines in 1942. The Germans had sunk at least 16 Brazilian ships by the time Brazil declared war on Germany on August 22, 1942. Throughout the war, Brazil made naval bases and airfields available to the United States, and before the war ended the Brazilian navy controlled all patrol activities in the South Atlantic. From 1944 until the end of the war, a Brazilian expeditionary force fought with the Allies in the Italian campaign, suffering at least 448 dead.

Bulgaria

At the beginning of World War II, Bulgaria was a neutral nation. In September 1940, with help from Hitler, Czar Boris III reclaimed some territories Bulgaria had lost following World War I. In March 1941, Bulgaria joined the Axis powers and declared war on Greece and Yugoslavia, eventually occupying all of Yugoslav Macedonia, Grecian Thrace, Eastern Greek Macedonia, and the Greek districts of Florina and Kastoria. In December 1941, after Hitler declared war against the United States and Britain, Bulgaria also declared war on the Americans and British, but it did not declare war on the Soviet Union. During the war, Bulgarian troops aided Hitler in Yugoslavia and elsewhere in the Balkans.

After Anglo-American bombing raids and the

threat of invasion by the Soviet Union (and the mysterious death of Czar Boris III in August 1943), the new government severed ties with Germany. The Soviet Union declared war on Bulgaria on September 5, 1944, and the new Bulgarian Communist government asked for an armistice with the Soviets and then declared war on Germany on September 7. The armistice required that the Bulgarians evacuate Yugoslav Macedonia and the territories that they had taken from Greece. In the fall of 1945, tensions escalated with both the United States and Britain *and* the Soviet Union, partly because the Soviet-controlled Fatherland Front dominated Bulgarian politics and a Communist regime controlled the Bulgarian government.

Canada

When World War I began, Great Britain's foreign policy was also the foreign policy of Canada, including Britain's declaration of war against Germany. After World War I, Canada gained more independence and joined the League of Nations as a separate entity. In 1926, Great Britain acknowledged that the Dominions of the British Commonwealth were equal in stature to Great Britain itself, and this was codified in 1931 in the Statute of Westminster.

After Britain declared war on Germany on September 3, 1939, Canada followed suit on September 10. During the war, the Canadian armed forces fought in every major theater, and the Royal Canadian Navy contributed to the patrolling of the North Atlantic. Canadian forces formed a large contingent of the Allied invasion of Normandy, France, on June 6, 1944. Canadian losses included 17 warships and 59 merchant ships, and approximately 39,300 killed or missing. Canada also suffered 53,200 wounded and 9,000 prisoners of war.

China

The Republic of China was created in 1911 following the overthrow of the monarchy. The new government was weak and controlled only a small portion of the country, while the remainder was ruled by local warlords. By the 1930s, two parties had emerged to battle for control of China: the Nationalists, or Kuomintang, led by Chiang Kai-shek, and the Communists, headed by Mao Tse-tung.

This vast land, weakened by poverty and civil war, was ripe for attack by the Japanese, who wanted to control China's natural resources and expand their empire. In September 1931, the Japanese extended military control over all of Manchuria, transforming its three provinces into the Japanese puppet state of Manchukuo and later making Henry Pu Yi, the last ruler of the Manchu dynasty, its puppet emperor.

In July 1937, full-scale war broke out between China and Japan, and within a year Japan had seized control of most of northeast China, part of the Yangtze valley, and the area surrounding Guangzhou. In 1937, the Kuomintang and the Chinese Communists formed a united front against the Japanese and attempted to cooperate with each other until the end of the war. The United States considered Chiang's Nationalists as the legitimate government of China and provided arms, money, and materiel in the struggle against the Japanese. American volunteers formed the legendary Flying Tigers to carry supplies and troops within China and in Burma.

From 1931 through 1945, China's military casualties totaled 1.4 million killed or missing, 1.8 million wounded. It also suffered approximately 8 million civilian casualties. At least 200,000 died in Japan's attack on the civilian population of the city of Nanking alone in November 1937 (see Chapter 12, "Man's Inhumanity"). After the Japanese surrendered in August 1945, the Kuomintang and the Chinese Communists resumed their civil war, which resulted in a Communist victory in 1949.

Czechoslovakia

The Republic of Czechoslovakia was created out of the old Austro-Hungarian Empire from a collage of nationalities. Czechs made up only 51 percent of the national population; Slovaks, 16 percent; while the remainder were primarily Germans (concentrated in the Sudeten region of northern Bohemia), and Ukrainians and Hungarians. The relations among these peoples were strained from the beginning of the republic.

Hitler had resolved to bring all Germans in neighboring countries into the Third Reich. After annexing Austria in March 1938, he moved against Czechoslovakia. His obvious objective was the absorption into the Reich of the Sudeten Germans, but he also had a less-publicized military purpose: the capture of Czechoslovakia's mountainous military defenses in the Sudetenland (see Chapter 2, "Causes of War"). In an effort to preserve the peace in Europe, Britain's prime minister, Neville Chamberlain, flew to Germany in September 1938 to meet with Hitler. In the meetings that followed, Britain and France, eager to avoid war, coerced the Czechs into accepting Hitler's demand and ceding the Sudetenland to Germany. Great Britain, France, Germany, and Italy finalized the terms on September 29–30, 1938. As a result of the Munich Pact, Czechoslovakia lost its western and northern borders and with them its fortifications and natural defenses, as well as vast economic resources.

Poland and Hungary seized the opportunity to make their own demands against Czechoslovakia for territory. The Polish government demanded the frontier district of Teschen, and Hungary too presented ultimatums for long-disputed border territories. In March 1939, German troops occupied the remainder of Czechoslovakia and carved up the country. Slovakia became a puppet Fascist state headed by a Roman Catholic priest, Father Josef Tiso, while Bohemia and Moravia became protectorates of the German Reich. The shock of Hitler's betrayal of the promises he had made at Munich—namely that the Sudetenland would be his last territorial demand—made the British and French realize that Hitler's next seizure of neighboring land would mean war.

The Czechoslovak government-in-exile was reestablished in Czechoslovakia in April 1945. Although democratic forces in Czechoslovakia hoped to ally the country with the West, communism eventually won out, and Czechoslovakia fell into the Soviet orbit, where it remained until the collapse of the Soviet empire in 1989. In the war's aftermath, all the Sudeten Germans were expelled from the country.

Denmark

A small country on the northern border of Germany, Denmark had always hoped to preserve its national existence by a policy of neutrality. In 1939, the Danish government signed a nonaggression pact with Nazi Germany, but in April 1940, Hitler's forces invaded and occupied the country. In 1941, the British occupied the Danish-protectorate of the Faroe Islands north of Great Britain. Also that year, the United States established a temporary protectorate over another Danish possession, Greenland, and used Greenland's Atlantic coast to patrol U-boat activity (see also Iceland).

The Germans allowed the Danish civil service to maintain control of most of the country's legal and domestic affairs but an active resistance against Nazi occupation developed and engaged in acts of sabotage. In early 1943, Hitler curtailed Denmark's relative independence and ordered the SS to round up and deport the country's 8,000 Jews.

Denmark's Jews consisted of 6,500 assimilated Danes and about 1,500 émigrés from Germany, Austria, and Czechoslovakia. The Germans planned to seize these Jews on a single night, October 1, 1943. Working with extraordinary speed, the Danes smuggled virtually the entire Jewish population onto small vessels and transported them across the narrow Øresund Strait to neutral Sweden, where they were welcomed and kept safe until they were returned to their homes at the end of the war.

The Danes paid terribly for their kind act. The Germans set off a wave of terror, arresting scores of alleged saboteurs and rounding up and shooting Danish citizens without pretense of trial.

Estonia

Estonia, which had been part of Russia since 1729, was trying to break away when Germany invaded in February 1918. When Germany capitulated to the Allies in November, Estonia declared its independence, which it maintained until 1940. Although Estonia's independence was secured by the Soviet-Estonian Nonaggression Pact of 1932, the Nazi-Soviet Nonaggression Pact of 1939 secretly assigned Estonia to the Soviet sphere of influence. After the Soviets imposed a treaty of mutual assistance, the Red Army entered Estonia in June 1940 and declared it a Soviet Socialist Republic that August.

After the German invasion of the Soviet Union, Estonia became part of the German Reich Commissariat of Ostland. The Soviet Union reoccupied Estonia in January 1944 and reincorporated this smallest of the Baltic States into the USSR. The Soviet occupations, together with the German military draft and deportation of Estonia's Jewish population, decimated Estonia.

Finland

Finland, which shares its lengthy eastern border with Russia, had been an independent nation only since the end of World War I when the Nazi-Soviet pact of 1939 designated that Finland was to be within the Soviet sphere of influence. After the German-Soviet invasion of Poland in 1939, the Soviets made sweeping territorial demands against the Finnish government. The Finns were prepared to make significant concessions, but the Soviets attacked anyway, prompting what is known as the Winter War.

The Soviet leadership fully expected the Winter War to be an easy task. Yet Finland's small army of 135,000 troops first fell back to more secure lines, then held and succeeded in a hit-and-run harassment of the Soviet forces. As well, the massive failure of the initial Soviet assault against Finland had a significant effect upon the war; it strongly influenced Hitler's impression of Soviet might, encouraging Hitler to launch an attack the next year. During that winter, however, Stalin reorganized his forces, and the Soviets soon prevailed.

The Winter War ended with the Treaty of Moscow on March 11, 1940. The Finns suffered 24,900 killed or missing and 43,600 wounded; the Soviets suffered at least 200,000 dead and huge losses of war materiel: nearly 1,000 planes and 2,300 tanks and armored cars.

At the end of the Winter War, although Finland had technically lost, it was still a free country unoccupied by the Soviet Union, unlike the other nations in the Soviet sphere. When Germany attacked the USSR in June 1941, the Finns aligned themselves with Germany against the Soviet Union. In the conflict against the Soviet Union, Finland served as a "cobelligerent" of the Reich but only against the Soviet Union, not against the Western Allies.

Initial Finnish victories were swift, and the now-400,000 Finnish troops regained virtually all the land lost during the Winter War. The Western nations, principally Britain, implored the Finnish government to come to some agreement with the Soviet Union, which was now an ally, and the Finns halted their own offensive against the Soviets in July and August 1941.

Three years later, in June 1944, the Soviets made a surprise attack on the Finns and demanded that the Finns break relations with Germany and evict the German army from Finland. Under Soviet pressure, the Finns struck at the Germans, and the Germans struck back with savagery. As the Germans retreated, they destroyed every house, farm, school, and hospital in their path. By January 1945, the Germans were out, and Finland was still an independent nation. Since the autumn of 1939, 89,900 Finns had been killed or were missing, and 201,600 were wounded; civilian casualties numbered at least 3,400.

In the postwar years, Finland was able to maintain its independence in the shadow of the more powerful USSR through careful diplomacy.

For years Finland suffered the stigma of having been a German ally against the Soviet Union, although Germany and Finland fought their common foe for entirely different reasons.

France

France had fought two devastating wars with Germany in the late 19th and early 20th centuries: The Franco-Prussian War of 1870–71 saw German forces come within miles of Paris. In World War I (1914–18), grinding trench warfare scarred northeastern France and left millions of French soldiers dead and wounded. By the 1930s, the French government wanted to avoid war with Germany at any cost—to the point of allowing Germany to annex parts of Czech territory in return for a promise that Germany would have no further territorial demands in Europe.

In the wake of their shock at Hitler's absorption of the remainder of Czechoslovakia in March 1939, however, Great Britain and France pledged "all support in their power" to protect Poland against German aggression.

On September 1, 1939, Germany invaded Poland; Great Britain and France declared war against Germany on September 3. On May 10, 1940, Germany invaded France, leading to France's utter defeat within six weeks. The British Expeditionary Force in France consisted of 10 divisions, which were evacuated at Dunkirk by June 3 (see Chapter 7, "Campaigns and Battles: Europe and the Atlantic"), leaving the French army to fight alone. Paris fell on June 14, and on June 22, 1940, France signed an armistice with Germany.

France's losses have been estimated at 92,000 killed; 250,000 were wounded, and 1.45 million captured, versus Germany's 29,640 dead and total casualties of 163,213. Germany annexed Alsace and Lorraine and continued to occupy the north and west of France. While the German authorities remained in Paris, a puppet French government was set up in Vichy. The cooperation and collaboration of the French government at Vichy with the German victors contributed to the subjugation of the French people, and French administrators and police assisted Germany in its deportation of Jews and political enemies.

On November 11, 1942, Germany occupied the free zone in southern France and disbanded the Vichy army; the French navy scuttled the French fleet, some of which was sunk by gunfire from the British Royal Navy, to keep these warships from getting into German hands. On June 6, 1944 (D-Day), Allied forces invaded France at Normandy, and by August Paris had been liberated. The Vichy government collapsed with the liberation of France, and in August 1944 a provisional government under General Charles de Gaulle (see Chapter 5, "Politicians and Demagogues," Chapter 10, "Intelligence, Espionage, and Propaganda," and Chapter 11, "The Home Front") took power. The Allies formally recognized this government in October 1944.

Although France ended World War II as a victorious ally, the collaboration of the Vichy government from June 1940 through August 1944 left a shameful legacy: the official French government's general support of the Nazi regime.

Great Britain and Northern Ireland

Much of Britain's foreign policy after World War I focused on peace and avoiding another world conflagration. Great Britain helped lead the League of Nations and participated in several disarmament conferences that attempted to limit the size of the world's navies. As the German threat began to rise after Hitler's accession to power in 1933, the British government followed a policy of appeasement that ignored Germany's step-by-step repudiation of the Treaty of Versailles and accommodated Germany's territorial claims. By the time Great Britain pledged to defend Poland against German aggression in 1939, Germany had rearmed, reoccupied the Rhineland, annexed Austria, negotiated the cession of the Sudetenland, and annexed the balance of Czechoslovakia.

With France, Britain declared war on Germany after the invasion of Poland in September 1939 and stood alone against Nazi Germany after the surrender of France in June 1940. Under the inspired leadership of Prime Minister Winston S. Churchill, Britain mobilized against Germany, achieved air supremacy in the Battle of Britain, and thwarted Hitler's plans to invade the island nation. British cities were heavily bombed in 1940–41, and later in the war, German V-1 and V-2 rockets rained down on London, bringing terror and destruction to the population.

After the German invasion of the Soviet Union in June 1941, and the Japanese attack on the U.S. naval base at Pearl Harbor, in December 1941, Great Britain, the Soviet Union, and the United States forged the grand alliance to fight against the Axis. British troops were part of the Allied invasion force that stormed the beaches of Normandy on D-Day on June 6, 1944, and British bombers, along with the American Army Air Forces, flew missions over Germany, hitting German cities and industrial targets. Following the war, the British were given responsibility for a zone of occupation in northwestern Germany.

The war left the British economically exhausted and with over 100,000 civilians dead, and it was many years before the nation emerged from the tremendous devastation of the conflict.

ROBERT WILKINS, 149TH ENGINEER COMBAT BATTALION

Making Friends in Wartime

We boarded a train that took us to a little village in southern England in South Devon called South Brent. We were billeted at South Brent in little English army huts of the Quonset type. It was rainy, cold, and miserable. It seemed like it rained every day, and we were out marching and hiking in the moors on the highways. We certainly had our share of blisters.

From there, on January twenty-second they took us into the town of Paignton, England, in trucks. . . . I can remember the place that I went to, their name was Glover. He was a retired piano dealer from New Zealand and Australia. Our boots were muddy, and everything about us, I suspect, was offensive—certainly to Missus Glover. She made us remove our boots outside before she would even let us come in the house. We immediately thought that this was going to be a very difficult situation, and we certainly weren't happy with it at all. After we became acquainted with the Glovers, they treated us like we were their own sons. . . . At the time we were down in South Devon, they sealed off that part of the country, and they would not allow any of the people (such as the people that lived up in Birmingham or London) to come out to that area because they wanted to keep that secret, and they didn't want the Germans to know what was going on down there. But I'm sure from some of the things that happened that Germany did know pretty well what was going on, but the people that were in this part of the country, in South Devon—the southwest part of England—made a lot of sacrifices for the war effort. Many of them were not able to use their farms, and some had to sell off their herds of cattle. But they accepted the Americans quite well and were really good to the Americans. I have fond memories of this family that I lived with in England, and I made a trip back to England a couple of years ago and visited this part of the country. Of course, this family I think are deceased now because I haven't heard from them in years and years.

Each time we would leave to go on these mock invasions, we didn't really know whether it was the real thing or not. But then it came time for the real invasion. On May sixteenth we went to Dorchester near Weymouth. We were sealed in a camp. We knew then that this was the real thing. In fact, the British people in Paignton would not talk about it. But they also knew that it was the real thing. When we left the Glovers' home to go get on the train to be sealed into this camp, the Glovers cried just as if they were our parents. It was quite a touching thing for us.

—Eisenhower Center for American Studies Archives

Greece

Although Greece had signed a friendship pact with Italy in 1928, it fell victim to Mussolini's imperial ambitions when Italian troops invaded in October 1940. If Mussolini thought the Greeks would be an easy target, he learned quickly that the Greeks knew how to defend themselves. By December, the Greek army had driven the Italians out of their country. They were soon in possession of one-fourth of Albania, which had been under Italian occupation. In April 1941, German troops arrived to rescue the hapless Italians, and they soon overcame the Greek army. On April 23, 1941, Greece surrendered to the Germans.

Life during World War II brought famine and severe inflation to Greece, but the population remained determined to fight for independence. Several resistance groups arose during the war to fight the Germans. By October 1944 with the Russian army pushing westward toward the borders of Germany, the German army withdrew from Greece. Total Greek military casualties resulting from the Italian invasion, the German invasion and occupation, air raids, and famine have been estimated at 18,300 killed or missing and 60,000 wounded, and there were 415,000 civilian casualties.

Iceland

A dependency of Denmark, Iceland received Danish recognition of its independence in 1918, but the Danish king remained Iceland's head of state, and Denmark controlled Iceland's foreign policy. After the Nazis occupied Denmark in April 1940, British troops occupied Iceland (by invitation). In 1941, the Americans replaced the British in order to free the British troops for service elsewhere. In 1944, Iceland voted to sever all ties with Denmark and proclaimed itself a republic. Iceland, strategically located in the northern Atlantic, was an important base for the Allies throughout the war.

Iran (Persia)

At the turn of the 20th century, Iran's weak government was under continuing pressure from both Russia and Great Britain for economic control. In 1901, the government of Iran gave Great Britain a 60-year concession to exploit Iran's petroleum resources.

Iran was neutral during World War I, but because those petroleum resources were crucial to the Allied cause, the Allies and Turks fought several battles for control of the Iranian oil fields.

By the time World War II began, the Iranian government under Reza Shah Pahlavi was friendly to Germany and the Axis cause. By July 1941, 2,000 to 3,000 German nationals involved in different Iranian industrial projects were living in Iran, and Germany was Iran's biggest foreign trade partner.

On August 21, 1941, Great Britain and the Soviet Union made a joint demand that Iran expel all German nationals. Reza Shah refused, and on August 25, Britain and the Soviet Union invaded Iran, meeting scattered resistance. On August 28, Reza Shah surrendered to the British and Soviet invaders. The Soviet Union occupied northern Iran, and Great Britain occupied central and southern Iran. Reza Shah abdicated his throne in favor of his son, Mohammad Reza Pahlavi, who then severed diplomatic relations with Germany and Italy, expelled their nationals, and then severed relations with Japan on April 12, 1942.

Britain, the Soviet Union, and Iran signed an agreement under which the British and Soviets agreed to leave Iran within six months after the end of the war. The Allies also agreed not to interfere in Iran's internal affairs, but that promise was not kept. The Allies, including the United States after its entry into the war, made extensive improvements in Iran's transportation facilities. By the end of the war more than four million tons of Lend-Lease supplies—almost one-fourth of all Lend-Lease aid delivered to the Soviet Union—were shipped through the Persian Gulf and Iran.

Both the Soviets and the West had too many vested interests in the country to simply leave. The Soviets were deeply concerned about the internal politics of a nation on its border, and the West wanted access to Iranian oil.

Iraq

Iraq had been a Turkish province under the Ottoman Empire since 1534. After Turkey entered World War I as an ally of Germany, Britain invaded Iraq, and by the end of the war Iraq was under full British military control. In August 1921, the Iraqis selected Faisal al-Husein as Faisal I, the first king of Iraq. The British had maintained an army in the county, and in June 1922, at the request of King Faisal I, the British mandate became a 20-year treaty of alliance between the two countries. In October 1932, Britain granted Iraq full independence and it joined the League of Nations as an independent sovereign state.

After the deaths of King Faisal I in 1933, and his son, King Gahzi, in 1939, three-year-old Faisal II ruled Iraq under a regency government. When World War II began, Iraq broke off relations with Germany in accordance with a treaty it had with Great Britain to support that country. But in March 1940, a pro-Nazi military junta led by Rashid Ali al-Gailani replaced the pro-British government. Prime Minister Rashid Ali refused to allow the British to move troops through Iraq and instead ordered Iraqi troops to surround the British air base at Habbaniya, near Baghdad. German aircraft arrived in support and armed conflict broke out between Iraq and Britain in May 1941. Within a month, the British had prevailed, relieving their troops at Habbaniya and surrounding Baghdad. Britain and Iraq signed an armistice and Iraq formed a pro-British administration in October 1941. On January 17, 1943, Iraq declared war on the Axis powers and thus joined the Allies for the duration of the war.

Latvia

Latvia, part of the Russian Empire since 1795, had gained its independence from the Soviet Union in 1918, but didn't see true independence until World War I fighting was over. The Nazi-Soviet Nonaggression Pact of August 1939, however, secretly assigned Latvia to the Soviet sphere of influence. On October 5, 1939, the Soviet Union coerced Latvia into signing an agreement that permitted Soviet troops on Latvian territory. In June 1940, the Red Army entered Latvia, and the Soviets annexed Latvia on August 5, 1940.

As with Estonia and Lithuania, the Soviet occupation (June 1940–July 1941) resulted in the destruction of Latvia's political and social infrastructure.

After Germany invaded the Soviet Union, Germany occupied Latvia from July 1941 to May 1945, incorporating it into the German Reich Commissariat Ostland. The German occupation resulted in untold brutalities, including the mass murder of Jews and anyone else considered an enemy of the Reich. The Soviet Union partially reoccupied Latvia in 1944 but did not complete its occupation until the surrender of the German army in May 1945. The Soviet occupation resulted in the deportation of the German population and a postwar emigration of Russians, who soon became a majority in Latvia.

Lithuania

Lithuania obtained its independence from the Soviet Union after World War I but remained in a formal state of war against Poland over Lithuanian claims to Wilno, the historic capital of Lithuania, which Poland had annexed in 1922. In 1939, the Nazi-Soviet Nonaggression Pact initially assigned Lithuania to the German sphere of influence, but after the German invasion of Poland (1939), Lithuania was transferred to the Soviet sphere.

The entry of the Red Army into Lithuania in 1939 led to the Soviets' annexation of Lithuania on August 5, 1940. Like Latvia, Lithuania became part of the German Reich Commissariat Ostland after the German invasion of the Soviet Union in 1941. Under the German occupation, Jews and political opponents of the Germans were murdered and the country was plundered.

The Soviet Union reoccupied Lithuania in April 1944 and reannexed Lithuania into the Soviet Union. Lithuania lost 25 percent of its population as a result of the Soviet deportation of ethnic Germans and Poles, the German military draft, the murder of the Jews, and war casualties. Like the other Baltic States, Lithuania's geography was its destiny: Between two vast and warring nations, it was crushed first by one, then by the other, and was dominated by the Russians until their empire collapsed in the early 1990s.

Luxembourg

Luxembourg, a tiny principality nestled along the western border of Germany, was occupied by the Germans during World War I. Its history, for better and worse, was the result of this geographic reality. World War II began for Luxembourg on May 10, 1940, when Germany invaded the neutral nation without warning. The German goal was not to conquer Luxembourg, but to drive through it on the way to Paris. Resistance was nominal, and the reigning Grand Duchess Charlotte established a government-in-exile in London. In August 1942, Hitler announced that he had annexed Luxembourg into the German Reich and declared that Luxembourg's citizens were now German citizens. This made all young men eligible for conscription into the German army, and before the war was over about 20,000 of Luxembourg's men wore the German uniform. In 1939, Luxembourg had a total population of only 290,000, as many as 10,000 of whom died as a result of World War II. Of those, some were killed in German military service, others died in SS custody, and Luxembourg lost half its Jewish population.

Mexico

Mexico declared war on the Axis powers on May 22, 1942 and cooperated with the U.S. war effort by denying the Axis use of Mexico's ports and goods by patrolling the coast (German submarines sank six Mexican merchant ships) and by providing 250,000 Mexican troops to serve in the U.S. military (one received the U.S. Con-gressional Medal of Honor). A squadron of Mexican fighter planes joined the Allied air forces and saw action in the Philippines in the summer of 1945 by attacking Japanese ground forces on Luzon.

Netherlands

The Netherlands, a democratic monarchy, had remained militarily neutral during World War I and again declared its neutrality at the outbreak of World War II. By May 1940, however, German U-boats had sunk 31 Dutch merchant ships and had blown up a navy minesweeper, killing 30. A nation on the border of Hitler's Germany could not maintain its neutrality.

On the morning of May 10, 1940, without warning or a formal declaration of war, Germany bombed Dutch ports, airfields, and border defenses. The Dutch army mobilized, but by the sixth day of the attack, the Dutch navy and merchant fleet sailed for Britain and the Netherlands surrendered to Nazi Germany. As the Dutch government-in-exile, headed by Queen Wilhelmina, vowed to carry on the war from Britain, the Germans recruited the conquered Dutch into the German armed forces or to assist in the German war industry. The Dutch civil service remained in place to run the country, but by 1943, the Germans tightened their rule over the country and began to round up and deport Dutch Jews. The Dutch also developed a vibrant resistance that engaged in sabotage.

In 1944, as the Allies moved toward the border of Germany, the Germans stripped the Netherlands bare. The result was starvation on a mass scale and great suffering throughout the country. With war's end, the queen returned in triumph, but returned to a country devastated.

The Dutch military resistance in 1940 resulted in 2,900 killed or missing and 6,900 wounded. An additional 10,800 Dutch military personnel, including free Dutch and those wearing German uniform, died in exile, and the Netherlands and its possessions suffered 150,000 civilians killed or missing.

New Zealand

Although the Statute of Westminster gave New Zealand the option of not declaring war, it declared war on Germany within hours of Britain's declaration on September 3, 1939. Until the Pacific war began, New Zealanders fought alongside British troops in the Atlantic and in North Africa. After Pearl Harbor and the declaration of war against the Japanese, New Zealand was in a vulnerable position geographically and anticipated a Japanese invasion. New Zealand forces, including navy pilots who flew bombing missions, fought in parts of the Pacific theater until the end of the war in 1945.

Although New Zealand was not bombed by the Japanese, it suffered 12,200 killed or missing, 19,300 wounded, and 8,500 prisoners of war. Relative to New Zealand's population, this loss was 20 percent greater than that suffered by the British armed forces and double that suffered by the Americans.

Norway

Norway had stayed out of World War I and declared neutrality when World War II began in 1939. But Norway was a victim of its location. The iron mines in northern Sweden were the richest in Europe and were vital to the manufacture of war materiel. The most convenient port for the exportation of this ore was at Narvik, in northern Norway. At the beginning of the war, the Allied efforts to stop ore shipments that might reach Germany were so intense that Norwegian seamen were at risk. In the seven months following the declaration of war, 51 Norwegian ships were sunk and many others damaged. Norway, however, maintained its neutrality even after the Soviet Union invaded neighboring Finland. At this time, Norway rejected an Anglo-French request for troop transits to aid Finland in its war against the Soviets.

On April 8, 1940, Great Britain and France announced that they had mined Norwegian waters in the commercial route between the Norwegian coast and the coastal islands. The purpose was to prevent the Scandinavian countries from supplying any war materiel to Germany via commerce over those waters. The Norwegian government protested.

The next day, however, Germany invaded Norway; the Norwegian government sought help from Great Britain and France and the Allies delivered immediately. But the Allies were overwhelmed and evacuated Norway on June 8; the last Norwegian troops surrendered to the Germans on June 10. King Haakon VII (see Chapter 5, "Politicians and Demagogues") fled to Britain with three aircraft squadrons and 58 warships; 1,876 Norwegian merchant vessels escaped to Allied ports. The Germans set up a puppet government under the Norwegian Fascist Vidkun Quisling (see Chapter 6, "Officers and Soldiers"). Norway, like other countries under German occupation, was brutalized during the years 1940–45.

The total number of Norwegian military personnel killed or wounded is estimated at 2,000, with 3,800 civilian casualties.

Poland

Perhaps no other country suffered more from its location adjacent to Nazi Germany. Ethnic Poles occupied a landlocked territory bordered to the west by Germany and Czechoslovakia, to the south and southeast by the Ukraine and Belorussia, and to the east by Russia. After World War I, the Treaty of Versailles granted Poland a narrow belt of German land, popularly known as the Polish Corridor, which provided access to the Baltic Sea (see Chapter 2, "Causes of War"). The "free city" of Danzig (now Gdansk) was located on the Baltic inside this narrow strip. That treaty and a subsequent war with the new Soviet Union gave Poland some Ukrainian, Belorussian, and Russian territory.

With the Munich Pact in September 1938, which gave Germany the Sudeten region of Czechoslovakia, Poland made its own demands on Czechoslovakia. On September 30, the Polish government demanded that the Czechs immediately cede the frontier district of Teschen, which added about 1,036 square kilometers, or about 400 square miles, to Poland. But Poland's benefit from Germany's aggression in 1938 was to be short-lived.

Even as Germany was carving up and occupying Czechoslovakia in March 1939, Hitler was beginning his diplomatic offensive against Poland. The German government began by demanding the return of Danzig and the readjustment of the lines in the Polish Corridor. Poland refused, and on March 31, Britain and France pledged "all support in their power" to protect Poland against German aggression. On August 25, the British government confirmed the guarantees in a formal treaty with Poland.

On September 1, 1939, Germany attacked Poland at dawn. Britain immediately mobilized its forces. Germany attacked from five points on the frontiers, overwhelming and surrounding the Poles by pincer movements. On September 17, in accordance with the terms of the Molotov-Ribbentrop Pact signed in August 1939 (the Nazi-Soviet Nonaggression Pact; see Chapter 2, "Causes of War"), Soviet armies occupied eastern Poland. By September 19, the Polish army had ceased to exist as an organized force. The last bastion of resistance was Warsaw, but it fell on September 27.

About 100,000 Polish troops reached France, where they were regrouped into combat units. The Polish government-in-exile, led by General Władysław Sikorski, was also reorganized in France. After the fall of France in 1940, the Polish government moved to London.

During the German occupation of Poland, the German armies and the SS systematically exterminated millions of Polish citizens, including Jews, Gypsies, and other targeted groups, in concentration and extermination camps, which that dotted the landscape of the country. In April 1943, a Jewish uprising broke out in the ghetto in Warsaw and led to three weeks of fighting in the streets (see Chapter 12, "Man's Inhumanity"). Although brutally crushed in the end, the uprising in the Warsaw ghetto stands as a supreme moment of heroism in the face of Nazi barbarism.

After the Germans attacked the Soviet Union and the Soviets became allied with the British in the summer of 1941, Britain urged the Soviets to recognize the Polish government-in-exile and to nullify the German-Soviet partition of Poland. The British also requested the liberation of Polish prisoners of war deported to the Soviet Union after the Soviet occupation. Throughout July 1941, negotiations continued among the British, the Polish government-in-exile, and the Soviets, but to no avail—the Soviets wanted to install a postwar government in Warsaw that was pro-Soviet, and the British government chose to table the territorial future of Poland "until easier times."

In September 1944, the Red Army reentered Polish territory. The Polish resistance forces in Warsaw responded by initiating a full-scale attack against the German occupation forces. Instead of pushing forward to assist these forces, and despite Western entreaties to do so, Stalin halted his armies at the gates of Warsaw and allowed the Germans to annihilate the pro-Western Polish resistance. The Red Army then occupied Warsaw in January 1945 and finally drove the Germans out of Poland in March 1945.

In the meantime, a Soviet-sponsored Polish Committee of National Liberation, dominated by Communists, was established in the city of Lublin and proclaimed itself the provisional government of Poland in December 1944. In June 1945, the Polish government-in-exile in London and the Polish Committee of National Liberation in Lublin established a coalition government in Warsaw. The British and U.S. governments officially recognized the Polish government amid Soviet promises at the Yalta conference (see below and Chapter 13, "Aftermath") for free elections for Poland—elections the Soviets never allowed to take place.

After the defeat of Germany, Poland's boundaries were shifted westward into areas of eastern Germany, a region containing 8.9 million people, more than 7 million of whom were Germans. Poland subsequently expelled most of those Germans, who fled to the West. Poland's eastern boundary was also shifted westward, giving former Polish land to the Soviet Union. The nearly 4 million Poles living in these territories were resettled, mainly in the areas obtained from Germany.

Polish casualties in World War II were horrendous. Total military and civilian losses, including the almost total decimation of Poland's Jewish population, have been estimated at 5.5 million.

South Africa, Union of

South Africa's involvement in World War II was limited because of opposition from both the nation's black majority and the ethnic Dutch Afrikaners. Therefore, although the Union of South Africa declared war on Nazi Germany on September 6, 1939, it did not institute mandatory conscription and most black troops served in noncombatant roles. Although far removed from the battlefields of Europe, 334,224 South Africans served in World War II (roughly split between white and black). Casualties amounted to almost 9,000 dead and 8,000 wounded, with more than 14,000 captured.

Turkey

World War I destroyed the Ottoman Empire, leaving Turkey a poor and small country. In 1939, at the outbreak of the war, the Turkish government, led by Ismet Inonu, was fully aware that its armed forces were outmoded. The Turkish Republic immediately declared its neutrality, which it maintained throughout most of the war.

Turkey's status was rooted in a series of treaties with key warring countries. In 1925, the Soviet Union and Turkey signed a treaty of friendship after years of fighting, which was renewed in 1935; in 1939, Great Britain and Turkey entered into a treaty pledging to aid one another if either was the victim of an act of aggression. Turkey and France entered into a similar commitment that same year. The Nazi-Soviet Nonaggression Pact of August 1939, however, created a serious danger in the event that Hitler and Stalin combined to attack Turkey. In October 1939, France, Great Britain, and Turkey signed the Tripartite Treaty of Mutual Assistance pledging support should another European power attack any signatory. However, the treaty did not require Britain and France to come to the aid of Turkey if it was attacked by the Soviet Union. Italy's entry into the war on the Axis side in June 1940 and the German occupation of the Balkans in April 1941 brought the Axis powers to the Turkish frontier. Turkey, fearing an attack by Hitler, then signed the Treaty of Territorial Integrity and Friendship with Germany on June 18, 1941. Four days later, Hitler invaded the Soviet Union, which meant that Turkey escaped attack by Germany or the Soviet Union since both nations were now engaged in a death struggle with each other.

Nevertheless, Turkey faced pressure from Germany to enter the war on the German side. In 1943, with the tide of war turning in the Allies' favor, the Allies also pressed Turkey to join them, but Turkey managed to postpone doing so until February 23, 1945, when the war against Germany had entered its final phase. When it finally declared war on Germany and Japan, Turkey was elevated to the status of a founding member of the United Nations.

Union of Soviet Socialist Republics

By the time Russia became involved in World War I, it was a country weakened by war against Japan in 1904, by a revolution in 1905, and by a corrupt monarchy that was ripe to be overthrown. The Russian military, weak and inefficient, faced foreign armies and domestic unrest that culminated in the Russian Revolution of February 1917. Czar Nicholas II abdicated in March, and a weak provisional government attempted to rule the country. In the October Revolution of 1917, Vladimir Ilich Lenin and the Communists came to power. Lenin then negotiated a separate peace with Germany, entering into the Treaty of Brest-Litovsk on March 3, 1918. That treaty stripped Russia of

Latvia, Lithuania, and Estonia, as well as Finland, Poland, and the Ukraine. Russia found itself in civil war until late 1920. Meanwhile, the Allied powers defeated Germany in 1918 and stripped it of many of its acquisitions. The Baltic States, Finland, and Poland gained their independence, and the Ukraine was returned to Russian rule.

On December 30, 1922, the establishment of the Union of Soviet Socialist Republics united with Russia the ethnic territories of the former Russian Empire.

But Lenin's rule was short-lived. A stroke incapacitated him in May 1922 and he died in 1924. As Josef Stalin consolidated power, he created a social upheaval and wave of political terror unprecedented in history, starting by forcing agricultural laborers into state-owned collective farms and instituting rapid industrialization, beginning with the first Five-Year Plan in 1928.

From 1934 through 1938, Stalin conducted a series of purges of anyone he imagined to be a real or potential political opponent. These purges included high military commanders whose leadership Stalin would desperately miss in the early years of the coming war. The number of those purged between 1936 and 1938 is widely estimated at 1.5 million to 7 million. The forced collectivization of the Ukrainian peasants led to famine in 1932–33 and the deaths of 5 million to 7 million Ukrainians. This served Stalin by weakening a hotbed of opposition, but also weakened the Soviet army for the war to come.

On August 23, 1939, the Nazi-Soviet Nonaggression Pact shocked the world by creating an alliance between Germany and its avowed enemy, the Soviet Union. The purpose of this pact was to neutralize Germany's eastern flank when it invaded Poland a few days later; for the Soviets, its purpose was to protect them—for a time at least—against an immediate threat from Germany. A secret protocol gave Stalin a free hand in Finland, Estonia, Latvia, eastern Poland, and eastern Romania. In accordance with this agreement, when Hitler invaded Poland, Russia occupied the eastern section of Poland.

Less than two years later, however, on June 22, 1941, three million German troops smashed into the Soviet Union. Although the German mobilization had been going on for months, Stalin stubbornly refused to believe that the Germans would attack. In the months that followed, the German army drove the Soviets back to the suburbs of Moscow before the Red Army and the harsh Russian winter halted the German advance in December 1941.

From 1942 through late 1944, German and Soviet forces engaged in brutal combat across the length and breadth of western Russia. In February 1943, the German Sixth Army surrendered at Stalingrad—a major defeat that put the Germans on the defensive for the remainder of the war. In the summer of 1943, the largest tank battle in history occurred at Kursk, leading to another German defeat. From then on, the Red Army advanced relentlessly, until in late 1944, it

Published in the *Des Moines Register* on March 17, 1941, this political cartoon depicts Soviet Russia as a sleeping watchdog while Germany and Italy pursue their military ambitions in Southern and Eastern Europe.

stood within 100 miles of Berlin. In April 1945, the triumphant Red Army entered the German capital. The war was over a week later.

More than any other nation in World War II, the Soviets suffered horrific losses. Military and civilian deaths have been estimated at 17,700,000 (figures for the total number wounded are unavailable).

United States of America

Despite its decisive involvement in World War I, the United States government, reflecting the overwhelming sentiment of its citizens, remained profoundly isolationist in the 1920s and 1930s. The U.S. Senate refused to ratify the Treaty of Versailles and the country never joined the League of Nations. Reinforcing these strongly held beliefs was the Neutrality Act of May 1937, which stated that, in the event of any war that threatened U.S. security, the federal government would forbid the sale of arms to belligerents, and loans to them would likewise be illegal. Belligerents trading with the United States would have to pay cash for all nonrestricted items and transport them in their own ships. The act also banned U.S. citizens from traveling on the vessels of other warring nations.

When World War II began in Europe in 1939, President Franklin D. Roosevelt issued the Proclamation of Neutrality, in accordance with the act. But the president, an internationalist, understood that the United States at some point would have to become involved in the war. The November Congress lifted the ban on arms sales to allow France and Great Britain to purchase arms on a cash-and-carry basis. By March 1941, U.S. neutrality was further belied by the Lend-Lease Act, by which Roosevelt intended to "lend" U.S. warships and war materiel to beleaguered Great Britain. The United States also allowed its merchant ships to arm and to enter war zones, further diminishing the legitimacy of U.S. neutrality. U.S. naval vessels escorted British convoys, which resulted in an undeclared naval war between Germany and the United States.

Meanwhile, Japan's war effort against China required critical raw materials from the United States, particularly scrap metal and petroleum. Amid U.S. government protests against Japan's aggression in China, Japan considered alternative sources in French and Dutch possessions in Indochina and the East Indies, which would entail further conquest and aggression. The United States imposed an embargo on scrap metal exports to Japan on September 26, 1940, and after the Japanese occupied French Indochina in July

---

PRESIDENT HARRY S TRUMAN

Dropping the Bomb

This weapon is to be used against Japan between now and August 10th. I have told the Sec. of War, Mr. Stimson, to use it so that military objectives and soldiers and sailors are the target and not women and children. Even if the Japs are savages, ruthless, merciless and fanatic, we as the leader of the world for the common welfare cannot drop this terrible bomb on the old capital or the new.

He and I are in accord. The target will be a purely military one and we will issue a warning statement asking the Japs to surrender and save lives. I'm sure they will not do that, but we will have given them the chance. It is certainly a good thing for the world that Hitler's crowd or Stalin's did not discover this atomic bomb. It seems to be the most terrible thing ever discovered, but it can be made the most useful.

—From *Off the Record: The Private Papers of Harry S Truman* (New York: Harper & Row, 1986).

1941, the United States froze all Japanese assets in the United States and halted all shipments to Japan, including oil.

On December 7, 1941, Japan attacked the United States naval base at Pearl Harbor, and on December 8, 1941, the United States declared war on Japan. Germany declared war on the United States three days later.

The vast resources of the United States were mobilized to fight a war on two fronts. In the fall of 1942, U.S. forces invaded North Africa and within a year had defeated the German Afrika Korps. In the Pacific, the U.S. Navy began an island-by-island campaign that moved ever closer to the main Japanese islands; by 1944, U.S. forces had begun to retake the Philippines, and Japanese cities were being bombed regularly. In Europe, U.S. amphibious forces spearheaded the invasion of Normandy, in France, on June 6, 1944—the beginning of the march that would lead into the heartland of Germany by the spring of 1945. In the summer of 1945, the United States dropped two atomic bombs on Japan, and within days, the Japanese surrendered. World War II ended with the United States a colossal world power in both Europe and Asia.

The United States suffered approximately 405,400 military deaths and 670,800 wounded, and had 139,700 prisoners of war taken, during World War II.

Yugoslavia

After World War I, the Paris Peace Conference created the Kingdom of Yugoslavia, initially called the Kingdom of the Serbs, Croats, and Slovenes, which joined various portions of the dissolved Austro-Hungarian Empire under the general domination of Serbia. From the start there was political strife. The nation's population included 6.6 million Serbs, whose religion was primarily Eastern Orthodox and who used the Cyrillic alphabet; 4 million Croats, who were primarily Roman Catholic and used the Roman alphabet; 870,000 Bosnian Muslims, Slovenians, Macedonians, Germans, Albanians, Hungarians,

Montenegrins, Romanians, Italians, and Bulgarians; 100,000 Gypsies; and 78,000 Jews.

Ethnic and religious tensions simmered in Yugoslavia throughout the 1920s and early 1930s. On October 9, 1934, a Macedonian connected with Croatian separatist groups assassinated Yugoslavia's King Alexander (who was a Serb). He was succeeded by Peter II, at the time still a minor, and the government was controlled by a three-person regency council. In 1939, Yugoslavia instituted a federalist system, which created (seven) separate states under the Yugoslav federal government, largely to placate the separatist Croats.

When World War II began in September 1939, Yugoslavia at first declared its neutrality but then, in March 1941, succumbed to German pressure and entered into the Tripartite Pact with Germany, Italy, and Japan. This action led to a revolution and coup d'état. The regency was deposed, and a new government was formed that again declared Yugoslavia's neutrality. In retaliation, the German army, aided by Italian, Hungarian, and Bulgarian forces, invaded Yugoslavia in April 1941. King Peter and the government fled and the nation disintegrated into a three-way civil war. The Chetniks, Serbian nationalists under General Draza Mihajlovic, waged guerrilla warfare against the Germans and their puppet state in Croatia. Nationalist Croats, called the Ustasa, retaliated with a campaign of extermination against the Serbs. The Communists, led by Josip Broz (also called Tito), a Croatian, campaigned against the Germans and against the Croatian Fascists.

In September 1944, Allied armies, operating in conjunction with Tito's forces, launched an offensive against the German occupation army in Yugoslavia and largely cleared the Germans from Yugoslavia by the end of October. A new government was formed in March 1945 with Marshal Tito as premier and with Communists in key positions. Yugoslavia abolished its monarchy in August 1945, and the king remained in exile.

During the war, 276,000 Yugoslavs wore a Croat uniform, and 246,000 wore a German uniform. At least 120,000 more served on the side of other Axis armies or against other Yugo-slavs. It is unknown how many Yugoslavs died in the war, but the total has been estimated between 1.5 million and 1.7 million.

NEUTRAL NATIONS

Republic of Ireland

The Republic of Ireland remained neutral throughout World War II—a by-product of its long history of hostile relations with the British, who had dominated and exploited the island for centuries.

In December 1920, the British Parliament had enacted the Government of Ireland Bill, which provided for the partition of Ireland into two states. The six counties of the Protestant north (Northern Ireland) would elect a separate parliament, remain unified with Great Britain, and have limited home rule. The southern 26 counties, called the Irish Free State, would elect a parliament and be provided with status equal to that of Canada and Britain's other Dominions. But the status of Ireland remained disputed throughout the 1920s and 1930s, with civil war raging between the official Irish government and those who favored complete independence from the British.

The Irish Free State joined the League of Nations in 1923 and sent its own ambassador to Washington, D.C. Under Prime Minister Eamon De Valera, the Irish Free State continued to chip away at British control and influence. In 1937, Irish voters approved a new constitution that declared Eire (as the Irish called Ireland) to be a "sovereign independent democratic state." In 1938, Great Britain abandoned control of the "treaty ports" in Ireland. This act brought loud protest from members of Parliament, including Winston Churchill. Britain would sorely miss those ports during the coming war. Ireland had no intention of giving them back.

When war broke out in 1939, Ireland now had the status to declare war along with Great Britain or to remain neutral. Ireland became the only British Commonwealth nation to declare neutrality, a position it maintained throughout the war. But although Ireland was officially neutral, its people were not. Sixty thousand southern Irish enlisted in the British armed forces, others joined the British merchant fleet, and thousands went to Britain to work in manufacturing plants. Northern Ireland, with almost half of the population of the south, was exempted from British conscription but still provided the British armed forces with 30,000 enlistees.

> His Majesty's government never laid a violent hand, although at times it would have been quite easy and quite natural, and we left the De Valera government to frolic with the Germans and later with the Japanese representatives to their heart's content.
> —British Prime Minister Winston Churchill, May 13, 1945, on potentially occupying Ireland

> Mr. Churchill is proud of Britain's stand alone after France had fallen and before America entered the war. Could he not find in his heart the generosity to acknowledge there is a small nation that stood alone not for one year or two but for several hundred years against aggression, that endured spoliation, famines, massacres, in endless succession, that was clubbed many times into insensibility but that each time upon returning consciousness took up the fight anew, a small nation that could never be got to accept defeat and has never surrendered her soul?
> —Irish Prime Minister Eamon De Valera, May 16, 1945, responding to Churchill

Prime Minister De Valera was often outraged by British and American criticism of Irish neutrality and argued that although his government's policy was to preserve its essential neutrality, it had demonstrated time and again its sympathy for the Allied cause. But De Valera lost credibility when after learning of Hitler's death on April 30, 1945, he walked to the German embassy and expressed to the German minister his official condolences at Germany's loss. Although diplomatically correct given Ireland's neutrality, this action was, in light of events, extremely shortsighted. This incident, coupled with Ireland's neutrality during the war, served to prevent Ireland from joining the United Nations for another 10 years.

Portugal

During World War I, Portugal, an ally of Great Britain since the 14th century, was a cobelligerent against Germany. After the war, the Portuguese economy was in shambles when Antonio de Oliveira Salazar became Portugal's minister of finance in 1928 and revived the country's economy. As the country's most powerful political figure, he became prime minister and dictator in 1932 and established the state with a planned economy, yet his regime more closely resembled those of Germany, Italy, and Spain than the Western democracies.

Salazar supported Franco during the Spanish Civil War and in 1939 signed the Friendship and Nonaggression Pact with Spain. He was instrumental in helping to keep Spain from becoming an ally of Hitler; Salazar feared that a Spain allied with Germany would lead to an occupied Portugal.

Throughout World War II, Portugal's neutrality afforded it an important position far beyond its small size. Lisbon was the focus of international intrigue, with Allied and German agents finding themselves side by side in the city, at restaurants, and at the airport.

In October 1943, Portugal's neutrality was compromised when the government allowed the Allies to base planes and ships in the Portuguese-controlled Azores. By this time in the war, however, the Germans were in no position to take any action against the country.

Spain

Spanish dictator Francisco Franco solidified his power as a result of the Spanish Civil War, which ravaged Spain from 1936 to 1939 (see Chapter 2, "Causes of War"). His regime received substantial support from Germany and Italy, to which he remained both practically and ideologically indebted.

In March 1939, Spain joined the Anti-Comintern Pact (see Chapter 2, "Causes of War") and signed a treaty of friendship with Nazi Germany. Although Spain declared its neutrality at the beginning of World War II, it officially supported the Axis and changed its "neutral" status to that of "nonbelligerent" after Italy entered the war.

During the war, Franco met with Hitler several times to pledge his support and assure Hitler that Spain would enter the war on the Axis side when the time was right. Spain permitted German ships to refuel in Spanish harbors, allowed widespread German espionage, and allowed the recruitment of the volunteer Blue Division, initially numbering 17,692 officers and men. The latter fought alongside the Germans on the Eastern Front for "the extermination of Russia." After the Allies instituted an oil embargo against Spain in 1944, Spain banned the export of wolfram (used in the production of tungsten steel) to Germany, expelled certain German spies, withdrew the Blue Division from the Eastern Front, and released to the Allies three Italian ships interned in Spanish ports. Franco, however, was very crafty in his dealings with Hitler, and by never fully embracing Germany, he probably spared Spain the same fate suffered by Italy.

In April 1945, Spain severed diplomatic relations with Germany and Japan, but at the Potsdam Conference (see Chapter 15 "Documents, Organizations, and Monuments") the United States, Great Britain, and the Soviet Union specifically disallowed Spain's membership in the United Nations. Spain was not admitted to the United Nations until 1955.

WERE THEY REALLY NEUTRAL?

Any nation attempting to remain neutral during World War II found itself under pressure from both sides as well as its own citizens. There were, in fact, various degrees of "neutrality" and some nations stretched the definition to the breaking point.

For example, at the end of the Spanish Civil War and the beginning of World War II, Spain was indebted both ideologically and financially to Germany and Italy for the military aid and war materiel that helped put Franco's Nationalist regime into power in 1939. Throughout the war, Spain proceeded gingerly, pledging its friendship to Germany but pleading war weariness and poverty. For years, Germany would pressure Spain or demand its participation in the war, and Spain would respond with requests for aid and protection in amounts far beyond Germany's ability to give. Meanwhile, Spanish fascism was in an ideological war with Soviet communism, and Spain did, in fact, send an entire division (the Spanish Blue Division) to the Russian front to fight with the Germans against the Soviets. Spain finally withdrew the Blue Division in 1943 under Allied pressure that questioned Spain's neutrality. War trauma and casualties on the Russian front must have influenced Franco's decision to "postpone" a declaration of war by Spain against the Allies. Franco, in fact, had played his hand very shrewdly, avoiding an embrace of Hitler that might have invited Allied invasion but at the same time keeping the Germans satisfied enough not to take drastic action against the Spanish for their reluctance to get more involved in the fighting.

Other countries such as Sweden and Switzerland found that their proximity to Germany caused diplomatic crises. Both countries maintained their neutrality by accommodating Nazi Germany to a point. In fact, both countries used strength tempered by accommodation in dealing with Germany. Each sought to convince Germany that a German attempt at occupation would be militarily expensive and that Germany would face opposition and substantial force; the militaries of both Sweden and Switzerland remained mobilized to some degree throughout the war. Meanwhile, both nations tested the limits of true neutrality by increasing their trade in war materiel with the Germans as well as by allowing limited German troop movements across their territory. Both Sweden and Switzerland were under imminent danger of occupation by Nazi Germany several times, and the Nazi military had thoroughly prepared plans to invade them.

For nations of strategic importance, neutrality provided no security from German attack. Denmark, the Netherlands, Belgium, and Luxembourg, for example, all attempted to find comfort behind a declaration of neutrality after Britain and France declared war on Germany, and early in the war the German army attacked, invaded, and occupied each nation.

As the Allies began to succeed, they pressured the European neutrals. By mid-1944, Germany's trade with Sweden, Switzerland, and even Spain had all but ceased. No neutral nation was under more Allied pressure and scrutiny, however, than Ireland, which declared its neutrality at the beginning of the war and maintained it throughout the conflict. Great Britain sorely missed the Irish "treaty ports" of Cobh, Castletown Bere, and Lough Swilly, and Ireland's refusal to allow British use of them remained a grave concern to Britain (as was Irish neutrality itself). It seemed to the Allied world, as Irish Prime Minister Eamon De Valera as much as stated, that Irish hatred of English domination exceeded Ireland's fear of invasion by Nazi Germany. During the Battle of Britain in 1940, Ireland remained resolute in its neutrality and absolute in its refusal to allow Great Britain use of the treaty ports. After the United States entered the war, American-Irish diplomatic relations became frigid.

Perhaps the most interesting "neutral" was the United States. For the first two years (1939–41), the United States was officially neutral, although it provided Great Britain with war materiel, ships, and every imaginable supply for its survival. The United States patrolled the North Atlantic against German submarines, supplied aid to China (including an entire fighter squadron), and embargoed both Japan and Germany.

Before Pearl Harbor, the Americans and the British entered into the Atlantic Charter, which planned a grand military strategy and announced to the world the U.S. intention to halt German aggression. The United States and Germany were in a de facto sea war in the Atlantic Ocean for four months before Japan attacked Pearl Harbor. President Franklin Roosevelt cautiously directed U.S. foreign policy with the intention of guiding the United States into the war when public support would be assured. His strategy worked.

Sweden

Sweden declared its neutrality in World War I and did the same when World War II broke out in 1939. Sweden was able to maintain its neutrality and resist invasion—while Finland to the east was devastated and Norway to the west was occupied by the Germans—because of its military strength. Sweden was able to convince Germany that it would resist any aggression with such force that Germany would be tied down while its paramount interests remained elsewhere.

Germany, on the other hand, was content to leave Sweden unscathed so long as the country met Germany's ever-increasing trade and military demands, primarily for iron ore from Sweden's rich mines (see Chapter 2, "Causes of War," and Chapter 3, "The Economics of World War II") and, as time passed, for access to troop transit via Sweden's railroads to places in Finland and Norway.

Sweden's acquiescence to these demands waned as Germany began to lose the war in 1943. By the end of the war, Sweden had cut off all iron transport to Germany and was refusing to allow German troop movements across Swedish territory. By the last months of the war, Sweden's shift away from Germany was so complete that the nation could be termed a "pro-Allied nonbelligerent state." Sweden maintained diplomatic relations with the Third Reich until its last day as a sovereign power. On May 7, 1945, the Swedish foreign minister informed the German minister in Stockholm that diplomatic relations between the two countries had ceased to exist.

Although Swedish war casualties were comparatively low, 202 Swedish merchant vessels were sunk during the war and many more damaged. So many mines were laid about Sweden's coast that they sank seven more ships after the war.

Switzerland

Switzerland managed to maintain its neutral status throughout World War II through a pattern of accommodation to Axis demands (see Chapter 3, "The Economics of World War II") and a simultaneous show of military strength. In addition to mobilizing its army, the Swiss government formulated a plan by which it would retreat to a national redoubt in the southern Alps if the Germans invaded. The Swiss had prepared their railroad tunnels through the Swiss Alps for demolition in the event of invasion, a powerful deterrent to the Germans.

Throughout much of the war, Switzerland allowed German and Italian troops to use its railways and traded essential food and war materiel with the Germans. During the war, Switzerland was a refuge for escaped prisoners, members of the French resistance, and other parties seeking political asylum. But Switzerland closed its borders to 170,000 French Jews in early 1942. According to some estimates, 400,000 refugees passed through Switzerland during World War II. Swiss neutrality allowed it to serve as a go-between for belligerent nations. Switzerland did not withstand the war unscathed, however. Allied aircraft mistakenly bombed the Swiss city of Schaffhausen in April 1944 as well as the towns of Rafz and Stein.

In recent years information has surfaced describing an active role played by Swiss banks in the financial dealings of the Nazi government. Particularly disturbing was the revelation that Swiss banks refused—until pressured by negative press accounts and lawsuits—to return money deposited for safekeeping by Jews subsequently murdered in the Holocaust to their survivors and heirs.

Lend-Lease Aid

The table that follows shows the amounts of war materiel (in millions of dollars) supplied to nations opposing Axis forces through the U.S. Lend-Lease program. Lend-Lease was created at a time when the United States was officially neutral. The program allowed for the shipment of U.S. goods, such as arms and related war materiel, and services, such as financial aid, as a means of providing assistance to the British in their struggle against the Germans.

	Monthly Goods	Services	Total	CUMULATIVE FROM JANUARY 1943		
				Goods	Services	Total
1943						
January	627	55	682	7,175	1,760	8,035
February	656	41	697	7,831	1,801	9,632
March	663	24	687	8,494	1,825	10,319
April	720	63	783	9,214	1,888	11,102
May	716	74	790	9,930	1,962	11,892
June	954	77	1,031	10,884	2,039	12,923
July	1,018	32	1,050	11,902	2,071	13,973
August	1,114	147	1,261	13,016	2,219	15,235
September	1,121	76	1,197	14,137	2,294	16,431
October	1,028	73	1,101	15,165	2,368	17,533
November	971	105	1,076	16,136	2,473	18,609
December	1,300	77	1,377	17,436	2,550	19,986
1944						
January	1,214	45	1,259	18,650	2,595	21,245
February	1,124	226	1,350	19,774	2,821	22,595
March	1,406	224	1,630	21,180	3,045	24,225
April	1,266	18	1,284	22,446	3,063	25,509
May	1,160	239	1,399	23,607	3,301	26,908
June	1,212	150	1,362	24,819	3,451	28,270

	Monthly Goods	*Services*	*Total*	Goods	Services	Total
July	1,308	82	1,390	26,127	3,533	29,660
August	1,009	156	1,165	27,136	3,689	30,825
September	1,116	82	1,198	28,252	3,771	32,023
October	1,048	97	1,145	29,300	3,868	33,168
November	856	39	895	30,156	3,907	34,063
December	1,254	65	1,319	31,410	3,972	35,382
1945						
January	997	179	1,176	32,407	4,151	36,558
February	1,407	55	1,462	33,814	4,206	38,020
March	993	−411[1]	952	34,807	4,165	38,972
April	902	68	970	35,709	4,233	39,942
May	846	33	879	36,555	4,266	40,821
June	886	314	1,200	37,441	4,580	42,021

[1] Negative figure results from adjustment to reflect downward revision in ship charter rates.
Source: "Twentieth Report to Congress on Lend-Lease Operation (on the period ending 30 June 1945)," (Washington, D.C.: U.S. Government Printing Office, 1945).

Treaties

The following is an alphabetical listing of the major treaties leading up to World War II and entered into during the war. It includes principal treaties between and among both the Axis powers and the Allied nations.

ANGLO-SOVIET TREATY The Anglo-Soviet Treaty created the alliance between Great Britain and the Soviet Union; the British foreign secretary, Anthony Eden, and his Soviet counterpart, Vyacheslav Molotov, signed it in London on May 26, 1942. It pledged a mutual alliance against Germany and its Axis allies, and the signatories agreed that neither would negotiate or conclude a separate peace without the consent of the other. Great Britain and the Soviet Union agreed that they were not fighting the war to seek territorial aggrandizement for themselves, and they pledged noninterference in the internal affairs of other states. In negotiating this treaty, Stalin had demanded recognition of the Soviet Union's earlier acquisition of eastern Poland and the Baltic States, which the Soviets had occupied while allied with the Germans. The British refused to recognize these acquisitions and the matter was left unresolved.

ANTI-COMINTERN PACT This was originally an agreement between Germany and Japan signed in November 1936; the governments agreed to exchange information about the activities of Soviet-backed international Communist parties. Italy joined in November 1937, and in 1939, Spain, Hungary, and the Japanese puppet state of Manchukuo joined. In November 1941, Bulgaria, Croatia, Denmark, Finland, Romania, and Slovakia joined, along with the pro-Japanese "reformed government of the Republic of China" located in Nanking. The pact was anti-Communist (and later anti-British), but it was not a military alliance (see Chapter 2, "Causes of War").

ATLANTIC CHARTER This was a joint declaration by the United States and Great Britain, made and signed on August 14, 1941, by U.S. President Franklin D. Roosevelt and British Prime Minister Winston Churchill. Although the United States had not yet entered the war, the Atlantic Charter expressed common principles and a list of common national policies to be followed in the postwar era (see Chapter 15, "Documents, Organizations, and Monuments," for more details).

CZECH-SOVIET TREATY OF ALLIANCE In July 1941, the Soviet government, with the consent of Great Britain, entered into a treaty with the Czech government-in-exile under Edvard Beneš; it gave Czechoslovakia the status of an Allied fighting power.

DANISH-GERMAN NONAGGRESSION PACT Denmark was alone among the Scandinavian countries in accepting Hitler's offer of a nonaggression pact; Germany and Denmark signed a 10-year agreement in March 1939. It guaranteed Denmark's right to trade with other nations, and Denmark's primary trading partner was Great Britain until the German occupation of Denmark in April 1940.

FINNISH-SOVIET ARMISTICE OF MARCH 12, 1940 Entered into at the end of the Winter War, on March 12, 1940, this treaty ceded to the Soviet Union a military base at Hanko as well as the Karelian Isthmus.

FINNISH-SOVIET ARMISTICE OF SEPTEMBER 19, 1944 At the end of the Continuation War, Finland entered into a treaty with the Soviet Union, returning lands to the Soviet Union previously reclaimed by Finland, substituting Parkkala for Hanko as a Soviet military base, and providing for Finland to pay reparations to the Soviet Union.

FOUR-POWER TREATY OF 1922 Japan, France, Great Britain, and the United States agreed to respect each other's territories and possessions in the Pacific Ocean and to consult each other and negotiate if such rights were threatened.

FRANCO-SOVIET TREATIES On November 28, 1942, the Soviet Union signed an agreement with the Free French, recognizing the Free French government and pledging mutual assistance against the Germans. On December 10, 1944, France and the Soviet Union signed a 20-year treaty of friendship and mutual assistance. This military alliance required that neither party enter into a separate peace with Germany and that each remain allied against Germany until total victory was achieved.

KELLOGG-BRIAND PACT This treaty was also called the Pact of Paris, and its official name was the Treaty for the Renunciation of War. Fifteen nations signed it in Paris on August 27, 1928, and other nations later ratified it, bringing the total to 62, including all the great powers of the day and nearly every independent nation in the world. Drafted by U.S. Secretary of State Frank B. Kellogg and French Foreign Minister Aristide Briand, the pact bound its signatories to renounce war as an instrument of national policy and committed them to settle international disputes by peaceful means. Signers included Japan, Italy, and Germany. In 1931, Japan waged war in Manchuria, and Italy invaded Ethiopia in 1935. Although by this time the treaty had become discredited as a means for halting aggression, it did establish the concept that war was an outlaw act and that aggression was morally reprehensible under international law. In doing so, it weakened the tradition of war as foreign policy by other means and laid a basis for Allied indignation at neutral nations that maintained their neutrality in the face of aggression against their neighbors.

LATERAN TREATY In 1929, Italy and the Roman Catholic Church ended almost 60 years of hostility revolving around the incorporation of the former Papal States into the unified nation of Italy in the 19th century. The treaty created the small independent nation of Vatican City in Rome in return for the church's acceptance of the loss of the Papal territories.

LITTLE ENTENTE This alliance among Czechoslovakia, Romania, and Yugoslavia was aimed primarily at discouraging the resurgence of Hapsburg power in Eastern and Central Europe. The Little Entente was a political and economic alliance formed to maintain the territorial integrity of the three nations whose boundaries were established by the Treaty of Versailles, the Treaty of Saint-Germain, and the Treaty of Trianon after World War I. Throughout the 1920s and the 1930s, the Little Entente maintained a common foreign policy and acted as a diplomatic bloc in the League of Nations. German claims against Czechoslovakia, which culminated in the Munich Pact of 1938, effectively dissolved the power of the Little Entente.

MUNICH PACT Germany, Italy, France, and Great Britain signed the Munich Pact in Munich on September 29, 1938. Britain and France acquiesced in the cession of the Sudetenland in Czechoslovakia to Germany after Hitler promised that this would be his last territorial demand in Europe. British Prime Minister Neville

Chamberlain and French Premier Edouard Daladier, as well as Hitler and Mussolini, signed the pact. Under its terms the Germans were to occupy the Sudetenland as of October 1, 1938, and the parties agreed to convene a new conference if Hungarian and Polish claims were not settled in three months. All parties agreed to guarantee the new boundaries of Czechoslovakia. Poland and Hungary then seized Czech territory, and in March 1939 the Germans marched into Czechoslovakia and made most of the country a German protectorate, effectively nullifying the Munich Pact.

The Munich Pact has since become a symbol for the ineffectiveness of the policy of appeasing aggression in the hope of avoiding war.

NAVAL DISARMAMENT CONFERENCE In 1920 and 1921, Britain and the United States held the Naval Disarmament Conference in Washington, D.C. They invited Japan as the third major naval power, France and Italy as medium-sized naval powers, and Belgium, Holland, Portugal, and China as minor powers. All agreed to reduce naval tonnage and impose limits on the size of each nation's navy in order to avoid an arms race. The ratio set for Britain, the United States, and Japan was 5:5:3 in battleship and aircraft carrier tonnage. Although the Japanese figure was smaller, Japan had a naval interest only in the Pacific Ocean, versus U.S. naval interests in both the Atlantic and Pacific and British interests worldwide. One result of the conference was that it tended to make Japan supreme in the Pacific.

NAZI-SOVIET NONAGGRESSION PACT This general term encompasses the German-Soviet Treaty of Nonaggression of August 23, 1939, as well as the secret protocols that accompanied it (and remained secret until the capture of German documents at the end of the war). The published terms of the pact established trade agreements and committed each nation not to go to war against the other. The secret protocols were as follows: Each nation agreed to distinct

Soviet Foreign Minister Vyacheslav Molotov signs the infamous Nazi-Soviet nonaggression pact on August 23, 1939, as German Foreign Minister Joachim von Ribbentrop and Soviet Premier Josef Stalin look on.

Bulgaria signed the Treaty of Neuilly at Neuilly, France. Under this treaty, Bulgaria lost most of what it had gained in the Balkan wars of 1912 and 1913 as well as all of its World War I conquests. Bulgaria recognized the independence of and ceded territory to Yugoslavia and gave up part of Thrace to Greece and part of Dobruja to Romania.

NINE-POWER TREATY OF 1922 The following nations agreed to respect the territorial integrity and sovereignty of China: the United States, Great Britain, Japan, France, Italy, Portugal, the Netherlands, Belgium, and China.

PACT OF STEEL On May 22, 1939, the foreign ministers of Italy and Germany, Galeazzo Ciano and Joachim von Ribbentrop, signed a pact that declared that each country would come to the aid of the other if it were attacked. The Italians signed the Pact of Steel on the verbal understanding that neither party would provoke war before 1943.

RAPALLO, TREATY OF This was a secret treaty that Germany and the Soviet Union entered into in 1922. In addition to various trade agreements, the treaty allowed Germany to secretly produce weapons in the Soviet Union. In return, Germany recognized the Soviet government, the first nation to do so.

SAINT-GERMAIN, TREATY OF The Allies and Austria executed the Treaty of Saint-Germain, the peace treaty ending World War I, at Saint-Germain-en-Laye, France, on September 10, 1919. It provided that Austria would make financial reparations for war damages and would never join in any future union with Germany. The treaty required Austria to recognize the sovereignty of Hungary and cede territories to Yugoslavia, Czechoslovakia, Poland, Romania, and Italy.

spheres of influence within which each side would be free to operate without interference from the other party. The pact provided for the partition of Poland between Germany and the Soviet Union along the Vistula, Narew, and San Rivers; the Soviet sphere of influence included the eastern portion of Poland, as well as Bessarabia, Estonia, and Latvia. The German-Soviet Treaty of Friendship, Cooperation, and Demarcation of September 28, 1939, amended the original treaty. This new agreement, entered into near the end of the German invasion of Poland, gave the Germans the portion of Poland between the Vistula and the Bug Rivers in return for adding Lithuania to the Soviet sphere of influence. Germany ultimately betrayed the terms of the treaty and invaded the Soviet Union in June 1941.

NEUILLY, TREATY OF On November 27, 1919, the World War I Allies and the defeated

TRIANON, TREATY OF The Treaty of Trianon, signed at the Grand Trianon Palace at

Versailles, France, on June 4, 1920, constituted the treaty of peace between the World War I Allies and Hungary. It provided for Hungary to pay reparations in part by May 1, 1921, with the remainder to be paid in 66 semiannual installments. It limited the Hungarian army to 35,000 men, and Hungary lost about two-thirds of its territory and half its population. Hungary ceded Slovakia and Carpathian Ruthenia to Czechoslovakia, and Transylvania and part of the Banat region to Romania. Yugoslavia gained the remainder of the Banat region and Croatia-Slavonia. Austria received the Gurgenland and the treaty gave other territory to Italy and Poland.

TRIPARTITE PACT Germany, Italy, and Japan signed this pact in Berlin on September 27, 1940. The terms included a promise of mutual aid if any signatory was attacked by a power not already involved in the existing European or Asian war, a provision clearly directed at the United States and intended to forestall U.S. intervention. The pact contained a secret protocol allowing Japan to use its withdrawal from the pact as a bargaining point with the United States. The pact did not intimidate the United States, which in fact increased its aid to China, and Japanese negotiations with the United States foundered. In November 1940, the original signatories asked the Soviet Union to join, but they ended negotiations after Hitler found Stalin's conditions unacceptable. That same month, Romania, Hungary, and Slovakia signed the pact, and in March 1941 Bulgaria and Yugoslavia joined. Yugoslavia's decision led to a revolution and coup d'état, and the new government repudiated Yugoslavia's signing. The Nazi puppet state of Croatia, however, entered into the pact on June 15, 1941. Unlike the grand alliance of the United States, Great Britain, and the Soviet Union, the Tripartite Pact and the coalition of the Axis powers had no agreed-upon strategy for the prosecution of the war.

UNITED NATIONS DECLARATION On January 1, 1942, the 26 nations at war against the Axis powers adopted and accepted the terms of the Atlantic Charter in this joint declaration. They also agreed to use their full resources against the Axis powers until the Axis was defeated, to cooperate, and to not make a separate peace (see Atlantic Charter).

VERSAILLES, TREATY OF At the end of World War I, the Paris Peace Conference was held at Versailles, France, on January 18, 1919. The United States, Great Britain, France, and Italy represented the Allied nations. The treaty put full responsibility for the war and the payment of its total cost on Germany and required Germany to reduce its army to 100,000 and abolish compulsory military service. It also required Germany to stop importing, exporting, and producing nearly all war materiel and to limit its navy to 24 ships with no submarines. It limited the German navy to a force of 15,000. The treaty forced Germany to agree to permit former Kaiser Wilhelm II to be tried on the charge of "a supreme offense against international morality" (although the trial never took place). The treaty also placed the Saar Basin under a League of Nations commission for up to 15 years, required Germany to cede Eupen-et-Malmédy and Moresnet to Belgium, and mandated the cession of Alsace-Lorraine to France and of West Prussia to Poland. It further required an election to determine the status of northern and central Schleswig. Northern Schleswig was returned to Denmark in 1920, but central Schleswig remained with Germany. Poland received large parts of the provinces of Posson and West Prussia and a portion of Silesia. Czechoslovakia gained a portion of Upper Silesia, the port of Mimmil went to Lithuania, the port of Danzig became a free city, and Germany lost its entire colonial empire. Germany signed the Treaty of Versailles on June 28, 1919. The U.S. Senate, however, never ratified the agreement; it signed the separate Treaty of

Berlin with Germany on July 2, 1921 (see Chapter 2, "Causes of War").

Conferences

The following list of the principal Allied conferences illustrates the changing dynamics of the Grand Alliance as well as the development of the United Nations into a global allied force.

PANAMA CONFERENCE On September 23, 1939, the United States and 20 other Pan-American nations issued the Panama Declaration, which confirmed their neutrality, demanded that the belligerent nations cease subversive activities within their boundaries, banned belligerent submarines from their ports, and created a security zone extending 480 kilometers (300 miles) offshore.

HAVANA CONFERENCE At this conference held on July 22, 1940, Argentina, Brazil, Chile, Peru, Uruguay, and the United States declared the Havana Act in anticipation of the transfer of European colonies in the Western Hemisphere from one belligerent nation to another as a result of the war. The act declared that the signatories would be trustees of any territory in danger of changing hands. The act decreed that should a belligerent nation lose control of its territory and a trusteeship be declared, that territory or colony would have the right of future self-determination.

HYDE PARK DECLARATION On April 20, 1941, Canada and the United States agreed to provide each other with war materiel and that Canada could transfer such materiel to Great Britain under the Lend-Lease Act.

PLACENTIA BAY CONFERENCE At this conference, held off the coast of Newfoundland from August 9–12, 1941, Churchill, Roosevelt, and their advisers drafted and published the Atlantic Charter.

THREE-POWER CONFERENCE As a follow-up to the Placentia Bay Conference, representatives of Great Britain and the United States met with Stalin in September of 1941 in Moscow to offer materiel aid to the Soviet Union. Although Stalin demanded much more than the Allies felt they could provide, the parties did agree to aid the Soviet Union for the period from October 1941 through June 1942.

ARCADIA CONFERENCE Churchill and Roosevelt met in Washington, D.C. from December 22, 1941, to January 14, 1942, to coordinate war strategy for the foreseeable future. Principal topics were the extension of Lend-Lease to the Soviet Union, assistance to MacArthur in the Philippines, production targets, placing U.S. personnel in Northern Ireland and Iceland, and the wording of the United Nations Declaration.

RIO DE JANEIRO CONFERENCE (OR RIO CONFERENCE) Held on January 15, 1942, the United States attempted to obtain a declaration of war from those Latin American states that had not yet pledged their support. Chile and Argentina were the principal holdouts, although Chile did finally sever diplomatic relations with the Axis powers in 1943.

ANGLO-SOVIET TREATY CONFERENCE This conference on May 26, 1942, led to the treaty signed in London by the British foreign secretary, Anthony Eden, and Soviet foreign minister, Vyacheslav Molotov, in which both nations agreed that neither would enter into a separate peace with Germany or the Axis without the consent of the other.

SYMBOL CONFERENCE AT CASABLANCA This conference held from January 14–24, 1943, was attended by Churchill, Roosevelt, and their military staffs, and centered on war strategy. Roosevelt declared the policy of requiring

British Prime Minister Winston Churchill, U.S. President Franklin D. Roosevelt, and Free French leader Charles de Gaulle pose with members of their staffs during the Casablanca Conference in January 1943.

unconditional surrender by the Axis powers. Stalin did not attend because of the raging battle at Stalingrad.

TRIDENT CONFERENCE IN WASHINGTON, D.C. Churchill, Roosevelt, and their advisers attended from May 11–25, 1943. The leaders agreed to delay the invasion of France until May 1944 and confirmed the policy of requiring the unconditional surrender of Italy, although General Eisenhower had requested that they soften it. Roosevelt and Churchill also agreed to pressure Portugal to allow Allied air bases in the Azores Islands.

QUADRANT CONFERENCE IN QUEBEC Attended by Churchill, Roosevelt, and their advisers from August 17–24, 1943 this conference proposed landings on the French Riviera to coincide with the Normandy invasion, and the parties agreed to pressure Spain to remove its Blue Division from the Eastern Front. Churchill and Roosevelt agreed to keep all research information about the atomic bomb secret within their respective countries and to use such a weapon only with the consent of the other.

SEXTANT CONFERENCE IN CAIRO Churchill, Roosevelt, and their staffs were joined

Notes:

1 Austria separated from Germany regains its independence.

2 Vienna, like Berlin, is divided into four occupational zones.

3 Trieste is an "International City," and later returns to Italy.

Territory lost by Germany to Poland and the Soviet Union

Territory gained by the Soviet Union

- - - Boundaries in 1945

—— Boundaries in 1939

Zones of Occupation

American

British

French

Soviet

0   300 Miles

Scale for main map

Berlin

Airfields   Checkpoints

0   5 Miles

STATUS OF EUROPE POST–WORLD WAR II

by a Chinese delegation in order to negotiate further aid to China in its war against Japan from November 23–26, 1943, and again from December 3–7, 1943. Churchill and Roosevelt assured the Chinese that territory taken from China by Japan would be returned. Roosevelt informed Churchill that he had appointed Eisenhower to command the Normandy invasion.

EUREKA CONFERENCE IN TEHRAN November 8–December 1, 1943, marked the first time that Churchill, Roosevelt, and Stalin (along with their advisers) had met together, and it resulted in Stalin's agreement to declare war on Japan as soon as Germany was defeated. Also, Stalin continued to press the United States and Great Britain to mount a Western invasion, and Roosevelt and Churchill pledged to do so in May 1944.

OCTAGON CONFERENCE IN QUEBEC At this conference of Churchill, Roosevelt, and their advisers, held from September 12–16, 1944,

Churchill offered, and Roosevelt accepted, a British fleet to operate with the Americans against Japan. The parties also agreed to divide Germany into postwar occupation zones.

TOLSTOY CONFERENCE IN MOSCOW Churchill, Stalin, and their staffs attended, and Averell Harriman, the U.S. ambassador to the Soviet Union, headed the U.S. delegation on August 9, 1944. They discussed the timetable by which the Soviet Union would declare war on Japan, the relative degree of influence the countries would exert on the various nations in the Balkan Peninsula, and Poland's future.

ARGONAUT CONFERENCE IN YALTA After a preliminary conference between U.S. and British representatives from January 30 to February 3, 1945, at which Churchill and Roosevelt met only twice, Churchill, Roosevelt, and Stalin met for the Argonaut Conference from February 4–11, 1945. The predominant topics were postwar political concerns, the occupation of Germany

The Big Three, British Prime Minister Winston Churchill, U.S. President Franklin D. Roosevelt, and Soviet Premier Josef Stalin (left to right), pause on a patio during the conference at the Crimean resort town of Yalta in February 1945.

and Austria, the participation of France in the German and Austrian occupation, and the nature of Polish boundaries and frontiers. Without Churchill's knowledge, Roosevelt and Stalin entered into secret agreements that addressed Soviet territorial demands in return for the Soviet Union's declaring war on Japan.

INTER-AMERICAN CONFERENCE IN MEXICO CITY At this conference on February 21, 1945, the Latin American nations signed the Chapultepec Act, whereby they agreed not to harbor any Axis leader or agent guilty of war crimes. The Pan-American nations agreed that aggression against one would be considered aggression against all. Although the governments of the United States and Great Britain did not recognize the government of Argentina, a final protocol allowed Argentina to declare war against the Axis powers. Subsequently, the United States and Great Britain recognized Argentina's government.

SAN FRANCISCO CONFERENCE This was the first meeting of the United Nations, held on April 25, 1945, attended by delegates from 50 Allied nations. Because of disagreement between the United States and the Soviet Union regarding the legitimacy of the Polish government, the seat reserved for Poland remained vacant.

TERMINAL CONFERENCE IN POTSDAM The heads of the governments of the United States, Great Britain, and the Soviet Union attended from July 17 to August 2, 1945. Harry S Truman was now U.S. president, and Churchill gave up his seat at the conference on July 26, after he was defeated in the British general election. His replacement was Clement R. Attlee of the British Labour Party. The three governments issued the Potsdam Declaration, which called for the unconditional surrender of Japan, the limitation of Japanese sovereignty to its four main islands, Japan's disarmament, and the establishment of a democratic government. The leaders also discussed postwar boundaries in Europe, especially those of Poland.

CHAPTER 5

Politicians and Demagogues

The leaders of World War II included democrats and tyrants, eccentrics and geniuses, patriots and puppets. They made brilliant decisions and they made foolish, destructive decisions. For better or worse, they shaped the conduct of the war and helped determine their nations' place in the postwar world.

The Allies were led to victory by two commanding eloquent figures. Britain's Prime Minister Winston Churchill's soaring rhetoric and stubbornness rallied his dispirited nation when it stood alone facing the Nazi threat. The United States's Franklin Delano Roosevelt was elected president in 1932 in the depths of the Great Depression, and, like Churchill, the popular and charismatic Roosevelt almost single-handedly rallied his people at a time when it seemed that the nation might disintegrate. A politician of vision, he understood that the Germans represented a threat not only to Europe but to the United States as well.

Churchill and Roosevelt were products of democratic societies. Their unlikely ally in World War II was Stalin—leader of the Soviet Union—a repressive dictator who had ordered the murder of millions of his own people. But the Soviet Union was a major power, fighting Germany in the East, and Stalin was a necessary ally for the British and Americans, who alone could not have defeated the Axis.

113

British Prime Minister Winston Churchill tips his hat to an adoring crowd in Quebec as he arrives to meet President Franklin D. Roosevelt in August 1943.

France had produced few leaders of distinction in the years immediately preceding the conflict. Once the war came, however, one emerged: Charles de Gaulle, self-proclaimed head of Free France, a demanding leader who insisted that the French be treated as equals. De Gaulle became the supreme French military and political hero, the incarnation of the courage and defiance of France's resistance movement while under occupation.

The Axis leaders were almost all the products of authoritarian cultures with little or no tradition of democratic rule. Adolf Hitler was a poverty-stricken Austrian who had fought as a private in the German army in World War I. In a few short years he had fashioned himself into the leader (*Führer*) of a small political party—the National Socialist German Workers Party, the Nazis—dedicated to the overthrow of the weak postwar democratic regime set up after World War I. His ambitions—to conquer all Europe and to eliminate all European Jews—were not taken seriously by most political leaders, but by 1941, Germany dominated Europe. As the war continued, Hitler seemed to lose the deft touch of the early years of his rise to power, leading his armies from one disaster to another. His suicide in 1945 was carried out against the backdrop of the total destruction and the inevitable surrender of Germany.

Hitler's principal ally in Europe, Benito Mussolini of Italy, Il Duce ("The Leader"), had come to power in the early 1920s. At first, Mussolini was wary of Hitler's ambitions, but he eventually came to see Hitler as a vehicle through which Italy could achieve greater imperial power and embraced Nazi Germany in alliance. Italy joined the war in 1940—a move that proved to be a catastrophic mistake. At war's end, Italy was in ruins, and Mussolini was placed against a wall and executed by Italian partisans.

With the possible exception of the Emperor Hirohito, few Japanese wartime leaders are familiar today in the West. The beloved emperor of Japan, Hirohito's life was spared after Japan's surrender to prevent a possible uprising among the Japanese people. Other Japanese leaders, such as General Hideki Tojo and Admiral Isoruku Yamamoto, were not as fortunate.

Biographical sketches of the major players in World War II follow:

The Leaders

BENEŠ, EDUARD (1884–1948) Beneš was president of the Czech government-in-exile during the war. Forced to resign under pressure from Adolf Hitler after the 1938 Munich Pact that carved up his country and gave the Sudetenland to Germany, Beneš left for France. In 1939, after the Nazis occupied all of Czechoslovakia, Beneš formed the Czech National Committee in Paris, moving it to London in 1940. He promoted the formation of Czech army and air units within the British armed forces. The British recognized his provisional government in 1941, as did all the Allies in 1942. After the war, Beneš returned to Czechoslovakia, where he was elected president by the parliament in 1946. He resigned, however, in 1948 as Communist pressure eventually drove Czechoslovakia into the Soviet sphere of influence.

BERNADOTTE, FOLKE (1895–1948) The nephew of King Gustav V of Sweden, Bernadotte was vice chairman of the Swedish Red Cross Committee, which enabled him to arrange prisoner exchanges between Britain and Germany. Negotiating with Nazi SS chief Heinrich Himm-

ler in 1945, he forwarded peace proposals to the Allies (they were rejected). He was assassinated by Jewish extremists in Palestine in 1948 while on a peacekeeping mission for the United Nations.

BERNHARD, PRINCE (1911) Married to Princess Juliana, the heir to the Dutch throne, German-born Prince Bernhard fled to London in 1940, flew for the Royal Air Force, and coordinated the Dutch resistance movement. He reorganized the Dutch intelligence service, became commander in chief of the Dutch armed forces in 1944, and returned secretly that year to the Netherlands to organize resistance groups.

CHAMBERLAIN, NEVILLE (1869–1940) Chamberlain was British prime minister from 1937 to 1940. He led Allied negotiators to the infamous 1938 Munich Conference that carved up Czechoslovakia and gave its Sudeten region to Hitler's Germany. His policy of appeasement bought time for Britain and France to prepare to meet Hitler's threat but tarnished Chamberlain's reputation when Germany annexed the remainder of Czechoslovakia in 1939 (see Chapter 2, "Causes of War," and Chapter 4, "Allies, Enemies, and Bystanders").

Often adversarial, General Joseph Stilwell, commander of American and Chinese troops in the China-Burma-India theater, and Generalissimo and Madam Chiang Kai-shek, leaders of the Nationalist Chinese, manage to smile for a photographer. When the war was over, Chiang became the first elected president of China under a new constitution.

Ill at ease directing the war, Chamberlain resigned in May 1940, a broken and sick man, after the disastrous Norway campaign. He was succeeded by Winston Churchill.

CHIANG KAI-SHEK (1897–1975) The leader of the Kuomintang and head of Nationalist China found himself at open war with the invading Japanese in 1937. Generalissimo Chiang then transferred his capital from Nanking to Chungking in the interior and with U.S. support maintained the fight in China and Burma until war's end. His land forces were largely ineffectual but kept more than a million Japanese tied down in China. Defeated after the war by Mao Tse-tung's Communists, Chiang moved his Nationalist government to Taiwan in 1949, where he continued to rule until his death in 1975 (see Chapter 4, "Allies, Enemies, and Bystanders").

CHURCHILL, WINSTON S. (1874–1965) Churchill, the son of an English father and an American mother, was a war correspondent, member of Parliament, and World War I cabinet minister. In the 1930s he was almost the sole voice warning his country of the danger of Nazi Germany and denouncing the appeasement of the Munich Pact of 1938. As a result of his unpopular views, he was kept out of government. But when war broke out in 1939, he returned to government and became First Lord of the Admiralty (a post he had held early in World War I). He succeeded Chamberlain as prime minister in May 1940.

During the dark days of the Battle of Britain and the German bombing of British cities, Churchill's stirring speeches and stubborn courage inspired his people to carry on their fight against Germany. During the war, he was one of a triumvirate that included Roosevelt and Stalin, the Big Three who shaped the Allied victory. In July 1945, an electorate exhausted by war and eager to improve living conditions at home, turned Churchill's party out of office. He was named prime minister once again during the postwar period (1951–55) and is remembered as the outstanding statesman of the 20th century (see Chapter 14, "World War II and the Arts," and Chapter 15, "Documents, Organizations, and Monuments").

> We have sustained a defeat without a war.
> —Winston Churchill,
> after the signing of the Munich Pact

CURTIN, JOHN (1885–1945) The leader of Australia's Labour Party became prime minister and defense minister in October 1941 with a one-vote majority and led the country through World War II. He declared war on Japan in December 1941, stepped up conscription, ensured the defense of Australia by recalling troops from the Middle East, and cemented relations with the United States. Curtin suffered a fatal heart attack in 1945, just weeks before the Allies' victory over Japan.

DARLAN, JEAN-FRANÇOIS (1881–1942) After commanding the French navy at the beginning of the war, Admiral Darlan collaborated with

THE DILEMMA OF FRANCE

Clouds of despair tinged the bright skies across northwestern Europe in May 1940 as it yielded before the panzer-led juggernaut of the Wehrmacht. Rumbling out of the Ardennes Forest, General Paul von Kleist's armored columns tore a 50-mile gap in the Allied right flank and sped toward the French coast at the English Channel. The Netherlands surrendered on May 15, and in Germany a general observed, "The Führer is beside himself with joy."

That same day French Prime Minister Paul Reynaud telephoned British Prime Minister Winston Churchill and said, "We have been defeated. We are beaten—we have lost the battle." An alarmed Churchill rushed to Paris the next day to try to instill his fighting spirit in the French leaders and found that "utter dejection was written on every face."

The situation was hopeless. Although the Allies had held a solid, broad front of 102 divisions, mostly French, stretching from the Channel to Switzerland, their operations were uncoordinated, troop distribution was uneven, and indecision gripped the high command. Friction and distrust between the French commanders and the British Expeditionary Force complicated the situation, and memories of the carnage of 1914–18 undermined French patriotic fiber.

In the field, the French army retreated before the panzers, knowing that French leaders were powerless to lead. Yet individual units and soldiers fought bravely against great odds. One such implacable foe was a six-foot-five tank brigade colonel named Charles de Gaulle, the son of a Jesuit school headmaster, a veteran of Verdun, and a fervent advocate of mobile, mechanized warfare. Appointed a brigadier general and given command of the half-formed Fourth Armored Division, he fought valiantly to stem the German tide that May.

With about 200 tanks, de Gaulle attacked the southern flank of General Heinz Guderian's panzer group near Montcornet on May 17. But outclassed and lacking artillery or air support, the division's two-day operation did little more than annoy the Germans. De Gaulle made another counterattack, north of Laon, on May 19, and came close to wiping out the enemy bridgehead across the River Somme on May 27–29. He was the only French general to force any German withdrawals during the Battle of Flanders.

Meanwhile, after the miraculous evacuation from Dunkirk of the British Expeditionary Force, along with 112,000 French, Belgian, and Polish soldiers, the German armies regrouped and smashed through crumbling resistance as they moved toward Paris.

Long impressed by de Gaulle's writings on defense and strategy, Premier Reynaud appointed him war minister on June 6. Events on the battlefield were moving swiftly, however, and on June 14, German columns marched into Paris. Reynaud appealed to U.S. President Franklin D. Roosevelt for "clouds of airplanes," but it was too late. The Germans soon reached the Swiss frontier and boxed the French in at their vaunted Maginot Line. It was all over. Once-proud France was prostrate again before the Hun. Reynaud resigned on June 16 and was replaced by aging Marshal Henri Pétain. The honored defender of Verdun in 1916, now a pessimist and a collaborator, surrendered France without asking for terms.

Many in France were ready to accept and make the best of the German occupation, but Charles de Gaulle was not. His personal mission, as he saw it, was to flee and rally the Free French in England and the colonies to his side. In defiance of the new collaborationist regime and in real danger of arrest, de Gaulle flew to London from Bordeaux on June 17 with Major General Edward Spears, Churchill's representative in Paris. The following day, de Gaulle made a historic broadcast, calling on the French people to continue the fight. France had lost a battle, he said, but not the war.

De Gaulle's emotional appeal divided the French in their hour of humiliation, and the problem would fester. De Gaulle placed himself at the head of the new Free French movement, headquartered in London, and adopted the Cross of Lorraine as its symbol. On June 28, Prime Minister Churchill officially recognized the towering, melancholy soldier as "chief of the Free French."

The British government authorized de Gaulle to announce the formation of the French National Committee and to issue proclamations denying the legitimacy of the Pétain government. The latter promptly outlawed de Gaulle, reduced him to the rank of colonel, and placed him on the retired list. On July 4, 1940, a French court-martial in Toulouse sentenced him to four years in prison, and on August 2, a court-martial sitting in Clermont-Ferrand sentenced him to death. He was later stripped of his citizenship, but all these punishments were the fantasies of collaborators and were, ultimately, meaningless. As leader of the Free French and eventually president of the French Committee of National Liberation in Algiers, de Gaulle became the symbol of French resistance to occupation and an unwavering ally of the Western powers.

In his homeland, the Germans annexed Alsace and part of Lorraine and occupied the northeastern two-thirds of the country. The Germans declared southern France a "free zone," and the Chamber of Deputies and the Senate made Pétain chief of state. He set up a collaborationist government in the spa town of Vichy, 200 miles south-southeast of Paris. Recognized by the then-neutral United States, the curious regime adopted as its slogan "Work, Family, Country" and claimed to seek a "national revival."

Pétain insisted later that he played a "double game" with the Germans, but the Vichy government had adopted repressive measures against French Jews, including property confiscation, dismissals from government service, and exclusions from professions and higher education. Vichy interned thousands of foreign Jews and handed many over to the Germans. About 3,000 died in French camps. In April 1942, Marshal Pétain, then 85, turned the Vichy government over to the widely despised Hitler sympathizer and French politician Pierre Laval, who pursued an openly collaborationist policy.

Meanwhile, General de Gaulle's stormy relations with the British and later with the U.S. government grew out of his insistence that he was head of the legitimate French government thereby demanding being treated as an equal. He was suspicious of British motives and was outraged when the Allies excluded Free French units from Operation Torch, the Allied invasion of French North Africa, in November 1942. His haughty manner and intransigence infuriated President Roosevelt, and Churchill, a lifelong Francophile, would admit later, "Of all the crosses I have had to bear, the heaviest one has been the Cross of Lorraine." To the French, however, he was a towering figure and a heroic leader.

De Gaulle's finest hour came in August 1944, when, after the French Second Armored Division supported by the U.S. Fourth Armored Division had liberated Paris, he strode along the Avénue des Champs Elysées amid delirious throngs. In the aftermath of liberation, the legitimacy of his leadership was popularly confirmed, and he led the Fourth Republic until 1946. After a period of political exile, he emerged in 1958 to lead the Fifth Republic—a newly structured government that gave the president—de Gaulle—far more powers than presidents had had under the Fourth Republic.

the German occupiers as vice premier in Marshal Henri Pétain's Vichy government. Darlan became high commissioner of French North Africa in 1942 and was recognized by the U.S. government, in direct conflict with the British recognition of General Charles de Gaulle, as leader of the Free French Forces. A young French monarchist assassinated Darlan on Christmas Eve, 1942.

> We shall fight on forever and ever and ever.
> —British Prime Minister Winston Churchill, in a message to French Prime Minister Paul Reynaud after the fall of France, 1940

DE GAULLE, CHARLES (1890–1970) A veteran of Verdun (1916), an instructor at the Saint-Cyr Military Academy, and an outspoken prewar advocate of mobile mechanized warfare, General de Gaulle fought gallantly in the 1940 Battle of Flanders before fleeing the collaborationists to set up the headquarters of the Free French Forces in London. A proud and prickly patriot, de Gaulle insisted that the French be treated as an equal partner by the Allies, although France, under occupation, had few assets to offer in the war. De Gaulle had a stormy relationship with Churchill and Roosevelt, but his courage and determination made him the supreme political figure of wartime

France. He became prime minister of France in 1944 and, after more than a decade out of politics, returned as president of the Fifth Republic in 1958.

EDEN, ANTHONY (1897–1977) Anthony Eden won the Military Cross for heroism in World War I and served as foreign secretary in 1935–38. He resigned because of his disagreement with Neville Chamberlain on appeasement. Eden, an internationalist like Churchill, believed that the nations of Europe needed to confront Hitler, not appease him. When Churchill became prime minister in 1940, he recalled Eden to government, first as dominions secretary, then as war secretary, and finally as foreign secretary. Eden enjoyed Churchill's full confidence and harbored no illusions about Soviet ambitions in Eastern Europe. He succeeded Churchill as prime minister in 1955 but served only two years before resigning in the wake of the Suez Crisis of 1956.

EICHMANN, KARL ADOLPH (1906–62) This former laborer and traveling salesman rose through the Nazi ranks to head the Gestapo Department for Jewish Affairs. Known as a "Jewish specialist," Eichmann was responsible for the concentration camp deaths of millions of Jews. He escaped an American internment camp after Germany's surrender and lived for years in Argentina. He was found by Israeli agents in 1960 and brought to trial for his war crimes. Found guilty on all counts, he was hanged on May 31, 1962.

FORRESTAL, JAMES V. (1892–1949) A former World War I naval aviator and banker, the intense, retiring Forrestal was a driving force as undersecretary of the U.S. Navy in providing the navy with ships, aircraft, and ordnance during World War II. He succeeded Frank Knox as navy secretary in 1944 and spent much time in the war theaters. He later became the first U.S. defense secretary from 1947 to 1949. Unhappy with Forrestal's performance, Truman forced him to resign. Forrestal committed suicide that same year.

FRANCO, FRANCISCO (1892–1975) Promoted to general in the Spanish army in Morocco in 1916, Franco became deputy commander of the Spanish Legion and army chief of staff. He returned from duty in the Canary Islands in July 1936 to capture Medilla, touching off the bloody three-year Spanish Civil War, and emerged as the country's absolute dictator. During World War II, Franco trod a path of nonbelligerence, if not strict neutrality (see Chapter 4, "Allies, Enemies, and Bystanders"), and skillfully brushed off Hitler's designs on the British bastion at Gibraltar. Franco grew cooler to the Axis powers, though he did send Spanish volunteers, the Blue Division, to fight with the Germans on the Russian front.

GEORGE VI, KING (1895–1952) Shy and unassuming, George VI ascended to the British throne when his elder brother, Edward VIII, abdicated in 1936. The king won the undivided affection of his people during the war by tirelessly visiting the armies in the field and, with his popular Queen Elizabeth and two daughters at his side, sharing with Londoners the ordeal of German air raids.

GOEBBELS, PAUL JOSEPH (1897–1945) Goebbels received his doctorate from Heidelberg University, joined the Nazi Party in 1924, and

Hitler stands with (left to right) Luftwaffe leader Hermann Göring, Propaganda Minister Joseph Goebbels, and Deputy Führer Rudolf Hess during a Nazi Party gathering. In the spring of 1941, Hess piloted an aircraft to Great Britain on an unauthorized peace mission.

became Adolf Hitler's minister for public enlightenment and propaganda. A skilled administrator and orator, Goebbels rallied German public morale throughout the war. He introduced the almost-mandatory salutation "Heil Hitler," perfected the "great lie" doctrine that a continually repeated falsehood—the bigger the better—eventually will be believed, and used the Allies' "unconditional surrender" pronouncement to stiffen the German will to fight on. A day after Hitler's suicide in the Berlin bunker on April 30, 1945, Goebbels had his children poisoned and himself and his wife shot by an SS officer (see Chapter 6, "Officers and Soldiers").

GÖRING, HERMANN WILHELM (1893–1946) A World War I air ace, Göring joined Adolf Hitler's National Socialist Party in 1922 and was an original storm troop commander. Named Prussian minister of the interior in 1933, he organized the Gestapo and set up the first concentration camps. He became aviation minister and then head of the German air force in 1935 and also held the titles of Reichsmarshal and president of the Council of Defense. Corpulent, drug addicted, and dissolute, though popular with the German people, Göring remained loyal to Hitler. At war's end, however, the Führer turned against Göring because he suspected him of trying to usurp his power. After he was convicted on four counts of war crimes at the Allied tribunals in Nuremberg, the senior surviving Nazi swallowed potassium cyanide in 1946—a few hours before he was scheduled to be hanged.

HAAKON VII, KING (1872–1957 Haakon, the former Prince Charles of Denmark, was elected king of Norway in 1905 when the country gained its independence from Sweden. Haakon rallied his people when German troops invaded in April 1940. He refused to recognize the authority of Vidkun Quisling's collaborationist government and withdrew with the retreating British forces in 1940 after their abortive attempt to dislodge the Germans (see

Chapter 2, "Causes of War"). From London, Haakon promoted the formation of Free Norwegian forces and supported the resistance movement in his country. He returned home in 1945 to great acclamation.

HESS, RUDOLF (1894–1987) Born in Alexandria, Egypt, Hess became an aviator in World War I and then a political science student in Munich. He joined the Nazi Party in 1920 after hearing Adolf Hitler speak. After taking part in the 1923 Munich Beer Hall Putsch, Hess spent seven months in Landsberg Prison, where he helped Hitler write his bestselling *Mein Kampf*. Hitler dedicated the book to Hess, who became the Führer's private secretary. Introverted and subservient, Hess served as deputy führer until September 1939, when Hermann Göring replaced him. Hess made world headlines in May 1941 when he flew alone to Scotland, ostensibly on an unofficial peace mission. The British ignored his proposals and held him as a prisoner of war; Hitler declared him insane. Sentenced at the Nuremberg tribunals to life imprisonment, Hess spent 35 years in Spandau Prison. The Soviets, unlike the other Allies, were unwilling to free Hess once he had become an aged and ailing man. Hess committed suicide in Spandau in 1987, the last remaining major war criminal in captivity (see Chapter 6, "Officers and Soldiers").

HIMMLER, HEINRICH (1900–1945) Once Hitler's bodyguard, Himmler rose through the ranks to become Nazi secret police chief, head of the SS, and lead engineer of the "final solution." He set up the first concentration camp in Dachau and in January 1943 pleaded with the Reich minister of transport: "If I am to wind things up quickly, I must have more trains for transports. . . . Help me get more trains." Himmler was arrested in 1944, but he committed suicide before he was brought to trial.

HIROHITO, EMPEROR (1901–89) Revered as both god and father of the Japanese people, Emperor Hirohito, who reigned from 1926 until his death, was a seemingly mild and ineffectual man who yielded to the demands of his militaristic cabinet, although the degree of Hirohito's involvement in the policies that led to war has been a subject of debate among scholars since his death. As the tide turned against Japan from 1942 on, Hirohito became more involved in state affairs, calling upon the nation to make sacrifices in his name. When Japan surrendered on August 15, 1945, and Hirohito made the announcement in a radio speech, it was the first time the Japanese people had heard his voice. The United States agreed to allow Hirohito to remain on the throne at the time of Japan's surrender, although he was required to publicly renounce his divinity. Under the U.S. occupation, he worked with U.S. General Douglas A. MacArthur in rebuilding his country, and at the time of his death in 1989 he was a widely revered and respected figure.

HITLER, ADOLF (1889–1945) Enraged by the perceived humiliation of Germany by the 1919

ASCENT OF THE CORPORAL: HITLER'S RISE TO POWER

For Adolf Hitler, founder and leader of the Nazi Party and the guiding spirit of the Third Reich from 1933 to 1945, the rise to power was a long path marked by legitimate elections, conspiracy, persuasion, terror, and bloodshed.

A moody, lazy, and unstable man born in poverty in Austria, Hitler served in the German army in World War I and was awarded the Iron Cross First Class in 1918 for bravery on the Western Front. Hitler was deeply affected by the German surrender in 1918 and was incensed by the 1919 Versailles Treaty. After the war he lived a listless life in Munich and dreamed of being an artist or an architect, but he was unable to gain entrance into any school to pursue his dreams. Instead, he wallowed in resentment and eventually drifted into the twilight world of radical politics, in this case, of those fringe groups espousing a nationalistic, anti-Semitic ideology. He convinced himself that his destiny was to rescue a humiliated Germany from bolshevism and Jewry and to restore its greatness.

Assigned by the Reichswehr (Defensive Land Forces) to spy on political parties in postrevolutionary Munich, Hitler joined the 40-member German Workers Party in September 1919 and soon displayed a powerful talent for oratory and manipulation. By July 1921, he had imposed himself as its chairman, changed its name to the National Socialist German Workers Party (NSDAP), and provided it with a symbol—the swastika—and its greeting, *"Heil!"*

In the unstable political and social atmosphere of postwar Germany, the movement grew to 3,000 members, who recognized the persuasive Hitler as their Führer ("leader"). To keep order at meetings and intimidate opponents, he organized strong-arm squads, out of which grew the brown-shirted storm troopers (Sturmabteilungen, the SA) and his black-shirted personal bodyguard, the SS (Schutzstaffel).

The NSDAP announced a 25-point program in February 1920, emphasizing Aryan supremacy, nationalism, profit sharing and nationalization, and the exclusion of Jews, who were believed to be responsible for Germany's economic and social chaos. By November 1923, Hitler was convinced that the Weimar Republic was on the verge of collapse, so the NSDAP, aided and abetted by General Erich Ludendorff of World War I fame and local nationalist groups, sought to overthrow the Bavarian government in Munich by force.

But Hitler had misread public sentiment, which, although responsive to much of his message, still craved order and peace in the wake of the war: 1923 Munich The Beer Hall Putsch failed when, instead of joining Hitler and his group, the police opened fire and killed 16 Nazis. Hitler was arrested, tried, and sentenced to Landsberg Prison for five years. Treated like an honored guest there, he dictated to his aide Rudolf Hess his turgid, best-selling "bible" of racial myth and anti-Semitism, *Mein Kampf* (My Struggle).

Released after nine months, Hitler, aided by Hermann Göring and Joseph Goebbels, set about reassembling his followers and rebuilding the movement, which had disintegrated in his absence. Following the abortive Beer Hall Putsch, the Nazi Party was officially banned by the Weimar government. This ban, however, was lifted in 1925, and Hitler regained permission to speak in public.

In the 1928 national elections, the Nazi Party gained only 810,000 votes out of 31 million, and 12 seats out of 491 in the Reichstag. But the following year, as the worldwide economic depression devastated the German middle class, Hitler began to win increasing support from agricultural laborers, craftsmen, traders, intellectuals, industrialists, national conservatives, and army circles. The masses longed for a movement that would give political voice to their social anxieties and a deep-seated yearning for order.

Hitler was a messiah for many, but the former lance corporal was also a "small man," a man of the people. He shared their desire for strong government and social order and played skillfully on their resentments, feelings of revolt, and nationalism. At the same time, the great industrial magnates, fearing socialism and communism, contributed liberally to the coffers of the NSDAP. Skirting rigid definitions of national socialism that would have undermined his charismatic popularity and his claim to absolute leadership, Hitler extended his appeal beyond Bavaria and attracted both right- and left-wing elements. The Beer Hall Putsch, however, had taught him that he should seek power by constitutional means. He would use the system in order to eventually undermine and destroy it.

In the 1930 elections, the party won 107 seats in the Reichstag. After Hitler acquired German citizenship and ran unsuccessfully in the April 1932 presidential elections, the Reichstag elections of July 1932 proved to be the turning point for him and his party.

Emerging as the largest political party in Germany, the National Socialists garnered almost 14 million votes (37.3 percent) and 230 seats. The party, however, slipped back in November 1932 to 11 million votes and 196 seats, but Hitler was helped to power by a cabal of conservative politicians led by Franz von Papen, who persuaded the aging, reluctant Reich President Paul von Hindenburg to nominate "the Bohemian corporal" as Reich chancellor on January 30, 1933. These conservatives were convinced they could control Hitler and advance their own agendas. It was a mistake of monumental dimensions.

Once in office, Hitler hastened to outmaneuver his rivals, virtually ousting the conservatives from any real government participation by July 1933. He abolished the trade unions; eliminated Communists, Social Democrats, and Jews from any role in political life; and swept opponents into concentration camps. With support from the nationalists, Hitler gained a majority in the last "democratic" elections in March 1933.

Fearing the rising power of the paramilitary SA, Hitler ordered the assassination of the SA leadership, including Ernst Röhm, in June 1934. This tightened Hitler's grip on Germany and guaranteed the allegiance of the army, which had been threatened by Röhm's paramilitary hordes. By that August, when he united the positions of president and chancellor upon the death of Hindenburg, Hitler became the undisputed Führer of Germany. The rabble-rousing genius with the toothbrush mustache held all the powers of state.

Treaty of Versailles (see Chapter 2, "Causes of War," and Chapter 4, "Allies, Enemies, and Bystanders"), Austrian-born Hitler used persuasive oratory, brutality, and skilled propaganda to lead his National Socialist (Nazi) Party to power. Hitler's first grab at power was the failed Munich Beer Hall Putsch in 1923 (see Chapter 2, "Causes of War"), which landed him in prison at Landsberg for nine months, during which time he wrote his memoir, *Mein Kampf*. Thereafter, Hitler used the electoral process to climb to power. Although the Nazis never became the majority party, they were able to become the largest party in Germany, and in 1933, Hitler was appointed chancellor by President Paul von Hindenburg. When Hindenburg died in 1934, Hitler proclaimed himself head of state and commander in chief of the German armed forces. Hitler never hid his goal of eliminating Europe's Jews, and to take territories in the East, principally in the Soviet Union, for *Lebensraum* ("living space") for the German people. After outmaneuvering the irresolute French and British governments in the late 1930s, he started World War II by invading Poland, crushed much of Western Europe in lightning campaigns, and retained the initiative for two years. After the Royal Air Force's defeat of the Luftwaffe in 1940, he called off a plan to invade England and then gazed eastward toward an invasion of the Soviet Union. But the former World War I infantry corporal was no great strategist. His invasion of the Soviet Union in June 1941 would prove his undoing. He was unable to manage a war on two fronts, especially after the United States joined the Allies following Hitler's reckless declaration of war against the Americans in 1941. From then on, he clung stubbornly to a strategy of holding every inch of ground and left his able general staff with little or no room to maneuver. Long after an Allied victory was inevitable, he ranted and raged in a fantasy world. Yet he maintained his hold on the German people until the end and, despite several attempts on his life during his reign of terror, remained unchallenged until he committed suicide in his Berlin bunker on April 30, 1945, as the Allies closed in.

HOPKINS, HARRY L. (1890–1946) The son of an Iowa harness maker, Harry Hopkins became President Franklin D. Roosevelt's closest and most trusted adviser. In the early years of the

---

FIELD MARSHAL ERWIN ROMMEL, AFRIKA KORPS

Meeting with the Führer, Rastenburg, November 28, 1942

At about 1700 I was ordered to the Führer. There was a noticeable chill in the atmosphere from the outset. I described all the difficulties which the army had had to face during both the battle and the retreat. It was all noted and the execution of the operation was described as faultless and unique.

Unfortunately, I then came too abruptly to the point and said that, since experience indicated that no improvement in the shipping situation could now be expected, the abandonment of the African theater of war should be accepted as a long-term policy. There should be no illusions about the situation and all planning should be directed towards what was attainable. If the army remained in North Africa it would be destroyed.

I had expected a rational discussion of my arguments and intended to develop them in a great deal more detail. But I did not get so far, for the mere mention of the strategic question worked like a spark in a powder barrel. The Führer flew into a fury and directed a stream of completely unfounded attacks upon us.

—From *The Rommel Papers*, ed. B. H. Liddell Hart (New York: Collins, 1953), as published in *A Mammoth Book of Eyewitness World War II*, ed. Jon E. Lewis (New York: Carroll & Graf, 2002).

New Deal, Hopkins worked mainly on domestic programs and was a principal architect of many work programs such as the WPA. After the United States entered the war in 1941, Hopkins was appointed Roosevelt's special assistant, and his responsibilities shifted to foreign affairs. He worked energetically to coordinate Lend-Lease programs, chair war committees, attend high-level conferences, and advise Prime Minister Winston Churchill and Soviet Premier Josef Stalin.

HULL, CORDELL (1871–1955) Born in a Tennessee log cabin, Cordell Hull was a circuit judge and U.S. congressman and senator before becoming Franklin Roosevelt's secretary of state in 1933. A confirmed internationalist, Hull spent much of his time from 1937 to 1941 in protracted and ultimately fruitless negotiations with the Japanese. Roosevelt conducted foreign policy himself, and Hull often complained about being left out of major decisions—which he was. (Roosevelt often relied more on Hull's undersecretary of state, Sumner Welles.) Hull served longer than anyone else in the post, resigning in November 1944.

KING, WILLIAM MACKENZIE (1874–1950) The Canadian prime minister from 1921 to 1930 and from 1935 to 1946, MacKenzie King was a scholar, author, and shrewd politician who abandoned an isolationist stance to lead his country to Britain's side in 1939. Seeking to avoid conscription, he built up Canada's naval and air services before expanding the army and committing it to overseas duty. He worked for Canadian-American amity and was an effective war leader.

KNOX, FRANK W. (1874–1944) One of the most effective secretaries the U.S. Navy ever had, Boston-born Frank Knox—a former Rough Rider, World War I artillery colonel, Chicago publisher, and 1936 Republican vice presidential nominee—served from July 1940 until his death in April 1944. He investigated the failure of the Pearl Harbor defenses and worked harmoniously

with Fleet Admiral Ernest J. King, the irascible navy commander.

LEOPOLD III, KING (1901–83) Leopold, who was educated at Eton and Ghent University, became Belgium's monarch when his father was killed in a climbing accident in 1934. When German forces invaded Belgium in May 1940, Leopold took command of the army and received French and British support. Believing that the Belgian position was hopeless, he surrendered 18 days after the invasion, contrary to the wishes of his government, which wanted to continue fighting. The surrender rendered the French-British position untenable and made the Dunkirk evacuation of the British army an urgent necessity. Leopold refused to cooperate with the German occupiers, who held him under house arrest. Although the Belgians eventually exonerated him from any responsibility for the 1940 defeat, he abdicated in favor of his son in 1951 (see Chapter 4, "Allies, Enemies, and Bystanders").

MENZIES, ROBERT G. (1894–1978) As Australia's prime minister from April 1939 to August 1941, Robert Menzies, a minority government leader, led his country into World War II, introduced compulsory military service, and quickly sent three crack divisions to the Middle Eastern theater. After resigning in 1941, he headed a new defense coordination ministry.

MOLOTOV, VYACHESLAV (1890–1986) Molotov served as the Soviet commissar for foreign affairs from 1939 to 1952. Formerly Stalin's right-hand man on the central committee, Molotov negotiated the nonaggression pact with Germany in August 1939 and in April 1941 concluded a similar accord with Japan. After the Germans invaded the Soviet Union, he assumed many of Stalin's foreign policy responsibilities. He pressed the Western Allies to open a second front and increase Soviet aid and attended all major Allied conferences. He was the Soviet Union's first delegate to the United Nations in 1945. Like many in Stalin's entourage,

Molotov's fortunes waxed and waned over the years. Throughout the war, his wife, who was Jewish, was under arrest in a labor camp in Siberia. Molotov survived the worst of Stalin's purges, but after Stalin's death in 1953, he faded into obscurity.

MUSSOLINI, BENITO (1883–1945) Raised in one of the poorest regions in Italy, Mussolini worked as a laborer and teacher before starting his political career. Kicked out of the Socialist Party for supporting Italy's entry into World War I, Mussolini declared war on socialism and founded the Fascist party. The Fascists gained power and the bombastic Il Duce (Leader) ruled Italy as a dictator from 1922 to 1943 (see Chapter 4, "Allies, Enemies, and Bystanders"). He had come to power in the chaotic years immediately following World War I, when Italy was in a state of economic and political collapse. Mussolini, who was popular in the early years of his rule, sought to restore Italy's lost military glory, even though the nation was weak and impoverished. He launched a number of campaigns (Ethiopia, North Africa, Greece, and East Africa) that proved disastrous, was a participant in the

During the summer of 1940, a beaming Hitler sits in a staff car beside Italian dictator Benito Mussolini as the pair rides triumphantly through the Bavarian city of Munich.

Munich Conference in 1938 that carved up Czechoslovakia, and declared war on the Western Allies in June 1940, when a German victory in France was certain. Mussolini's military failures became a burden on Hitler, who was forced to rescue his army in Greece, Albania, and North Africa. Mussolini was deposed by the Fascist Grand Council in July 1943 as the Allies prepared

CAPTAIN OTTO SKORZENY, WAFFEN SS

Rescuing Mussolini from Gran Sasso, September 12, 1943

Sounds of firing could now be heard in the distance and I put my head into the corridor and shouted for the officer-in-command at the hotel. A colonel appeared from nearby and I summoned him to surrender forthwith, assuring him that any further resistance was useless. He asked me for time to consider the matter. I gave him one minute, during which Radl turned up.

The Italian colonel returned, carrying a goblet of red wine which he proffered to me with a slight bow and the words: "To the victor!"

A white bedspread, hung from the window, performed the functions of a white flag.

After giving a few orders to my men outside the hotel I was able to devote attention to Mussolini, who was standing in a corner with Untersturmführer Schwerdt in front of him. I introduced myself:

"Duce, the Führer has sent me! You are free!"

Mussolini embraced me: "I knew my friend Adolf Hitler would not leave me in the lurch," he said.

—From Otto Skorzeny, *Special Mission* (Robert Hale Ltd., 1957), as published in *A Mammoth Book of Eyewitness World War II*, ed. Jon E. Lewis (New York: Carroll & Graf, 2002.

to invade the Italian mainland. He was interned, rescued by Nazi paratroopers, and headed a puppet government in German-occupied northern Italy. As Italy fell to the Allies, Communist partisans executed Mussolini and his mistress, Clara Petacci, in April 1945.

PÉTAIN, HENRI (1856–1951) Marshal Henri Philippe Pétain, defender of Verdun in 1916, was a French national hero who became president in June 1940 as the German army rolled into Paris. Pétain believed that the only way to save France was to cooperate with the more-powerful Germans; he headed the collaborationist Vichy government (see Chapter 4, "Allies, Enemies, and Bystanders"), but the Germans continued to strip away what small powers it had, and in 1944 Pétain was taken to Germany. A French court sentenced him to death in August 1945, but General Charles de Gaulle, taking into account Pétain's great age and his status as a hero of World War I, commuted the penalty to life imprisonment.

PETER II, KING (1923–70) Peter II was eleven and had just begun school in England in 1934, when his father, King Alexander I of Yugoslavia, was assassinated by a Croatian fanatic while in Marseilles, France, and the boy assumed the throne. After the Germans invaded Yugoslavia in April 1941, Peter and his ministers escaped through Greece to London, where they established a government-in-exile (see Chapter 4, "Allies, Enemies, and Bystanders"). He made a serious error of judgment in backing Dragoljub Mihailovic, a Serb who headed the Chetniks, antimonarchist guerrillas who had battled the German occupiers. Although Peter reached an accommodation in 1944 with Communist Partisan leader Josip Broz Tito, who had British support, Peter's influence had by then sharply declined, especially after Tito had Mihailovic executed. Tito also had no intention of ever allowing the monarchy to be reestablished in Yugoslavia. Peter never returned to Yugoslavia, and Tito declared the country a republic in November 1945.

QUEZON, MANUEL (1878–1944) The son of Luzon teachers, a soldier who fought the Spanish and the Americans at the turn of the century, a lawyer, and a member of the Philippine Assembly, Manuel Quezon served as president of the Philippine Commonwealth from its founding in 1935 to his death from tuberculosis in August 1944. A staunch ally of the United States, he took General Douglas A. MacArthur's advice and moved to the island bastion of Corregidor, in Manila Bay, when Japanese forces invaded the mainland in December 1941. After the Japanese conquest of the Philippines, Quezon went to the United States to plead his country's cause and head a government-in-exile. Less than three months after he died, the U.S. Sixth Army landed on Leyte.

REYNAUD, PAUL (1878–1966) Nicknamed "Mickey Mouse" and "the Cat" by his enemies, the diminutive, agile Paul Reynaud was a maverick politician and devout foe of appeasement who served as France's finance minister and tried to prepare the economy for war. He succeeded Edouard Daladier as prime minister in March 1940. The Germans invaded in May, and Reynaud resigned in June rather than make peace with Hitler. The Vichy authorities (see Chapter 4, "Allies, Enemies, and Bystanders") arrested him in September, tried him in 1942, and deported him to Germany in 1943. He was released in 1945 but never resumed a role in French politics.

RIBBENTROP, JOACHIM VON (1893–1946) Nazi Germany's foreign minister from 1938 to 1945 was a suave, vain, and loquacious man, who sold champagne and had worked briefly as a journalist in New York and Boston. He joined Hitler's National Socialist Party in 1932 and served as German ambassador in London in 1936–38. He signed pacts with Italy and the Soviet Union in 1939, and he played an important role in the diplomacy surrounding the Munich Pact of 1938 and the German invasion of Poland in September 1939. During the war,

NIGHT OF THE LONG KNIVES

A stocky, red-faced man who had had half of his nose shot away as an army major in World War I, Ernest Röhm was the only man in Adolf Hitler's early career capable of opposing him or negotiating with him on equal terms.

Röhm began his association with the future Führer in 1919. A founder of the German Workers Party, Röhm helped Hitler to win the support of the army in Bavaria and provided him with the services of his own brown-shirted strong-arm squads. These became the Sturmabteilungen (SA).

Hitler wanted the SA to remain subordinate to his National Socialist (Nazi) Party, but Röhm, a genuine radical, wanted it to be on equal terms with the party and eventually to absorb or replace the Wehrmacht (regular armed forces). Röhm resigned his leadership of the SA in 1925. But after the spectacular Nazi electoral successes in 1930, Hitler persuaded Röhm to return and reorganize the SA. For the next three years, Röhm provided an organized army of gangsters and thugs that filled an indispensable role in Hitler's rise to power. They beat up and killed political opponents, and they marched by the thousands through the streets in intimidating displays of numbers and power. By the end of 1933, the SA had swelled to almost 4.5 million men.

Röhm dreamed of a military state and the primacy of the soldier over the politician, and when Hitler became chancellor, Röhm deplored his delay in continuing the revolution. For a time, Hitler compromised by bringing Röhm into his cabinet, but then the chancellor reduced the SA to the status of a subordinate body so that its power would not rival his and to keep it from making trouble with the Wehrmacht. Hitler, looking ahead, knew that Germany could not restore its status as a big power without the support of the regular army. He was also concerned that the army, if disgruntled, could be a source of a potential coup. The SA, in short, had outlived its usefulness.

Röhm, meanwhile, had become a populist demagogue and had antagonized two dangerous rivals, Hermann Göring, commander of the Gestapo (secret state police), and Heinrich Himmler, then leader of the Bavarian political police. Both Göring and Himmler pressured Hitler to deal with the Röhm problem. Röhm's conduct and that of his entourage—dissolute homosexual orgies, drinking bouts, and other loutish behavior—also contributed to the SA leader's downfall and were cited as reasons justifying murder, even though Hitler had long known about and tolerated Röhm's homosexuality. The officer corps of the Germany Army was threatened by Röhm's paramilitary SA and removing this obstacle could solidify the Army's loyalty to Hitler.

Hitler was still reluctant to kill his oldest comrade-in-arms, to whom he felt a debt of gratitude. Nevertheless, on the pretext that the SA was preparing a putsch, Hitler ordered a purge of Röhm and his closest followers on June 30, 1934, "the Night of the Long Knives."

The guileless Röhm, who suspected nothing, was surprised that day in a private hotel at Bad Wiessee, a small spa south of Munich where he was taking a month's leave with other SA leaders. Hitler and a detachment of SS troops awoke Röhm and took him to the Munich-Stadelheim Prison. Still solicitous toward his old friend, Hitler ordered that Röhm be given a loaded pistol with which to shoot himself. The SA leader was unable to do so and was executed two days later, gasping, "My Führer, my Führer!"

In addition to Röhm, 77 other leading SA members and at least 100 others who were not members of the SA were liquidated, including Gregor Strasser, leader of the social-revolutionary north German wing of the Nazi Party; General Kurt von Schleicher, last chancellor of the Weimar Republic; and Schleicher's wife.

The ringmaster of the brutal purge was Göring, resplendent in a full-dress uniform. Röhm was posthumously branded a traitor, and by the end of 1934 his brownshirts had lost any political function in the new Nazi state. After the Night of the Long Knives, no one inside or outside Germany had any doubt that the regime would resort to the most brutal force—even against its own people—to achieve its objectives.

Ribbentrop helped pressure the Vichy French and the Italians to deport their Jews to Nazi concentration camps. After the defeat of Germany, Ribbentrop was arrested and put on trial at Nuremberg. He was convicted of crimes against peace and humanity and was hanged in October 1946.

RÖHM, ERNST (1887–1934) During the Nazi rise to power and the early years of Hitler's regime, Röhm headed the SA (Sturmabteilung), commonly known as the "brownshirts." Hitler feared the growing power of the paramilitary SA and ordered the SS to assassinate Röhm and other SA leaders during the Night of the Long Knives, June 30, 1934.

ROOSEVELT, ELEANOR (1884–1962) Anna Eleanor Roosevelt, the tall, energetic, gregarious wife of President Franklin D. Roosevelt, played an active role in boosting U.S. and Allied morale during World War II. She served as a special envoy for her husband to Great Britain, Australia, and other countries; toured war plants, military bases, and hospitals all over the country, and visited U.S. military personnel overseas. She made many friends for the United States and later became a highly respected delegate to the United Nations, where she chaired the UN Commission on Human Rights (1946–51).

> This nation will remain a neutral nation, but I cannot ask that every American remain neutral in thought, as well. . . . Even a neutral cannot be asked to close his mind or his conscience.
> —U.S. President Franklin D. Roosevelt, radio address, September 3, 1939

ROOSEVELT, FRANKLIN DELANO (1882–1945) Although disabled by polio, the patrician Harvard graduate and onetime assistant secretary of the navy overcame his illness to be elected governor of New York (1928) and then president (1932). As president, he rallied his

nation during the Great Depression and made it the great military and economic "arsenal of democracy" that ensured victory in World War II. He had the foresight to support the British when they stood alone in 1940 and understood the danger of Japanese militarism in Asia and the Pacific. Although legally bound by U.S. neutrality laws, Roosevelt found ways to ship materiel to the British through the Lend-Lease program, and he attempted to prepare the American people for what he knew was inevitable—U.S. entry into World War II. As a wartime leader, Roosevelt was one of the architects of the winning military strategies that were needed to fight a war on two fronts. Elected to an unprecedented four terms as president of the United States, Roosevelt championed Chinese interests, aided the Soviets, and insisted upon the "unconditional surrender" of Germany and Japan. Charismatic and occasionally devious, he was a generous and idealistic leader whose unwavering advocacy of freedom and dignity inspired millions. Although Roosevelt usually appeared healthy and vigorous, he had suffered, in fact, from congestive heart failure for many years. By the time of the Yalta Conference in February 1945, he was physically exhausted. He died at Warm Springs, Georgia, on April 12, 1945, on the eve of the European victory for which he had toiled. Roosevelt is remembered as one of the great presidents of the United States.

SALAZAR, ANTONIO DE OLIVEIRA (1899–1970) Reclusive and hardworking, Portugal's leader from 1932 to 1968 was the mildest of European dictators. The former economics professor skillfully maintained neutrality throughout World War II, though both the Germans and Allies used tungsten and wolfram from Portuguese mines (see Chapter 4 "Allies, Enemies, and Bystanders"), while Portugal's alliance with Britain, which dated to 1386, remained intact. Neutrality notwithstanding, Salazar eventually recognized the need to favor the Allies and granted the United States base rights in the Azores in 1943. Meanwhile, Portugal was a haven for refugees and the Portuguese capital, Lisbon, a hotbed of Allied and Axis espionage.

SELASSIE, HAILE (1892–1975) The feisty emperor of Abyssinia (now Ethiopia) was an early hero of World War II. After Italian forces invaded his country in 1935 (see Chapter 2, "Causes of War"), the "Lion of Judah" fled to England and made a futile plea to the League of Nations. He remained in exile until 1940 when, with the entry of Italy into World War II, Britain agreed to help restore him to his throne. He formed a patriot army in the Sudan, and, aided by guerrilla brigade leader Orde C. Wingate and British units advancing from Somaliland and Eritrea, reentered his capital, Addis Ababa, in May 1941. He stabilized his government and joined the United Nations. Haile Selassie was deposed by Marxists in 1974, and he died the following year in prison, most likely at the hand of his captors.

SMUTS, JAN C. (1870–1950) After fighting the British in the Boer War (1901–2), commanding British troops in East Africa in 1916, and representing his country in David Lloyd George's war cabinet, Prime Minister Smuts led South Africa into World War II at its outset. He

---

RED TERROR

In the late 1920s and through much of the 1930s, after Communist Party Secretary Josef Stalin introduced his five-year program of forced agricultural collectivization in 1928, an estimated nine million peasants were shot or starved to death, or died while being hauled to labor camps in Siberia. The next year, Stalin began a major cleansing of the party and government apparatus. He demanded constant vigilance against anyone who deviated from party plans and harsh punishment for anyone deemed to have done so. These harsh policies and Stalin's blood purges of political opponents and the Red Army officer corps were fueled by Stalin's desire for complete control of the government and his paranoia.

The victims came from all walks of life, and an enemy of the state was anyone who was defined as such or denounced as such. Many were simply poorly trained officials or managers who could not cope with the demands of industrialization and modernization. Stalin and his henchmen regarded anyone who was technologically incompetent as a saboteur: peasants who drove their tractors too hard, foremen who could not read the instructions on American-made machinery, and managers who failed to meet their quotas. A child could be apprehended for picking up off the road some food that had fallen off a truck. Remorseless officials of the NKVD (the secret police) hunted down these enemies of the state. In the end, the purges were mostly a product of Stalin's paranoid imagination and not rooted in any legitimate reasons.

The victims included former Premier A. I. Rykov, two former presidents of the Communist International, many former diplomats, cabinet ministers, and economic executives, and, eventually, seven Red Army generals and thousands of other officers.

The NKVD arrested, summarily tried, and executed large sections of the party, the civil service, and the armed forces. Confessions extorted in torture chambers implicated friends and associates. For those lucky enough to evade firing squads or the noose, exile in the bleak Siberian labor camps invariably meant a slow death from starvation, exposure, or cruel treatment. The Soviet Communist Party became locked into a vicious spiral of suspicion, denunciation, betrayal, and vengeance; only Stalin and his grim inner circle were immune—and many in the inner circle were themselves consumed by the purge after having persecuted others.

During the height of Stalin's purges, 1936 to 1938, the NKVD arrested about eight million Russians, one million of whom were executed, and as many as two million died in concentration camps. In addition, millions were arrested and died before and after the major purges.

was a loyal supporter of Churchill and one of his closest confidants. Smuts was the only national leader to attend both the 1919 and 1945 peace conferences.

STALIN, JOSEF VISSARIONOVICH (1879–1953) Roosevelt called him "Uncle Joe" and tried to reason with him, but the Soviet Union's "Man of Steel" was one of the most cunning and ruthless leaders in history. After having outmaneuvered his opponents in the Soviet government following Lenin's death in 1924, Stalin soon gathered all power in his hands by a willingness to use breathtakingly brutal tactics. Millions of opponents—real or imagined—were executed or sent to exile in work camps in Siberia. In the 1930s, he purged additional millions, including the top echelons of the Soviet armed forces, leaving the military dangerously weakened in its forthcoming confrontation with Germany. Stalin's cold brutality was summed up in his own words, "One death is a tragedy; a million deaths is a statistic." [When German forces invaded his vast country in June 1941, the Red Army performed badly as it had in the forcible annexation of eastern Poland in 1939 and the 1939–40 Winter War with Finland (see Chapter 4, "Allies, Enemies, and Bystanders"]. Stalin had ignored warnings from Churchill that the Nazis were preparing to invade the Soviet Union (he considered the warnings a British plot to drive a wedge between the Soviet Union and Germany). After a series of early disasters, Stalin rallied the Russian people to superhuman effort and built up his forces dramatically by moving armaments production east of the Urals. His armies waged several great counteroffensives that were aided by the bitter Russian winters and ultimately broke the German army. Britain and the United States sent Stalin massive amounts of aid, but Stalin remained suspicious of the Allies' motives throughout the war; he pressured the British and Americans to open a second front long before they were capable of it, and at times threatened to make a separate peace with Hitler. Eventually, as his soldiers battered their way into Berlin, Stalin turned his attention to spreading his remorseless, totalitarian regime across all of Eastern Europe. Stalin died of a cerebral hemorrhage in 1953.

STIMSON, HENRY L. (1867–1950) Republican Henry Lewis Stimson was 72 when President Franklin Roosevelt asked him to serve as secretary of war in July 1940. Stimson already had an illustrious career: he had been a field artillery colonel in World War I, district attorney, secretary of war under President William Howard Taft, and secretary of state under President Herbert Hoover (1929–33). As Franklin Roosevelt's war secretary, Stimson oversaw mobilization and conscription, established the autonomy of the U.S. Army Air Corps (later Army Air Forces), and staunchly supported the Lend-Lease program and increased aid to Britain. Known in Washington as "the Colonel," the courtly Stimson was responsible for arming U.S. merchant ships against Axis attacks, backed the Allies' "Germany first" strategy, and recommended the use of the atomic bomb against Japan.

TITO, JOSIP BROZ (1892–1980) A Croatian-born veteran of the Austro-Hungarian army and the Russian and Spanish civil wars, Communist Marshal Tito became a celebrated symbol of resistance as his well-organized partisan guerrilla bands fought German occupation troops in Yugoslavia from 1941 to 1944. With British assistance, they tied down enemy units and weathered seven major German offensives. Tito eventually mustered an army of 250,000 and obtained recognition from the Yugoslav government-in-exile, which abandoned royalist General Draza Mihailovic's rival Chetniks in May 1944 (see Chapter 4, "Allies, Enemies, and Bystanders"). Tito liberated Belgrade that October, set up a provisional government, and became prime minister and eventually president of Yugoslavia, administering a Communist regime that was friendly to the West. He remained in power until his death in 1980, whereupon the Yugoslav confederation disintegrated into civil war.

TOJO, HIDEKI (1884–1948) A hard-nosed militarist, Hideki Tojo was the third son of a Japanese army lieutenant. A totally dedicated soldier, he rose through the ranks after overseas service in Switzerland and Germany and was consumed by a burning desire to establish Japan's military supremacy. He served as war minister, army chief of staff, and prime minister, forcing the Vichy regime in France to admit Japanese troops to Indochina and presiding over a government that sent a carrier strike force to Pearl Harbor. After the December 7, 1941, sneak attack, Tojo's image, with his spectacles and inscrutable grin, became a kind of racial stereotype of the Japanese enemy that was widely seen in American media. After the fall of the Mariana Islands in 1944 (see Chapter 8, "Campaigns and Battles: Asia and the Pacific"), the emperor replaced Tojo as premier with the less fanatical Lieutenant General Kuniaki Koiso. After Japan surrendered, Tojo made a failed suicide attempt. After his recovery, he was tried as a war criminal and hanged in December 1948.

TRUMAN, HARRY S (1884–1972) Less than three months after his inauguration in 1945, Vice President Harry Truman, a World War I artillery officer, failed haberdasher, and former senator from Missouri, was sworn in as president on the death of President Franklin D. Roosevelt. Though unschooled in foreign policy, Truman competently completed Roosevelt's mission of guiding the nation to victory over the Axis powers. Truman attended the Potsdam Conference (see Chapter 4, "Allies, Enemies, and Bystanders") with new British Prime Minister Clement Attlee and Soviet Marshal Josef Stalin and did not flinch in making the awesome decision to drop two atomic bombs on Japan. In

foreign policy, Truman understood that the United States was a superpower and could never retreat into isolationism, as it had after World War I. His administration presided over the creation of the Marshall Plan, NATO, and the national security apparatus (including the CIA) that is an integral part of U.S. military and diplomatic policy today. His second term was consumed by the Korean War (1950–53). Honest and plainspoken, he stood up boldly to the Soviet threat during the early years of the cold war and is remembered today as a significant president whose administration shaped the direction of modern U.S. foreign policy.

VICTOR EMMANUEL III (1869–1947) The prince of Naples ascended to the Italian throne in 1900, was a soldier during World War I, and began a cordial relationship with future Fascist dictator Benito Mussolini. Victor Emmanuel opposed Italian involvement in World War II and, as the war turned against Italy, eventually opposed Mussolini. He ratified the terms of Italy's surrender to the Allies in September 1943, but because of his long association with fascism, he responded to public opinion and abdicated in May 1946, at which time Italy became a republic.

Milestones in Political History

The section that follows details major political events in which key Allied and Axis powers were involved in World War II. The milestones begin with the end of World War I in 1918 and continue through World War II. Because many events involved more than one country, it is necessary to read the entire section for a complete picture. The countries are listed in alphabetical order.

GERMANY

1918

Germany accepts an armistice, ending World War I. In the enduing postwar chaos, Kaiser

Wilhelm II abdicates and flees to Holland, and Germany becomes a republic.

1919

SEPTEMBER: A young German army officer named Adolf Hitler attends a meeting of a small right-wing political party in Munich, the German Workers Party (DAP). He becomes its leader and changes its name to the National Socialist German Workers Party (NSDAP), Nazis, for short.

1923

NOVEMBER: Hitler and fellow Nazis attempt to take over a meeting at the Munich Beer Hall to state the Nazis would take over the Bavarian government. The coup fails and Hitler is arrested.

NOVEMBER: Inflation destroys the savings of Germany's middle class, creating great political unrest that benefits radical parties, including Hitler's Nazis.

1924

DECEMBER: Hitler is paroled after spending nine months (of a five-year sentence) in jail for the Munich Beer Hall incident.

1925

APRIL: Field Marshal Paul von Hindenburg is elected president of Germany.

1926

SEPTEMBER: Germany joins the League of Nations.

1930

SEPTEMBER: In the German elections, the Nazi Party receives 20 percent of the vote and becomes the second-largest party in the Reichstag (the German parliament).

1932

MARCH–APRIL: Hitler runs unsuccessfully against Hindenburg in the presidential elections.

JULY: After widespread intimidation of opponents, the Nazis become the largest party in the Reichstag, with 230 of 608 seats.

1933

JANUARY: Hitler is appointed chancellor of Germany by Hindenburg.

FEBRUARY: The Reichstag is set on fire, and four suspected Communists are publicly tried and executed, though the fire probably was the work of the Nazis.

MARCH: The Reichstag passes a special constitutional law, the Enabling Act, which gives Hitler wide-ranging emergency powers in the wake of the Reichstag fire. Hitler uses his new powers to arrest opponents and crush political opposition.

OCTOBER: Hitler withdraws Germany from the League of Nations and ends German participation in disarmament conferences.

1934

JANUARY: Germany and Poland conclude a nonaggression pact.

JUNE: On the "Night of the Long Knives," Hitler orders the execution of more than 1,000 of his enemies, including the top leadership of the SA (Sturmabteilungen) (see sidebar Night of the Long Knives on p. 127).

AUGUST: President Hindenburg dies, and Hitler proclaims himself supreme leader (Führer), abolishing the office of president. He orders the armed forces to swear personal allegiance to him.

1935

JANUARY: In an important success for the Nazis, the people of the Saar region vote overwhelmingly in a referendum for union with Germany.

MARCH: Hitler introduces compulsory military service and announces the creation of a German air force (Luftwaffe). This buildup is in direct contravention of the 1919 Versailles Treaty. The Nuremberg Laws (see Chapter 2, "Causes of War") increase the persecution of Jews in Germany, including the denial of civil liberties and the barring of Jews from most professions.

JUNE: The Anglo-German Naval Agreement is signed, allowing Germany to build a fleet as large as 35 percent of the Royal Navy. U-boats are permitted.

1936
MARCH: German troops reoccupy the demilitarized Rhineland. The French and British briefly protest Hitler's first foreign-policy triumph but take no action.

1937
JANUARY: Hitler formally revokes all provisions of the Versailles Treaty during a Reichstag speech.

NOVEMBER: At an important conference, Hitler outlines his aims for Germany, particularly the policy of procuring *Lebensraum* ("living space") in Eastern Europe, including the Ukrainian breadbasket. He lets it be understood that the use of force will be necessary to achieve his goals.

1938
MARCH: The Germans annex Austria in the Anschluss ("union") and proclaim Austria a province of the German Reich.

The Reichstag erupts in thunderous shouts of "Sieg Heil!" as Hitler announces the successful *Anschluss,* or union, with Austria in March 1938.

SEPTEMBER: Hitler, British Prime Minister Neville Chamberlain, French Premier Edouard Daladier, and Italian dictator Benito Mussolini agree in Munich to Germany's acquisition of the Sudetenland, a region of Czechoslovakia. The Czechs are not consulted about the dismemberment of their country. This, says Hitler, is his last territorial claim in Europe.

DECEMBER: France and Germany sign a friendship agreement.

1939

MARCH: Hitler's army invades the remainder of Czechoslovakia. Bohemia and Moravia (Czech provinces) become protectorates of Germany; Slovakia becomes a puppet state ruled by Father Tiso, a Slovakian Fascist-priest. This action induces Britain and France to guarantee the territorial integrity of Poland, the next likely victim of Hitler's aggression.

AUGUST: Germany and the Soviet Union sign a nonaggression pact in Moscow, defining the countries' spheres of interest. They are to divide Poland in half; Germany will control Lithuania, and the Soviet Union will control Finland, Estonia, and Latvia. A later revision places Lithuania in the Soviet sphere and gives more of Poland to Germany. Chamberlain warns Hitler that Britain is prepared to help Poland with force.

SEPTEMBER: German forces invade Poland without a declaration of war. A British ultimatum to Germany expires, and Britain declares war on Germany. France follows suit.

OCTOBER: Hitler issues a directive telling Britain and France that if they do not bring the war to an end, he will "go over to the offensive."

1940

FEBRUARY: Germany and the Soviet Union sign a trade agreement.

MARCH: Hitler and Mussolini meet at the Brenner Pass, and the Italian leader vows to join Germany and its allies in a war against Britain and France.

APRIL: Germany invades and occupies Denmark and Norway.

MAY: German forces invade the Low Countries (Belgium, Holland, and Luxembourg) and then France in an armor-tipped, lightning offensive that would become known as *Blitzkrieg* ("lightning war").

JULY: Hitler issues a directive outlining a plan to invade England.

AUGUST: The Luftwaffe Blitz of London and other British cities begins.

SEPTEMBER: Germany, Italy, and Japan agree that each will declare war on any third party that joins the war against one of the three.

OCTOBER: Hitler and Mussolini confer, and the Führer warns the Italian dictator against undertaking any new campaigns. Hitler meets Generalissimo Francisco Franco of Spain at Hendaye on the French-Spanish border and offers the British colony of Gibraltar and French territory in North Africa as a lure for Franco to join the war. Franco successfully evades making a commitment.

1941

MAY: Nazi Party deputy Rudolf Hess flies to Scotland on a bizarre peace mission. Hitler declares that Hess is insane. The British take him as a prisoner of war.

JUNE: German forces invade the Soviet Union in Operation Barbarossa. Germany and Turkey sign a friendship agreement in Ankara.

DECEMBER: Germany and Italy declare war on the United States three days after the United

States declares war on Japan following the attack on Pearl Harbor. German forces are halted in the suburbs of Moscow as Russian winter sets in and the Soviets mount a furious counteroffensive.

1942
JANUARY: Nazi officials meet at the Wannsee conference in Berlin and put into action plans for the "final solution"—the extermination of all Jews in Europe.

APRIL: Hitler and Mussolini meet at Salzburg, discuss the worsening situation in North Africa, and decide that they must hold on.

JULY: Hitler and Mussolini meet at Feltre in northern Italy, and the Führer demands more effort from the Italians.

1943
FEBRUARY: The huge German Sixth Army surrenders at Stalingrad, a decisive defeat that marks the turning point in the war in the Soviet Union and the beginning of the end for the Germans.

NOVEMBER: Allied bombers conduct massive air raids on the German capital of Berlin.

1944
JUNE: Operation Overlord, the Allied invasion of Western Europe, begins.

JULY: Hitler survives an assassination attempt at his forest headquarters in Rastenburg, Prussia. In Berlin, the Nazis shoot several leading conspirators, including Count Claus von Stauffenberg, who planted a briefcase bomb. Several thousand more executions follow.

1945
MARCH: Hitler orders a scorched-earth policy for all fronts. In the west, Allied armies enter Germany and cross the Rhine. In the east, Soviet forces move within a hundred miles of Berlin.

APRIL: With Soviet forces pushing into the capital and the war hopelessly lost, Hitler retreats to his bunker beneath the Chancellery garden in Berlin. On April 29 he marries his mistress, Eva Braun, and the following day both commit suicide. Before his suicide, Hitler appoints Admiral Karl Dönitz as his successor.

MAY: Germany surrenders to the Allies and is divided into four military occupation zones. The city of Berlin is also divided into four zones.

GREAT BRITAIN
1918
DECEMBER: Campaigning on a platform calling for full reparations by Germany, the rehabilitation of those broken in World War I, and the need to make Great Britain a land "fit for heroes to live in," Prime Minister David Lloyd George and his coalition win a resounding victory in the national elections.

1919
JUNE: The Treaty of Versailles disarms Germany and substantially redraws the map of Europe. Britain receives most German colonies as mandated territories of the newly founded League of Nations, while in the Middle East, Britain and France divide the remnants of the Turkish Ottoman Empire. Britain assumes control of mandates in Palestine, Jordan, and Iraq. The British and French empires reach their zenith, occupying almost one-third of the world's land area and administering more than a third of the world's population. The Sinn Fein rebellion erupts in Ireland, and Mohandas Gandhi begins a passive resistance movement in British-ruled India.

1920
Britain fights a civil war in Ireland.

1921

NOVEMBER: The leading naval powers meet in Washington to discuss limiting their forces and halting a battleship-building race. Britain and the United States accept parity in their main fleets.

DECEMBER: The Irish Free State is established.

1922

AUGUST: Palestine becomes a British League of Nations protectorate.

1925

OCTOBER: Britain and Italy conclude the Locarno treaties, which seek to guarantee and stabilize the French-German frontier. Britain also seeks better relations with Germany and seeks to avoid entanglements in order to keep defense spending low.

1929

OCTOBER: The New York Stock Exchange collapses and the resulting depression cripples Britain's declining economy and shakes the stability and security of the empire. By 1932, unemployment has risen sharply. Fighting begins between Arabs and Jews in Palestine.

1930

APRIL: Britain, the United States, France, and Italy agree at the London Naval Conference not to build any battleships before 1937. The Japanese withdraw rather than sign.

1931

Under Ramsay MacDonald's minority Labour government, Britain abandons the gold standard, centerpiece of the 19th-century free-trade system, and devalues sterling. The British Empire becomes the British Commonwealth.

1935

APRIL: British, French, and Italian officials meet at Stresa, Italy, to condemn breaches of the Ver-

sailles Treaty and show united opposition to German rearmament under Hitler.

JUNE: The Anglo-German Naval Agreement is signed, permitting Germany to build a fleet as large as 35 percent of the Royal Navy.

OCTOBER: Italian forces invade Abyssinia (Ethiopia), and Britain and France lead the League of Nations into imposing sanctions against the Mussolini regime.

1936

DECEMBER: King Edward VIII of England abdicates in order to marry American divorcée Wallis Simpson. He is succeeded by his brother, who takes the name George VI.

1937

MAY: King George VI of England is crowned. Neville Chamberlain succeeds Stanley Baldwin as prime minister.

1938

FEBRUARY: Foreign Secretary Anthony Eden resigns over Chamberlain's appeasement of Mussolini and Hitler.

SEPTEMBER: Chamberlain and French Prime Minister Edouard Daladier confer with Hitler and Mussolini at Munich and sanction the German dismemberment of Czechoslovakia. Hitler says that this is his last territorial claim in Europe, and Chamberlain says that he believes the Führer will keep his word. Churchill calls the agreement a "defeat" and warns that Europe is now in more danger than before.

1939

MARCH: Britain and France issue guarantees to Poland that they will help to defend it against German aggression. The change comes about after Germany, in violation of the Munich Pact, occupies the remainder of Czechoslovakia.

MAY: Britain introduces conscription. The government proposes to limit Jewish entry to Palestine and to work for a joint Arab-Jewish government, but the Zionists oppose it.

SEPTEMBER: After the German invasion of Poland, Britain and France demand that the Nazis withdraw. The British mobilize the army and, because of fear of German bombing raids, begin to evacuate children from London and other potentially vulnerable areas. Parliament opposes the passive line that Chamberlain's government is taking, and the cabinet presents an ultimatum to Germany, as do the French. After a frantic series of talks in London and Paris, the British ultimatum expires, and Chamberlain solemnly broadcasts that a state of war exists with Nazi Germany. The French follow suit. Australia and New Zealand declare war immediately. Chamberlain forms a war cabinet that includes Winston Churchill as first lord of the Admiralty (navy secretary). A message goes out to ships of the British Fleet: "Winston is back." (Churchill, who had vigorously opposed Chamberlain's appeasement of Hitler, was first lord during World War I.) Canada also declares war on Germany. Sir John Simon, chancellor of the exchequer, presents his first war budget and raises income taxes.

1940

FEBRUARY: The British announce they are arming merchant ships in the North Sea.

MARCH: The British-French Supreme War Council decides that neither country will make a separate peace with Germany.

MAY: The House of Commons debates the conduct of the ill-fated British campaign to attack the Germans in occupied Norway, and Chamberlain resigns, although some blame for the failure of the campaign belongs to Churchill. After the popular Lord Halifax is considered but rejected because he sits in the House of Lords, Churchill becomes prime minister. He visits King George VI and officially takes office on May 10. He makes the first of a series of inspirational radio speeches to mobilize Britain and the free world against fascism: "I have nothing to offer but blood, toil, tears and sweat." Recruiting begins for the Local Defense Volunteers, a home-defense militia that will be renamed the Home Guard. Churchill visits Paris to discuss plans for an Allied offensive. Parliament passes the Emergency Powers Act, giving the British government sweeping powers over citizens and property. General Sir John Dill heads the Imperial General Staff. The evacuation of the battered British Expeditionary Force from Dunkirk, France, begins. Invasion fears prompt a series of home-front precautions, including the removal of direction signs from road junctions.

JUNE: Churchill delivers his most famous wartime speech: "We shall fight on the beaches. . . . We shall never surrender." The prime minister returns to France but is unable to instill his fighting spirit in the disorganized French leaders. In response to telegram pleas from Churchill, President Franklin D. Roosevelt ignores U.S. neutrality laws and orders the export of surplus artillery and rifles to Britain. Churchill tells the people that the Battle of France is over and that the Battle of Britain is about to begin: "Let us so bear ourselves that, if the British Empire and its Commonwealth last for a thousand years, men will still say, 'This was their finest hour.'"

JULY: The Battle of Britain begins with a German bomber raid on South Wales. General Alan Brooke is appointed commander of Home Forces. The British Purchasing Commission in the United States is allowed as much as 40 percent of the aircraft that the Americans are producing. British fighter production increases by 50 percent.

AUGUST: Churchill pays tribute to the outnumbered Hurricane and Spitfire pilots of the Royal Air Force Fighter Command who are defeating the Luftwaffe and preventing a German invasion of England: "Never in the field of human conflict was so much owed by so many to so few." The British government decides to lease bases to the United States.

SEPTEMBER: The British government officially allows Londoners to use the subway system as air raid shelters during the Blitz. The Battle of Britain climaxes and subsides, with heavy losses to the Luftwaffe.

OCTOBER: Chamberlain resigns from the War Cabinet, and Churchill becomes head of the Conservative Party.

NOVEMBER: German bombing raids extend to Coventry, Birmingham, Liverpool, Bristol, and Southampton.

DECEMBER: Lord Halifax becomes ambassador to the United States, and Eden takes over as foreign secretary. President Roosevelt outlines his Lend-Lease program to aid Britain.

1941
MAY: The British intern Rudolf Hess, deputy leader of the Nazi Party, after his bizarre peace-mission flight to Scotland.

JUNE: Churchill promises help to the Soviet Union after the invasion by German forces.

JULY: Britain freezes Japanese assets.

AUGUST: Churchill meets Roosevelt for the first time aboard the battleship HMS *Prince of Wales* and the cruiser USS *Augusta* in Placentia Bay, Argentia, Newfoundland. They agree on the Atlantic Charter, which calls for all nations to have the right to conduct free elections and be free from foreign threats.

SEPTEMBER: Fifteen governments, including Britain, the United States, the USSR, and the British Empire countries, sign the charter in London and Washington.

NOVEMBER: General Alan Brooke replaces General John Dill as chief of the Imperial General Staff, and Dill heads the British Military Mission in Washington.

DECEMBER: Parliament passes a new national service bill that includes compulsory conscription for female labor. Britain, Australia, and New Zealand join the United States in declaring war on Japan. Churchill, Roosevelt, and their staffs meet at the Arcadia Conference in Washington, D.C., and agree that the defeat of Germany is their top priority. They establish the U.S. Joint Chiefs of Staff as the directing body for the Allied war effort.

1942
JANUARY: The first U.S. troops arrive in Britain. Churchill wins a vote of confidence on the conduct of war.

APRIL: The British government accepts the U.S. plan "Bolero" for a military buildup in Britain. King George awards the George Cross to Malta for its valiant defense against Axis air attacks.

JUNE: In Washington, Churchill and Roosevelt discuss a second front and atomic research.

AUGUST: Churchill goes to Cairo to investigate the conduct of the Western Desert war and to rally the British Eighth Army. Churchill and Roosevelt agree that an able but obscure staff officer, General Dwight D. Eisenhower, should lead Operation Torch, the invasion of North Africa, set for November.

1943
JANUARY: Churchill and Roosevelt meet at Casablanca and agree on priority for the offensive against U-boats, supplies for the Soviet Union, the invasions of Sicily and Italy, and the strategic bombing of Germany. Stunned when Roosevelt

announces that the Allies will demand the "unconditional surrender" of Germany, Italy, and Japan, Churchill swiftly endorses the move.

MAY: The Trident Conference sets a target date of May 1, 1944, for the Allied invasion of northwestern Europe. Churchill and General George C. Marshall, U.S. Army Chief of Staff, visit North Africa to discuss the upcoming Italian campaign with Eisenhower.

JUNE: King George visits the troops in North Africa.

JULY: Churchill and Roosevelt call for Italy's surrender. Labour Minister Ernest Bevin orders women aged 50 and younger to register for war work, a sign of the strain on British manpower resources.

AUGUST: Churchill, Roosevelt, and their staffs confer in Quebec and agree that the commander of the cross–English Channel invasion should be an American.

NOVEMBER: Churchill and Roosevelt meet Soviet Marshal Josef Stalin for the first time at

Teheran, and the Russian leader vows to join the war against Japan after Germany's defeat.

DECEMBER: General Eisenhower is named supreme commander for Operation Overlord, the invasion of northwestern Europe, with Arthur Tedder, marshal of the Royal Air Force, as his deputy.

1944

JUNE: British, U.S., and Canadian armies invade Normandy, in northern France. Churchill visits the beaches six days after the June 6 landings. He had pleaded in vain with Eisenhower and the king to let him go ashore with the assault troops. German V-1 buzz bomb and V-2 rocket attacks on Britain begin.

AUGUST: Sir Alexander Cadogan leads a British delegation at the Dumbarton-Oaks Conference, in Washington, D.C., where plans are made for postwar security.

SEPTEMBER: Churchill and Roosevelt meet in Quebec, and the British leader insists that the Royal Navy take part in the final campaigns against Japan.

OCTOBER: The prime minister and Foreign Secretary Eden talk with Stalin in Moscow on the future of Eastern Europe. Stalin insists that Bulgaria and Romania remain in the Soviet sphere of influence.

NOVEMBER: Churchill and General Charles de Gaulle, the Free French leader, receive a tumultuous welcome in liberated Paris.

1945

JANUARY: The prime minister rises in the House of Commons to praise the "great American victory" in the Battle of the Bulge. The prime minister and Roosevelt meet at Malta to prepare for their upcoming talks with Stalin.

On the south portico of the Soviet embassy in Teheran in November 1943, Stalin, Roosevelt, and Churchill are seated in front of members of their diplomatic entourages. At Teheran, Stalin agreed to declare war on Japan after the defeat of Germany.

FEBRUARY: The Big Three and their staffs confer at Yalta, in the Crimea. Stalin redraws the map of Poland; Churchill and Roosevelt believe he gives assurances that elections will be held in Eastern Europe. Churchill, who strongly distrusts the Soviet leader, seeks to limit Soviet influence in postwar Europe but receives no support from the ailing Roosevelt.

APRIL: The constitution for the United Nations Organization is drawn up at a conference in San Francisco.

MAY: Churchill, King George, and new U.S. President Harry S Truman make special broadcasts announcing the Allied victory in Europe.

JULY: Churchill, Truman, and Stalin meet at Potsdam, Germany, and demand the unconditional surrender of Japan. Before the conference ends, Churchill's government is voted out of office in a general election, and he is succeeded by his able wartime deputy, Clement Attlee of the Labour Party. Ernest Bevin becomes foreign secretary.

SEPTEMBER: The Japanese officially surrender aboard the battleship USS *Missouri* in Tokyo Bay, and Admiral Sir Bruce Fraser signs on behalf of Great Britain. The surrender of Japanese forces in Southeast Asia is concluded in Singapore before Admiral Lord Louis Mountbatten.

ITALY

1919

Benito Mussolini, a wounded World War I veteran, former laborer and teacher, and an agitator, begins to form the nationalistic Fasci di Combattimento, which would become the Fascist Party. Italy, devastated by the war and on the verge of economic and social collapse, is ripe for the appeals of political extremists like Mussolini.

1922

OCTOBER: In an audacious bluff, Fascists march on Rome to demand power; they succeed. King Victor Emmanuel III invites Mussolini to form a government, and the party blackshirts begin operations to eliminate opposition.

1928

Mussolini, popularly known as Il Duce ("The Leader"), suspends parliamentary government to become the absolute dictator of a Fascist corporate state. He raises national confidence by reclaiming land, boosting wheat production, stabilizing the currency, building a modern navy and air force, and "making the trains run on time." He respects the monarchy, which helps to give him a broad popular base.

1929

FEBRUARY: Mussolini signs the Lateran Treaty, recognizing the Vatican, the seat of the Catholic Church, as a separate and independent entity within the city of Rome. The treaty settles a 60-year-old dispute going back to the unification of Italy, when the former Papal States were incorporated into a united Italy over the objections of the pope.

1934

MARCH: Mussolini signs an agreement with Hungary and Austria. He fears any union among the German-speaking nations and supports Austrian Chancellor Engelbert Dollfuss in opposing both socialism and Nazism.

1935

OCTOBER: In an effort to restore Italian glory and build an overseas empire, Italy invades Abyssinia (Ethiopia) in force.

NOVEMBER: Great Britain and France lead the League of Nations into imposing sanctions against Italy, but these are halfhearted. The failure to strongly counter the invasion becomes the most important single factor in the dissolution of the League of Nations.

1936

MAY: The Abyssinian war ends with the occupation of Addis Ababa and the flight of Emperor Haile Selassie. The Italians formally annex the country.

JULY: The League of Nations ends its sanctions against Italy. The Spanish Civil War begins, and Mussolini enters it belatedly after Adolf Hitler sends German planes to bomb on behalf of Franco. The conflict draws Italy and Germany closer.

1938

MARCH: The German annexation of Austria disturbs Mussolini, but then he earns Hitler's gratitude by condoning the act.

SEPTEMBER: Il Duce proves invaluable to Hitler by arranging and conducting the Munich Conference, at which Germany, Italy, Britain, and France agree to the dismemberment of Czechoslovakia.

1939

MAY: Italy and Germany sign, in Berlin, the "Pact of Steel"—a formal alliance creating the Rome-Berlin Axis.

SEPTEMBER: Mussolini announces Italy's neutrality when Britain and France declare war against Germany.

1940

MARCH: Mussolini and Hitler meet at the Brenner Pass in the Alps, and Il Duce says he is prepared to join Germany and its allies in the war against Britain and France.

JUNE: Once the Germans have crushed the French, Italy declares war on Britain and France, although neither the Italian people nor the economy is well prepared for extended conflict.

AUGUST: Italian forces invade British Somaliland in East Africa, forcing the vastly outnumbered British to evacuate. Eventually, Italian opposition crumbles in the face of British and South African reinforcements.

SEPTEMBER: Italy, Germany, and Japan sign the Tripartite Pact, promising that each will declare war on future enemies of any of them.

OCTOBER: The Italian War Council decides to attack Greece, without alerting Hitler. The invasion becomes another debacle that requires the German army to intervene and occupy Greece.

1941

DECEMBER: Italy, along with Germany, declares war on the United States.

1943

FEBRUARY: Mussolini forms a new government and takes over from Count Galeazzo Ciano as foreign minister.

APRIL: Mussolini and Hitler meet at Salzburg, Austria, and the Italian leader urges the Führer to settle with the Soviet Union. Hitler, making plans to occupy Italy in the event of an Italian military collapse, will not consider it.

JULY: Mussolini and Hitler meet at Feltre, in northern Italy, and the German leader demands more effort from the Italians. On July 10, Allied forces invade Sicily and prepare to attack the Italian mainland. In the wake of this defeat, Mussolini is ousted by the Grand Fascist Council. The Grand Council chooses Marshal Pietro Badoglio to form a new government. Mussolini is arrested while leaving the palace and eventually interned at Gran Sasso in the Apennines. Badoglio forms a cabinet and declares martial law throughout Italy.

SEPTEMBER: Italy signs an armistice with the advancing Allies. German paratroopers led by Colonel Otto Skorzeny dramatically rescue Mussolini and fly him to see Hitler, who installs him under heavy SS protection as head of a puppet regime, "Salo Republic," in German-occupied northern Italy.

OCTOBER: Marshal Badoglio's government declares war on Germany.

1944

JUNE: Marshal Badoglio resigns, and Ivanoe Bonomi, a former prime minister from pre-Fascist times, forms a new government.

1945

APRIL: As Allied forces are about to start overrunning the Po Valley, Mussolini moves his rump government to Milan. After seven days, he flees northward in a German army truck, in the hope of taking refuge in the Tyrol. Partisans catch Mussolini and his mistress, Clara Petacci, near Lake Como, shoot them, and hang their bodies upside down at a gasoline station in Milan. The surrender of the German forces in Italy is signed at Caserta.

JAPAN

1919

JUNE: At the Versailles peace conference, Japan takes its place among the Western Allies and gains a mandate over the Marshall, Mariana, and Caroline island groups, all former German territories in the Pacific. This fails to gratify Japanese ambitions and upsets the balance of domestic politics. It reinforces the view of a growing number of radical nationalists that Japan can expect nothing from the international community and that only its own strength and resources will guarantee the future.

1921

NOVEMBER: Japan takes part in the Washington disarmament conference, which seeks to guarantee the stability of the Pacific, secure the future of China, and place limits on naval forces. Great Britain and the United States accept parity in their main forces, and the Japanese are to have about two-thirds this strength. Britain, the United States, France, and Japan sign a four-power treaty, recognizing each other's rights in the Pacific. In a sign of increasing political instability, Japanese Prime Minister Hara Takashi is stabbed to death at the Tokyo railroad station.

1922

FEBRUARY: In Washington, five powers—the United States, Britain, Japan, France, and Italy—agree to respect Chinese sovereignty and place limits on naval arms. They place a 10-year moratorium on construction of capital ships, which are limited to 35,000 tons and 16-inch guns. A nonfortification clause, whereby the United States and Britain pledge not to strengthen the fortifications of their Pacific possessions (except Australia, New Zealand, and Singapore), compensates for the Japanese inferiority in tonnage, and the Japanese are free to increase the defenses of their home islands.

1926

Hirohito succeeds his insane father, Emperor Taisho, to become Japan's 124th emperor.

1928

AUGUST: By signing the Kellogg-Briand Pact, the United States, Britain, France, Germany, Italy, and Japan agree to renounce aggressive war.

1930

APRIL: At a Washington naval conference, the signatories of the London Naval Treaty agree to extend its terms—no new battleships—for five years. The United States, Britain, and Japan also limit cruiser tonnage to a ratio of 10:10:7, respectively.

MAY: A group of young army officers assassinates Japanese Prime Minister Tsuyoshi Inukai because of his support for the London treaty. The militants had hoped for parity with Britain and the United States. The slaying is one of many and a sign of growing anarchy within the Japanese ruling class as lawless junior officers become involved with pressure groups and "patriotic" societies. (From 1912 to 1941, six premiers are murdered and many other politicians killed or wounded.)

1931

SEPTEMBER: Following alleged sabotage by Chinese soldiers at Mukden on the South Manchurian Railroad, Japanese forces invade the Chinese portion of south and central Manchuria. They brush aside weak Chinese resistance, and within days much of Manchuria is in Japanese hands.

1932

FEBRUARY: Japan declares the independence of the former Manchuria as the puppet state of Manchukuo, and Henry Pu Yi, the last emperor of China, is installed as figurehead leader. Economic exploitation follows, and Japan encourages the opium trade. The United States refuses to recognize the new kingdom. The Japanese invasion of Manchuria is the first major international act of aggression since World War I.

1933

FEBRUARY: After an investigation, the League of Nations censures Japan for its actions in Manchuria. Japan withdraws from the League. Japan allocates money to modernize its army.

MARCH: Japan, China, the Dutch East Indies, and Siam form the Great Asia Association to create a coherent trading bloc—later known as the Greater East Asia Co-Prosperity Sphere. Under Japanese leadership, its aim is for the peripheral nations to supply raw materials to Japanese core industries, which in return will export finished goods.

MAY: Japan and China sign a truce that gives Japan control north of the Great Wall and that sets up, to the south, a demilitarized zone to keep the Chinese and Japanese armies apart.

1934

DECEMBER: Japan abrogates the Washington Naval Treaty.

1936

FEBRUARY: A group of young army officers, modeling themselves on the heroic 45 Ronin (dispossessed samurai warriors), launch a full-scale campaign to assassinate their military and civilian enemies and impose a new cabinet on the emperor. Not all the killings are carried out, and after a few days' confusion, senior politicians regain control. The army begins to purge itself, retiring the hotheads or dispatching them to distant commands on the mainland.

NOVEMBER: Japan and Germany sign the Anti-Comintern Pact, whose main purpose is to threaten the USSR from both west and east and to strengthen Germany as a way to distract Britain from Asian affairs.

1937

JULY: After a minor incident probably provoked by junior officers on both sides at the Marco Polo Bridge near Peking, Japanese forces invade China proper. The fighting spreads throughout northern China, beginning a conflict that will flow into World War II. Prince Fujimaro Konoye, the strongly nationalist prime minister, announces to the parliament that Japan has taken the first steps toward the creation of a new order in Asia.

DECEMBER: Japanese planes sink the Yangtze River gunboat USS *Panay,* killing two crewmen and wounding 43. Japan apologizes to the United States, calls it an unfortunate error, and pays a substantial indemnity. Japanese soldiers commit atrocities on a grand scale in the Chinese city of Nanking, killing as many as 200,000. The horror becomes known as the "Rape of Nanking."

1938

NOVEMBER: Japan announces the establishment of the New Order for East Asia to create peace in East Asia under the leadership of Japan. This declaration stiffens British and U.S. opposition to Japanese expansion.

1940

FEBRUARY: A record budget is presented to the Japanese diet (parliament), with almost half earmarked for military expenditure.

MARCH: The Japanese set up a puppet Chinese government in Nanking.

JULY: Prime Minister Yonai resigns because of military pressure, and Prince Konoye heads a new cabinet that includes General Hideki Tojo as minister of war.

SEPTEMBER: The United States clamps controls on the export of war materiel and prohibits the sale of oil and scrap metal to Japan. President Franklin D. Roosevelt's aim is to "slip a noose around Japan's neck and give it a jerk now and then." The Japanese react with defiance and believe the U.S. actions are an act of war that threatens the existence of Japan. Japanese troops enter Indochina after an "invitation" from the French Vichy government. Germany, Italy, and Japan agree that each will declare war on any third party that joins the war against one of them.

1941

APRIL: Japan and the Soviet Union sign a five-year neutrality agreement.

JULY: Britain and the United States freeze Japanese assets in those countries.

AUGUST: The United States presents a formal warning to Japan to cease its aggression in Asia.

SEPTEMBER: The Japanese cabinet accepts a document from naval planners that states that, unless diplomats can restore the supply situation interrupted by the U.S. embargoes, Japan should contemplate seizing the East Indies oil fields from the Dutch and "immediately decide to commence hostilities against the United States, Britain, and the Netherlands."

OCTOBER: Roosevelt rejects Premier Konoye's request for a summit conference. Konoye, who had hoped to avoid war, resigns and is replaced by the bellicose Tojo, who assumes the offices of prime minister, war minister, and home affairs minister.

NOVEMBER: The Japanese decide to make further peace attempts, but Washington rejects their terms. Roosevelt and Secretary of State Cordell Hull present the Japanese with a stiff 10-point note demanding that they leave China and Indochina and recognize the Chinese Nationalist government. The Americans promise in return to negotiate new deals on trade and raw materials. The Japanese do not respond. A Japanese carrier force leaves its bases to move across the Pacific toward Hawaii.

DECEMBER: President Roosevelt makes a final appeal to Emperor Hirohito for peace but receives no reply. Japanese negotiators at their embassy in Washington conduct talks with the State Department. On December 7, Japanese carrier planes attack and maul the U.S. Pacific Fleet at Pearl Harbor, Hawaii, propelling an outraged and unified United States into World War II. The United States and Britain declare war on Japan, as do Australia, New Zealand, and the Netherlands.

1942

FEBRUARY: General Tojo outlines Japanese war aims to the Diet, speaking of "a new order of coexistence and co-prosperity on ethical principles in Greater East Asia."

JUNE: Japanese forces are stopped at the Battle of Midway, a major turning point that puts Japan on the defensive for the remainder of the war.

1943

Japanese forces in the Pacific continue to retreat as the U.S. island-hopping strategy brings the U.S. Navy closer and closer to the Japanese main islands.

1944

AUGUST: The Japanese government introduces measures to conscript females aged 12 to 40 for war work.

OCTOBER: The U.S. deals a major defeat to the Japanese navy at the Battle of Leyte Gulf and begins the reconquest of the Philippines.

1945

APRIL: The United States invades and occupies Okinawa, in the Ryukyu Islands, a few hundred miles from the Japanese main islands.

JULY: U.S. President Truman decides to use the atomic bomb on Japan if it does not soon come to terms.

AUGUST: The United States drops atomic bombs on Hiroshima and Nagasaki, killing an estimated 120,000 people. The Soviet Union declares war on Japan. Emperor Hirohito orders that the war should end and broadcasts the decision to the Japanese people.

SEPTEMBER: Foreign Minister Shigemitsu leads a Japanese delegation in signing the surrender terms aboard the battleship USS *Missouri* in Tokyo Bay. General Douglas A. MacArthur signs on behalf of the Allies. Japanese forces in Southeast Asia surrender to Admiral Lord Louis Mountbatten. U.S. forces occupy Japan, which is to be ruled by MacArthur for the next five years.

SOVIET UNION

1922

Josef Stalin becomes general secretary of the Soviet Communist Party. As commissar of nationalities, he is instructed to draw up a plan of federation.

DECEMBER: The first Congress of Soviets of the Union of Soviet Socialist Republics meets in Moscow and confirms the pact for the formation of a union.

1923

JULY: The Central Executive Committee of the Congress of Soviets accepts the constitution of the USSR. Stalin launches a campaign against Leon Trotsky, political heir-apparent to Vladimir Lenin, architect of the October 1917 revolution. Lenin regards Stalin as power-hungry and "too crude" for top leadership.

1924

JANUARY: Lenin dies. As party secretary, Stalin builds his power base, and the 13th party conference cannot muster the votes to oust him.

1927

Stalin becomes sole leader of the party, having ousted Trotsky and triumvirate members Lev Borisovich Kamenev and Grigory Zinoviev. Although Stalin has no official position in the government, he is a cunning manipulator and shrewd negotiator, who dominates it as head of the Politburo. He continues and extends Lenin's New Economic Policy, which includes the abolition of private property and the breaking up of vast estates.

1928

The New Economic Policy has brought some agricultural prosperity, but Stalin changes course and orders a campaign of forced collectivization. During the course of the program (1928–33), an estimated nine million peasants suffer. Many are shot for resisting resettlement, many die en route to Siberia, and hundreds of thousands starve to death. They are stripped even of seed for the next crop. Stalin launches the first Five-Year Plan, giving priority to military production but without sufficient capital. A man-made famine of staggering proportions grips the Soviet Union.

1929

Stalin begins a major cleansing of the party and government apparatus to remove his many enemies. Political purges and terror intensify throughout the 1930s, and he has hundreds of thousands arrested, tortured, dispatched to Siberian labor camps, or summarily executed.

1932

NOVEMBER: Stalin's second wife, Nadzezhda (Nadya) Alliluyeva, commits suicide, and he is genuinely saddened.

1933

NOVEMBER: The United States grants diplomatic recognition to the Soviet regime. Great Britain had done so in 1924 but severed relations in 1927.

1934

SEPTEMBER: Sensing the threat of Nazi Germany to Eastern Europe, and particularly the Ukraine breadbasket, Stalin joins the League of Nations.

1935

MAY: The USSR and France conclude a mutual assistance pact. British Foreign Secretary Anthony Eden visits Moscow later in the year, but the British government is still reluctant to regard the Soviet Union as an ally against Germany.

1936

JULY: The Spanish Civil War breaks out, and fear of fascism prompts Stalin to send tanks, aircraft, and advisers to aid the Republicans in opposing Generalissimo Francisco Franco and his German and Italian allies.

1937

JUNE: Stalin's continuing party purges extend to the Red Army, and during the next months he has about 35,000 officers from various ranks arrested, tortured, executed, or banished to Siberia. This leaves the army disorganized and demoralized.

1939

JUNE: Formal talks start in Moscow between the Soviets and British and French representatives. Britain and France try to arrange help for Poland and Romania, but Stalin, prepared to fight Germany if granted a free hand in the future of Eastern Europe, wants to station Soviet troops in Poland. Little progress is made.

AUGUST: The Soviet Union and Germany sign an economic agreement. The Soviets and Germans also sign their nonaggression pact in Moscow, its secret terms defining the countries' spheres of influence. They will divide Poland, Germany will control Lithuania, and the USSR will control Finland, Estonia, and Latvia. A later revision places Lithuania in the Soviet sphere and apportions more Polish territory to Germany. British Prime Minister Neville Chamberlain tells German dictator Adolf Hitler that Britain is prepared to help Poland with force.

SEPTEMBER: Soviet troops enter eastern Poland in the wake of the German invasion that begins September 1.

NOVEMBER: Relations between the Soviet Union and Finland deteriorate, and the Kremlin renounces the two countries' nonaggression pact.

Soviet troops and aircraft invade Finland, and a costly, four-month Winter War ensues during which the outnumbered but determined Finns inflict a series of defeats on the poorly equipped and led Red Army before being finally overwhelmed. Soviet losses are heavy.

DECEMBER: The League of Nations agrees to intervene in the settlement of the dispute between Finland and the Soviet Union, but the Soviets refuse the offer and are expelled.

1940
FEBRUARY: The USSR and Germany sign a further trade and economics agreement whereby the Soviets will supply oil and food in return for arms.

MARCH: The Soviet Union and Finland sign a peace treaty in Moscow, ending their Winter War.

1941
APRIL: The Soviet Union and Japan sign a five-year neutrality agreement. In what becomes a fortuitous event for Stalin, the pact enables him to transfer forces from Siberia when Germany invades the Soviet Union in June.

JUNE: Hitler launches Operation Barbarossa, the invasion of Russia. Three German army groups, including 3,332 tanks, supported by four air fleets, take the Soviets by surprise and make rapid advances. Six months of catastrophes follow for the retreating, ill-prepared Red Army, which loses 4.5 million: 1.5 million killed and 3 million taken prisoner.

JULY: After a period in which Stalin suffers a mental breakdown, raging at subordinates, making senseless demands in the Kremlin, and retreating to his dacha, cronies persuade him to take the position of commander in chief. While not an orator, he makes an effective radio address rallying the country for the "great patriotic war."

OCTOBER: Stalin announces that he will remain in Moscow, although most of the government has moved away from the combat zone, and that the city will be defended with every means.

DECEMBER: The German advance is halted in the suburbs of Moscow. The brutal Russian winter takes its toll on the German troops and equipment. As the German offensive stalls, the Soviets launch a massive counteroffensive led by Marshal Zhukov that drives the Germans into retreat.

1942
SEPTEMBER: The five-month Battle of Stalingrad commences, during which the Red Army surrounds and crushes the German Sixth Army and thwarts the enemy effort to take Transcaucasia. The epic Soviet victory is a turning point of World War II. Stalin gains confidence in his generals and follows up with a westward drive, remaining largely on the offensive for the rest of the war.

1943
NOVEMBER: Stalin, British Prime Minister Winston Churchill, and U.S. President Franklin D. Roosevelt meet at Teheran. They confirm plans to invade Western Europe (for which Stalin has long been pressing London and Washington in order to take pressure off the Eastern Front) and southern France, and the Soviet leader promises to join the war against Japan after Germany's defeat.

1944
OCTOBER: Churchill and Eden confer with Stalin in Moscow on arrangements for the political future of Eastern Europe, but no one makes real concessions.

1945
FEBRUARY: Stalin, Churchill, and Roosevelt meet at Yalta in the Crimea. Churchill and Roosevelt agree at Stalin's insistence, that Stalin retain Polish territory seized in 1939, with Poland to gain land in the west at Germany's expense.

At Potsdam in July 1945, President Harry Truman greets Soviet Premier Josef Stalin. The group includes (left to right) Stalin, Truman's interpreter Charles Bohlen, Stalin's interpreter V. N. Pavlov, President Truman, Soviet Ambassador to the United States Andrei Gromyko, U.S. Press Secretary Charles Ross, and Soviet Foreign Minister Vyacheslav Molotov.

The Soviet leader gives assurances that he will permit elections in Eastern Europe.

APRIL: The Soviets attend the conference in San Francisco that draws up the charter for a United Nations organization. The conferees agree that the major powers—the United States, Great Britain, the USSR, France, and China—will constitute the permanent members of the Security Council, with veto power.

JULY: Stalin, Churchill, and new U.S. President Harry Truman meet at Potsdam, Germany, and demand an unconditional surrender by Japan. Truman informs Stalin of a "new and powerful weapon" ready for use against Japan, without specifying its nature. Stalin already knows about the atomic bomb from his spies in the United States.

AUGUST: The Soviet Union, as promised at Yalta, declares war on Japan 90 days after the end of the war in Europe.

1946
The Soviets consolidate their position in Eastern Europe, stationing millions of troops and making

sure that Communist regimes are installed in all the nations that are on their western borders. Relations with the United States continue to deteriorate, as the former Allies become adversaries.

UNITED STATES

1920
MARCH: The U.S. Senate refuses to ratify the Treaty of Versailles ending World War I and creating the League of Nations. In a move to further U.S. isolationist policies, the U.S. refuses to join the League, which is a major blow to the new organization.

> I ask you to look at the map of Europe today and see if you can suggest any way in which we could win this war if we entered it. —Charles A. Lindbergh, speech in New York, 1941

1921
JULY: President Warren G. Harding signs separate peace treaties by approving a joint congressional resolution declaring peace with Germany, Austria, and Hungary. (The treaties are signed in August.)

NOVEMBER: At the arms limitation conference in Washington, the leading naval powers agree to curtail warship construction, outlaw poison gas, restrict submarine attacks on merchant ships, and respect the integrity of China. Great Britain and the United States accept parity in their main forces. The agreements are ratified in 1925.

1928
AUGUST: The United States, Britain, France, Germany, Italy, and Japan sign the Kellogg-Briand Pact, agreeing to renounce aggressive war.

1929
OCTOBER: The New York Stock Exchange collapses and triggers a worldwide economic depression that worsens over the next four years.

1930

APRIL: In London, the United States, Britain, Italy, France, and Japan sign a treaty mandating that no battleships will be built before 1937. The treaty also places limitations on cruisers, submarines, and destroyers.

1933

MARCH: Newly-elected President Franklin D. Roosevelt introduces a wide array of innovative social and economic legislation (collectively known as the New Deal) designed to revive the American economy.

APRIL: The United States drops the gold standard.

DECEMBER: The United States forswears armed intervention in the Western Hemisphere.

1935

AUGUST: Congress passes the Neutrality Act (designed to keep the United States out of a European war), which prohibits the shipment of war materiel to belligerents and forbids U.S. citizens from traveling on belligerent vessels.

1936

NOVEMBER: Roosevelt is reelected to a second term in a landslide.

1938

MAY: The Naval Expansion Act authorizes a significant increase in the strength of the U.S. Navy and the procurement of 3,000 aircraft.

1939

JANUARY: Roosevelt, realizing that war may break out in Europe, asks for an increase in the defense budget.

SEPTEMBER: The United States declares its neutrality after the outbreak of World War II in Europe. Roosevelt proclaims a limited national emergency and asks Congress to repeal the neutrality laws prohibiting the sale of arms and ammunition to warring nations on a cash-and-carry basis. He also requests authority to prohibit U.S. ships from entering "danger zones."

OCTOBER: Upon the advice of scientist Albert Einstein, President Roosevelt sets up the Advisory Committee on Uranium to explore the possible military uses of atomic energy.

OCTOBER: Meeting in Panama, the Congress of American States establishes a "neutral zone" extending 300 miles from the coast of the Americas.

1940

MAY: President Roosevelt asks Congress to appropriate $1.18 billion for defense and to authorize the production of 50,000 airplanes a year. He also asks for an extraordinary credit of $900 million. He recommissions 35 destroyers that had been mothballed after World War I.

JUNE: The president signs the Naval Expansion Act of 1940, authorizing an 11 percent increase in fleet strength. Congress approves $4 billion to build a two-ocean navy and procure 15,000 naval aircraft. In an effort to create bipartisan support for his foreign policy, Roosevelt appoints prominent Republicans to his cabinet—Henry L. Stimson as secretary of war and Frank Knox as secretary of the navy.

JULY: Congress grants the president the authority to control the export of war materiel. He immediately bars the sale of such goods to Japan. Roosevelt signs a further Navy bill providing for the construction of 45 more ships and appropriating $550 million to finance these and other projects.

SEPTEMBER: Roosevelt and British Prime Minister Winston Churchill of Great Britain conclude an agreement whereby the United States will transfer 50 World War I destroyers to the Royal Navy in exchange for 99-year leases to British bases in the West Indies, Bermuda, and Newfoundland. Signing the Selective Training Service Act, Roosevelt establishes the first peacetime draft in U.S. history. All males aged 21 to 35 become subject to induction into the armed forces.

NOVEMBER: Roosevelt defeats Wendell Willkie of Indiana and wins an unprecedented third term.

DECEMBER: The president declares in a "fireside chat" radio broadcast that he wants the United States to become the "arsenal of democracy" and to give full aid to Britain, then standing alone against Germany.

1941

JANUARY: Roosevelt unveils a program to produce two hundred 7,500-ton freighters to be called Liberty ships. In his State of the Union message to Congress, the president outlines the four essential freedoms—of speech and worship, and from fear and want. The budget he presents to Congress outlines a total expenditure of $17.5 billion, with $10.8 billion for defense. The Lend-Lease Bill, providing $7 billion worth of military credits for Britain, is introduced in Congress; Roosevelt signs it in March. British and U.S. representatives conduct secret talks in Washington and agree that Allied policy in the event of war with Germany and Japan should have as its priority Germany's defeat.

MAY: When a German U-boat sinks the U.S. merchant ship *Robin Moor* in the Atlantic, President Roosevelt calls the attack "an act of intimidation" to which "we do not propose to yield."

JUNE: The Army Bill for 1942 is introduced in Congress and calls for appropriations of $10.4 billion. Congress enacts a law allowing the government to take over foreign ships laid up in the United States. The president freezes German and Italian assets in the United States.

JULY: After the United States agrees to provide U.S. naval forces to defend Iceland, U.S.

Marines land at Reykjavik. Roosevelt asks Congress to extend the draft period from one year to 30 months and to make similar increases in the terms of service for the national guard. The measure squeaks through the House by one vote (203–202) and passes in the Senate. In response to the occupation of Indochina, Roosevelt freezes Japanese assets in the United States. Britain does likewise.

AUGUST: President Roosevelt forbids the export of oil and aviation fuel, except to Britain, the British Empire, and the countries of the Western Hemisphere. The decision hits Japan hard. Roosevelt, Churchill, and their staffs meet for the first time aboard the battleship HMS *Prince of Wales* and the cruiser USS *Augusta* in Placentia Bay, Argentia, Newfoundland, and agree on the eight principles set forth in the Atlantic Charter.

SEPTEMBER: After a U-boat attacks the destroyer USS *Greer* off Iceland, Roosevelt issues an order to U.S. warships to "shoot on sight" any German ship.

OCTOBER: After deliberating for almost two months, President Roosevelt rejects moderate Japanese Prime Minister Fuminaro Konoye's request for a summit conference. A U-boat sinks the USS *Reuben James*, which was on convoy escort duty in the Atlantic; 100 die.

NOVEMBER: While its military prepares for war with the United States, the Japanese government makes further peace attempts, setting the deadline for the end of any negotiations at the end of November. Washington rejects the terms offered. Roosevelt announces a loan of $1 billion to the Soviet Union to finance the acquisition of Lend-Lease supplies. Congress amends the neutrality laws to allow for the arming of U.S. merchant ships and for their entry into war zones. Japanese special envoy Saburo Kurusu presents Secretary of State Cordell Hull with a final negotiating program, proposing a free hand for Japan in the Far

East. Hull rejects it and hands Japanese Ambassador Kichisaburo Nomura a stiff 10-point U.S. counterproposal for a general Far East settlement, calling on Japan to pull out of China and Indochina. The Japanese do not respond. Led by Vice Admiral Chuichi Nagumo, a Japanese strike force of six aircraft carriers, two battleships, nine destroyers, three submarines, and tankers sails secretly from the Kurile Islands toward Hawaii. Unless Japan reaches an agreement with the United States by December 5, the force is to attack the U.S. Pacific Fleet at Pearl Harbor, Hawaii.

DECEMBER: Bombers, torpedo bombers, dive-bombers, and fighters from the Japanese strike force attack the anchored U.S. fleet at Pearl Harbor with complete tactical and strategic surprise. The U.S. losses are 2,403 killed and 1,178 wounded. Roosevelt addresses Congress and describes December 7 as "a date which will live in infamy." The United States and Britain declare war on Japan. Germany and Italy declare war on the United States four days later. British and U.S. leaders and their key staffs gather at the three-week Arcadia Conference in Washington to plan joint conduct of the war and affirm the strategic priority of "Germany first."

1942

JANUARY: Roosevelt submits his 1943 budget to Congress calling for appropriations of $59 billion for planes, tanks, and shipping. He names Donald Nelson to head the new War Production Board.

MARCH: In compliance with an executive order from President Roosevelt, 120,000 Japanese Americans, including 75,000 U.S. citizens, are transported from their homes on the West Coast to internment camps in the interior of the country.

JUNE: Roosevelt and Churchill meet in Washington to discuss operations in the European theater and rule out a second front for 1942. Churchill suggests an invasion of French North

Africa for later in the year. They discuss atomic research, and the two countries agree to share knowledge.

OCTOBER: Congress gives the president the power to control wages and agricultural prices. Congress passes the largest tax bill in U.S. history, designed to raise $6.9 billion.

NOVEMBER: Allied forces invade northwest Africa and begin their engagement of Axis forces across the breadth of North Africa.

DECEMBER: The president confirms a policy, recommended by his advisers, of not cooperating with the British on atomic research. His goal is to have the United States develop the atomic bomb on its own.

1943

JANUARY: Roosevelt, Churchill, and their combined staffs meet at Casablanca and agree to postpone an invasion of northwestern Europe until 1944. They decide to invade Sicily and the Italian mainland, give priority to the U-boat offensive and the supplying of the Soviet Union, intensify the strategic bombing of Germany, and push on through the Pacific toward Japan. Roosevelt surprises the other conferees by announcing that the Allies are fighting for the "unconditional surrender" of the Axis powers. Although taken aback, Churchill supports Roosevelt. (Churchill and others were opposed to unconditional surrender because they thought it would stiffen the resistance of the enemy and prolong the war.)

MARCH: Congress extends Lend-Lease for another year.

MAY: Roosevelt, Churchill, and their chiefs of staff meet in Washington for the Trident Conference, agree to invade Italy and force that country out of the war, and reach a compromise decision to land 29 divisions in France in May

1944. Roosevelt bars war contractors from racial discrimination.

JUNE: Roosevelt signs the pay-as-you-go income tax bill.

AUGUST: At the Quadrant Conference in Quebec, Roosevelt, Churchill, and their combined staffs confirm May 1, 1944, as the target date for an invasion of Normandy and decide that the supreme commander should be an American.

NOVEMBER: With 530,000 coal miners out on strike, Roosevelt orders Secretary of the Interior Harold Ickes and his Solid Fuels Administration to take over the running of U.S. mines. Roosevelt, Churchill, and Chinese Generalissimo Chiang Kai-shek meet for the Sextant Conference in Cairo to finalize plans for 1944. Shortly after, Roosevelt and Churchill meet Soviet Premier Josef Stalin at the Eureka Conference in Teheran. They confirm May 1944 as the date for the invasion of Europe and agree upon landings in northern France. Stalin vows to enter the war against Japan when Germany has been defeated.

DECEMBER: At their second Cairo parley, Roosevelt and Churchill discuss their plans for the invasion of southern France.

1944

JANUARY: President Roosevelt appeals to Congress for a new national service law to prevent damaging strikes and to mobilize the entire adult workforce for war work. The major railroad unions accept Roosevelt's terms and avert a strike. The United States, Britain, and Australia protest ill treatment of prisoners by the Japanese.

JUNE: Roosevelt signs the GI Bill of Rights providing benefits to returning veterans.

JUNE: Allied forces land in Normandy (D-Day) and begin liberation of France and march toward Germany.

JULY: Delegates of 44 countries attend a monetary conference at Bretton Woods, New Hampshire, at which the International Bank for Reconstruction and Development is created and the postwar world financial system is discussed.

AUGUST: Allied representatives meet at Dumbarton Oaks, Washington, D.C., to plan the maintenance of postwar security. This will be the basis for the United Nations organization.

SEPTEMBER: Roosevelt, Churchill, and their staffs meet for the Octagon Conference in Quebec, and Roosevelt agrees with Churchill that the Royal Navy should support the U.S. Fleet in the Pacific.

NOVEMBER: Though ailing, Roosevelt runs for a fourth term and wins handily over Thomas E. Dewey.

1945

FEBRUARY: The Big Three—Roosevelt, Churchill, and Stalin—confer at Yalta, in the Crimea. Stalin agrees to declare war on Japan in August 1945, promises to conduct "free and unfettered" elections in Eastern Europe, and agrees to send delegates to the United Nations charter meeting in San Francisco.

APRIL: President Roosevelt dies of a cerebral hemorrhage at the "Little White House" in Warm Springs, Georgia, and is succeeded by Vice President Harry S Truman.

MAY: The Allies celebrate victory in Europe.

JUNE: The text of the United Nations Charter is completed, formally approved, and signed in San Francisco.

JULY: The United States successfully tests the world's first atomic bomb at Alamogordo, New Mexico. President Truman, Churchill, and Stalin meet at Potsdam, Germany, and call upon Japan to surrender unconditionally or face "utter destruction." The Japanese government rejects the ultimatum. The United States informs Stalin that the Americans have a new and powerful weapon but does not specify its nature. (Stalin, who has had spies in the atomic program, is already aware of the weapon's existence.) Congress ratifies the Bretton Woods economic agreement. Truman decides to use the atomic bomb against Japan if the country does not soon come to terms. Churchill's government is voted out of office, and Clement Attlee is named prime minister during the conference.

AUGUST: B-29 Superfortress heavy bombers drop atomic bombs on the Japanese cities of Hiroshima and Nagasaki, killing an estimated 120,000 people. The Soviet Union declares war on Japan. Emperor Hirohito orders that the war should end, and the Allies celebrate victory in the Far East. President Truman orders Lend-Lease aid to halt immediately.

SEPTEMBER: The Japanese surrender aboard the battleship USS *Missouri* in Tokyo Bay. General Douglas A. MacArthur accepts the surrender on behalf of the Allies. MacArthur takes over as military ruler of occupied Japan.

Columns of American soldiers stretch down the Champs Elysées toward the Arc de Triomphe, passing in review for a throng of celebrating Parisians on August 28, 1944.

OCTOBER: The UN Charter takes effect.

NOVEMBER: The trial of major German war criminals opens in Nuremberg.

DECEMBER: A war crimes trial commences in Japan.

1948

At the request of President Truman, Congress approves a $14 billion economic recovery package for the war-ravaged countries of Europe. It is popularly known as the Marshall Plan, after Secretary of State George C. Marshall, who described the plan at a speech at Harvard University in June 1947.

RISE OF THE NAZI PARTY

This table shows the ascendancy of the Nazi Party as its support among the German electorate increased. In August 1934, when Germany's President Paul von Hindenburg died, Hitler was able to proclaim himself supreme leader of Germany.

Election	NSDAP percent of total votes	NSDAP Reichstag seats	Comments
1928 (Reichstag national elections)	<3	12	54 Communists gain seats
1930 (Reichstag national elections)	20	107	77 Communist seats; Hitler's is the second largest party in Germany
March 1932 (presidential election)	>30	N/A	Hitler's opponents are the aging incumbent Field Marshal Paul von Hindenburg, army officer Theodor Duesterberg, and Communist Party leader Ernst Thaelmann
April 1932 (presidential runoff)	37	N/A	Hindenburg reelected
July 1932 (Reichstag national election)	37	230	Nazis are largest party in Germany
November 1932*	33	196	100 Communist seats
March 1933**	44	288	Hitler has 53 percent majority

*In January 1933, a reluctant Hindenburg names Hitler German chancellor, with a coalition cabinet, but refuses him extraordinary powers.
**In March 1933, a special constitutional law, the Enabling Act (the Law to Remove the Distress of People and State) takes away from the Reichstag legislative powers, budget control, the initiation of constitutional amendments, and approval of treaties with other nations, and gives them to Hitler's Reich Cabinet for a four-year period.
Source: Fischer, *Nazi Germany: A New History* (New York: Continuum, 1996)

NAZI ORGANIZATIONS

The National Socialist German Workers Party (NSDAP) set up many organizations to promote Nazi ideals and philosophy during the 12 years of the Third Reich. This table outlines those groups.

Organization	Function
National Political Training Institutes	Established by Adolf Hitler to develop a Nazi elite
National Socialist Fliers Corps	Special aircraft unit
National Socialist German Doctors Alliance	Monolithic physicians' group; superseded all previous medical associations of the Weimar Republic
National Socialist German Secondary School	Special school for future leaders
National Socialist German Students League	Dedicated to furthering the Nazi way of life among young people
National Socialist German Workers Party	National labor union—the Nazi Party
National Socialist Lawyers Association	Composed of all practicing lawyers and with its own honor courts
National Socialist League of Ex-Servicemen	Veterans organization
National Socialist Lecturers Alliance	Designed to keep university teachers in line with Nazi ideology
National Socialist Monthly	Propaganda organization
National Socialist Motor Corps	Paramilitary formation overseeing the premilitary training of army recruits
National Socialist People's Welfare Organization	Devoted to the welfare of party members and their families
National Socialist Relief Fund	Accident and insurance plan
National Socialist Shop Cell Organization	Industrial propaganda units; replaced the old labor unions
National Socialist Teachers Alliance	Monolithic party organization of educators
National Socialist Women's Groups	Auxiliary organization promoting the rearing of children as patriots

CHAPTER 6

Officers and Soldiers

Despite the advances in military machinery—from artillery to precision bombing and from aircraft carriers to the atomic bomb—World War II was decided ultimately by men fighting men. The foot soldiers who stormed ashore at Normandy, in France, surprising the Germans; the marines who endured the jungles of Guadalcanal fighting the Japanese for months before victory was certain; the sailors who experienced the kamikaze suicide attacks in the closing days of the war—these were some of the citizen soldiers, nameless individuals who, in the end, fought bravely for their respective countries and defeated the enemy.

War, as experienced from 1939 to 1945, was a drawn-out slugging match that demanded maximum endurance from its combatants. Military forces of millions of men are run by officers, and both the Allies and the Axis produced many fascinating and brilliant military leaders, who like chess players strategized war plans and directed millions of men in battle. They were men like Admiral Isoroku Yamamoto, the visionary planner of the Pearl Harbor attack who had studied at Harvard University; or General Erwin Rommel, who led his German troops, the Afrika Korps, to near-victory in the North African theater; or General Dwight D. Eisenhower, who organized the complex D-Day landings in Normandy; or flamboyant types like General George Patton and Admiral William "Bull" Halsey.

These leaders—however diverse their styles and personalities—were products of their cultures, and the ways they ran their military forces were a reflection of different cultural traditions. The Japanese and Germans, for example, created more rigid military hierarchies managed from the top; underlings were not encouraged to improvise on the battlefield. Germans, especially, were reluctant to change the order of battle until Hitler had given permission, and such delays in the command structure were fatal at Normandy. By contrast, the American forces were encouraged to improvise when necessary, and subordinate officers responded to shifting events on the battlefield with innovation and bravery.

Warriors and Heroes

Generally speaking, the Allied and Axis military leaders of World War II fought a different kind of war than their World War I counterparts because of technological advances. The Western Front generals and field marshals of 1914–18, their tactics rooted in 19th-century technology, needed to dispatch wave after wave of young men to frontlines in order to win a battle. Top-ranking officers of World War II had the potential of modern weapons available to them and with this brought a different kind of challenge—an ethical one. They would have to fight a more subtle war of maneuver because with technological advances governments and people would no longer tolerate indiscriminate slaughter.

There would be lapses, as on the Eastern Front, where slaughter was wholesale, such as in the Hurtgen Forest, where elements of eight U.S. divisions were mauled in a wasteful campaign in late 1944. But by and large it would be a war of machine against machine, although the human cost was nevertheless tremendous.

The German high command was an efficient organization with many dedicated, innovative captains at its disposal. They and their well-disciplined armies fought hard and long, even after their inevitable defeat became obvious. Battle-hardened Japanese land and naval forces, under Yamamoto, Nagumo, Ozawa, Yamashita, Homma, and others conquered vast territories across Asia and the Pacific.

By comparison, Great Britain and the United States both entered the war woefully unprepared and fielding small professional armies that great numbers of citizen soldiers would have to supplement. But the Allies, like their German and Japanese foes, had the benefit of cadres of capable generals to mold their armies, after early blunders and reverses, into highly able combat forces.

Led ably by British Prime Minister Winston Churchill and U.S. President Franklin D. Roosevelt and guided by such men of genius as Field Marshal Alan Brooke, chief of the British Imperial General Staff, and General George C. Marshall, U.S. Army chief of staff, the Allied generals and admirals directed momentous campaigns that inevitably wore down their enemies. Soviet dictator Josef Stalin's great peasant armies were aided in no small measure by the Russian

Smiling and confident, well equipped German soldiers move toward a new assignment after fighting for three straight days in another area.

winters, but in the end, the courage of the average Soviet soldier and the superb generalship of leaders like Georgi Zhukov and Ivan Konev were an essential ingredient in Allied victory.

ALLIED COMMANDERS

ALEXANDER, SIR HAROLD (1891–1969), FIELD MARSHAL, GREAT BRITAIN A veteran of World War I and the Northwest Frontier, the handsome, gallant officer was the last British soldier to leave Dunkirk, France, as the Germans closed in on the British Expeditionary Force in June 1940. He led the Middle East Forces and was Eisenhower's deputy in North Africa (1943) and later supreme Allied commander in the Mediterranean theater (1943–45).

ANDERS, WLADISLAW (1892–1970), GENERAL, POLAND A former cavalryman, General Anders led the Polish II Corps at Tobruk (Libya) and in the Western Desert, in the bloody May 1944 capture of Monte Cassino, Italy, and in the liberation of Bologna in April 1945.

ANTONOV, ALEKSEI (1896–1962), GENERAL, SOVIET UNION Antonov was the Red Army chief of staff and head of operations in 1942–45, kept Stalin informed of the overall situation, and helped to plan the Belorussian campaign and the Berlin offensive of 1945.

ARNOLD, HENRY H. (1886–1950), GENERAL OF THE ARMY, UNITED STATES Good-natured General Henry "Hap" Arnold oversaw the mass production of aircraft and training programs, argued for precision bombing, led the U.S. Army Air Forces from 1941 to 1946, and served on the Joint Chiefs of Staff. He was one of a handful of officers to achieve five-star rank and is considered one of the founders of the modern U.S. Air Force.

JAMES EIKNER, SECOND RANGER BATTALION

Preparing for D-Day

About three o'clock on D-Day morning we were roused and went up and had a light breakfast—our medical officer had ordered a light breakfast because the ocean was still quite [rough] and . . . if we ate too heavily, too many of us would become seasick. Following breakfast we were busy little beavers, making sure that everyone had the right equipment and the boats or landing craft were being loaded up properly. And I can recall that Colonel Rudder and I, just before getting into the landing craft, made a change in that we decided to split up the small HQ group into two boats—it would be much safer for the operation if we were split up into two boats. . . .

We put it into the water, and of course it was pitch black and nothing could be seen, the waves were rough. . . . Before too long we lost one entire boat, and this was about twenty-six to twenty-seven people, plus one of the most gung-ho captains of the Rangers. Most of these men were picked up later and taken back to England, and we got them back in about three weeks. We also lost a supply craft that went down, and all six hands on board were lost. A second supply craft had to throw off about half of its load to stay afloat.

In my own boat and many others I discovered we had to rip up the floorboards and use our helmets to bail out the water, and on top of that some of the fellows were vomiting. . . . A little later on, while being shot at, you can imagine the situation there—with the bailing water with your helmet, dodging bullets, and vomiting all at the same time. Not much fun, I can assure you.

—Eisenhower Center for American Studies Archives

AUCHINLECK, SIR CLAUDE (1884–1981), FIELD MARSHAL, GREAT BRITAIN Replacing Field Marshal Archibald P. Wavell as British Middle East commander, Auchinleck took personal command of the Eighth Army and defeated the Afrika Korps at the first battle of El Alamein in July 1942. But British Prime Minister Winston Churchill's son replaced him when he was defeated at the Libyan port of Tobruk.

BEDELL SMITH, WALTER (1895–1961), LIEUTENANT GENERAL, UNITED STATES Walter Bedell Smith rose through army ranks to become secretary of the Allied Combined Chiefs of Staff and General Dwight D. Eisenhower's chief of staff. He negotiated the Italian armistice in 1943 and arranged the German surrender in Northwest Europe in 1945.

BLAMEY, SIR THOMAS (1884–1951), GENERAL, AUSTRALIA Blamey led Australian ground forces in Greece and the Middle East and then in the grueling 1942 New Guinea campaign.

BRADLEY, OMAR N. (1894–1982), GENERAL OF THE ARMY, UNITED STATES A former West Point instructor and Infantry School commandant, unassuming but able General Bradley ("the GIs' general") directed the logistical buildup for Operation Overlord (the June 1944 Allied invasion of Normandy) and led the U.S. First Army and then the 12th Army Group to victory in Europe. He rose to five-star rank and was later Army chief of staff and chairman of the Joint Chiefs of Staff in the years following World War II.

BRERETON, LEWIS M. (1890–1967), GENERAL, UNITED STATES Brereton commanded the U.S. Ninth Air Force in Tunisia and England and then led the First Allied Airborne Army into Holland for the ill-fated Operation Market-Garden in September 1944.

BROOKE, ALAN F. (1883–1963), FIELD MARSHAL, GREAT BRITAIN As chief of the Imperial General Staff from 1941 to the war's end, the dour Irish-born Field Marshal Brooke directed British field operations, complemented the irrepressible Prime Minister Winston Churchill, and negotiated tactfully with the Americans over tactics and logistics and the coordination of British and American forces on the battlefields of Western Europe.

CHENNAULT, CLAIRE L. (1890–1958), LIEUTENANT GENERAL, UNITED STATES "Old Leather Face" Chennault became Generalissimo Chiang Kai-shek's air adviser and in 1940 recruited 200 ex-service pilots for the American Volunteer Group ("Flying Tigers"). Chennault went on to lead the U.S. 14th Air Force in China.

CLARK, MARK W. (1896–1983), GENERAL, UNITED STATES After helping to plan the 1942 North African invasion and negotiating with the Vichy French, General Clark led the U.S. Fifth Army in Italy in 1943–45 and commanded the 15th Army Group.

Field Marshal Sir Alan Brooke, General Dwight D. Eisenhower, Field Marshal Bernard Montgomery, Major General John B. Anderson, and Lieutenant General Omar Bradley gather at XVI Corps headquarters in Germany, March 25, 1945. The group was awaiting the arrival of British Prime Minister Winston Churchill.

CRERAR, HENRY (1888–1965), GENERAL, CANADA Crerar was chief of the Canadian General Staff, organized the training of Canadian troops in England, and led the First Canadian Corps in the 1943 Sicily campaign.

CUNNINGHAM, SIR ANDREW (1883–1963), ADMIRAL, GREAT BRITAIN As commander in chief of the British Mediterranean Fleet in 1939–42, Admiral Cunningham defeated Italian naval forces, defended the supply routes to Malta and Suez, directed the air attack on strategic Taranto and the British evacuation from Crete, and led naval operations in the North Africa and Sicily invasions. He was appointed First Sea Lord in October 1943.

DE LATTRE DE TASSIGNY, JEAN (1889–1952), GENERAL, FRANCE A division commander in the 1940 Battle of France, the nonpolitical general escaped to England and led the French First Army in the invasions of Italy and southern France. He then directed its operations in Alsace and southern Germany and was posthumously made a marshal.

DEMPSEY, SIR MILES (1896–1969), LIEUTENANT GENERAL, GREAT BRITAIN Quiet, unassuming, and able, British Army Lieutenant General Dempsey fought a rearguard action with his 13th Infantry Brigade at Dunkirk in 1940, commanded XIII Corps in Sicily and Italy, and led the British Second Army through the toughest battles of the 1944 Normandy campaign.

DEVERS, JACOB L. (1887–1979), GENERAL, UNITED STATES After being appointed to command U.S. forces in Britain in 1943, General Devers commanded the Allied landings in southern France (Operation Dragoon) in August 1944.

DONOVAN, WILLIAM (1883–1959), BRIGADIER GENERAL, UNITED STATES "Wild Bill" Donovan was an unofficial observer in Britain in 1939–40, and from 1942 to 1945 headed the newly created Office of Strategic Services (OSS), forerunner of the Central Intelligence Agency (CIA).

DOOLITTLE, JAMES H. (1896–1993), LIEUTENANT GENERAL, UNITED STATES Jimmy Doolittle won the Medal of Honor for leading the famous B-25 raid on Japan in April 1942. At the time a colonel, Doolittle and his courageous raiders flew the large B-25 bombers off the deck of an aircraft carrier in a storm and surprised the Japanese by dropping bombs on Tokyo. The Doolittle raid stunned the Japanese, who had known only success up to that point and believed their home islands were invincible. Doolittle later commanded the 12th, 15th, and Eighth Air Forces.

DOWDING, SIR HUGH (1882–1970), AIR MARSHAL, GREAT BRITAIN "Stuffy" Dowding took command of the Royal Air Force's newly formed Fighter Command in 1936. His foresight and skill enabled the RAF to defeat the German Luftwaffe in 1940 and win the pivotal Battle of Britain.

EAKER, IRA C. (1896–1987), GENERAL, UNITED STATES A vigorous advocate of daylight precision bombing, Eaker led the first U.S. raids against Nazi-occupied Europe in 1942 as commander of the Eighth Air Force.

EICHELBERGER, ROBERT L. (1886–1961), LIEUTENANT GENERAL, UNITED STATES Eichelberger led the U.S. I Corps in defeating the Japanese in New Guinea in 1942–43. He later commanded the U.S. Eighth Army in recapturing the Philippines in 1945.

EISENHOWER, DWIGHT D. (1890–1969), GENERAL OF THE ARMY, UNITED STATES A West Point graduate, Dwight David Eisenhower, known as "Ike," rose to lieutenant general in July 1942 and was chosen to command Operation Torch, the Allied invasion of North

Africa, in November. (Operation Torch was the first Allied invasion of Axis-occupied territories.) After he was promoted to full general in 1943, Ike led his polyglot British-U.S.-French force in completing the conquest of Tunisia and then directed the Allied invasions of the Italian island of Sicily and the Italian mainland at Salerno in 1943. In December 1943 he was appointed supreme Allied commander of Operation Overlord, the invasion of northern France scheduled for June 1944. Eisenhower was chosen for this position by Roosevelt because of his unique ability to work harmoniously with diverse personalities. He was a successful staff officer in the best sense of the word: He was able to motivate all kinds of men, including those with difficult egos. Meticulously planned and successfully executed, the greatest invasion in history, launched on June 6, 1944, bore his personal stamp and was his greatest achievement. Promoted to five-star general of the Army in December 1944, he commanded U.S. occupation forces in Germany, retired from the Army to become president of Columbia University, and directed NATO forces in Europe in 1950–52. In 1952 he was nominated for the presidency by the Republican Party and was overwhelmingly elected the 34th president of the United States. He was easily reelected in 1956 and left office in 1961 after eight successful years as president.

FLETCHER, FRANK J. (1885–1973), ADMIRAL, UNITED STATES Fletcher was in tactical command of U.S. naval units in the Battle of the Coral Sea in May 1942. He was also in nominal command during the Battle of Midway the following month but deferred to Admiral Raymond Spruance, who made most of the critical decisions. In 1943, Fletcher took over operations in the northern Pacific.

FRASER, SIR BRUCE (1888–1982), ADMIRAL, GREAT BRITAIN As commander in chief of the Royal Navy Home Fleet, Fraser

JOSEPH A. DRAGOTTO, FIRST INFANTRY DIVISION

Meeting General Eisenhower

I was drafted into the army in March of 1943. I spent a few months in the United States before I was sent to the United Kingdom with the First Infantry Division, Company C, Sixteenth Infantry, First Battalion. I was stationed in the United Kingdom to train for the invasion of Normandy and was billeted in a small coastal village called Lyme Regis from January 1944 to May 1944. On the first of June 1944, the entire division, The Red One, was assembled in a staging area north of London.

On the third day, Captain Briggs, our company commander, assembled the entire company, ordered trucks, and drove to a large field. In the field [were] assembled many thousands [of] American troops, and over a loudspeaker, I heard the word "Attention!" I, with the other troops, snapped to attention, and in the corner of my eye, I could see two men—one wearing an American uniform, the other a British uniform. As they came closer, I recognized them. The American was General Eisenhower, the Supreme Allied Commander, and the other was Field Marshal [Bernard] Montgomery.

Both men stepped onto the platform and spoke to the men. General Eisenhower said we were about to embark on a great cause: "The liberation of Europe and God be with you." Montgomery said almost the same thing but added that he was grateful for the help, and the troops, talking to them. And then General Eisenhower stopped in front of me. I thought [to] myself, "My God, the supreme commander of all the Allied forces in Europe is going to talk to me!" The general asked where I was from and how long I was in the service. After talking a few minutes, we saluted, and he went down the line. I then returned to our area, getting ready for what was ahead.

—Eisenhower Center for American Studies Archives

directed the pursuit and destruction of the German battle cruiser *Scharnhorst* in December 1943. He later led the Eastern Fleet in the Indian Ocean and took over the British Pacific Fleet in 1944.

FREYBERG, SIR BERNARD (1889–1963), GENERAL, NEW ZEALAND The gallant leader of New Zealand forces throughout World War II, Freyberg led his forces in North Africa, Greece, and Crete, and at Monte Cassino, Italy, as part of the U.S. Fifth Army.

GHORMLEY, ROBERT L. (1883–1958), VICE ADMIRAL, UNITED STATES Guadalcanal proved the undoing of Vice Admiral Ghormley, who was ordered to take charge of the August 1942 invasion of Guadalcanal and Tulagi in the Solomon Islands. He was replaced by Admiral William F. Halsey, returned to a staff post in Washington, D.C., and held no significant command thereafter.

GORT, JOHN (1886–1946), FIELD MARSHAL, GREAT BRITAIN Gort led the British Expeditionary Force to France in 1939 and skillfully directed its withdrawal from Dunkirk in May 1940 following the German invasion.

GOVOROV, LEONID (1897–1955), MARSHAL, SOVIET UNION Govorov commanded the Soviet Fifth Army outside Moscow in November 1941 and in the December counteroffensive against the invading Germans; he then directed the defense of beleaguered Leningrad, which was under German siege from 1941 to 1944.

HALSEY, WILLIAM F., JR. (1882–1959), FLEET ADMIRAL, UNITED STATES "Bull" Halsey commanded U.S. Task Force 16, which launched the famous Doolittle raid in April 1942, won the naval battle of Guadalcanal that November, and took command of the U.S. Third Fleet in June 1944 for the advance to the Philippines. While taking part in the great Battle of Leyte Gulf, he fell for a Japanese ruse and led

his 64-ship fleet after 17 decoy ships, leaving the San Bernardino Strait unprotected. Nevertheless, he destroyed the remnants of enemy naval airpower. In December 1945, he was promoted to the rank of fleet admiral.

> Cease firing, but if any enemy planes appear, shoot them down in a friendly fashion.
>
> —U.S. Admiral William F. Halsey,
> in a message to his Third Fleet
> in August 1945

HARMON, MILLARD F. (1888–1945), GENERAL, UNITED STATES Harmon commanded U.S. forces in the South Pacific and was responsible for the invasion of the Solomon Islands and the Guadalcanal campaign. From July 1944, he led the Army Air Forces in the entire Pacific Ocean area and directed the strategic air offensive against the Japanese home islands.

HARRIS, SIR ARTHUR (1892–1985), MARSHAL, GREAT BRITAIN When he took over the Royal Air Force Bomber Command in February 1942, Air Chief Marshal Harris injected new confidence and an aggressive spirit into a command that had been experiencing heavy losses and disappointing results. Harris was the creator of the campaign of strategic area bombing of Germany, under which scores of German cities were reduced to rubble and thousands of civilians killed. Many argued that the area bombing was not only inhuman but militarily unnecessary, since it did not stop war production or affect enemy morale. After the war, he was the only senior British commander not to be given a peerage, and no campaign medal was struck for his men.

HEWITT, H. KENT (1887–1972), ADMIRAL, UNITED STATES Hewitt was an expert in amphibious operations who put General George S. Patton Jr.'s Western Task Force ashore at Casablanca in 1942, led the U.S. Eighth Fleet in North African waters, and then directed naval operations in the invasions of Sicily, Italy, and southern France.

HODGES, COURTNEY H. (1887–1966), GENERAL, UNITED STATES Hodges was deputy commander of the U.S. First Army under General Omar N. Bradley. He organized the landings at Utah and Omaha Beaches on D-Day and succeeded Bradley in August 1944. Hodges's army took the brunt of the German Ardennes offensive in 1944–45 and then seized the Ruhr dams, crossed the Rhine at Remagen, and linked up with the Ninth Army to encircle the strategic Ruhr pocket in Germany.

JUIN, ALPHONSE (1888–1967), MARSHAL, FRANCE Juin led Vichy forces in North Africa until joining the invading Allies in November 1942 as commander of the Free French forces. He was posthumously named a marshal of France.

KENNEY, GEORGE C. (1889–1977), GENERAL, UNITED STATES As commander in chief of the U.S. Far East Air Forces in the Southwest Pacific Area, General Kenney, a U.S. Air Service squadron commander in France in World War I, was General Douglas A. MacArthur's principal air officer in World War II.

KIMMEL AND SHORT: SCAPEGOATS OF PEARL HARBOR

Hours after Japanese carrier planes swept in and decimated the U.S. Pacific Fleet and Army installations in Hawaii on the fateful early morning of Sunday, December 7, 1941, attempts to affix responsibility began. Why had the main U.S. bastion in the Pacific Ocean been caught flat-footed, considering the decade-long aggressive posture of the Japanese in the Far East and that war had been raging in Europe for more than two years?

The attack led to eight investigations between December 22, 1941, and July 15, 1946, to establish responsibility. On January 24, 1942, a presidential commission headed by Supreme Court Justice Owen J. Roberts attributed the success of the Japanese attack to the failure of the U.S. military leaders in Hawaii—Admiral Husband E. "Hubby" Kimmel, the Pacific Fleet commander, and Lieutenant General Walter C. Short, the army commander—to coordinate adequate defensive measures.

The Roberts Commission concluded that advance warnings—including those to Kimmel—had been numerous enough that the Hawaii commanders should have been on alert instead of maintaining the Sunday routine. In addition, as the crisis with Japan had mounted, Washington had notified Kimmel, Short, and all other Pacific commanders on November 27 that war was imminent. Kimmel and Short assumed that this meant that they should be alert to sabotage, which both regarded as the main threat, considering Hawaii's sizable Japanese population. They did not think it was possible for the Japanese to strike the Hawaiian Islands given the logistical difficulties of transporting a large attack force thousands of miles from the Japanese home islands.

As a result of the findings, the panel found both guilty of "dereliction of duty." Kimmel was relieved of command and succeeded on December 17 by Admiral Chester W. Nimitz, and Short was replaced by Lieutenant General Delos C. Emmons. Both Kimmel and Short were forced into retirement but were never court-martialed.

With the benefit of additional testimony and declassified information about the deciphering of Japanese diplomatic codes and monitoring of naval radio traffic, a joint Democratic-Republican committee conducted a Pearl Harbor investigation from November 1945 to July 1946. In their final report, the minority Republicans criticized the Roosevelt administration, the army and navy secretaries, and General George C. Marshall, army chief of staff, for misjudgments, interservice rivalry, and poor communications; the majority Democrats blamed Kimmel and Short for errors of judgment rather than dereliction. Like its predecessors, the Capitol Hill inquiry failed to resolve who was ultimately responsible for what scholars have generally concluded was an unforeseen tragedy. All the reports, however, refrained from excessive criticism of President Roosevelt, who some scholars believe bore the ultimate responsibility for Pearl Harbor.

KIMMEL, HUSBAND E. (1882–1968), **REAR ADMIRAL, UNITED STATES** "Hubby" Kimmel had the misfortune to be commanding the U.S. Pacific Fleet at Pearl Harbor, Hawaii, on December 7, 1941. He was relieved of his duties 10 days after the attack. (See sidebar, p. 163.)

KING, ERNEST J. (1878–1956), **FLEET ADMIRAL, UNITED STATES** Irascible, arrogant, and brilliant, King was both commander in chief of the U.S. Navy and chief of naval operations. After his initial failure to mobilize adequately against German U-boat operations along the East Coast in 1942, he masterfully helped plan the great naval offensives in the Pacific theater until 1945. King was the Washington-based naval commander behind the great Pacific campaigns such as the conquest of the Marianas (1944), the U.S. return to the Philippines (1944–45), and the Battles of Iwo Jima (1945) and Okinawa (1945).

KINKAID, THOMAS C. (1888–1972), **ADMIRAL, UNITED STATES** Kinkaid led U.S. Task Force 16 in the 1942 Battle of Santa Cruz in the Pacific, defended Guadalcanal with Task Force 67, commanded the Seventh Fleet off New Guinea, and staved off disaster from a Japanese fleet during the Battle of Leyte Gulf in October 1944.

KIRK, ALAN G. (1888–1963), **ADMIRAL, UNITED STATES** Kirk led the Central Task Force in the 1943 Sicily invasion and, with his flag aboard the cruiser USS *Augusta,* commanded the 1,000-vessel fleet that landed Bradley's U.S. First Army in Normandy on D-Day in June 1944.

KONEV, IVAN S. (1897–1973), **MARSHAL, SOVIET UNION** Konev was considered one of the best Soviet field commanders of World War II. He commanded a corps on the Russian southern front in 1942, helped Zhukov to encircle two German corps near Korsun in 1944, linked up with the U.S. 12th Army Group on the

River Elbe in April 1945, and joined Zhukov to seize Berlin in May 1945.

KRUEGER, WALTER (1881–1967), **GENERAL, UNITED STATES** Krueger commanded the U.S. Sixth Army in 1943–45 in the Pacific theater.

LECLERC, PHILIPPE (1902–47), **GENERAL, FRANCE** Leclerc formed the crack French Second Armored Division, which fought in Normandy with Patton's U.S. Third Army, liberated Paris in August 1944, and advanced as far as Hitler's "Eagle's Nest" at Berchtesgaden.

LEESE, SIR OLIVER (1894–1978), **LIEUTENANT GENERAL, GREAT BRITAIN** Leese was one of Field Marshal Bernard L. Montgomery's most trusted corps commanders. He led XXX Corps at the Second Battle of El Alamein, fought in Sicily and Italy, and took over the Eighth Army in 1943.

LEIGH-MALLORY, SIR TRAFFORD (1892–1944), **MARSHAL, GREAT BRITAIN** Leigh-Mallory commanded the Royal Air Force's 12th Fighter Group in the Battle of Britain, took over Fighter Command in 1942, and headed the Allied Expeditionary Air Forces in the 1944 Normandy invasion.

LEMAY, CURTIS E. (1906–90), **GENERAL, UNITED STATES** LeMay was a strategic air warfare pioneer. From July 1944, he headed the 20th and 21st Bomber Commands in the Far East and directed devastating bomber raids against Formosa and Japan. He is considered one of the founders of the modern U.S. Air Force.

MACARTHUR, DOUGLAS A. (1880–1964), **GENERAL OF THE ARMY, UNITED STATES** After being caught by surprise by the Japanese in the Philippines in 1941, MacArthur, a World War I hero and former West Point superintendent, redeemed himself with a brilliant, hard-hitting island-hopping campaign in the Pacific theater that wore down enemy resistance. He conducted the Japanese surrender ceremony in Tokyo Bay (September 1945), was the military ruler of Japan (1945–50) and won great acclaim for his fairness and gentle touch from the Japanese people, and went on to lead United Nations forces in the first year of the Korean War (1950–51). He disagreed with the war policies of President Harry S Truman—a disagreement that he aired in the press—and, as a result, was removed from his command for insubordination. A difficult and egotistical personality (Roosevelt called him "one of the most dangerous men in America"), MacArthur was widely loved in his time and was a genuinely brilliant and charismatic leader.

MANNERHEIM, BARON CARL G. (1867–1951), MARSHAL, FINLAND Retired Marshal Mannerheim was recalled to service when the Red Army invaded Finland in November 1939. He brilliantly led the Finns in a heroic, four-month Winter War until being forced to surrender in March 1940.

MARSHALL, GEORGE C. (1880–1959), GENERAL OF THE ARMY, UNITED STATES Appointed U.S. Army chief of staff before the outbreak of World War II, General of the Army Marshall had the foresight and planning genius to ensure that the U.S. Army was able to expand rapidly, eventually to eight million men, when war came in 1941. He chaired the Joint Chiefs of Staff and became indispensable to President Roosevelt. (Marshall had hoped to command Operation Overlord, the invasion of Normandy, but Roosevelt refused to let him leave Washington and gave the command to Eisenhower instead.) Marshall later served as secretary of state (1947–49) and secretary of defense (1950–51), and helped war-ravaged Europe to recover with his unprecedented economic assistance package known as the Marshall Plan. Marshall was the quintessential military planner—although not experienced on the field of battle,

he provided the organization, brains, and political skill necessary to create a massive fighting machine that won the war.

MCAULIFFE, ANTHONY C. (1898–1975), BRIGADIER GENERAL, UNITED STATES McAuliffe found his niche in military history by gallant leadership and the utterance of one word. During the Battle of the Bulge (1944), when his unit of the 101st Airborne Division was surrounded at Bastogne, a strategic road and rail junction in Belgium, McAuliffe, the assistant commander of the 101st, responded to a German surrender ultimatum with a now-famous reply: "Nuts!"

MCCREERY, SIR RICHARD (1898–1967), GENERAL, GREAT BRITAIN McCreery planned the final stage of the Second Battle of El Alamein in October 1942, led X Corps at Salerno and Monte Cassino (Italy), and took over the Eighth Army in November 1944.

MITSCHER, MARC A. (1887–1947), ADMIRAL, UNITED STATES Marc Andrew "Pete" Mitscher commanded the carrier USS *Hornet* during the Doolittle raid over Tokyo in April 1942 and served as air commander at the Battle of Guadalcanal. In 1944–45, he led the great Task Force 58 (also designated TF58), which provided air cover for the invasions of islands of the Pacific and vanquished the Imperial Japanese Navy.

MONTGOMERY, BERNARD L. (1887–1976), FIELD MARSHAL, GREAT BRITAIN Montgomery led the Eighth Army to victory over the Afrika Korps at El Alamein in October 1942 and then led them into Sicily and the Italian mainland in 1943. After helping to plan the Normandy invasion, he led the British 21st Army Group across northwestern Europe and the Rhine River. A notoriously difficult personality, Montgomery, who was second to Eisenhower, disagreed with the Eisenhower plan to proceed across Germany on a broad front, favoring instead pinpoint thrusts into northwestern Germany.

MORGAN, SIR FREDERICK (1894–1967), LIEUTENANT GENERAL, GREAT BRITAIN Morgan was chief of staff to the supreme commander and drew up the initial plans for Operation Overlord (the Allied invasion of Normandy), which were accepted in July 1943.

MOUNTBATTEN, LORD LOUIS (1900–1979), FLEET ADMIRAL, GREAT BRITAIN Mountbatten, the uncle of Phillip, the husband of the future Queen Elizabeth II, headed Combined Operations in 1941–43. He worked on the St.-Nazaire and Dieppe raids and the North African invasion before becoming the supreme Allied commander in Southeast Asia. He oversaw the successful British offensives in Burma and later served as First Sea Lord. After the war, Mountbatten served as the last British viceroy of India and oversaw the transition of that country from British colony to an independent nation. He was assassinated by the Irish Republican Army (IRA) in 1979 in a blow aimed at the British royal family.

NIMITZ, CHESTER W. (1885–1966), FLEET ADMIRAL, UNITED STATES Nimitz, one of the outstanding naval strategists of the war, assumed command of the U.S. Pacific Fleet in the wake of the disaster at Pearl Harbor. He directed the Pacific Fleet's great offensive across the central Pacific and later served as chief of naval operations. Nimitz's hand was behind all the major Central Pacific battles, from Midway (1942) to Tarawa (1943) to the Marianas (1944), Iwo Jima (1945), and Okinawa (1945). He often opposed the strategic plans of Douglas MacArthur, whose campaigns were oriented across the Southwest Pacific toward the liberation of the Philippines. In the end, Roosevelt adopted a plan that combined both Nimitz's and MacArthur's recommendations.

> Among the men who fought on Iwo Jima, uncommon valor was a common virtue.
> —U.S. Admiral of the Fleet Chester W. Nimitz, in March 1945

PATCH, ALEXANDER M., JR. (1889–1945) MAJOR GENERAL, UNITED STATES Patch led army forces to a final victory on Guadalcanal in February 1943. He then masterfully led the U.S. Seventh Army in its advance from southern Germany.

PATTON, GEORGE S., JR. (1885–1945), LIEUTENANT GENERAL, UNITED STATES "Blood and Guts" Patton was one of the most colorful combat commanders of World War II. After restoring discipline to II Corps in Tunisia, he led the Seventh Army across Sicily in 1943, beating British Field Marshal Bernard L. Montgomery to Messina while the latter faced the

Lt. General George S. Patton, Jr., instructs his troops in Sicily. They capture Messina on August 17, 1943, clearing the way for Allied shipping in the Mediterranean.

main concentration of Axis resistance. In July 1944, Patton led the hard-driving Third Army across France and over the River Meuse. During the Battle of the Bulge, his army cut the southern flank of German penetration and relieved besieged Bastogne. In March 1945, he directed a brilliant Rhine crossing. Patton was a spit-and-polish soldier who loved war but was egocentric, outspoken, and profane. He died in an auto accident in Germany in 1945.

PORTAL, SIR CHARLES (1893–1971), AIR CHIEF MARSHAL, GREAT BRITAIN As chief of the British Air Staff from 1940 to 1945, Portal built and directed the Royal Air Force, advocated area bombing, and worked closely with Prime Minister Churchill and the U.S. Army Air Forces. He was one of Britain's most important strategic planners.

POUND, SIR DUDLEY (1877–1943), FLEET ADMIRAL, GREAT BRITAIN He was First Sea Lord in the early years of World War II. A tireless worker, he suffered from an undetected brain tumor that affected his judgment.

RIDGWAY, MATTHEW B. (1895–1993), GENERAL, UNITED STATES Ridgway led the crack U.S. 82nd Airborne Division with distinction in Sicily, Italy, and Normandy, and then commanded the 18th Airborne Corps through the Market-Garden, Ardennes-Alsace, and Rhineland campaigns of late 1944 and 1945. He later led United Nations forces in Korea.

ROKOSSOVSKY, KONSTANTIN (1896–1968), MARSHAL, SOVIET UNION Red Army Marshal Rokossovsky led the decisive breakthrough at Stalingrad in December 1942, directed the central front in the decisive Battle of Kursk in July 1943, and then pushed the First Belorussian Front through Lublin and Brest-Litovsk. He swept north through Poland, trapped the German armies in eastern Prussia in January 1945, and linked up with British forces at Lübeck that May.

SHORT, WALTER C. (1880–1949), MAJOR GENERAL, UNITED STATES Short was the Army commander in Hawaii at the time of the attack on Pearl Harbor on December 7, 1941. He, along with Admiral Husband Kimmel, was held responsible for the lack of preparedness and was recalled 10 days after the attack. (See sidebar, p. 163.)

SIKORSKI, WLADYSLAW (1881–1943), MARSHAL, POLAND Sikorski became prime minister of the Polish government-in-exile and commander in chief of the free forces. He moved his 100,000-man army to England when France fell in 1940.

SIMPSON, WILLIAM H. (1888–1980), GENERAL, UNITED STATES "Big Simp" Simpson ably led the U.S. Ninth Army through the Brest, Lorient, Loire, Orléans actions in France and the Rhine and Ruhr campaigns in Germany in 1944–45.

SLIM, SIR WILLIAM (1891–1970), FIELD MARSHAL, GREAT BRITAIN Slim took over the First Burma Corps in March 1942 and conducted its long retreat from Rangoon to the Indian frontier before brilliantly leading the newly formed 14th ("Forgotten") Army in reconquering Burma in 1944–45.

SMITH, HOLLAND M. (1882–1967), GENERAL, UNITED STATES "Howlin' Mad" Smith of the U.S. Marine Corps was largely responsible for developing the amphibious warfare tactics used in the Pacific theater. He commanded the V Amphibious Corps in capturing the Aleutian Islands, Tarawa, Makin, Kwajalein, Eniwetok, Saipan, Tinian, Guam, and Iwo Jima in 1943–45.

SPAATZ, CARL A. (1891–1974), GENERAL, UNITED STATES "Tooey" Spaatz served as the first commander of the U.S. Eighth Air Force. He initiated its daylight precision bombing offensive against German-occupied

Europe. Spaatz later coordinated air operations in the Mediterranean theater, commanded the U.S. Strategic Air Forces in Northwest Europe in 1944, and directed the final air assault on Japan.

SPRUANCE, RAYMOND A. (1886–1969), ADMIRAL, UNITED STATES Spruance became the most effective American carrier commander of the Pacific war. Spruance assumed tactical command at the Battle of Midway (1942) and inflicted a crushing defeat on the Imperial Japanese Navy. He later led offensive operations against the Gilbert and Marshall Islands and was in command of U.S. naval forces during the Battle of the Philippine Sea.

STARK, HAROLD R. (1880–1972), ADMIRAL, UNITED STATES A friend of President Franklin D. Roosevelt, Admiral "Betty" Stark served in London during both world wars, became chief of naval operations in 1939, and placed the U.S. Navy on a war footing when relations with Japan deteriorated in 1940–41. From March 1942, he commanded U.S. naval forces in Europe, readying them for the Normandy landings.

STILWELL, JOSEPH W. (1893–1946), GENERAL, UNITED STATES "Vinegar Joe" Stilwell became Chinese Generalissimo Chiang Kai-shek's chief of staff in 1942. He led the Chinese Fifth and Sixth Armies in a difficult withdrawal to India during the 1942 campaign and commanded U.S. forces in the China-Burma-India theater. He was recalled in October 1944 and succeeded General Simon Bolivar Buckner as commander of the 10th Army on Okinawa.

TEDDER, SIR ARTHUR W. (1890–1967), MARSHAL, GREAT BRITAIN Tedder built up the British Western Desert Air Force in 1941–43, coordinated land and air operations during the invasions of Sicily and Italy, and served as a deputy supreme Allied commander in Normandy. He successfully coordinated the tactical and strategic air forces in the campaigns in Western Europe.

TOVEY, SIR JOHN (1895–1971), ADMIRAL, GREAT BRITAIN As commander of the Royal Navy's Scapa Flow–based Home Fleet from 1940 to 1943, Admiral Tovey protected the Atlantic and Soviet convoys, directed the epic pursuit and sinking of the German battleship *Bismarck* in May 1941, and tried unsuccessfully to draw out and sink the *Tirpitz.* He later protected Allied convoys to Amsterdam.

TRUSCOTT, LUCIAN K., JR. (1895–1965), GENERAL, UNITED STATES Truscott led the U.S. Third Infantry Division in Sicily and at Salerno and Anzio in 1943–44 and then took over VI Corps for the breakout toward Rome and the invasion of southern France in August 1944. He returned to Italy in December 1944 to take over the Fifth Army and eventually commanded the Third Army.

TURNER, RICHMOND K. (1885–1961), ADMIRAL, UNITED STATES Turner was known in the U.S. Navy as "Terrible Turner" and to the Japanese as "the Alligator" because of his expertise in amphibious warfare. He was appointed commander of the South Pacific Amphibious Force in July 1942.

VANDEGRIFT, ALEXANDER A. (1887–1972), GENERAL, UNITED STATES Vandegrift was the first marine to hold four-star rank. He took the First Marine Division ashore at Guadalcanal in August 1942 and later became the 18th commandant of the Marine Corps.

VASILEVSKY, ALEXANDR M. (1895–1977), MARSHAL, SOVIET UNION Vasilevsky was chief of the Red Army General Staff for most of the war. He planned the counteroffensive that trapped the German Sixth Army at Stalingrad in November 1942, fortified the Kursk salient, and coordinated the advance of the Second and Third Belorussian Fronts across Poland in 1944.

VATUTIN, NIKOLAY F. (1901–44), MARSHAL, SOVIET UNION Vatutin commanded the Southwest Front in 1942 and encircled the German Sixth Army at Stalingrad. He successfully defended the southern half of the Kursk region during the huge tank battle of 1943, captured Kharkov, and liberated much of the Ukraine.

WAINWRIGHT, JONATHAN M. (1883–1953), LIEUTENANT GENERAL, UNITED STATES Wainwright conducted a fighting retreat against superior Japanese forces down the Bataan Peninsula in the Philippines, holding out until April 1942. He retired to the fortress of Corregidor but was forced to surrender in May and was held as a prisoner of war until 1945.

WAVELL, SIR ARCHIBALD (1883–1950), FIELD MARSHAL, GREAT BRITAIN Wavell was given impossible tasks and subjected to British Prime Minister Winston Churchill's meddling. After brilliantly defeating the Italians in North and East Africa, Wavell's understrength forces were beaten in Greece, Crete, and Cyrenaica. Next, with few resources at his disposal, he was unable to push back the Japanese in Southeast Asia. Churchill lost confidence in him and appointed him viceroy of India in 1943, where he served under his replacement by Lord Louis Mountbatten.

WILSON, SIR HENRY M. (1881–1964), FIELD MARSHAL, GREAT BRITAIN "Jumbo" Wilson conducted a masterful delaying action in Greece in 1941, invaded Vichy-controlled Syria that year, succeeded Field Marshal Harold Alexander as Middle East commander in 1943, and was appointed supreme Allied commander in the Mediterranean in 1944.

ZHUKOV, GEORGI K. (1896–1974), MARSHAL, SOVIET UNION As commander in chief of the Red Army for most of the war, Zhukov prevented the Germans from capturing Leningrad (now St. Petersburg), coordinated the defense of Moscow and Stalingrad, and directed the defense of the Kursk salient during the massive German tank counteroffensive. He led the advance across the Ukraine, smashed German Army Group Center in Operation Bagration, captured Warsaw, pushed through Prussia at the rate of 100 miles a week, and encircled Berlin in April 1945. Zhukov was one of the few high-ranking officers who, for reasons that are unknown to this day, survived Stalin's purges in the 1930s. Considered by some historians to be the greatest general of the war, Zhukov was economical in the expenditure of his forces, unwilling to sacrifice large numbers of casualties without sound military reasons. Yet he was a ruthless and relentless adversary of the Nazis.

AXIS COMMANDERS

ARNIM, HANS J. VON (1889–1962), GENERAL, GERMANY Arnim led a panzer division and the 39th Panzer Corps in Russia in 1941–42 and then was given command of the Fifth Panzer Army in North Africa. He succeeded Field Marshal Erwin Rommel in December 1942 as commander of Army Group Afrika and was captured by the British in May 1943.

BADOGLIO, PIETRO (1871–1950), MARSHAL, ITALY Badoglio led Italian forces in the 1935 invasion of Abyssinia (Ethiopia) and was appointed army chief of staff in 1940. After the overthrow of Mussolini in 1943, he briefly served as prime minister and helped negotiate Italy's surrender.

BOCK, FEDOR VON (1885–1945), FIELD MARSHAL, GERMANY Bock was an outstanding army group commander in World War II. Relieved of command in the Wehrmacht purge after the Soviet counteroffensive of December 1941, Bock was reinstated to take over Army Group South. He held this post until July 1942, when he was again relieved.

BRAUCHITSCH WALTHER VON (1881–1948), FIELD MARSHAL, GERMANY Commander in chief of the German army in 1938–41, Brauchitsch was dismissed after the German army was halted in the suburbs of Moscow in December 1941.

DIETRICH, JOSEF (1892–1976), GENERAL, GERMANY In 1928, "Sepp" Dietrich became commander of Hitler's bodyguard, which became known as the Leibstandarte SS Adolf Hitler. Dietrich led the Sixth Panzer Army in the Ardennes counteroffensive in December 1944. He staged a daring rescue of Mussolini from the Italian Alps in 1944.

DÖNITZ, KARL (1891–1984), GRAND ADMIRAL, GERMANY As commander in chief of the *Kriegsmarine* (German navy), Admiral Dönitz was responsible for the devastating U-boat operations in the Atlantic that reached their peak early in 1943. Chosen as Hitler's successor in April 1945, Dönitz negotiated the capitulation of German forces in the West. He was tried as a war criminal at Nuremberg and sentenced to 10 years' imprisonment.

GRAZIANI, RODOLFO (1882–1955), MARSHAL, ITALY Graziani, a long-serving veteran, led the Italian army in Libya before being soundly defeated by the British Eighth Army and halted at Benghazi.

GUDERIAN, HEINZ W. (1888–1954), FIELD MARSHAL, GERMANY Guderian was a pioneer of armored tactics and a master of strategy. He built the German army's panzer force in the face of opposition from the general staff and created blitzkrieg warfare. Guderian personally led the XIX Panzer Corps into Poland in 1939 and into France in May 1940. He then commanded the Second Panzer Group in the June 1941 invasion of the Soviet Union. Hitler dismissed him and made him inspector general of panzer troops. Guderian became army chief of staff and was dismissed after a blazing row with the Führer in March 1945.

HALDER, FRANZ (1884–1971), GENERAL, GERMANY Halder conducted the 1939 Polish campaign, planned the 1941 invasion of the Soviet Union, and served on the Eastern Front before being dismissed after arguing with Hitler about plans that led to the disaster at Stalingrad (1943).

HOMMA, MASAHARU (1888–1946), GENERAL, JAPAN Homma led the surprise attack on Luzon (Philippines) that culminated with the surrender of 65,000 Filipino and 15,000 U.S. troops at Bataan in April 1942. The Allies held him responsible for the Bataan Death March, during which several American and Filipino prisoners of war were murdered by their captors or died of exposure, heat exhaustion, or starvation, and executed him in 1946 for war crimes.

HONDA, MASAKI (1889–1964), LIEUTENANT GENERAL, JAPAN Commanding the Japanese 33rd Army in Burma in 1944–45, Honda conducted a skillful fighting retreat after the British victories at Kohima and Imphal, held off U.S. and Chinese forces attempting to open the Burma Road in January 1945, and failed to dislodge the British at Meiktila.

JODL, ALFRED (1890–1946), GENERAL, GERMANY Jodl was appointed German army chief of staff in 1939 and effectively led operations in all theaters except Russia. He signed the unconditional German surrender at Rheims (France) in May 1945. He was convicted of war crimes at the Allied tribunals at Nuremberg and hanged in 1946.

KEITEL, WILHELM (1882–1946), FIELD MARSHAL, GERMANY Appointed chief of the Wehrmacht high command in 1938, efficient, servile Keitel dictated the terms of the French armistice in 1940, signed orders for the execution of prisoners, and acted as Hitler's military mouthpiece. Convicted of war crimes at the Allied tribunals at Nuremberg, he was hanged in 1946.

KESSELRING, ALBERT (1885–1960), FIELD MARSHAL, GERMANY "Smiling Albert" Kesselring was appointed chief of the German air staff in 1936 and conducted Luftwaffe operations against Poland, France, and England and in North Africa. He then led a brilliant two-year defense of Italy against the Anglo-U.S. armies.

KLEIST, EWALD VON (1881–1954), FIELD MARSHAL, GERMANY Retired Field Marshal Kleist was recalled to duty at the outbreak of World War II and commanded the XXII Army Corps in Poland in 1939 and a panzer group in France in 1940. He then led the First Panzer Group in the Balkans, the First Panzer Army in the June 1941 invasion of the Soviet Union, and Army Group A in the long retreat from the Ukraine in 1943–44.

KLUGE, GÜNTHER VON (1882–1944), FIELD MARSHAL, GERMANY Kluge led the German Fourth Army in Poland, France, and the Soviet Union and became army commander in Normandy in July 1944. As Allied armies overran France, Kluge committed suicide.

MANSTEIN, ERICH VON (1887–1973), FIELD MARSHAL, GERMANY Manstein was probably the German army's most brilliant strategist and field commander of World War II. As commander of Army Group A on the Western Front, he devised the lightning panzer thrust from the Ardennes to the English Channel coast that severed the French and British armies in

May 1940. His 11th Army captured the Crimea in 1941, advanced into the Caucasus, and came close to relieving the trapped Sixth Army at Stalingrad in December 1942. His greatest feat on the Eastern Front was the capture of Kharkov in February 1943.

MANTEUFFEL, BARON HASSO VON (1897–1978), GENERAL, GERMANY Manteuffel developed German armored forces, led panzer divisions in Tunisia, commanded the Fifth Panzer Army in the 1945 Ardennes offensive, and later headed the Third Panzer Army. He is remembered as one of the chief architects of Germany's armor-driven blitzkrieg.

MODEL, WALTHER (1891–1945), FIELD MARSHAL, GERMANY Model became one of the Wehrmacht's best World War II commanders. During the Russian campaign in 1941–42, he led both the Second and Ninth Panzer Armies during Operation Citadel and its aftermath and restored the stability of the Eastern Front. Later, as commander of Army Group B, he was responsible for the Allied failure in Holland in September 1944, and mounted the great German counteroffensive through the Ardennes the following December. In the wake of the German defeat, he committed suicide.

NAGUMO, CHUICHI (1886–1944), VICE ADMIRAL, JAPAN Nagumo led the fateful Japanese attack on the U.S. Pacific Fleet at Pearl Harbor and mauled the Royal Navy's Eastern Fleet in April 1942 before being defeated in the climactic Battle of Midway that June. He was demoted and posted to the Mariana Islands, where he organized the defense of Saipan. He committed suicide in July 1944.

OZAWA, JISABURO (1886–1966), VICE ADMIRAL, JAPAN An early advocate of the importance of aircraft carriers, Ozawa believed that carriers should be deployed aggressively and in large numbers. He was responsible for operations in the South China Sea and took over the Combined Fleet, which the Americans decimated at the Battle of the Philippine Sea in June 1944. At the Battle of Leyte Gulf in October 1944, he came the closest of any Japanese commander to inflicting a reverse on the U.S. Pacific Fleet, but success eluded him.

PAULUS, FRIEDRICH (1890–1957), FIELD MARSHAL, GERMANY Paulus planned Operation Barbarossa, the German invasion of the Soviet Union in June 1941. He led the Sixth Army to Stalingrad during the 1942 summer offensive and was trapped there that November and later surrendered the Sixth Army. Paulus made anti-Nazi propaganda broadcasts during his captivity in the Soviet Union, testified for the Soviets at Nuremberg, and, after his release, lived in Dresden, East Germany.

RAEDER, ERICH (1876–1960), GRAND ADMIRAL, GERMANY Raeder commanded the Kriegsmarine (German navy) from 1935 to 1943. At the Allied tribunals at Nuremberg in 1946, he received a life sentence.

REICHENAU, WALTHER VON (1884–1942), FIELD MARSHAL, GERMANY Reichenau was a fervent Nazi and an outstanding field commander. He led the 10th Army in Poland and the Sixth in Belgium, France, and the Soviet Union and succeeded Rundstedt as commander of Army Group South in December 1941.

ROMMEL, ERWIN (1891–1944), FIELD MARSHAL, GERMANY The famed Desert Fox, Rommel was a dashing exponent of mobile warfare and forward leadership. He commanded the Seventh Panzer Division with flair in France in May–June 1940 and built a reputation as a first-rate tactician and leader of the Afrika Korps. Ordered next to France as commander of Army Group B, he worked to build the English Channel coast defenses. He blunted early Allied attempts to break out of the Normandy beach-

head. While recuperating from wounds, he came under suspicion of complicity in the July 1944 plot to kill Hitler and was offered the choice of committing suicide or standing trial. Rather than put his family through a trial whose outcome was preordained, he chose suicide and was given a hero's funeral.

> What difference does it make if you have two tanks to my one, when you spread them out and let me smash them in detail? —German Field Marshal Erwin Rommel to a captured British officer in 1941

RUNDSTEDT, GERD VON (1875–1953), FIELD MARSHAL, GERMANY Rundstedt was 64 when he was recalled to service in 1939. He commanded Army Group A in Poland, and his armored spearheads inflicted blitzkrieg on the Low Countries and France in May–June 1940. He later led Army Group South in the Soviet Union, disagreed with Hitler, and tendered his resignation in November 1941. By the spring of 1942, he was reinstated, and then, in 1942, he was made responsible for building the Atlantic Wall against an Allied invasion. By then pessimistic about Germany's fate, he reluctantly executed Hitler's Ardennes offensive (the Battle of the Bulge) in December 1944.

SENGER UND ETTERLIN, FRIDOLIN VON (1891–1963), MAJOR GENERAL, GERMANY One of the war's best commanders at the division and corps levels, General Major Senger und Etterlin directed the crack 17th Panzer Division in its abortive attempt to relieve Stalingrad in 1942. He skillfully conducted the extrication of German forces from Sicily in the summer of 1943 and then led the 14th Panzer Corps in Italy, distinguishing himself by his stubborn defense of the Monte Cassino sector early in 1944.

SPEIDEL, HANS (1897–1984), LIEUTENANT GENERAL, GERMANY Speidel served with the German Sixth Army in France in

1940 and acted as chief of staff to the military governor of Paris. After spending almost two years on the Russian front, Speidel returned to France as chief of staff of Rommel's Army Group B. Part of the officers' conspiracy against Hitler, Speidel tried unsuccessfully to win over Rommel.

STUDENT, KURT (1890–1978), COLONEL GENERAL, GERMANY Student commanded the world's first airborne division. After recovering from a head wound, Student directed the successful airborne assault on Crete in May 1941. Because of heavy losses, Hitler forbade further large-scale parachute operations. Student's men then fought as elite infantry, stubbornly opposing Montgomery's push through Holland in 1944–45.

TOYODA, SOEMU (1885–1957), ADMIRAL, JAPAN As commander in chief of the Japanese Combined Fleet from March 1943, Admiral Toyoda lured the U.S. Pacific Fleet from the Marianas to a point near the Palaus; this resulted in the Battle of the Philippine Sea in June 1944 and the virtual destruction of Japanese naval airpower. Toyoda then stubbornly mounted a complex series of actions that culminated in the great Battle of Leyte Gulf in October 1944 and heavy losses that effectively crippled the Imperial Navy.

YAMAMOTO, ISOROKU (1884–1943), ADMIRAL, JAPAN Yamamoto, Japan's brightest naval tactician, was the architect of the Pearl Harbor attack. Immediately after the attack—which failed to destroy the U.S. carrier fleet—he became pessimistic about Japan's ability to win the war and feared that the Japanese had "awakened a sleeping giant." After the defeat of a major part of his carrier force at Midway in June 1942, he waged a defensive war and attempted unsuccessfully to hold the Solomon Islands. He died when his plane was shot down in April 1943, an action that was planned and approved by President Roosevelt.

YAMASHITA, TOMOYUKI (1885–1946), LIEUTENANT GENERAL, JAPAN Yamashita earned the nickname "Tiger of Malaya" when his 25th Army landed in Malaya in December 1941, outmaneuvered the British defenders, captured all of Malaya, and then forced the surrender of the British colony of Singapore. He later conducted a skillful delaying action in the Philippines following the U.S. counterattack in 1944. After the war, the Allies found him guilty of war crimes, mainly for his actions in the Philippines, and executed him.

The Armed Forces: The Growth of Military Power

The armed forces of each combatant nation were in varying states of readiness at the outset of the war. Germany and Japan—the two nations that initiated hostilities—were generally far better prepared than were Great Britain, the United States, or the Soviet Union.

WAR IN EUROPE

Few armies in history have gone to war less prepared than the British in 1939 and the United States in 1941, the result of Depression-constricted defense budgets, wrong-headed planning, and national isolationism. One marvel of the great conflict of 1939–45 is that, once thrust into war, the British and U.S. military establishments were able to survive the grim early months, build up strength and resolve, and emerge victorious to preserve global freedom and justice.

While Adolf Hitler's arsenal grew, the British and American armies remained small professional forces, without the mechanization they would need for any modern war and led mostly by officers unwilling to adapt to new strategies and tactics. Shortly after the declaration of war on September 3, 1939, the first four divisions of the British Expeditionary Force (BEF) crossed the English Channel to support the French. The operation was smooth, but the BEF was inadequately trained and short of everything, particularly tanks, guns, and ammunition. Its transport was augmented with civilian vehicles.

In 1939, the Allies—Britain, France, and Poland—were together superior in industrial resources, population, and military manpower, but the Wehrmacht, because of its armaments, training, and doctrine, was the most efficient fighting force for its size in the world.

Against Germany's 100 infantry divisions and 6 armored divisions, France had 90 infantry divisions, Britain had 10 infantry divisions, and Poland had 30 infantry divisions, 12 cavalry brigades, and an armored brigade.

> Overpaid, overfed, oversexed, and over here.
> —British saying about the American buildup
> in Britain in 1942–44
>
> Underpaid, underfed, undersexed, and under Eisenhower.
> —American response

But a review of the regular infantry divisions of the British field force in July 1939 showed that only 72 of 240 heavy antiaircraft guns and 144 of 240 antitank guns were available. The Royal Artillery had not yet used the 25-pound gun, which would prove to be one of the most effective field guns of the war.

The six German armored (panzer) divisions consisted of some 2,400 tanks. The Allies had almost as many tanks but no armored divisions. In August 1939, the British army had only 60 infantry support tanks; it needed 1,646.

The German air force (Luftwaffe) was the strongest force of its kind in 1939, and its planes were qualitatively superior to almost all Allied types. The Allies had more planes, but many were obsolete. Germany had an operational force of 1,000 fighters and 1,050 bombers in September 1939.

At sea, the odds against Germany were much greater than at the outbreak of World War I in August 1914. The Royal Navy still dominated, and World War II would see no Jutland-style clash of Allied and German fleets.

Meanwhile, the German army, with more than a million men under arms and 3.5 million more available for immediate activation, subdued Poland in September 1939, then swept through the Low Countries and into France in

KARL FUCHS, 25TH PANZER REGIMENT, SEVENTH PANZER DIVISION

A German Trains for War

The intensity of training is tremendous and there is no rest for anyone. All of us are eager to make progress and no one complains, least of all your son. You won't ever have to be ashamed of me; you can depend on me.

Several days ago I had to report to the captain of our company and speak to him about my plans for officer training. Today for the first time we had to practice pistol shooting—five shots and five bull's-eyes for me! Next week we have training in shooting with rifles and machine guns. The recruits are looking forward to this training. All of us tank gunners need to be crack shots.

Next week we'll be able to climb into our tanks for the first time. Operating the vehicle will have to become second nature to us. Tanks are really awesome!

For the time being we will have no furlough, at least not until New Year's Christmastime will be spent in our barracks. I hope that all is well at home.

—Extract From *Seig Heil!*, ed. Horst Fuchs Richardson, (New York: Anchor, 1987), as published in *A Mammoth Book of Eyewitness World War II*, ed. Jon E. Lewis (New York: Carroll & Graf, 2002).

the spring of 1940. Remnants of the British army escaped at Dunkirk and France fell by the end of June. The campaign in the West was over.

After Dunkirk, the British could barely muster 14 divisions, most of which were sparsely equipped and lacking mobility. While enduring a series of calamities from Greece to Tobruk and from Singapore to Burma, the British army had to simultaneously fight a defensive war and rebuild itself into a modern force capable of fighting the German and Japanese armies on equal terms.

The Soviet armed forces were plagued by a uniquely devastating event: Stalin's purges of the 1930s. With few exceptions, almost all general and field grade officers were shot or sent to Siberia. Stalin, notoriously paranoid that he would be overthrown or killed by enemies, focused not only on potential political rivals but also on the military, with the result being that the purges left the armed forces leaderless at a time when they needed leaders the most. When the Soviet Union was attacked by Germany in 1941, the Soviet military suffered staggering losses numbering in the millions in just the first four months. But because of the nation's seemingly inexhaustible supply of manpower and

the courage of its people, the Soviet Union struggled back from these early catastrophes and built up one of the great fighting forces in history.

The rise of militarism in Japan was a relatively rapid phenomenon. Following the opening of the nation to trade by U.S. Navy Commodore Matthew C. Perry in the 1850s, the nation began to embrace elements of Western culture, and its feudal society modernized to an extent. Due to a lack of natural resources, including arable land, and a steadily growing population, Japan began to seek territories that could supply these necessities.

It had become apparent to the Japanese leadership early in the 20th century that expansion was the key to the survival of the nation, particularly if it wished to occupy a place of preeminence in Asia and among the traditional world powers. In 1910, Japan annexed Korea. After fighting on the side of the Allies in World War I, the country was given a mandate over numerous Pacific islands. The defining moment, however, for the future of Japan was its astounding victory over Russia in the Russo-Japanese War of 1904–5. An upstart Asian nation had defeated a centuries-old European power. This emboldened the Japanese to further advances of their expansionist aims.

Decades before World War II began, Japan had embarked on a military modernization and improvement program that would position the country as a global force with which to be reckoned. The Imperial Japanese Navy became one of the most powerful in the world, and its command structure was based upon that of the British Royal Navy. The army and air forces also grew substantially in strength during the years leading up to the war.

During the 1930s, Japanese army forces occupied the Chinese province of Manchuria without the consent of their government as warmongers and right-wing radicals eroded the power of the

The horses of a Red Army cavalry troop thunder across the Russian steppes to stem the tide of Operation Barbarossa. The German offensive rolled forward on a 1,000-mile front, June 22, 1941. Twenty million Soviets died in what is remembered as the Great Patriotic War.

government in Tokyo. The Japanese installed a puppet ruler in Manchuria and renamed it the state of Manchukuo. While the army ranged unchecked on the Asian mainland, a wave of terror and assassination further unsettled the Tokyo government and paved the way for the ascendance of prowar ministers, many of whom were career army and navy officers.

In 1937, the Japanese fabricated an incident at the Marco Polo Bridge in northern China and used it as a pretext for a full-scale invasion of their vast neighbor. During that year, Japanese aircraft mistakenly bombed the U.S. gunboat *Panay* on the Yangtze River, and they also deliberately ravaged Chinese cities. Nanking was occupied and then subjected to a horrendous orgy of rape and murder conducted by Japanese soldiers. This incident came to be known as the Rape of Nanking. The government of Generalissimo Chiang Kai-shek was forced to relocate to Chungking.

U.S. diplomatic pressure on the Japanese seemed to have little or no effect, and they marched unopposed into the French colony of Indochina after the fall of France to Nazi Germany. Eventually trade sanctions and embargoes imposed by the United States would cause the Japanese to conclude that they had no other course but war in achieving their goals.

For example, Japan imported roughly 88 percent of its oil, and 80 percent of that came from the United States. An American oil embargo would grind the Japanese war machine to a halt. The seizure of the oil fields of the Dutch East Indies appeared to be the only solution. This would require military action, and the U.S. Pacific bases and warships in Hawaii were a threat that had to be neutralized.

The Japanese aircraft carrier force that was to attack Pearl Harbor on December 7, 1941, set sail from the waters of the home islands in late November. At the time the attack commenced, Japanese diplomats were continuing to negotiate in Washington, D.C.

THE UNITED STATES: GROWTH OF A SUPERPOWER

Like its British counterpart, the U.S. Army in the prewar years was small and professional but out-of-date and sadly lacking in modern equipment. Congress would not appropriate enough money to maintain a peacetime level of 200,000 men, and the army's strength remained at about 132,000 for a decade. Pay was dismal, living conditions shoddy, and officer morale low.

But improvements came, thanks to the vision and energy of men like Major General Douglas A. MacArthur, Army chief of staff in 1930–35; General Malin Craig, MacArthur's successor, and Colonel George C. Marshall of the general staff.

In September 1939, as war broke out in Europe, President Franklin Roosevelt proclaimed a "limited national emergency" and immediately authorized an increase of 17,000 regulars in the army and increased the National Guard by 35,000 to a strength of 200,000. The Army Air Corps had already been authorized to expand to 50,000 men and 6,000 aircraft.

In the fall of 1939, the U.S. Army numbered 190,000 men. It maintained three square infantry divisions in the United States at half strength (15,000 men instead of 28,000) and a half-strength division in Hawaii and the Philippines. Because of unemployment during the Depression, more men had enlisted in the army, pushing its numbers up somewhat in the late 1930s, but even the outbreak of war in Europe did not push the manpower ceiling beyond 227,000.

However, a new man was in charge of the U.S. Army. On the afternoon of September 1, 1939, as German panzers and Stuka dive-bombers unleashed misery in hapless Poland, Marshall, now a general, stood in the Munitions Building in Washington, D.C., and was sworn in as chief of staff by the adjutant general. Congress and even Roosevelt, however, were still not convinced that the United States needed a larger army. As the Battle of France reached its climax in May 1940, Marshall asked the president for an emergency appropriation of $657 million. Roosevelt sought an additional appropriation, and Marshall got a large percentage of his request. Then, with the fall of France a month later, the army found itself drowning in money. Congress appropriated $9 billion to the army in 1940, more than all the money spent by the War Department since 1920.

On September 16, 1940, the president signed the Selective Service Act, authorizing the induction of 900,000 men for a year, federalizing the National Guard, and raising the regular-army strength to 500,000. Civilian-run draft boards were operating within a month.

Marshall's army grew and trained. During large-scale maneuvers in the South in 1940 and 1941, the army learned valuable lessons about logistics, communications, movement, and artillery tactics and analyzed and reevaluated its needs. The Pearl Harbor attack in December 1941 and U.S. entry into the European war a few days later accelerated its recruitment and preparation. Eventually, the U.S. Army reached a peak

WALTER MARTINI, SIXTH NAVAL BEACH BATTALION

Fighting the D-Day Battle

D-Day, June 6th. About two in the morning, I heard the anchor chain clang over the side, and I couldn't stay below any longer. I got dressed and went topside. And though it was dark, I could make out the outline of the coast of France. It wasn't long before the fireworks began.

First, the only gunfire and explosion was from the air force bombing the coast. The shore batteries were sending up a lot of flak, and I saw three big fortresses go down in France. When the daylight began to show through a bit, the battlewagons opened up with a terrific barrage from their big guns. It was quite a sight to see the shells lobbing inland from the *Texas*, the *Nevada*, and some of the French and British battleships fifteen or so miles out at sea. Then a line of cruisers moved in closer and, together with the big ships, kept up broadside after broadside for at least an hour.

When it was nearly daylight, and close to H-Hour, six-thirty, about fifteen or more destroyers moved in to about a mile off the beach and began picking off shore batteries and pillboxes. By this time, the beach was just a mass of flames and smoke, and vision was very poor. We had loaded into a small landing craft, so I was on an LCP, which carried us to the beach. After doing some rendezvousing, we managed to dash onto the beach. Minesweepers had already cleared three channels of mines leading to the beach, and a smoke screen had been laid, which afforded a lot of protection, but shells were dropping close by all the way onto the beach.

When the craft hit the shore, we dashed into the water and headed for the beach. The water in some places was over my head, but my life preserver kept me on top. When I finally made the beach, we were greeted with a hail of machine-gun fire and a terrific shelling. My boat caught a direct hit, and I saw it blown up. We didn't make it with much to spare. The next problem was to dig in and keep low to the ground as well as we could. I fired my carbine at a pillbox, which was firing at us, but to no avail. I didn't think it would help, but it lifted my morale a bit to be able to shoot back.

The next few hours I spent ducking shells, and each time one landed close by, I dug a little deeper into my foxhole. The sight of human suffering about me wasn't pretty, but after an hour or so, it became evident that we were in a tough fight.

—Eisenhower Center for American Studies Archives

Bunked in the cramped crew quarters of a landing ship tank, sailors head for an Allied port in North Africa and eventually to participation in Operation Husky, the Sicily campaign.

U.S. Ranks

Army, Army Air Forces, Marine Corps

General of the Army
General
Lieutenant General
Major General
Brigadier General
Colonel
Lieutenant Colonel
Major
Captain
First Lieutenant
Second Lieutenant

Navy

Fleet Admiral
Admiral
Vice Admiral
Rear Admiral
Commodore
Captain
Commander
Lieutenant Commander
Lieutenant
Lieutenant Junior Grade
Ensign

British Ranks

Army

Field Marshal
General
Lieutenant General
Major General
Brigadier
Colonel
Lieutenant Colonel
Major
Captain
Lieutenant
Second Lieutenant

strength of 91 divisions and 5.9 million men—less than half the size of the Red Army, slightly smaller than the German army, and not much bigger than Japan's. The U.S. Army Air Forces totaled 2.3 million men.

Marshall's army, mainly a draftee force but trained and led by a cadre of able professionals, matured in the crucible of combat, used its technological resources fully, and, while striving to hold down losses, defeated its stubborn enemies on its own terms.

The American and British armies were created out of necessity from societies that were loathe to maintain large full-time military establishments. The Soviet armies were also a product of necessity—first from a weakness created by purges and then by the need to respond to an overwhelming invasion. Ironically, these armies—all of which had to be expanded and trained while under grave attack—were able to overcome the hard-driven professional armed forces of the Axis powers.

ARMED FORCES RANKS

These tables list the ranks of the major armed forces in World War II.

Navy

Admiral of the Fleet
Admiral
Vice Admiral
Rear Admiral
Commodore
Captain
Commander
Lieutenant Commander
Lieutenant
Sub-Lieutenant; Acting Sub-Lieutenant

Air Force

Marshal of the RAF
Air Chief Marshal
Air Marshal
Air Vice Marshal
Air Commodore
Group Captain
Wing Commander
Squadron Leader
Flight Lieutenant
Flying Officer
Pilot Officer

German SS Ranks

Reichsführer
Obergruppenführer
Gruppenführer
Brigadeführer
Oberführer
Standartenführer
Obersturmbannführer
Hauptsturmführer
Obersturmführer
Untersturmführer

German Ranks

Army

Generalfeldmarschall
Generaloberst

General
Generalleutnant
Generalmajor
Oberst
Oberstleutnant

Navy

Grossadmiral
Generaladmiral
Vizeadmiral
Konteradmiral
Kapitän zur See
Fregattenkapitän
Korvettenkapitän
Kapitänleutnant
Oberleutnant zur See
Leutnant zur See

Air Force:

Reichsmarschall
Generaloberst
General der [unit concerned]
Generalleutnant
Generalmajor
Oberst
Oberstleutnant
Major
Hauptmann
Oberleutnant
Leutnant

Soviet Ranks

Army

Marshal of the Soviet Union
Chief Marshal of Artillery
Marshal of Engineers
General
Lieutenant General
Major General
Brigadier General
Colonel

Lieutenant Colonel
Major
Captain
Senior First Lieutenant
First Lieutenant
Second Lieutenant

Stalin's War with the Red Army

Western military observers watched in the mid-1930s as the Red Army displayed state-of-the-art tactics and operational originality. In contrast to the French army, the Workers and Peasants Red Army had made a distinct effort in the 1920s to break with the past, which included the oppression of the Czarist regime and crushing defeat in World War I. Despite its failing economy in the interwar period, exacerbated by World War I and the civil war, the Soviet state and its armed forces pushed ahead to address their difficulties in organization, equipment, and morale.

The Five-Year Plan (1928–33), a massive industrialization program introduced by Stalin, provided the Soviet Union with the economic structure to build a great military force. At the same time, Soviet military thinkers displayed considerable imagination in pushing for innovations in the ground forces.

The Soviets established their first mechanized corps in the autumn of 1932, three years before the first German panzer divisions appeared, and Red Army paratroops made the first mass jump in 1936 maneuvers, again well ahead of the Germans. By the mid-1930s, Soviet industry was producing vast amounts of war-making materiel, and the Soviet Union had become a major military power.

The weakness of this emerging modern army lay in a lack of education among the bulk of its forces, but reforms in recruiting deemphasized its territorial system and increased the Red Army in numbers. By early 1938, the Red Army had 1.5 million men in its ranks.

In 1937, Stalin's heavy hand fell on the Red Army. Political purges that had already eroded Soviet professional elites now reached the military. In June, Marshal Mikhail N. Tukhachevskii and seven other distinguished officers were tried and executed on false charges of treason. A full-blown purge of the officer corps ensued as Stalin ordered about half of his 70,000 officers either shot or dispatched to Siberian exile.

Of approximately 40,000 officers arrested (36,761 army and 3,000 navy), about one-third, 15,000, were executed. The rest served prison terms and eventually returned to the army, still as officers, in time to fight in World War II (the Great Patriotic War, as the Soviets called it). Stalin's precise rationale for the purge is still unknown—perhaps the reason can be found only in the obscure recesses of his paranoid mind—but its undeniable effect was to cripple the Red Army while Adolf Hitler was gearing up to plunge Europe into war.

The Home Guard

As German panzer and infantry columns rampaged across Belgium, Holland, and northern France in May 1940, the British people watched with great apprehension from across the narrow English Channel.

The rapid German advance split the retreating French and British armies, and the outlook for Western freedom was bleak. Soon the mauled British Expeditionary Force would be compelled to evacuate Dunkirk without its heavy equipment, and the dispirited French would capitulate, leaving Britain alone to face the Germans.

Britons watched the skies for the first signs of German paratroops; the British hastily established antiaircraft emplacements on golf courses, in parks, and other likely landing fields, sent bartage balloons aloft, and blacked out road and railway station signs to confuse potential invaders.

On May 14, 1940, Secretary for War Anthony

Eden broadcast to the nation, appealing for men aged 17 to 65 to join the Local Defense Volunteers. Overnight, lines formed outside police stations, and in six weeks 1.5 million men and boys signed up, eager to do their part. Prime Minister Winston Churchill redesignated the force the Home Guard in July 1940.

Although the butt of many jokes, the Home Guard took its role seriously during the stern early months of World War II. Ironically, as the Home Guard's professionalism increased, the need to deploy it waned. By March 1943, the Home Guard was 1.8 million strong and was performing a real wartime role, but the successful Allied invasion of Normandy spelled the demise of Britain's Home Guard, and it was officially disbanded on December 3, 1944.

The Volkssturm

Germans truly were desperate as Soviet armor and infantry battered relentlessly through the suburbs of Berlin in the spring of 1945. When Adolf Hitler appointed General Karl Weidling commander of Berlin on April 26, 1945, he faced as daunting a task as had confronted any officer in history. He had to defend Berlin with the remnants of his own 56th Panzer Corps, Luftwaffe ground troops, Hitler Youth boys, and some Volkssturm (People's Army) units, Germany's equivalent of the British Home Guard.

Raised as a last line of German defense against the advancing Allied armies, the Volkssturm was established by a decree from Hitler on September 25, 1944. It was under the direct control of the Nazi Party.

All able-bodied males aged 16 to 60 who were not in the armed forces but capable of bearing arms were eligible for service. The ranks of the Volkssturm were filled mostly with youths and with World War I veterans, men who had been invalided out of the regular services or who were otherwise considered unfit for duty.

Among the most poignant photographs of the last days of the war are those of young teenage boys—children—the last remnants of the Volkssturm defending Berlin, being taken into captivity by the Soviets.

Wings of the Eagle: The U.S. Army Air Forces

In January 1939, with Japanese armies rampaging through China, and with war in Europe becoming all but certain, President Franklin D. Roosevelt asked Congress to strengthen U.S. airpower. The U.S. Army Air Corps (USAAC) had only 22,287 personnel and barely 13 operational new B-17 Flying Fortress heavy bombers, and this, said Roosevelt, was "utterly inadequate." The USAAC would have been no match for a well-armed aggressor such as the powerful Luftwaffe, soon to rain death and destruction on northwestern Europe and Great Britain.

In April 1939, after much wrangling and horse trading, Congress passed the expansion bill authorizing a ceiling of 5,500 aircraft for the air corps. Five years later, the U.S. Army Air Forces (USAAF), which had been renamed on June 21, 1941, had become a powerful fighting machine.

By 1944, the USAAF had reached peak strength with 2.4 million personnel, and by the end of World War II, 24,000 aircraft. The U.S. Air Force was established as an armed service separate from the U.S. Army in 1947.

THE RESISTANCE

When German armies overran and occupied Denmark, Norway, Luxembourg, the Netherlands, Belgium, and France between April and June 1940, citizens of these countries were stunned, frightened, and powerless. Yet resistance began almost at once in all the occupied nations. The early resistance was passive and mostly spur-of-the-moment; eventually, the various Resistance networks—supported, supplied, and armed by the British Special Operations Executive (SOE), the British Special Air Service, and later the U.S. Office of Strategic Services (OSS)—expanded and grew increasingly skilled at sabotage and guerrilla harassment.

The cumulative activities of the Resistance—the Army of the Shadows, as the French called it—eventually took on strategic importance, pinning down hundreds of thousands of enemy troops and greatly diminishing the plunder that Germany had expected to reap from the factories, farms, and resources of the occupied countries.

Nazi reprisals against Resistance members and acts of sabotage were swift and brutal, with whole villages wiped out after a single sabotage act in more than one instance. But the resisters hung on, and when liberation finally came, the shadow warriors emerged into the open and played a vital supporting role beside the Allied armies.

Similarly, across the world, Chinese shadow groups maintained a lasting, if fragmented, resistance to their ruthless Japanese occupiers from 1931 to 1945, while in Burma, Indonesia, the Philippines, and on many Pacific islands, citizens attacked Japanese outposts, severed communications, helped prisoners and liberating forces, and reported on enemy dispositions.

The following is a list of significant acts of resistance between 1941 and 1944:

AUGUST 1941 Vichy Foreign Minister Pierre Laval and a prominent German newspaper editor are shot and wounded near Versailles.

OCTOBER 1941 The German commander in Nantes is shot and killed. The Nazis execute 50 hostages in reprisal.

MAY 1942 SOE-supported Czech agents assassinate Reich's Protector Reinhard Heydrich in Prague. In retaliation, the Nazis destroy the nearby village of Lidice and murder its inhabitants.

NOVEMBER 1942 Greek Resistance fighters and SOE agencies destroy an important viaduct on the Athens–Salonika railroad at Gorgopotamus, severing Field Marshal Erwin Rommel's main supply line to North Africa.

FEBRUARY 1943 Parachuted in from Britain, Norwegian soldiers badly damage the Norsk hydro power station near Ryukan where "heavy water" is being produced for German atomic research.

JUNE 1943 French patriots and SOE operatives badly damage the Michelin tire plant at Clermont-Ferrand.

JULY 1943 French saboteurs attack the roundhouse at Troyes, 100 miles southeast of Paris, and destroy six locomotives and seriously damage six others.

SEPTEMBER 1943 The citizens of Naples rise against their German occupiers and fight them for three days, with heavy losses. The battle ends when the British and U.S. armies approach.

NOVEMBER 1943 After an unsuccessful raid by Royal Air Force bombers, Resistance fighters set bombs in the Peugeot factory at Sochaux, France, where German tank turrets and aero engine components are made. When the Germans bring in new machinery, that too is sabotaged, halting production for many weeks.

JANUARY 1944 French patriots and SOE agents blow up the Ratier aircraft plant near Figeac in southern France, ending the production of propellers for the Luftwaffe.

JUNE 1944 French partisans in Toulouse sabotage a train carrying tanks of the Reich Waffen

SS Division to Normandy and fire on the Germans. In retaliation, the SS massacres more than 600 residents of the village of Oradour-sur-Glane.

JUNE 1944 In conjunction with the Allied invasion of Normandy on June 6, French patriots cut telephone lines, block roads, blow up bridges and canal locks, torch fuel dumps, and sabotage hundreds of railroad lines to hamper German operations.

AUGUST 1944 The Resistance in Paris begins open warfare against the German garrison, and, after a bitter struggle, the capital is largely freed.

A Woman's War, Too

World War II was a woman's war, as no other conflict in history had ever been. In steadily increasing numbers, the women of several nations went to war and performed a wide variety of duties, on home fronts and on battlefields. Many donned uniforms, and many endured the rigors and perils of combat.

ALLIED WOMEN

Great Britain

Despite the immediacy of the German threat in 1940, Great Britain was slow to mobilize its women for war. At first, the country depended on volunteerism to fill its women's auxiliaries, but a low response convinced Parliament to pass a law in December 1941 requiring young unmarried women to register for national service. Most went to work in munitions plants, but 125,000 were drafted into the armed forces. Another 430,000 volunteered.

The largest of the women's units, the Auxiliary Territorial Service (ATS), began as a women's auxiliary in 1938 and received military status in 1941. (It was later renamed the Women's Royal Army Corps.) When German air raids on Britain started in 1940, the ATS provided women to serve alongside men on antiaircraft guns and searchlight batteries. The first mixed unit fired in action in November 1941 and tallied its first "kill" in April 1942.

Meanwhile, other British women served in the Women's Royal Naval Service (WRENS) as plotters, code breakers, radar and radio operators, drivers, cooks, clerks, and telephonists and in the Women's Auxiliary Air Force (later Women's Royal Air Force) in similar functions. Women also served as ambulance drivers during the Blitz, nursed the wounded at British hospitals at home and in the war theaters, and toiled on farms as members of the Women's Land Army. Others joined the Air Transport Auxiliary, which ferried 120 types of aircraft, from biplane trainers to four-engine bombers, all over the British Isles.

The British women's service components expanded to a wartime high of 470,000.

United States

As the great American war machine gained momentum and men flocked to recruiting stations early in 1942, U.S. leaders were quick to perceive the potential resources available among the female population.

General George C. Marshall, Army chief of staff, had been monitoring the British services' experience in using women and was impressed. At his request and at the urging of First Lady Eleanor Roosevelt and other women leaders, Congress passed a law on May 15, 1942, creating the Women's Auxiliary Army Corps (WAAC). Congress upgraded the women's auxiliary into the Women's Army Corps (WAC), with full military status, in June 1943. WACs performed 200 noncombatant jobs from running switchboards to driving staff cars to sorting mail at 400 mainland bases and in every theater of operations, from Australia to North Africa and from Italy to Normandy. The WAC reached its peak strength of 100,000, including 6,000 officers, in April 1945.

The Navy bypassed the auxiliary stage in July 1942 and created the Women Accepted for Voluntary Emergency Service (WAVES). They had the same status as male reservists and did not serve overseas. By November, the Coast Guard had created the SPARs (an acronym derived from the Coast Guard motto "Semper Paratus, Always Ready"), and the Marine Corps followed in February 1943.

Women were not allowed to fly combat missions, but the Women's Airforce Service Pilots (WASPs) ferried planes, tested fighters, and towed targets in 1942–44. Another group of intrepid American women, 4,000 in all, spent the war in a more clandestine fashion, serving with Major General William J. Donovan's Office of Strategic Services (OSS).

A total of 350,000 American women served in uniform during World War II. They were all volunteers and, on average, were older and better educated than their male counterparts. About 5 percent of U.S. nurses served overseas, and 30 were killed in action.

One of the enduring symbols of the contribution of women in World War II was Rosie the Riveter, a smiling girl in overalls and a ban-

American Red Cross workers distribute candy bars to Womens Army Corps (WACs) members soon to depart for Europe. As the war progressed, WACs began replacing male soldiers in noncombat roles. By mid-1945, the number of WACs in service in the Pacific theater neared 7,000.

dana who represented the many thousands of women toiling in war plants from coast to coast, and who exhorted others to join them. These women, who filled the ranks of civilian jobs left empty by men serving in the armed forces, were an essential element in Allied victory.

Soviet Union

When the Germans invaded the Soviet Union in June 1941, the Soviets mobilized their women swiftly. In addition to the thousands of women who dug ditches, unloaded supply ships, and erected street barricades and other defenses in threatened cities, an estimated 800,000 women served in the Soviet armed forces. The Soviet Union was the only country in World War II to send uniformed women into combat. About a third of the women soldiers received instruction in handling mortars, machine guns, or automatic rifles; another 300,000 served in antiaircraft batteries, in which they performed all duties, while still others fought as tankers, field artillery gunners, and even snipers.

Although the Red Army had a few all-female ground combat units, most army women served in integrated formations. More than 100,000 Soviet servicewomen were decorated during the war, including 91 who received the highest award for valor.

While Soviet women on the ground fought and suffered through the great, bitter campaigns against the German army on the Eastern front from 1941 to 1945, others made history as fighter and bomber pilots. They were the first women to fly in combat.

Women in Occupied Europe

Women played crucial roles, with many emerging as leaders, in the Resistance movements across German-occupied Western and Eastern Europe from 1940 to 1945. Tens of thousands of women joined the Resistance, and they came from all walks of life—housewives, businesswomen, students, stage performers, and princesses.

They fought bravely with guerrilla bands, helped to sabotage enemy installations and communications lines, carried messages, gathered intelligence, and organized escape routes for refugees and downed Allied fliers.

In Poland, for example, women fought and died in the tragic Warsaw uprisings of 1943 and 1944. Some 100,000 Yugoslav women were in the ranks of Marshal Josip Broz Tito's famed Partisans in Yugoslavia. Of these, 25,000 died.

In Western Europe, French women in the Communist and Free French underground units performed a wide range of subversive functions that were duplicated on a smaller scale in Belgium, Holland, Denmark, and Norway.

AXIS WOMEN

Germany

Unlike Britain and the United States, Adolf Hitler's Third Reich was slow to consider women for active roles in the war effort much less put them in uniform. The main reason was that Nazi ideology saw a woman's primary role as a mother, and as a result, the government was loath to use women in any industrial or military setting.

In 1935, the Nazi hierarchy set up the Lebensborn ("fountain of life") program to produce a "master race" of pure Aryans (tall, blond, and light-skinned). Members of the League of German Girls were encouraged to mate with officers and men of the Schutzstaffel (SS), Hitler's elite bodyguard, and their offspring were nurtured in a series of baby farms at resort hotels and villas in idyllic Bavarian settings.

In 1939, on the eve of the war, most of Germany's 14 million working women were either unpaid hands on family farms or bottom-level industrial workers. But, as they began to lose the war, the Nazis were forced to reconsider the role of women. By 1941, seven million German men

were in military service, and the only way to sustain the war effort was to put more women to work.

The first response to the government recruiting drive was tepid, but by 1943 the labor shortage was critical. The government called up three million women aged 17 to 45 for factory work. Women volunteers were enrolled, civilian nurse units were organized, and 450,000 women joined military auxiliary services to aid the war effort. Wehrmacht regulations prohibited women from bearing arms. Some German women joined the army and navy, primarily as nurses and secretaries, whereas others joined the Helferinnen (SS auxiliary services) to perform administrative duties and serve as matrons and guards in concentration camps.

Japan

As in Nazi Germany, the leaders of the Land of the Rising Sun did not initially regard women as a wartime resource. That feudalistic society looked upon women strictly as functional wives or pliable daughters. Their social status was lower even than that accorded German women by the Nazi regime.

Japanese society permitted a young woman to teach, nurse, or work in the textile industry, but once her marriage was arranged, she was expected to quit work and concentrate on raising a family. But by the summer of 1943, after Japanese military expansion in Asia had been halted and the Allies were gaining the upper hand, tradition fell victim to military necessity.

Once the ancient social barriers had fallen, Japanese women and schoolgirls performed hard and sometimes hazardous physical labor in steel mills and coal mines. They often worked 12- to 16-hour shifts in unheated factories and slept on the job.

However, a combat role was never contemplated for Japanese women until the spring of 1945, when American B-29 formations were incinerating Japanese cities, Allied task forces were standing off the home islands, and an invasion was feared imminent. The war ended suddenly, however, in August 1945, and an expanded role for Japanese women never materialized.

African Americans in the U.S. Military

At the beginning of World War II, the American military was segregated. African Americans and whites fought side by side but in different units. Blacks, like whites, responded with patriotism and enlisted to defend their country, but many white military leaders believed they could not perform adequately and didn't want to use them in combat. These racist notions were quickly disproven on the battlefields.

For example, during the costly two-month struggle by U.S. Marine and Army units to capture Peleliu in the Pacific Palau Islands in the fall of 1944, a platoon of black leathernecks saw its first combat and won praise for gallantry. When deadly Japanese crossfire trapped the Third Battalion of the Fifth Marine Regiment, First Marine Division, on Bloody Nose Ridge, a runner dashed back to the command post to call for reinforcements, medical corpsmen, water, and stretchers. But all reserve units were committed across the island, with heavy casualties. No help was available.

A top sergeant and two marines then dashed to the beach area to recruit anyone available and ran into a black marine sergeant and his platoon. The black sergeant said his men had finished their beach work and would volunteer

---

THE PORT CHICAGO EXPLOSION

A tragic explosion in 1944 shocked the United States, embarrassed the navy, and threatened to derail the hesitant development of racial parity in the U.S. armed forces.

On Monday, July 17, 1944, black sailors who were part of a black ordnance unit working as stevedores were loading 860,000 tons of fragmentation and incendiary bombs onto the freighters *E. A. Bryan* and *Quinault Victory*, at the Port Chicago, California, ammunition depot when the ordnance suddenly exploded. A tremendous blast equal to five tons of TNT destroyed the ships and leveled most of the base.

The accidental explosion killed 320 men, including the naval armed guards on the ships and 202 black sailors (15 percent of all black naval casualties during World War II).

The surviving members of the unit were ordered to return to work at the nearby Vallejo ammunition depot on August 9. Three hundred fifty-eight refused. Admiral Carleton H. Wright, commander of the 12th Naval District in San Francisco, threatened to have them arrested and executed for mutiny. Instead of such harsh punishment, the navy dishonorably discharged 208 men but decided to court-martial the remaining 50.

After just an hour's deliberation on October 24, 1944, the court-martial found the strikers guilty of mutiny, sentenced them to 15 years in prison, and gave them dishonorable discharges.

The Port Chicago incident was a setback for race relations in the navy, which had admitted blacks into its ranks only in 1942. The navy, seeking to put the incident behind it, released most of the men from prison in January 1946 and gave them the opportunity to apply for an honorable discharge. Nonetheless, the Port Chicago court-martial remained an irritant in race relations in the postwar world, a reminder of what many believed were racially motivated double standards that punished blacks more harshly than whites. In 1999, President Bill Clinton granted executive clemency to Freddie Meeks, one of the few surviving men of the original 50 who had been tried. In doing so, the president hoped to further heal the wounds and to acknowledge without saying so directly that the government had been excessively harsh in its punishment.

where needed. The top sergeant was puzzled. How could he send in an all-black unit to rescue members of the famous all-white First Division?

But the black unit had armed themselves heavily and were lined up and ready. They went into action, carrying stretchers and firing automatic weapons as they broke through the surrounding enemy. That night, they helped to repel an enemy counterattack, and the next morning they took part in a bloody fight to take the ridge. A company of the army's 81st Infantry Division relieved them. As the soldiers passed, they asked sarcastically, "Who are the black guys in your outfit?" The white top sergeant bellowed back, "Why, some of our company's best damn marines, that's who!"

On several other occasions black marines served in combat, but they were never officially assigned to such duty. The Corps had stoutly resisted even enlisting blacks until 1942. And it was much the same story in the other services.

The Navy relegated black sailors to support roles, but in order to appease critics, it did graduate a handful of blacks from officer training programs. The USS *Mason,* a destroyer escort with an all-black crew, served with distinction in the North Atlantic convoys.

The Army enrolled the most blacks, but at first it too was reluctant to commit them to combat, as it had been in World War I. In 1940, the Army had only 5,000 black soldiers (2 percent of the force) and five black officers. But eventually, after pressure from civil rights leaders, 900,000 blacks served in the armed forces in World War II. (See the sidebar on the Tuskegee Airmen in Chapter 7, "Campaigns and Battles: Europe and the Atlantic.") Most were in segregated units, chiefly in the army, and they included black women in segregated sections of the Women's Army Corps and the army and navy nurse corps.

Racial tensions plagued the army's two black infantry divisions, the 92nd and 93rd, from the start. The 92nd fought as part of General Mark W. Clark's Fifth Army in Italy and was commanded by a white southerner, Major General Edward M. Almond, an able officer but one who lacked faith in his men. Although individual soldiers and small units performed credibly, the 92nd achieved mixed success in combat, and white officers and enlisted personnel sabotaged its reputation.

Hurried into action in the Pacific theater, the 93rd Infantry Division fought at Bougainville but was unable to live down the performance of the green K Company of its Third Battalion, which broke and ran while supporting the Americal Division. Regiments of the 93rd were spread around the Pacific as garrison troops, and it did not function as a division until it reached the Philippines in June 1945.

Meanwhile, black service troops kept the war effort rolling. They unloaded ammunition and gasoline from cargo ships, drove most of the DUKWs (amphibious vehicles) across the invasion beaches, provided much of the manpower that built the Alcan Highway through the

A pilot of the famed Tuskegee Airmen stands at his base in Ramitelli, Italy. More than 450 black pilots experienced combat in the Mediterranean. Airmen trained at Tuskegee flew nearly 1,600 missions with the 322nd Fighter Group and 99th Fighter Squadron, destroying 261 enemy aircraft.

Northwest Territories and the Ledo Road in Burma, and set records unloading Liberty ships in the Iran port of Khorramshahr.

The most spectacular contribution made by black service troops was the famed Red Ball Express, organized by the army's Service of Supply in August 1944 to rush fuel, food, and ammunition to the rapidly advancing U.S. First and Third Armies. Red Ball drivers, three-quarters of whom were black, hauled 412,193 tons of supplies during 81 days from August 25 through November 16, 1944.

During the Allied pursuit across Europe, U.S. artillery, armored, and tank-destroyer units were integrated, although there were distinguished all-black formations. The most successful black units were those of battalion size; the 761st Tank Battalion was outstanding.

Blacks were not committed to combat in significant numbers until the Battle of the Bulge,

JAPANESE AMERICAN SOLDIERS

Their average height was five-foot-four, their average weight was 125 pounds, and they were a quartermaster's nightmare. They wore shirts with 13½-inch necks, trousers with 26-inch waists, and the shoe size 2½ EEE. They were the smallest soldiers in the U.S. Army during World War II, and they were among the best. Their tenacity and fighting spirit became legendary from Salerno to Cassino, from Anzio to Rome-Arno, and from the Vosges Mountains to Champagne.

Thousands of young Americans of Japanese and Hawaiian ancestry served in the 100th Infantry Battalion and the 442nd Regimental Combat Team. While their families languished in 10 bleak guarded relocation camps in California, Arizona, and Wyoming (see Chapter 11 "The Home Front"), they volunteered for army service and underwent basic training at Camp McCoy, Wisconsin, and Camp Shelby, Mississippi.

Their motto was "Go for Broke!"—an indication of their determination to succeed in the military against great odds.

Shipped in 1943 to the Mediterranean theater, where the U.S. Fifth Army and the British Eighth Army were struggling up the boot of Italy against German Field Marshal Albert Kesselring's hard-fighting 10th and 14th Armies, the Nisei (Japanese American) GIs distinguished themselves. But glory came at a high cost. The 442nd Regimental Combat Team suffered an overall casualty rate of 30 percent by the war's end, and its members received 9,486 Purple Hearts. In fact, the outfit became the most decorated unit in U.S. Army history. Its decorations included 8 Presidential Unit Citations, 52 Distinguished Service Crosses, 1 Distinguished Service Medal, 560 Silver Stars, 22 Legion of Merit medals, and 4,000 Bronze Stars.

Even though their families had been removed from the West Coast to relocation camps, the young Japanese American men who volunteered for military service were intent on showing their fellow Americans that they were indeed loyal Americans, and their service in Europe proved their valor and determination.

Members of the 442nd Regimental Combat Team parade at Camp Shelby, Mississippi. Along with the 100th Infantry Battalion, the 442nd was composed of Nisei, Japanese Americans born in the United States. The two units were among the most highly decorated of the U.S. Army during the war.

when the infantry faced a critical shortage of riflemen. During the historic siege of Bastogne in December 1944, half the field artillery battalions were black, and the 969th won a Distinguished Unit Citation.

Segregation in the military was ended by the order of President Harry S Truman in 1948.

Native Americans at War

Native Americans had served with distinction in World War I. When World War II began, Native American enlistment was high, at a rate greater than that of the Caucasian population. Some 25,000 men served in the armed forces, and thousands of Native American women took jobs in factories and volunteered in other sectors of the economy to help the war effort. One such Native American, Ira Hamilton Hayes, gained immortality as one of six marines to raise the Stars and Stripes atop Mount Suribachi on the Pacific island of Iwo Jima on February 23, 1945 (see Chapter 8, "Campaigns and Battles: Asia and the Pacific").

Although the number of American Indians in the Marine Corps never exceeded 800 during the war, 375 to 420 of them performed a unique service in the Pacific theater, beginning at the battle of Guadalcanal in 1942. Military leaders decided to use the Navajo language—a language virtually unknown except to the relatively small number of people who spoke it—as a code. Navajo code talkers (see Chapter 10, "Intelligence, Espionage, and Propaganda") were communications personnel who transmitted messages between air and ground units, between ships and shore stations, between frontline armor or artillery positions and rear headquarters, and among infantry command posts—all in the Navajo language. The Japanese were never able to decipher the code, and the Navajo code talkers became a legendary group of men who performed a crucial service that protected American military secrets from the Japanese.

The Pale Blue Ribbon

At 7:55 A.M. on Sunday, December 7, 1941, Chief Aviation Ordnanceman John W. Finn was lying in bed at the Kaneohe Naval Air Station on the windward side of the Hawaiian island of Oahu. Suddenly, Japanese aircraft swept in over Hawaii to attack the U.S. Pacific Fleet anchored in Pearl Harbor, as well as other U.S. naval and army bases. Finn grabbed a .50 caliber machine gun, set it up on an instruction stand, and hammered away at the enemy planes. His was the only gun at Kaneohe to return fire during the attack.

At his exposed post, Finn was painfully wounded, but he kept firing, remaining for more than two hours. He tracked a Zero fighter in his sights and smiled as the plane trailed smoke and crashed.

For his bravery, Finn was awarded the Medal of Honor, the coveted bronze-and-enamel, five-pointed star hung on a pale blue ribbon. He was one of 15 heroes to be honored with the distinction but only five of them had survived that day.

Instituted in 1861 for the navy and in 1862 for the Army, the Medal of Honor is the highest U.S. decoration, which is awarded to the nation's "bravest of the brave." Between 1861 and 1990, only 3,398 people received it. It is the most honored American decoration for valor, similar to Great Britain's Victoria Cross.

Of the estimated 13 million men who served in the U.S. armed forces during World War II, only 433 received the Medal of Honor (294 Army, 57 Navy, 81 Marine Corps, and 1 Coast Guard). Only 190 World War II recipients survived to have the pale blue ribbon placed around their necks.

Its recipients during the 1941–45 conflict included:

GUNNERY SERGEANT "MANILA JOHN" BASILONE, who fought with the First Battalion, Seventh Marines at Guadalcanal, and helped to dispatch an estimated 1,200 fanatical Japanese attackers one night in October 1942.

ARMY LIEUTENANT COLONEL ROBERT G. COLE, commander of the Third Battalion, 502nd Parachute Infantry Regiment, 101st Airborne Division, who led the first U.S. bayonet charge in the European theater at Carentan, Normandy, in June 1944.

ARMY AIR FORCES LIEUTENANT COLONEL JAMES H. DOOLITTLE, who led 16 B-25 Mitchell medium bombers from the carrier USS *Hornet* against targets in Japan in April 1942.

NAVY COMMANDER HOWARD W. GILMORE, who sacrificed himself to save his submarine, the USS *Growler,* while on a Pacific patrol in February 1942.

The Congressional Medal of Honor is the highest decoration for bravery that is awarded by the U.S. government. Fewer than 500 of them were awarded during all of World War II.

MARINE LIEUTENANT WILLIAM D. HAWKINS, who, despite being wounded, persistently attacked Japanese pillboxes with grenades on the Pacific atoll of Tarawa in November 1943 until he was killed by an explosive shell.

ARMY AIR FORCES LIEUTENANT JACK W. MATHIS, who was the bombardier in the lead plane of a B-17 Flying Fortress over Vegesack, Germany, in March 1943. Although wounded, Mathis crawled to his bomb sight, lined up the crosshairs, and shouted, "Bombs away!" Then he died at his post as the bombs fell on target.

ARMY PRIVATE HAROLD H. MOON, a machine-gunner in the 34th Infantry Regiment during the Leyte campaign in October 1944. After everyone else in his platoon had been killed or wounded, he held off Japanese onslaughts for four hours.

CANADIAN-BORN SIGNALMAN FIRST CLASS DOUGLAS A. MUNRO of the Coast Guard, mortally wounded by the Japanese while rescuing wounded marines with his Higgins boat on a Guadalcanal beach.

ARMY PRIVATE FIRST CLASS SADAO S. MUNEMORI, of the 100th Infantry Battalion of the famed 442nd Regimental Combat Team, who led several heroic assaults on German defenses near Seravezza, Italy, in April 1945 and then died while smothering an enemy hand grenade with his body.

ARMY LIEUTENANT AUDIE L. MURPHY of the 15th Infantry Regiment, Third Infantry Division, who jumped onto a burning tank destroyer in the Colmar Pocket of northeastern France in January 1945 and used its .50-caliber machine gun to single-handedly turn back a German task force. He was the most decorated U.S. soldier in World War II. (See sidebar.)

ARMY LIEUTENANT ALEXANDER R. "SANDY" NININGER, who, despite several bullet wounds, used a captured light machine gun and his .45-caliber pistol to kill an undetermined number of Japanese infiltrators on Bataan in January 1942.

NAVY LIEUTENANT COMMANDER JOSEPH T. O'CALLAHAN, the Roman Catholic chaplain aboard the carrier USS *Franklin* in the Pacific theater. He tended to wounded and dying sailors, led firefighting crews, and helped to throw live bombs, rockets, and ammunition off the deck.

NAVY LIEUTENANT EDWARD H. "BUTCH" O'HARE, a Grumman F4F Wildcat pilot, who single-handedly shot down five Japanese bombers to save his ship, the carrier USS *Lexington,* in February 1942.

NAVY LIEUTENANT JOHN J. POWERS, a dive-bomber pilot who, during the Battle of the Coral Sea, plunged to within 200 feet of the Japanese carrier *Shokaku* to make sure that he did not miss, released his bomb, and was engulfed in the resulting explosion in May 1942.

AUDIE MURPHY, BABY-FACED HERO

When the Japanese attacked Pearl Harbor on December 7, 1941, 17-year-old Audie L. Murphy marched off to the local recruiting station. But the seventh of 12 children born to a poor Texas sharecropper's family was rejected by every branch of the service. He stood but five-feet-five inches tall and weighed only 110 pounds.

During the next few months, Murphy put on weight, and he finally was able to enlist in the army in June 1942. By the time he shipped out to North Africa in February 1943, he was a corporal. In North Africa he joined the Third Infantry Division and took part in its campaigns from North Africa to Germany.

When the Third Division hit the beaches of southern France on August 15, 1944, Murphy earned his first of many combat decorations for attacking a German machine-gun nest with his automatic weapon, killing more than five enemy soldiers and capturing five. For this action the army awarded him the Distinguished Service Cross.

Murphy was wounded in September 1944, returned to his company in less than a week, and earned Silver Stars for gallantry at Cleurie on October 2 and 5. While his company was attacking through the Montagne Forest near Les Rouges Eaux, Murphy suffered his most serious wound of the war when a sniper shot him in the right hip.

Murphy rejoined his company in January 1945, in time for the bloody Colmar Pocket campaign in northeastern France, where the Third Division was part of Lieutenant General Alexander M. Patch's Seventh Army. Early on the afternoon of January 26, six German tanks and about 250 German infantrymen advanced toward B Company's position. A U.S. tank destroyer slid into a ditch while trying to maneuver into a firing position, and its crew fled to the rear. Murphy ordered his men to go deeper into the safety of the woods as he fired his carbine at the German infantry, now less than 200 yards away.

When he ran out of ammunition, Murphy dashed to the burning tank destroyer, dragging his telephone line, and climbed aboard. He loaded the tank's machine gun and fired at the Germans, all the time calling down artillery fire on the position. Eventually, the German tanks, denied the protection of their infantry, withdrew. Single-handedly, Murphy had beaten off an armored task force. For his heroism, Murphy was awarded the Medal of Honor by General Patch on June 2, 1945.

Murphy received a total of 33 medals and citations and was the most decorated U.S. soldier of World War II. After the war, at the urging of the actor James Cagney, Murphy went to Hollywood and eventually starred in almost 30 movies, most of them Westerns.

ARMY BRIGADIER GENERAL THEODORE ROOSEVELT JR., son of the 26th president of the United States and assistant commander of the Fourth Infantry Division, who strode about Utah Beach, armed only with a small-caliber pistol and a walking stick, to "steady the boys" on D-Day.

ARMY AIR FORCES STAFF SERGEANT MAYNARD H. "SNUFFY" SMITH, the first of only three enlisted airmen to win the Medal of Honor in the European theater. Smith distinguished himself when his plane was crippled by German Focke-Wulf 190 fighters over Nazi-occupied France in May 1943.

ARMY PRIVATE FIRST CLASS WILLIAM A. SODERMAN, a radio operator in the Ninth Infantry Regiment, Second Infantry Division who was pressed into frontline duty near Rocherath, Belgium. After disabling two tanks with a bazooka and scattering an enemy skirmish line, he faced a column of 17 panzers with a single remaining bazooka projectile.

ARMY LIEUTENANT GENERAL JONATHAN M. WAINWRIGHT, who directed the hopeless defense of Bataan and Corregidor in 1942 and then spent the rest of the war in captivity.

ARMY CAPTAIN MATT URBAN of Buffalo, New York, who went ashore at Utah Beach leading F Company of the 60th Infantry Regiment, Ninth Infantry Division, and rescued a wounded man from a burning tank in July 1944. Urban did not receive the Medal of Honor until 1980.

NAVY COMMANDER CASSIN YOUNG of the repair ship, USS *Vestal,* who, blown overboard when the magazines of the nearby battleship USS *Arizona* exploded during the Pearl Harbor raid, swam back to his damaged ship and conned it out of danger to a beaching.

ARMY SERGEANT RODGER W. YOUNG, who was a rifle squad leader in the 37th Infantry Division during the bloody fighting on the Pacific island of New Georgia. Bleeding after being hit by Japanese bullets, he crawled forward to toss grenades into a troublesome machine-gun nest and then died on the jungle trail.

The Bronze Cross

Captain Philip L. Vian, skipper of the sleek destroyer HMS *Cossack,* was patrolling with the Royal Navy's Fourth Destroyer Flotilla off German-occupied Norway on February 16, 1940, when he received instructions directly from Winston Churchill, First Lord of the Admiralty, in London. Vian's urgent assignment was to steam into Jossing Fjord and rescue British prisoners of war from the German supply ship *Altmark.* Violating Norwegian neutrality, the *Cossack* slipped into the fjord in one of the most daring exploits of World War II.

The destroyer drew up beside the *Altmark,* which was bound for Germany with 299 sailors and merchant seamen who had been captured by the pocket battleship *Admiral Graf Spee* in the South Atlantic. A boarding party, armed with revolvers and drawn cutlasses, jumped onto the *Altmark,* killed four German sailors, and freed the prisoners. The *Cossack* then quickly sailed away. Vian was awarded the Victoria Cross (the VC), Britain's highest decoration for valor.

Established by Queen Victoria in 1856 as an award open without distinction to all ranks of the army and navy "who had performed some signal act of valour," the decoration is a pattee bronze cross hung on a dull crimson ribbon.

Since 1857, almost 1,300 VCs have been awarded to British and Commonwealth officers, soldiers, sailors, and airmen. During the six years that Britain was engaged in World War II, only 171 members of the military received Victoria Crosses.

Its recipients during the conflict included:

RAF PILOT OFFICER CYRIL BARTON, who crashed his crippled Halifax bomber in a Durham coal-mine yard to avoid hitting four rows of miners' cottages.

GUARDSMAN EDWARD C. CHARLTON, who rescued crewmen from a trapped tank in the German village of Wistedt in April 1945 and died of his wounds after being captured.

MAJOR DAVID CURRIE, a Canadian who led 175 men in destroying seven German tanks, killing or wounding 800 of the enemy, and capturing 1,000 at St.-Lambert-sur-Dives during the Battle of Mortain in France in August 1944.

ARMY SERGEANT THOMAS DERRICK, an Australian, who, after an eight-day battle, led the capture of the Sattelberg summit on the Kokoda Trail in New Guinea in November 1943.

CORPORAL JACK EDMONDSON, an Australian, died helping repel German infiltrators from besieged Tobruk all while badly wounded in the stomach and neck in April 1942.

CAPTAIN EDWARD S. FOGARTY FEGEN, who was skipper of the armed merchant cruiser *Jervis Bay*. With his left arm torn off by a shell fragment, he faced hopeless odds in protecting an Atlantic convoy against the German pocket battleship *Admiral Scheer* in November 1940.

LIEUTENANT IAN FRASER, commander of a Royal Navy midget submarine, and **Leading Seaman Mick Magennis**, who blew holes in the Japanese cruiser *Takao* with limpet mines in the Singapore dockyard in July 1945.

WING COMMANDER GUY GIBSON, who led the famous 18-plane "Dam Busters" skip-bombing raid that seriously damaged the Ruhr dams in May 1943.

GANJU LAMA, a Gurkha who, though wounded in both arms and a leg, knocked out two Japanese tanks in India during the siege of Imphal in 1944.

RAF FLIGHT LIEUTENANT D. S. A. LORD, who died while flying his burning Dakota (C-47) transport over Arnhem, Holland in September 1944, to drop desperately needed supplies to besieged British paratroopers.

SQUADRON LEADER JOHN DERING NETTLETON, a South African, who led 12 Lancaster bombers on a daring daylight raid at an altitude of only 500 feet over Augsburg, Germany, in April 1942.

ROYAL AIR FORCE FLIGHT LIEUTENANT ERIC J. NICOLSON, who shot down a Messerschmitt fighter over Southampton in August 1940, even though he was wounded and his Hurricane's cockpit was on fire.

LIEUTENANTS B. C. G. PLACE AND D. CAMERON, Royal Navy commanders of midget submarines, who disabled the German battleship *Tirpitz* at Alta Fiord, Norway, in September 1943.

CAPTAIN P. A. "PAT" PORTEOUS of the British Commandos, who led attacks on German gun batteries during the disastrous assault on Dieppe, France, in August 1942.

CAPTAIN ROBERT ST. V. SHERBROOKE of HMS *Onslow,* who after he had been hit in the face and was losing an eye, repelled a four-hour attack by a German naval squadron.

SQUADRON LEADER LEONARD H. TRENT, who led 12 bombers of an RAF New Zealand squadron on a raid against a power station near Amsterdam in May 1943.

LIEUTENANT CHARLES UPHAM of New Zealand, who led a gallant but unsuccessful attempt to recapture the Maleme airfield in Crete in May 1941. He later won a second Victoria Cross in the Western Desert and was the only British or Commonwealth serviceman to receive it twice during the war.

PANZER PRIDE: MICHAEL WITTMANN

The strategically vital French town of Caen—on the Orne River only nine miles from the English Channel coast—was an immediate objective of the British Second Army during the Normandy invasion. The Allied landings in Normandy had gone well on the fateful Tuesday morning of June 6, 1944, and the British, American, and Canadian armies had started pushing inland. But the Germans swiftly drew the bulk of their panzer units to the Bayeux-Caen-Falaise area, where the bocage, small fields bounded by ditches and thicketed earthen embankments, strongly favored defense. A bloody slugging match developed, a series of frontal assaults by the British produced heavy losses, and the Allies did not capture the devastated town of Caen until July 9.

One man had held up the British timetable by a month in one of the most remarkable feats of World War II. He was Obersturmführer (Lieutenant) Michael Wittmann, commander of the Second Company of the 101st Heavy Tank Battalion, First Panzer Corps.

Wittmann was already a legend in the Waffen SS and its leading panzer ace. He fought in Greece and served with distinction for a year in Russia, where he was credited with 66 tank kills, was wounded twice, and won the Iron Cross First Class in 1941 and then the Knight's Cross. He attended an SS officers' school and was commissioned in 1942. In 1944, Wittmann was promoted to lieutenant, and 10 days later he received Oak Leaves to add to his Knight's Cross. Also that month, he received command of the Second SS Panzer Company in the 101st Heavy Panzer Battalion. Wittmann and his gunner, Bobby Woll, had been credited with destroying 119 armored fighting vehicles on the Eastern Front.

After the Normandy invasion, the British Seventh Armored Division (the famed Desert Rats) managed, in a bold stroke, to penetrate as far as the town of Villers-Bocage by June 13. At 8 A.M. a spearhead tank-infantry force of Brigadier Robert "Looney" Hinde's 22nd Armored Brigade rolled virtually unopposed into Villers-Bocage and received an enthusiastic welcome from its gaily dressed citizens. The reception astonished the tank crews, but the mutual joy was short-lived.

Leading a company of four 57-ton Tiger tanks and a 25-ton Mark IV Special, Wittmann spotted a squadron of British armor leaving Villers-Bocage to occupy positions to the south and decided to act on his own without waiting for support. He had no time to deploy his other Tigers but ordered them "not to retreat a step but to hold their ground."

While the British tankers dismounted to stretch their legs and brew tea, Wittmann's Tiger burst from cover on the south side of the Caen road, knocked out a tank, and drove along a parallel cart track, blasting Rifle Brigade vehicles as he went. Wittmann swung through the town, knocking out three Stuart reconnaissance tanks and antitank guns. Wittmann was then able to prudently withdraw into the woods southeast of Villers-Bocage. In about five minutes, Wittmann had created havoc in the British ranks; it would take a month's hard fighting before the British returned to Villers-Bocage.

Wittmann was awarded Swords for his Knight's Cross for his actions on June 13 and was promoted to captain. His kills now totaled 138 enemy tanks and 132 antitank guns. The most successful tank commander of the war was killed in action near Falaise, France, in August 1944.

Cross of Valor

The Iron Cross was originated by King Frederick William III of Prussia on March 10, 1813. As was customary at the beginning of a war, Adolf Hitler revived the Iron Cross decoration for heroism on September 1, 1939, the day his troops invaded Poland. To put his own stamp on the decoration, the Führer changed the grading, design, and ribbon and abolished award of the medal for noncombatant service. He also established a new grade, the Ritterkreuz (Knight's Cross), to bridge the gap between the Iron Cross First Class and the Grand Cross. The ascending grades of the Knight's Cross were:

Knight's Cross.
Knight's Cross with Oak Leaves.
Knight's Cross with Oak Leaves and Swords. The first to receive this decoration was Luftwaffe Lieutenant General Adolf Galland after 20 kills in the Battle of Britain. A later recipient was Lieutenant Michael Wittmann, the famed panzer ace who was killed in the 1944 Normandy campaign (see sidebar).

Knight's Cross with Oak Leaves, Swords, and Diamonds. The first to receive this medal was Luftwaffe Major Werner Moelders, who was credited with 115 kills. Other Luftwaffe officers given this decoration included General Adolf Galland, Colonel Gordon Gollob, Captain Hans-Joachim Marseille, Major Walther Nowotny, and Major Erich Hartmann.

FEARLESS "PADDY" MAYNE

"Paddy" Blair Mayne was a boyish former sportsman from Ireland who joined the elite Special Air Service (SAS) at its inception, and his specialty was destroying grounded aircraft. The SAS was the brainchild of Scots Guard Captain David A. Stirling, who was stationed in Egypt and who believed that a highly trained and motivated group of commandos could be dropped well behind enemy lines in North Africa and wreak havoc equal to or greater than that of a larger military unit. Mayne was his second-in-command.

During a raid on the Italian airfield at Tamet, Libya, in December 1941, Mayne put 24 planes out of action. Two weeks later he went back and destroyed 27 more. When Stirling's unit was expanded as the First SAS Regiment, Mayne took command of A Squadron and was awarded the Distinguished Service Order in recognition of his "special services."

When Shirling was captured by the Germans, Mayne was promoted to lieutenant colonel and assumed command of the regiment until it was reorganized into two units, the Special Raiding Squadron (SRS) and the Special Boat Section (SBS). He subsequently led the SRS when both units fought in the Sicilian and Italian campaigns in 1943–44.

Mayne led the Raiding Squadron in the Allied invasion of Sicily on July 10, 1943. After being put ashore by landing craft and scrambling up a cliff, Mayne and his men drove spikes into the Italian guns at Capo Murro di Porco and took the 700 men in the garrison prisoner within minutes.

The final action in the Mediterranean theater for the Special Raiding Squadron came on October 4, 1943, when it landed with Royal Marine commandos at Termoli on the eastern Italian coast. The SRS advanced into the town, secured it, and then faced a fierce German counterattack during which 22 of Mayne's men were blown to pieces in the back of a truck. The shaken SRS hung on grimly for three days before beating back the Germans, and Mayne was awarded a bar for his Distinguished Service Order (DSO).

The gallant Paddy Mayne led his regiment during operations in northern France, the Low Countries, Scandinavia, and Germany and won two more bars for his DSO. When the Special Air Service was disbanded in October 1945, he returned to civilian life.

Knight's Cross with Golden Oak Leaves, Swords, and Diamonds. This medal was awarded only once, to Colonel Hans-Ulrich Rudel, a legendary Stuka pilot, the most highly decorated soldier in the Third Reich.

Grand Cross of the Iron Cross. The only recipient in World War II was Reich Marshal Hermann Göring.

German decorations awarded in World War II were, in descending order: Iron Cross (6,973); Knight's Cross with Oak Leaves (853); Knight's Cross with Oak Leaves and Swords (150); Knight's Cross with Oak Leaves, Swords, and Diamonds (27); Knight's Cross with Oak Leaves; Swords, and Diamonds (1); Grand Cross of the Iron Cross (1).

Decorations

World War II saw acts of bravery and heroism like no other. The medal system of each country is one way to recognize the soldiers of distinction. The following list shows the order of military decorations in descending order for each country

U.S. Decorations

Medal of Honor
Distinguished Service Cross (army)
Navy Cross
Distinguished Service Medal (army)
Silver Star
Distinguished Flying Cross
Legion of Merit
Soldier's Medal
Navy and Marine Corps Medal
Bronze Star
Air Medal
Purple Heart

British Decorations

Victoria Cross
George Cross

Distinguished Service Order
Distinguished Conduct Medal
Distinguished Service Medal
Military Cross
British Empire Medal
1939–45 Star
Distinguished Flying Cross
War Medal, 1939–45
Defense Medal

German Decorations

Grand Cross of the Iron Cross
Knight's Cross with Golden Oak Leaves, Swords, and Diamonds
Knight's Cross with Oak Leaves, Swords, and Diamonds
Knight's Cross with Oak Leaves and Swords
Knight's Cross with Oak Leaves
Knight's Cross
Iron Cross First Class
Iron Cross Second Class

Soviet Decorations

Order of Lenin
Order of Victory
Order of Glory
Order of Kutozov
Order of Suvorov
Order of Alexander Nevsky
Gold Star
Leningrad Medal
Moscow Medal
Sevastopol Medal
Stalingrad Medal
Arctic Medal
Odessa Medal
Caucasus Medal

> There are no atheists in foxholes.
> —U.S. Army Chaplain William T. Cummings, on Bataan in March 1942

CHAPTER 7

Campaigns and Battles: Europe and the Atlantic

W orld War II in Europe was fought across a vast expanse of land and sea, from the Atlantic in the west to the Urals in Russia in the east, and from the Barents Sea near the North Pole to the blisteringly hot deserts of North Africa. It was the quest for expansion that moved the battles from country to country during the war's turbulent years.

Powerful German invasions—first into Poland, then a lightning thrust into Norway and Denmark, followed a month later by the crushing defeats of the Low Countries and France—left the British reeling and isolated; the only bright spots were their amazing rescue of most of their army from the beaches of Dunkirk, France, in 1940, and the Royal Air Force's triumph over the Luftwaffe in the Battle of Britain later that summer.

The next German hammer blow was to the Soviet Union in June 1941, a massive invasion that took the German armies to the outskirts of Leningrad and Moscow before being stopped by the brutal Russian winter.

> Close your hearts to pity. Act brutally. Eighty million Germans must obtain what is their right.
>
> —German Chancellor Adolf Hitler
> to his troops

Although Germany's ground forces were at first undefeated, the British Royal Navy and Royal Air Force (RAF) were formidable threats. The Royal Navy was the most powerful in the world in 1939, and it provided the first Allied victories. Unable to compete on the ocean surface, the German Kriegsmarine began an unrestricted submarine campaign against Allied shipping. The Allies responded by developing convoy and antisubmarine tactics that decided the Battle of the Atlantic in the Allies' favor in 1943.

The airplane, first used offensively over Europe during World War I, emerged as a powerful weapon in World War II. Without air supremacy a combatant's ability to wage war on the ground or at sea was severely limited. From the evacuation at Dunkirk in June 1940 until the D-Day landings four years later, a great aerial battle raged in the skies as the Allies fought to achieve air supremacy over the Continent. The campaign began after the Battle of Britain in the late summer of 1940, in which the Royal Air Force defeated the Luftwaffe's plans to control the air over England. The RAF initially fought the air war alone and was joined by the U.S. Army Air Forces only after the United States entered the war in Europe in 1942.

Although the United States became the world's arsenal, the Soviet Union provided the man—and woman—power to prevent the German juggernaut from rolling through Russia as it had through Western Europe and Poland. The Battle of Stalingrad in the winter of 1942–43 saw the war turn in the Allies' favor. From this point on, the German forces remained on the defensive. Soviet troops began advancing westward, while U.S. and British forces expelled the Germans from North Africa in 1943, and in the same year, invaded Sicily and the Italian mainland. In June 1944, the Allies invaded Western Europe with the D-Day assault at Normandy. By August, Paris was liberated and the Allied armies were on the march toward Germany. The war in Europe—more than five years old—finally ended when Soviet troops captured Berlin, forcing the Germans to capitulate.

The European Theater

The battles waged in the European theater ranged from quick small-unit actions to massive campaigns involving clashes of armies over weeks and months. Air attacks and occasional commando-style raids by both sides were more common from May 1940, when the Allies were driven out of France, until their return on June 6, 1944, although large-unit actions were being fought during this time in North Africa, Italy, and the Soviet Union. On the Atlantic, Allied convoys sailed through waters infested with German U-boats and surface raiders. Until 1943, when the Allies finally got the upper hand over the U-boats, German submarines sank hundreds of ships and threatened the lifeline of men and materiel between the United States and the British Isles.

The airplane played a major role throughout the European theater, not only as a bomber and fighter but as transportation as well, ferrying troops from place to place and into battle. In May 1941, German forces attacked and occupied

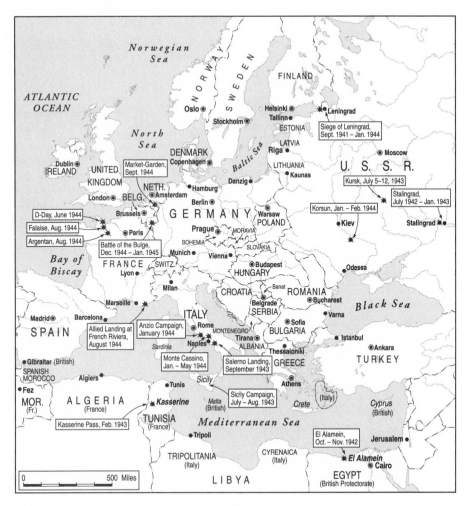

MAJOR ENGAGEMENTS IN THE EUROPEAN THEATER OF OPERATIONS

the Aegean island of Crete in an invasion carried out almost entirely from the air—the first major parachute assault in wartime. The Allies later employed massive parachute drops in Normandy and, in 1945, when crossing the Rhine in western Germany.

Yet the war was finally won for the Allies by conventional ground forces. Germany was crushed not by bombs or commando actions, but by the weight of the U.S., British, and Soviet armies entering German territory, seizing cities and rural areas, and destroying the remnants of the German army. In the end, the common foot soldier liberated Europe from Nazi tyranny.

The war in Europe consisted of numerous campaigns—extended strategic battles waged over long periods of time. The table below provides information about the most significant campaigns.

Name/Date	Commanders	Objectives	Troops Engaged	Casualties	Consequences
Battle of France/ May–June 1940	*German:* Von Bock, Von Rundstedt, Von Leeb *French:* Gamelin *British:* Gort	German invasion of France, designed to defeat the French military	Germany: 94 divisions France: 100 divisions Belgium: 18 divisions *Britain:* 9 divisions	*German:* 30,000–40,000 *Allies:* 390,000	The Allied forces are defeated, leading to German domination of the European continent.
Africa/1940– spring 1943	*Italian:* Graziani *German:* Rommel *British:* Wavell, Auchinleck, Montgomery	To defend Egypt, protect the Suez Canal, and gain control of oil fields	Germany: Afrika Korps Italy: Various divisions Britain: Eighth Army U.S.: Seventh Army	Axis Losses: More than 950,000 men killed and captured Allied Losses: "Moderate" exact numbers (unknown)	With the surrender of the Afrika Korps, North Africa is in Allied hands, paving the way for the invasion of Sicily.
Italy/July 1943– May 2, 1945	*German:* Kesselring *British:* Alexander *U.S.:* Mark Clark	To defeat Axis troops in Italy	Germany: 10th Army Britain: Eighth Army U.S.: Fifth and Seventh Armies	Exact numbers unavailable	The Allies place pressure on German forces from the south, allowing Allied bombers to operate from Italian bases.
Eastern Front/ June 1941–May 2, 1945	*German:* Von Rundstedt, Von Leeb, Von Bock *Soviet:* Timoshenko, Voroshilov, Zhukov	Possession of Russia	Germany: 180 divisions Soviet Union: 158 divisions	*German:* >3 million Soviet: 7.5 million	After two years on the offensive, the war on the Eastern Front turns at the Battle of Stalingrad, putting Germany on the defensive. The war ends after the Battle of Berlin.
Western Front (D-Day; Operation Overlord)/June 6, 1944–May 2, 1945	*German:* Von Rundstedt, Model *British:* Montgomery *U.S.:* Eisenhower, Bradley, Devers	To liberate Western Europe	U.S.: 57 divisions Britain: one army group Canada: One army group Germany: N/A	*German:* 263,000 KIA Allies: 186,900 KIA	Allied forces defeat Germans. The war ends with Germany's surrender.

The following engagements are some of the more famous events of the war in Europe (including North Africa), from the initial fighting in Poland in 1939 to the turning point in Stalingrad in 1943 to the decisive Battle of Berlin in the spring of 1945. They are listed alphabetically.

Anzio, Italy (January 22–May 24, 1944)

When the Germans halted the Allied advance north from Salerno, Italy, the Allies planned a second landing behind German lines at Anzio, a port city southwest of Rome. German defenses at Anzio were strong, and heavy fighting elsewhere in central Italy allowed the Germans to reinforce their defenses at Anzio. The Allied forces were trapped on the Anzio beachhead for more than four months. What had been intended as a lightning maneuver to outflank strong German defenses had become a bitter battle of attrition. Eventually, the Allies were able to break the German defenses and proceed northward to Rome. Anzio is significant not only because of the stalemate that resulted, but because it showed that even late in the war the Germans could mount a stiff resistance to Allied advances.

> I had hoped we were hurling a wildcat onto the shore, but all we got was a stranded whale.
> —British Prime Minister Winston Churchill on the landings at Anzio

Arnhem-Nijmegen, Holland (Operation Market-Garden; September 17–25, 1944)

Following a plan conceived by British Field Marshal Bernard Montgomery, Allied paratroopers jumped into Holland to seize bridges

EISENHOWER'S BROAD FRONT STRATEGY

Once the Allied forces managed a breakout from the Normandy beachhead, the Supreme Headquarters, Allied Expeditionary Forces (SHAEF), under the command of General Dwight D. Eisenhower, adopted a "broad front strategy." His plans called for an advance over a wide front, with one major force advancing into Germany north of the Ardennes region of Belgium and Luxembourg into the Ruhr Valley, and the other going south through France. British Field Marshal Bernard Montgomery commanded the northern army; the southern group was under U.S. General Omar Bradley. Montgomery's 21st Army Group eventually advanced into northern Germany as far as the Elbe River, the demarcation line between the British/American and Soviet advances. Bradley's 12th Army Group advanced into central and southern Germany and Czechoslovakia, while the Sixth Army Group under U.S. General Jacob Devers broke off and moved from the south of France into southern Germany and then Austria.

While Eisenhower's generals followed his basic strategy, they made some deviations. After the Allied breakout from Normandy, the U.S. Third Army under General George S. Patton advanced so far into France that it outran its lines of ground supply. But the biggest philosophical disagreement about how to defeat the Germans was between Montgomery and Eisenhower. Montgomery pressed for a concentration of forces on a single front for a massive drive into northern Germany followed by an encircling of the industrial Ruhr region—this tactic, he believed, would end the war quickly. Eisenhower disagreed, believing such a move was too risky and stuck to his basic plan, although he allowed a diversion of forces to support Montgomery's planned advance into the Rhine region of Holland, a plan that came to disaster in Operation Market-Garden.

After the war, Montgomery continued the debate, arguing that Eisenhower's strategy prolonged the war unnecessarily and creating bitterness between the two. Most military historians disagree strongly and believe that Eisenhower's plan was the sounder strategy.

so that advancing British armored troops could cross the Lower Rhine River, move rapidly into the Ruhr (the industrial heart of Germany), and, they hoped, end the war by Christmas 1944. The airborne portion of the plan went well initially, but the ground advance was held up, forcing the British and Polish paratroopers at Arnhem to withdraw. The Germans mauled the British First Airborne Division at Arnhem, killing, wounding, and capturing thousands, although the British put up gallant resistance. The operation, code-named Operation Market-Garden, involved U.S. paratroopers of the 82nd and 101st Airborne Divisions. The campaign is often described as having attempted

to reach "a bridge too far," which later became the title of a book about the operation by Cornelius Ryan.

Ardennes Offensive/Battle of the Bulge (December 1944)

On December 16, 25 German divisions launched a fierce attack on a thinly defended area in the Allied lines in the frigid and snow-covered region of the Ardennes Forest of Belgium. The surprise attack came in an area held by six newly arrived U.S. divisions, and the panzers advanced rapidly, held up only by the courageous defense of scattered pockets of U.S. troops, including the 101st Airborne Division in

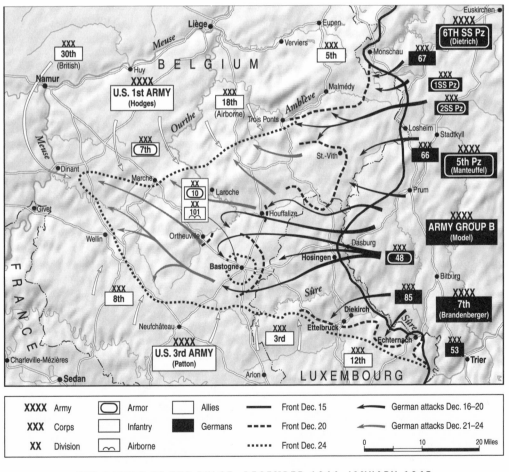

THE BATTLE OF THE BULGE, DECEMBER 1944–JANUARY 1945

the strategic crossroads town of Bastogne. German special troops infiltrated the lines by wearing U.S. uniforms, although the Allies quickly discovered the ruse. They finally defeated the Germans by a combination of counterattacks by elements of the U.S. First and Third Armies and heavy air attacks by British and U.S. fighter-bombers, and because the Germans eventually ran out of fuel. By January 1945 they had reduced the German penetration, which had planned to cross the River Meuse and reach the major Belgian seaport of Antwerp. The Battle of the Bulge, so named due to the pocket of penetration achieved by the Germans, was the largest battle fought by U.S. troops in Europe and was a shock to the Allies, who did not believe the Germans had the resources or will to mount such a massive attack at a time when they seemed all but defeated.

> This time the Kraut has stuck his head in a meat grinder, and this time I've got hold of the handle.
> —General George S. Patton Jr.,
> during the Battle of the Bulge

Berlin, Germany (April 16–May 2, 1945)

The Battle of Berlin was the last battle of World War II and one of the most costly. Despite heavy casualties, Soviet troops in two massive army fronts managed to break through the German defenses and surround the capital on April 24 as the city saw fierce house-to-house fighting. The assault killed more than 100,000 German civilians and left the already battered city in rubble. On April 30, Hitler committed suicide in his bunker beneath the Reich chancellery. Two days later, Soviet riflemen stormed the Reichstag and raised the Soviet flag over Berlin.

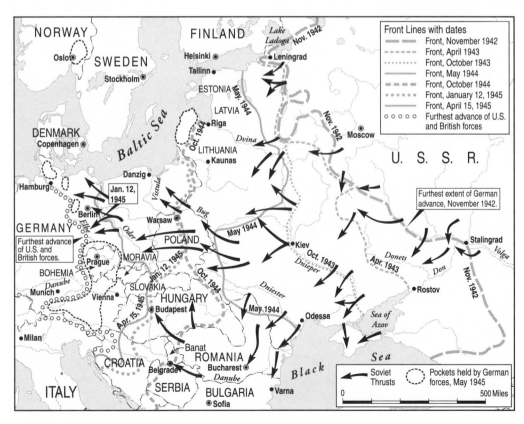

SOVIET ADVANCES AGAINST THE NAZIS, 1945

Bulge, Battle of

See Ardennes Offensive.

Cassino, Italy (Winter–Spring, 1943–44)

The Allied advance north from Salerno was held up by stiff German opposition centered on Monte Cassino, a hill topped by an ancient Benedictine abbey that some Allied officers thought the Germans were using for artillery observation. Bombers turned the abbey into rubble, which the Germans then turned into defenses. The Germans were eventually routed, and the Allied armies proceeded northward. The destruction of such a revered religious shrine made many of the Allies uneasy, but in the end, most believed it was unavoidable given the battlefield situation.

Crete (May 20–31, 1941)

In a daring air assault, German paratroops captured the Aegean island of Crete and seized airfields that had been used by troop-carrying airplanes to bring in reinforcements. Although Germany overcame the British and New Zealand defenders, the invasion was so costly that Hitler forbade future large-scale airborne operations. Crete was the first massive use of paratroopers in battle. The loss of the island was a major embarrassment to the British government.

D-Day (Operation Overlord; June 6, 1944)

The liberation of Western Europe from Nazi occupation began June 6, 1944, and ended with

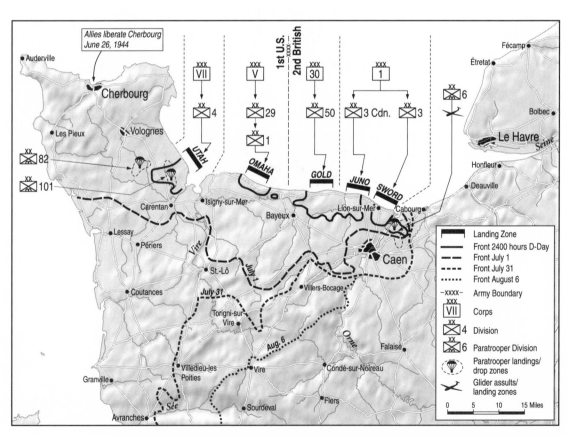

D-DAY LANDINGS, JUNE 6, 1944

OPERATION OVERLORD/NORMANDY (JUNE 6–AUGUST 31, 1944)

After years of planning, Allied troops, with General Dwight D. Eisenhower in overall command, landed on five beaches (Gold, Juno, Sword, Utah, and Omaha), in the French region of Normandy on June 6, 1944, beginning Operation Overlord, the invasion of Western Europe. The invasion had been postponed 24 hours due to bad weather. The objective of the D-Day landings was to secure a beachhead so the invading Allied armies could pass into Western Europe in the long-awaited front that would relieve the Soviets in the East. Early that morning paratroopers jumped inland behind the beaches in an attempt to secure bridges and other objectives for the amphibious landings that were to follow. At the end of the first day of ferocious fighting, casualties, although lighter than expected, were some 2,500 dead. Most deaths occurred at Omaha Beach, where German defenses were much stronger than at the other beaches.

Confusion among the Germans aided the Allies. Hitler believed the "real" invasion would take place at the Pas de Calais and refused to allow his commanders to reinforce their defenses in Normandy until late in the day. This was due largely to the success of an Allied plan of deception called "Fortitude," which involved fictitious military units, radio traffic, and more. But the major factor in the success of the landings undoubtedly was the Allies' complete air superiority over the beaches.

Once the Germans realized that the Normandy invasion was no diversion, they rushed troops in to try to force the Allies back into the English Channel. Between June 6 and August 31, more than 30,000 Germans and 45,000 Allied troops died in battle, while hundreds of thousands on both sides were wounded or missing. The Allies realized one of their first goals—securing the Cotentin Peninsula and capturing the port at Cherbourg—on June 24. Cherbourg was especially important, because a storm had inflicted severe damage on the portable ports off the beachhead.

Once the Allies were ashore in Western Europe, the Germans mounted furious counterattacks that prevented the Allies from extending their lines eastward for several weeks. In late July, U.S. General Omar Bradley launched Operation Cobra, an attack on the German lines near Avranches, in an attempt to force an opening. After initial attacks on July 25, the Allies began breaking the German line three days later. Avranches fell to the Allies on July 31, and the next day General George S. Patton's Third Army began pouring through the break and advancing into France.

Thanks to Allied code breakers, Bradley learned of a planned German counterattack to cut off the advancing Americans. When the German attack stalled near Argentan, Bradley ordered elements of the U.S. First and Third Armies to attack the Germans from the east, while British troops advanced off the beachhead from the west. Inexplicably, British and Canadian troops failed to close a 25-mile-wide gap at Falaise that would have cut off the German Seventh Army. The Allies finally closed the Falaise Gap on August 20, and the battle lines began moving out of Normandy. Less than a week later, Paris was liberated and the battle began moving eastward, toward Germany.

Viewed from the landing craft they have just exited, American soldiers wade toward the beach under fire on D-Day, June 6, 1944. The long-awaited Allied invasion of Nazi-occupied France occurred in Normandy, while Hitler had expected it elsewhere, at the Pas de Calais.

total victory eleven months later. Allied planners originally picked May 1, 1944, as the date for invasion of the Norman coast of France. When it was decided that too few landing craft would be available to invade on that date, June 5 was chosen. Storms on June 5 caused the delay of D-Day until June 6, 1944, when the Allied troops landed on the beaches of the French province of Normandy, beginning the invasion of Western Europe and the launching of a third front. Omaha, one of two beaches assigned to the U.S. Army, saw the heaviest fighting.

Thanks in part to German confusion and Hitler's refusal to believe that the Normandy landings were not a ruse, the Allies secured beachheads on all five beaches, and by nightfall reinforcements were coming ashore. (See Operation Overlord sidebar.)

> The war will be won or lost on the beaches. The first 24 hours of the invasion will be decisive.
>
> —Field Marshal Erwin Rommel
> on the expected D-Day invasion

THOMAS VALANCE, SERGEANT, COMPANY A, 116TH REGIMENT, 29TH DIVISION

Surviving D-Day

As we came down the ramp, we were in water, I guess about knee high, and started to do what we were trained to do. That is, move forward and then crouch and fire. One of the problems was [that] we didn't quite know what to fire at. I saw some tracers coming from a concrete emplacement, which to me looked mammoth. I never anticipated any gun emplacements being that big. I guess it was known commonly as a pillbox. I attempted to fire back at that, but I had no concept of what was going on behind me. There was not much to see in front of me, except a few houses that we knew were to be there . . . from the . . . mock-up.

It became evident rather quickly that we weren't going to accomplish very much. I remember floundering in the water with my hand up in the air, I guess trying to get my balance, when I was first shot. I was shot through the left hand and suffered from a broken knuckle, which still has not been replaced properly. And I was shot through the palm of the hand. I remember feeling nothing but a little sting at the time, but I was aware that I was shot.

Next to me in the water a fellow named Hank Witt—Private Henry G. Witt, actually—was rolling over towards me. I remember him very clearly saying, "Sergeant, they're leaving us here to die like rats. Just to die like rats." I don't know why I remember that statement so clearly. I certainly wasn't thinking the same thing, nor did I share that opinion. I didn't know whether we were being left or not. It turns out that he either had great perception of what was going on or made a statement that coincidentally was factual, because it turns out that subsequent waves did not come in behind us as was planned originally.

At any rate, I made my way forward as best I could. There was no way I was going to knock out a German concrete emplacement with a thirty-caliber rifle. But I was hit several other times, once in the left thigh, which broke a hip bone. I didn't know it at the time, but I found it out later, and several other bits that were not injurious. I remember being hit in the pack a couple of times, feeling a tug, and my chin strap on my helmet which was not around my chin . . . was severed by a bullet. I worked my way up onto the beach and staggered up against a wall and sort of collapsed there, and as a matter of fact I spent the whole day in the same position.

Eventually, the bodies of the other guys washed ashore, and I was one live body in amongst so many of my friends, all of whom were dead. In many cases, very severely blown to pieces, which was not a very pleasant way to spend a day.

—The Eisenhower Center for American Studies Archives

Dieppe, France (August 19, 1942)

Accompanied by a few U.S. Rangers, British and Canadian commandos landed at the French port of Dieppe in a probe of German defenses. More than half the force was killed or captured, but Allied high commanders regarded the raid, code-named Operation Jubilee, as a learning experience for the Normandy invasion of June 1944. Above all, the Allies learned that massive numbers of men and materiel would be needed to overcome the fierce German defenses along the coast of the English Channel.

Dunkirk, France (May 26–June 3, 1940)

As the Allied forces in France retreated toward the English Channel and the invading Germans encircled them, it became apparent that control of France would be lost to the Nazis. England organized a 900-vessel flotilla of warships, barges, fishing boats, skiffs, and yachts to bring out the remnants of the British Expeditionary Force (BEF) and some French and Belgian troops who were trapped on the beaches near Dunkirk. In a move that many historians point to as one of the greatest blunders of the war, Hitler had decided to halt his ground troops and allow the Luftwaffe to administer the final blow against the enemy. Although German planes killed or wounded many soldiers massed on the beach and hampered rescuing ships, they failed to annihilate the BEF. The British rescue mission saved about 338,000, thus preserving the bulk of the British army. Dunkirk is remembered as one of the greatest rescues in military history, but also as a triumph amidst defeat as ordinary Britons took their small boats and ventured across the Channel to bravely save their fellow countrymen.

East Africa (Summer 1940–May 1941)

After Italian troops invaded British territory in Africa and moved into Egypt, the British built up forces to defeat the Italian threat. Using mostly colonial troops, Britain began a campaign that culminated in the surrender of Italian troops in Ethiopia.

El Alamein, Egypt (October 1942)

The North African campaign turned in the Allies' favor when British and Australian troops of the Eighth Army broke through the German lines at El Alamein, on the Mediterranean coast of Egypt. As Sir Winston Churchill said, "Up to Alamein, we survived. After Alamein, we conquered." Indeed, the German Afrika Korps had pushed the Eighth Army from Lbyia to the Egyptian frontier. With the British victory, led by Field Marshal Bernard Montgomery, the forces of German Field Marshal Erwin Rommel began

---

CAPTAIN RICHARD AUSTIN, BRITISH EXPEDITIONARY FORCE

Awaiting Evacuation from Dunkirk

From the margin of the sea, at fairly wide intervals three long thin black lines protruded into the water, conveying the effect of low wooden breakwaters. These were lines of men, standing in pairs behind one another far out into the water, waiting in queues till boats arrived to transport them, a score or so at a time, to the steamers and warships that were filling up with the last survivors. The queues stood there, fixed and almost as regular as if ruled. No bunching, no pushing, nothing like the mix-up to be seen at the turnstiles when a crowd is going to a football match. Much more orderly, even than a waiting theater queue.

—From *Return Via Dunkirk* (London: Hodder & Stoughton, 1940), as published in *A Mammoth Book of Eyewitness World War II*, ed. Jon E. Lewis (New York: Carroll & Graf, 2002).

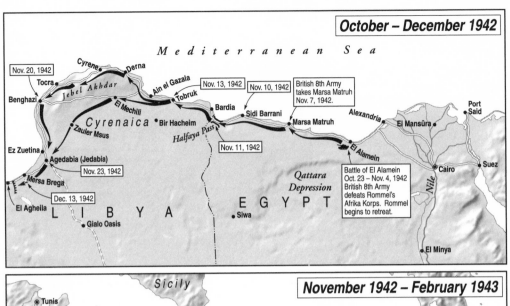

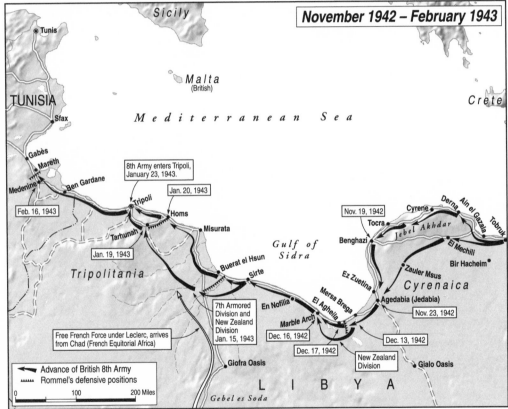

ROMMEL'S RETREAT AND HIS PURSUIT BY THE BRITISH EIGHTH ARMY

a retreat of hundreds of miles that ended with their capitulation to British and U.S. forces in Tunisia in May 1943.

France, Battle of (May 1940)

On May 10, 1940, Germany attacked France, Belgium, and Holland on a front from the North Sea south to Luxembourg. Using blitzkrieg tactics, German mechanized and armored divisions advanced quickly across the Lowlands and into France, defeating the Allied forces within a month.

Kasserine Pass, Tunisia (February 19–20, 1943)

The first major action for U.S. ground troops in the ETO was a disaster as German forces under Field Marshal Erwin Rommel drove through the Kasserine Pass in the Tebessa Mountains in an attempt to flank the Allied armies. The inex-perienced U.S. troops suffered more than 6,000 casualties, about half of whom were reported missing in action. Despite his success against the Americans, Rommel withdrew his forces through the pass on February 23 in the face of superior Allied forces.

Kiev, Ukraine (July 1941)

Advancing German forces encircled the Ukrainian capital and killed or captured some 750,000 Soviet soldiers. The fall of Kiev was one of the greatest losses suffered by the Red Army in the early weeks of the war.

Kursk, Russia (July–August 1943)

After losing the city of Kursk to a Russian attack in early 1943, the Germans mounted a massive campaign to retake it in what is believed to have been the largest tank battle ever. A thunderstorm halted the huge force of German armor when

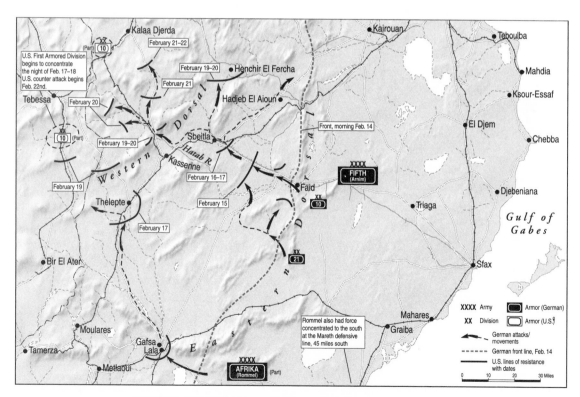

BATTLES OF KASSERINE PASS, FEBRUARY 14–22, 1943

the battlefield became a sea of mud. The battle seesawed back and forth until August 6, ending in defeat for Germany when Hitler called off the offensive. Kursk is remembered as a titanic battle of armored units and as one of the most significant German defeats of 1943 (see Chapter 9, "Arms and Equipment").

Leningrad, Russia (August 1941–January 1944)

German forces advancing into Russia reached the outskirts of Leningrad in August 1941 and, supported by Finnish troops attacking from the north, immediately began an attack to capture the city. The Soviets managed to halt the Axis advance by late September, and the Germans

A destroyed home on Leningrad's (now St. Petersburg) Nevsky Prospekt is mute testimony to the savagery and privations endured during a Nazi siege that lasted nearly 900 days. As many as 1.5 million Russian civilians were killed during the city's agony.

began a siege that lasted for approximately 900 days, during which time they shelled the city and hoped to starve its population into surrender. The only supply routes into the city were by water (over Lake Ladoga) and by air. When the lake froze, the Soviets built a road over the ice. In January 1943, a Soviet advance broke the German lines but failed to lift the siege. Finally, in January 1944, Soviet forces managed to drive the Germans away. The siege of Leningrad resulted in the deaths of some 900,000 civilians, most through starvation and artillery bombardment, but it became a symbol of the absolute courage and willpower of the Soviet people who, despite unspeakable hardships and suffering, held out against the Germans.

Malta (April–August 1942)

Located off the southern tip of Italy, the two islands that make up Malta were important to the British Royal Navy's control of the Mediterranean. Although England was enduring constant air attack, the British reinforced their positions on the islands and held off German attacks, thus ensuring their dominance in the Mediterranean.

Moscow, Russia (Winter 1941–42)

Hoping to capture the Soviet capital of Moscow before winter, the German army began an attack in early October 1941. But winter came early, and by December snow made roads impassable. Extremely cold temperatures poured down from the Arctic, bringing misery and death to the ill-prepared troops, who had been issued summer coats only and froze in the cruel Russian winter. With the Germans only 10 or so miles from Moscow (they could see the domes of the Kremlin), the Soviets began a counteroffensive after bringing troops back from the Far East. By the end of January, the Soviets had pushed the German front lines 40 miles back from Moscow. The Germans never advanced again toward Moscow and instead began their three-and-one-half-year retreat that ended in the Soviet advance into Berlin.

Norway (April 1940)

On April 9, 1940, German ships began landing small detachments of troops at several points along the Norwegian coast while paratroops seized airfields. Despite the numerical superiority of the invading Germans, Norwegian forces continued to resist while British and French expeditionary forces landed troops in the central and northern regions of the country. Allied forces managed to retake the town of Narvik, but the deteriorating situation in France led to their withdrawal in early June and forced Norway's surrender.

Poland (September 1–October 6, 1939)

The German invasion of Poland on September 1, 1939, sounded the opening guns of World War II and introduced the world to the German form of battle called blitzkrieg. Using fast-moving light infantry supported by aircraft and armor, the German forces quickly advanced toward Warsaw, which fell on September 27 after a two-week siege. The German defeat of the Poles was hastened by the invasion of the Soviet Union (with whom the Germans had a nonaggression pact that provided for the division of Poland), on September 17.

BLITZKRIEG

The term *Blitzkrieg* ("lightning war") originally referred to special shock troops whose job was to break through Allied lines in World War I, is now used to describe the tactics of the Germans in the opening months of the war. Moreover, it is actually a misnomer because most German actions were conventional. The term, however, evoked fear and was probably coined by the Germans for that effect.

Between the wars, Germany developed a form of warfare built around rapid movement of ground forces supported by air. On September 1, 1939, the German army revealed its new tactics to the world as General Heinz Guderian's Panzer Corps spearheaded the advance into Poland. He combined the rapid advance of ground forces with devastating air attacks on Polish airfields, communications links, and railroads. The combination of fast-moving armor and intense air attack threw the Polish defenses into chaos on the first day of the war.

The Germans used blitzkrieg tactics again when they bypassed the Maginot Line and invaded France through Belgium and the lowlands of the Netherlands. Ten armored panzer divisions and eight motorized infantry divisions led the larger force of infantry into Belgium over bridges that had been seized by airborne troops who had landed by parachute and glider. As in Poland, the Luftwaffe played a major role as Stuka dive-bombers attacked Belgian and French positions and cut supply lines. Allied forces in Holland collapsed quickly under the German onslaught, but French forces were able to move into Belgium without opposition. The Germans sprang a trap in mid-May when panzer forces attacked the mostly French defenders and quickly threw the whole Allied defense into disarray. In less than two weeks, the Germans had pushed the Allied defense lines west by more than 60 miles at their most eastern point, while German forces had driven to the English Channel in the south. The Germans needed less than a month to destroy Allied resistance in France.

Blitzkrieg tactics were most successful in the west. (The term "Blitz" was coined by the English to refer to the German air raids on their cities in 1940–41.) The Eastern Front, however, demonstrated the limitations of blitzkrieg warfare. The strategy worked best against a weak enemy who could be defeated in the early weeks of the attack. It also worked best in good weather, a lesson learned on the Eastern Front. During the summer and early fall of 1941, the Germans were able to use their fast-moving armored divisions with great effect, but the severe Russian winter of 1941–42 brought the mechanized forces to a standstill. Many panzer divisions outran their supply lines, and were cut off by Soviet forces operating to the rear of the Germans. The war on the Eastern Front became a war of attrition with heavy casualties inflicted on both sides.

Rhine River Crossing, Germany (March 23, 1945)

Although U.S. troops had crossed the Rhine River over the bridge at the town of Remagen on March 7, 1945, British Field Marshal Bernard Montgomery prepared to mount an operation to cross the river. The Rhine represented the last natural obstacle facing the Allied armies as they advanced eastward into Germany. Mont-

AIRBORNE FORCES

Soldiers from many Allied and Axis forces underwent extensive training to learn how to parachute from airplanes and then function as shock troops after reaching the ground, a mode of operation that led to heavy casualties, but proved valuable at times in securing vital bridges, beach exits or transportation centers, as well as spreading confusion among the enemy. Although conceived during World War I, the idea of landing troops by parachute or in troop carrier aircraft was developed in the 1920s by the Soviet military. It fell to the Germans to make use of the concept in combat initially. The success of German paratroops and glider troops in the opening campaigns of World War II, especially in the Low Countries and France, led most of the world's military to experiment with airborne units of their own.

The most successful Axis airborne operation was the invasion of Crete (1941), which was carried out almost entirely from the air. Paratroops and glider troops landed and captured three airfields, which Luftwaffe transports then used to deliver reinforcements. Although the invasion and occupation of Crete were successful, more than 4,000 of the 15,000 troops who took part were killed, and thousands were wounded, leading Hitler to forbid further large-scale paratroop operations.

Allied airborne forces made their debut in North Africa (1942), where U.S. and British paratroops conducted a few small-scale operations to capture airfields and other installations. The invasion plan for Sicily (1943) called for massive use of paratroop and glider units. Although the operations in Sicily were plagued with problems—including high winds that caused scattered drops, premature glider releases, and "friendly fire"—the overall determination was that they were a success because they seized designated objectives and the presence of the airborne forces caused confusion among the Axis defenders. Airborne operations in support of the Normandy landings (1944) were as problematic as those in Sicily, but they too were considered successful for many of the same reasons.

By September 1944, the Allied airborne forces were better organized and the troop carrier pilots better trained. Drops in the Netherlands in Operation Market-Garden were successful; all the troops landed where they were supposed to despite heavy ground fire. The U.S. troopers captured the bridges in their assigned sectors, and the British and Polish troops did likewise, although heavy German fire caused heavy casualties among the latter. But the ground forces that were supposed to use the seized bridges failed to reach the area in time to cross before the Germans brought up heavy reinforcements. The final airborne operation of World War II in Europe took place in March 1945 in support of the British 21st Army's crossing of the Rhine.

In the opening phase of Operation Market-Garden, Allied paratroopers drop in Holland in September 1944. Developed by British General Bernard Montgomery, the plan called for a lightning thrust into the Ruhr, the industrial heart of Germany. It failed with heavy losses.

gomery's plan called for a massive two-week aerial and artillery bombardment of the intended crossing area in northern Germany near the town of Wesel. The airborne Operation Varsity began the campaign on March 23 with massive paratroop drops on the eastern side of the Rhine.

Salerno, Italy (September 1943)

Troops of the U.S. Fifth Army landed at Salerno, the port south of Naples, during the Allied invasion of Italy. Massive German resistance led U.S. General Mark Clark to ask that plans be made for evacuating his troops; the request led headquarters to send him reinforcements from the 82nd Airborne Division. Naval gunfire knocked out much of the German resistance, allowing the Fifth Army to link up with the British Eighth, further inland, on September 15, six days after the landings.

Sicily (Operation Husky; July 10–August 17, 1943)

The invasion of Sicily placed Allied ground troops on European soil on a second front and led to Italy's surrender. U.S. and British troops landed on July 10 and secured the island after a 38-day campaign. British troops under Field Marshal Bernard Montgomery advanced through the interior of the island, while the U.S. Seventh Army under General George S. Patton drove along the northern coast, with both forces aimed toward the town of Messina. Italian troops suffered high casualties. The Sicily campaign knocked Italy out of the war.

Smolensk, Russia (Summer 1941)

German panzer divisions attacked the Russian city of Smolensk in an attempt to open the way to Moscow. Despite heavy casualties of their own, Soviet forces inflicted severe losses on the Germans and brought the offensive to a halt, but the Germans managed to take the city in early August. Soviet forces recaptured it in September 1943, once again suffering heavy losses.

A pair of American soldiers approaches a group of Sicilians, one waving a U.S. flag. In the summer of 1943, Allied forces landed on Sicily to capture the island as a prelude to the invasion of the Italian mainland.

Southern France (Operation Dragoon; August 15, 1944)

After Allied troops were ashore in Normandy, a second invasion in the south of France was mounted in August 1944. On August 15 troops of the U.S. Seventh Army made an amphibious landing against light opposition on the French Riviera, while a British and American airborne force landed a few miles inland. French and Algerian troops landed the following day. German forces in the area began retreating northward.

Stalingrad, Russia (August 1942–January 1943)

The German Sixth Army and Fourth Panzer Army attacked Stalingrad on August 23, 1942, but met stiff Soviet resistance. The Germans did not reach the outskirts of Stalingrad until mid-September. By mid-November, despite heavy losses, the Germans had captured the city, which they had virtually destroyed by bombing and shelling. The Soviets, however, mounted a powerful and sustained counterattack, and the Germans soon had no avenue of escape. In mid-December, Soviet attacks halted a German relief operation 30 miles short of the city. More than 200,000 German soldiers died of starvation and from enemy action as the Soviets placed the

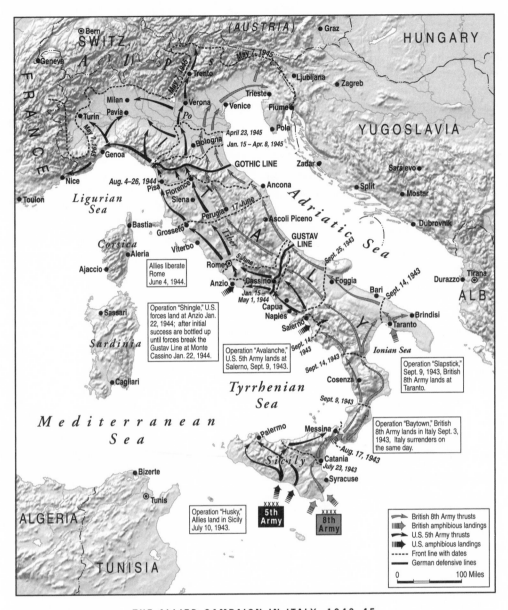

THE ALLIED CAMPAIGN IN ITALY, 1943–45

city under siege before capturing it, following a horrendous battle that involved house-to-house fighting. Stalingrad is considered the turning point of the war on the Eastern Front.

Tobruk, Egypt (June 1942)

Although Italian troops initially occupied Tobruk, on the North African coast, British forces took it and turned it into a major supply base. They rebuffed an attempt by Germany to retake the city in 1941, but in June 1942 Erwin Rommel's forces found the defenses at Tobruk much weaker than before, and the city fell to the Germans after a one-day battle on June 21. More than 35,000 British troops surrendered, and the Germans gained thousands of tons of supplies.

Tobruk remained in German hands until November 13, 1942, when they abandoned it after their defeat at El Alamein.

Tunisia (April–May 1942)

After failing to deliver a crippling defeat of the Allies at Kasserine Pass, Erwin Rommel's Afrika Korps retreated into northwest Tunisia. Although Rommel had left Africa and returned to Germany because of illness, his men put up a stubborn defense. Bizerte and Tunis fell to the Allies on May 7. Five days later, on May 12, the last Germans in North Africa surrendered, thus ending all Axis involvement in North Africa.

Warsaw, Poland (August–October 1944)

After Soviet troops reached the outskirts of Warsaw, Polish Resistance fighters rose up against the occupying German forces. The Germans sent SS forces to counter the rebellion. They wiped out the Resistance while the Soviets watched from a distance.

CASUALTIES

Determining exact casualties for specific battles and campaigns is difficult for a number of reasons, including different methods of accounting, lost records, and incomplete record-keeping by defeated units. Still, there is no doubt that the heaviest casualties occurred on the Eastern Front, where German losses were close to 1 million by the end of November 1941, and Soviet losses close to 3 million. Records for the Western Front are more precise—between D-Day and the German surrender, 263,000 Germans died, 49,000 were permanently disabled, and 8.1 million were captured (apparently including civilians), whereas the Allies suffered 186,900 dead, 545,700 wounded, and 109,600 missing. The table that follows lists losses for several battles of the European theater in decreasing order of severity.

Name of Battle/Date	Casualties (KIA, MIA, POW)*
Battle of Berlin/May 1945	1,500,000 (German: 1,000,000, Soviet: 480,000)
Stalingrad/November 1942–January 1943	1,000,000 (Axis: 600,000; Soviet: 400,000–600,000)
Sicily/July–August 1943	180,672 (Allied: 16,672 KIA; Axis: 164,000, of which 132,000 were Italian and mostly POWs)
Kursk/July 5–August 17, 1943	150,000 (German: 70,000 KIA/wounded; Soviet: estimated at roughly the same)
Ardennes (Bulge)/December 16, 1944–January 28, 1945	110,000 (German: 30,000 KIA, 40,000 MIA; American: 20,000 KIA, 20,000 MIA)
Normandy/June 6–August 14, 1944	75,000 KIA (German: 30,000, U.S.: 29,000, U.K./Canada: 16,000)
Crete/May 20–June 1, 1941	19,628 (German: 2,000 KIA, 2,000 MIA; British: 3,628 KIA, 12,000 POW)

*KIA = killed in action; MIA = missing in action; POW = prisoner of war

COMMANDO OPERATIONS

Although large-scale battles dominated the war in Europe, both sides conducted commando raids designed to create confusion in the enemy's rear and/or to destroy specific targets and gain intelligence. Here are details of the major commando raids, arranged alphabetically.

Location/Date	Details
Appennino, Italy/September 12, 1943	German commando team rescues the Italian dictator Benito Mussolini from a mountain redoubt where he was being held.
Bardia, Libya/April 1942	Raid by British commandos.
Beda Littoria, North Africa/June 7–8, 1942	British commandos raid what is thought to be the headquarters of German General Erwin Rommel. Rommel is not located and only two commandos return to Allied lines.
Benghazi, Libya/May 20–21, 23, 1942	British commandos attack airfields, railroads, and other targets around Benghazi.
Bordeaux, France/December 1942	British Royal Marine commandos paddle up the Garrone River to attack German ships at Bordeaux. Though the attack is successful, only two marines escape.
Boulogne harbor, France/1942	Two-man raid sinks a German ship with a limpet mine.
Boulogne, France/June 23-24, 1940	British commando raid near Boulogne–Le Touget meets with inconclusive results.
Budapest/October 1944	German commandos under Otto Skorzeny organize the capture of Hungarian Admiral Horthy to prevent his capitulation to the Allies.
Dieppe, France/August 19, 1942	Large-scale British commando raid with some Canadian and American participation: The attackers are detected and more than half of the 6,000-man force is killed or captured. Casualties are greatest among the Canadians. The Dieppe raid is an effort to test German coastal defenses and preparedness to resist a full-scale invasion.
Eban Emael, Belgium/May 10, 1940	Specially trained German airborne commandos land on the top of and capture the Belgian Fort Eban Emael.
Elojem, Tunisia/December 24, 1942	Detachment of American paratroopers jump behind enemy lines to attack and blow up a railroad bridge.
Flore, Norway/February 14–15, 1943	Norwegian commandos raid German ships.
Glomfjord, Norway/September 20–21, 1942	British commandos attack a power station for an aluminum plant.
Guernsey/July 14–15, 1940	British conduct a small raid on German garrison on Guernsey.

Location/Date	Details
Iran/June 1940	German commandos carry out operations against the Abadan oil refineries.
Island of Stord, Norway/January 23–24, 1943	The British and Norwegians attack a pyrite mine.
Lofoten Island, Norway/February and December 1941	British commandos raid Lofoten Island twice, attacking fish oil factories that produced glycerine.
Mayiop, Soviet Union/August 1942	German commandos seize Soviet oil fields and refineries.
Murmansk, Soviet Union/July 25, 1942	German "Brandenburg" special forces attack Soviet railroads leading out of Murmansk.
Sidi Bu Baker, Tunisia/December 26, 1942	German commandos attack and destroy a key bridge defended by French troops.
Spitzbergen, Norway/September 3, 1941	British commandos set fire to 450,000 tons of coal and 275,000 gallons of petroleum products.
St.-Nazaire, France/March 27–28, 1942	British commandos ram the gates of a German dry dock with an explosives-laden obsolete destroyer while a motor torpedo boat places explosives on the lock gates of the St.-Nazaire Basin, where the battle-ship *Tirpitz* is moored.
Vaagso, Norway/December 27, 1941	British commandos raid German headquarters.
Vagsey, Norway/December 27, 1941	British commandos conduct raids against shipping, warehouses, docks, and fish-oil plants.
Vemork, Norway/November 19–20, 1942	Royal Engineers attack a German "heavy water" plant.

CODE NAMES OF OPERATIONS

To preserve secrecy, Allied and Axis planners assigned code words to each operation. Here are the code names used for some European operations:

Name	Details
ACHSE	German plan to control Italy after the Italian surrender to the Allies
ALARICH	German plan to occupy northern Italy after a political collapse of the Italian Axis party
ALSOS	Allied intelligence plan to gather information about developments in German experiments with nuclear fission

Name	Details
ANTON	German occupation of southern France that took place after the Allied invasion of French North Africa and the collapse of the Vichy forces there
ANVIL	Original Allied plan to invade southern France. Later changed to DRAGOON
ARGUMENT	U.S. Army Air Forces plan for air operations against the German aircraft industry, beginning in February 1942
AUSLADUNG	German secondary attack near Tunis
AVALANCHE	Allied invasion of Italy at Salerno, September 9, 1943
BARBAROSSA	German plan for the invasion of the Soviet Union
BAYTOWN	British plan for invading Italy at Reggio di Calabria from Sicily
BIG WEEK	Series of intensified U.S. Army Air Forces attacks on German aircraft factories that kicked off Operation ARGUMENT
BLACKCOCK	British operations between the Meuse and Roer-Wrum Rivers in the spring of 1945
BLOCKBUSTER	Canadian II Corps offensive in the vicinity of Calcar-Udem-Xanten
BOLERO	1942 plan for a buildup of U.S. forces and supplies in preparation for a cross-Channel attack, combined with an air offensive against German targets on the European mainland
BRIMSTONE	Allied plan to capture Sardinia
BUFFALO	Allied plan to break out of the Anzio Beachhead
CAMEL	36th Infantry Division task force for the invasion of southern France
CITADEL	German operation to recapture the city of Kursk after it was taken by the Soviets
CARPETBAGGER	Allied name for clandestine operations using American and British aircraft to insert agents and resupply underground forces operating in Western Europe
CASANOVA	Diversionary operation by the U.S. 96th Infantry Division during operations in the vicinity of Metz
CENT	Allied word for the beaches of Sicily

Name	Details
CHESTNUT	Four airborne missions sent by British Field Marshal Bernard Montgomery to reinforce his army in Sicily
CLIPPER	British offensive against German forces in the Geilenkirchen salient
COBRA	Operation by the U.S. First Army to break out of the Normandy Beachhead
CROSSBOW	Allied air operations against experimental V-weapon sites
CROSSWORD	Allied covert operation conducted at the end of the war to induce Germany to surrender
DELTA	Used to identify the role of the U.S. 45th Infantry Division during the invasion of southern France
DIADEM	Allied offensive in Italy
DIME	The beaches at Gela during the Sicily invasion
DRAGOON	Final plan for the invasion of southern France, originally named ANVIL
ECLIPSE	Allied plan for early operations in Germany after the cessation of hostilities; originally named TALISMAN
ELIBOTE	German operation to capture the Kebir River dam during an offensive against French forces in Tunisia in January 1943
FELIX	1940 German plan to capture Gibraltar
FIREBRAND	Allied invasion of Corsica
FLASHPOINT	U.S. Ninth Army's crossing of the Rhine River as part of Field Marshal Montgomery's Operation PLUNDER
FLAX	Allied air operation aimed at German transports operating from Italy to Sicily and Tunisia
FRANTIC	U.S. Army Air Forces shuttle-bombing by English-based B-17s operating between their home bases in England and turnaround points in Italy and the Soviet Union
FRÜHLINGSWIND	German Fifth Panzer attack against Allied positions around Sidi Bou Zid during the North African Campaign in February 1943

(*continued*)

Name	Details
GARDEN	Ground portion of the Allied combined airborne/armor attack on key bridges in Holland
GOLD	Normandy beaches on which the British XXX Corps landed
GOLDFLAKE	Movement of Canadian I Corps up from Italy
GRENADE	Large-scale offensive by the British 21st Army Group from the Roer River to the Rhine
GYMNAST	Allied invasion of French northwest Africa
HARDIHOOD	Allied aid provided to Turkey in an effort to induce the country to enter the war
HERSTENEBEL	German plan for a withdrawal beyond the Po River
HUSKY	Allied invasion of Sicily
INDEPENDENCE	French offensive in the vicinity of Belfort, France
JOSS	Beaches in the vicinity of Licata, Sicily
KAPUT	Ninth Army operation along the Elbe River
KONSTANTIN	German reinforcement of the Balkans and Greece
KOPENHAGEN	German plan to seize the Mount Cenis Pass while attempting to take control of Italy after the Italian surrender
LEHRGANG	Evacuation of German troops to the Italian mainland after the Allied invasion of Sicily
LEVER	Allied operation in the vicinity of Reno, Italy
LUMBERJACK	Converging offensive of the U.S. First and Third Armies to trap Germans in the Eifel (a German mountain range) in the spring of 1945
MAGNET	Movement of the first U.S. troops into Northern Ireland in 1942
MALLORY MAJOR	Air offensive against bridges on the Po River in Italy
MANNA	British occupation of southern Greece

Name	Details
MARKET	Airborne phase of Field Marshal Montgomery's plan to capture bridges on the lower Rhine and advance into Germany in September 1944
MORGENLUFT	German attack against Gafsa during the North African Campaign in February 1943
NEPTUNE	Secret word used for the planning of actual operations of the Normandy invasion
NORDWIND	German offensive against the U.S. Seventh Army in Alsace in January 1945
OCHSENKOPF	German offensive operation in Tunisia in February 1943
OLIVE	Allied attack on the Gothic Line in Italy in September 1944
OMAHA	Normandy beach on which the U.S. Army V Corps landed during OVERLORD
OVERLORD	Allied landings in Normandy
PANTHER	British operation involving the crossing of the Garigliano River in Italy
PERPETUAL	Allied Eastern Task Force landings in North Africa
PLUNDER	Field Marshal Montgomery's plan for crossing the Rhine—it involved massive aerial and artillery bombardment and the largest airborne operation of the war
POINTBLANK	Combined Allied bomber offensive against Germany using long-range bombers based in England
PUGILIST-GALLOP	Allied attack to outflank the German Mareth Line in Tunisia
QUEEN	Operation conducted by 12th Army Group between the Wurm and Roer Rivers
RAINBOW	Collection of U.S. war plans that were developed prior to the U.S. entry into the war. Each plan was named for a color; the collection was published in October 1941
RAINCOAT	Allied assault on German positions around the Camino Hills in Italy
RESERVIST	American landings at Oran during the North African invasion
RETRIBUTION	Allied plan to prevent Axis forces from reaching Italy if they attempted to evacuate Tunisia

Name	Details
ROAST	Allied operations to clear Comacchio Spit, Italy
ROMEO	French commando operations at Cap Negre, North Africa
ROSE	Allied operations in the Ruhr in April 1945
ROSIE	French naval forces who landed in southern France
ROUNDHAMMER	Part of an early plan for a cross-Channel invasion of France
ROUNDUP	1943 plan for a cross-Channel operation in France
RUGBY	Allied airborne forces who jumped into southern France
SCIPIO	British Eighth Army attacks on Axis positions at Akarit wadi on April 6, 1942
SEELÖWE (Sea Lion)	Adolf Hitler's planned invasion of the British Isles. Sea Lion was canceled after the failure of the Luftwaffe to gain air supremacy during the Battle of Britain
SHINGLE	Allied amphibious landings at Anzio on January 22, 1944
SIEGFRIED	German plan to occupy southern France after the Italian surrender to the Allies
SITKA	Allied task force that captured the Mediterranean islands of Levant and Port Cros
SLAPSTICK	Landing by British paratroopers at Taranto, Italy, on September 9, 1943
SPARK (Iskra)	Soviet offensive to breach the German lines around Leningrad
STRANGLE	Allied air operation to interdict Axis supply lines in Italy
STURMFLUT	Field Marshal Erwin Rommel's attack against Allied positions around the Kasserine Pass and the Sibiba Gap
SUPERCHARGE	British breakout in Eygpt in November 1942; part of the Eighth Army's offensive in the Western Desert
SUPER-GYMNAST	Plan combining American and British plans for the invasion of French North Africa

Name	Details
SWORD	One of the Normandy beaches; SWORD was assaulted by the British Third Division
TALISMAN	Early plan for postwar Allied activities in Germany
TERMINAL	Allied operation in the harbor of Algiers on November 8, 1942
THESUS	German plan for operations in Libya in 1942
THUNDERBOLT	Allied offensive in the vicinity of Metz
TIDALWAVE (formerly SOAPSUDS)	Daring low-level attack by American B-24 Liberator heavy bombers on the Ploesti oil fields on August 1, 1943
TORCH	Allied invasion of northwest Africa, November 1942
UNDERTONE	Offensive by the U.S. Third and Seventh Armies to break through the West Wall and clear the Saar-Palatinate region and to secure a bridge-head east of the Rhine in the vicinity of Worms
UTAH	Normandy beach that was assaulted by the U.S. Army VII Corps
VARSITY	First Allied airborne army operation near Wesel, Germany, in support of Field Marshal Montgomery's Operation PLUNDER
VERITABLE	Operation by the Canadian First Army to clear the region between the Maas and Rhine Rivers
VULCAN	Final Allied offensive in Tunisia in May 1943
WINTERGEWITTER	German counterattack against the U.S. Army IV Corps on December 26, 1944
WOP	Opening attack by U.S. Army II Corps against Gafsa on March 17, 1943

Source: U.S. Army Historical Office

Military Organizations

The armies of both sides were organized along similar lines. On the Allied side, British and U.S. forces were organized into numbered "army groups" (for example, British Eighth Army, U.S. First Army), each of which was made up of divisions. The German Wehrmacht was organized the same way. Soviet forces followed a somewhat different scheme: they were organized into "fronts" named after specific regions of the country. The following tables list U.S., German, and British divisions and Soviet fronts and where they saw combat.

Division	Combat
First Infantry	Landed in North Africa and Sicily; moved to England for the Normandy landings
First Armored	North Africa, Sicily, Italy
First Air Division	Eighth Air Force heavy bomber unit
Second Infantry	Landed in Normandy and fought across Europe
Second Armored	North Africa, Sicily, Normandy, European campaigns
Second Air Division	Eighth Air Force heavy bomber unit
Third Infantry	North Africa, Sicily, Anzio, southern France, Germany campaigns
Third Armored	Landed in Normandy and spearheaded attacks across France
Third Air Division	Eighth Air Force heavy bomber unit
Fourth Infantry	Normandy, Battle of the Bulge, Ardennes, Germany
Fourth Armored	Normandy, France, Ardennes, Germany
Fifth Infantry	Normandy, France, Germany
Fifth Armored	France, Germany
Seventh Armored	Normandy to Germany
Eighth Armored	Germany, Holland
Eighth Infantry	Normandy, France, Germany
Ninth Infantry	Normandy, France, Germany
Ninth Armored	Ardennes, Alsace, Rhine; seized Ludendorff Bridge at Remagen, Germany
10th Mountain	Italy
10th Armored	France, Germany
11th Armored	France, Germany
12th Armored	France, Central Europe

Division	Combat
13th Airborne	Only U.S. division to see no action
13th Armored	France, Belgium, Germany
14th Armored	France, Central Europe
16th Armored	France, Belgium, Germany, Czechoslovakia
17th Airborne Infantry	Rhineland, Ardennes, Germany
20th Armored	Germany
26th Infantry	northern France, Rhineland, Ardennes, Central Europe
28th Infantry	Normandy, France, Germany
29th Infantry	Normandy, France, Germany
30th Infantry	Normandy, northern France, Alsace-Lorraine, Central Europe
34th Infantry	Italy
35th Infantry	Normandy, northern France, Rhineland, Ardennes-Alsace, and Central Europe
36th Infantry	Italy, southern France, Germany, Austria
42nd Infantry	France, Germany
44th Infantry	northern France, Rhineland, Central Europe
45th Infantry	Sicily, Anzio, southern France, Germany
63rd Infantry	France, Germany
65th Infantry	Germany
66th Infantry	northern France (many members lost in sinking of HMS *Leopoldville*)
69th Infantry	Rhineland, Central Europe
70th Infantry	Rhineland, Central Europe
71st Infantry	Germany

(*continued*)

Division	Combat
75th Infantry	Belgium, France, Netherlands, Germany
76th Infantry	Belgium, Germany
78th Infantry	Belgium, France, Germany
79th Infantry	Normandy, Belgium, Germany
80th Infantry	northern France, Belgium, Germany
82nd Airborne Infantry	Sicily, Italy, Normandy, Holland, Germany
83rd Infantry	Normandy, Brittany, Ardennes, Rhineland, Central Europe
84th Infantry	Ardennes, Rhineland, Central Europe
85th Infantry	Italy
86th Infantry	Central Europe
87th Infantry	France, Belgium, Luxembourg, Central Europe
88th Infantry	Italy
89th Infantry	Rhineland, Central Europe
90th Infantry	Normandy, France, Ardennes, Germany
91st Infantry	Italy
92nd Infantry	Italy
94th Infantry	Normandy, France, Germany
95th Infantry	France, Germany
97th Infantry	Germany
99th Infantry	Belgium, Germany
100th Infantry	France, Germany
101st Airborne Infantry	Normandy, Holland, Germany

Division	Combat
103rd Infantry	Belgium, Germany
104th Infantry	France, Belgium, Germany

GERMAN ARMY AND WAFFEN (ARMED) SS DIVISIONS (SELECTED)

Division	Combat
Afrika Korps (Fifth Light Infantry, 15th Panzer)	North Africa
Grossdeutschland Division	Romania, East Prussia
Hermann Göring Division	Sicily, Italy
Panzer Lehr	Normandy, Battle of the Bulge, Ruhr
First Panzer Division	France 1940
First SS Panzer Division (Leibstandarte Adolf Hitler)	Poland, Eastern Front, Low Countries and France, Battle of the Bulge (responsible for the Malmédy Massacre)
Second Panzer Division	Battle of France, Battle of the Bulge
Second Paratroop Division	Defended the French town of Brest
Second SS Panzer Division (Das Reich)	Eastern Front, France, Normandy (responsible for massacre of French civilians at the village of Oradour-sur-Glane)
Third Panzer Division	France 1940, Eastern Front
Third SS Panzer Division (Totenkopf)	France, Eastern Front
Fourth Panzer Division	Poland 1939, France 1940, Russia, Germany
Fifth Light Infantry/ 21st Panzer Division	North Africa
Fifth Panzer Division	France 1940
Fifth SS Panzer Division (Wiking)	Russia, Ukraine, Hungary
Sixth Panzer Division	Battle of the Bulge
Seventh Panzer Division	Belgium, France 1940, Eastern Front

(*continued*)

Division	Combat
Eighth Panzer Division	France 1940
Ninth Panzer Division	France 1940
Ninth SS Panzer Division (Hohenstauffen)	Holland, Germany
10th Panzer Division	France 1940, North Africa, Holland
11th Panzer Division	southern France, Western Front
12th SS Panzer Division (Hitler Youth)	Normandy, Western Front
15th Panzer Division	North Africa, Sicily
17th Panzer Division	Eastern Front
20th Panzer Division	Eastern Front
21st Panzer Division (formerly Fifth Light Infantry)	North Africa
24th Infantry Division	Poland, Eastern Front
33rd Waffen-Grenadier Division (also known as Charlemagne Division, made up of Frenchmen)	Eastern Front, Battle of Berlin
90th Light Infantry Division	North Africa
116th Panzer Division (Greyhound)	Western Front, Battle of the Bulge

BRITISH ARMORED AND INFANTRY DIVISIONS

Division	Combat
Coldstream Guards	France, North Africa, Italy, Normandy, Western Europe
First Infantry	Battle of France, 1940
First Airborne	Sicily, Italy, Arnhem
First Armored	North Africa
First Canadian Infantry	Sicily, Italy, Germany

Division	Combat
Second Canadian Infantry	Dieppe, Western Europe
Third Infantry	Battle of France, evacuated from Dunkirk, Normandy, Western Europe
Third Canadian Infantry	Normandy
Fifth Canadian Armored	Western Europe
Sixth Airborne Infantry	Normandy, crossing of the Rhine, Germany
Sixth Armored	North Africa, Italy, Po Valley
Seventh Armored	North Africa, Normandy, France, Germany
12th East African	Kenya
49th Infantry	Norway
50th Infantry	North Africa, Normandy, Western Europe
51st Highland Infantry	Normandy, France, Western Europe
56th Infantry (London)	Anzio, Italy
78th Infantry	North Africa
81st West African	Somalia, Ethiopia
82nd West African	Somalia, Ethiopia

SOVIET FRONTS

Division	Combat
First Baltic	Balkans, East Prussia
Second Baltic	Balkans
Third Baltic	Balkans
First Belorussian (White Russian)	Baltic, Poland, Berlin
Second Belorussian	Prussia, Berlin

(c o n t i n u e d)

Division	Combat
Third Belorussian	Minsk, Berlin
Bryansk (renamed Second Belorussian)	Moscow, Kursk
Central	Kursk
Don	Stalingrad
Karelian	Unknown
Leningrad	Leningrad
Northwest	Finland
Reserve	Moscow
Southeast	Stalingrad
Southern	Kursk
Southwest	Kursk, Volga, Ukraine
Special Baltic	Crimea
Steppe	Kursk
Transbaikal	Siberia
Transcaucasus	Caucasus
First Ukrainian	Ukraine, Prague, Poland, Berlin, Elbe
Second Ukrainian	Ukraine, Budapest, Vienna
Third Ukrainian	Ukraine, Belgrade, Vienna
Fourth Ukrainian	Carpathians, Sevastopol, Crimea, Czechoslovakia
Volkhov	Leningrad, Novgorod
Vornezh	Kursk, Vornezh
Western	Moscow, Kursk, Smolensk

The Battle of the Atlantic

Unlike the Pacific war, World War II in Europe was primarily land based, but control of the Atlantic and Mediterranean determined the Allies' ability to move supplies from the United States to Europe and to supply their forces in the field. The Battle of the Atlantic (1940–43) primarily involved the Allied effort to defeat the German U-boat (submarine) threat, but other battles saw the sinking of capital ships on both sides as well as actions by heavily armed raiders preying on merchant shipping.

Although Germany controlled most of Western Europe by mid-1940, the British Royal Navy was in control of the surface of the Atlantic. The Kriegsmarine (German navy) chose to raid shipping rather than battle the Royal Navy. German surface raiders such as the pocket battleship *Admiral Graf Spee* took their toll among Allied shipping in both the North and South Atlantic. The fall of France allowed Germany to establish submarine pens on the French coast of Brittany, thus extending its area of operations. By the time the United States entered the war in December 1941, U-boats were capable of operating all the way to the Caribbean and the Gulf of Mexico, and attacks on shipping soon became a regular occurrence right off the East Coast of the United States. Convoy tactics to protect

Ships of a convoy protected by vessels of the U.S. Coast Guard press on toward their destination, a British port. Seaborne supplies were vital to the survival of Great Britain, and marauding packs of German U-boats nearly succeeded in severing the lifeline from North America.

shipping, and the increasing availability of long-range radar-equipped patrol bombers to find and sink U-boats, decided the Battle of the Atlantic in the Allies' favor in early 1943. Nevertheless,

BATTLE OF THE RIVER PLATE, URUGUAY

After several weeks of successful commerce-raiding operations in the South Atlantic, the German pocket battleship *Admiral Graf Spee* encountered the British South America Division at the mouth of the River Plate off Uruguay on December 13, 1939. Although the *Graf Spee* was badly outnumbered, its superior firepower and speed made it a dangerous adversary. Commodore Henry Harwood divided his force, ordering the HMS *Exeter*, a heavy cruiser, to attack from one side, while two light cruisers, the *Ajax* and *Achilles*, would attack from the other, forcing the German captain to split his fire. German fire crippled the *Exeter*, but the German captain, Hans Langsdorff, ordered his crew to break off the battle, perhaps because he was confused after suffering a heavy blow to the head. He took his ship into the harbor of Montevideo, Uruguay. Since Uruguay was a neutral nation, the *Graf Spee* was not permitted, under international law, to remain longer than four days. With the British forces waiting outside the harbor, Langsdorff decided to scuttle his ship rather than surrender it or fight the British. Several days later, he committed suicide.

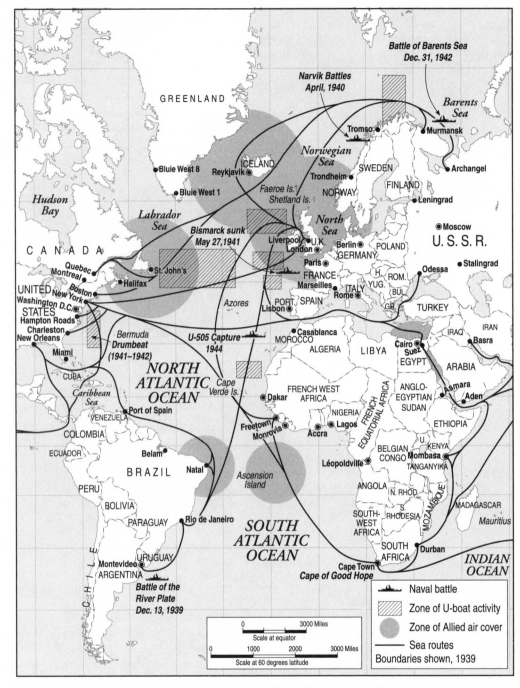

MAJOR NAVAL ENGAGEMENTS IN THE ATLANTIC

Battle of Barents Sea
Dec. 31, 1942

Narvik Battles
April, 1940

GREENLAND

Barents
Sea

Tromson

Murmansk

Bluie West 8

Reykjavik

ICELAND

Norwegian
Sea

SWEDEN

Archangel

Bluie West 1

Faeroe Is.
Shetland Is.

Trondheim

NORWAY

FINLAND

Leningrad

Hudson
Bay

Labrador
Sea

Bismarck sunk
May 27,1941

Liverpool

North
Sea

U.K.

London

POLAND

Moscow

U.S.S.R.

CANADA

Quebec
Montreal

St. John's

Berlin

GERMANY

Paris

Odessa

Stalingrad

Halifax

Boston

FRANCE

ROM.

UNITED

New York

Washington D.C.

STATES

Hampton Roads

Charleston

New Orleans

Azores

Marseilles

ITALY

Rome

YUG.

BUL.

GR.

TURKEY

IRAN

Lisbon

PORT.

SPAIN

Miami

U-505 Capture
1944

Casablanca

MOROCCO

Cairo

Suez

Basra

IRAQ

Bermuda
Drumbeat
(1941–1942)

ALGERIA

LIBYA

EGYPT

ARABIA

Asmara

Aden

CUBA

Caribbean
Sea

NORTH
ATLANTIC
OCEAN

Cape
Verde Is.

FRENCH WEST
AFRICA

Dakar

ANGLO-
EGYPTIAN
SUDAN

ETHIOPIA

Port of Spain

VENEZUELA

NIGERIA

COLOMBIA

Freetown

Monrovia

Lagos

Accra

FRENCH EQUATORIAL AFRICA

U.

KENYA

ECUADOR

Belam

BRAZIL

Natal

Ascension
Island

Léopoldville

BELGIAN
CONGO

Mombasa

TANGANYIKA

PERU

ANGOLA

N. RHOD.

MADAGASCAR

BOLIVIA

PARAGUAY

Rio de Janeiro

SOUTH
ATLANTIC
OCEAN

SOUTH-
WEST
AFRICA

S.
RHODESIA

MOZAMBIQUE

Mauritius

URUGUAY

Montevideo

ARGENTINA

SOUTH
AFRICA

Durban

INDIAN
OCEAN

Cape Town

Cape of Good Hope

Battle of the
River Plate
Dec. 13, 1939

0   3000 Miles
Scale at equator

0   1000   2000   3000 Miles
Scale at 60 degrees latitude

Naval battle

Zone of U-boat activity

Zone of Allied air cover

Sea routes

Boundaries shown, 1939

MAJOR NAVAL ENGAGEMENTS IN THE ATLANTIC

Germany continued to build and deploy large numbers of U-boats until the end of the war.

SHIPS AND ENGAGEMENTS AT SEA

The opening months of the war saw several engagements between Allied—mostly British—and German and Italian ships. The names of several ships became household words as newspapers around the world followed their operations.

ADMIRAL GRAF SPEE A German pocket battleship that raised havoc in the South Atlantic and Indian Ocean at the outbreak of the war, the *Graf Spee* was intercepted by British ships off Uruguay, and it took sanctuary in Montevideo, where it was scuttled and abandoned in December 1939. (See sidebar on p. 231.)

HMS ARK ROYAL Planes from the British aircraft carrier *Ark Royal* played a major role in the sinking of the German battleship *Bismarck* on May 27, 1941. A German submarine sank the *Ark Royal* on November 14, 1941.

BARENTS SEA, BATTLE OF (DECEMBER 31, 1942) Hoping to sink several ships, the German navy dispatched a surface task force to attack an Allied convoy sailing through the Barents Sea en route to the Russian town of Murmansk. The tenacious defense put up by the British destroyer screen prevented the Germans from attacking the convoy. German Admiral Karl Dönitz, realizing that the Allies were now able to defend against U-boat attacks, declared that Germany had lost the Battle of the Atlantic.

SINKING OF THE *BISMARCK*

The pursuit of the German battleship *Bismarck* was one of the most dramatic events of the war in the Atlantic. The ship was intended to be a giant commerce raider. Its maiden voyage occurred in early May 1941, when the *Bismarck* sailed toward the Denmark Strait accompanied by the heavy cruiser *Prinz Eugen*.

When aerial reconnaissance photographs revealed that the ship had sailed, the British organized a fleet of several battleships, cruisers, and aircraft carriers to intercept the two ships before they reached the Atlantic sea lanes. The British cruisers *Norfolk* and *Suffolk* made contact with the *Bismarck* and *Prinz Eugen* on May 23 and shadowed the pair during the night, attacking early the next morning. In the raging battle that developed, the *Bismarck* and *Prinz Eugen* sank the British battlecruiser *Hood* and severely damaged the *Prince of Wales*. Shells from the British guns damaged the *Bismarck*, and the German captain withdrew to the north, shadowed by the *Norfolk* and *Suffolk*. Toward nightfall the *Bismarck* turned and fired on the cruisers, creating a diversion for the *Prinz Eugen* to escape. Then the *Prinz Eugen* disappeared into the darkness.

The two cruisers kept radar contact with the *Bismarck* until the following morning, when the ship disappeared from their radar screens. Fearful that the German ship would reach the protection of port, the British organized a massive air-sea hunt to locate it. Late the next evening, the U.S. Coast Guard cutter *Modoc* spotted the battleship, and a U.S. Navy patrol plane on loan to the British was dispatched to search the area (at the time, the United States was still supposedly neutral; U.S. participation was kept secret).

The Consolidated PBY Catalina flying boat found the ship the next morning. Later in the day British torpedo aircraft from the carrier *Ark Royal* attacked the ship and scored two hits. One torpedo struck the *Bismarck*'s steering mechanism, knocking out the rudder and severely crippling the ship. The British battleship *Rodney* attacked the *Bismarck* again the following day and sent the now-helpless ship to the bottom of the North Atlantic.

The sinking of the *Bismarck* was a dramatic, high-stakes cat-and-mouse game that eliminated the pride of the German surface fleet. It was as much a psychological victory as it was a military success, and it demonstrated the weakness of large capital vessels such as battleships, which were vulnerable to a combination of air and sea power.

BISMARCK (MAY 1941) A large, powerful German battleship that the British navy was determined to sink, the *Bismarck* became the subject of a massive air-sea search that led to its interception and destruction. (See sidebar on p. 233.)

DRUMBEAT (DECEMBER 1941–EARLY FALL 1942) Immediately after declaring war on the United States on December 11, 1941, Germany began dispatching U-boats to seek out targets along the East Coast of the United States and in the Gulf of Mexico. Supported by long-distance supply submarines known as "milk cows," the small force of U-boats—never more than a dozen—wreaked havoc among Allied ships in U.S. waters with minimal cost to themselves. The development of convoy tactics, which offered greater protection to shipping and made detection of U-boats more likely, led to the termination of Operation Drumbeat, but its few months of operations cost the Allies almost 500 ships.

GERMAN MERCHANT RAIDERS In addition to naval vessels and submarines, Germany outfitted several merchant ships as armed, auxiliary cruisers known as "Q Ships" and sent them out against Allied shipping. Disguised as ordinary freighters, the raiders could sneak up on their unsuspecting targets and open fire. The table lists the most prominent German raiders:

Name of Ship	Tonnage Sunk	Ultimate Fate
Atlantis	145,697	Sunk November 1941 by HMS *Devonshire*
Komet	31,005	Sunk October 14, 1942
Kormoran	68,274	Scuttled after battle with Australian ship, November 1941
Michel	27,632	Took sanctuary in Japan

Name of Ship	Tonnage Sunk	Ultimate Fate
Orion	48,477	Damaged in air raid; retired
Pinguin	136,551	Sunk May 8, 1941, by HMS *Cornwall*
Stier	29,409	Sunk by U.S. Liberty Ship *Stephen Hopkins* on September 27, 1942
Thor	96,602—first voyage 56,037—second voyage	Burnt out after accident
Widder	58,644	Survived the war, became British prize

HMS GLORIOUS (JUNE 8, 1940) A British aircraft carrier, the *Glorious* was returning from the unsuccessful Allied action in Norway when the German battleships *Scharnhorst* and *Gneisenau* intercepted and sank it.

GNEISENAU The German battle cruiser *Gneisenau* was sister ship to the *Scharnhorst,* with which it participated in the invasion of Norway (where they sank HMS *Glorious*) and in commerce raiding in the North Atlantic. The two ships went into port at Brest, in occupied France, where they were watched closely and attacked repeatedly by the British Royal Air Force. On February 11, 1942, along with the *Scharnhorst* and *Prinz Eugen,* the *Gneisenau* made a daring daylight dash down the middle of the English Channel to make port in Wilhelmshaven, Germany. The ship was decommissioned in July 1942 after it suffered severe damage from RAF bombs.

USS GUADALCANAL (JUNE 1944) The *Guadalcanal* was an escort carrier that served as the flagship of Captain Daniel V. Gallery, commander of the U.S. Navy task force that captured the German submarine U-505 off the coast of Africa. (See sidebar on p. 235.)

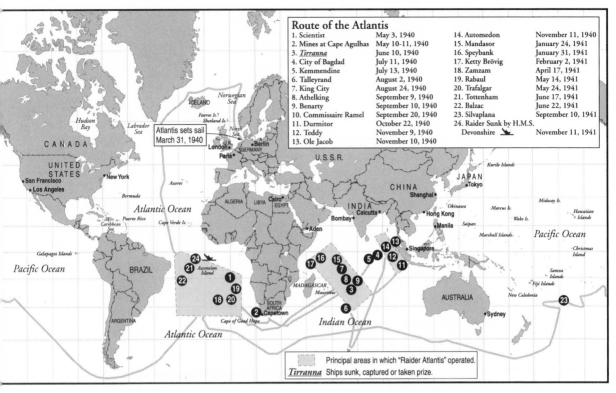

Route of the Atlantis

1. Scientist	May 3, 1940	14. Automedon	November 11, 1940
2. Mines at Cape Agulhas	May 10-11, 1940	15. Mandasor	January 24, 1941
3. *Tirranna*	June 10, 1940	16. Speybank	January 31, 1941
4. City of Bagdad	July 11, 1940	17. Ketty Brövig	February 2, 1941
5. Kemmendine	July 13, 1940	18. Zamzam	April 17, 1941
6. Talleyrand	August 2, 1940	19. Rabaul	May 14, 1941
7. King City	August 24, 1940	20. Trafalgar	May 24, 1941
8. Athelking	September 9, 1940	21. Tottenham	June 17, 1941
9. Benarty	September 10, 1940	22. Balzac	June 22, 1941
10. Commissaire Ramel	September 20, 1940	23. Silvaplana	September 10, 1941
11. Durmitor	October 22, 1940	24. Raider Sunk by H.M.S.	
12. Teddy	November 9, 1940	Devonshire	November 11, 1941
13. Ole Jacob	November 10, 1940		

Principal areas in which "Raider Atlantis" operated.

Tirranna Ships sunk, captured or taken prize.

TRAVELS OF THE NAZI COMMERCE RAIDER *ATLANTIS*

CAPTURE OF THE U-505

The German submarine U-505 was the first enemy warship that the U.S. Navy had captured on the high seas since the War of 1812. In May 1944, a U.S. Navy task force made up of the escort carrier *Guadalcanal,* commanded by Captain Daniel V. Gallery, and five destroyers set sail from Norfolk, Virginia. After patrolling off Africa, where Allied intelligence had determined a number of U-boats were operating, the task force had just turned north for a refueling stop in Casablanca, French North Africa, when it made sonar contact with a submarine.

A pair of F-4M Wildcat fighters were launched from the carrier, while the destroyers set up for a depth charge attack. From high above the clear water, the fighter pilots could see the silhouette of the submarine beneath the surface. They began making strafing runs over the spot to show the destroyers the submarine's location. A depth charge attack caused the German captain to decide to surface. The fighters continued to strafe while the deck guns of the U.S. fleet fired at the conning tower of the surfacing submarine.

Believing his ship was damaged beyond repair, the captain ordered his men to abandon ship, an order that the crew carried out so quickly that sailors failed to follow all the scuttling procedures and left the engines running. U.S. sailors from the destroyers boarded the still-running submarine, which the carrier towed until it transferred it to the care of an oceangoing tug, which towed it to the U.S. naval base at Bermuda. The U-505 is now on display at the Museum of Science and Industry in Chicago, an intact relic of the war and of submarine technology of the 1940s.

MATAPAN, MEDITERRANEAN SEA (MARCH 27–28, 1941) When the main Italian battle fleet sailed from its home port in Italy into the Mediterranean into battle, a British naval force set out and intercepted it off Cape Matapan, Greece. A five-minute gun battle inflicted heavy damage on the Italian fleet, which quickly returned to port and never ventured into Mediterranean waters again.

NARVIK, NORWAY (APRIL 10–13, 1940) Two sea battles early in the war off the Norwegian coast resulted in the destruction of a German flotilla of 10 destroyers. Every German ship was sunk or scuttled. The Allied victory allowed British and French troops to land and retake the town of Narvik, although it was soon abandoned because of the German invasion of France, which required forces to be pulled back from the Norwegian operation to defend the British Isles.

Narvik was an early attempt by the British to confront German power, but at this stage, the Germans still had superior forces.

SCHARNHORST (1940–DECEMBER 1943) The German battle cruiser *Scharnhorst* began its career in the invasion of Norway, then became a commerce raider with its sister ship, the *Gneisenau*. Damaged by Royal Air Force bombers while in port at Brest, France, the *Scharnhorst* suffered additional damage from mines in early February when it made a dash through the English Channel; it remained out of action until spring 1943. Repaired, the ship operated against Allied shipping in the North Atlantic. On December 26, 1943, the *Scharnhorst* single-handedly engaged a force of British ships, including the battleship *Duke of York*, in the Battle of North Cape. The *Scharnhorst* was sunk, and 1,864 men went down with it.

NAVAL ENGAGEMENTS

Naval engagements between surface ships occurred with some frequency during the early years of the war but declined as the German navy lost most of its surface fleet. The table that follows lists the more significant naval engagements of the European war.

Battle/Date	Participants	Commanders	Ships Sunk	Casualties
Battle of the River Plate/December 13, 1939	German: pocket battleship *Admiral Graf Spee* British: cruisers, *Ajax*, *Exeter*, *Achilles*	German: Langsdorff British: Harwood	*Admiral Graf Spee* scuttled	German: 37 killed, 50 wounded British: *Exeter*–61 killed, 23 wounded *Ajax*—7 killed, 5 wounded *Achilles*–4 killed
Narvik/April 9–13, 1940	British: Battleship *Warspite*, destroyers *Hardy*, *Hotspur*, *Havock*, *Hunter*, *Hostile* German: 10 destroyers	British: Admiral Whitworth, Captain Warburton-Lee German: Commodore Bonte	All German ships sunk or scuttled	Not available
Sinking of *Glorious*/June 8, 1940	British: aircraft carrier *Glorious*; destroyers *Ardent*, *Acasta* German: battleships *Gneisnau*, *Scharnhorst*	British: Captain D'Oyly-Hughes German: Admiral Marschall	*Glorious*, *Ardent*, *Acasta* sunk	British: 1,519 men lost

Battle/Date	Participants	Commanders	Ships Sunk	Casualties
Cape Matapan/ March 27–28, 1941	British: Battleships *Warspite, Barnham, Valiant, Fomidable*; cruisers *Orion, Ajax, Perth, Gloucester, Havock, Jervis, Nubian* Italian: battleship *Vittorio Veneta*; cruisers *Fiume, Pola Zara*; destroyers *Alfieri, Carducc, Garibaldi, Abruzzi, Trieste, Trento, Bozanoi*	British: Admiral Cunningham Italian: Admiral Iachinio	*Pola, Fiume, Zara*; two Italian destroyers	British: none Italian: 2,400 men
Pursuit of the *Bismarck*/May 1941	German: battleship *Bismarck*; cruiser *Prinz Eugen* British: battleships *Hood, Prince of Wales, King George V*; carriers *Ark Royal, Victorious*; cruisers *Suffolk, Norfolk*	British: Admiral Tovey German: Vice Admiral Lutjens	HMS *Hood, Bismarck*	British: 1,416 men on *Hood* German: 2,091 men on *Bismarck*
Stier—Stephen F. Hopkins/September 27, 1942	German: Q-Boats *Stier, Tannenfels* U.S. Liberty Ship *Stephen Hopkins*	German: Horst Gerlach U.S.: Captain Paul Buck	*Stier, Hopkins* both sunk	U.S.: 30 men lost, 30 more died in lifeboats while sailing to Brazil German: 3 KIA, 31 wounded
North Cape/ December 26, 1943	German: battleship *Scharnhorst* British: battleship *Duke of York*; cruisers *Belfast, Norfolk, Sheffield, Jamaica*	British: Admiral Fraser German: Admiral Bey	*Scharnhorst* sunk	German: 1,927 men went down with the ship; 36 survived to become POWs
Barents Sea/ December 31, 1942	German: pocket battleship *Lutzow*: cruiser *Hipper*; seven destroyers British: cruisers *Jamaica, Sheffield*; destroyers *Obdurate, Onslow, Achates,*	German: Vice Admiral Kummetz British: Rear Admiral Burnett	German: destroyer *Friedrich Eckholdt* British destroyer *Achates*	German: all hands on *Friedrich Eckholdt* British: 40 killed and wounded on *Onslow*, 100-plus lost with *Achates*

ALLIED SHIPPING LOSSES

Allied shipping losses were tremendous during the first years of the war as German U-boats and surface raiders roamed the seas. But by mid-1942, the British and U.S. navies had begun to develop effective convoy and antisubmarine tactics that resulted in a rapid decline in losses.

Year	Total Allied Losses* (Ship Tonnage)	German U-Boats	German Surface Raiders
1939	755,392	421,156	61,337
1940	7,805,360	3,801,095	277,028
1941	4,921,792	3,111,051	205,966
1942	6,266,207	6,266,207	325,086
1943	3,220,137	1,189,833**	7,040**
1944	1,045,629	N.A.	N.A.
1945	438,821	N.A.	N.A.

*Total is for all losses, including those to mines, aircraft, E-boats, and other causes.
**Submarine and raider losses for first three months of 1943.
Note: "Raider" losses include warships and converted merchant ships.

TIME LINE: THE BATTLE OF THE ATLANTIC

The Battle of the Atlantic raged from the beginning of hostilities until virtually the end of the war. This time line relates events during the crucial fight for control of the Atlantic sea lanes and the ultimate Allied victory.

1939

SEPTEMBER: The German navy dispatches U-boats and sinks the British passenger ship *Athena* on the first day of the war and the HMS *Courageous* about two weeks later. The British sink their first U-boat on September 14. The German

U-BOAT LOSSES

From the outbreak of the war through 1942, the German U-boats (*Unterseeboot,* German for submarine) inflicted a terrible toll on Allied shipping in comparison with their own relatively light losses. But as the war continued, the Allies developed ever more effective antisubmarine tactics, particularly the use of the long-range land-based Liberator bomber, to hunt down and sink submarines. From 1943 until the end of the war, life aboard a German U-boat was the most hazardous duty imaginable, and few U-boat crews survived the war.

Year	U-Boats Sunk
1939	9
1940	24
1941	35
1942	87
1943	237
1944	242
1945	151

surface raiders *Admiral Graf Spee* and *Deutschland* begin operations.

OCTOBER: HMS *Royal Oak* is sunk on October 13 in the anchorage at Scapa Flow off Scotland.

NOVEMBER: The German navy begins unrestricted submarine warfare. The *Gneisenau* and *Scharnhorst* go to sea to raid British shipping.

DECEMBER: The British and Germans fight the Battle of the River Plate in the South Atlantic off the coast of Uruguay. The *Graf Spee* is trapped in the harbor at Montevideo, and the captain

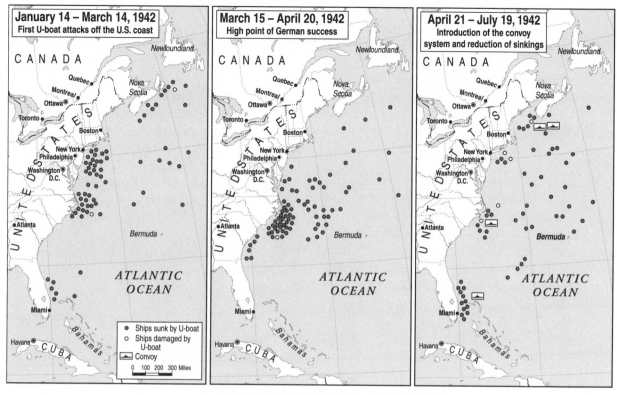

OPERATION "DRUMBEAT," 1942

decides to scuttle the ship rather than surrender to the British.

1940

MARCH: The German raider *Atlantis* embarks on her maiden voyage.

APRIL: Germany invades Norway, and the British Royal Navy destroys a German flotilla off Narvik on April 13.

MAY: The British evacuate Dunkirk, May 29–June 1. *Atlantis* claims its first victim: the British freighter *Scientist*.

JUNE: The *Scharnhorst* and *Gneisenau* sink HMS *Glorious* and two escorts on June 8.

JULY: British ships fire on the French fleet at Oran, North Africa. British ships engage the Italian fleet in the Mediterranean and sink the battleship *Giulio Cesare*.

SEPTEMBER: U.S. President Franklin Roosevelt signs an executive order on September 2 transferring 50 U.S. destroyers to the Royal Navy in return for leases on bases in British possessions. A U-boat "wolf pack" sinks 11 merchant ships from Convoy HX 72 on September 21.

OCTOBER: U-boats sink 20 ships from the 34-ship Convoy SC 7 on October 17–18, the "Night of the Long Knives." Royal Navy Swordfish torpedo planes attack Italian naval vessels at Taranto.

1941

JANUARY: The German raiders *Scharnhorst* and *Gneisenau* sortie against British shipping.

FEBRUARY: German U-boats, aircraft, and the cruiser *Hipper* make the first coordinated air, surface, and U-boat attack on British Convoy HG 53, sinking nine of 16 ships. The *Scharnhorst* and *Gneisenau* sink five ships on February 22.

MARCH: U-boats sink five ships on March 9 in the Atlantic Ocean. German raiders and U-boats sink 13 ships and capture three tankers on March 15. British ships sink several Italian ships in the Battle of Cape Matapan, March 27–28. German U-boats sink 43 ships in the Atlantic. The U.S. Congress approves the Lend-Lease Act.

APRIL: U-boats sink 45 ships in the North Atlantic. The U.S. Navy transfers ships from the Pacific to the Atlantic Fleet.

MAY: The Royal Navy loses HMS *Hood* in a battle with the *Bismarck* and *Prinz Eugen,* then pursues and sinks the *Bismarck*. U-boats sink 58 ships.

JUNE–JULY–AUGUST: U-boat successes against Allied convoys decline as convoy tactics become more effective. German Admiral Dönitz orders U-boats to avoid attacking U.S. ships.

SEPTEMBER: Allied convoys begin arriving in Soviet ports. Unaware that his boat had been depth-charged by a British patrol plane, the captain of U-652 fires three torpedoes at the USS *Greer* on September 4, provoking an incident that gave President Roosevelt the excuse to order U.S. Navy ships to defend convoys.

OCTOBER: U-boats attack U.S. destroyers on escort duty on October 16. A German torpedo sinks the *Reuben James,* a U.S. destroyer, killing 115 sailors.

NOVEMBER: A U-boat sinks British carrier HMS *Ark Royal.*

DECEMBER: German navy dispatches U-boats to operate off the U.S. East Coast after Hitler declares war on the United States.

1942

JANUARY: German navy sets January 13, 1942, as the opening date for Drumbeat campaign against Allied shipping off the U.S. East Coast, with tankers as the highest priority. On January 12, the British ship *Cyclops* becomes the first ship sunk in U.S. waters. Thirty-five ships are sunk before the end of the month.

FEBRUARY: Relief arrives for initial German U-boat force off North America. The *Scharnhorst, Prinz Eugen,* and *Gneisenau* make a daring dash down the English Channel on February 11–15.

MARCH: A U.S. Navy patrol plane off Newfoundland claims the first U-boat sinking by American forces on March 1. The Germans begin their campaign to capture Malta.

APRIL: Germany dispatches large "milk cow" submarines to resupply and refuel U-boats operating in U.S. waters.

MAY: U-boats sink 45 ships in the Gulf of Mexico alone. The British reinforce the strength of the Royal Air Force on Malta, reducing the threat to the island.

JULY: Germans attack Convoy PQ-17 after escorts are withdrawn by the British Admiralty. Only 11 of the 33 ships that left New York make port in England. Admiral Dönitz recalls U-boats from American waters and launches a new campaign in the North Atlantic.

AUGUST: The first relief convoy sent to Malta battles with German aircraft to reach the island. Despite heavy losses, five merchant ships arrive. British aircraft on Malta join with British submarines in the attack on German supply lines to North Africa.

SEPTEMBER: The German raider *Stier* attacks the U.S. Liberty ship *Stephen Hopkins,* which then sinks the *Stier* before it founders, in the South Atlantic. U.S. Navy begins using convoy tactics along the American East Coast.

NOVEMBER: Allied ships land U.S. and British troops in Northwest Africa.

DECEMBER: Allies resume convoys to the Soviet Union. British navy fights off attack on convoy by German surface ships in the Battle of the Barents Sea.

1943

JANUARY: Hitler orders the liquidation of the German surface navy and an increase in U-boat production.

MARCH: U-boats sink 21 of 40 ships in Convoy HX-229 in the North Atlantic. German ships, aircraft, and surface ships sink 97 ships.

APRIL: Allied losses to U-boats decline as new escort tactics are implemented. U-boat losses begin mounting.

MAY: Admiral Dönitz ends U-boat attacks on North Atlantic convoys because of heavy losses. The Battle of the Atlantic ends.

SEPTEMBER: Royal Navy commandos attack the German battleship *Tirpitz* with limpet mines.

DECEMBER: The *Scharnhorst* squares off against a British force in the Battle of North Cape on December 26. The Royal Navy sinks the *Scharnhorst.*

1944

JUNE: U.S. Navy task force captures U-505 (see below). Allied naval operations support D-Day landings.

NOVEMBER: RAF bombers sink the battleship *Tirpitz.*

THE MERCHANT MARINE

U.S. merchant shipping played the central role in ferrying men and materiel across the Atlantic from the United States to the British Isles. To better coordinate efforts, in February 1942 President Franklin D. Roosevelt established the War Shipping Administration, which took control of 131 U.S. operators of merchant shipping, recruited and trained personnel, and dealt with the labor unions representing the seamen serving aboard the Liberty and Victory ships.

During the first months of U.S. participation in the war, merchant ships were not armed and set out alone rather than in convoys.

Losses were particularly heavy in the North

"YOU BET I'M GOING BACK TO SEA!"
Register at your nearest U.S. Employment Service Office
U.S. MERCHANT MARINE
War Shipping Administration
MAN THE VICTORY FLEET

A 1942 poster encourages veterans of the U.S. Merchant Marine to return to sea and continue contributing to the war effort. It was not until decades after the war's end that former members of the Merchant Marine gained veterans status from the U.S. government.

Atlantic, as well as off the U.S. East and Gulf coasts. Almost 1,100 ships were lost in the North Atlantic in 1942 alone and it was soon learned that convoys were safer than solo travel. The run to the Russian city of Murmansk, the main supply port to the Soviet Union, was the most dangerous—the route exposed them to both U-boat and air attacks from German bases in Norway. In the summer of 1942 alone, 24 ships from a 35-ship convoy were sunk while en route to Murmansk. Because of news that the German battleship *Tirpitz* had sailed (which later proved to be false), the British Admiralty ordered the convoy's escorts to disperse, thereby making the ships vulnerable to attack.

German U-boats and surface raiders did not always win their sorties against the merchant ships. When the German raider *Stier* attacked the U.S. Liberty ship *Hopkins,* its crew put up such a valiant fight that the raider sank along with its victim. The *Stier's* sinking was attributed to the final actions of Midshipman Edwin O'Hara of the U.S. Merchant Marine, who fired the last five shells of the gun under his command and set fire to the German ship as his own ship was sinking.

In addition to transatlantic convoys, merchant mariners participated in all the Allied invasions of the war, and more than 5,600 merchant mariners died as a result of enemy action worldwide. More than 2,500 Allied merchant ships took part in the first wave of the Normandy invasion. U.S. seamen volunteered to sail 22 obsolete merchant ships across the English Channel to be sunk off the Normandy beachheads to serve as anchors for an artificial harbor.

Air Operations in Europe

Supremacy of the air was critical in almost all major engagements throughout the European theater. Both the Axis and Allied forces attempted to retain or achieve air supremacy in order to protect land-based forces from bombing and strafing. Whoever controlled the air also, ultimately, controlled the ground war. Germany controlled the skies over France in June 1940, but the Luftwaffe was unable to defeat the British Royal Air Force, and their loss in the Battle of Britain saved the British from a German invasion. By war's end, the Americans and British in the West, and the Soviets in the East, completely dominated the Germans—and, as a result, their armies were protected from German attack as they progressed through the heartland of Europe.

USES OF MILITARY AVIATION IN EUROPE

Military aviation developed rapidly in World War II and was used in many different ways. Powerful bombers devastated cities from England to Germany and the Soviet Union on a scale never seen before. Airpower was also used against shipping and submarines. Smaller fighters were used to protect British and American bombers on their runs deep into Germany, and they also engaged their counterparts in the Luftwaffe in dogfights over Europe. Aircraft were also used in a less dramatic but no less important area of simple transportation—the movement of men and materiel to staging areas and directly to the battlefield.

Air Transportation

The problems presented by combat and terrain in World War II were major factors in the rapid evolution of military air transportation between 1939 and 1945. The rapid tempo and often landlocked nature of conflict in the European theater created the need for reliable, safe, and speedy transportation of men and materiel over long distances. Both Axis and Allied forces used air transport for logistical purposes: airplanes could fly over impassable mountains, cross rivers, and operate in areas that had no roads or rail lines.

Although air transportation was costly and more dangerous than more traditional means of travel (in the early 1940s, airplanes were far less sophisticated pieces of machinery than they are today), it was rapid and versatile. Both sides used gliders and planes to facilitate airborne assaults because they could bypass heavily fortified areas and deliver paratroopers behind enemy lines, as was done in Normandy in 1944 and when Montgomery's forces crossed the Rhine River in 1945. Logistical air transportation moved critical aircraft parts and other materiel to combat units. The Allies also used the air to supply the French Resistance and other partisan movements, resupply beleaguered troops in isolated garrisons, and airlift critically injured troops to hospitals in the rear.

Air Assaults on Shipping and Submarines

The Allies in the European theater relied heavily on ocean transportation to supply their war needs. Great Britain was particularly dependent on open sea lanes across the Atlantic, and the Soviet Union, under the Lend-Lease agreements, began receiving convoys from the United States as well over the northern route through the Barents Sea. Germany's submarines and commerce raiders were formidable obstacles to safe shipping in the Atlantic, forcing the Allies to create air units that could attack German warships and, later in the war, cut supply lines between Italy and Africa.

The Allies developed specialized bombers and patrol planes to carry bombs, depth charges, rockets, and torpedoes against German sea power. They could patrol, provide cover for convoys, or be scrambled and directed to a particular location by ground-based equipment that intercepted radio communications. One early example that proved the worth of antishipping air patrols occurred in May 1941 when a Catalina flying boat detected the German battleship *Bismarck,* which had just sunk HMS *Hood.* After the carrier-based planes damaged the *Bismarck,* surface ships closed in and sank it. (See sidebar on p. 233.)

Airpower was also vital in the defeat of the German submarine forces in the Atlantic. Because aircraft early in the war had limited ranges and could not fly far out into the Atlantic, Allied convoys were unprotected in the air when they were in the mid-Atlantic region. By 1943, however, newer models of aircraft had greater ranges, and this, along with the development of better radar and depth charges, doomed the German U-boats.

Blitzkrieg Airpower

Blitzkrieg, the "lightning war" tactic that Germany used against Poland and France, required close coordination of air and ground assault forces. While the Luftwaffe made strategic bombing runs against industrial and military centers in the enemy rear, its tactical air units, mostly dive-bombers, worked closely with panzer divisions to strike quickly and fiercely against the front lines. The tactic was first used to great effect in the assault on Poland in September 1939. As the panzers advanced, they were accompanied by diving fighters, whose unmistakable high-pitched whine as they homed in on their targets created fear in the hearts of all who heard them. The Junkers Ju-87 Stuka dive-bomber was by far the most effective aircraft in the German arsenal; it could carry nearly two tons of bombs for use against enemy tanks, troops, and lines of communication. Regular army troops then mopped up and held the ground taken by the lead elements.

Blitzkrieg airpower was used again in the campaign in France in 1940 and in the early months of the invasion of the Soviet Union in 1941. Once the Germans had lost the battlefield initiative and were thrown back on the defensive (1943), the blitzkrieg airpower was no longer a tactical possibility.

Strategic Bombing

Strategic bombing involved the use of hundreds, sometimes thousands, of heavy bombers to drop high-impact explosives on the enemy's population centers. This type of bombing originally was aimed at industrial and military targets, but because the technology was imprecise, strategic bombing soon became wholesale area bombing.

The Allied strategic bombing campaign against Germany grew from a minor, imprecise harassment into an offensive program that rained bombs on Germany around the clock, devastating industrial and population centers alike. After initial daylight raids proved too costly, in the fall of 1940 the Royal Air Force's bombers switched tactics to nighttime bombing, which although imprecise, was less costly in terms of planes and crews. On the night of May 30, 1942, the new RAF Bomber Command launched the first "Thousand Plane Raid" against Cologne, Germany, and burned much of the city to the ground.

When the United States entered the war, it embarked on a program to produce thousands of planes and put its crews into position to mount a strategic bombing offensive. The Combined Bomber Offensive, which the Allies decided upon at the Casablanca conference in early 1943, gave the RAF the task of night bombing German cities, while by day the U.S. Army Air Forces struck oil refineries and factories deemed critical to the German war effort. The U.S. bombing of Schweinfurt in 1943 was a campaign to eliminate the ball-bearing industry concentrated in that city. It was painfully costly, with the loss of some 120 bombers. The United States also participated in area bombing, which was utilized to drop bombs over a much wider area than the precision daylight bombing raids conducted by the Americans. One such controversial air raid was on the city of Dresden in February 1945. It killed thousands of German citizens when the war was already nearing the end.

Jet Power

Although strategic bombing with four-engine behemoths and the buzzing of propeller-driven fighters characterized the air war in Europe, both sides made a concentrated effort to develop a new generation of military aircraft propelled by jet engines. German engineers saw jets, with their speed and agility, as the best bet for attacking Allied bombers. (However, Hitler stressed the use of jet engines in heavy bombers to attack ground forces and stifled the production of the smaller jet fighters until it was too late.)

Later in the war, as Allied and Axis forces demolished each other's oil production facilities, both sides tried to develop nonpetroleum fuels to power jets and rockets. German technology in this field was clearly superior to the Allies', but it was no match for the numerical superiority that the Allies enjoyed with traditional airpower: German jets just could not shoot down enough fighters and bombers to change the course of the war. At war's end, German technology, like other spoils of war, went to the victors, and Soviet, U.S., and British researchers exploited the Nazi-developed technology in rebuilding their air forces.

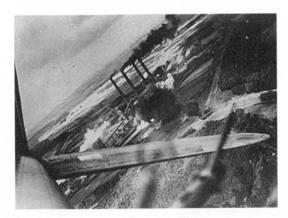

Taken from aboard a bomber of the British Royal Air Force, this photograph details an air attack against the Fortuna power station in Cologne, Germany, in August 1941.

ACES

No group captured the imagination of the public more than the young Axis and Allied airmen who managed to down five or more enemy aircraft in aerial combat. These were the airmen known as "aces." This table lists several of the most successful aces on both sides of the conflict.

Country	Name	# of Victories
Germany	Erich Hartmann	352
	Gerhard Barkhorn	301
	Guenther Rall	275
	Otto Kittel	267
	Walter Nowotny	258

Country	Name	# of Victories
Italy	Adriano Visconti	26
	Teresio Martinoli	22
	Leonardo Ferrulli	21
	Franco Lucchini	21
	Franco Bordoni Bisleri	19
Australia	Clive Caldwell	28.5
	C.C. Scherf	23.5
	Keith Truscott	17
	John Waddy	15.5
	Pat Hughes	14
Canada	G.F. Beurling	31.5
	V.C. Woodward	21.8
	H.W. McLeod	21
	W.L. McNight	15
	R. Bannock	11
France	Pierre Closterman	33
	Marcel Albert	23
	Jean Demozay	21
	Edmond Marlin la Meslee	20
	Pierre LeGoan	20
British Commonwealth		
South Africa	M.T. St. J. Pattle	51

Country	Name	# of Victories
England	James Johnson	38
Ireland	Brendon Finucane	32
South Africa	A.G. Malan	32
England	Robert Braham	29
England	Robert Stanford Tuck	29
England	F.R. Carey	28
Poland	Stanislaw Skalski	21
	Witold Urbanowicz	17
	Eugeniusz Horbaczewski	16.5
	Boleslaw Gladych	14
	Jan E. L. Zumbach	12.5
United States	Francis S. Gabreski	28
	Robert Johnson	28
	George E. Preddy	26
	Lance Wade (flew with RAF)	25
	John C. Meyer	24
USSR	Ivan N. Kozhedub	62
	Aleksandr I. Pokryshkin	59
	Grigori A. Rechkalov	58
	Nokolai Gulayev	57
	Arsenii V. Vorozheikin	52
	Kirill A. Yevstigneyev	52

AIRCRAFT PRODUCTION

Although aircraft losses were heavy on all sides, aircraft production replaced those lost in combat. The United States enjoyed a high production rate because its factories were out of range of enemy bombers and because its strong American economy allowed an almost limitless output of goods.

Country	Number of Aircraft Produced						
	1939	1940	1941	1942	1943	1944	1945
Germany	8,295	10,247	11,776	15,409	24,807	39,807	7,540
Italy	1,800	1,800	2,400	2,400	1,600	N/A	N/A
Great Britain	7,940	15,049	20,094	23,672	26,263	26,461	12,070
United States	5,856	12,804	26,277	47,836	85,898	96,318	49,761
USSR	10,382	10,565	15,735	25,436	34,900	40,300	20,900

MAJOR AIR BATTLES

Allied and Axis aircraft fought hundreds of battles during the war. Some were between bombers and attacking fighters and antiaircraft, while others were between fighters only. In many—if not most—instances, fighter battles were fought in conjunction with bomber attacks. The following are some of the major air battles fought in Europe from 1940 to 1945.

The Battle of Britain (July–October 1940)

The Battle of Britain (July 10–October 31, 1940) ultimately put a stop to German expansion in Western Europe. Hitler originally planned to whittle away at the Royal Air Force thereby giving the Germans air superiority during Operation Sea Lion, the proposed cross-channel invasion of Britain.

As the battle progressed, the Luftwaffe suddenly changed its tactics. It stopped attacking airfields and other military installations and instead began bombing industrial centers and,

finally, on September 7, the city of London. The Germans' goal was to crush the will of the British people so they would call for a truce. But the attacks inadvertently spared the RAF, allowing it time to regroup and replace its lost aircraft. By late September the intensity and scope of the air battle had diminished greatly because the RAF was on patrol in full force. British cities continued to be bombed nightly, but the Luftwaffe did not control the skies by day, and, as a result, an invasion was no longer practical. Hitler abandoned plans for an amphibious assault against Great Britain and turned his ambitions toward the Soviet Union.

> This is London, ten minutes before five in the morning. Tonight's raid has been widespread. London is again the main target.
> —Journalist Edward R. Murrow during the Blitz, October 10, 1940

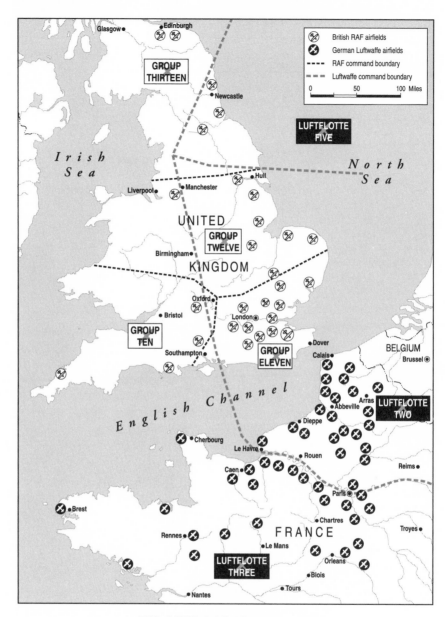

THE BATTLE OF BRITAIN, 1940

Regensburg/Schweinfurt (August–November 1943)

In the summer and fall of 1943, the U.S. Eighth Army Air Force mounted a series of air raids on the German cities of Regensburg and Schweinfurt. The most important target was the ball-bearing factory at Schweinfurt. Ball bearings were vital components of all kinds of machinery, including tanks and other military vehicles. The destruction of the ball-bearing facilities in Germany would, the Allies believed, seriously set back the German war effort.

Date	Targets	No. of Planes	Results	Losses–RAF	Losses–Luftwaffe
July 10, 1940	Shipping in English Channel	120 in largest formation, plus smaller harassing raids	Some airfields damaged, convoy attacked	6	13
August 8, 1940	Channel convoy	300 in 3 main attacks	2 ships sunk	20	31
August 13, 1940	Raids on several towns and airfields	1,485 German sorties	Damage to aircraft factories and some airfields	13	45
August 15, 1940	Airfields, coastal towns, some factories	Up to 800 planes throughout the day	Damage to some airfields	34	75
August 24, 1940	Airfields	700	Extensive damage to airfields	22	38
August 26, 1940	Factories and airfields	700	Airfields damaged, large railway junction destroyed	31	41
September 7, 1940	London and surrounding area	820	Damage to docks and gasworks	28	41
September 15, 1940	London	680	Bridges destroyed, residential areas hit	26	60
September 27, 1940	London, Bristol	1,200	Factories, aircraft production slowed	28	55
September 30, 1940	London, factories	830	Last mass daylight raids on London	20	48

The raids proved very costly to the Allies. In bombing runs on August 17 and October 14, 1943, the United States lost more than 120 B-17 bombers to German fighters and antiaircraft fire. More than 60 percent of all ball-bearing production in Germany was disrupted by these two raids, and aircraft production at Regensburg was also seriously disrupted, but the price was too high to pay for any return engagements to finish off the factories. Within a few months, the ball-bearing production was almost back to normal. Regensburg/Schweinfurt showed that strategic bombing could be effective but the resulting heavy losses were too high a cost.

Smoke billows skyward from the blazing docks area on London's Thames River. The British capital sustained the first of many heavy German air raids on September 7, 1940. Hitler hoped to break the will of the British people in preparation for a German invasion.

Battle of Berlin (November 1943–March 1944)

In the fall of 1943, the British began a series of major air assaults to cripple and destroy the German capital city of Berlin. Berlin had been bombed as early as 1940, but it was not until late 1943 as the Germans lost their advantage that massive raids could be launched that would, the British hoped, break the morale of the German people. The Allies' goal was to destroy the capital of Berlin and also to force German workers off the assembly lines to focus on rebuilding the city instead. The British bombed by night, flying through antiaircraft fire and the defense of German fighters, to drop their loads of bombs over the city. The raids continued on an intermittent basis until the spring of 1944, when they were halted in order to pull back all aircraft for the impending invasion of Normandy.

Military analysts and historians have debated the military effectiveness of the bombing of cities with large civilian populations for the bombings resulted in the destruction of almost all of the central part of the city and the deaths of tens of thousands of civilians. While some historians argue that the raids tied up thousands of workers who would otherwise have been used in war production or on the front, others maintain that the

Targeting the Enemy

Crossing the south coast [of England], we began descending in order to get in under the clouds and [to] sight over our course and target when the time came. The sky was full of airplanes, and below the water [was] covered with streams of surface vessels. Closing in on the French coast, we could see battleships belching fire from their shelling of the shore. Down on the water below, we saw landing craft leaving streaks of white-churned water behind. Down at this altitude, the assault force was in full view. We kept expecting to see German fighters as we neared the coast but so far so good. We had heard all along [that] we had mostly destroyed the airpower. We believed we were right.

Steady now as we approached the target. The bomb bay doors are opening. Bombs away. The bombardier says he believes we have a hit. Light flak coming up and getting more intense—out over the French countryside, scattered everywhere, were parachutes and patches of huge crashed gliders. I don't believe I saw an undamaged one in the lot. We had a sickening feeling that things were not going well, and it's just started.

We made a sweeping turn back towards the coast; formations were tightening, pulling back together, and [we] could see the aircraft everywhere and landing craft approaching the coast. Weather had improved some, but the sea looked terribly rough. We flew back over the sea full of vessels of our types, making our landfall over the chalk-white cliffs at Beachy Head. This is a prominent point on England's south coast, perfect for a landfall. . . . At our base, we headed for debriefing with a cup of coffee [from] the Red Cross truck. The mission had gone well, except for [the] loss of one aircraft and a crew at the base. Hope it saved some of our boys' lives by silencing these big guns.

The ships would be reloaded, and we would be making another trip with almost the same type of targets later in the day.

—The Eisenhower Center for American Studies Archives

raids on cities did not break morale but in fact may have strengthened it.

Berlin remained quiet for most of the remainder of 1944, but in early 1945, the United States joined the British—the Americans bombed by day and the British again by night. By the time the Allies entered the city in May 1945, little was left of Berlin. The beautiful capital of imperial Germany, with its Baroque architecture and elegant boulevards, had been reduced to a moonscape.

MAJOR AIR BATTLES

The following is a list of the major air battles that were waged over Europe between 1940 and 1945.

Date	Location	Description/Casualties
August 15, 1940	Britain	Largest day of the Battle of Britain. Germans claim 99 RAF aircraft; RAF claim 180 Germans. Actual losses are 30 RAF, 75 Luftwaffe.
April 5, 1943	Mediterranean/Operation FLAX	Allied fighters and B-25s launch major assault on German transports in Italy and Sicily. More than 200 German aircraft are destroyed, 40 in the air, against losses of 3 Allied aircraft and 6 missing.

Date	Location	Description/Casualties
August 1, 1943	Ploesti, Romania	USAAF B-24s attack oil fields; 54 bombers lost to fighters and flak. Axis aircraft losses unknown.
August 17, 1943	Regensburg and Schweinfurt	Eighth Air Force B-17s attack ball-bearing factories and are intercepted by German fighters. Sixty B-17s are lost; aerial gunners claim shooting down 288 German fighters, but that figure is probably exaggerated.
October 9, 1943	Münster	German fighters shoot down 29 B-17s; German losses 14 shot-down, 9 damaged.
October 14, 1943	Schweinfurt	Eighth Air Force B-17s attack; 60 B-17s are lost, mostly to fighters. U.S. gunners claim 186 fighters. Actual German losses are 38 fighters destroyed, 20 damaged. Eighth halts deep penetration missions into Germany.
January 11, 1944	Halberstadt-Oschersloben	USAAF P-51s escort Eighth Air Force bombers into Germany for the first time. Sixty bombers, mostly B-17s, are lost to German fighters; P-51 claim 15 fighters with no losses to themselves.
February 22, 1944	Germany	Eighth and Fifteenth Air Force bombers attack German targets in a major offensive known as "Big Week." Eighth loses 41 B-17s and B-24s, Fifteenth, 14; but escort fighters claim 60 German aircraft.
February 24, 1944	Gotha, Schweinfurt, Steyr	Eighth Air Force B-17s attack Schweinfurt while B-24s go to Gotha and 15th Air Force attacks Steyr. Twenty-eight B-17s and 33 B-24s are shot down; gunners claim 108 Germans. Escort fighters claim 37 Germans against 10 lost.
February 25, 1944	Augsburg, Regensburg, Stuttgart, Fürth	German fighters shoot down 64 U.S. bombers. Gunners claim "large numbers" of fighters.*
March 4, 1944	Berlin	The first major USAAF mission to Berlin resulted in the loss of 69 bombers and 11 escorting fighters. Aerial gunners claim 97 German fighters, while escort fighters claim 82.
March 8, 1944	Berlin	German fighters and flak claim 37 bombers and 17 fighters. U.S. fighters claim 87 Germans.
November 27, 1944	Germany	P-51s claim 98 Germans while losing 11 aircraft.
December 5, 1944	West of the Rhine	Four U.S. bombers lost, 90 German fighters claimed destroyed.
December 23, 1944	Germany	USAAF loses 31 bombers and 12 fighters; claims 84 German fighters.

Date	Location	Description/Casualties
January 1, 1945	Western Europe	More than 700 German aircraft attack Allied installations and destroy 156 airplanes.
January 14, 1945	Germany	Allied fighters claim 175 German fighters while losing 5 fighters and 9 bombers.
March 2, 1945	Berlin	Allied fighters and bomber crews claim 35 German fighters; Allies lose 6 bombers.
March 3, 1945	Germany	German jets shoot down 6 U.S. fighters and 3 bombers without loss.
March 18, 1945	Germany	German jets shoot down 24 bombers and 5 fighters.

*Note: Allied claims for the six days of "Big Week" were more than 600 German fighters, with one-third credited to fighters and two-thirds to aerial gunners.
Source: U.S. Army Air Forces in World War II

THE NIGHT WITCHES

The Soviet Union was the first country in the world to use female pilots in combat. The decision was based primarily on necessity, after Hitler's murderous assault had reduced USSR manpower by the millions. In 1942, Major Marina Raskova was assigned to form three regiments of women fighter pilots, with female mechanics, supply troops, and other support personnel.

Using a hodgepodge of antiquated biplanes and other fighters, the women bombed German positions, participated in dogfights, and provided cover for cargo transports. One of the most distinguished women fliers was Lily Litvak, the "White Rose of Stalingrad," who was credited with 12 enemy kills. At 22 she had survived three shoot-downs when a squadron of eight Messerschmitts attacked and killed her. Although her body was never recovered, a monument to her memory stands in Volgograd (formerly Stalingrad).

The 588th Night Bomber Regiment, which flew ancient Polikarpov PO-2 biplanes, became known as the Nachthexen, or Night Witches, a name given to them by the German soldiers against whom they flew daring night attack missions. Their mission was primarily psychological, because the PO-2s could carry only two 1,000-pound bombs. To avoid detection the female pilots would fly close to the German positions at high altitude and cut their engines, then make a gliding attack over the enemy lines. Unless radar detected them, the fabric-covered airplanes gave no warning until the sound of the wind in the rigging wires between the wings reached the ground. The women were often able to release their bombs, restart their engines, and make their way back over the Soviet lines at low altitude before the Germans could intercept them. The women of the 588th are said to have flown more than 24,000 sorties, dropping 23,000 tons of bombs.

THE TUSKEGEE AIRMEN

Still segregated in World War II but feeling political pressure to admit African Americans into all positions in the army, and facing a serious manpower shortage, the U.S. Army set up the 66th Air Force Flying School in November 1941 at the Tuskegee Institute, a black college in Tuskegee, Alabama. The first graduates were assigned to the 99th Fighter Squadron, which trained for combat under the command of Lieutenant Colonel Benjamin O. Davis. On May 31, 1943, the 99th arrived in Africa for combat as a "separate" (segregated) fighter squadron with the Northwest African Tactical Air Force. But the squadron was poorly prepared for combat, and its lack of discipline provoked the ire of veteran U.S. Army Air Forces pilots who had several months' combat experience in North Africa. After pilots from the 99th engaged fighters escorting a flight of German JU-88 ground attack bombers instead of going after the bombers, which where their primary targets, General Henry H. Arnold, commander of the Army Air Forces, received a report expressing dissatisfaction with the performance of the 99th.

When Arnold saw the report, he withdrew the 99th from combat operations. His decision attracted the attention of the White House, and the War Department held a hearing. Davis testified that while the other squadrons had been in combat for several months, the 99th was led by officers with little or no combat experience; furthermore, no replacements had come in for those lost in combat, and morale was low.

Davis's testimony saved the 99th and convinced the War Department to continue the training of black airmen at Tuskegee. During the war nearly 1,000 black aviators graduated from the school, won more than 850 medals, and destroyed 261 enemy planes. A new fighter group, the 332nd, was formed and sent to Italy under Davis; the 99th Fighter Squadron became part of the group. Tuskegee graduates cumulatively flew 15,553 sorties with the 12th Tactical and 15th Strategic Air Forces. Composed of four squadrons of Tuskegee graduates, the 332nd Fighter Group, known as the "Red Tail Angels," started out by flying ground support missions, then received P-51s and served as escorts—and became the only escort group never to lose a bomber to the enemy. Other graduates staffed a medium bomber group equipped with B-25s, but that group never went overseas.

The Tuskegee airmen proved that blacks could perform their duties with courage and skill, just as any other group in the military. Their success became an emblem for those African Americans struggling for equality.

TACTICAL AIRPOWER

While strategic bombing operations concentrated on factories and population centers, the Allied Tactical Air Forces provided troops with close-in support—by severing lines of communication and providing air cover for ground operations. Tactical airpower relied on bomb- and rocket-carrying fighter planes and light and medium bombers, such as the A-20 Havoc and B-26 Marauder, and was instrumental in the Allied successes in North Africa, Sicily, and Italy. It was also important in preparations for the D-Day landings.

Bombers systematically destroyed railroads, forward air bases, and tanks throughout the Normandy area in the months before June 6, 1944. After the successful landing in France, tactical fighters strafed the enemy positions and advancing ground columns, providing aerial artillery to frontline troops. After the Allied forces broke out of the Normandy beachhead, tactical air squadrons moved forward with the troops, using captured airfields or hastily fashioned airstrips.

The effectiveness of tactical airpower led General George Patton to comment that he didn't worry about his flanks because he could depend on General Pete Quesada's 18th Tactical Air Command to protect them. Allied ground forces on all fronts depended heavily on tactical air units to pound German defenses as they advanced. Although snow and fog temporarily

From 1942 until nearly the end of the war, the Allied Combined Bomber Offensive maintained constant pressure on Germany and German forces in the occupied countries. The following are some of the major air raids mounted against Germany and its interests in Europe between 1942 and 1945.

Date	Target	Units	Losses	Results
May 30–31, 1942	Cologne	RAF	41 planes lost to night fighters	Most of city center destroyed
July 24, 1943	Hamburg	RAF and B-17s from Eighth Air Force	Unavailable	Firestorm in city, 50,000 civilian casualties
August 1, 1943	Refineries at Ploesti	Units from Eighth and Ninth Air Forces	50 planes lost to antiaircraft and fighters.	Major damage to refineries
August 17, 1943	Schweinfurt and Regensburg	Eighth Air Force	60 bombers lost, 122 heavily damaged	Damage to aircraft factory at Regensburg
August 17, 1943	Peenemunde, V-2 launch facilities	RAF Bomber Command	69 heavy bombers lost	Severe damage to V-2 launch and production facilities
October 14, 1943	"Black Thursday," Schweinfurt again	Eighth Air Force	60 bombers lost, 138 damaged	Destruction of ball-bearing plants
November 18, 1943–March 31, 1944	Battle of Berlin 35 major raids of 500-plus aircraft	RAF Bomber Command	1,047 bombers lost during campaign	Considerable damage to city, loss of civilian morale
February 20–26, 1944 ("Big Week")	German aircraft production facilities	Eighth, Ninth, 15th Air Forces	226 bombers lost	Destruction of half of German fighter production facilities
March 11, 1944	Essen	RAF Bomber Command	Few losses	Oil and railroad facilities wiped out
February 13–14, 1945	Dresden	RAF Bomber Command and U.S. Army Air Forces	6 bombers	Firestorm that destroyed city, up to 135,000 civilian casualties

ALLIED AIRFIELDS IN ENGLAND, AND GERMAN RADAR SITES AND FIGHTER BASES IN EUROPE, 1943

grounded fighters during the opening days of the Battle of the Bulge in late 1944, clearing weather allowed tactical airpower to play a major role in the defeat of the Germans.

Ploesti, Romania

The Romanian oil fields at Ploesti were the major source of oil for Germany and Italy. If the Allies could cut oil production, the Axis would be short on much-needed fuel, which would aid the Allies in the campaigns planned for Sicily and Italy and would take some pressure off the Eastern Front. Colonel Jacob Smart of the U.S. Army Air Forces was in charge of planning Operation Soapsuds; the name was later changed to Operation Tidal Wave. Smart determined that a low-altitude attack would carry the element of surprise and would greatly increase bombing accuracy. Because of the distances involved, the Consolidated B-24 Liberator bomber was the only Allied aircraft capable of flying the mission. The three Eighth Air Force B-24 groups then in England were ordered to Africa to supplement the two that made up the Ninth Air Force Bomber Command under Brigadier General Uzal Ent.

A formation of 179 Liberators began taking off early on Sunday, August 1, 1943. One was lost in a takeoff accident, and another inexplicably plunged into the sea. The success of the attack

A U.S. B-24 Liberator bomber flies low over partially obscured installations of the oil refinery complex at Ploesti, Romania. On August 1, 1943, American planes mounted Operation Tidal Wave, a costly attempt to cripple the production of oil for the Nazi war machine.

heavy losses. The unprecedented low-level attack exposed the bombers to fierce antiaircraft fire, and losses exceeded 30 percent, with more than 500 airmen killed or missing. Five Medals of Honor were awarded to Ploesti airmen, three posthumously. The Ploesti raid damaged oil production facilities but did not knock them out. The 15th Air Force began an extended campaign in the spring of 1944 to use high-level bombing to flatten the refineries. Ploesti was finally taken out of the war when Soviet troops captured the region in August 1944.

Hamburg and Dresden, Germany

The firebombings of Hamburg (1943) and Dresden (1945) were the most destructive air attacks on civilian populations in the European theater. For four nights in July 1943, Allied heavy bombers pounded Hamburg, creating a firestorm that gutted 80 percent of the city. About 30,000 civilians died as a result of the Hamburg raids. On February 13–15, 1945, British and U.S. bombers hit Dresden, dropping several thousand tons of high-explosive and incendiary bombs. The resulting firestorm produced casualty rates similar to the Hamburg raids. The Dresden raid was among the most controversial air operations in Europe. Critics say the city had little strategic importance and at the time of the bombing was crammed with refugees fleeing the advancing Soviet armies. Advocates of the raid point out that Dresden was a legitimate target and that the western Allies needed to demonstrate support for their Soviet counterparts, who were less than 100 miles away.

was threatened when the lead plane, flown by General Ent and the 376th's commander, Colonel Keith Compton, turned for the target early. The lead pilot of the second element in the formation, 93rd Bomb Group commander Lieutenant Colonel Addison Baker, recognized the error. Seeing the refineries to the left of their path, he decided to turn toward the target, taking his group with him. Baker and his crew died when their burning Liberator crashed after he led his formation over the target.

All the groups on the Ploesti mission suffered

CHAPTER 8

Campaigns and Battles: Asia and the Pacific

W orld War II in the Pacific was fought from East and Southeast Asia to the shores of Hawaii, and from the frozen tundra of Alaska's Aleutian Islands in the north, through the tropical islands of the Central and South Pacific, to the doorsteps of the Australian continent. Japan dominated the first phase of the Pacific war, which started with the thunderous surprise attack at Pearl Harbor on December 7, 1941, that temporarily knocked out the U.S. Pacific Fleet. In those early months of the war, Japan's naval and armed forces swept to victory in the Philippines, Malaya, Singapore, Hong Kong, Wake Island, Guam, and the Netherlands East Indies (now Indonesia). Allied forces sustained heavy losses before they were able to slow the Japanese juggernaut in the spring of 1942.

The Pacific war was mainly an American war. The British fought to defend their colonies in Southeast Asia and valiantly attacked the Japanese in Burma; and the Australians committed thousands of troops to the effort in Asia and China. But it was the vast resources of men and materiel from the United States that ultimately crushed the smaller nation of Japan.

Of course, since military strategy also played a huge part in Allied victory, the United States embarked on a two-pronged strategy in its drive toward Japan. While one immense effort—largely supervised by the U.S. Navy—began against the Japanese in the Gilbert Islands in the Central Pacific, a second—largely organized by the army under General Douglas MacArthur—pushed northward and westward along the coast of New Guinea toward the Philippines. The two military machines ground through the Pacific, wresting the Gilberts, Marshalls, and Marianas from the Japanese in the Central Pacific, and New Guinea and the Philippines in the Southwest. At the same time, U.S. submarines decimated the Japanese merchant fleet, causing severe shortages of vital war materiel in Japan, while the U.S. Navy won a lopsided victory in the climactic Battle of Leyte Gulf. With the American victories at Iwo Jima and Okinawa, the Allies were at the gates of the Japanese homeland by early 1945.

In the final phase of the Pacific war, U.S. military might inflicted lethal wounds from land, sea, and air. A destructive air offensive, which relied on devastating firebombings of Tokyo and other major Japanese cities, instilled terror in the Japanese civilian population and left Japanese industry in shambles.

Finally, in August 1945, the crews of two U.S. bombers ended history's most destructive war by dropping atomic bombs at Hiroshima and Nagasaki. With his military reeling in defeat and his cities and industry in ruins, Emperor Hirohito told his countrymen that they would have to "endure the unendurable"—they would surrender, their dreams of conquest and the domination of Asia and the Pacific shattered.

> I have given serious thought to the situation prevailing at home and abroad and have concluded that continuing the war can only mean destruction for the nation and a prolongation of bloodshed and cruelty in the world. . . . . I cannot bear to see my innocent people struggle any longer. . . . The time has come when we must endure the unendurable.
>
> —Japanese Emperor Hirohito
> to his top government advisers
> after atomic bombs destroyed Hiroshima and Nagasaki,
> August, 15, 1945

The Pacific Theater

From the war's first days, when Japanese troops rushed down the jungle-clad Malaysian coastline, to the final year, when U.S. forces stormed heavily fortified island chains on the road to Japan, islands and jungles were the stage for bitter combat between Japanese and Allied soldiers. Japan had a hold on these jungles and islands early in the war. It wasn't until early 1943 that the United States saw success against the Japanese on land.

The U.S. Army and Marine Corps advanced across the Pacific in two giant offensives. To the south, General Douglas MacArthur led his forces over the Owen Stanley Mountains in New Guinea, through dense jungles to the northern coast and on to the Philippine Islands. Meanwhile, Admiral Chester Nimitz's Central Pacific drive consisted of a series of assaults against island fortifications whose names are now associated with images of valor and horror: Guadalcanal, Tarawa, Saipan, Peleliu, Iwo Jima, and Okinawa each exacted a bloody price for its seizure.

Only the United States could have mounted such an enormous endeavor. Armed by the continual flow of tanks, artillery, rifles, ammunition, trucks, and other items pouring out of U.S. factories, army, navy, and marine personnel shoved the enemy back more than 2,000 miles to their homeland and stopped only when the Japanese asked for peace.

The table that follows provides basic information about 12 crucial campaigns of the Pacific war.

Campaign	Allied Commander	Troops Engaged	Total Casualties	Japanese Commander	Japanese Troops Engaged	Total Casualties	Consequences
Malay Peninsula (December 1941– February 1942)	General Arthur Percival	140,000 (British)	138,708 (of which 130,000 were prisoners)	General Tomoyuki Yamashita	35,000	9,824	Great Britain lost control of Southeast Asia, and suffered great embarrassment when it had to surrender "invincible Singapore" to Japanese troops the British had deemed inferior.
Hong Kong (December 1941)	British Major General C.M. Maltby	12,000	4,400	Lieutenant General Takashi Sakai	18,000	2,754	Great Britain absorbed a blow to its prestige; Japan gained a valuable port in Southeast Asia.
Japanese invasion of the Philippines (December 1941–April 1942)	General Douglas MacArthur	120,000	120,000	Lieutenant General Masaharu Homma	43,000	Unknown	Japan controlled the Philippine Islands; the United States was at its lowest point in the war.
Netherlands East Indies (January– March 1942)	Major General Hein ter Poorten	125,000	15,958	Lieutenant General H. Imamura	50,000	900	Japan controlled the resource-rich Dutch East Indies.
Guadalcanal (August 1942– January 1943)	Major General Alexander A. Vandegrift	36,000	5,775, plus 4,900 Navy dead	Lieutenant General Haruyoshi Hyakutake	36,000	23,000	The Japanese advance into the Southwest Pacific was halted; security of U.S.-Australia line of communications ensured.
New Guinea (1942–44)	General Douglas MacArthur, General Sir Thomas Blamey	30,000	8,546	Major General Tomitaro Horii	Unknown	43,000	Australia was free from invasion; MacArthur possessed a staging area for his leap to the Philippines.
Tarawa (November 1943)	Major General Holland Smith	12,000	3,348	Rear Admiral Keiji Shibasaki	4,836	4,819 (17 prisoners)	The U.S. military learned valuable lessons on how to assault island fortresses.

Campaign	Allied Commander	Troops Engaged	Total Casualties	Japanese Commander	Japanese Troops Engaged	Total Casualties	Consequences
Marshall Islands (February 1944)	Major General Holland Smith	53,000	848	Rear Admiral Monzo Akiyama	13,500	11,900	The United States pushed Japan farther back toward its inner line of defenses.
Mariana Islands (June 1944)	Vice Admiral Raymond A. Spruance; Marine Lieutenant General Holland Smith	105,859	22,800	Lieutenant General Hideyoshi Obata; Admiral Chuichi Nagumo	55,208	55,208	The campaign led to the fall of the government of Hideki Tojo; handed the United States air bases from which to attack the home islands.
Return to Philippines (October 1944)	General Douglas MacArthur	202,500	62,000	General Tomoyuki Yamashita	327,000	320,000	Japan was cut off from valuable Southeast Asian resources; U.S. troops possessed a staging area for the assault on Japan proper.
Iwo Jima (February 1945)	Major General Harry Schmidt	60,000	6,821 dead, 20,000 wounded	General Tadamichi Kuribayashi	21,000	21,000	U.S. forces moved closer to the home islands; stricken B-29 bombers possessed an airfield upon which to land following bombing raids over Japan.
Okinawa (April– June 1945)	Lieutenant General Simon Bolivar Buckner	180,000	12,000, dead 38,000 wounded	General Mitsuru Ushijima	100,000	70,000 dead	Outside of China, Japanese forces now controlled only the home islands.

Sources:
John Costello, *The Pacific War, 1941–1945* (New York: Quill, 1982).
Norman Colmar and Thomas B. Allen, *World War II: The Encyclopedia of the War Years, 1941–1945* (New York: Random House, 1996).

MAJOR LAND BATTLES

The following are the major land engagements of the Pacific theater, including the South Pacific, Central Pacific, and the Asian mainland.

Attu and Kiska (May–August 1943)

As part of their complex Midway operation in 1942, the Japanese occupied Attu and Kiska in the Aleutian Islands of Alaska. This invasion of the islands, considered U.S. soil, outraged the American people, who demanded the expulsion of the Japanese.

On May 11, 1943, the U.S. Army's Seventh Infantry Division landed in two locations on Attu Island and advanced through the muddy, frigid terrain. For the next 15 days, army units forced the retreating Japanese into the island's northeast corner. Recognizing that defeat was unavoidable, the Japanese mounted a terrifying suicidal night attack on May 29, engaging in furious hand-to-hand combat until the Americans prevailed.

The Americans took prisoner 29 of the 2,600 Japanese who defended Attu in a battle that, in proportion to the number of troops involved, was the second most costly in the Pacific after Iwo Jima: 550 of 11,000 American soldiers participating in the operation died there.

The Japanese withdrew their garrison from Kiska in late July while thick fog shielded the operation from U.S. scout planes. When 35,000 American and Canadian soldiers rushed ashore on Kiska on August 15, they found an abandoned post.

Attu and Kiska were the northernmost territories occupied by the Japanese. Although they had little strategic value to the Japanese, their occupation was a psychological blow to the U.S. side in the early months of the war.

Bataan (January–April 1942)

The 30-mile-wide Bataan Peninsula along the western edge of Manila Bay, the Philippines—home to thick jungles, steep cliffs, and deep ravines—was meant to be the spot where General Douglas MacArthur's units would wait, following the Japanese invasion of December 1941, as the U.S. Navy transported reinforcements from the mainland. About 15,000 American and 65,000 Filipino troops evaded the Japanese elsewhere in the Philippines and poured into Bataan, but food, ammunition, and medical supplies soon ran dangerously low.

The Japanese offensive to capture Bataan opened on January 9, 1942. MacArthur's men fought valiantly, but after two weeks of repeated attacks by the Japanese, MacArthur pulled his men back to a new defensive line that stretched

---

FRANK HALL, FOX COMPANY, SECOND BATTALION, 21ST MARINE REGIMENT, THIRD MARINE DIVISION

Fighting the Japanese

Every time I ask myself what I am doing, strolling through the jungle, carrying a rifle, and hunting Japs, a little voice in my head asks: "Did you not rush over to 299 Broadway in New York City to sign up soon after the Japanese attack on Pearl Harbor?" I always answer yes, but it is all Red Meany's and Goldie's fault. They decide they want to join the marines and talk me into going with them. They both fail the physical, but I do not, and I wind up a marine. Red is now in the [Army] Air Corps learning how to fly a plane, and Goldie is in the SeaBees eating all that good chow, while I am looking for Japanese behind every bush.

We know there are several companies of Japs dug in just ahead of us. These are what are left of a battalion or more after our artillery worked them over this morning. Now we must find them and root them out of their foxholes. The problem is, what with the dense woods we walk through and the skill of the Japanese at camouflage, we cannot spot them until they shoot at us. This is very spooky.

The whole skirmish line, with scouts out in front, walks forward until the Japs open up. Then everybody hits the deck, in this case the mud, until the guys nearest to the shooting spot the Japs and wipe them out. As I walk along, I can barely see Louie behind me but can see no one else—we stay far enough apart so one mortar or grenade does not get more than one of us. I hear much crashing through the bushes, however, because this is no time to be subtle. We are attacking, and the Japs know it and are very determined to bump us off.

—Eisenhower Center for American Studies Archives

across the peninsula. When U.S. resistance temporarily stiffened along this line, Lieutenant General Masaharu Homma halted his offensive for two months and asked Tokyo to send reinforcements.

The lull handed the besieged American and Filipino troops a reprieve, but malaria, lack of supplies, and dwindling hope aggravated an already serious situation. After a five-hour bombardment on April 3, fresh Japanese reinforcements punched holes all along the thin American defensive line. On April 9, 12,000 U.S. and 63,000 Filipino soldiers on Bataan laid down their arms and surrendered. Some evaded capture and fled to the island of Corregidor, off the southern coast of Bataan, where they held out for another month. Those captured were sent by foot on a horrendous march to prison camps that killed thousands of Americans and Filipinos. The infamous "Bataan Death March" became a symbol of Japanese cruelty toward prisoners of war.

Burma (December 1941–April 1942)

The Japanese invaded Burma because it lay on their route to British India, which they hoped to conquer and occupy, and because it was a major Allied supply route to nearby China. A six-day bombing of Rangoon started on December 23, 1941, in preparation for a massive invasion by Japanese troops. They advanced from Thailand toward the city, easily overwhelming a series of British defenses. General Harold Alexander, the British commander, ordered his men to disappear into the jungles and join forces commanded by U.S. Major General Joseph Stilwell. Together, they were to mount guerrilla operations to harass the enemy.

Rangoon fell on March 2. By the end of April, Japanese troops had pushed into northern Burma and closed the Burma Road, the main Allied supply route to China. For the next two years, the Japanese controlled much of the region, although they were constantly harassed by American and British guerrilla campaigns mounted from jungle hideaways.

China-Burma-India Theater (February 1944–May 1945)

The first major Allied counteroffensive in Burma occurred in February 1944, when a unit known as Merrill's Marauders embarked on a series of commando operations to take the town of Myitkyina. Headed by Major General Frank Merrill, the 5307th Composite Unit (Provisional) plunged into the forbidding Burmese jungles to harass the Japanese. Resupplied by airdrops, Merrill's men battled leeches, 20-foot pythons, hunger, and unbearable heat in a successful drive to oust Japanese defenders from Myitkyina and help secure supply routes to China.

British forces also fought in Burma. Brigadier Orde Wingate's Chindits lived off the jungle as they sabotaged Japanese installations (see sidebar).

THE CHINDITS

The Chindits, named after an animal in an ancient Hindu myth whose statues guarded Burmese temples, were a brigade of guerrilla fighters who battled the Japanese in Burma. Made up of men from India, Burma, and Great Britain, and commanded by the brilliant yet eccentric Brigadier Orde C. Wingate, the unit harassed the enemy by attacking supply areas and communications lines and by destroying bridges and outposts. The Chindits melted into Burma's jungles for months on end, supplied mainly through aerial drops, and kept the Japanese off balance in Burma in 1943 and 1944, effectively tying up troops that could have been transferred to other parts of the Pacific.

Eventually, Wingate commanded three brigades called Long-Range Penetration Groups. In March 1944 he was killed in a plane crash in the Burma jungle. The Chindits proved that Allied soldiers could best the Japanese in jungle warfare.

In a separate drive, the British launched the second Arakan campaign to seize the Maungdaw Ridge in April 1944 and advance toward Akyab. A Japanese offensive against British bases at Imphal and Kohima in India, however, stopped Wingate's guerrillas.

The Japanese quickly surrounded the outnumbered British troops in India, but General William J. Slim turned them back. He maintained a steady flow of supplies by air, ordered heavy bombing sorties against Japanese concentrations, and dispatched relief forces to the area.

An American B-24 Liberator bomber is seen during an attack against Japanese bridges in Burma on January 27, 1945. After the U.S. aircraft departed, a destroyed bridge was photographed with its railroad tracks bent and twisted.

Slim then shifted to the offensive. After surprising their foe by crossing the large Irrawaddy River and swinging behind the Japanese, by March 1945 Slim's British forces controlled Mandalay. Slim then turned his attention south, and when British troops swept into Rangoon in May 1945, the Japanese had been ousted from Burma.

Corregidor (April–May 1942)

The Malinta Tunnel on Corregidor, an island off the Bataan Peninsula at the entrance to Manila Bay, provided shelter for the last group of American and Filipino survivors battling the invading Japanese. A one-month bombardment by the Japanese had softened Corregidor for their final attack. During the night of May 5–6, Japanese forces crossed over from Bataan (see pp. 261–262), fought through minor resistance at the beaches, and defeated the Allied troops. With the collapse of resistance in the Philippines, the Japanese controlled the Pacific from Hawaii to India.

Dutch East Indies (January–March 1942)

Because of its rich supply of precious resources, especially rubber and oil, the Japanese planned to conquer the Dutch East Indies, a 3,000-mile string of resource-laden islands north of Australia that now form most of the nation of Indonesia. They opened a three-pronged attack on January 11, 1942. In the next three months, one Japanese force seized the islands of Amboina and Timor and cut off communications and supply lines with Australia, a second attacked Borneo and the Celebes in the middle region, and a third group struck western Sumatra and Java. As occurred elsewhere in the Pacific during the early months of 1942, Japanese forces easily dislodged Allied opposition from the Dutch East Indies.

Guadalcanal (May 1942–January 1943)

On May 2–3, 1942, Japanese troops landed in the Solomon Islands, northeast of Australia. U.S. military leaders reacted quickly, because an airfield on the island of Guadalcanal and the proximity of the enemy threatened U.S. supply lines to Australia.

In early August, 11,000 marines landed at five different locations throughout the Solomons, including Guadalcanal, where they seized the airfield (Henderson Field) and established a defensive perimeter. For the next five months, U.S. and Japanese forces waged a bitter contest for control of Guadalcanal. The first battle occurred at the Ilu River on August 21. More than 1,000 Japanese charged straight into heavy marine fire and failed in their attempt to take the airfield.

On September 12 marines turned back a second offensive by 3,000 Japanese. Lieutenant Colonel Merritt Edson rallied his men on top of a ridge barely 1,000 yards from the airfield, and from there the surrounded marines held on. One hundred fifty marines and 1,500 Japanese died at Bloody Ridge.

Among the Guadalcanal marines, who had been fighting a determined enemy since August with few reinforcements, morale plunged as food supplies and ammunition dwindled. In late October, Admiral William F. Halsey rushed supplies to the marines and ordered his naval commanders to adopt a more aggressive stance. His efforts helped turn the tide. In late October the marines registered a victory at the Matanikau River. Gradually, the reinforced marines were able to enlarge the defensive perimeter, and by the end of the month they had eliminated the threat to Henderson Field. Recognizing that the fighting had turned irretrievably against them, the Japanese withdrew from Guadalcanal in January 1943.

Guam (December 8, 1941, and July 21, 1944)

An island in the Marianas chain in the Central Pacific, Guam was the setting for two invasions. On the same day that other Japanese forces raided Pearl Harbor, 6,000 Japanese troops overwhelmed the tiny American garrison of 500 men on Guam. After two days of fighting, the Americans surrendered.

Marine units commanded by Major General Roy Geiger returned on July 21, 1944, as part of a massive Marianas invasion that also targeted Saipan and Tinian. Fierce combat on the beach and inland preceded a suicide charge by 5,000 Japanese soldiers on the night of July 25–26.

U.S. Marines survey the bodies of dead Japanese soldiers littering a Guadalcanal beach after an abortive attempt to dislodge the Americans from strong defensive positions. Following a savage six-month struggle, Guadalcanal was secured by marines and troops of the U.S. Army in February 1943.

Hand-to-hand fighting broke the attack, and by August 10 the Americans held the island.

Hong Kong (December 1941)

After a weeklong bombardment, Japanese units advanced onto the British-held island of Hong Kong on December 18, 1941. The understrength British units attempted to stall the Japanese, but they could do little. The outlook deteriorated as the Japanese systematically reduced each pocket of British resistance. On Christmas Day, British forces surrendered. Hong Kong was the first defended British territory that the Japanese took in World War II.

Iwo Jima (February–March 1945)

Iwo Jima, an eight-square-mile island of sulfuric sand and ash only 700 miles south of Tokyo, had two airfields that could support the expected U.S. invasion of Japan and serve as emergency landing fields for damaged B-29 bombers as they returned from bombing runs over Japan. Japanese General Tadamichi Kuribayashi placed his 21,000 men in elaborate underground complexes tied together by miles of trenches to face the landing by 10,000 marines on February 19, 1945.

On the black sands of Iwo Jima, marines of the Fourth Division shell Japanese positions further inland. The marines landed on the island February 19, 1945, and suffered 6,000 casualties before Iwo Jima was secured more than a month later.

The initial wave scrambled out of amtracs (landing craft with the ability to crawl over sea obstacles) onto soft, black volcanic sand. The Japanese held their fire until the beach was choked with men and equipment. Then, in a mind-numbing barrage of Japanese fire, the marines suffered 2,400 casualties that first day, including 600 dead.

THE FLAG RAISING ON IWO JIMA

The battle to wrest the small volcanic island of Iwo Jima from the Japanese proved more difficult than American planners imagined. Most appalling was the number of casualties inflicted by enemy guns employed on Mount Suribachi, which dominated the island with its view from the southern tip. Taking fire from an almost invisible enemy that emerged from underground complexes, marines used hand grenades, satchel charges, and flamethrowers to move toward Suribachi's crest.

When they finally reached the top on February 23, a group of marines first raised a small American flag to signal to the men fighting on the beaches and elsewhere on Iwo Jima that they had reached the top. This tiny flag was difficult to spot from below, so Lieutenant Colonel Chandler W. Johnson ordered Private First Class Rene Gagnon to take a larger flag from the beach to the summit.

As Gagnon worked his way up Suribachi, five other marines joined him: Private First Class Ira Hayes, Private First Class Franklin Sousley, Hospital Corpsman John Bradley, Corporal Harlon Block, and Sergeant Mike Strank. The group attached the larger flag to a 20-foot piece of pipe and raised it for the entire island to see. Joe Rosenthal of the Associated Press stood off to the side where, with his camera, he recorded the historic moment. The photograph became the most reproduced picture of the war and one of the most lasting symbols of the American fight for freedom. Three of the six men who raised the flag—Strank, Sousley, and Block—perished on Iwo Jima.

If the marines were to clear the island and limit casualties, they had to scale Mount Suribachi on the southern end and remove the deadly Japanese mortars and artillery. Four days of bloody combat ensued. During the next few weeks the marines pushed the Japanese into Iwo Jima's northern end, where the Americans eventually wiped out all sources of opposition. The Americans finally declared the island secure on March 16, at a cost of 6,000 dead marines. Only 200 Japanese soldiers survived, the remainder having been killed in combat or by committing suicide.

The raising of the U.S. flag atop Mount Suribachi stands as one of the defining moments in the war. (See sidebar on p. 265.) The Associated Press photographer Joe Rosenthal captured the scene on film as marines raised a second flag, larger than one they had raised a few hours earlier, that was too small to be seen by troops elsewhere on Iwo Jima; his photograph, perhaps the most enduring image of the Pacific war, served as the model for the Marine Corps Memorial in Washington, D.C.

Malaya and Singapore (December 1941–January 1942)

On December 7, 1941, 60,000 Japanese troops of the 25th Army, commanded by Lieutenant General Tomoyuki Yamashita, landed in Malaya, intent on sweeping south to clear the Malay Peninsula and overrun the British island bastion at Singapore. Yamashita sent one force across the Kra Isthmus, then south along Malaya's west coast toward Singapore. A second group swept down the east coast with orders to meet the first group in front of Singapore for the final attack.

Many of the 88,000 British soldiers defending Malaya were poorly trained native units with inferior ammunition and equipment. Despite this, the British believed that they could hold out until relief arrived. Confident that no army would be foolish enough to invade through the swampy, jungle-infested Malay Peninsula, the British contended that Singapore, separated from the mainland by the Johore Strait, could never be taken, especially by what they regarded as inferior Asian troops.

The British were wrong. Yamashita's men swept down the Malay Peninsula in 70 days, often using bicycles to advance and willingly plunging into murky swamps to cut behind British defenders. Although the British stiffened their defenses, the Japanese readily broke through. Near the end of January, the British destroyed the narrow causeway connecting the island fortress with the mainland and withdrew into Singapore.

On February 8, Japanese soldiers crossed the Johore Strait after bombing the city. Within a week Yamashita, who earned the nickname the "Tiger of Malaya," had forced his foe to surrender. The entire surviving British garrison was marched into captivity. The loss of Singapore was a devastating blow to British morale and a triumph for the Japanese.

The Marianas (June 1944)

Americans expected tough fighting during the assault of the Marianas, a group of islands only 1,200 miles from Japan that could provide locations for air bases from which B-29 bombers could attack the Japanese home islands. Two marine divisions landed on Saipan on June 15, 1944. Following stiff opposition, most of Saipan was in American hands five days later.

A July 7 banzai suicide charge by Japanese troops did not surprise the Americans, but the ensuing civilian reaction stunned war-hardened marines. As marines inched closer to seaside cliffs and caves, thousands of men, women, and children jumped to their deaths or exploded hand grenades to kill themselves and their families. Japanese propagandists had warned them falsely that American soldiers would rape and murder indiscriminately.

After taking Guam in three weeks in late July, marines assaulted the island of Tinian and secured it by mid-August. Tinian became the main base for B-29 bombers attacking Japanese cities. The *Enola Gay,* the B-29 that dropped the atomic bomb on Hiroshima, took off from Tinian on its mission on August 6, 1945.

The Marshalls (February 1944)

The Marshalls were an important chain of Japanese-occupied islands in the Central Pacific that the Americans needed to take on their road to Japan. Kwajalein, an atoll in the Marshall chain, posed problems for attacking U.S. forces: nestled into its crags and bunkers were 8,700 defenders eager to fight for what was the major Japanese communications center for the Marshalls.

When army infantry and marines stormed ashore on February 1, 1944, however, the Japanese could not coordinate a successful defense because a preinvasion bombardment had destroyed their communications network. Within four days the Americans had secured Kwajalein Atoll, killing all but 35 of the defenders. On February 18, a combined army-marine force assaulted Eniwetok, an island in the northern Marshalls some 360 miles northeast of Kwajalein. More than 3,000 Japanese died defending the island, which the Americans secured by February 23.

New Guinea (July 1942–September 1944)

The island of New Guinea, north of Australia, provided the setting for some of the war's most difficult fighting. Stretching across the island's midsection, the practically impassable jagged peaks of the Owen Stanley Mountains rise 13,000 feet from the thick jungle foliage.

The Japanese landed troops at Buna on New Guinea's northern coast on July 21, 1942. Soldiers under Major General Tomitaro Horii immediately headed inland toward the Owen Stanleys and pushed the Australians across the mountains. Because the Japanese were losing ground elsewhere in the Pacific, Horii received orders to halt his drive when victory appeared in sight. Australian forces rebounded near the end of October and forced Horii to fall back on positions around Buna, Gona, and Sanananda.

In November, soldiers of the U.S. 32nd Infantry Division attacked Japanese strong points at Buna. The brutal fighting in humid, steamy swamps finally ended in a U.S. victory on December 14. Twenty miles to the north, Australian troops absorbed ghastly casualties in taking Gona, while a combined force of American and Australian soldiers drove against Sanananda. When the Japanese fell back to other positions at Lae and Salamaua to the northwest, Sanananda fell on January 22, 1943.

General Douglas MacArthur, the Allied commander in the Southwest Pacific, now turned to clearing the Japanese out of northern and western New Guinea. Salamaua fell on September 9, 1943, four days before Allied soldiers overran Lae. The two victories forced the remaining Japanese in the area into a peninsula on the island's northern coast.

On January 2, 1944, units of the 32nd Infantry Division landed near Saidor on the northern coast and seized its airfield. MacArthur then moved to protect his flanks by securing the Admiralty Islands, north of New Guinea. U.S. soldiers rushed ashore at Los Negros on February 29, 1944, and methodically pushed the Japanese out of the islands by the end of May.

MacArthur masterfully neutralized the opposition to clear the remainder of New Guinea. Aided by Allied intelligence, he bypassed many Japanese strong points to hit vulnerable areas to their rear. Fighting in New Guinea continued until late September, when MacArthur completed his conquest. In a remarkable campaign, he brought U.S. forces 1,400 miles closer to the Philippines and built support for plans to return to the scene of his 1941 retreat.

Okinawa (April–June 1945)

American strategists targeted the island of Okinawa, 700 miles from Japan and administratively a part of the Japanese home islands, as a location from which to sever the enemy supply routes to Southeast Asia. It was also yet another island from which the Allies could bomb Japanese cities with

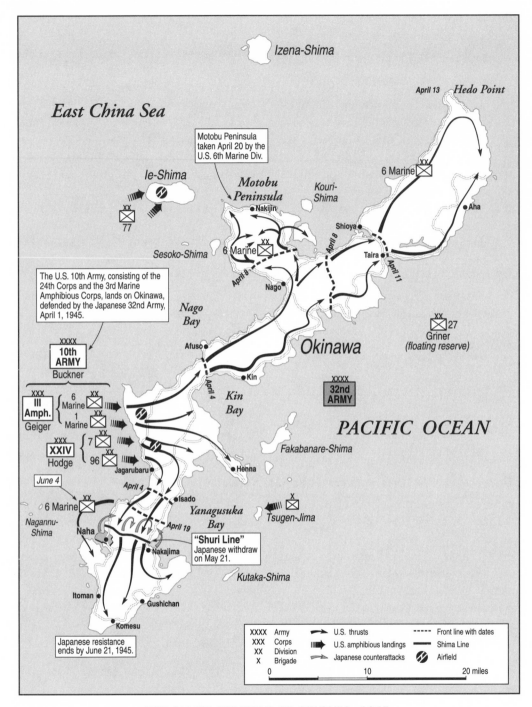

Izena-Shima

East China Sea

April 13   Hedo Point

6 Marine [XX]

Aha

Motobu Peninsula taken April 20 by the U.S. 6th Marine Div.

Ie-Shima

77 [XX]

Motobu Peninsula

Kouri-Shima

Nakijin

Shioya

April 8

6 Marine [XX]

Taira

April 8

April 11

Sesoko-Shima

The U.S. 10th Army, consisting of the 24th Corps and the 3rd Marine Amphibious Corps, lands on Okinawa, defended by the Japanese 32nd Army, April 1, 1945.

Nago

Nago Bay

Okinawa

27 [XX]
Griner
(floating reserve)

[XXXX]
10th ARMY
Buckner

Afuso

Kin

[XXXX]
32nd ARMY

[XXX]
III Amph.
Geiger

6 Marine [XX]

1 Marine [XX]

Kin Bay

PACIFIC OCEAN

[XXX]
XXIV
Hodge

7 [XX]

96 [XX]

Fakabanare-Shima

Jagarubaru

Henna

June 4

April 4

6 Marine [XX]

Isado

Nagannu-Shima

Naha

April 19

Yanagusuka Bay

Tsugen-Jima [X]

Nakajima

"Shuri Line" Japanese withdraw on May 21.

Kutaka-Shima

Itoman

Gushichan

Komesu

Japanese resistance ends by June 21, 1945.

XXXX	Army	→ U.S. thrusts	---- Front line with dates
XXX	Corps	▶ U.S. amphibious landings	—— Shima Line
XX	Division	Japanese counterattacks	Airfield
X	Brigade		

0   10   20 miles

THE ALLIED INVASION OF OKINAWA, 1945

Advancing U.S. Marines stride past the bodies of dead Japanese soldiers on Okinawa. More than 100,000 Japanese troops were killed during the fighting on the island, which lasted nearly three months in the spring of 1945.

Pearl Harbor (December 7, 1941)

This major U.S. naval base, located on the Hawaiian island of Oahu, was the site of the surprise Japanese attack of December 7, 1941, that brought the United States into World War II. Two waves of more than 350 Japanese aircraft swooped down in complete surprise on the hapless ships and men. Within hours, U.S. battleships either lay on the harbor's bottom or were enveloped in smoke from numerous bomb hits. The Japanese sank or damaged 18 ships and killed more than 2,000 U.S. sailors at the loss of 29 Japanese aircraft. (See sidebar on p. 270 for other military targets on Oahu that the Japanese attacked that day, as well as Chapter 2, "Causes of War," Chapter 5, "Politicians and Demagogues," and Chapter 6, "Officers and Soldiers.")

relative ease. Japanese General Mitsuru Ushijima stationed his 100,000 soldiers along three lines in Okinawa's southern portion, hoping to wear down the Americans as they fought among the slopes and ravines that peppered the terrain.

Two marine and two army divisions landed on April 1, 1945. While the marines veered north, the army turned to the south and met tougher resistance than the marines did. The marines eventually joined from the north, and the combined force dislodged the Japanese by early May.

Ushijima fell back to a second line of defense, where a litany of bloody encounters entered the pages of war history. Dakeshi Ridge, Wana Ridge, and Wana Draw evoke haunting memories of their own, but no battle produced more misery than that for Sugar Loaf Hill: in seven days of combat 2,662 marines were killed or wounded. Ushijima retreated to his final defense line on April 21. Army and marine troops finally forced the Japanese out by the middle of June.

Okinawa was the bloodiest battle of the Pacific. Almost 50,000 Americans were wounded or killed, and few Japanese survived.

> Yesterday, December 7, 1941—a date which will live in infamy—the United States of America was suddenly and deliberately attacked by naval and air forces of the Empire of Japan.
>
> —President Franklin D. Roosevelt
> in his December 8, 1941,
> speech to Congress

Peleliu (September–October 1944)

The First Marine Division and 81st Army Division landed on the southern beaches of Peleliu, an island in the Palau group east of the Philippines, on September 15, 1944. The small island, which was to be used as a base of operations for MacArthur's drive into the Philippines, hid coral ridges that offered the Japanese defenders superb natural fortifications. Marines and army infantry had no choice but to scale cliffs honeycombed with enemy bunkers to eliminate the positions. Seven brutal weeks of fighting in 105-degree heat finally cleared Peleliu's caves. The United States suffered 1,750 dead and 8,000 wounded, giving Peleliu the highest casualty rate of any amphibious landing during the war. Peleliu is considered one of the most controversial battles of the

PEARL HARBOR

Led by Captain Mitsuo Fuchida, 182 Japanese bombers, torpedo planes, dive-bombers, and fighters sped over the northern tip of Oahu in the Hawaiian Islands, veered right, flew down the west coast, and entered their final approach to the huge U.S. naval base at Pearl Harbor. It was Sunday morning, December 7, 1941. A peaceful calm greeted the raiders intent on destroying U.S. naval power in the Pacific; 94 ships floated leisurely at their moorings, including seven battleships along Battleship Row. At 7:49 A.M., Fuchida sent the coded message to headquarters, "Tora! Tora! Tora!" signaling that he had achieved a complete surprise.

Fuchida's torpedo planes peeled off, dipped low to skim the water's surface, and dropped their torpedoes into the water, aimed at the stationary ships dead ahead. Within moments Pearl Harbor was a blazing cauldron as every ship on Battleship Row absorbed hits. The *Oklahoma* capsized; the *West Virginia* and *California* settled to the harbor's bottom; the *Arizona* sank in a gigantic explosion that killed more than 1,100 of its crew.

Other components of Fuchida's first wave struck nearby airfields, barracks, and storage facilities. Japanese bombs systematically destroyed the U.S. aircraft that had been lined up in neat rows, wingtip to wingtip, to guard against sabotage. Such a formation, however, was disastrous, because it allowed the planes to be easily destroyed in an air attack. At Ford Island Naval Air Station only one U.S. aircraft managed to lift off the runway.

Less than one hour after the first Zeros (Japan's best fighter aircraft) hit Pearl Harbor, a second wave of 171 aircraft swooped down to complete the devastation. In the two waves, the Japanese destroyed 188 aircraft and damaged 159 more; sank or damaged 18 ships, including all eight battleships in the harbor; and killed 2,403 U.S. sailors and soldiers and wounded another 1,178. The cost to the Japanese was 29 aircraft and pilots, 5 midget submarines, and 1 large sub.

But the Japanese missed opportunities that would have handed them an even more stunning victory. They ignored oil storage tanks and repair facilities at Pearl Harbor, because they had failed to realize that without fuel or the ability to repair fighters and bombers, the United States might just as well have no ships. Japanese Admiral Isoroku Yamamoto had hoped to catch the valuable U.S. aircraft carriers at anchor, but all three had been out on missions—and these carriers proved crucial in turning the tide of the war against the Japanese only months later.

Yamamoto had not counted on the effect of the surprise attack on the American people. In his own words, he feared that Japan's attack had "awakened a sleeping giant." Americans rallied to the cry of "Remember Pearl Harbor!" and the smoldering wreckage at Pearl Harbor united the nation in a way that nothing else could have achieved. (See page 269, as well as Chapter 2, "Causes of War," Chapter 5, "Politicians and Demagogues," and Chapter 6, "Officers and Soldiers.")

Ammunition magazines aboard the destroyer USS *Shaw* erupt in a ball of fire during the attack on Pearl Harbor, December 7, 1941.

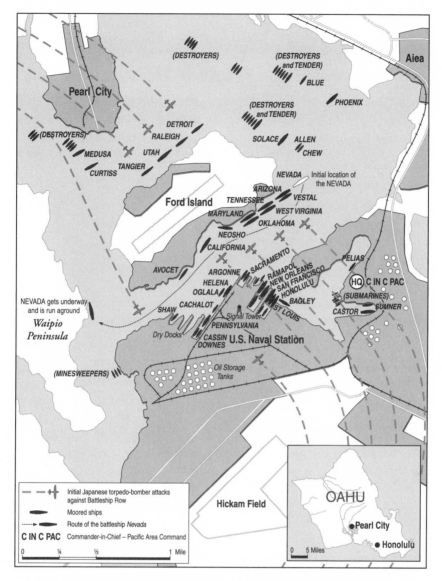

THE LAYOUT OF PEARL HARBOR ON DECEMBER 7, 1941

Pacific war, with some historians arguing that the operation was ill-conceived and was an unnecessary waste of life and resources.

The Philippine Invasion (December 1941)

Five hours after Pearl Harbor, more than 200 Japanese aircraft approached U.S. military installations in the Philippines. Because of the earlier strike against Hawaii, the Japanese avia-tors expected stiff resistance, but in a surprise even more astonishing than Pearl Harbor, they encountered none. Fliers dove on American bombers and fighters neatly arranged in rows and inflicted a second major blow to U.S. forces stationed in the Pacific. The commander of Allied forces in the Philippines, General Douglas MacArthur, lost much of his air capability in a matter of minutes.

On December 22, 43,000 Japanese soldiers under Lieutenant General Masaharu Homma landed at Lingayen Gulf, on Luzon, north of Manila. The Japanese army raced behind MacArthur's soldiers and closed in from the rear. At the same time a second invasion force landed 70 miles south of Manila at Lamon Bay and headed toward the capital. Caught in this predicament, MacArthur had no choice but to order a hasty retreat into Bataan to avoid being trapped by the two forces. After four months, all the forces on Bataan and the offshore island of Corregidor had surrendered to the Japanese.

The Philippines: MacArthur's Return (October 1944–March 1945)

Douglas MacArthur's campaign to free the Philippines entailed three operations—securing Leyte, a large island in the center of the Philippines; heading north into Luzon and freeing Manila; and driving south to clear other pockets of resistance. Because losing the Philippines would mean that Japan would be cut off from Southeast Asian oil and other products, Japan intended to wage all-out warfare to retain it.

Four divisions of the U.S. Sixth Army, commanded by General Walter Krueger, landed on Leyte on October 20, 1944. General Tomoyuki Yamashita placed his 70,000 men along Leyte's Central Mountains 30 miles away, from where he conducted an effective defense from well-concealed positions.

A large American drive stalled in the Ormoc Valley, but U.S. superiority in numbers and weaponry gradually wore down Yamashita's men. The Americans successfully repelled an attack in December 1944, then switched to the offensive and forced the Japanese out of the mountains. By the end of the month, the main operations on Leyte had ended.

For the fighting in Luzon, Yamashita stationed his men along the mountains that flanked MacArthur's likely route to Manila. Krueger's Sixth Army landed unopposed on January 9, 1945, but quickly slowed once it encountered Yamashita's determined men dug into the rugged hillsides. The struggle to take Manila lasted three months and produced thousands of casualties, including as many as 100,000 Filipino civilians killed by vengeful Japanese soldiers or

American artillery. Krueger finally gained control of the city in mid-March.

After Manila fell, U.S. forces assaulted 10 other locations spread throughout the Philippines to remove the last vestiges of Japanese strength. The entire Philippine invasion produced 62,000 American casualties, including 14,000 deaths, and 320,000 Japanese dead. The Japanese, cut off from their supply sources in the south and reeling in defeat elsewhere in the Pacific, could not hope to win the war after the loss of the Philippines.

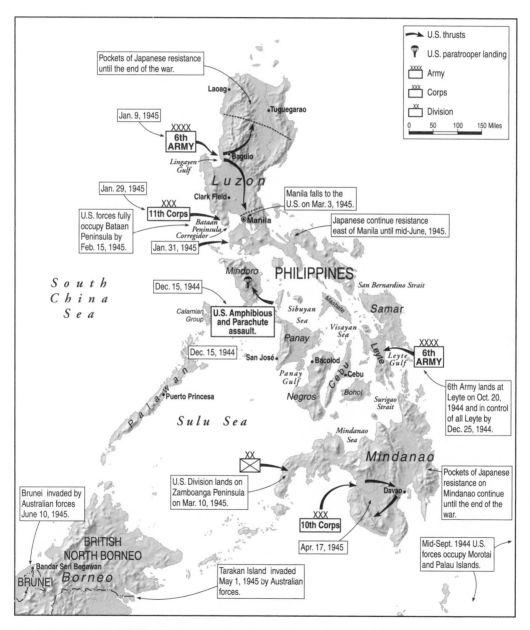

THE LIBERATION OF THE PHILIPPINES, 1944–45

MACARTHUR'S RETURN

From the moment he left the Philippines in 1942 on the orders of President Franklin D. Roosevelt, Douglas MacArthur made it his goal to return as quickly as possible. He argued that the United States had a moral obligation to liberate the Philippines from Japanese rule because the inhabitants had been so loyal to the United States. A successful reconquest of the region would also sever Japan's supply lines for the sorely needed oil and other resources of Southeast Asia.

Four divisions of the Sixth Army, commanded by General Walter Krueger, landed on the island of Leyte in the central Philippines on October 20, 1944. With the attack barely four hours old, General MacArthur, accompanied by the president of the Philippines, Sergio Osmeña, stepped into a landing craft for the ride toward Leyte's beaches. When the barge ran aground 50 yards from shore, an excited MacArthur readily jumped into knee-high water and waded ashore in front of a throng of cameramen who were present to record the moment. Like a Hollywood actor trying to perfect his scene, MacArthur repeated his walk a number of times so the cameras could capture it for posterity, then broadcast to the Filipinos that he had made good his vow to return.

"People of the Philippines, I have returned," uttered the general. "By the grace of Almighty God, our forces stand again on Philippine soil—soil consecrated by the blood of our two peoples. . . . Rally to me. . . . For your homes and hearths, strike! For future generations of your sons and daughters, strike! In the name of your sacred dead, strike!"

Osmena ended the episode in less dramatic fashion. He stuck a Filipino flag in the shore and announced that democracy had returned to his beloved land.

Making good on his promise to return, General Douglas MacArthur wades ashore on the Philippine island of Leyte in October 1944.

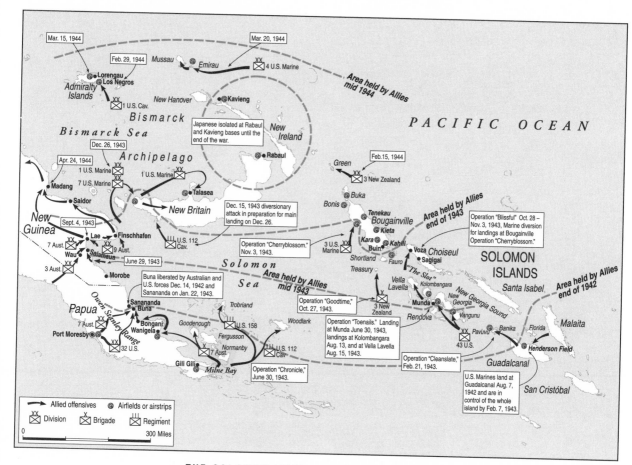

THE SOLOMON ISLANDS CAMPAIGN, 1942–44

The Solomons (1943–44)

With Guadalcanal secured, the Americans had to dislodge the Japanese from the other islands that made up the Solomons. Beginning in early 1943, Admiral William F. Halsey organized successful campaigns to seize Rendova, New Georgia, Kolombangara, and Vella Lavella. By late October he faced the last, and largest, island—Bougainville.

American forces rushed ashore on Bougainville on November 11, 1943. In some of the most bitter fighting since Guadalcanal, the Americans secured the island by March 1944. Their victory set the stage for the next phase in the American march to Japan—the invasion of other island groups in the Central Pacific.

Tarawa and Makin Assaults (November 1943)

The U.S. assaults of Tarawa and Makin, islands in the Gilbert chain 2,500 miles southeast of Hawaii, showed how difficult it would be to defeat Japan. Forced to wade 700 yards through deadly fire when the amphibious tractors ferrying them could not climb over a surrounding coral reef, many of the 5,000 marines who attacked Tarawa on November 20 never made it to shore. By the end of the first day, 1,500 marines were dead or wounded; it took three days of bitter fighting before the island was declared secure. The frightful carnage in taking Tarawa shocked the American

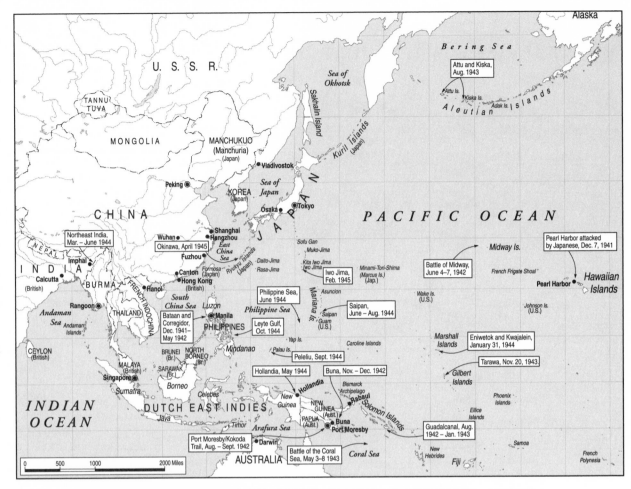

MAJOR ENGAGEMENTS IN THE PACIFIC THEATER OF OPERATIONS, 1941–45

public and warned that hard times lay ahead in the Pacific war. The landings at Tarawa also provided valuable lessons for future amphibious landings.

At the same time, army units assaulted Makin Island to the north. Four days of combat wrenched the island from the Japanese but not before a Japanese submarine sank the escort carrier *Liscombe Bay*, killing 642 sailors.

Wake Island (December 1941)

Defended by 502 U.S. military personnel and situated 2,300 miles west of Hawaii, Wake Island was the scene of a courageous American battle against overwhelming odds. After bom-

barding Wake for four successive days, the Japanese sent an invasion force toward the beach on December 11. After U.S. artillery and marine fighter aircraft hit one cruiser and sank two destroyers, the Japanese turned away without attempting to land.

Newspapers in the United States heralded the victory, but the battle was far from over. On December 23 a more potent invasion flotilla disgorged 2,000 crack Japanese troops, who quickly overran Wake's defenses and forced the Americans to surrender. With the conquest of Wake, the Japanese hoped to move farther eastward to take Midway Island, thus expanding their reach well into the North-Central Pacific.

MAJOR NAVAL BATTLES

The watery terrain of the Pacific islands meant that mighty sea battles were the milestones of the Pacific conflict. Aircraft, launched from carriers that never saw the enemy targets, delivered much of the devastation. In these actions, as in other Pacific fighting, U.S. factories handed a decisive advantage to the American military by producing an overwhelming stream of ships and aircraft. Listed below chronologically are some of the major naval battles of World War II.

Name/Date	Commanders	Casualties	Consequences
PEARL HARBOR December 7, 1941	U.S.: Admiral Husband E. Kimmel Japanese: Vice Admiral Chuichi Nagumo	U.S.: 18 ships sunk or heavily damaged; 200 aircraft destroyed; 2,403 killed, 1,178 wounded Japanese: 5 midget submarines destroyed; 29 aircraft destroyed; 64 killed	The United States entered World War II; Japan attained temporary naval dominance in the Pacific.
JAVA SEA February 27, 1942	U.S.: Dutch Admiral K.W.F. M. Doorman Japanese: Rear Admiral Takeo Takagi	U.S.: 5 cruisers and 6 destroyers sunk Japanese: 1 destroyer damaged	The Japanese gained control of the approaches to the Netherlands East Indies.
CORAL SEA May 7–8, 1942	U.S.: Rear Admiral Frank Jack Fletcher Japanese: Vice Admiral S. Inouye	U.S.: 1 carrier sunk, 1 destroyer sunk Japanese: 1 carrier sunk, 2 carriers damaged	United States halted the Japanese invasion of Port Moresby and secured the approaches to Australia.
MIDWAY June 3–6, 1942	U.S.: Rear Admiral Raymond A. Spruance Japanese: Admiral Isoroku Yamamoto	U.S.: 1 carrier sunk, 1 destroyer sunk; 307 dead Japanese: 4 carriers sunk, 1 cruiser sunk; 3,500 dead	Japanese navy lost 4 irreplaceable carriers and numerous pilots; the tide in the Pacific war began shifting to the United States.
PHILIPPINE SEA June 19–21, 1944	U.S.: Rear Admiral Raymond A. Spruance Japanese: Admiral Jisaburo Ozawa	U.S.: 130 aircraft lost, 76 men killed Japanese: 3 aircraft carriers sunk; 476 aircraft lost, 450 aviators killed	Japanese naval strength, especially her experienced carrier aviators, suffered irreplaceable losses.
BATTLE OF LEYTE GULF October 23–25, 1944	U.S.: Admiral William F. Halsey, Rear Admiral Clifton Sprague, Rear Admiral Jesse Oldendorf Japanese: Admiral Jisaburo Ozawa, Admiral Takeo Kurita, Admiral Kiyohide Shima, Admiral Shogi Nishimura	U.S.: 1 light carrier, 2 escort carriers, 3 destroyers sunk; 200 aircraft lost; 3,000 men killed Japanese: 4 aircraft carriers, 3 battleships, 6 cruisers, and 12 destroyers sunk; 10,000 men killed	Japanese naval power was decisively crushed; the path to Japan was now open to an American assault.

Sources:
John Costello, *The Pacific War, 1941–1945* (New York: Quill Books, 1982).
James F. Dunnigan and Albert A Nofi, *The Pacific War Encyclopedia* (New York: Checkmark Books, 1998).

TURNING POINTS IN THE PACIFIC LAND CAMPAIGN

Five Pacific land campaigns were turning points in the war with Japan advancing the Allied effort to defeat an enemy that had so swiftly piled up victories in late 1941 and early 1942: New Guinea, Guadalcanal, Tarawa in the Gilbert Islands, the China-Burma-India theater, and the Marianas.

New Guinea

The first campaign occurred in the dense jungles of New Guinea, north of Australia, where Australian and U.S. soldiers battled the Japanese, jungles, rivers, mountains, and wild beasts in 1942. Invincible to date, Japan now turned its forces toward New Guinea's Port Moresby and toward the continent of Australia. Should Australia fall, Great Britain would forfeit a valuable portion of its empire, and the United States would lose a priceless base.

While Australian civilians and U.S. military strategists waited tensely, the bitter fighting on New Guinea seesawed for much of 1942 and 1943. For a moment, Japanese soldiers advanced to within 30 miles of Port Moresby, but by September 1943, Allied troops had forced Japan back across the Owen Stanley Mountains and away from Australia. They had avoided a catastrophic defeat, and the United States could embark on its gigantic buildup for the march across the Pacific.

Guadalcanal

Another threat to the U.S. supply lines to Australia developed in 1942, when Japan started to build an airstrip on Guadalcanal in the Solomon Islands. Both sides immediately recognized the importance of Guadalcanal—if it fell to the Japanese, Australia and the supply lines to that continent would be in danger; if the Americans held it, the path to the Japanese bastion of Rabaul in New Britain lay open. Five months of harsh fighting produced a U.S. victory that laid the groundwork for succeeding triumphs.

Tarawa

With the threat to Australia extinguished, the American effort veered northeast to the Gilbert Islands. Though small in comparison to other Pacific battles, the invasion at Tarawa, the first U.S. assault against a heavily fortified, small Japanese-held island, yielded significant lessons that altered the procedures for future island assaults and saved lives. U.S. military planners studied the November 1943 invasion of Tarawa and concluded that the preinvasion bombardment had to be longer and carried out with more potent shells; that they needed more amtracs, the landing craft with the ability to crawl over sea obstacles; and that they needed to assemble an overwhelming force.

The carnage at Tarawa helped alert U.S. civilians to the realities of Pacific combat. Images of dead marines bobbing in Tarawa's waters and of destroyed vehicles littering the beaches stunned the nation. Bloody Tarawa, as it came to be called, also taught valuable lessons to military strategists.

China-Burma-India theater

Meanwhile, in the China-Burma-India theater, U.S. and British commandos halted a Japanese effort to interrupt supply routes to China. Troops commanded by Major General Frank Merrill, called Merrill's Marauders, ousted Japanese defenders from the town of Myitkyina in August 1943, while British commander Orde C. Wingate and his Chindits harassed Japanese concentrations elsewhere in Burma. The two groups ensured that American supplies continued to pour into troubled China, which was partly occupied by millions of Japanese troops, and they tied down elements of the Japanese army that could have been deployed in other parts of the Pacific. Had Merrill and Wingate failed, China might have been removed as a force in the war, a development that would have freed Japanese soldiers to fight elsewhere.

Marianas

The June 1944 attack on the Mariana Islands—Saipan, Tinian, and Guam—heralded the U.S. advance into the inner line of Japanese defenses. By taking these islands, U.S. bombers could hit Japan from airfields on Saipan and Tinian and thus bring the war home to Japanese civilians. The loss of such a crucial stronghold in Japan's Pacific defenses so stunned the Japanese people that Prime Minister Hideki Tojo resigned.

The following are descriptions of the major naval engagements of the Pacific theater.

Coral Sea, Battle of the (May 7–8, 1942)

Partly in reaction to the April 1942 Doolittle air raid against Japan, which stunned the Japanese military and public, the Japanese dispatched three naval groups to the Southwest Pacific to support new operations in New Guinea. In this potent armada were the small carrier *Shoho* and the aircraft carriers *Shokaku* and *Zuikaku*, accompanied by two heavy cruisers and six destroyers.

The Japanese felt confident of success, for their intelligence picked up no signs of U.S. aircraft carriers. Unknown to them, however, Admiral Chester W. Nimitz, commander of naval forces in the Pacific, had rushed two carriers—the *Yorktown* and *Lexington*—to the South Pacific.

Both carrier task forces entered the Coral Sea in early May. On May 7, a Japanese pilot spotted the U.S. tanker *Neosho* and its escorting destroyer *Sims* and directed an attack on the targets. Both ships sank in the action. Later in the day American aircraft sank the carrier *Shoho*.

The battle resumed on May 8. Although American aircraft failed to sink either of the remaining Japanese carriers, U.S. pilots caused enough damage to keep both carriers out of the war for two months. The Japanese would sorely miss the two vessels during the coming battle at Midway.

In the meantime, Japanese torpedoes slammed into the *Lexington* and a bomb hit the *Yorktown*, but both limped away from the battle. The *Lexington* was abandoned and sank later in the day. The *Yorktown* survived to fight again, while both the *Zuikaku* and *Shokaku* missed the fighting at Midway because of repairs and heavy aircraft losses. The Battle of the Coral Sea gave a slight edge to the Americans. They also proved they could meet and face down a substantial Japanese naval force.

Guadalcanal Battles (August–November 1942)

While U.S. marines and Japanese soldiers battled on Guadalcanal for three months in late 1942, their navies participated in a series of slugfests for dominance of the waters surrounding the island. The Japanese landed the first punch. In the early morning hours of August 9, seven cruisers and one destroyer led by Admiral Gunichi Mikawa raced down the Slot, the narrow channel that rests inside the Solomon Islands, and hit Allied forces near Savo Island. Superb Japanese night gunnery and accurate torpedoes ripped into five surprised Allied ships that prowled the waters off Savo. The Australian cruiser *Canberra* and three American cruisers— the *Quincy, Vincennes,* and *Astoria*—were sunk, and the cruiser *Chicago* was damaged—a substantial U.S. defeat.

On August 24, 1942, in the Battle of the Eastern Solomons, the U.S. Navy partially atoned for its previous poor performance. Carrier aircraft disrupted a Japanese resupply convoy by sinking the Japanese light carrier *Ryujo* and its 90 aircraft at the cost of 15 U.S. planes and damage to the carrier *Enterprise*.

The Japanese landed the next blow on September 15, when a Japanese submarine sent two torpedoes into the U.S. carrier *Wasp*. The ship quickly turned into an inferno, and the crew abandoned it. The *Wasp*, along with 200 crew members still aboard, sank shortly afterward.

The Americans and Japanese clashed again the next month in the Battle of Cape Esperance, during which Rear Admiral Norman Scott sank one Japanese cruiser and a destroyer.

The Battle of the Santa Cruz Islands on October 26 ended in a draw after two Japanese carriers were damaged and the U.S. carrier *Hornet* sank. Within weeks U.S. Admiral D. J. Callaghan intercepted a reinforcement convoy of 13,000 Japanese soldiers. In the ensuing Naval Battle of Guadalcanal in mid-November,

Callaghan's force sank two Japanese destroyers and one battleship while losing two cruisers and four destroyers. In subsequent naval combat over the next few days, the Japanese lost one battleship, one destroyer, two cruisers, and seven transports.

These final defeats helped seal Japan's fate at Guadalcanal. After losing control of the waters around the island, the Japanese could not adequately supply their men ashore. In January 1943, the Japanese withdrew from Guadalcanal. The U.S. victory on the island was an early example of the need for combined land and naval forces required in island-hopping warfare.

> Kill Japs, kill Japs, and keep on killing Japs.
> —U.S. Admiral William F. Halsey's plan
> for defeating the Japanese at Guadalcanal, 1942

Indian Ocean Raid (April 1942)

Admiral Chuichi Nagumo led five large carriers and their accompanying screen into the Indian Ocean. For one week in April 1942, he attacked the British bases at Colombo and Trincomalee in Ceylon. He withdrew after sinking the British heavy cruisers *Dorsetshire* and *Cornwall* on April 5 and the small carrier *Hermes* on April 9.

Java Sea, Battle of the (February 27, 1942)

An Allied flotilla of five cruisers and nine destroyers under Dutch Rear Admiral Karel Doorman steamed out to intercept a Japanese invasion force heading toward Java on February 27, 1942. In the clash in the Java Sea, the Japanese navy proved to be more than a match for the hastily assembled Allied unit. In a daylong battle, the Japanese sank two cruisers and four destroyers.

Leyte Gulf, Battle of (October 23–25, 1944)

In an attempt to halt the retaking of the Philippines by the United States, the Japanese navy created one of the most complex schemes in the history of naval warfare. The plan, called SHO-1, involved four separate naval units that would strike during the first days of the U.S. invasion of the Philippines. While one force lured U.S. carriers away from the region, the other three would steam into Leyte Gulf, eliminate any surface vessels that remained, and destroy the forces landing on Leyte's beaches. What emerged from the elaborate scheme was the Battle of Leyte Gulf, the largest naval battle in history.

Admiral Jisaburo Ozawa commanded the Main Force, consisting of four carriers shorn of aircraft. His task was to lure Admiral William F. Halsey from the Leyte region and leave the invasion forces open to attack. The Second Striking Force under Admiral Kiyohide Shima was to join with Admiral Shoji Nishimura's First Striking Force, race through the Surigao Strait, burst from the south into Leyte Gulf, and attack the amphibious forces at anchor.

Admiral Takeo Kurita wielded the real power, however. His Central Force included the two superbattleships *Yamato* and *Musashi,* three older battleships, 12 cruisers, and 15 destroyers. He planned to head through the Sibuyan Sea west of the Philippines, dart through the San Bernardino Strait to the north of Leyte Gulf, and head down the coast of Samar Island into Leyte Gulf, where he could use his potent guns against helpless American targets.

Disaster struck before the Japanese even reached their intended destinations. On October 23, two U.S. submarines intercepted Kurita west of the Philippines, sank two cruisers, and damaged a third. The next day was no better. Aircraft from Halsey's carriers located Kurita in the Sibuyan Sea and inflicted more damage.

The next victims—Shima and Nishimura—now took center stage. As their two forces approached the Philippines, U.S. submarines and scout aircraft reported their position. On the night of October 24–25 an impressive array of U.S. vessels met Nishimura at the exit of Surigao

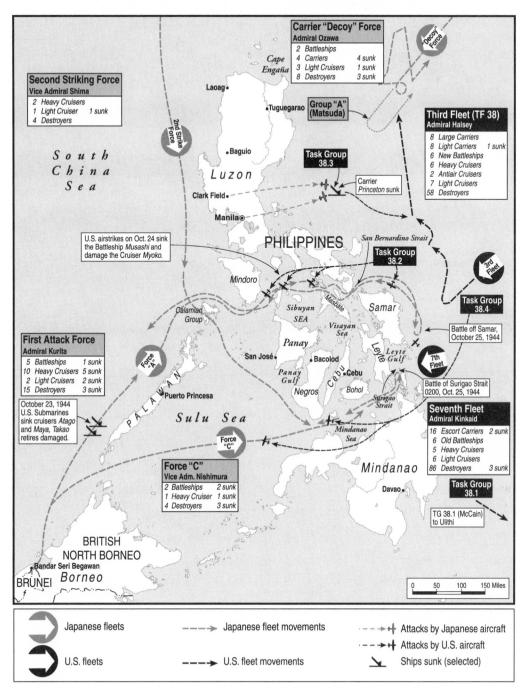

Carrier "Decoy" Force
Admiral Ozawa

2	Battleships	
4	Carriers	4 sunk
3	Light Cruisers	1 sunk
8	Destroyers	3 sunk

Cape Engaña

Laoag

Tuguegarao

Group "A"
(Matsuda)

Second Striking Force
Vice Admiral Shima

2	Heavy Cruisers	
1	Light Cruiser	1 sunk
4	Destroyers	

South China Sea

Baguio

Third Fleet (TF 38)
Admiral Halsey

8	Large Carriers	
8	Light Carriers	1 sunk
6	New Battleships	
6	Heavy Cruisers	
2	Antiair Cruisers	
7	Light Cruisers	
58	Destroyers	

Luzon

Task Group 38.3

Carrier
Princeton sunk

Clark Field

Manila

San Bernardino Strait

U.S. airstrikes on Oct. 24 sink
the Battleship *Musashi* and
damage the Cruiser *Myoko*.

PHILIPPINES

Task Group 38.2

3rd Fleet

Mindoro

Calamian Group

Sibuyan SEA

Masbate

Samar

Task Group 38.4

Battle off Samar,
October 25, 1944

First Attack Force
Admiral Kurita

5	Battleships	1 sunk
10	Heavy Cruisers	5 sunk
2	Light Cruisers	2 sunk
15	Destroyers	3 sunk

Panay

San José

Visayan Sea

Leyte Gulf

7th Fleet

Bacolod

Leyte

October 23, 1944
U.S. Submarines
sink cruisers *Atago*
and *Maya*, *Takao*
retires damaged.

Puerto Princesa

PALAWAN

Panay Gulf

Negros

Cebu

Cebu

Bohol

Surigao Strait

Battle of Surigao Strait
0200, Oct. 25, 1944

Seventh Fleet
Admiral Kinkaid

16	Escort Carriers	2 sunk
6	Old Battleships	
5	Heavy Cruisers	
6	Light Cruisers	
86	Destroyers	3 sunk

Sulu Sea

Force "C"

Mindanao Sea

Force "C"
Vice Adm. Nishimura

2	Battleships	2 sunk
1	Heavy Cruiser	1 sunk
4	Destroyers	3 sunk

Mindanao

Davao

Task Group 38.1

TG 38.1 (McCain)
to Ulithi

BRITISH NORTH BORNEO

Bandar Seri Begawan

BRUNEI *Borneo*

0	50	100	150 Miles

Legend:

Japanese fleets — Japanese fleet movements — ···▸+ Attacks by Japanese aircraft

U.S. fleets — - -▸ U.S. fleet movements — ···▸+ Attacks by U.S. aircraft

Ships sunk (selected)

THE BATTLE OF LEYTE GULF, OCTOBER 21–25, 1944

On October 25, 1944, at the eastern exit of San Bernardino Strait off the Philippine island of Samar, the brave crews of 13 U.S. ships selflessly placed themselves in the path of a much larger Japanese force in order to protect U.S. soldiers and ships in Leyte Gulf.

Japanese Admiral Takeo Kurita steamed through the strait with 32 battleships, cruisers, and destroyers, intent on stopping the U.S. invasion of the Philippines. Instead, he encountered 13 ships commanded by Rear Admiral Clifton Sprague (see Leyte Gulf, p. 280). Called Taffy 3, the unit consisted of six small aircraft carriers, known as escort carriers, and their screen of seven destroyers and destroyer escorts. Kurita could have easily shoved aside Sprague's force, for the lightly armed ships were designed to ferry supplies and scout for submarines, not to fight in a surface engagement.

Upon sighting the Japanese, Sprague's initial thought was that his ships could last no more than 15 minutes against the massive guns of Kurita's battleships and cruisers. But he knew that he had to try to keep the Japanese ships from turning into Leyte Gulf and attacking the land forces. Sprague issued a series of bold orders: to launch every aircraft, telling his pilots to swoop down on the Japanese ships, even when they had no ammunition, and sending his destroyers and destroyer escorts in suicidal charges straight at the enemy. Sprague allowed that "we might as well give them all we've got before we go down."

Miraculously, the 13 ships turned back Kurita, who believed that the American unit was much stronger than it was and would not fight in such a foolhardy fashion unless additional naval units were rushing to their aid.

Sprague and the rest of Taffy 3, battered, bruised, yet alive, watched in wonderment as the larger Japanese ships turned around and steamed away. Taffy 3 lost one escort carrier and three escorting ships, along with a substantial portion of their crews, but the group saved the invasion force in one of war's most glorious examples of an underdog's refusal to yield.

Strait and sank all but one of his ships. Shima reversed course and fled.

The other two portions of the Battle of Leyte Gulf unfolded north of Leyte. Ozawa lured Halsey from the eastern exit of San Bernardino Strait, although the Japanese admiral subsequently lost all four carriers and three destroyers when Halsey caught him in what is known as the Battle of Cape Engaño. Ozawa's sacrifice opened a path through the strait for Kurita, but when Kurita emerged, he found his way into the gulf blocked by thirteen small escort carriers and destroyers commanded by Rear Admiral Clifton Sprague (see sidebar). Kurita, believing that the American force was much stronger than it actually was, turned back.

The fighting off Samar concluded the Battle of Leyte Gulf. Shima and Kurita limped back to Japan with the remnants of their fleets. The Battle of Leyte Gulf finally eliminated the Japanese navy as a major factor in the Pacific war.

Midway, Battle of (June 4, 1942)

Admiral Isoroku Yamamoto's elaborate operation involving the island of Midway, a U.S. base 1,100 miles northwest of Hawaii, used 16 different groups in the hope of drawing out the U.S. fleet in a decisive battle. Yamamoto believed that the United States would dispatch its fleet to protect the island, so he devised a trap. Lurking behind an invasion force were four aircraft carriers of Admiral Chuichi Nagumo's Striking Force, followed 300 miles behind by Yamamoto's own Main Force of powerful battleships and one carrier. These ships would destroy the unsuspecting U.S. fleet before it could inflict significant damage on the Japanese. Faced with a

U.S. Navy Douglas Dauntless dive-bombers attack Japanese warships during the Battle of Midway, the turning point of the Pacific war. A stricken enemy vessel burns in the background. The Imperial Japanese Navy was devastated by the loss of four aircraft carriers during the battle.

second devastating attack in six months, the United States, the Japanese hoped, might agree to peace negotiations.

The U.S. forces, however, held a significant advantage. Although outnumbered, they knew where and when to position themselves because U.S. code breakers had delivered most of the Japanese plan to American commanders before the battle. Admiral Chester Nimitz ordered his commander, Admiral Frank Jack Fletcher, who later relinquished tactical command to Rear Admiral Raymond A. Spruance, to wait with his carriers northeast of Midway until scout planes located the Japanese, then to unleash an all-out attack on the four carriers.

On the morning of June 4, 1942, Nagumo launched the first Midway strike wave. He held back 126 aircraft, loaded with armor-piercing bombs and torpedoes, to use against any U.S. ships that might draw near.

Eighteen minutes later, a U.S. scout plane reported Nagumo's position, and Spruance immediately ordered aloft three different groups of torpedo planes, dive-bombers, and fighters. Still unaware of the U.S. presence, Nagumo pondered a different problem. The first Midway attack wave radioed that it needed a second air strike to fully knock out the island's airfields, so Nagumo ordered his reserve aircraft moved below decks so that crews could replace the armor-piercing bombs and torpedoes, used against light-skinned ships, with high-explosive bombs normally used against land targets.

MITSUO FUCHIDA, ZEROS COMMANDER

Witnessing the Battle of Midway

The terrifying scream of the dive-bombers reached me first, followed by the crashing explosion of a direct hit. There was a blinding flash and then a second explosion, much louder than the first. I was shaken by a weird blast of warm air. There was still another shock, but less severe, apparently a near miss. Then followed a startling quiet as the barking of guns suddenly ceased. I got up and looked at the sky. The enemy planes were already gone from sight. The attackers had gotten in unimpeded because our fighters, which had engaged the preceding wave of torpedo planes only a few moments earlier, had not yet had time to regain altitude. Consequently, it may be said that the American dive-bombers' success was made possible by the earlier martyrdom of their torpedo planes. Also, our carriers had no time to evade because clouds hid the enemy's approach until he dove down to the attack. We had been caught flatfooted in the most vulnerable condition possible—decks loaded with planes armed and fueled for attack.

—From Mitsuo Fuchida and Masataka Okumiya *Midway: The Battle That Doomed Japan: The Japanese Navy's Story*, intro. Thomas B. Buell, ed. Clarke H. Kawakami, Roger Pineau (and Raymond A. Spruance Annapolis, MD: United States Naval Institute, 2001).

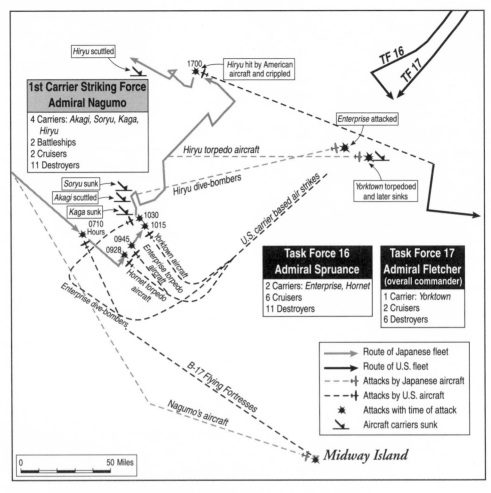

THE BATTLE OF MIDWAY, JUNE 4, 1942

Map labels:

Hiryu scuttled

1700 — *Hiryu* hit by American aircraft and crippled

TF 16
TF 17

Enterprise attacked

1st Carrier Striking Force
Admiral Nagumo

4 Carriers: *Akagi, Soryu, Kaga, Hiryu*
2 Battleships
2 Cruisers
11 Destroyers

Hiryu torpedo aircraft

Hiryu dive-bombers

Yorktown torpedoed and later sinks

Soryu sunk
Akagi scuttled
Kaga sunk

1030
1015
0710 Hours
0945
0928

Yorktown aircraft
Enterprise torpedo aircraft
Hornet torpedo aircraft

U.S. carrier based air strikes

Task Force 16
Admiral Spruance

2 Carriers: *Enterprise, Hornet*
6 Cruisers
11 Destroyers

Task Force 17
Admiral Fletcher
(overall commander)

1 Carrier: *Yorktown*
2 Cruisers
6 Destroyers

Enterprise dive-bombers

B-17 Flying Fortresses

Nagumo's aircraft

Legend:
→ Route of Japanese fleet
→ Route of U.S. fleet
–┤ Attacks by Japanese aircraft
–┤ Attacks by U.S. aircraft
✳ Attacks with time of attack
⤵ Aircraft carriers sunk

0   50 Miles

Midway Island

As Japanese sailors made the switch, Nagumo received stunning news that a U.S. carrier had been spotted. At almost the same moment the aircraft from his first Midway attack wave, now low on fuel, returned and radioed that they needed to land. Nagumo had to decide whether to continue preparing the planes below decks, and risk losing some of his Midway planes to low fuel, or to halt the switch, recover the Midway force, then ready the group for a strike against the U.S. carriers. He chose the latter, even though that meant the

carrier decks would be jammed with aircraft for a short time. This decision doomed the Japanese carriers.

Minutes later, U.S. aircraft attacked. Japanese antiaircraft fire downed many U.S. planes, but the surviving American pilots continued toward their foe. In six minutes, a period that Nimitz described as "the attack that in minutes changed the whole course of the war," the *Akagi, Kaga, Hiryu,* and *Soryu* were blazing wrecks that would soon slide beneath the waves as a direct result of attacks by American dive-bombers. Yamamoto's potent Main Force remained, but when Yamamoto realized that Spruance had not taken the bait, he canceled the Midway operation.

In addition to the four carriers, Japan lost one heavy cruiser, 3,500 sailors, 322 aircraft, and hundreds of skilled aviators. It never recovered from this blow, and after Midway fought a defensive war while the United States switched to the offensive.

Philippine Sea, Battle of the (June 19–21, 1944)

The Battle of the Philippine Sea was an attempt by the Japanese to smash the U.S. fleet in a huge engagement off the Mariana Islands. Japan hoped that the United States would then ask to negotiate a settlement to end the Pacific war so the Americans could focus on Hitler and Europe. Admiral Jisaburo Ozawa commanded a flotilla of five separate groups, each centered on aircraft carriers.

In the opening act, Japanese aircraft made a series of four sorties against U.S. ships. In one of the most lopsided meetings of the war, American carrier aircraft shot down most of the attacking Japanese before they reached their targets (see Air War in the Pacific, pp. 249–302). This action is often referred to as the "Great Marianas Turkey Shoot" because of the ease with which the U.S. planes destroyed the Japanese aircraft.

As the aerial massacre unfolded, U.S. submarines glided toward Ozawa. In a three-hour period the submarine *Cavalla* sank the carrier *Shokaku* and the *Albacore* sank the carrier *Taiho*. Japan lost two priceless carriers, hundreds of aircraft, and irreplaceable pilots.

Rabaul and Truk (1942–45)

Rabaul, a Japanese stronghold on New Britain, and Truk, a major naval base in the Caroline Islands, were subject to some of the most intense bombing attacks of the Pacific clash. Rather than invade with land forces, U.S. mili-

tary planners neutralized the two locations by constantly hitting them by air. U.S. pilots flew thousands of sorties against Rabaul and Truk, whose garrisons were cut off from resupply, bypassed by American ground troops, and allowed to "wither on the vine" in their island fortresses. Japanese at both fortresses surrendered at war's end.

Repulse and Prince of Wales (December 10, 1941)

On December 8, 1941, Britain sent the powerful battle cruiser *Repulse* and the majestic battleship *Prince of Wales* from Singapore to intercept the Japanese invasion force heading toward Malaya. Before the ships could inflict any damage, Japanese aircraft attacked on the morning of December 10 and sank both vessels. The loss left the Allies without a battleship in the Pacific and was a catastrophic psychological blow to the heretofore invincible British navy.

> In all the war I never received a more direct shock. Over all the vast expanse of waters Japan was supreme, and we everywhere were weak and naked.
> —British leader Winston Churchill, about receiving news that the Japanese had sunk two prize warships, the *Repulse* and the *Prince of Wales* December 10, 1941

THE CARRIER WAR

Naval airpower dominated the naval war in the Pacific. It was responsible for the devastating American defeat at Pearl Harbor in 1941, formed the backbone for the vast majority of naval clashes from 1942 to 1944, and played a key role in determining the outcome of the Battle of Leyte Gulf, the largest naval action in world history.

Traditional naval warfare, in which opposing battleships, cruisers, and destroyers blasted away in surface engagements, sometimes occurred in the Pacific war. For example, the Japanese victo-

One of the most remarkable displays of courage and accurate gunfire in the Pacific war occurred off Okinawa on May 11, 1945, when the crew of the U.S. destroyer *Hugh W. Hadley* shot down 22 Japanese kamikaze planes. The first suicide planes appeared shortly before 8 A.M., and for the next 90 minutes the *Hadley* battled five waves of aircraft totaling 151 planes.

Kamikazes attacked from all quarters in groups of four to six planes. Despite being hit by two bombs and two suicide aircraft, the ship gamely plowed on, its crew firing every gun. They downed 12 aircraft in the initial onslaught, and 10 more in the battle's last moments when, simultaneously, four Japanese aircraft attacked on the port bow, four on the starboard bow, and two astern. As the ship's Action Report stated, "All ten planes were destroyed . . . and each plane was definitely accounted for."

Although the ship listed from many shell holes and settled from a flooded fireroom and engine rooms, a group of officers and men succeeded in keeping the ship afloat until help arrived. The *Hadley* eventually was towed to Ie Shima.

---

ries in the Java Sea and in some engagements off Guadalcanal were waged without the benefit of naval airpower.

Most Pacific battles relied on airpower to deliver the punishment and guarantee the margin of victory. In the war's opening months, the U.S. Navy, battered and bruised at Pearl Harbor, fought simply to prevent the Japanese from adding more triumphs. Outnumbered in both ships and aircraft, the U.S. Navy relied on courage, bold leadership, and information received through intelligence to register wins in the Battle of the Coral Sea and at Midway.

But from that time on, the Japanese navy fought a losing war. U.S. factories produced ships and planes in record numbers, while Japan's manufacturing capacity plummeted as a result of U.S. bombing raids and the effective American submarine campaign. As the war ground through 1944, fresh U.S. pilots arrived to complement those already fighting in the Pacific, while the numbers of skilled Japanese aviators dwindled. Consequently, each battle wore down Japan's ability to mount naval operations. U.S. victories in the Battle of the Philippine Sea and at Leyte Gulf—both of which used airpower in record numbers—sealed Japan's doom.

Carriers of the U.S. Navy

U.S. aircraft carriers played a prominent role in Japan's defeat. The alphabetical list that follows includes information about the carriers, the battles in which they were involved, and whether they were sunk or survived the war. The designation CV refers to larger fleet carriers; CVL refers to smaller light aircraft carriers. A third designation, CVE, was used for escort carriers, which are not listed here. Japan had 11 aircraft carriers on December 7, 1941, 10 of which were sunk during the war. The Japanese added another 16 after Pearl Harbor, 13 of which were sunk.

BATAAN, CVL-29 Served from early 1944 until war's end. Scrapped in 1960.

BELLEAU WOOD, CVL-24 Served from late 1943 until war's end. Participated in Battle of the Philippine Sea and the Philippine invasion, where it absorbed a kamikaze suicide hit. Scrapped in 1960.

BENNINGTON, CV-20 Served from early 1945 until war's end. Participated in Okinawa

KAMIKAZE SUICIDE ATTACKS

As the war continued to turn against them, the Japanese adopted desperate tactics, the most feared of which became the kamikaze aircraft that flew suicide missions against the U.S. Navy. The word *kamikaze*, meaning "divine wind," referred to the 1281 typhoon that destroyed Mongol ruler Kublai Khan's invasion fleet, which was headed to Japan. Vice Admiral Takejiro Onishi organized the kamikaze unit as a last-ditch attempt to impede the U.S. drive toward Japan. He recruited volunteer pilots to join the Special Attack Corps with the understanding that these men would fly aircraft loaded with explosives directly into U.S. warships.

Kamikazes first struck on October 25, 1944, sinking the escort carrier *St. Lo* off Samar Island in the Philippines. While occasional forays plagued American assaults from then on, the unit caused its worst destruction off Okinawa, where more than 1,500 kamikaze missions in two months sank or knocked out of the war 64 Allied ships and damaged 60 others. U.S. Admiral Marc Mitscher's ship was hit three times in four days, the destroyer *Laffey* absorbed six kamikaze attacks, and five aircraft carriers were damaged. The navy suffered 5,000 dead and 7,000 wounded in these frightening assaults, a total that surpassed navy casualties during the Spanish-American War and World War I. In the end, however, the kamikaze attacks could not stop the overwhelming force and firepower of the U.S. Navy, and although they exacted a high toll in human life, they could not affect the outcome of the war.

> We were living twenty-four hours a day on a floating target. We constantly thought of being an open target. You never knew when you would be under attack and if you would be alive tomorrow. It's terrifying to see a kamikaze coming down. They keep boring in on you on a sharp angle, and it's either him or you. It was like living on a large bull's-eye.
>
> —Seaman Second Class William Rowe, who was aboard the aircraft carrier *Bunker Hill* when two kamikazes crashed into the ship

campaign and helped sink the *Yamato*. Scrapped in 1980s.

BON HOMME RICHARD, CV-31 Served from early 1945 until war's end. Participated in Okinawa campaign. Scrapped in 1980s.

BUNKER HILL, CV-17 Fought from 1943 until March 1945, when two kamikaze suicide attacks knocked it out of action off Okinawa.

Returned to the United States for repairs but saw no further action. Scrapped in 1966.

CABOT, CVL-28 Served from late 1943 until war's end. It endured two kamikaze suicide hits, once off the Philippines and another off Okinawa. Scrapped in the 1980s.

COWPENS, CVL-25 Served from early 1943 until war's end without suffering major damage. Scrapped in 1959.

ENTERPRISE, CV-6 Fought in numerous campaigns as Admiral William F. Halsey's flagship, including the Doolittle Raid, Midway, Guadalcanal, and Okinawa. Scrapped in 1958.

ESSEX, CV-9 Saw action from 1943 on, was hit by a kamikaze suicide attack off the Philippines in November 1944. Scrapped in 1975.

FRANKLIN, CV-13 Served in 1944 and 1945. On March 19, 1945, while on a bombing mission against the Japanese islands, the ship was hit by two 500-pound bombs, which caused immense damage to its hangar deck. Returned to the United States for repairs but never again saw action.

HANCOCK, CV-19   In operation from late 1944 until war's end. Damaged by a kamikaze suicide attack. Scrapped in 1976.

HORNET, CV-8   Launched the bombers that hit Japan in the 1942 Doolittle raid; participated in the Battle of Midway. Sunk by enemy aircraft during the Battle of the Santa Cruz Islands on October 26, 1942.

HORNET, CV-12   Constructed after the original carrier, *Hornet*, CV-8, was sunk at the Battle of the Santa Cruz Islands, it served from 1944 to 1945. It avoided serious damage and is under consideration for use as a war memorial.

INDEPENDENCE, CVL-22   Served from January 1943 until war's end. Participated in Gilbert Islands invasion, where it absorbed a torpedo hit. Sunk in a weapons test in 1951.

INTREPID, CV-11   Involved in many actions in the Pacific, where it was hit by a torpedo in February 1944 and four kamikaze suicide aircraft in subsequent attacks. It survived the war to become a museum in New York.

LANGLEY, CVL-27   Served from early 1944 until war's end. Scrapped in 1963.

LEXINGTON, CV-2   Revered ship that participated in the war's opening actions. Sunk during the Battle of the Coral Sea on May 8, 1942.

LEXINGTON, CV-16   Named in honor of the *Lexington* sunk in the Battle of the Coral Sea, it participated in the Battles of the Philippine Sea and Leyte Gulf. Hit by a torpedo in December 1943, a kamikaze suicide attack in January 1945, and a bomb in March 1945. Now a war memorial in Texas.

***MONTEREY*, CVL-26**   Served from late 1944 until war's end. Scrapped in 1970.

***PRINCETON*, CVL-23**   Served from late 1943 until October 24, 1944, when it was sunk during the Battle of Leyte Gulf.

***RANDOLPH*, CV-15**   Damaged off Ulithi Atoll in March 1945 but survived the war. Scrapped in 1973.

***SAN JACINTO*, CVL-30**   Served from early 1944 until war's end without suffering major damage. Scrapped in 1959.

***SARATOGA*, CV-3**   Revered ship that participated in the war's early actions along with the *Lexington*. Participated in the Guadalcanal campaign (Battle of the Eastern Solomons, assaults on the Gilbert Islands, the Marshall Islands, and Iwo Jima). Hit by two torpedoes in 1942 and a kamikaze suicide attack in 1945 off Iwo Jima. Sunk in the atomic bomb tests at Bikini Atoll in July 1946.

***SHANGRI-LA*, CV-38**   Served from early 1945 until war's end. Took part in raids against Japan. Scrapped in 1980s.

***TICONDEROGA*, CV-14**   Saw action from November 1944. Absorbed two kamikaze suicide hits in early 1945 off Luzon but returned in April for the remainder of the war. Scrapped in 1973.

***WASP*, CV-7**   Participated in the ferrying of aircraft to Malta in the Mediterranean and the Guadalcanal landings in the Pacific before being sunk by a Japanese submarine on September 15, 1942.

***WASP*, CV-18**   Fought from 1944 to war's end. Scrapped in 1973.

***YORKTOWN*, CV-5**   Sustained severe damage in the Battle of the Coral Sea but was repaired in time for the Battle of Midway, where it was sunk on June 6, 1942.

***YORKTOWN*, CV-10**   Replaced the ship of the same name that was sunk at Midway. Saw service throughout the Pacific war and participated in the destruction of the Japanese battleship *Yamato*. Currently floats as a war museum in South Carolina.

SUBMARINE WARFARE (1942–45)

In the war's first two years, Japanese submarines inflicted far more damage than did those of the United States. The Japanese Long Lance torpedoes sent many enemy ships to the bottom because of their accuracy, speed, and range, while frustrated U.S. submarine commanders watched as their technically less advanced torpedoes either failed to explode because of faulty firing mechanisms or swerved off course and missed the target.

Improvements in 1944 reversed the situation. U.S. factories doubled the number of American submarines, each carrying efficient radar-sonar equipment and accurate torpedoes, and the United States quickly gained the advantage. As a result, in 1944 and 1945, Japanese tankers delivered a mere 10 percent of the oil produced in Southeast Asia, and the Japanese army and navy suffered from shortages in cotton, rubber, sugar, lumber, and other essential items.

Near the end of 1944, U.S. submarine commanders had difficulty locating new targets because they had destroyed so many Japanese ships. By war's end, U.S. submarines had claimed 1,300 merchant vessels, 8 aircraft carriers, 1 battleship, 12 cruisers, 42 destroyers, and 22 Japanese submarines. At the same time, they suffered a 20 percent casualty rate, making service in submarines the most dangerous of any military branch.

In the early years of the war, the U.S. Navy needed time to reorganize and build its strength. In 1943–44 the submarine fleet inflicted mortal wounds on the Japanese, leaving fewer Japanese targets for submarines to sink.

	Warships Sunk	Merchantmen Sunk
1941–42	2	180
1943	22	325
1944	104	603
1945	60	186

Source: James F. Dunnigan and Albert A. Nofi, *The Pacific War Encyclopedia* (New York: Checkmark Books, 1998).

AMPHIBIOUS ASSAULTS

Amphibious landings were one of the main methods of advancing across the Pacific. In these operations landing craft shuttled marines or army units to the assault beaches from ships offshore. This table includes the most important Allied and Japanese amphibious operations.

Date	Location	Importance	Results
December 1941	Japanese landings in the Philippines, Wake Island, Malaya, Guam, Dutch East Indies	Asserted Japanese control throughout the Pacific	Japan dominated the area west of the Hawaiian Islands and Midway.
May 1942	Japanese landings in New Guinea	Threatened Australia	Combined U.S.–Australian force defeated the Japanese.
June 1942	Japanese landings in the Aleutian Islands	Stunned the United States by taking American soil; established air bases	Japan remained in the Aleutians until forced out in 1944.
August 7, 1942	American invasion of Guadalcanal	Prevented Japan from threatening lines of communication with Australia	The United States forced the Japanese out of Guadalcanal.
1943 into 1944	A series of American landings in the Solomon Islands, culminating in the assault on Bougainville	Removed the Japanese from the Solomons; threatened the island bastion of Rabaul	The United States secured the Solomon Islands and removed Rabaul as a threat to U.S. forces.

Date	Location	Importance	Results
November 1943	American landings in the Gilbert Islands (Tarawa)	Commenced the attack against the Japanese defense perimeter; tested American amphibious doctrine against a strongly held island	After a three-day battle, U.S. Marines eliminated Japanese resistance on Tarawa and the U.S. Army secured Makin Island.
February 1944	American assault against the Marshall Islands	Continued the U.S. advance through the Central Pacific	The United States forced the Japanese out and constructed air bases.
June 1944	American assault against the Mariana Islands	Proved to be the first major threat against the Japanese inner defense line	Japan was shoved back farther toward the home islands; American bombers based in the Marianas could hit targets in Japan proper.
October 1944	American assault against the Philippine Islands	Reestablished American control of the islands; isolated Japan from its supply sources in Southeast Asia	The United States defeated the Japanese, who now could only fight a holding war and hope for a beneficial peace offer.
February 1945	American assault against Iwo Jima	Established air bases from which to attack Japan and on which crippled American bombers could safely land	The United States defeated the Japanese and intensified its bombing campaign of the home islands.
April 1945	American assault against Okinawa	Established air bases from which to attack Japan; established a base of operations for the expected invasion of Japan	The United States defeated the Japanese and now faced only the invasion of the Japanese home islands.

Sources:
John Costello, *The Pacific War, 1941–1945* (New York: Quill, 1982).
Norman Polmar and Thomas B. Allen, *World War II: The Encyclopedia of the War Years, 1941–1945* (New York: Random House, 1996).

MAJOR COMMANDO RAIDS

Pacific commando raids were confined mainly to the China-Burma-India theater, where British and U.S. commandos fought behind Japanese lines. Three units, in particular, contributed to the war behind the scenes, mainly by destroying bridges and enemy communications.

Commando Unit	Commander	Where Fought	When Fought
Chindits	Orde Wingate	Burma	1943
511th Parachute Infantry Division	Major Henry Burgess	Freed 2,000 Allied prisoners of war at Los Banos, in the Philippines	February 23, 1945

(*continued*)

Commando Unit	Commander	Where Fought	When Fought
Merrill's Marauders	Brigadier General Frank D. Merrill	Burma, where they seized the airfield at Myitkyina	1943–44
OSS Detachment 101	Captain Carl Eifler, Colonel William R. Peers	Burma	1942–45

Sources:
William B. Breuer, *Retaking the Philippines* (New York: St, Martin's Press, 1986).
Francis Russell, *The Secret War* (Alexandria, VA: Time-Life Books, 1981).

COMPARATIVE NAVAL STRENGTH IN THE PACIFIC, DECEMBER 1941

This table, of comparative naval strength in the Pacific in December 1941, shows that although the United States and its allies had as many traditional ships (battleships, cruisers, and destroyers) as the Japanese did, the Allies held an edge in submarines, while the Japanese enjoyed an advantage in aircraft carriers. As the war continued, the United States greatly expanded its number of submarines and carriers, whereas Japan experienced difficulty replacing naval losses, which ultimately led to Japan's defeat.

	U.S.	Allies	Japan
Aircraft Carriers	3	0	10
Battleships	9	2	11
Heavy Cruisers	13	1	18
Light Cruisers	11	10	17
Destroyers	80	20	104
Submarines	73	13	67

Source: James F. Dunnigan and Albert A. Nofi, *The Pacific War Encyclopedia* (New York: Checkmark Books, 1998).

MAJOR COMBAT LOSSES OF THE JAPANESE NAVY

The Japanese navy possessed a potent armada during the war and dominated the fighting in the early stages. As the table shows, American might wore down the opposition with such devastating efficiency that few Japanese ships remained at war's end.

Name of Ship	Fate
Carriers	
Akagi	Sunk, Midway, June 4, 1942
Amagi	Sunk, July 24, 1945
Chitose	Sunk, Battle of Leyte Gulf, October 25, 1944
Chiyoda	Sunk, Battle of Leyte Gulf, October 25, 1944
Chuyo	Sunk by submarine, December 4, 1943
Hiryu	Sunk, Midway, June 5, 1942
Hiyo	Sunk, June 20, 1944
Hosho	Survived
Hyuga	Sunk, July 24, 1945

Name of Ship	Fate
Ise	Sunk, July 28, 1945
Junyo	Survived
Kaga	Sunk, Midway, June 4, 1942
Kaiyo	Sunk, July 18, 1945
Katsuragi	Survived
Ryuho	Survived
Ryujo	Sunk, Battle of the Eastern Solomons, August 24, 1942
Shinano	Sunk by submarine, November 29, 1944
Shinyo	Sunk by submarine, November 17, 1944
Shoho	Sunk, Battle of the Coral Sea, May 7, 1942
Shokaku	Sunk, Battle of the Philippine Sea, June 19, 1944
Soryu	Sunk, Midway, June 4, 1942
Taiho	Sunk by submarine, June 19, 1944
Taiyo	Sunk by submarine, August 18, 1944
Unryu	Sunk by submarine, December 19, 1944
Unyo	Sunk by submarine, September 16, 1944
Zuiho	Sunk, Battle of Leyte Gulf, October 25, 1944
Zuikaku	Sunk, Battle of Leyte Gulf, October 25, 1944
Battleships	
Fuso	Sunk, Battle of Leyte Gulf, October 25, 1944

Name of Ship	Fate
Haruna	Sunk, July 27, 1945
Hiei	Sunk, Battle of Guadalcanal, November 13, 1942
Kirishima	Sunk, Battle of Guadalcanal, November 15, 1942
Kongo	Sunk by submarine, November 21, 1944
Musashi	Sunk, Battle of Leyte Gulf, October 24, 1944
Mutsu	Sunk, June 8, 1943
Nagato	Survived
Yamashiro	Sunk, Battle of Leyte Gulf, October 25, 1944
Yamato	Sunk, April 7, 1945
Cruisers	
Abukuma	Sunk, October 26, 1944
Agano	Sunk by submarine, February 16, 1944
Aoba	Sunk, July 28, 1945
Ashigara	Sunk by submarine, June 8, 1945
Atago	Sunk, Battle of Leyte Gulf, October 25, 1944
Chikuma	Sunk, Battle of Leyte Gulf, October 25, 1944
Chokai	Sunk, Battle of Leyte Gulf, October 25, 1944
Furutaka	Sunk, Battle of Cape Esperance, October 11, 1942
Haguro	Sunk, May 16, 1945

(continued)

Name of Ship	Fate
Isuzu	Sunk by submarine, April 7, 1945
Jintsu	Sunk, Battle of Kolombangara, July 13, 1943
Kako	Sunk by submarine, August 1942
Kashii	Sunk, January 12, 1945
Kashima	Survived
Katori	Sunk, February 17, 1944
Kinu	Sunk after the Battle of Leyte Gulf, October 26, 1944
Kinugasa	Sunk, Battle of Guadalcanal, November 14, 1942
Kiso	Sunk, November 13, 1944
Kitakami	Survived
Kuma	Sunk by submarine, January 11, 1944
Kumano	Sunk, November 25, 1944
Maya	Sunk, Battle of Leyte Gulf, October 23, 1944
Mikuma	Sunk, Battle of Midway, June 6, 1942
Mogami	Sunk, Battle of Leyte Gulf, October 25, 1944
Myoko	Survived
Nachi	Sunk, November 5, 1944
Nagara	Sunk by submarine, August 7, 1944
Naka	Sunk, February 17, 1944
Natori	Sunk by submarine, August 18, 1944

Name of Ship	Fate
Noshiro	Sunk, October 26, 1944
Oi	Sunk by submarine, July 19, 1944
Oyodo	Sunk, July 28, 1945
Sakawa	Survived
Sendai	Sunk, Battle of Empress Augusta Bay, November 2, 1943
Suzuya	Sunk, Battle of Leyte Gulf, October 25, 1944
Takao	Survived
Tama	Sunk, Battle of Leyte Gulf, October 23, 1944
Tatsuta	Sunk by submarine, March 13, 1944
Tenryu	Sunk by submarine, December 18, 1942
Tone	Sunk, July 24, 1945
Yahagi	Sunk, April 7, 1945
Yashoshima	Sunk, November 25, 1944
Yubari	Sunk by submarine, April 27, 1944
Yura	Sunk off Savo Island, October 25, 1942

Source: Paul S. Dull, *A Battle History of the Imperial Japanese Navy, 1941–1945* (Annapolis, MD: Naval Institute Press, 1978).

THE AIR WAR IN THE PACIFIC

The Pacific air war followed the same pattern as the carrier war—the United States fought a holding action until its factories and training centers produced aircraft and proficient aviators in such numbers that the Japanese could not keep pace.

The war's first year offered desperate moves on

the part of the United States. In April 1942, the Doolittle raid on Tokyo, inflicting little real damage on Japan itself, delivered a stunning boost to American morale and shocked the Japanese military and public. Naval aviators selflessly flew to their deaths in the Battle of Midway in June 1942 to ensure a crucial victory, and U.S. aircraft lay in wait to intercept and shoot down a Japanese airplane carrying Admiral Isoroku Yamamoto in 1943.

The preponderance of airpower asserted itself in 1943 and 1944. American bombers smashed the Japanese navy in the Battle of the Bismarck Sea, and naval aviators shot down opposing Japanese pilots in record numbers in the Marianas Turkey Shoot. Two steps—a new tactic that was implemented in 1944, and a new weapon in 1945—guaranteed U.S. victory in the air war. Beginning in November 1944, U.S. bombers destroyed Japanese cities and killed thousands of civilians in a terrifying firebombing campaign, while American scientists delivered a weapon of unequivocal destructiveness in 1945—the atomic bomb—used at Hiroshima and again at Nagasaki.

The following were the major engagements of the air war in the Pacific.

Bismarck Sea, Battle of the (March 1–4, 1943)

In early March 1943, aircraft from General George Kenney's Fifth Air Force attacked a Japanese convoy of eight destroyers and nine troop transports in the Bismarck Sea, northeast of New Guinea. Kenney armed his B-25 bombers with additional machine guns so they could pepper enemy ships with lethal fire. He also trained the crews in a technique called "skip-bombing," whereby the aircraft approached from low altitude and released bombs that skipped across the water's surface and smashed into the hulls of their targets. In this decisive sea-air battle, Kenney's aircraft destroyed 14 of 17 Japanese ships at the cost of only two American aircraft.

Death of Yamamoto (April 18, 1943)

In April 1943, American code breakers intercepted a message indicating that Admiral Yamamoto, who was despised in the United States for his role in planning Pearl Harbor, intended to inspect Japanese bases in Bougainville. The message included the date and time that the Japanese admiral would arrive.

On April 18, 18 American fighters waited near Bougainville for Yamamoto's twin-engine bomber and nine escorting aircraft. When they appeared, the U.S. aircraft surprised the group of Japanese and shot down the plane bearing Yamamoto, which crashed in Bougainville's jungle. One of Japan's premier military thinkers, Yamamoto's death was a devastating loss.

Doolittle Raid (April 18, 1942)

A bold action to take the war directly to the Japanese homeland and give the American people a

The Flying Tigers officially was a group of volunteer American pilots the U.S. government recruited to assist China in its war against the Japanese in the days before Pearl Harbor. The isolationist American public had opposed direct intervention on behalf of China, so the U.S. government quietly collected 100 pilots from the army, navy, and marines for the mission.

Named the American Volunteer Group (AVG) and commanded by Major General Claire Lee Chennault, the aviators quickly came to the attention of the public. Reporters christened the group the "Flying Tigers," and Walt Disney cartoonists created the menacing tiger-shark-grin logo, which covered each aircraft's nose. The unit assembled before Pearl Harbor, but it was not officially activated until December 18, 1941. It then flew against the Japanese during the invasions of Burma and during China operations.

The group was disbanded on July 4, 1942, and absorbed into the U.S. Army Air Forces. In its brief existence, the AVG shot down almost 300 Japanese aircraft at the loss of only 12 Flying Tigers.

much-needed injection of optimism, the Doolittle raid was a bombing attack on Japan by sixteen B-25 Mitchell medium bombers led by Army Lieutenant Colonel James H. Doolittle. Aircraft carriers under the command of Admiral William F. Halsey transported the bombers to within 600 miles of Japan, from where they launched and bombed the enemy capital on April 18, 1942, before flying on to friendly bases in China.

For weeks before the operation, U.S. pilots practiced takeoffs on Florida runways to match the short distance they would have to face aboard aircraft carriers. Until the actual day of attack, however, they never actually attempted takeoffs from the deck of a carrier.

Doolittle's force successfully lifted off from the carriers during heavy seas and headed toward Tokyo. The aircraft surprised the Japanese and dropped their bombs, then proceeded toward China, where most bombers crash-landed far short of their airfields. One crew alighted in Soviet-controlled territory and was held by the Russians, and more than 60 members, including Doolittle, reached the safety of friendly Chinese guerrillas.

PAUL "PAPPY" GUNN

One of the most innovative aviation experts of the Pacific war, Paul Gunn, contributed to General George Kenney's successful 1942 air campaign in the South Pacific. Given the nickname "Pappy" because he was older than the pilots with whom he worked, Gunn altered the A-20 and the B-25 bombers so that they would be more effective in attacks.

Both bombers had proved ineffective at higher altitudes, so Gunn adapted them to work at lower levels. He replaced the clear nose of the B-25, and, to make room for four additional .50-caliber machine guns in the front, he removed the aircraft's bombardier and added a mechanism that allowed the pilot to release the bombs. A bottom gun turret had slowed the B-25 to a dangerous speed, so Gunn removed it.

His changes both made the aircraft more deadly in attacks against Japanese airfields, whose pilots were sometimes surprised by the sudden appearance of the low-level bombers, and made the planes more effective against enemy barges and troop transports. When U.S. pilots learned how to skip-bomb their missiles toward the Japanese ships, their raids proved still more productive.

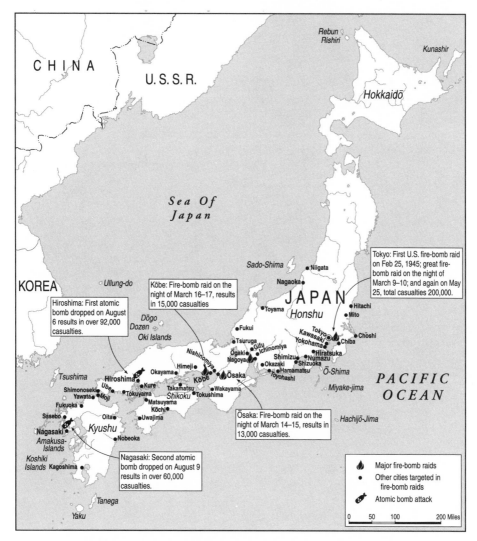

Hiroshima: First atomic bomb dropped on August 6 results in over 92,000 casualties.

Kōbe: Fire-bomb raid on the night of March 16–17, results in 15,000 casualties

Tokyo: First U.S. fire-bomb raid on Feb 25, 1945; great fire-bomb raid on the night of March 9–10; and again on May 25, total casualties 200,000.

Ōsaka: Fire-bomb raid on the night of March 14–15, results in 13,000 casualties.

Nagasaki: Second atomic bomb dropped on August 9 results in over 60,000 casualties.

Major fire-bomb raids
Other cities targeted in fire-bomb raids
Atomic bomb attack

0   50   100   200 Miles

MAJOR ALLIED BOMBING RAIDS AGAINST JAPAN, 1945

However, the Japanese captured eight other crewmen and executed three of them. A total of 71 of Doolittle's 80 airmen survived the war.

Japanese morale absorbed a heavy shock with this raid, because the military had repeatedly assured the people that they never had to worry about being attacked. Meanwhile, American morale soared with the knowledge that U.S. pilots had attacked Japanese soil so soon after the Pearl Harbor disaster.

The Doolittle mission so humiliated Japanese navy officials that they hastened their plans for an operation in the South Seas and approved a daring offensive against American-held Midway Island. This rushed decision, coupled with the work of American code breakers, led to the catastrophic Japanese defeat at Midway that helped turn the tide in the Pacific.

Hiroshima (August 6, 1945)

A crew piloting an American B-29 bomber, the *Enola Gay*, dropped the world's first atomic

BOMBING OF JAPAN (1944–45)

The Japanese spread terror with kamikaze suicide attacks, but the United States answered with its own devastating weapon—the bombing of Japan by the B-29 Superfortress bombers. Searching for a way to bring the war to the Japanese civilian population, U.S. military strategists selected the new bomber, which could fly the immense distances required to reach Japan from U.S. bases in the western Pacific. Because numerous Japanese factories stood amid residential sections, the bombers hit civilian as well as military targets, resulting in large conflagrations and thousands of deaths.

Initial raids in late 1944 proved disappointing. The 16-hour round trip to Japan from bases in the Marianas left no more than a 30-minute margin for finding and attacking the target. The B-29s had to fly without fighter escort because no fighter had the range to accompany them. If the bombardiers flew above the antiaircraft range, dropping the bombs accurately was impossible. If they wanted to be more accurate, the planes had to drop to lower altitudes, but that put them at the mercy of Japanese antiaircraft fire.

The first B-29 attack on Japan occurred in November 1944. More than 100 bombers left Saipan, but fewer than 30 reached the target and dropped bombs. The remainder had to turn back because of low fuel, or they flew off course and never located the target or were shot down.

Results improved when General Curtis LeMay took over. He ordered the bombers to attack at night from lower altitudes, and he placed incendiary bombs—bombs that purposely spread fire—aboard each aircraft. He said that although more American pilots might die because of the new tactics, widespread destruction would result in Japan and thereby shorten the war. His purpose was to blanket an entire area of an enemy city with the firebombs and destroy anything that existed, including military, industrial, and civilian targets.

On March 9, 1945, more than two hundred B-29s dropped 2,000 tons of incendiaries on Tokyo in what LeMay called "the biggest firecracker the Japanese have ever seen." In moments, fire engulfed 16 square miles of the city's midsection, destroying 250,000 homes and buildings and killing some 80,000 people. The intense conflagration reached 1,800 degrees Fahrenheit. LeMay continued these tactics from March until the war's end in August. In all, nearly 300,000 civilians perished, and eight million were left homeless. But it wasn't until after two atomic bombs were dropped on Japan that they surrendered.

bomb on this Japanese port city at 8:15 A.M. on August 6, 1945. The enormous explosion demolished the city and killed at least 80,000 people. (The casualty figures are rough estimates. In addition to those killed in the explosion, tens of thousands of others died of radiation poisoning in the weeks and months ahead, and others were maimed for life.) The Hiroshima bombing, followed three days later by the atomic bombing of Nagasaki, helped persuade the Japanese government to surrender. Critics today say the United States didn't sufficiently warn Japan of the force of the weapons it possessed and give Japan

> There was the mushroom cloud growing up, and we watched it blossom. And down below it the thing reminded me more of a boiling pot of tar than any other description I can give it. It was black and boiling with a steam haze on top of it.
>
> —Colonel Paul Tibbets,
> pilot of the *Enola Gay*,
> after dropping the atomic bomb
> on Hiroshima, August 6, 1945

DEVELOPMENT OF THE ATOMIC BOMB

Scientists had been working to develop the atomic bomb since early in the 20th century. In 1904, two British scientists claimed that radiation could yield a source of energy that might be harnessed into a bomb. Leo Szilard, a Hungarian physicist, said that if anyone could produce a nuclear chain reaction, the result would create an enormous source of energy.

As Hitler added to his European conquests, more scientists left Europe for the United States, where they would be free to research atomic power. Albert Einstein departed Germany in 1933 because he was Jewish, and Enrico Fermi and his Jewish wife abandoned Italy for the United States in 1938.

When Fermi learned that German scientists had made startling discoveries in developing atomic power, he and a small team worked to produce a chain reaction before the Germans. He enjoyed the support of the world's foremost thinker, Einstein, who in 1939 wrote to President Franklin D. Roosevelt, convincing him to create the Uranium Committee to fund Fermi's experiments. On December 2, 1942, working in a former squash court at the University of Chicago, Fermi and a group of scientists achieved history's first controlled, self-sustaining nuclear chain reaction.

The U.S. government quickly organized the Manhattan Project, a program of hundreds of scientists and military officers working to develop an atomic bomb. The Manhattan Project turned out to be one of the costliest and most secret activities of the war. Two huge complexes—at Hanford, Washington, and Oak Ridge, Tennessee—produced the ingredients for the atomic warheads, while workers at a third facility at the remote desert location of Los Alamos, New Mexico, worked to develop the hundreds of parts into a deliverable bomb.

The work benefited from the organizational and inspirational genius of Major General Leslie R. Groves, a military engineer. Although he was accustomed to military preciseness and order, Groves faced the specter of working with what he called a "collection of crackpots"—scientists whose minds were focused more on solving abstract problems than on concrete organizational issues. Despite the difficulties, Groves pulled the project through to completion.

One of Groves's skills was the ability to select highly competent subordinates. The most controversial—and brilliant—appointment was of the physicist J. Robert Oppenheimer, who supervised the scientific end of the Manhattan Project. Oppenheimer's past included mild flirtations with the Communist Party, but Groves stoutly defended the scientist against any attack.

On July 16, 1945, scientists, top military officers, and invited visitors gathered in fortified bunkers at Alamogordo in the New Mexico desert for the test of an atomic device. The bomb was placed on top of a 100-foot steel tower 10,000 yards from the bunkers in a spot called Ground Zero.

When the bomb ignited, a blinding flash lit the sky for a radius of 20 miles and an enormous ball of fire and smoke billowed to a height of more than 10,000 feet before it dimmed. People more than 100 miles away saw the light from the explosion, while windows rattled in Gallup, New Mexico, 235 miles away. The cloud eventually reached a height of 41,000 feet, causing Oppenheimer, a mystic who would become deeply conflicted about his role in developing the bomb, to quote from Hindu scripture: "Now I am become Death, the destroyer of worlds."

When informed of the test's success, President Harry S Truman issued an ultimatum to the Japanese government. He warned that unless the Japanese surrendered immediately, they would face horrible consequences. When he received no reply, Truman gave the Army Air Forces permission to drop the world's first atomic bomb any time after August 3. Truman's overriding concern was the horrible number of anticipated casualties that could be expected on both sides in the event that Japan was invaded. Allied casualties alone were estimated at one million. Truman believed that the use of the atomic bomb would ultimately save lives.

DROPPING OF THE ATOMIC BOMBS (AUGUST 6 AND AUGUST 9, 1945)

A special Army Air Corps unit, the 509th Bombardment Group (Composite), was formed to fly the aircraft containing the atomic bombs to Japan and drop them over the targets. Commanded by Colonel Paul W. Tibbets, a 29-year-old pilot who had flown missions over Germany, the airmen trained for the assignment without being told specifically what their mission—or their payload—would be.

Of 71 major Japanese cities, four had escaped major damage in the war—Kyoto, Kokura, Hiroshima, and Nagasaki. Because Kyoto housed sacred religious shrines, President Truman removed it from consideration as a site. In the end, the target that was chosen was Hiroshima, a manufacturing city of 350,000 residents, because of a vast military installation, a large T-shaped bridge that the bombardier could use as a target, and the supposed absence of Allied prisoner-of-war camps in the area. In the days preceding the bomb drop, U.S. bombers blanketed the city with leaflets warning the inhabitants to leave.

On August 6, Tibbets lifted his B-29, which he had named the *Enola Gay,* after his mother, from the island of Tinian and headed toward Japan. At 8:15 A.M. local time, the bombardier released the atomic bomb, called Little Boy because of its smaller size in relation to the second atomic bomb, and Tibbets veered the *Enola Gay* away from the blast center.

The bomb exploded 1,900 feet above Shima Hospital in Hiroshima's midsection with a force equal to 12,500 tons of TNT. A blinding light brightened the sky, and a dark cloud spread for three miles in diameter. From the midst arose a white mushroom cloud. Within one second, four square miles of Hiroshima disappeared and 80,000 people died. City residents were vaporized by the intense 300,000-degree Centigrade heat, which imprinted their shadows on sidewalks and bridge structures. Shortly after the explosion, a radioactive black rain started falling on the city.

In the *Enola Gay,* crew members sat in silent awe at the spectacle. A few cheered at first because they assumed this bomb would bring the war to an end, but their joy died quickly when they thought of the residents trapped by the churning black cloud. The copilot, Captain Robert A. Lewis, stared at the frightening explosion and muttered, "My God, what have we done?" Postwar estimates put the number of dead anywhere from 140,000 to 200,000. Half died in the explosion, and the other half perished within one month from radioactive poisoning.

When informed of what occurred at Hiroshima, Emperor Hirohito told an adviser that the nation must accept its fate and ask for peace. The Soviet Union declared war on Japan two days later and opened a huge offensive into Manchuria. When no word of surrender came from Japan, Truman ordered the use of the second bomb. On August 9, Major Charles W. Sweeney and his crew in *Bock's Car* dropped an atomic bomb on Nagasaki, a port city and shipbuilding center. Within months, 70,000 people had died as a result. Concerned that the United States possessed an arsenal of atomic bombs to devastate the entire country, and shocked by Soviet declaration of war, Japanese leaders asked for peace.

It is my earnest hope—indeed, the hope of all mankind—that from this solemn occasion a better world shall emerge out of the blood and carnage of the past, a world founded upon faith and understanding, a world dedicated to the dignity of man and the fulfillment of his most cherished wish for freedom, tolerance and justice. Let us pray that peace be now restored to the world and that God will preserve it always.

—General Douglas MacArthur
at the official ceremony marking Japan's surrender
aboard the battleship USS *Missouri*
September 2, 1945

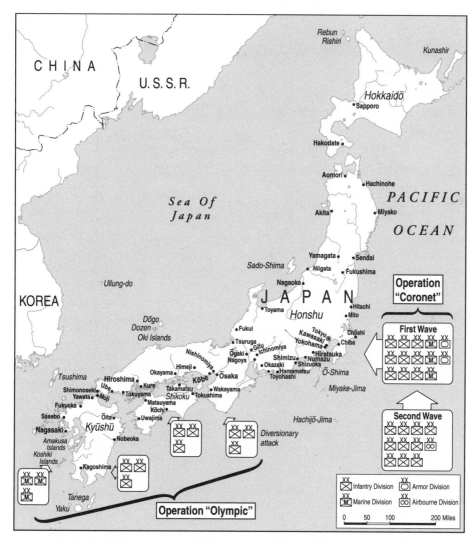

THE PLANNED ALLIED INVASION OF JAPAN (NEVER EXECUTED)

enough opportunity to surrender before unleashing such destruction.

Marianas Turkey Shoot (June 19, 1944)

The opening salvo of the Battle of the Philippine Sea involved a series of four sorties by Japanese aircraft against U.S. ships. In one of the most lopsided meetings of the war, U.S. carrier aircraft shot down most of the attacking Japanese before they reached their targets: 49 of 69 aircraft in the first wave, 98 of 130 in the second

wave, and 73 of 82 in the fourth. The third wave avoided serious harm, but only because it flew off course and failed to locate the Americans. U.S. pilots so easily outperformed the less experienced Japanese aviators that one compared it to a turkey shoot back home, where hunters leisurely bagged a string of turkeys in succession as they walked by. The Marianas Turkey Shoot effectively eliminated a large portion of the Japanese carrier aircraft force.

Nagasaki (August 9, 1945)

The Japanese port city of 250,000 became the second target of an American atomic bomb on August 9, 1945. Nearly 75,000 people perished in the explosion, which, combined with the damage inflicted at Hiroshima by the first atomic bomb, prodded the Japanese government to end the war.

Torpedo Squadron 8 (June 4, 1942)

A 15-plane torpedo-bomber unit from the U.S. aircraft carrier *Hornet* bravely attacked Japanese naval forces in the Battle of Midway. The aircraft dove in an attempt to hit enemy carriers, but Zeros (Japanese fighter aircraft) swarmed on them from all sides. One by one the planes exploded and crashed into the ocean. Only one U.S. airman, Ensign George H. Gay Jr., survived. Their acts of heroism, however, diverted Japanese attention from other U.S. dive-bombers that soon arrived and sank three Japanese carriers. A fourth Japanese carrier was later sunk.

TOP FIGHTER ACES

The top Japanese aces registered a high number of kills because they remained in combat much longer than their U.S. counterparts. However, while the Americans continually rotated a fresh group of aviators into the war and brought home experienced pilots to train other men, the ready supply of top Japanese pilots dwindled as the war ground on. Once those men were gone, their replacements proved no match for the better-prepared U.S. fliers.

U.S. ACES

Pilot	Number of Kills
Richard I. Bong	40
Thomas McGuire Jr.	38

Pilot	Number of Kills
David McCambell	34
Gregory Boyington	28
Charles W. MacDonald	27
Joseph J. Foss	26
Robert M. Hanson	25
Cecil E. Harris	24
Eugene A. Valencia	23
Gerald R. Johnson	22
Neil E. Kearby	22
Jay T. Robbins	22

JAPANESE ACES

Pilot	Number of Kills
Hiroyoshi Nishizawa	87
Tetsuzo Iwamoto	80
Shoichi Sugita	70
Saburo Sakai	64
Takeo Okumura	54
Toshio Ota	34
Kazuo Sugino	32
Shizuo Ishii	29
Kaneyoshi Muto	28
Jun-ichi Sasai	27

Source: James F. Dunnigan and Albert A. Nofi, *The Pacific War Encyclopedia* (New York: Checkmark Books, 1998), p. 4.

CHAPTER 9

Arms and Equipment

World War II ushered in the refinement of the weapons and forms of warfare in ways that combatants of previous wars could never have imagined. When the war began in Europe in 1939, some countries still relied on horse-drawn artillery, yet by August 1945 the world saw a weapon so powerful that a single detonation could destroy an entire city.

World War II was fought with such technologically advanced weapons as rocket bombs and jet aircraft. Radar, sonar, and other systems were refined. These weapons were taken to higher levels of technological sophistication in World War II and created a new kind of warfare—one in which firepower far exceeded anything ever before experienced.

At the end of World War I (1918), established militaries had developed the use of airplanes and dirigibles to bomb military and civilian targets. But these early aircraft were small, flimsy, and incapable of delivering much ordnance on their targets, and were easily shot down. By the beginning of World War II, however, the bomber had become a major weapon in most arsenals, and interceptor aircraft became its defensive counterpart.

Tanks, named for their boilerlike construction, became the standard battlefield weapon for armies in World War II. Armor combined with infantry permitted potent, knifelike thrusts into enemy territory. The aircraft carrier and the submarine changed the face of naval warfare. Submarines had played a role in previous wars, but the aircraft carrier was entirely new. Both carried war to the shores of far-away enemies that once would have been immune to direct attack. The aircraft carrier, in particular, projected airpower far beyond any previous capabilities. Great sea battles, which in the previous world war had been waged directly between battleships and cruisers, could now be fought by aircraft from carriers while the ships themselves were out of sight.

As with weapons, the variety of ordnance was wide, ranging from lightweight hand grenades to 20,000-pound "blockbuster" bombs dropped from four-engine land-based bombers. A variety of artillery shells, bullets, and bombs—of weights ranging from a few ounces to thousands of pounds—became efficient vehicles of destruction.

Aircraft

World War II is sometimes termed "the war of the airplane"—and with some justification. It began with aerial attacks and ended dramatically after a single airplane was shown to be capable of leveling a city. Several types of planes played a major role in Germany's blitzkrieg form of warfare—fighters to destroy the enemy's air forces, bombers to attack ground targets, and transports to provide mobility to ground forces and paratroops. Germany attempted to use the airplane as a strategic weapon, but its efforts were thwarted by the Luftwaffe's failure to destroy the British Royal Air Force during the great aerial campaign now known as the Battle of Britain.

Great Britain and the United States managed to wage a successful strategic bombing campaign against Germany but only after they developed long-range escort fighters that could accompany the bombers to and from their targets. Another strategic bombing campaign against Japan became possible after the development of the long-range Boeing B-29 Superfortress heavy bomber and the capture of Pacific islands close enough to Japan to serve as bases.

The capsule descriptions that follow outline key aircraft used by the major participants.

BRITAIN AND THE BRITISH COMMONWEALTH

Britain used several U.S.-supplied aircraft, and the British aircraft industry produced aircraft designs of its own, some of which proved outstanding.

AVRO LANCASTER A four-engine heavy bomber used primarily on night missions into Germany. The Royal Air Force's 617 Squadron used the huge bombers on special missions such as low-level attacks on the Ruhr dams.

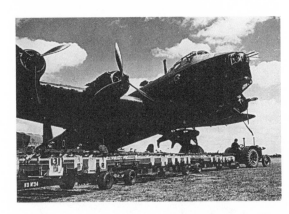

Ground crewmen load incendiary bombs aboard a bomber of the Royal Air Force in preparation for a night attack against an industrial target in Germany. Many of Germany's major cities also suffered greatly under a rain of American bombs by day and British by night.

AVRO YORK   A large, four-engine transport.

BLACKBURN FIREBRAND   Single-engine fighter/attack aircraft designed for the Royal Navy.

BOULTON-PAUL DEFIANT   Single-engine fighter equipped with a mechanically operated gun turret. Defiants were first used as day fighters—one squadron was credited with destroying 37 German aircraft over Dunkirk without loss—then adapted for the night fighter role.

BRISTOL BEAUFIGHTER   A twin-engine multifunctional aircraft that served as a night fighter, fighter, and attack aircraft using bombs, rockets, and torpedoes.

BRISTOL BEAUFORT   Light attack bomber and torpedo bomber, used with success by Australian forces in the southwestern Pacific.

COMMONWEALTH BOOMERANG   An Australian-produced single-engine fighter.

COMMONWEALTH WIRRAWAY   Australian-produced single-engine airplane.

DE HAVILLAND MOSQUITO   One of the most famous British aircraft of the war, the "Mossie" was a multifunctional aircraft that saw service in a variety of roles, including attack bomber, fighter, and reconnaissance. A unique feature of the Mosquito was its wooden construction.

FAIREY BARRACUDA   Single-engine torpedo bomber used in an attack on the German battleship *Tirpitz* in April 1944. Also used by Royal Navy forces in Southeast Asia.

FAIREY FIREFLY   Single-engine, two-seat naval reconnaissance aircraft and fighter.

FAIREY SWORDFISH   Single-engine biplane torpedo bomber that was the primary torpedo aircraft in the Royal Navy at the outbreak of the war. Although slow and antiquated by 1940 terms, the Swordfish played crucial roles in many naval actions, including the sinking of the *Bismarck*.

GLIDERS   The Royal Air Force and the British army used the British-built Airspeed Horsa and the American Waco to deliver airborne troops and supplies behind enemy lines. Gliders were a successful but somewhat risky means of transport.

HANDLEY-PAGE HALIFAX   Four-engine medium/heavy bomber and transport.

HAWKER FURY AND SEA FURY   Single-engine fighter and attack aircraft developed late in the war.

HAWKER HURRICANE   One of the first modern fighters, the single-engine Hurricane played a major role during the Battle of Britain. A versatile aircraft, the Hurricane also saw service as a ground attack aircraft and as a fleet fighter with the Royal Navy.

HAWKER TYPHOON AND TEMPEST   The Typhoon was designed as a fighter but was most successful as a ground attack aircraft. The Tempest was an advanced development of the Typhoon.

SHORT STIRLING   Four-engine heavy bomber, also used as a troop transport and glider tug.

SUPERMARINE SPITFIRE AND SEAFIRE
The most famous British aircraft of the war and one of the best known in aviation history, the Spitfire played a major role in the Battle of Britain. The single-engine fighters were very successful, but their limited range ruled out their use as deep-penetration escort fighters. Spitfires

also operated in the reconnaissance role. The Seafire was a naval adaptation.

VICKERS-ARMSTRONG WELLINGTON
Known by its crews as "Wimpy," the Wellington was a twin-engine land-based bomber that was used extensively by the Royal Air Force Bomber Command on night missions over Germany and by the RAF and Commonwealth forces all over the world.

> The jet plane was not the only effective new weapon that could have been slated for mass production in 1944. We possessed a remote-controlled flying bomb, a rocket plane that was faster than the jet plane, a rocket missile that homed on an enemy plane by tracking the heat rays from its motors, and a torpedo that reacted to sound.
>
> —German Armaments Minister Albert Speer

GERMANY
The German aircraft industry, in violation of the armistice terms that ended World War I, was revived in the 1920s and 1930s and produced some of the world's finest modern aircraft, including the first jet combat aircraft to see action.

ARADO AR-234
After producing the 232 transport, Arado developed the AR-234 as a twin-engine jet reconnaissance bomber. Instead of conventional landing gear, the 234 used an auxiliary cart for takeoff, then landed on skids.

DORNIER DO-217
A twin-engine bomber that saw wide service in Luftwaffe squadrons, the Dornier was one of the principal German bombers used against targets in the British Isles.

FIESELER STORCH
A light, three-piece, single-engine monoplane, the Storch was used extensively as a utility transport and in German special operations.

FOCKE-WULF FW-190
A single-engine fighter with a large radial engine, the Fw-190 was a primary Luftwaffe fighter.

FOCKE-WULF 200C CONDOR
Large, four-engine commercial transport converted to military use as a bomber and reconnaissance aircraft.

HEINKEL HE III
Extensively used twin-engine heavy bomber. Primarily a bomber, the He-III was also used as a torpedo bomber, a transport, and glider tug.

HEINKEL HE-II7
Long-range bomber and reconnaissance aircraft first used in cooperation with the German navy to attack convoys.

HENSCHEL HS-I26 AND HS-I29
The Hs-126 was used initially as a reconnaissance and close air support airplane, then was adapted for towing gliders. The Hs-129 was designed only for use as a ground attack plane on the Eastern Front.

JUNKERS 52
A trimotored transport originally produced for the German commercial airline industry, the Ju-52 was adapted to serve as the primary Luftwaffe transport.

JUNKERS 87 STUKA
A single-engine dive-bomber, the Stuka was one of the most feared German aircraft of the war's early years. Diving Stukas often signaled the beginning of a German advance. But as Allied air defenses improved, the slow speeds of the Ju-87, which had a fixed landing gear, made it an easy target for fighters.

JUNKERS 88
A highly maneuverable twin-engine airplane, the Ju-88 was a multifunctional design that saw service as a day and night fighter, bomber, and close-air support and reconnaissance aircraft.

JUNKERS 263
A small, rocket-propelled interceptor used to attack Allied bomber formations.

MESSERSCHMITT 109 Designed in the mid-1930s, the Me-109 was the primary Luftwaffe fighter at the outbreak of the war and one of the most famous fighter planes in history. Produced in large numbers, Me-109s served in the West and on the Eastern Front, and were a primary defensive aircraft against Allied bombers.

MESSERSCHMITT 110 A twin-engine fighter, the Me-110 saw wide service in roles that included day and night fighter, bomber, ground attack aircraft, and long-range reconnaissance aircraft. Although later aircraft were supposed to replace it, the Me-110 remained in production throughout the war. Variants of this aircraft were also produced for ground support and bombing roles and designated the Me-210, Me-310, and Me-410.

MESSERSCHMITT 163 An ultra-short-range rocket-powered interceptor that featured a delta-wing design and was used to attack Allied bombers.

MESSERSCHMITT 262 The Me-262 was the first truly successful operational jet fighter. A twin-engine jet fighter, it was a highly successful airplane that could create havoc among Allied bombers. Although Hitler's generals advised that it be produced as an interceptor, he concentrated on producing the attack version.

MESSERSCHMITT 323 A large, six-engine transport capable of carrying large vehicles because of its visorlike forward opening door.

ITALY

During the 1920s and 1930s, the Italian aviation industry was a world leader, but Italian designers were eventually outclassed by Great Britain, Germany, Japan, and the United States at the outbreak of the war. Several Italian-produced aircraft saw service.

CANT Z.506B Three-engine bomber-torpedo reconnaissance aircraft mounted on floats.

CANT Z.1007 Land-based derivative of the Z.506B.

CAPRONI CA-313 Twin-engine light reconnaissance bomber.

FIAT R.S. 14 Twin-engine reconnaissance/torpedo bomber configured as a seaplane.

MACCHI C.202 Single-engine fighter similar in appearance to the German Me-109, the C.202 was considered to be the best of the Italian fighters.

REGGIANE 2001 Single-engine fighter.

SAVOIA-MARCHETTI 70 Three-engine reconnaissance bomber, also used by the Germans as a transport.

SAVOIA-MARCHETTI 82 Armed transport derivative of the SM-70.

JAPAN

Between the world wars, the Japanese army and naval air forces evolved into one of the largest and most modern in the world. The Mitsubishi A6M2 fighter, as well as modern torpedo and bomber aircraft, in the hands of skilled pilots, provided Japan with the means to dominate the skies over Asia and the Pacific early in World War II. However, staggering losses in the naval battles of 1942, rapidly improving American aircraft development, and, later, the bombing of Japanese industry, spelled the demise of Japanese army and navy aircraft as effective fighting forces.

AICHI B7A1 RYUSEI (SHOOTING STAR) Designated by the Allies as "Grace," the Ryusei was a two-place single-engine carrier-based dive/torpedo bomber.

AICHI D3 VAL   Although it was considered obsolete before the war began, the Japanese used this dive-bomber successfully at Pearl Harbor and in other actions. It served as the main Japanese dive-bomber early in the war.

AICHI E16AI ZUIUN (AUSPICIOUS CLOUD) (ALLIED DESIGNATION: "PAUL")   A single-engine two-seat dive/torpedo bomber seaplane.

KAWANISHI H6K5 (ALLIED DESIGNATION: "MAVIS")   A large, four-engine reconnaissance/bomber flying boat.

KAWANISHI H8K2 (ALLIED DESIGNATION: "EMILY")   A four-engine flying boat used for reconnaissance and as a transport.

KAWANISHI NIK2-J SHIDEN (VIOLET LIGHTNING) (ALLIED DESIGNATION: "GEORGE")   Land-based derivative of the NiK1.

KAWASAKI TYPE 99 (ALLIED DESIGNATION: "LILY")   Twin-engine light bomber.

KAWASAKI KI-45 TORYU (DRAGON SLAYER) (ALLIED DESIGNATION: "NICK")   Twin-engine, two-seat fighter.

KAWASAKI KI-61 (ALLIED DESIGNATION: "TONY")   Single-engine, single-seat fighter.

MITSUBISHI A7MI ROPPU (HURRICANE) (ALLIED DESIGNATION: "SAM")   Single-engine, single-seat carrier-based fighter.

MITSUBISHI J4MI JINRAI (THUNDERCLAP) (ALLIED DESIGNATION: "LUKE")   Single-engine, twin-boom interceptor.

MITSUBISHI J2M2 RAIDEN (THUNDERBOLT) (ALLIED DESIGNATION: "JACK")   Single-engine land-based fighter.

MITSUBISHI A6M5 TYPE 0 (ALLIED DESIGNATION: ORIGINALLY "ZERO," THEN "ZEKE")   Carrier-based single-engine fighter; initial version was used in Pearl Harbor attack. The Zeke was greatly feared by Allied airmen flying underperforming aircraft. The Zero was one of the legendary aircraft to emerge from the war. (See sidebar on p. 309.)

MITSUBISHI KI-462 (ALLIED DESIGNATION: "DINAH")   Twin-engine reconnaissance aircraft.

MITSUBISHI KI-67 (ALLIED DESIGNATION: "PEGGY")   Twin-engine bomber, used as an attack, heavy, and torpedo bomber.

MITSUBISHI G4M2 (ALLIED DESIGNATION: "BETTY")   Twin-engine land attack bomber used by the Japanese navy from land bases.

MITSUBISHI KI-213 (ALLIED DESIGNATION: "SALLY")   Twin-engine army bomber.

NAKIJIMA KI-84 HEIN (FLYING SWALLOW) (ALLIED DESIGNATION: "FRANK")   Single-engine army bomber.

NAKIJIMA KI-44 SHOKI (FORMIDABLE) (ALLIED DESIGNATION: "TOJO")   Single-engine army fighter.

NAKIJIMA B6N2 TENZAN (HEAVENLY MOUNTAIN) (ALLIED DESIGNATION: "JILL")   Navy carrier-based torpedo bomber, also used for reconnaissance.

NAKIJIMA B5N2 TYPE 97 (ALLIED DESIGNATION: "KATE")   Navy carrier-based torpedo bomber.

NAKIJIMA KI-49 DONYA (DRAGON SWALLOW)   Twin-engine army heavy bomber.

YOKOSUKA D4Y5 AND D4Y2 (ALLIED DESIGNATION: "JUDY") Navy carrier-based bomber, also used for reconnaissance.

YOKOSUKA P1Y1 AND P1Y1S GINKA (MILKY WAY) AND HAKKO (WHITE LIGHT) (ALLIED DESIGNATION: "FRANCES") Originally designed to be a twin-engine land-based navy bomber, it was adapted for use as a night fighter.

SOVIET UNION

The Soviet Union had a thriving aircraft industry and produced and used several designs of its own. However, the Soviet military was also a recipient of several types of U.S.-manufactured aircraft.

Fighters

LAVOCHKIN LA-5 Single-engine fighter.

MIKOYAN/GUREVICH MIG-3 Single-engine fighter.

YAKOVLEV YAK-1 Single-seat fighter.

YAKOVLEV YAK-9 Later designation of the YAK-1.

THE ZERO

During the opening months of the war, the Japanese Mitsubishi A6M Type "0" fighter attained near-mythical status among both Allied and Japanese airmen. The Zero, as it came to be known, was an extremely light and agile fighter that achieved a large degree of success against Allied fighters early in the war in the Pacific.

To some degree, the success of the Zero was more the result of the inadequacies of the opposition than its own superiority. In 1941 the primary U.S. Navy fighter was the Grumman F4F Wildcat, a single-engine fighter that was obsolete when it entered service. It could climb only 1,900 feet per minute and had a ceiling of 34,000 feet, making it no match for the Zero, which could climb 3,000 feet per minute. The Zero was also considerably faster, But its one disadvantage was that it was extremely vulnerable and would come apart when hit by heavy-caliber machine-gun fire.

Until mid-1942, the U.S. Army depended on Curtiss P-40s and Bell P-39s in the Pacific. While the heavier P-40 was successful against the Zero in a diving attack, the Zero's maneuverability gave the Japanese pilots the advantage in a dogfight. The P-39 was an extremely agile airplane that could hold its own at lower altitudes, but its short wings gave it limited performance above 16,000 feet. The higher experience level of the Japanese pilots—some of whom had been fighting in China since 1937—also contributed to their success.

In November 1941, just before Pearl Harbor, a Zero had made a forced landing in Chinese territory. Claire Chennault, a retired U.S. Army captain working as an adviser to the Chinese, flew the airplane and made notes on its performance that were useful in the later success of his American Volunteer Group and the 23rd Fighter Group in China.

In the summer of 1942, the U.S. Navy was blessed with finding an intact Zero. A wounded pilot had landed the plane on a remote island in the Aleutians and died in the cockpit. The find allowed the navy to study the airplane and make design changes in the Grumman F6F Hellcat, a single-engine fighter under development to replace the Wildcat.

Even before the Hellcat, the days of Japanese air supremacy in the Pacific were ending. On December 27, 1942, nearly a year before the Hellcat entered combat operations, 12 American P-38s flew their first major mission against the Japanese. The Lightnings shot down 11 of the 27 Japanese bombers and fighters that they engaged and suffered only minor battle damage. Three days later, on January 1, 1943, a formation of 11 P-38s engaged a 12-plane formation of Zeros, shooting down nine, claiming another probable, and damaging two more. The indefatigable zero had finally been defeated.

Bombers

ILYUSHIN DB-3F   Twin-engine bomber/torpedo bomber.

ILYUSHIN IL-2 SHTURMOVIK   Single-engine attack bomber, one of the most successful Soviet aircraft of the war. It was most popular as a tank buster, because it was armed with heavy cannon, antitank rockets, and machine guns.

ILYUSHIN IL-4   Improved version of the IL-2.

PETLYAKOV PE-2   Twin-engine long-range multipurpose aircraft, used as a fighter, low-level attack aircraft, and dive-bomber.

TUPOLEV TB-7   Four-engine heavy bomber.

UNITED STATES

Although the U.S. aviation industry was somewhat behind those of Europe and Japan in 1939, by 1945 the United States had caught up and its airplanes had literally won control of the world's skies. Utilizing a tremendous manufacturing capability, the United States produced thousands of aircraft in its role as "the arsenal of democracy," whereby U.S.-built aircraft played not only deciding roles in every American campaign, but they also aided the Allies in their battles.

> Shoot them down in a friendly fashion.
> —Order to U.S. fighter pilots approached by Japanese planes in August 1945

BELL P-39 AIRACOBRA AND P-63 KINGCOBRA   The single-engine P-39 lacked the power to serve as an interceptor, but it could hold its own with Japanese fighters in New Guinea, where it fought as a primary escort fighter and attack aircraft in the early months of the Pacific war. The Soviet Union received P-39s and used them as ground attack aircraft. The P-63 was an upgrade of the P-39 that saw service primarily with the Soviets.

BELL P-59 AIRACOMET   Although it did not see action, the P-59 was the first operational U.S. jet fighter.

BOEING B-17 FLYING FORTRESS   Of all the U.S. aircraft used in the war, the Flying Fortress was the most famous. Designed in the early 1930s as a four-engine heavy bomber, this B-17 equipped U.S. bombing squadrons before the war and was involved in combat in the Pacific from the beginning. Most served with the Eighth and Fifteenth Air Forces on daylight bombing raids over Europe. A handful of early B-17s served with the Royal Air Force.

BOEING B-29 SUPERFORTRESS   A large high-altitude four-engine heavy bomber originally designed to strike Germany from bases in Northern Ireland, the B-29's service was confined to the Pacific because the war in Europe ended prior to its deployment there. Operations from China proved inefficient because of logistical problems, and all B-29s were based in the Marianas in 1944. Stripped of their armament, the B-29s carried large payloads of incendiary bombs that were dropped on Japanese cities during medium-level night raids. B-29s assigned to the 509th Composite Group dropped on Hiroshima and Nagasaki the only nuclear weapons to be used in combat.

BOEING PT-17 KAYDET   The biwinged Stearman trainer served both the U.S. Army and the U.S. Navy as a primary trainer for thousands of aviation cadets.

CHANCE VOUGHT F4U CORSAIR   One of the best fighters of the war, the Corsair served navy and marine squadrons in the Pacific, where it was used as a fighter, ground attack aircraft, and dive-bomber.

CHANCE VOUGHT OS2U KINGFISHER A large single-engine seaplane designed to be carried on large naval vessels. Kingfishers also served in the Royal Navy.

CONSOLIDATED MODEL 28 CATALINA Produced for the U.S. Navy, which used it as a patrol bomber and search-and-rescue aircraft, the twin-engine amphibious Catalina also saw service with the U.S. Army and with the British Royal Navy.

CONSOLIDATED MODEL 32 LIBERATOR Designated the B-24 by the U.S. Army, the Liberator was the most versatile and widely produced aircraft in history. First flown in 1940, Liberators were just entering service when the Japanese attacked Pearl Harbor, but by war's end they had served in all theaters. The B-24 was the mainstay of Allied bomber operations in the Pacific except for the attacks on the Japanese home islands by the B-29s. Liberators also served with the Eighth Air Force, where they made up about one-third of the bomber force, and with the 15th Air Force. The range, speed, and payload of the Liberator led to the conversion of several thousand to transport roles, where they were designated the C-87 Liberator Express.

CURTISS P-40 WARHAWK Although considered obsolete by some in 1941, the P-40 remained in production until 1944 and saw wide service with U.S. and Allied squadrons. P-40s entered combat on December 7, 1941, when pilots in Hawaii intercepted Japanese aircraft and shot several down, although the P-40s were badly outnumbered. The most famous P-40s were those fighting with the American Volunteer Group, the famed Flying Tigers, in China during the opening months of the war in the Pacific. With several variants, the P-40 also saw service

in North Africa, the Mediterranean, and the Aleutians.

CURTISS COMMANDO Designated the C-46 by the U.S. Army, the twin-engine Commando was a large transport capable of hauling heavy payloads over long distances. Although initially plagued with design problems that led to a worldwide grounding, C-46s became a mainstay of air transportation, particularly over the famous Himalayan Hump.

CURTISS HELLDIVER Designated the SB2C by the navy, the Helldiver was a single-engine carrier-based dive-bomber used in large numbers aboard U.S. Navy fast-attack carriers.

DOUGLAS BOSTON/HAVOC Designated the A-20, it was originally designed as a light bomber called Boston by the Royal Air Force, which used it both as a bomber and as a night fighter. Major Paul I. Gunn, a former U.S. Navy petty officer–pilot, developed a package of .50-caliber machine guns for a nose installation. The A-20 became a deadly weapon when carrying the machine guns and parachute fragmentation bombs. Factory-produced models of this modification, the A-20G, became known as the Havoc.

A U.S. Liberator bomber retracts its landing gear as it takes flight from a Chinese airfield. In the foreground are Curtiss P-40 Tomahawk fighters, their noses painted to resemble the mouths of sharks.

DOUGLAS C-47 SKYTRAIN Designed in the early 1930s, the twin-engine Douglas DC-3 was quickly adapted as a commercial transport all over the world. When war broke out, the U.S. Army adapted the DC-3 to serve as a military transport, giving it the designation C-47, often called "Gooney Bird." A special version built for paratroop operations was designated the C-53. General Dwight Eisenhower referred to the C-47 as one of the most important weapons of the war.

DOUGLAS C-54 SKYMASTER Under development as the DC-4 when the war broke out, the four-engine C-54 first entered military service in 1942, although it did not become the primary long-range transport in the army's Air Transport Command until 1944. By war's end, C-54s were a regular sight at airfields worldwide as they operated along the far-flung routes of the Air Transport Command.

DOUGLAS DAUNTLESS Designated by the navy as the SBD and by the army as the A-24, the Dauntless was the primary dive-bomber in the U.S. inventory in 1942. SBDs struck the deciding blow in the Battle of Midway, destroying four Japanese aircraft carriers. Its main weakness was lack of defense against enemy fighters.

DOUGLAS DEVASTATOR A single-engine torpedo bomber, the Devastator was obsolete at the beginning of the war. This craft suffered severe losses in combat against Japanese fighter defenses and antiaircraft fire before it was replaced.

GRUMMAN WILDCAT U.S. Navy F4F, the single-engine Wildcat, was the navy's primary fighter in the early days of the war. Wildcats were less maneuverable than the Japanese Zero and proved to be less than a match.

GRUMMAN F6F HELLCAT This was the primary U.S. carrier-based plane of the war. It car-ried either six .50-caliber machine guns or two 20mm cannon and four .50-caliber guns, as well as up to 2,000 pounds of bombs. It was widely successful and decimated Japanese airpower.

GRUMMAN TBF AVENGER The single-engine, three-seat Avenger was a large, carrier-based torpedo bomber. Also produced by General Motors as the TBM, Avengers saw wide service in the Pacific theater.

GRUMMAN GOOSE AND WIDGEON High-wing, twin-engine amphibians used by the navy as light transports and by the coast guard for search and rescue.

LOCKHEED P-38 LIGHTNING The twin-engine P-38 was a preferred fighter in the Far East where it was flown by three of the war's top-scoring U.S. aces: Major Thomas McGuire, Major Tommy Lynch, and Major Richard I. Bong, the top American ace of all time. The unarmed photo-reconnaissance version was designated as the F-5.

LOCKHEED HUDSON A twin-engine transport modified as an attack bomber and designated as the A-28 and A-29. Hudsons were

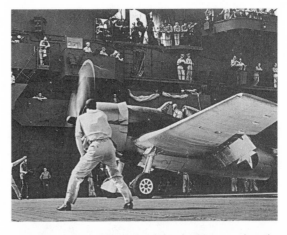

A U.S. Navy Grumman F6F Hellcat fighter begins to roar down the flight deck of an aircraft carrier. Part of a new generation of American fighter planes, the Hellcat was the dominant carrier-borne aircraft of its type from 1943 until the end of the war.

produced for the Royal Air Force and China, as well as for several other Allied air forces.

LOCKHEED CONSTELLATION A four-engine high-altitude transport, the military version of the Constellation served with the Air Transport Command as the C-69.

LOCKHEED LODESTAR Designated the C-60, the twin-engine Lodestar saw service as a troop carrier transport in the southwestern Pacific early in the war. It was also used by the navy.

LOCKHEED P-80 SHOOTING STAR A single-engine jet fighter, the P-80 did not become operational in time to enter combat.

MARTIN MARINER Large twin-engine flying boat, designated the PBM, used as a patrol bomber.

MARTIN B-26 MARAUDER A twin-engine medium bomber, the B-26 had a reputation for being difficult to fly but had the lowest incidence of combat loss—thanks more to tactics than design—of any U.S. Army bomber in Europe.

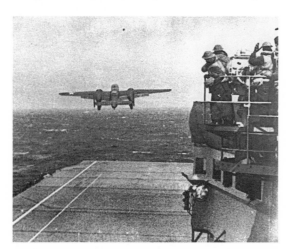

A B-25 Mitchell bomber of the U.S. Army Air Corps strains skyward from the deck of the aircraft carrier USS *Hornet*. The bomber was one of 16 led by Lieutenant Colonel Jimmy Doolittle, which attacked the Japanese capital of Tokyo on April 18, 1942.

NORTH AMERICAN P-51 MUSTANG Probably the most famous American airplane of the war, the Mustang was originally designed for the British. An Army Air Forces demand for a long-range escort fighter led to a redesign of the airframe to accommodate additional fuel. The Mustang became the preferred fighter in Europe after mid-1944 but entered service in the Pacific in large numbers only in the war's final months.

NORTH AMERICAN B-25 MITCHELL A twin-engine medium bomber, the Mitchell is best known as the aircraft used in the Doolittle raid on Japan in 1942. A field modification of a squadron of B-25s turned the Mitchell into a devastating ground and sea attack weapon.

REPUBLIC P-47 THUNDERBOLT A large, durable single-engine fighter equipped with a radial engine, the P-47 achieved an admirable record in both Europe and the southwestern Pacific. After D-Day, P-47s were a mainstay of the Ninth Air Force, a special unit created to provide tactical support for ground troops in Normandy.

STINSON L-5 A light, two-seat single-engine utility aircraft used for liaison and observation.

WACO GLIDERS The CG-4 was the only American-produced glider used in large numbers during the war. CG-4s participated in both the Sicily and Normandy invasions. They were followed by the CG-13 and then the CG-15.

Armor, Artillery, and Vehicles

With few exceptions, this war was not to be fought in the trenches. World War II began with the German blitzkrieg, a lightning-fast attack that relied heavily on mobile troops, tanks, armored cars, and self-propelled artillery. Germany used a force that depended on speed

ROBERT BUTLER, GLIDER PILOT

Learning to Glide

. . . When I found out that they were looking for volunteer glider pilots, I immediately applied. The qualification for becoming a glider pilot at that time was that you had to have a pilot's license in civilian life, which I did have, at a rather tender age.

Our training started in Victorville [California], and we promptly became staff sergeants in order to get larger flight pay, I believe, and graduated as flight officers, which was a new designation and rank alongside a warrant officer. We were accorded the privilege of going into officers' clubs and eating in the officers' mess and that sort of thing but really were never totally accepted as a full-fledged officer.

Our training after graduation from Victorville was in various areas of the United States, from Arizona to Texas to Louisville, Kentucky, and one of the first was at Tucumcary, New Mexico, where the air force had taken over a dude ranch which had a landing strip, and there were about twenty of us that lived very exclusively in the dude ranch facilities, with their French chef and that sort of thing.

We had as our instructor a German defectee who was a world-famous glider pilot and had trained many German troops and pilots prior to their entering World War II. As you will recall, the Germans were not allowed after World War I to have any power planes, so they instead became very proficient in gliders. We learned a great deal from this German instructor, who was very strict and taught us a great deal about clouds and thermal activities from mountain to mountain, cloud to cloud, and desert to desert.

We had as our training glider Sweitzer gliders, which were our finest soaring glider at that time, and they could stay up for literally hours, gliding from thermal to thermal, cloud to cloud, and mountain tip to mountain tip. It was really a great experience. However, we were to find out later on that this soaring-type glider had little or nothing to do in relation to military gliders.

Eventually, we got into the CG-4 military gliders, which carried fifteen full-laden airborne troops, and practiced for many, many months throughout the country under every condition imaginable. I eventually became an instructor in North Carolina for nighttime training, and I must say that this experience was equally as exciting as combat duty, in that we had to land by smudge pots at night, in very small areas, and we instructors of course had to wait until the very last second to take over in case of emergencies, and there were many. It was a nerve-racking job, and I was almost elated when I received word that I was being transferred to England.

—Eisenhower Center for American Studies Archives

and mobility to occupy most of Europe. These same tactics were used by the Allies to drive the Germans back. From Normandy in the west to Stalingrad in the east, Allied forces on wheels and treads literally drove the Germans into ever-shrinking pockets of resistance.

In the Pacific, the Allies faced a different kind of enemy. The Japanese empire across the Pacific consisted of many places that were little more than fortified slabs of coral and rock. Combat operations in the Pacific involved amphibious vehicles, pack howitzers, and a more limited use of armor. Vehicles and weapons once considered experimental became paramount as the island-hopping campaigns slogged their way toward Japan.

BRITAIN AND BRITISH COMMONWEALTH

The British land forces used a wide complement of vehicles and artillery. Some were prewar models that were obsolete even as they rolled off the lines. Others were imports, such as the famous

40mm Bofors antiaircraft gun designed by Sweden. Britain had little heavy artillery but did have well-designed tanks, howitzers, armored cars, and other vehicles.

> Tanks are very blind and cannot reconnoitre by themselves. In mobile war they will normally move forward by bounds in support of the advancing infantry.
> —Field Marshal Bernard Law Montgomery

Armor

TANKS

MK VII TETRARCH This was Britain's attempt to develop a tank capable of transport aboard aircraft with airborne troops. Armed with either 40mm or three-inch cannon, they proved adequate.

MK VI CRUSADER Another early tank, it was technically obsolete even as it was built. It saw action in North Africa as a frontline tank and later was relegated to such tasks as towing artillery.

MK III VALENTINE This excellent tank saw service in all theaters throughout the war. The chassis of this vehicle normally sported a turret-mounted 75mm main gun, but it was also used for self-propelled artillery, mine-clearing devices, and in engineer battalions. Well suited to upgrades, its drawback was its slow speed.

CHURCHILL TANKS If the Valentine provided the bulk of the frontline force at the war's beginning, the Churchill stood ready in the second wave. Usually equipped with a 75mm main gun, this tank had many variants, including a flamethrower version.

ARMORED CARS

Although far behind the United States in tank development, the British had a clear edge in armored car design as a result of the early engagements of British Field Marshal Bernard Montgomery in the deserts of Africa.

AEC ARMORED CARS Basically a wheeled tank, these privately built vehicles were armed with a variety of weapons, including a main gun as large as a 75mm or an antiaircraft cannon. Although not widely used, they were similar in many respects to modern armored cars.

DAIMLER ARMORED CARS Many reconnaissance troops considered these four-wheeled vehicles to be the best. They were armed with a 40mm cannon in the turret and coaxial 7.62mm machine guns. Their top speed was about 50 mph with a range of more than 200 miles.

HUMBER ARMORED CARS Although produced in larger numbers than the Daimler variants, this vehicle was not as successful in its intended role of scouting and reconnaissance. It originally relied on a heavy machine gun and smaller .30-caliber weapons. Redeployed as an assault vehicle and festooned with light machine guns to provide covering fire, it advanced with the troops, using its armor to shield them.

SELF-PROPELLED ARTILLERY AND TANK DESTROYERS

ARCHER Built on a converted Valentine tank chassis, this was Britain's only self-produced antitank weapon, with a three-inch long-barreled cannon. It was unique in that its fixed gun faced to the rear so it could fire and pull back rather than reverse itself in a sticky situation.

BISHOP This was Britain's only attempt at producing self-propelled artillery. It was armed with a powerful 3.5-inch gun but was slow, cramped, and could not fire its cannon at a high trajectory.

TRUCKS AND CARS

Commonwealth forces used several British-designed trucks, such as the Matador, a modified tractor, and the Bedford QL and Humber models, which did well in a variety of roles. After Dunkirk, British forces relied mainly on American-supplied trucks.

AMPHIBIOUS VEHICLES

DD SHERMAN An amphibious version of the ubiquitous M4 Sherman, it used air tubes, a collapsible screen, and snorkel gear. Along with the Terrapin, which was the British equivalent of a DUKW, the DD Sherman was the only British amphibious vehicle of note used during the war.

Artillery

HOWITZERS, 7.2-INCH The variants of the 7.2-inch howitzer were the only organic pieces of heavy artillery that Commonwealth troops used throughout the war. They could lob a 200-pound shell more than 14 miles. They were phased out by 1944.

HOWITZER, QF 4.5-INCH Developed in 1910, this gun was valued for its elevation, which enabled it to drop shells onto dug-in positions. It could deliver a 35-pound shell 7,000 yards.

MK I 60-POUNDER This five-inch gun was Britain's main long-range weapon and could send a 60-pound shell at a flat trajectory more than 12,000 yards.

BRITISH MORTARS

For close infantry support, the British leaned toward mortars, which use plunging fire at close range to drop relatively small projectiles on enemy positions or troops.

2-INCH ML Carried by one man who was assisted by an ammo bearer, this was used at the platoon level for close support.

3-INCH ML This weapon could be broken into loads and carried by three men. It could fire a 10-pound shell 2,800 yards.

4.2-INCH, SB A crew-served weapon that fired a 20-pound shell 4,000 yards.

ANTIAIRCRAFT ARTILLERY

The German air raids on British cities (the Blitz) offered British forces plenty of opportunity to hone their antiaircraft skills. Along with the 40mm Bofors gun, two other designs formed the backbone of British air defense.

QF 3.7-INCH MK III This main British air defense weapon could hurl a 28-pound shell as high as 32,000 feet. It could be fired alone or from a fire-control center, which often used radar to help aim.

QF 4.5-INCH AA MK II This heavy weapon played a dual role as an antiaircraft and coastal defense piece. It could throw a 54-pound shell higher than 42,000 feet and featured automated ammunition handling.

LIGHT ANTIAIRCRAFT ARTILLERY

Great Britain had only one native light antiaircraft artillery piece, the Polsten. This 20mm gun could fire 450 rounds per minute and was inexpensive to manufacture. Other low-level antiaircraft artillery that British forces liked to use included the Swiss 20mm Oerlikon and the American Maxson Mount.

FRANCE

The "French 75," the world's first quick-firing mobile cannon, set the standard of battlefield supremacy in World War I. By 1939, French generals were ready to fight the same war again. But their static defenses along the Maginot Line were outflanked, and in a short time Paris fell. But the Free French Army escaped the occupation, and both the Axis and Allies pressed French weapons into service.

Armor

TANKS

CHAR BI-BIS HEAVY TANK This monstrous tank was armed with a 40mm cannon in the turret and a 75mm main gun in the hull. It was quite modern for its time and did well in the fight for France in early 1940.

RENAULT R-35 This light tank had a crew of two, a 37mm cannon, and a 7.5mm machine gun. Produced in large numbers, it was an ideal scout vehicle.

S-35 MEDIUM TANK This tank was well suited for the early stages of the war, with a 47mm main gun, radio, and maneuverability.

ARMORED CARS

PANHARD 178 This, the only significant French armored car, was a four-by-four car armed with either a 25mm cannon or machine guns. The Germans pressed Panhard 178s into service. They were also used by the Allies and issued to Free French cavalry units.

THE BATTLE OF KURSK

After the defeat of the German Sixth Army at Stalingrad in the winter of 1942–43, the German high command planned a massive counteroffensive to halt the Soviet advance and to reduce a 150-mile bulge, a salient jutting from Soviet lines around the city of Kursk into German territory. This bulge was a weak spot in the German lines, and the high command feared that Soviet forces would break through. Code named Citadel, what ensued was what is considered to be the largest tank battle in history, in which more than 6,000 tanks were engaged. Fifty divisions, including 16 panzer and motorized divisions, assembled for the attack. By the end of June, Germany had more than 2,700 tanks and assault vehicles, 10,000 guns, and 2,000 planes facing the Soviet forces at Kursk. German forces totaled more than 900,000 men. Soviet forces were stronger, with more than a million troops, 3,400 tanks and assault vehicles, and 2,100 planes.

The attack began on July 5, and within two hours the German forces had managed to break through the Red Army lines. But the German success was short-lived. A massive summer thunderstorm broke over the battlefield, slowing the German thrust. Then the advancing troops encountered minefields. By July 8, the Soviets had halted the Germans on every front and were beginning to push them back. Three German divisions advanced toward the town of Prokhorovka and a Soviet trap. As the panzers emerged from the town on July 12, Soviet forces launched a counterattack. This epic clash ended in a stalemate, as the German losses were offset by two corps of panzers that caught a sizable Soviet force between them in a pincer movement. But unlike the Germans, the Soviets had reserves, and the tactical draw was a strategic victory for the Red Army.

Upon learning of Allied landings in Sicily, Hitler ordered that Citadel be terminated the same day. German forces tried to advance in an attempt to inflict at least a partial defeat on the superior Soviet force. The battle took on what has been described as a "seesaw" effect until August 6, when German forces began withdrawing into defensive positions. After Kursk, the Germans could never again muster the necessary force to go on the offensive against the Soviets, and from 1943, Germany remained on the defensive all along the Eastern Front.

Artillery

FRENCH 75 Many countries used this venerable cannon throughout World War II. They were obviously no match for overwhelming German firepower, and the Germans captured many from surrendering French artillery companies. Then the Germans adapted the 75 for antitank use, and the United States used a modified version of it aboard B-25 Mitchells as a "ship-buster."

ANTIAIRCRAFT ARTILLERY

25MM HOTCHKISS Useful against both ground and air targets, this rapid-fire gun was crucial in France's defense network but was not available in sufficient numbers by 1940.

GERMANY

The German army was an army of contrasts. Its image was one of charging tanks and halftracks that outflanked obsolete static defensive positions. Yet in reality the bulk of its artillery was horse drawn, and most troops were foot soldiers, marching from one position to another. While many German weapons were state-of-the-art, basic shortcomings in command and control, coupled with the tremendous funneling of resources to Hitler's pet projects, meant that when faced with a competent, prepared enemy, the German soldier and his aura of invincibility crumbled.

Armor

TANKS

Throughout World War II, no other nation expended more effort to build the perfect tank than did Germany. The evolution of modern tanks can be traced from small lightly armed and armored vehicles to the monstrous Tiger II.

PZKPFW I Built mainly for training purposes, these armored fighting vehicles were adapted before the attack on Poland and sent into combat, where they quickly became obsolete.

PZKPFW II Armed with a 20mm cannon and machine gun, this proved to be an adequate reconnaissance tank in the early years of the war. After the PzKpfw II became obsolete, its chassis was used in a multitude of roles.

PZKPFW III Germany's first true combat tank had a 50mm main gun and was well suited for action in the West and Africa but was no match for the Soviet T-34.

PZKPFW IV This was Germany's standard battle tank—quite modern and armed with a 75mm cannon that could fire different types of rounds, including high explosive and armor piercing. Produced in large numbers, it was used throughout the war.

PZKPFW V Hitler's answer to the T-34, this tank, known to the troops as the "Panther," featured a long-barreled 75mm main gun and carried a crew of four. It operated throughout the European theater.

PZKPFW VI The Panzer VI, or Tiger, was armed with the dreaded 88mm gun. Greatly feared by the Allies in Normandy, it could easily outgun a Sherman.

PZKPFW VI TIGER II Representative of the German war machine and its basic flaws, this tank, so good on paper, did not perform well on the battlefield. It was too large to move without attracting Allied air patrols and used so much fuel that many were simply abandoned intact for lack of petrol. Armed with an 88mm gun and heavily armored, it was a formidable foe but a logistical nightmare.

ARMORED CARS

PANZERSPÄHWAGEN SDKFZ This eight-by-eight chassis formed the base of most German armored car variants. Versions included antiaircraft, antitank, and reconnaissance, as well as command-and-control vehicles.

PZKW SDKFZ 222 This four-by-four light armored vehicle was used throughout the war in a variety of roles, and a version was built as a halftrack.

SELF-PROPELLED ARTILLERY AND TANK DESTROYERS

BRUMMBÄR This 150mm self-propelled howitzer was unique in providing adequate armor protection for the crew as well as machine guns to fend off infantry attacks.

HETZER This vehicle's 75mm gun could knock out all but the heaviest vehicles that it encountered; it was a difficult adversary because of its low height and maneuverability.

HUMMEL Crewed by five, this tracked howitzer with a 150mm gun could fire a 95-pound projectile 14,000 yards.

JAGDPANTHER This was Germany's best run at an antitank weapon. Its powerful 88mm gun could take down anything on the battlefield, and its heavy armor protected its crew. Production fell behind, though, as it did for so many other German projects, and by war's end relatively few had been built.

KARL A series of siege mortars, these self-propelled giants sported 540mm or 600mm howitzers and could fire shells weighing as much as 2 tons.

MARDER This series of tank destroyers was built as German troops ran up against stiffening opposition in the East, specifically the Soviets' T-34. Most versions were equipped with a 76.2mm long-barreled cannon.

PANZERJÄGER Built on the chassis of a Panzer 1 tank, it was equipped with a 47mm cannon.

STURMTIGER This was a rocket projecter, not an actual self-propelled gun, that could hurl naval depth charges modified for use against hard, reinforced targets.

WESPE A 105mm self-propelled gun with a crew of five that either used direct fire or radio instruction for indirect-fire missions.

Other Vehicles

HALFTRACKS Although halftracks were expensive to build and maintain, the German army used them extensively as troop carriers, antiaircraft platforms, rocket launchers, and mobile artillery. They performed quite well on the muddy and frozen Russian plains.

SDKFZ This line was by far the most prolific, with nine different models of vehicles used mainly for purposes similar to American halftracks, and many variations of each. Some were well armored and armed, such as the 251; others were open and unarmed, like the SdKfz8, which was basically a flatbed tractor.

TRUCKS

OPEL BLITZ The most common German truck of the war had many variants, including uses as ambulance, cargo hauler, and mobile radio post. It had a range of 255 miles and was produced in four-by-two and four-by-four versions.

Artillery

HEAVY ARTILLERY

HAUBITZE M. 1 This 355mm behemoth was a siege weapon. Used only at Sevastopol in the Soviet Union, it took such a large crew to operate that it diverted manpower and resources from the main effort.

KRUPP HEAVY CANNON Arms maker Krupp created huge 180, 210, and 240mm cannons, which could discharge a 150-pound shell 32,000 yards or a 300-pound shell nearly 24 miles.

150MM GUNS Considered division-level weapons, the 150mm cannon had several variants, including the Kanones 18 and 39, which lobbed 94-pound shells more than 26,000 yards.

FIELD ARTILLERY

75MM FELDKANONE These World War I–vintage guns were updated and put to adequate use, able to fire a 12-pound armor-piercing or high-explosive shell as far as 10,000 yards.

105MM HOWITZER The 105mm gun was the German standard in field artillery and was quite formidable against France in 1940. However, in the vastness of the Eastern Front, it was considered too heavy and likely to bog down. It was also outgunned after D-Day, and although this class of weapons stayed on the line, the infantry disliked it.

ANTITANK AND SUPPORT WEAPONS

GERMAN MORTARS The Germans had 50mm and 80mm mortars, referred to as light or heavy grenade launchers.

PAK 35/36 This early antiarmor weapon was effective in the opening stages of the war but was quickly outclassed.

PAK 38 A 50mm long-barreled gun, it could defeat the Soviet T-34 but just barely.

PAK 40 This 75mm gun, intended as field artillery, found its true calling as an antitank weapon.

ANTIAIRCRAFT ARTILLERY

20MM FLAK The Germans had a number of 20mm rapid-fire guns, in all manner of mounts and combinations. Quad 20mm Flak 38s, Flak 30s, and a hodgepodge of captured and redesignated weapons completed this class.

37MM FLAK Like the 20mm series, this caliber weapon came in many versions and combinations. It had naval mountings, self-propelled and towed versions, as well as static emplacements at strategic locations.

FLAK 38 A 105mm cannon that was too heavy to be used in a mobile role, it provided adequate air cover from static positions.

FLAK 40 This heavy five-inch gun was relegated to homeland security and was prevalent in flak towers near centers of population and industry.

FLAK 88 Germany's most versatile piece of artillery, the 88mm gun was a plane killer and tank destroyer but could just as easily fire on ships or infantry with deadly accuracy, and it found its way into every theater of the war, on every mounting system imaginable. One of World War II's most famous and effective field guns, it had no comparable match in any other arsenal.

LIGHT ANTIAIRCRAFT ARTILLERY WEAPONS Like many other endeavors, this area of armament lacked standardization. The German arsenal included a host of rapid-fire weapons.

ITALY

By far the weakest and most ill-equipped of the Axis powers, Italy had little in the way of armor, artillery, or other vehicles. When Italy surrendered in 1943, German troops occupied the country and seized whatever equipment they could.

Armor

TANKS

FIAT 6/40 This light tank had a crew of two and was armed with a 37mm or 47mm main gun, as well as light machine guns.

FIAT MEDIUM TANKS Armed with a 47mm gun, Italy's most powerful tank was the M 15/42. Other models had similar complements of weapons and machine guns but were not suited to heavy combat. Plans were under way to develop a Fiat with a 75mm cannon, but after Italy surrendered, the Germans seized these prototypes.

ARMORED CARS

AUTOBLINDA MODELS 40 AND 41 These were successful designs, fitted with armament and kit based upon their area of operation. They usually featured 20mm dual-purpose antiartillery aircraft or antiarmor main guns, as well as light machine guns. With a top speed of 50 mph, they were an effective weapon.

SELF-PROPELLED ARTILLERY AND TANK DESTROYERS

L.40 DA 47/32 Italy was among the first countries to develop the tank destroyer, and several vehicles loosely fit this category. The main version was armed with a 47mm gun, but later models, including the M.41M, had a 90mm gun. Either version could be used against armor, but they were mainly used as artillery.

SEMOVENTE These assault guns carried either 75mm or 105mm long guns. These models afforded no protection for their crews and were basically gun tractors rather than actual self-propelled artillery.

Trucks and Cars

Although it had a number of light vehicles in service, Italy's premier truck was the OM Autocarretta, which handled the desert and mountains equally well. Other models included the Dovunque, or "Go Anywhere," and the Fiat TL37, a four-by-four carrier.

Artillery

45/5 MODELLO 35 The "Bixia" was Italy's idea of a mortar-grenade launcher. Complicated and inaccurate, it delivered far too little firepower for the energy that went into deploying it.

CANNONE DA 75/27 These throwbacks to World War I proved to be useful, although they did not have the same modern look and sophisticated fire control of comparable pieces.

CANNONE DA 75/32 A good field weapon and one of Italy's few successful prewar designs, this 75mm gun was quite versatile. It had sufficient elevation (−10 to +45 degrees) to be used as an antitank or direct-fire gun.

OBICE DA 75/18 This was an excellent mountain gun and among the last of a dying style of weapon. It could be carried by eight men up steep slopes or provide standard battery fire.

OBICE DA 210/22 Italy's only native heavy artillery, this 210mm howitzer could fire a shell nearly 17,000 yards. For transport it could be broken into two loads, and even after Italy's surrender, the Germans kept the gun in production.

ANTIAIRCRAFT ARTILLERY

20MM BREDA Comparable to the Scotti, it was equipped to deal with ground or air targets and was much more mobile.

20MM SCOTTI This was the main light anti-aircraft artillery gun of the Italian army. It had a high rate of fire and could be emplaced in static positions or towed by truck.

CANNONE DA 75/46 C.A. MODELLO 34 This was an effective gun that could send a 14-pound shell higher than 27,000 feet. Problems were with deployment and production, and in the end the Germans absorbed it into their arsenal.

CANNONE DA 90/53 Otherwise a good weapon, production problems prevented this 90mm antiaircraft artillery piece from meeting its full potential.

JAPAN

Japan's military focused on conquest from 1937 to 1942, traveling light and subduing disorganized and weak resistance. After the battle for Guadalcanal (1942) its focus shifted to fortifying and holding islands, atolls, and jungle airstrips. This shift presented an interesting challenge: how could an army successfully execute the transition from tactics that emphasized light, rapid advances to dug-in, traditional siege warfare? A look at Japanese armament throughout the war shows the shift in attention.

Armor

TANKS

Japan had only two tank models, neither of which was competitive by the time the United States entered the war. Yet tanks played an integral part in Japanese defensive strategy and served their purpose in holding up the U.S. advances. The Type 95 light tank was fitted with a 37mm cannon and two machine guns. The Type 97 medium tank, armed with a 57mm main gun, was completely outclassed by U.S. armor.

SELF-PROPELLED ARTILLERY

TYPE 4 HO-RO Japan's only true self-propelled gun, this tracked vehicle carried a 150mm howitzer. Crudely built and based on old designs, it had poor armor and was never engaged in large numbers.

Trucks and Cars

During the war, the Japanese military was required to hop from island to island and to trek across expanses of jungle. Supplies were generally ferried by boat and then carried by hand or rail. The few trucks and cars in most Japanese garrisons were usually knockoffs of U.S. vehicles, bought before the war or looted from seized territories. The only mass-produced light Japanese vehicle of note was the Type 95 Scout Car, which was used mainly for reconnaissance.

Amphibious Vehicles

TYPE 2 KA-MI Japanese troops used this amphibious light tank armed with one 37mm gun and two machine guns.

Artillery

Japan had virtually no heavy artillery. Its army was equipped with 75mm field guns, 70mm Battalion Gun Type 92, the 47mm Antitank Gun Type 1, and mortars. When the Japanese turned to siege warfare, they used a hodgepodge of weapons, including a wide variety of naval cannon, weapons scavenged from Allied ships, guns stripped from downed fighters, huge rockets, and spigot mortars.

SOVIET UNION

Like the United States, the Soviet Union had many natural resources and a large population from which to pull soldiers and workers. However, for the first few grim months of the war in 1941, Stalin was paralyzed militarily as the German offensive thrust deep into Russia. Only U.S. Lend-Lease aid stabilized the front and allowed the Soviets time to regroup.

> The Russian tanks are so agile, at close range they will climb a slope or cross a piece of swamp faster than you can traverse the turret.
>
> —A German tank soldier

Armor

TANKS

The first several rounds of Soviet tanks, including the T-40, T-60, T-26, and T-28, were all basically cannon fodder: something to throw at the Germans while the Soviets developed a real weapon.

IS-2 HEAVY TANK This monster, with a 122mm gun and heavy armor, was effective in battle and influenced postwar design for quite some time.

KV-1 A heavy tank, armed with either a 76.2mm gun or, in the case of the KV-2 variant, a 152mm howitzer. It was plagued with engine problems, and its high turret made it less stealthy than other contemporary tanks.

T-34 The T-34 was the Soviet Union's first tank that could hold its own against the Germans. Armed with a 76.2mm gun and two light machine guns, it was considered by many to be the best tank of the war, combining speed and maneuverability with armor and firepower.

ARMORED CARS

The BA-10 was the only Soviet armored car of any importance in the war. The six-wheeled vehicle sported a 37mm gun or heavy machine gun as its main armament. Later versions were fitted with a 45mm cannon.

SELF-PROPELLED ARTILLERY AND TANK DESTROYERS

ISU-122 AND ISU-152 These were 122mm and 152mm guns mounted on a KV-2 heavy-tank chassis. They debuted at the great tank battle at Kursk (1943), where they blasted German tanks from beyond range of enemy weapons. They became a fixture throughout the rest of the war.

SU-76 This was the Soviet Union's first-response vehicle in the early days of the war. Basically a three-inch howitzer slapped onto a tank chassis, it provided direct-fire support during the early days of the war as Stalin tried to slow the Germans.

Trucks and Cars

The Soviet Union used Lend-Lease vehicles from the United States.

Artillery

MODEL 1903 203MM This tractor-mounted behemoth of a howitzer was the premier Soviet heavy weapon. It could fire a 220-pound shell almost 20,000 yards.

MODEL 1937 152MM This howitzer was capable of firing a 95-pound shell a distance of 18,500 yards.

MODEL 1942 45MM This antitank gun was effective early in the war but grew obsolete as German armor gained power. It could be effective at ranges up to 330 yards.

MODEL 1943 152MM This howitzer was unique in that it served as a flat trajectory weapon and provided plunging fire. It could drop a 110-pound HE shell 13,000 yards away just as easily as it could flatten a tank on the horizon.

SOVIET MORTARS Like the United States, the Soviet Union had a series of mortars, ranging from the 50mm 50-PM 40 to the 107mm

107PBHM 38. Each weapon varied in crew size and performance, much as U.S. mortar teams did, but the Soviets also had the 120-HM 38, which was a crew-served, towed mortar that could lay down a devastating barrage of 35-pound HE shells anywhere within 6,500 yards.

THREE-INCH FIELD GUNS The keep-it-simple Soviet world had virtually no mid-range field artillery. As for the smaller guns, from the 00/02 designs through to the Model 1942, each improved upon the one before it, and the three-inch Model 1942 was the most-produced cannon of the war. It was a field and antitank gun. On the broad Eastern Front, the Soviets merely lined their cannons wheel to wheel to achieve massed fire.

SOVIET ANTIAIRCRAFT ARTILLERY DEFENSES

85MM AA GUN MODEL 1939 This 85mm cannon and others like it formed the backbone of Soviet air defenses. This particular model could fire a shell weighing 20 pounds to an altitude of 34,000 feet. The Soviets heavily supplemented their organic defenses with captured German 88mm guns.

UNITED STATES

The United States was ill prepared militarily for World War II. Isolationists and budget-conscious civil servants ignored world events, and by the time the country began to gear up for war in 1940, it had lost a lot of time. However, with vast natural resources, a large and eager labor pool, many top scientists and designers, and a huge industrial capacity, U.S. war production reached staggering levels by the end of the conflict.

Armor

TANKS

SHERMAN TANK M4 Nothing sums up the spirit of American production better than the M4 Sherman tank. Americans turned out about 40,000 of these fighting machines, which were armed with a 75mm main gun, two light machine guns, and one heavy machine gun for antiaircraft purposes. Even when the Sherman was outgunned, which it often was, its numbers tipped the balance in favor of the Allies.

MEDIUM TANK M3 The "General Grant" tanks first saw action with the British as part of the Lend-Lease program. Armed with a 37mm gun in the turret and a sponson-mounted 75mm cannon, as well as light machine guns, these were bulky and slow but were at the right place at the right time to help stop German advances in North Africa.

LIGHT TANK M3 Although lightly armored, the "Stuart" was well liked and proved to be excellent as a scout vehicle, rear guard, or radio carrier, and it also served as a weapons platform. Its original armament, a 37mm main gun and as many as five light machine guns, remained throughout the war.

HEAVY TANK M26 PERSHING Arriving in 1945, this tank was the basis for later U.S. heavy-

In the shelter of a Sherman tank, U.S. soldiers advance cautiously through the streets of a Belgian town. Note the blades welded to the hull of the tank. These were used to break through the thick, earthen mounds in the hedgerow country of France.

tank designs. With a 90mm main gun, it was devastating the few times it was used on the battlefield. It also had secondary weapons, including three machine guns.

ARMORED CARS

M8 "GREYHOUND" This six-by-six vehicle carried a crew of four, a 37mm cannon, and two machine guns. Lightly armored, it served its purpose as a scout vehicle well.

T17E1 STAGHOUND This American-built vehicle went to other countries' forces and was not used in the field by the United States. It had a 37mm cannon and a 7.62mm machine gun. Several conversions, including an antiaircraft variation, were developed.

SELF-PROPELLED ARTILLERY AND TANK DESTROYERS

M7 PRIEST This was a self-propelled 105mm howitzer on a modified M3 chassis. It had a pulpit-mounted antiaircraft artillery gun, hence the name. Many were diverted to British forces via Lend-Lease. They could fire a 33-pound shell 12,500 yards.

M10 GUN MOTOR CARRIAGE Equipped with a three-inch high-velocity main gun, this was the first U.S. tank destroyer. Built on a Sherman M4 hull, it had an open turret and less armor but was fast and worked well either with other M10s or integrated into a regular armored element.

M18 GUN MOTOR CARRIAGE This was the first antitank weapon in the U.S. arsenal built specifically for that purpose. It had a powerful three-inch gun and was quite mobile. Known as the Hellcat, its main weakness was lack of armor. The carriage was put to use widely in other roles.

155MM GUN, M40 The "Long-Tom," which combined firepower with accuracy and maneu-

verability, was one of the best self-propelled guns of the war. However, it did not appear in combat until early 1945.

Trucks and Cars

A number of different U.S. companies produced trucks for the war effort. Studebaker produced thousands of six-by-six trucks, many of which were diverted to the Soviet Union.

DEUCE AND A HALF Another "war winner," this six-by-six truck could carry troops and supplies or tow artillery. Churned out in huge numbers, it was used in all theaters of war by Allied forces and was one of the most famous and best trucks of the war.

DIAMOND T 968 This six-by-six truck could carry four tons 150 miles on a tank of gas, and it was produced in several types.

HALFTRACKS With wheels in front and tracks in the rear, designs such as the M3 could be used to haul troops, as antiaircraft platforms (such as the famous Maxson mount), or as self-propelled artillery. They were popular in the Soviet Union, which acquired them through Lend-Lease, and could maneuver easily through ice, snow, or mud.

JEEP A workhorse of the American military, the sturdy-wheeled vehicle transported personnel near the frontlines and in the rear echelons alike. Thousands were built, and the Jeep became an icon of American military transport.

Amphibious Vehicles

The unique nature of the Pacific war, as well as the need for amphibious landings in Africa, Italy, Normandy, and southern France, dictated that the U.S. develop amphibious assault vehicles.

DUKW Half boat, half ship, this craft operated in all theaters of the war and proved most effective. It could carry more than 5,000 pounds through water and onto land.

LVTS   The landing vehicle, tracked program had just one purpose: deliver marines forward from the sea, under hostile conditions, and support them as much as possible. The LVT 2 was adequate, although it leaked and was hard to unload. The LVT 4 had a cargo ramp at the rear, so that equipment or machinery could roll off, instead of being hoisted over the side. All LVTs were armed, and later in the war amphibious vehicles provided direct-fire support.

Artillery

During the course of the war, the United States perfected the science of artillery. By using forward observers, radio, timed fuses, and so forth, the military could time a barrage so that every round in the first salvo would drop almost simultaneously, to great effect. The U.S. arsenal was large but uncomplicated, and this uniformity was crucial in attaining superiority.

HOWITZER, 8-INCH M1   The largest field gun deployed by the United States, it could lob a 200-pound shell with devastating accuracy as far as 18,000 yards. It was the main battery weapon for the division and the corps. A 240mm variant based on the same design and carriage appeared later in the war.

M1 GUN 155MM   The "Long Tom," the standard heavy gun of U.S. ground forces in the war, could fire a 92-pound shell as far as 25,000 yards.

M2A1 AND M2A2   This 105mm howitzer was the standard field gun of U.S. troops and is still the standard medium artillery used by U.S. forces. Capable of delivering a 33-pound shell 12,000 yards, it was used in all theaters of combat and could fire high explosive, smoke, or even shells stuffed with propaganda leaflets.

M3 37MM ANTITANK GUN   Although too light to be of much use in Europe, it did find a place in the Pacific, where it could knock out Japanese tanks and fortifications.

M5 3-INCH ANTITANK GUN   This new design was popular as an antitank weapon but was phased out soon after the war.

M1A1 75MM PACK HOWITZER   Originally designed as a mountain gun, this small weapon found its place in the Pacific, where it could be manhandled into place to blast Japanese fortifications, providing direct fire at close range.

MORTARS   U.S. forces were issued one of three mortars. The M2, a 60mm design, was issued to airborne and other forward units. The M1 was 81mm and was heavier, requiring a crew of three to handle the weapon and its seven-pound bombs. The third was the 4.2-inch "chemical mortar," so called because it was originally designed to launch gas or smoke; it was soon issued with HE rounds.

ANTIAIRCRAFT ARTILLERY

M1 90MM GUN   The main U.S. heavy antiaircraft weapon during World War II could fire a 23-pound shell as high as 39,000 feet, fitted

Its crew at the ready, an American 90mm antiaircraft gun points skyward from a reinforced emplacement on Okinawa.

with either altimeter or radar proximity fuses. A well-trained crew could deliver 27 rounds per minute.

MI 37MM ANTIAIRCRAFT ARTILLERY GUN Firing up to 120 rounds per minute at targets as high as 18,000 feet, it was quite an effective medium antiaircraft gun.

MAXSON MOUNT Four .50-caliber Browning machine guns, mounted on an electrically powered central pedestal for elevation and traverse, were used for close antiaircraft artillery support. Together the four guns could deliver as many as 2,400 rounds per minute, which would bring down any plane within range.

Ships

During World War II, domination and superiority was gained not only on land and in the air, but on the sea. It became clear during this time that carrier-based aircraft were a primary source for destroying enemy forces. Due to this, by 1939, the aircraft carrier was rising to prominence among the world's major navies. The Imperial Japanese Navy, in particular, was built around carriers, with traditional ships in supporting roles. The exception was the German navy, which still emphasized battleships and submarines, due to restrictions placed on them in the Treaty of Versailles.

The battleship was still considered the most powerful weapon in the world, despite its vulnerability to air attack, as demonstrated by U.S.

Army bombers shortly after World War I. Heavily clad in armor to protect against enemy shells, most battleships sported 14- or 16-inch main guns, as well as secondary five- or six-inch batteries, and sophisticated antiaircraft defenses, such as quick-firing 40mm cannon.

Cruisers were smaller and faster than battleships but still powerful. Heavy cruisers usually had eight-inch main batteries, while light cruisers generally had six-inch main guns. The next level was the destroyer. Smaller, lighter, and less heavily armed but fast, they were used as screens for larger vessels and for convoy duty and generally carried five-inch main guns. Other types of ships included minelayers, minesweepers, and patrol boats such as the U.S. Navy Patrol Torpedo (PT) boats and the German E-boats, which were also torpedo boats. Submarines were a mainstay of the larger navies.

As World War II progressed and airpower more exact, aircraft carriers became preeminent. British aircraft carriers had heavily armored flight decks and hangars, which reduced the number of planes they could carry but made them much more durable. In contrast, the United States built carriers with lightly armored wooden decks that could carry more planes (as many as 83 in the Essex class) but were more vulnerable to damage and sinking. In the carrier battles of the early Pacific war, and facing kamikaze suicide attacks toward the end, crews aboard U.S. carriers suffered more casualties because the ships did not have armored decks. Japanese aircraft carriers were also lightly armored but were generally smaller and carried fewer planes than the Allied carriers that they faced. Supporting these capital ships was an array of oilers, tenders, and other service ships.

BRITISH ROYAL NAVY AND COMMONWEALTH FORCES

The Royal Navy was one of the most powerful naval forces in history, and at the outbreak of World War II it was the most powerful naval force in the Atlantic. For centuries, its navy had protected the British Isles from invasion and showed the Union Jack around the globe. Although aircraft carriers were beginning to find a niche, the Royal Navy was built around the battleship and included hundreds of lesser craft, ranging from cruisers to landing boats. Ships of the Canadian, Indian, South African, and New Zealand navies supplemented the Royal Navy.

Royal Navy

BATTLESHIPS

Some Royal Navy battleships were built as part of a specific class, indicated by the first ship of the class to be constructed. Others were in a class by themselves.

HOOD   The largest British battle cruiser of the war at 42,000 tons, the *Hood* was the pride of the British fleet. But its designers fatally sacrificed armor protection to give the vessel a greater cruising speed. This "glass-jawed" giant, as surviving crew members referred to it, was sunk in a duel with the German battleship *Bismarck* and the heavy cruiser *Prinz Eugen* on May 24, 1941.

NELSON   Launched in 1927, it played an important role in the war. An Italian torpedo bomber damaged the *Nelson,* but it survived the war.

PRINCE OF WALES   Launched in early 1941, the *Prince of Wales* fought the *Bismarck* along with the *Hood.* Sent to the Pacific with the battle cruiser *Repulse,* the *Prince of Wales* was sunk by Japanese aircraft off Singapore on December 10, 1941.

RODNEY   Launched in 1927, with the *Nelson,* it also played a major role early in the war. The *Rodney* was involved in the sinking of the *Bismarck.*

KING GEORGE CLASS   Consisted of four ships—the *King George V, Duke of York, Anson,* and the *Howe.*

QUEEN ELIZABETH CLASS Five ships—the *Queen Elizabeth, Valiant, Warspite, Malaya,* and the *Barham.* A U-boat sank the *Barham* in September 1941.

ROYAL SOVEREIGN CLASS Five ships—the *Royal Sovereign, Royal Oak, Resolution, Ramillies,* and the *Revenge.*

BATTLE CRUISERS, *RENOWN* AND *REPULSE* Japanese aircraft sank the *Repulse* off Malaya on December 10, 1941.

CARRIERS

Like the U.S. Navy, the Royal Navy was still built around the battleship when the war began, but it was developing carrier power. Most British carriers entered service too late to play major roles in the Battle of the Atlantic, but a handful of older carriers that were converted from cruiser hulls, as well as the *Ark Royal,* the first British carrier built from the keel up, did see action.

ARK ROYAL The *Ark Royal* became a hero of the battle with the *Bismarck* when the carrier's slow Swordfish torpedo planes struck the blow that damaged the German battleship's steering mechanism. The *Ark Royal* came to an inglorious end when sunk by a single torpedo off Gibraltar on November 13, 1941.

COURAGEOUS The *Courageous* was the first major British ship lost in the war, torpedoed by a U-boat off the Irish coast on September 17, 1939.

EAGLE A converted battleship, the *Eagle* served with the Mediterranean fleet until a U-boat sank it on August 11, 1942.

GLORIOUS Like the *Courageous,* the *Glorious* had a short-lived career. It fell victim to the guns of the German battle cruisers *Scharnhorst* and *Gneisenau* on June 8, 1940.

INDOMITABLE Launched on March 26, 1940, the *Indomitable* served in both the Atlantic and the Pacific. It survived a kamikaze attack off Okinawa.

ILLUSTRIOUS CLASS Three ships, the *Illustrious, Formidable,* and *Victorious,* all were launched in 1939 and served in both the Pacific and Atlantic.

IMPLACABLE CLASS The two ships in this class, the *Implacable* and *Indefatigable,* were launched in December 1942. Their construction used technology developed during the construction of the Illustrious class.

ESCORT CARRIERS The Royal Navy operated two classes of escort carriers. The first class, Ruler, consisted of 14 American-built ships made by the Kaiser Company. The Archer class consisted of 23 converted merchantmen, also built in U.S. shipyards.

CRUISERS

These were the backbone of the Royal Navy's surface fleet, which had no fewer than 12 different classes of cruisers—in all, about 30 ships—as well as 18 others of no particular class.

DESTROYERS

The destroyers were the smallest of the fleet combat ships, and the Royal Navy had 13 different classes of destroyers, ranging from as few as four Weapon class ships to 49 Hunt class ships.

SUBMARINES

The Royal Navy had 14 classes of submarines, including the midgets and large oceangoing boats. The three principal classes were S, T, and U.

Royal Australian Navy

The Royal Australian Navy was quite small, consisting of three nonclassed and five Queensborough-

and three Tribal-class cruisers. The rest of the fleet consisted of frigates, sloops, and minesweepers.

Royal Canadian Navy

The Royal Canadian Navy consisted of two light fleet carriers, 14 cruisers, and an assortment of frigates and minesweepers.

CHINA

At the outbreak of the war, the Japanese commandeered most of the Chinese navy, which consisted of two cruisers and other vessels, including gunboats.

FRANCE

When the war began, the French navy was the fourth largest in the world and was equipped with several modern vessels, including two battleships. Before the German victory in France in June 1940, the French navy fought alongside the British. With the French defeat, some French vessels and their crews made their way to British ports. The British considered the remaining French warships a threat and attacked the French at Mers-el-Kebir, Algeria. Eventually, some French ships operating under the Vichy government supported the Axis in the Mediterranean. When Allied forces landed in French North Africa, most of the Vichy French fleet was scuttled.

GERMANY

Partly because of treaty restraints, the German navy, or Kriegsmarine, was much smaller than the British Royal Navy. Although Hitler had made plans for a large surface navy, the plan did not call for it to take shape until 1944. Only two aircraft carriers had been built by September 1939, and neither played a role in the war. The principal German naval weapons of the war were its battleships and cruisers, which raided Allied shipping, and the U-boat force, which was the major threat of the Battle of the Atlantic. The German navy also built several surface raiders by converting merchantmen into armed ships.

Battleships

TIRPITZ CLASS This class consisted of two ships, the *Tirpitz* and the *Bismarck*. The *Tirpitz* was a major threat to Allied shipping in the North Sea and Arctic until Royal Navy midget submarines badly damaged it in an attack. The ship was a major target for Allied bombers and was eventually reduced to a floating hulk. The *Bismarck* was the object of a massive British search shortly after it was launched in early 1941. It was finally sunk a few months later after an epic naval chase (see Chapter 7, "Campaigns and Battles: Europe and the Atlantic").

"POCKET" BATTLESHIPS (BATTLE CRUISERS) Smaller than most battleships and larger than cruisers, Germany's "pocket" battleships were the terror of the seas during the war's opening months and major targets for the Royal Navy.

ADMIRAL GRAF SPEE This ship operated in the South Atlantic as a raider and sank nine merchant ships. Finally cornered by the Royal Navy off the coast of Uruguay, it was scuttled by its captain in Montevideo Harbor on December 17, 1939 (see Chapter 7, "Campaigns and Battles: Europe and the Atlantic").

ADMIRAL SCHEER After a successful career as a surface raider that sank 17 merchant ships and the cruiser HMS *Jervis Bay,* it was sunk in the Baltic Sea by Royal Air Force bombers in early 1945.

DEUTSCHLAND Renamed the *Lutzow* and assigned to the Baltic, the *Deutschland* sported 11-inch main guns, but it spent much of the war in dock and participated in few significant actions. It was scuttled in May 1945.

GNEISENAU AND SCHARNHORST Sister ships, the two battle cruisers operated as a team in the Atlantic and made the famous "Channel Dash" through the English Channel in early 1942. Damaged by bombs, the *Gneisenau* went into dry dock, where it remained at war's end. A Royal Navy force sank the *Scharnhorst* in December 1943 off the North Cape of Norway.

Carriers

Germany worked to develop two aircraft carriers. One, the *Graf Zeppelin,* was completed. However, it never saw service, in part because of political wrangling between the German navy and the Luftwaffe.

Commerce Raiders

The Germans converted a number of merchant ships into surface raiders to attack ships on shipping routes. The most famous of the class was the *Atlantis.* Others included the *Pinguin, Thor, Michel,* and *Komet.* They wreaked havoc in the Atlantic.

Cruisers

Germany had nine cruisers, several of which operated as surface raiders. The most famous were the *Admiral Hipper* and *Prinz Eugen.*

Destroyers

The German navy had plans to complete 70 destroyers by the end of 1947. Less than 50 were completed by war's end.

U-Boats (Submarines)

The Germans commissioned more than 1,100 U-boats during the war; U-boat strength rose from a mere 57 boats at the beginning of the war to 445 in early 1944. The main classes were the Type 7, Type 9, and Type 21 (the 21 never became operational in large numbers but was sophisticated for its day). U-boats prowled the Atlantic in the early war years, interrupting the flow of supplies from the United States to Britain. They were all sunk by the Allies and effectively eliminated as a force in 1943.

ITALY

The Italian navy was one of the most powerful sea forces in the world in 1939, with six battleships, 19 cruisers, and assorted smaller vessels, as well as more than 100 submarines. British Swordfish torpedo bombers disabled three of the battleships in an attack on the Italian base at Taranto in 1940. The most significant role of the Italian navy was defending Axis supply routes in the Mediterranean. Although significant in the number of vessels, the Italian navy was technologically backward; none of its ships, for example, had radar.

JAPAN

Japan emerged from World War I as the third most powerful navy in the world, but the 1922 naval arms limitation conference limited Japan to a tonnage of 60 percent of that of the United States. Consequently, Japan concentrated on the production of aircraft carriers and cruisers in order to develop a high power ratio in relation to size. Ultimately repudiating the treaty limits, the Japanese navy began a construction program in 1934 that included the two most powerful battleships ever built. By December 7, 1941, the Japanese navy consisted of 10 operational battleships, 10 carriers, and 28 cruisers supported by 112 destroyers. Japan also had 65 submarines, although 20 were obsolete.

Battleships

The Japanese navy possessed 12 battleships, of which 10 were operational. The *Yamato* and *Musashi* were the two largest battleships ever constructed, with 18-inch main batteries, and far outweighed the largest U.S. battleships of the day. U.S. Navy aircraft sank both during the final year of the war.

Carriers

Carriers were the backbone of the Imperial Japanese Navy until the Battle of Midway (June 1942), when all four carriers assigned to the attack force were destroyed. The loss was even more dramatic because the four made up two-thirds of Japan's large carrier force. Severe losses of both aircraft and carriers rendered Japanese carriers ineffective by mid-1944.

Cruisers

Cruisers were the mainstay of the Japanese surface navy. A force of 10 cruisers wreaked havoc among U.S. and Australian naval forces off Guadalcanal on August 7, 1942, sinking one Australian and three U.S. cruisers. Sixteen cruisers were part of the Japanese force that attacked Allied naval forces in Leyte Gulf in October 1944.

Destroyers

With more than 100 destroyers in the Japanese navy at the beginning of the war, the small, fast ships played a role in operations all over the Pacific. In addition to performing conventional duties such as screening task forces, they escorted troop ships and even served as troop transports.

Submarines

Japanese submarines sank fewer than 20 Allied warships and about 170 supply ships and merchant vessels. The Japanese subs operated briefly off the West Coast of the United States in the early war years. Allied forces sank 128 of the roughly 200 submarines that were built for the Imperial Japanese Navy during the war.

SOVIET UNION

The Soviet Union was in the process of upgrading the role of its naval forces when Hitler launched his attack in June 1941. Consequently, Soviet naval forces did not play a major role in the war. Compared with other Allied naval forces, those of the Soviet Union were fairly small, consisting of three battleships and about 50 destroyers. The Soviets did possess a large submarine force, with more than 200 operational boats, as well as almost 300 torpedo boats.

UNITED STATES

Between December 7, 1941, and August 8, 1945, the U.S. Navy underwent the greatest transformation of all navies in the world. Despite some movement toward the construction of carriers, the navy still emphasized capital ships in 1941, with 15 battleships and 18 heavy cruisers but only five aircraft carriers. By the war's end, the United States had produced an astounding 139 aircraft carriers, and the fast carrier task force had become the most powerful naval striking unit ever.

Battleships

The U.S. Navy began the war with 15 battleships that predated the 1921 naval treaty and two that were built in the 1930s, but the navy almost doubled that number by war's end. Although battleships were the focus of the navy's surface fleet in 1941, their role was actually more one of support because their big guns were used to shell enemy shore installations.

ARIZONA Commissioned in 1916, sunk at Pearl Harbor, now a national memorial.

ARKANSAS Launched in 1911, it served in the Atlantic until after the invasions of Western Europe, then moved to the Pacific.

PENNSYLVANIA Sister ship to the *Arizona,* also at Pearl Harbor when the Japanese attacked. Although badly damaged, it was refitted and served in the Aleutians and in the Pacific island offensives.

ALASKA CLASS Three ships, the *Alaska, Guam,* and *Hawaii,* made up the "battle cruiser" class.

COLORADO CLASS Composed of three ships that were launched in 1921: the *Colorado, Maryland,* and *West Virginia.* The *West Virginia* was sunk at Pearl Harbor but was salvaged and repaired.

IOWA CLASS Consisted of five ships, the *Iowa, New Jersey, Missouri, Wisconsin,* and *Kentucky,* all launched between 1942 and 1944, except the *Kentucky,* which was still under construction at the end of the war. The *Missouri* was the site of the signing of the Japanese surrender documents in Tokyo Bay in September 1945.

NEVADA CLASS Two ships, the *Nevada* and *Oklahoma*. Both were at Pearl Harbor on December 7, 1941. The *Nevada* was the only battleship to get under way during the attacks. The *Oklahoma* capsized and sank with heavy loss of life. Later refloated, it was never returned to active service and was sold for scrap after the war.

NEW MEXICO CLASS Three ships: the *New Mexico, Mississippi,* and *Idaho*. They were the most modern ships in the U.S. Navy in 1941. They went to the Pacific to replace ships lost at Pearl Harbor, serving there throughout the war, primarily providing fire support for invasion forces.

SOUTH DAKOTA CLASS Four ships, the *Alabama, Indiana, Massachusetts,* and *South Dakota,* served mostly with the Pacific Fleet.

Dive-bombers and torpedo planes, some with their wings folded, sit on the snow-covered deck of a U.S. aircraft carrier in the North Atlantic. Aircraft carriers extended the range of Allied airpower in offensive roles and in protecting convoys against submarines and surface raiders.

TENNESSEE CLASS Includes the *Tennessee* and *California,* both launched in 1920. Damaged at Pearl Harbor, they later rejoined the fleet.

TEXAS CLASS Two ships, the *Texas* and *New York.* Both served primarily in the Atlantic, providing support for amphibious operations, then moved to the Pacific late in the war.

WASHINGTON CLASS Included the *Washington* and *North Carolina.*

Carriers

The U.S. Navy entered the war with only five carriers and finished with more than 100. As the war continued, the navy developed three basic types: the large "fleet" carriers, which made up the striking force of the naval task forces that won control of the Pacific after 1943; the light carriers; and the small "escort" carriers, whose role was to provide aircraft for escorting merchant convoys and for other purposes.

PREWAR CARRIERS

At the outbreak of the war, the U.S. Navy had five carriers that were operational, with two others under construction.

ENTERPRISE Assigned to the Yorktown class, the *Enterprise* fought in nearly all the U.S. Navy carrier actions of the war in the Pacific and survived the war.

HORNET The navy's newest carrier at the outbreak of the war, the *Hornet* is most famous as the ship from which were launched the army B-25s for the Doolittle raid on Japan. The *Hornet* took part in the Battle of Midway and was sunk by U.S. Navy gunfire after being damaged beyond repair by Japanese air attack during the Battle of Santa Cruz in August 1942.

LEXINGTON One of the U.S. Navy's first carriers, the *Lexington* was badly damaged in the Battle of the Coral Sea in April 1942 and later was sunk. A new large fleet carrier was named in its honor.

SARATOGA After Pearl Harbor, the *Saratoga* was loaded with fighters and dive-bombers at San Diego and ordered to steam to Wake Island but was called back to defend Hawaii. Damaged by two torpedoes during the battle for the Solomon Islands, it participated in the invasion of Guadalcanal and the Solomons and campaigns in the Gilberts and Marshalls before being sent to the Indian Ocean to work with the British. It survived the war but was sunk during atomic bomb tests at Bikini Atoll in 1946.

WASP Initially assigned to the Atlantic Fleet, the *Wasp* ferried British Royal Air Force fighters to Malta in early 1942 and then joined the U.S. Pacific Fleet and covered marine operations at Guadalcanal and elsewhere in the Solomons. It was fatally torpedoed by a Japanese submarine while on convoy duty in the Solomons. An Essex-class carrier was named in its honor.

YORKTOWN This ship took part in the Battle of the Coral Sea and other U.S. carrier operations early in the war. One of three U.S. carriers in the Battle of Midway, the *Yorktown* was severely damaged by a Japanese air attack and then sunk by a Japanese submarine. An Essex-class carrier was named in its honor.

LARGE FLEET CARRIERS

ESSEX CLASS Consisting of 24 ships, the Essex class (CV) carriers were the backbone of U.S. naval power in the Pacific after 1943, when the first of the class were launched. Several bore names of other carriers—*Hornet, Lexington, Wasp,* and *Yorktown*—that had been lost earlier in the war.

Avoiding Japanese Bombs

Scared? No, I was only scared one night in all the years I was in the marines. We were sitting on some island, and them Jap Zeroes were comin' in there straight from the beach. 'Course the jungle was so damn thick we were camped along the beach. The Japs come through—voom . . . voom—straight from the beach. That night I—I dug a hole pretty deep. I got at least a foot deep before I hit water, and I buried my nose right down in it. Scared shitless.

And the only other time was on Okinawa when them Betty bombers, them Jap Betty bombers, was comin' in. They each carried fifty-five-hundred-pound bombs. That's all that the thing carried—and you don't worry about them. Only when they're comin' at ya. 'Cause when they drop their bombs, it's gotta go on a long glide, ya know, before it hits the ground. But then you hold your breath until he gets right up above you. Then you can start breathing again. Pretty quickly, you're soothed.

That was the only two times I was ever scared. That first night there when we slept on the beach and the first time we saw them Betty bombers (they had a voo . . . voo . . . voo [that] they'd throw out—always throbbin'—voo . . . voo . . . voo) and always all dark there at night—you couldn't see shit up there. Ya know, kinda eerie.

—Eisenhower Center for American Studies Archives

LIGHT FLEET CARRIERS AND ESCORT CARRIERS

BOGUE CLASS Made up of 10 carriers, all named after bodies of water known as "sounds."

COMMENCEMENT BAY CLASS Made up of 19 escort carriers (CVE).

CASABLANCA CLASS Made up of 37 light escort carriers, all constructed by the Henry J. Kaiser Company or the Oregon Ship Building Corporation. They were often referred to as "jeep carriers" because Kaiser also built jeeps.

INDEPENDENCE CLASS Consisted of nine converted cruisers, the *Independence, Belleau Wood, Cowpens, Monterey, Cabot, Langley, Bataan, San Jacinto,* and *Princeton.* They were designated CVL and were able to carry only 33 planes but made up for this relative lack of aircraft by being fast enough to keep up with larger carriers. The *Princeton,* the best-known ship of this class, performed admirably until shattered by Japanese bombs at the Battle of Leyte Gulf.

Cruisers

Far more numerous than battleships, cruisers did everything from convoy escort to shelling enemy shore installations. One of the more infamous incidents of the war was the loss in July 1945 of the cruiser *Indianapolis* and more than 800 of its crew to a Japanese submarine torpedo; it had just delivered components to Tinian in the Marianas for the two atomic bombs to be dropped on Hiroshima and Nagasaki.

Destroyers

Destroyers played a large role in every navy. U.S. destroyers were the first American naval vessels to see combat and to be lost. The most famous class of U.S. destroyer was the modern Fletcher class. Throughout the war, U.S. destroyers performed a variety of roles around the globe—escorting convoys, screening surface fleets, and searching for enemy submarines.

Landing Craft

By far the most famous landing craft of the war was the venerable Higgins boat, or LCM (Landing craft, mechanized). Built in New Orleans, these flat-bottomed landing craft were used in nearly every amphibious assault of the war. Nearly all assault troops arrived in Normandy aboard Higgins boats on D-Day (June 6, 1944). Other landing craft included LCTs (Landing Craft, Tanks), rocket-firing boats, and other assault craft.

PT Boats

Patrol torpedo boats were small, fast boats equipped with torpedo tubes and automatic weapons manned by the crew. Although their limited range restricted them to coastal operations, PT boats operated against Japanese shipping in the islands of the southwestern Pacific. One PT boat entered American folklore: PT-109, the boat commanded by the future President John F. Kennedy, which was sunk in action in 1943.

Submarines

Although defective torpedoes hampered the effectiveness of U.S. submarines until 1943, the "silent service" played a major role in the final years of the war. Gato-class fleet submarines were able to remain at sea for as long as 75 days and range more than 11,000 miles. Submarine commanders were noted for their spirit and willingness to take great risks to attack Japanese ships at periscope depth and even on the surface. U.S. submarines took a heavy—and decisive—toll on Japanese merchant shipping and warships.

Weapons and Arms Development

Infantry weapons saw few real advances during World War II. The basic weapon remained the rifle, with all combatants except the United States depending primarily on bolt-action mechanisms inspired by the German Mauser designs of the late 19th century. The United States had developed an effective and efficient semiautomatic rifle and had begun issuing it in large numbers to combat troops. Similarly, sidearms were based on tried and proven designs, although the larger armies used the newer semiautomatic weapons such as carbines and submachine guns. Aircrews and tankers sometimes received carbines, which were basically cut-down rifles. Infantry and other combat personnel sometimes carried submachine guns and other automatic weapons. The following is a list of infantry weapons used by each country.

Rifles and Carbines

ENFIELD NO. 4 AND NO. 5 RIFLES Both were essentially refinements of the Lee-Enfield rifle used in World War I. Each featured a 10-round magazine with a bolt action that fired .303-caliber cartridges.

DE LISLE SILENT CARBINE A .45-caliber bolt-action carbine based on the Lee-Enfield. It was equipped with a silencer for use by commando units.

Revolvers and Pistols

ENFIELD NO. 2 MARK I A .38-caliber six-shot revolver that came into use after World War I, it was redesigned as a double-action weapon just before the war began.

WEBLEY .38 MARK IV While the Enfield was the standard revolver of the British army, other branches of the service favored the Webley, a single-action six-shot revolver.

Automatic Weapons

OWEN MACHINE CARBINE An Australian weapon that came about largely because of the difficulty of receiving supplies from Britain after Japan allied with Germany. Similar to a Sten, the Owen featured a 32-round magazine and fired 9mm bullets at a rate of 700 rounds per minute.

STEN MARK I The most widely used British automatic weapon, the "Sten gun" fired 32 rounds of 9mm ammunition at a rate of 550 rounds per minute.

STEN MARK 2 Basically a stripped-down version of the Mark I, it was lighter and produced in two patterns distinguishable primarily by the design of the stock.

STEN MARK 6(S) An improvement of the Mark 2, with a wooden stock, it was used by British paratroops and Resistance fighters.

Machine Guns

BESA MARKS 1–3 Originally a Czech design, it was manufactured by the Birmingham Small Arms Company. The BESA fired 7.62mm rounds at a rate of 500 or 700 rounds per minute.

MKI BREN GUN This magazine-fed 7.62mm gun was an excellent light machine gun. It had a maximum rate of fire of 500 rounds per minute, was light enough to be used by frontline troops, and was powerful enough to be used in antiaircraft modes as well. The British army still uses variants of this design.

VICKERS ".303" A water-cooled, .303-caliber machine gun, the Vickers was widely used by British forces throughout the war. It fired at a rate of 500 rounds per minute.

Platoon Weapons

These weapons required a crew and were used primarily against tanks.

PROJECTER INFANTRY ANTITANK Similar to a mortar, the PIAT fired a single 2.5-pound bomb. As an antitank weapon, it had an effective range of 115 yards, but it was effective to 350 yards against structures.

FRANCE

Rifles and Carbines

FUSIL MAS36 7.5mm bolt-action rifle fed by a five-round box.

MLE 1886/93 This 8mm weapon was loaded from an eight-round tube.

MLE1907/15 M34 This old Berthier design held a five-round box of 7.5mm ammunition and represented France's attempt to update and standardize its military arsenal, a project cut short by the German invasion.

Machine Guns

FUSIL MITRAILLEUR MODELES 1924/29U Inspired by the Browning automatic rifle, this rifle, which fired a 7.5mm round from a 25-round box, became one of the standard French machine guns.

MITRAILLEUSE MLE 1931 This was a special version of the mle 1924/29 that was made specifically for tanks and other vehicles. It was modified to fire from a 150-round drum and had a higher rate of fire, 750 rounds per minute.

GERMANY

Rifles and Carbines

GEWEHR 41(W) Germany's first attempt at a self-loading rifle fired a 7.92mm round from a 10-round box, but it had drawbacks, including excessive weight and difficulty with loading and manufacture.

GEWEHR 43 This upgrade, which addressed the problems of the 41, was adopted almost immediately by front-line troops.

KARABINER 98K This 7.92mm shortened rifle was to serve as the basic frontline rifle for the German infantry. Originally built by Mauser, it was redesignated only after multiple modifications. It was fed from a five-round box and was accurate to about 200 yards without a scope.

Revolvers and Pistols

LUGER PISTOLE PO8 This sidearm, prized as a souvenir of war by American GIs, was based on an old design and fired a 9mm round from an eight-round clip.

WALTHER PP AND PPK Before the war civilian police throughout Europe adopted these pistols. During the war the 9mm regular (PP) and snub-nosed (PPK) were issued to aircrews and military police.

WALTHER P38 Another 9mm, the P38 was intended to replace the Luger but managed only to supplement it by war's end. It fired from an eight-round clip.

Automatic Weapons

MP18 The Machine Pistol Model 18 fired 9mm rounds from a 32-round clip and became the first effective operational submachine gun. All other models are variants of this one.

MP40 This submachine gun with a collapsible stock was given only to elite troops. Basically the same as its predecessors, it was the first submachine gun to be mass-produced.

STG44 This was the first true submachine gun, firing 7.92mm pistol rounds from a 30-round clip at a rate of 500 rounds per minute.

Machine Guns

MG34 During the early stages of the war, this was the standard machine gun issued at the platoon level and on armored vehicles. It fired a 7.92mm cartridge at the stunning rate of 800 to 900 rounds per minute. It could be fixed or carried by infantry into battle.

MG42 The mass-market version of the original Maschinengewehr 34, it differed only in being less expensive to manufacture and had nearly twice the rate of fire.

Platoon Weapons

PANZERFAUST Disposable, general-purpose rocket launchers. They could take out tanks and field fortifications and blow holes in buildings.

PÜPPCHEN   This close-range 88mm antitank weapon was generally manhandled into position and fired a hollow-charge rocket.

RAKETENPANZERBÜCHSE   This 88mm German knockoff of the American bazooka fired a seven-pound rocket that could take out any Allied tank.

ITALY

Revolvers and Pistols

BERETTA MODEL 1934   A much-sought war trophy, the 9mm Beretta fired from a seven-round box. Originally intended for Italian officers, it had a much longer career in the hands of Allied troops, who would wager their war trophies in high-stakes poker games.

Automatic Weapons

BERETTA MODEL 1938A   This submachine gun fired 9mm rounds from a 20- or 40-round box at 600 rounds per minute. It was quite accurate and could be used as a single-shot rifle at ranges up to 300 meters and as a mini–machine gun at closer ranges.

JAPAN

Rifles and Carbines

RIFLE, TYPE 38   The standard Japanese infantry rifle fired 6.5mm ammunition from a five-round box.

Revolvers and Pistols

PISTOL TYPE 94   A terrible pistol, this was the standard Japanese sidearm for officers. It fired 8mm rounds from a six-round box and is regarded as one of the worst pistols of the war.

Automatic Weapons

TYPE 100   Japan's only attempt to make a submachine gun, this 8mm weapon fired at a rate of 800 rounds per minute from a 30-round clip. It was a good weapon but failed to make a difference in the Japanese war effort.

Machine Guns

TYPE 11   This light machine gun, known popularly as a "Nambu" after its designer, fired 6.4mm ammunition from a 30-round hopper at 500 rounds per minute.

TYPE 96   This upgrade to the Nambu Type 11 featured a quick barrel-change system, choice of sights, and a bayonet.

Platoon Weapons

Japan had limited numbers of antitank grenade launchers that could be fitted to the muzzles of service rifles, as well as suicide antitank methods.

SOVIET UNION

Rifles and Carbines

MODEL 1891/30   A bolt-action 7.62mm rifle designed in the 19th century but updated by the Red Army. It drew rounds from a five-round box.

MODEL 1938 CARBINE   This shorter variant was fixed with a permanent bayonet that clipped back to the side.

Revolvers and Pistols

TT-33   The Tokarev 7.62mm pistol was the standard Soviet sidearm, replacing older revolvers and personal weapons. Drawing from an eight-round clip, it was a powerful sidearm.

Automatic Weapons

PPD-1934/38   This submachine gun fed from either a 71-round drum or 25-round clip. It shot 7.62mm submachine gun ammunition but was phased out as newer and better models came on line.

PPSH-41   Tough, inexpensive, and reliable, this was to become the standard Soviet submachine gun. Often the Germans used captured versions, finding it superior to their own arms. The weapon fired a 7.62mm standard round.

Machine Guns

DSHKI938   This .5-inch gun was wheeled into battle on carriages and fired at a rate of 550 rounds per minute from a metal-link belt.

SG43   This was to become the standard issue light machine gun of the Red Army. It fired a 7.62mm round at up to 600 rounds per minute from a metal-link belt. Like the DShK, and so many other Soviet arms, it was simple and tough.

TECHNOLOGICAL ADVANCES OF WAR

Throughout history, warfare has been the catalyst for great technological advances, and World War II was no exception. The rapid advance of aviation is one example. By 1945 military aviation had made such a huge leap forward that even the fast piston-engine fighters of the day were obsolete as the world entered the jet age. Tremendous advances in rocketry had been a hallmark of the German military, but the Allies had developed and deployed rocket-propelled artillery and aerial bombs. The most dramatic and deadly advance was in the development of the atomic bomb, which went from an idea in 1940 to the destruction of Hiroshima and Nagasaki in 1945.

Radar had evolved from the large screens used to detect formations of approaching aircraft to the comparatively tiny aircraft radar sets that night fighters used to bomb through clouds, targeting and navigating by the radar map. Radio beams that were first used to help Royal Air Force bombers find their way to targets in the night skies over Germany paved the way for radio navigation systems in later years. The principles of radio and radar also led to new artillery and antiaircraft proximity fuses that would cause the shells to detonate even if a direct hit was not obtained.

The war brought advances in other areas as well, especially medicine. Battlefield surgical units sometimes treated hundreds of wounded soldiers in one day, an experience that allowed medical personnel to gain vast knowledge in the treatment of wounds, burns, and infections. Although penicillin and sulfa drugs had been discovered in the 1930s, demand from military forces led to the production and use of vast quantities and established their prominence in the medical field.

> "I am become Death/The shatterer of worlds."
> —Physicist J. Robert Oppenheimer, quoting from the *Bhagavad Gita*, an ancient Hindu text, while observing the Alamogordo test of the atomic bomb on July 16, 1945

UNITED STATES

Rifles and Carbines

M1903\A1 The Springfield saw action primarily as a sniper rifle, firing standard 7.62mm rifle rounds.

M-I CARBINE This lightweight alternative to the Garand fired shortened 7.62mm rounds. It found its calling in the Pacific, where troops could use its 30-round clips to lay down fire at close range.

M-I RIFLE The war winner, as some called it. (See sidebar on p. 340.)

Revolvers and Pistols

COLT M-1911A1 Firing .45-caliber ammunition, this was the standard service pistol for the U.S. Army and was issued as a sidearm to officers, artillerymen, and armored crews.

Automatic Weapons

M-3 The 9mm "grease gun," as it was known, was well suited for dense jungle combat in the Pacific, as it could lay down high-volume fire at close quarters. The essence of mass production, it was easy to build, use, and maintain.

THOMPSON M-I The "tommy gun" found action in all theaters of war, mainly by U.S. and British forces. More complicated and expensive than the grease guns, production was stopped, and it became quite a coup later in the war to be issued or to acquire a tommy.

Machine Guns

BAR The Browning automatic rifle, made for World War I, became the standard squad automatic weapon. It fired 7.62mm rounds from a bottom-fed 20-round clip. A bipod was mounted underneath. The rifle, though awkward to march with, was indispensable in battle.

M-1919A4 An air-cooled, belt-fed light machine gun produced by Browning, it could sustain 400 to 500 rounds per minute and saw use on armored vehicles, jeeps, ships, and anywhere else it could be stuck. A water-cooled version was used for sustained suppressing or covering fire for ground troops. The most famous use of this gun was on Guadalcanal, where marine Al Schmid used just one to single-handedly repel a Japanese attack.

M-2HB The Browning .50-caliber heavy machine gun is a legend. Used in planes, on ships, tanks, and antiaircraft mounts, it was and remains one of the best firearms in the world. Firing armor-piercing, tracer, incendiary, or regular ball ammunition, the Browning heavy machine gun was a formidable weapon.

Platoon Weapons

ANTITANK GRENADES All Allied forces used the same basic type of grenade launcher that fitted to the end of service rifles and could propel rocket grenades. These included the Soviet RPG and several variants of U.S.-designed rifle grenades.

MIAI BAZOOKA Designed to take out tanks, this 60mm rocket launcher could be used from as far as 300 yards, but the effective range was within 100 yards. It not only bested most Axis armor but could blast pillboxes, field fortifications, and most anything else that was impeding the Allied advance in all theaters of war.

Arms and Armaments Time Line

The weapons of World War II were the product of two decades of political and military decisions made by major powers.

1918
World War I ends; the Versailles Treaty severely restricts Germany's military forces, abolishing compulsory military service, restricting the navy to 24 ships (no submarines), and banning military aviation.

1921
U.S. Army bombers sink old German battleships in trials conducted by the U.S. Navy off Chesapeake, Virginia, demonstrating for the first time that airpower can be used to sink large naval vessels.

1922
Washington Naval Arms Conferences limit the Japanese navy to one battleship for every three U.S. and British battleships and limit France and Italy to 1.75 (see Chapter 4, "Allies, Enemies, and Bystanders"). Also in 1922, Soviet troops drop from airplanes by parachute, introducing the concept of airborne warfare.

1925
A convention in Geneva prohibits the use of poison gas as a weapon of war.

1926
Dr. Robert Goddard, a U.S. scientist, launches the first liquid-fueled rocket.

1930
At a naval conference in London, the ratio of Japanese battleships increases to three for every five U.S. and British ships.

1932
A World Disarmament Conference is held in Geneva to discuss banning offensive weapons.

1935
Germany reveals to the world that it has been developing an air force. The U.S. Boeing B-17 Flying Fortress makes its first flight.

1936

A final naval conference is held in London. Japan withdraws from all further conferences and repudiates previous treaty requirements.

1937

The Panzer IV is introduced and quickly becomes Germany's standard battle tank.

1939

Production begins on the Japanese Mitsubishi A6M Type "o" fighter. The Zero became the symbol of Japanese air power in World War II.

1940

Expatriate Jewish scientists from Germany working in Britain conclude that it is possible to construct a nuclear bomb. The B-24 Liberator is designed and flown in less than a year. Development of the B-29 Superfortress begins. The semi-automatic M-1 Garand rifle becomes the standard infantry weapon in the U.S. military. Royal Air Force fighters defeat the Luftwaffe in the Battle of Britain.

1941

Japanese carrier aircraft inflict major damage on the U.S. Pacific Fleet at Pearl Harbor.

1942

Major General George C. Kenney uses airplanes to move troops into combat in New Guinea.

German U-boats inflict heavy casualties among Allied merchant ships in the Battle of the Atlantic.

Production begins on the M4 Sherman tanks at 11 facilities in the United States.

1943

The largest tank battle in history takes place at Kursk in the Soviet Union. The U.S. Navy fast carrier force enters combat in the Gilbert Islands campaign.

1944

B-29s enter combat from Chinese bases. German jet- and rocket-powered fighters attack Allied bombers. V-1 and V-2 rocket attacks against Belgium and Great Britain begin. Charles Lindbergh demonstrates his long-range cruise methods to army and marine pilots in the Pacific, allowing them to extend the combat range of the P-38 and F4U.

The first kamikaze attack takes place during the Battle of the Philippines.

1945

The first successful atomic bomb test is conducted in New Mexico. Atomic bombs are dropped from B-29s over Hiroshima and Nagasaki in August.

Books cannot be killed by fire.

People die, but books never die. No man and no force can put thought in a concentration camp forever. No man and no force can take from the world the books that embody man's eternal fight against tyranny. In this war, we know, books are weapons. *Franklin D. Roosevelt*

BOOKS ARE WEAPONS IN THE WAR OF IDEAS

CHAPTER 10

Intelligence, Espionage, and Propaganda

In war, intelligence and espionage exist in the shadows of secrecy, played not on the battlefront, but in back rooms and cafés. It is an integral and necessary part of warfare, especially in World War II—on both the Allied and Axis sides. The mission of those who served in the intelligence and espionage agencies was the covert acquisition of important military or political information about an enemy.

There were several methods used to gather intelligence and deceive the enemy during World War II, but three main methods stand out. The first—spying—had existed for centuries in Europe, and Axis and Allied powers alike relied on spies to unearth important information. A second and much newer form of espionage—cryptanalysis—involved the interception of coded radio messages sent by the enemy and the breaking of the elaborate codes in which the messages had been encrypted. The third— deceit, or deliberate misinformation—was intended to trick and mislead the enemy. As Churchill observed, "In wartime, truth is so precious that she should always be attended by a bodyguard of lies."

Because of the covert nature of intelligence gathering, many tactics were used to throw off the enemy. For example, spies were sometimes parachuted into enemy territory. Intelligence divisions established listening posts around the world to intercept enemy radio messages and hired teams of crack scientists, mathematicians, and college professors to unravel the complex codes. Armies sometimes dispatched subversion units to battle the enemy from behind the lines. A particularly ingenious tactic was used by the U.S. intelligence effort: Navajo marines were recruited to broadcast messages in their native tongue—an Indian language that had no written tradition and that was known by almost no one except the Navajos themselves. Navajo broadcasts were utterly undecipherable to the Japanese.

Results were mixed: the data led to either catastrophic failures or magnificent successes. The former often came not from a lack of knowledge but from leaders who refused to believe what they were told. In 1944, French generals scoffed at intelligence that predicted that German armies would attack through the Ardennes Forest. In 1941, Stalin refused to accept that Hitler was about to invade his nation, despite numerous warnings from his own intelligence services and from the British. The United States never seriously considered Pearl Harbor to be in any danger. In all three instances, agents had warned of the impending attacks, only to be ignored.

But for every failure, there were many more successes. For example, Great Britain convinced hundreds of arrested German spies to work as double agents. In 1944, with U.S. assistance, the British implemented a bold plan to trick the Germans into thinking the cross-channel invasion would occur at the Pas de Calais rather than at Normandy. And in the Pacific, U.S. intelligence helped turn the tide at the Battle of Midway (1942) and cracked the Japanese merchant shipping code.

Propaganda was also an important tool in the war to influence the thinking of both the enemy and the citizens of the warring nations. Propaganda came in many forms and was used for different purposes. Like the campaigns of deceit by the intelligence services, propaganda spread falsehoods about the enemy to damage its cause. On the other hand, propaganda promoted a nation or leader's ideology or unified a nation behind its leader and military forces. The racial propaganda of Dr. Paul Joseph Goebbels in Germany tried to stir the German population by dire warnings about their fate if the Soviet "beasts" won the war. On the Allied side, propaganda was not above using racial stereotypes, especially of the Japanese, but it also served to promote the sale of war bonds and to spread a patriotic message that appeared in war posters, Hollywood movies, and radio shows.

Covert Operations: Intelligence and Espionage

Often, the more important struggles of war occur behind the scenes, in confined rooms where people collect intelligence information and try to crack an enemy's code or in mysterious locales where men and women willingly place their lives on the line to surreptitiously gain information about their foes.

Numerous agencies employed these thousands of workers in the field and at home. The various agencies vied with each other to excel at gathering and interpreting information. At times ruthless, inefficient, and bumbling, they combined to form one of the war's most intriguing chapters. On the Allied side, the French Central Bureau for Information and Action (BCRA) worked out of London to assist the Free French forces battling Nazi subjugation, while the British Secret Service Bureau (MI5) and the Secret Intelligence Service (MI6) labored out of Bletchley Park near London. In the United States, the Office of Strategic Services (OSS), a precursor to the CIA, handled foreign intelligence operations, while the Federal Bureau of Investigation (FBI) concentrated on domestic surveillance and apprehension of enemy spies. The Soviet Union's secret police, the People's Commissariat for Internal Affairs (NKVD), joined with the Chief Intelligence Directorate of the General Staff (GRU) to keep track of developments in and outside the nation.

In Germany, the Abwehr tracked developments in other nations' military preparations, while the Sicherheitsdienst (SD) handled internal surveillance in Germany and conducted espionage in enemy nations. Japan relied on its naval intelligence and the Tokumu Bu (Special Service Organization) to relay crucial intelligence information to Tokyo.

THE INTELLIGENCE WAR

Described below are highlights of the organizations, operations, and people involved in the intelligence war. (For a more complete list of code operations, see Chapter 7, "Campaigns and Battles: Europe and the Atlantic.")

Intelligence Organizations

ABWEHR This German intelligence agency was responsible for spying on foreign military operations. Headed by Admiral Wilhelm Canaris until 1944, the agency contributed relatively little, in part because Great Britain was so successful in converting German agents in England to the Allied cause. Canaris, who often hired deaf mutes to sit in foreign restaurants to read the lips of diplomats and officers, frequently clashed with other German intelligence heads who questioned his loyalty, especially Reinhard Heydrich of the SD and with the Gestapo. The agency was absorbed into the SS RSHA during a reorganization in early 1944.

ALLIED INTELLIGENCE BUREAU (AIB) The Australian-American intelligence-gathering

---

RUSS JANOFF, U.S. ARMY

On Intelligence from the Air

We made topographical maps from aerial photography. It was a very unusual technique to be able to make a topographical map of an area without having anyone on the ground to do survey work and to study elevation and that type of thing. The way this was done, they would fly a photographic plane with three cameras mounted from horizon to horizon. They would fly it about a hundred miles up in one strip then it would make a U-turn and go about 20–25 miles adjacent and come back 100 miles and then it would do the same thing. It would cover whatever amount of land they wanted to map that way. And the cameras would click continuously as the flight was going through the hundred-mile run. What we were responsible for doing was linking . . . one run with the next run by finding the identical identifying points on the map. And once that was done, that's called tying it together and we tied together all of these various strips. Then they would create templates and determine by stereoscopic study what the elevations were. The templates were created to make the maps. It was rather a complex outfit.

—Rutgers Oral History Archives of World War II, http://fas-history.rutgers.edu

agency was established in the Southwest Pacific in July 1942 by General Douglas MacArthur, who preferred to rely on a department under his supervision for intelligence rather than depending on a Washington-based bureau or one controlled by the navy. The AIB provided such accurate information about Japanese troop dispositions that MacArthur was able to bypass enemy strongholds in New Guinea and land in relatively undefended areas. The most famous operation that outflanked the enemy was the acclaimed leap to Hollandia. The AIB was abolished after the war.

B-DIENST OBSERVATION SERVICE This German intelligence organization headed by Wilhelm Tranow contributed to early U-boat successes by providing accurate information on the location of British merchant and military ships during the Battle of the Atlantic. By April 1940, B-Dienst was so good at breaking into the British Merchant Navy code that it was able to read almost half the messages sent.

BUREAU CENTRAL DE RENSEIGNEMENTS ET D'ACTION (BCRA) The Free French intelligence organization was established by Brigadier General Charles de Gaulle. De Gaulle, with headquarters in exile in London, set up the agency to work with the Resistance in France and with British agents. De Gaulle also ordered the BCRA to compile files on those people inside France who could be considered friendly and those who would be opponents when de Gaulle returned to France after the war.

CAMBRIDGE SPY RING This was a group of British citizens recruited at Cambridge University by Soviet intelligence under the guise of forming a better understanding between the Soviet Union and the West. The most famous were the "Magnificent Five" of Harold "Kim" Philby, Donald Maclean, John Cairncross, Guy Burgess, and Anthony Blunt, who successfully infiltrated British and U.S. intelligence agencies. Their spying for the Soviets was not revealed to

the public until years after the war, by which time Burgess, Maclean, and Philby had defected to the Soviet Union. Blunt, who in his later years held the high-ranking position of keeper of the Queen's art treasures, was exposed in the 1980s and stripped of his knighthood.

COASTWATCHERS Coastwatchers was a group of missionaries, planters, and government workers stationed in various Southwest Pacific islands to radio information about Japanese troop movements to Allied headquarters. Started by Australia, the Coastwatchers came under the supervision of General Douglas MacArthur's Allied Intelligence Bureau in 1942. They gained fame during the U.S. advance up the Solomon Islands, where they risked their lives by broadcasting information from spots deep in the jungles or from behind enemy lines. They also rescued downed American aviators or sailors from sunken ships, including the young Naval officer John F. Kennedy, the future president of the United States, in 1943 after a Japanese destroyer rammed and sank his boat, the PT-109.

COMBAT INTELLIGENCE UNIT This U.S. cryptanalysis agency headed by Commander Joseph J. Rochefort succeeded in breaking the complex series of Japanese naval codes. Based at Pearl Harbor, the unit worked around the clock to decipher the Japanese naval codes, which relied on printed code books and cipher tables of five-digit numbers to represent words. By April 1942, Rochefort's unit could read almost one-third of the Japanese messages and was able to predict the approximate time, location, and composition of Japan's planned attack against Midway in 1942. Intelligence provided by this unit also helped in intercepting and shooting down the aircraft carrying Japanese Admiral Isoroku Yamamoto in 1943, and in directing U.S. submarines against Japanese shipping.

DETACHMENT 101 This U.S. Office of Strategic Services unit operated behind Japanese

In June 1942, Germany placed eight agents inside the United States to sabotage railroad lines and aluminum factories. After the volunteers had mastered American habits and slang by studying newspapers and magazines, German U-boats put four of the men ashore on Long Island, New York, and the other four in Florida. They were ordered to remain in the country and destroy whatever vital installations they could locate.

A U.S. Coast Guard member on Long Island spotted the first four and reported the information to superiors, who then alerted the Federal Bureau of Investigation (FBI). The German agents made their way to New York City, but the FBI kept close tabs on their activities.

Before the FBI closed in to arrest the group, one of the four Long Island agents, George Dasch, surrendered to authorities. Claiming to be anti-Nazi, Dasch revealed the details of the entire operation, and within two weeks the FBI had arrested the other seven members. Dasch and one other man who cooperated, Ernest Burger, received lengthy prison sentences, while the others—Werner Thiel, Edward Kerling, Hermann Neubauer, Richard Quirin, Heinrich Heinck, and Herbert Haupt—were executed.

lines in Burma. Conceived by Millard Preston Goodfellow in February 1942, and commanded by Captain Carl Eifler, Detachment 101 worked in the forbidding jungles of Burma, where it battled not only the Japanese but wild animals, giant leeches, poisonous snakes, and malaria. Detachment 101 enjoyed the superb assistance of the Burmese tribe known as the Kachins as it destroyed bridges and railways, severed Japanese communications lines, and rescued downed Allied aviators.

FEDERAL BUREAU OF INVESTIGATION (FBI) The U.S. agency was, and still is, responsible for internal security. After building a reputation for tracking criminals in the 1930s, the FBI expanded its operations in World War II to surveillance and apprehension of foreign spies working inside the United States as well as Latin America. The most renowned case occurred in June 1942, when eight German spies landed on the East Coast. After one spy surrendered to the FBI, the other members were quickly arrested and eventually executed.

FOREIGN ARMIES EAST Commanded by German Lieutenant Colonel Reinhard Gehlen

from 1942 until shortly before war's end, Foreign Armies East kept track of military intelligence in the Soviet Union. Foreign Armies East ultimately proved ineffective and committed major blunders. Most notable were the failure to spot Soviet intentions regarding a 1942 counteroffensive in Stalingrad that surrounded and ultimately destroyed the German Sixth Army, and the 1944 Soviet attack that annihilated Army Group Center, precisely where Gehlen had promised an attack would never come.

FOREIGN ARMIES WEST Similar to its counterpart in the East (see above), Foreign Armies West provided Germany with military intelligence pertaining to opponents in Western Europe. Partly because of deception spread by German double agents and partly because of incompetence, Foreign Armies West posted a dubious intelligence record, including misreading signs of the D-Day invasion of June 6, 1944.

GESTAPO Hitler established this powerful organization in 1933 to remove opposition to the Nazi Party and to maintain security inside Germany. An acronym for the organization's full name, Geheime Staatspolizei (secret state police), the Gestapo enjoyed the power of life and death over subject peoples in Germany and in conquered lands. By establishing a broad network of spies and by encouraging Germans to turn in anyone deemed disloyal, the Gestapo created an atmosphere of distrust and fear among civilians. First headed by Hermann Göring, the Gestapo was later directed by Heinrich Muller.

GRU (GLAVNOYE RAZVEDYVATELNOYE UPRAVLENIE) This was the Soviet Union's military intelligence organization. Like most Soviet spy agencies, the GRU was unable to convince Stalin of Hitler's intentions to invade the Soviet Union in the summer of 1941. However, its agents successfully penetrated the German general staff, while other operatives, such as the spy Klaus Fuchs, stole the secrets to the U.S. atomic bomb.

KEMPEITAI The Kempeitai was the Japanese military and intelligence agency responsible for both internal security and collecting information on other nations. Its intelligence work was far overshadowed by its efforts to suppress opposition at home and to instill fear in the population. Comparable to Germany's Gestapo, the Kempeitai was especially ruthless in suppressing civilians in occupied lands. After the war, the Allied occupation authorities abolished the organization.

MI5 The British agency was responsible for domestic security and uncovering enemy spying activities in the United Kingdom. Headed for most of the war by Sir David Petrie, MI5 (Military Intelligence, Division 5) attained amazing success in nabbing German spies, especially through the Double Cross operation and the Twenty Committee. Only one German spy is known to have operated out of England during the war and evaded capture. MI5 remains the United Kingdom's powerful defense security intelligence agency.

MI6 The British Secret Intelligence Service differs from the MI5 because it is responsible for foreign espionage and spying. Headed by then Colonel Stewart Menzies, MI6 (Military Intelligence, Division 6) achieved its most notable success in cracking the German Enigma machine code and intercepting thousands of German military and political messages.

NAVY COMMUNICATIONS INTELLIGENCE (COMINT) This was the U.S. Navy's agency for creating codes for naval use and for deciphering foreign coded messages. Called the OP-20-G, COMINT operations against the Japanese started in 1924, headed by Captain Laurence F. Safford. COMINT used a series of listening posts in the Pacific to intercept Japanese messages, which personnel in Washington and other posts then decoded. COMINT also used radio intelligence units aboard flagships at sea to intercept Japanese ship radio transmissions.

NKVD (NARODNYY KOMISARIAT VNUTRENNIKH DEL) The NKVD was the Soviet Union's internal and foreign intelligence agency. Headed by Lavrenti Beria, the agency

German Gestapo agents, arrested after the fall of the city of Liege, Belgium, are held in a cramped cell. As territory in Western Europe was liberated, German personnel and their collaborators often met with swift justice.

penetrated the British and U.S. militaries and relied heavily on the work of the "Magnificent Five"—five agents working out of England to gather information (see Cambridge Spy Ring, p.347). The NKVD spied on the Soviet Union's allies because the alliance was an uneasy one from the beginning, and it was clear to Stalin that the postwar years would be contentious. The NKVD also conducted internal security work for Stalin and, through an organization called SMERSH (later used by the former British intelligence officer Ian Fleming for his James Bond novels), investigated charges of disloyalty in the armed forces.

OFFICE OF NAVAL INTELLIGENCE (ONI)

The U.S. Navy agency was responsible for gathering intelligence and for protecting against foreign sabotage. Formed in March 1882, the ONI was the nation's first military intelligence organization. The ONI placed an intelligence officer aboard each vessel; he reported to the ONI about harbors, fortifications, and other valuable information as the ship plied the seas. The ONI also assigned naval attachés to the U.S. embassies in major nations to collect whatever data they could.

OFFICE OF STRATEGIC SERVICES (OSS)

This U.S. intelligence and espionage agency was headed by William J. ("Wild Bill") Donovan. Begun in June 1942, the Office of Strategic Services operated a spy ring from Switzerland that sent information about German defenses in Western Europe and sent teams to work behind enemy lines in the China-Burma-India theater. The OSS, under its research and analysis division, also conducted extensive studies of current magazines, speeches, and intelligence reports in an effort to predict German and Japanese moves. Its morale operations division focused on propaganda efforts.

RSHA (REICHSSICHERHEITSHAUPTAMT) The

Reich Central Security Office was the German secret police agency responsible for internal security. Established in 1939 under the command of Reinhard Heydrich, the agency coordinated the efforts of the Gestapo and the Sicherheitsdienst (SD), the intelligence and espionage section of the SS.

SAM BROUSSARD, U.S. ARMY, ATTACHED TO THE OFFICE OF STRATEGIC SERVICES (OSS)

Fighting with the Resistance

While in Brittany, I was sent to join a group of Resistance Maquis behind the German lines in the town of Kerien. While working with that group, we were notified that . . . a company of Germans . . . was headed towards the town of Kerien in order to take it over. Our Maquis kept us posted on the movement. Finally, when [the Germans] got close to the city, we took a position along the road with the understanding that at the proper time, when I felt that they were at the right range, I was to give the orders to fire. I positioned myself in a ditch . . . and [had] a good view of the Germans as they were coming in towards the town. They had mules and horse-driven carts.

The horses were pulling the wagons, and they had a bunch of Germans walking along the side. Finally, I gave the order to fire. They retreated at that time, and we killed a few Germans, and some of the wagons were left there, and then we pulled back in. . . . That afternoon we got some information from one of our Resistance workers that the Germans were coming back to make an attack on the town that night.

—Eisenhower Center for American Studies Archives

SICHERHEITSDIENST (SD) The German secret intelligence and security service was charged with unearthing plots against Hitler and exposing opponents to the Nazi regime. Headed by Reinhard Heydrich, the organization concentrated on espionage in other nations and internal surveillance in Germany. The SD frequently collaborated with the Gestapo but was often at odds with the Abwehr, headed by Admiral Wilhelm Canaris.

SIGNAL INTELLIGENCE SERVICE (SIS) This U.S. Army agency was established to coordinate army code-breaking efforts. Lieutenant Colonel William F. Friedman guided the SIS through the war years, but the agency failed to top its early triumph of breaking the Japanese Purple cipher. Hundreds of cryptanalysts worked at a secret headquarters in Arlington Hall, a former girls' school in Virginia.

TWENTY COMMITTEE This British organization was established on January 2, 1941, to recruit German spies who were found working in England (see Double Cross System, p. 352). The committee, chaired by J. C. Masterman, eventually had 120 double agents sending false information to Berlin, including reports pointing to the cross-channel invasion of June 1944 at Pas de Calais instead of Normandy.

Intelligence Operations

ATOMIC SPY RING The Soviets ran an operation to uncover the secrets behind the U.S. and British atomic bomb programs. By 1941, the Soviet Union had several spies placed in sensitive areas at Los Alamos, New Mexico, the top-secret laboratory and experimental ground where the atomic bomb was being built. U.S. Army Corporal David Greenglass stole a sketch of the Nagasaki bomb to turn over to the Soviets, while the British scientist Klaus Fuchs, among others, also provided valuable information to them.

BLETCHLEY PARK A large estate about 50 miles north of London, Bletchley Park was the headquarters of the British intelligence system. Military intelligence, spying, and code breaking and analysis work were all coordinated from Bletchley Park, which gained fame for its Ultra reports based on the interception of coded German messages. The work was so secret that once an individual was stationed at Bletchley Park, he or she remained there until war's end.

BODYGUARD Supervised by Colonel John Bevan and Lieutenant Colonel Sir Ronald Wingate and begun in early 1943, the code referred to the overall deception plan whose goal was to convince Germany that the cross-channel invasion of June 1944 would not occur in Normandy. This plan included Operation Fortitude, which focused specifically on deceiving the Germans into thinking the invasion would come ashore in the Pas de Calais region of France or in Norway. Bodyguard also enlisted the efforts of scores of British and U.S. spies as well as German double agents who sent disinformation to Berlin. Fake armies, one supposedly assembling in Scotland and another in England under Lieutenant General George S. Patton, sent radio messages to imaginary destinations and constructed thousands of wooden tanks and aircraft to divert attention from the actual force gathering in southern England. A professional English actor who looked amazingly like British General Bernard L. Montgomery was sent to the Mediterranean to fool the Germans into thinking that the top Allied commander was considering that area as an invasion site.

BODYLINE This was the British intelligence operation designed to determine German progress in rocket development. As a result of its findings, British bombers hit Peenemünde, where most of the German rocket industry was located. One raid targeted the homes of prominent German scientists working on rockets and jet engines and killed the scientist who had developed Germany's rocket jet design.

DOUBLE CROSS SYSTEM This British operation was run by the Twenty Committee (see p. 351) to capture and turn in German spies operating in England. Most were caught after they made mistakes because they were unfamiliar with British customs or were betrayed by cohorts who had been apprehended earlier. The name came from the Roman numeral designation for 20—XX—a double cross. Most of the captured spies cooperated, although 16 spies were executed in England.

ENIGMA This was the elusive German code machine used to send top-secret messages during the war. Developed in the 1920s by Arthur Scerbius, the machine looked much like a typewriter, but behind each key was an electric circuit that sent an impulse to a lampboard to illuminate a different letter. Interchangeable rotor wheels, which could be altered several times each day, made the task of breaking the Enigma code even more arduous. However, building on the work of Polish and French intelligence, British cryptologists at Bletchley Park solved the machine's workings. Of special assistance was a captured Enigma machine, complete with rotors and settings, from a German submarine.

FORTITUDE Operation Fortitude was the code name for that portion of the overall British-American invasion plan aimed at fooling the Germans into thinking that the cross-channel invasion of 1944 would occur somewhere other than Normandy. The plan had two parts. Fortitude North attempted to make the Germans believe that the invasion target was Norway, thereby tying down the 27 German divisions stationed there, while Fortitude South tried to divert German attention to the area around the Pas de Calais region, which was the shortest crossing point from England to France. German double agents transmitted false information to Berlin, and two fake armies were created in an attempt to deceive the Germans, including the nonexistent First U.S. Army Group commanded by Lieutenant General George S. Patton (see

Bodyguard, p. 351). The operation's success meant that 90 German divisions—almost a million men—were elsewhere when the invasion force hit Normandy's beaches on June 6, 1944.

JEDBURGH Operation Jedburgh planted 92 three-man teams in occupied Europe shortly before D-Day to work with the local underground forces and gather information about German troop dispositions. The teams, consisting of British, French, and U.S. agents, destroyed railways and communications centers to disrupt German movements on June 6, 1944.

LUCY SPY RING Operating out of Switzerland, Lucy was a Soviet spy ring that delivered information about the Germans with astonishing swiftness, sometimes within 24 hours of the German high command's having made a decision. Headed by Karl Sedlacek and Sando Rudolfi, the ring uncovered the German rocket program and forewarned the Soviet Union about a planned German offensive in the Kursk region in the summer of 1943. Armed with this information, Soviet tanks assembled near Kursk and turned back the attack in history's greatest tank battle.

MAGIC Before the war, Lieutenant Colonel William F. Friedman's Army Signal Intelligence Service had laboriously reconstructed a code machine that could read Japanese messages, This was code-named Magic. For much of World War II, top U.S. military commanders possessed crucial information about their Japanese foes. It even provided numerous indications that the Japanese would attack in the Pacific in December 1941, but few U.S. leaders seriously thought that Pearl Harbor would be the target (see Purple, p. 353).

MINCEMEAT This was the code name for the overall deception plan developed to convince Germany that the 1943 Allied invasion of Italy would occur on the island of Sardinia or somewhere in the Balkans rather than in Sicily.

Supervised by British Commander Ewen Montagu of British Naval Intelligence, the plan included floating to Spain's shores what was supposed to be the body of a deceased English soldier (thus the morbid operation name), which was dressed in an officer's uniform and carrying supposedly top-secret papers indicating the attack target (see "Martin, William," p. 355). German agents in Spain learned of the body and forwarded the fake military information to Berlin. As a result, some German troops were transferred from Sicily to Sardinia and the Balkans.

NAVAJO CODE TALKERS Because few people other than Navajos could use their language, which has no written tradition, and their messages did not have to be encoded, the U.S. Marine Corps used Navajos to transmit secret messages quickly (see Chapter 6, "Officers and Soldiers"). The first group of code talkers was recruited in September 1942 and reported for duty in the Pacific in early 1943. After that, Navajos participated in every marine operation for the duration of the war, including Iwo Jima, where six code talkers worked without rest for the first two days and handled more than 800 messages without a single error.

PURPLE Constructed by Lieutenant Colonel William F. Friedman and others in the Army's Signal Intelligence Service, the Purple decoding machine deciphered thousands of military and diplomatic important Japanese messages to U.S. political leaders. First used in 1940, the machine relied on a series of switches and a plugboard, unlike the German Enigma machine. Eventually, the United States sent three Purple machines to Bletchley Park in England (see Bletchley Park, p. 351).

ANTHONY BROOKS, BRITISH SPECIAL OPERATIONS EXECUTIVE (SOE)

Relaying Intelligence

I was trained by SOE after [an] interview. [I] trained in Scotland in parachuting, sabotage, and so on and trained in security and . . . resisting interrogation. . . . I was then parachuted into France at Blind on the first of July 1942 (so I was just over twenty), with one contact who was a Swiss and international trade unionist. . . . Through him I got in touch with French national trade unionists and progressively built up [a Resistance] organization [by] working mainly through French trade unionists but very seldom divided into cells and spreading from the Lyons area, which was my main HQ, to the Italian frontier area at Modane on the main river line to Italy and then down the [Rhône] valley as far as Avignon—always exclusively on railways—then 'round the Pyrenees, Toulouse, Montauban, and up to Limoges. It was a very, very, widely spread network. We received, I think, something like thirty-three tons of stores over the period, and we operated continuously from the beginning . . . until the autumn of 1944. Now in February 1944, I came back to England. I should say throughout [I had been] to England, [once] on a flight out [at] the end of August 1943 for briefing in London . . . and was given the D-Day messages for my own network . . . and for each area—we had four different areas—and [I was given] messages for different instructions [for] doing various things. . . . I should express that none of my groups was Maquis or that fighting Resistance. . . . I am not a soldier—I was a clandestine saboteur, and our network was small, tightly knit, urban, very much an urban organization. We did not shoot people, we did not throw grenades or anything like that. We concentrated entirely on operations in support of the Allied military effort.

—The Eisenhower Center for American Studies Archives

RED ORCHESTRA One of the most powerful spy rings during World War II, these Soviet spies worked in occupied Western and Central Europe. Germans called the network's radio operators "pianists," the transmitters "pianos," and the supervisors "conductors." The Red Orchestra achieved a number of successes, including placing an agent inside the German high command. However, Stalin dismissed its warning of the 1941 German invasion, because he refused to believe that the Germans would attack.

SPECIAL OPERATIONS EXECUTIVE (SOE) This British operation was established on July 22, 1940, to foment rebellion and encourage sabotage in occupied nations such as Poland and France. Prime Minister Winston Churchill told the division that he wanted it to "set Europe ablaze." This would force Hitler to switch more troops from the battlefronts to occupied nations, undermine the German economy, and lay the groundwork for large-scale uprisings to coincide with the 1944 cross-channel invasion of Normandy.

ULTRA After Hitler overran Europe in 1939–40, French and Polish mathematicians and scientists at Bletchley Park in England figured out how the Enigma code worked. Then British intelligence workers built machines called Bombes that could decode Enigma material. Ultra, for ultrasecret, was the code name given to all the intelligence yielded by German messages, and thereby played a crucial role in shifting the Battle of the Atlantic in England's favor.

VENLO INCIDENT On November 9, 1939, the Germans arrested two top British agents, Major R. Henry Stevens and Captain S. Payne Best. The pair, operating a spy ring inside Germany from their base in the Netherlands, were tricked into meeting a supposedly anti-Nazi German in a small Dutch town near Venlo on the German border. Instead, the two were apprehended and taken into custody in Germany and

tortured until they divulged top-secret information. Their loss eliminated much of Britain's intelligence network on the continent in the war's early years.

People in Intelligence

BERIA, LAVRENTI (1899–1953) Beria headed the NKVD, the Soviet Union's internal and foreign intelligence agency. Born in 1899, he supervised hundreds of executions of Stalin's opponents in the infamous 1930s purges. During the war, Beria directed Soviet attempts to infiltrate German, British, and U.S. military and political organizations. After Stalin's death in 1953, Beria was arrested by political foes, put on trial, and executed.

CANARIS, ADMIRAL WILHELM (1887–1945) Canaris headed the Abwehr (see p. 346) until 1944. A U-boat commander in World War I, he detested many of Hitler's policies after witnessing atrocities first-hand and was thus suspect in top Nazi circles. His organization appeared to have been involved in a number of plots against Hitler, including the July 1944 assassination attempt. After that operation failed, Canaris was arrested, sent to a concentration camp, and executed on April 9, 1945.

CICERO (1904–71) Cicero was the code name for Elyesa Bazna, a German spy who worked as a valet in the household of Britain's chief diplomat in Turkey. Bazna received the nickname because of the immense volume of material that he photographed and sent to Berlin evoking the memory of the ancient Roman orator Cicero's continual stream of oratory. Bazna stopped operating in 1944 out of fear of discovery. He was never caught by the British and lived until 1971, when he died in poverty.

DONOVAN, WILLIAM J. (1883–1959) A highly respected military officer who earned a Congressional Medal of Honor in World War I, Major General William J. ("Wild Bill") Donovan made several diplomatic trips to Europe and the Middle East for U.S. President Franklin D. Roosevelt shortly before the United States entered World War II. When Donovan returned, he was placed in charge of the Coordination of War Information, which became the Office of Strategic Services (see p. 350), the forerunner of the Central Intelligence Agency. Donovan supervised operations in most theaters of the war, including covert missions in Burma and Germany.

FRIEDMAN, WILLIAM F. (1891–1969) Lieutenant Colonel Friedman headed the U.S. Army's Signal Intelligence Service when it broke the Japanese Purple code in 1940. For the remainder of the war, Friedman directed intelligence efforts from the secret headquarters in Arlington Hall, a former girls' school in Virginia. His unit's work focused on decoding Japanese diplomatic messages, as opposed to the navy's Combat Intelligence Unit in Pearl Harbor, which worked with the Japanese naval code.

GARBO Juan Pujol Garcia, aka Garbo, was a Spaniard who sent volumes of disinformation to Berlin on behalf of the English. Originally recruited in his native Spain by the Abwehr, the antiFascist Garcia then contacted the British and offered his services as a double agent. He succeeded in creating a fictional network of fourteen agents who supposedly reported to him. His false information, particularly about the D-Day landings, so impressed the Germans that they awarded him the Iron Cross. That same year the British government handed Garcia the Order of the British Empire for his work.

JOSEPHINE This was the fictitious code name for an England-based source whose handler, Karl-Heinz Kramer, a member of the Abwehr who worked out of Stockholm, forwarded more reports to Berlin than any other German spy, with startling accuracy. Based on Josephine's information, Kramer notified Berlin of the Allied decision to postpone the cross-channel invasion from 1943 until 1944 and of troop dispositions. The British arrested Kramer after the war, and he confirmed that his source for the Josephine reports was a Swedish naval attaché in London.

LAYTON, EDWIN T. Captain Edwin T. Layton was the chief U.S. naval intelligence officer in the Pacific. In the days before the Pearl Harbor attack (December 7, 1941), Layton's unit at Admiral Husband E. Kimmel's headquarters in Pearl Harbor issued numerous bulletins containing crucial information culled from its readings of Japanese naval messages. Layton played such a prominent part in the war that at the end of the conflict, the highest-ranking naval officer in the Pacific, Admiral Chester Nimitz, asked him to attend the surrender ceremonies aboard the battleship USS *Missouri* in Tokyo Bay.

"MARTIN, WILLIAM" This was the name given to a dead man whose true identity was never determined. "Martin" became a courier of false information intended to deceive the Germans into believing that the Allies would invade the Balkans rather than Sicily in the summer of 1943. A briefcase filled with false topsecret information was handcuffed to the body, which was then—in Operation Mincemeat (see pp. 352–3)—deposited by a British submarine in the ocean off the coast of Spain. After the body was discovered, German agents in Spain transmitted the false information to Berlin. After the war, Martin became popularly known as "the man who never was."

MENZIES, STEWART GRAHAM (1890–1968) Major General Sir Stewart Graham Menzies was director of MI6 (see p. 349), the British Secret Intelligence Service, during the war years and until his retirement in 1953. He directed Britain's espionage efforts from headquarters at Bletchley Park.

ROCHEFORT, JOSEPH J. (D. 1976)
Captain Joseph Rochefort was the head of navy code breaking in the Pacific. Working from headquarters at Pearl Harbor, Rochefort and his team cracked the Japanese naval cipher in 1942, and the information helped the United States to victory at the Battle of the Coral Sea and at Midway.

ROSBAUD, PAUL Rosbaud was a German, code-named Griffin, who sent secret information to Great Britain. After being well treated by the British following his capture in World War I, Rosbaud agreed to help Great Britain when Hitler came to power. Rosbaud reported on the German rocket program, and his information proving Hitler's atom bomb program lagged behind that of the Allies eased British worries that they might be the target of such a weapon.

SCHELLENBERG, WALTER (1910–52)
General Walter Schellenberg headed foreign intelligence in the Reich Central Security Office (RSHA, see p.350) from 1944 to 1945. After the arrest of Admiral Wilhelm Canaris and the dissolution of the Abwehr, Schellenberg gained recognition for his direction of espionage raids earlier in the war, including the Venlo incident. As the war wound to its destructive conclusion, Schellenberg tried to arrange peace talks with the Allies. He was arrested at the war's end, tried at Nuremberg, and sentenced to six years' confinement. He was released in 1951.

STEPHENSON, WILLIAM (1896–1989)
A Canadian who represented British security interests in dealings with the United States, Stephenson was "the man called Intrepid." Appointed by Winston Churchill in 1940, he established the British Security Coordination as a cover for British operations in the United States before it entered the war in December 1941. After that, Stephenson acted as a liaison between British intelligence agencies and their U.S. counterparts.

INTELLIGENCE ORGANIZATIONS

Each major combatant in the war established its own intelligence-gathering and espionage organizations. These agencies enjoyed varying degrees of success and contributed to the conflict's final outcome in significant ways. The following is a tabular version of the organizations discussed above.

Organization	Director	Mission and Principal Activities
GERMANY		
Abwehr	Admiral Wilhelm Canaris	Foreign espionage, especially pertaining to the enemies' military capabilities
Foreign Armies East	Reinhard Gehlen	Collected intelligence on the Soviet Union
Gestapo	Hermann Göring, Heinrich Muller	Domestic security; incarceration of invaded non-German peoples
Reich Central Security Office (RSHA)	General Walter Schellenberg	Secret police agency responsible for internal security and foreign intelligence
Sicherheitsdienst (SD)	Reinhard Heydrich	Domestic surveillance and foreign espionage

Organization	Director	Mission and Principal Activities
GREAT BRITAIN		
British Secret Service Bureau (MI5)	Sir David Petrie	Domestic security; organized the Twenty Committee and Double Cross System to catch German spies
British Secret Intelligence Service (MI6)	Sir Stewart Menzies	Foreign espionage and spying; cracking of German Enigma machine code
JAPAN		
Kempeitai	Japanese Imperial Navy	Secret police organization to spy on civilians and suppress dissent in Japan
SOVIET UNION		
Chief Intelligence Directorate of the General Staff (GRU)	Five men from 1938 to 1946—I. I. Proskurov, F. I. Golikov, A. P. Panfilov, I. I. Ilichev, and F. F. Kuznetsov	Military intelligence organization designed to spy on foreign nations
People's Commissariat for Internal Affairs (NKVD)	Lavrenti Beria	Internal security and foreign espionage
UNITED STATES		
Allied Intelligence Bureau	General Douglas MacArthur	Intelligence gathering in the Southwest Pacific
Combat Intelligence Unit	Commander Joseph J. Rochefort	Deciphering of Japanese naval codes
Communications Intelligence (COMINT)	Navy Captain Laurence F. Safford	Set up listening posts in Pacific to intercept Japanese diplomatic and military messages; employed Radio Intelligence Units aboard ships at sea to intercept radio communications among Japanese vessels
Federal Bureau of Investigation (FBI)	J. Edgar Hoover	Domestic security
Office of Strategic Services (OSS)	William J. Donovan	Overseas intelligence gathering and spying; research and analysis of enemy journals and reports
Signal Intelligence Service (SIS)	William F. Friedman	Deciphered Japanese PURPLE code and other diplomatic messages

Time Line: Breaking the Japanese Diplomatic Code

Code-breaking operations against the Japanese began as early as 1921, but teams working on cracking codes did not see the impending attack on Pearl Harbor. The United States rebounded quickly from its defeats in the Pacific war's first six months by successfully breaking the enemy's codes through cryptanalysis. They redeemed themselves by gathering enough information to help determine the Japanese offensive threats that resulted in the battles of the Coral Sea and Midway, among others. Intelligence gained from reading decoded Japanese radio traffic allowed the Allies to amass forces to meet anticipated Japanese strikes and to plan strategic responses that would be most effective.

1921
U.S. Army code breakers provide information that helps the government achieve a favorable outcome in the Washington Naval Treaty.

1925
U.S. Navy establishes a cryptographic unit.

1929
Secretary of State Henry Stimson cancels code-breaking work, claiming it violates ethical standards.

1935
U.S. Army Signal Intelligence Service (SIS) restores its code-breaking teams under the guidance of William Friedman.

1937
Japan introduces a sophisticated code called "Alphabetical Typewriter 97." Friedman's teams work for four years to crack the code.

1939
Japanese Navy adopts the Japanese naval code, called JN-25.

1940
U.S. code breakers achieve the ability to read Japan's naval codes.

Japanese Imperial Navy revises its code and cipher system.

1941
A Combat Intelligence Unit, commanded by Lieutenant Joseph J. Rochefort, is established at Pearl Harbor to crack the Japanese naval code. Interceptions of the Japanese diplomatic code indicate that war is imminent, although where it will break out is uncertain.

1942
Rochefort's unit is able to read 30 percent of the Japanese naval code, enough to provide information in time for the Battles of the Coral Sea and Midway.

CODE BREAKERS OF ENIGMA

First produced in 1923 by engineer Arthur Scherbius, the German Enigma machine was marketed as a business tool to keep information from competitors. The German military quickly adapted it for military purposes, confident the complicated machine was foolproof. They were unaware, however, of different individuals whose hard work cracked Enigma's secrets. Polish scientists first worked to break the machine's secrets, later sharing their work with French and British code breakers. The following is a list of those who contributed to the deciphering of Enigma.

Name	Nation	Contributions
Brigadier General Gustave Bertrand	France	As head of the French decoding section, he received secret reports from Hans-Thilo Schmidt, a French agent who worked in the German military code section. The information helped solve Enigma's complex system. In 1939, he chaired a meeting of French, British, and Polish intelligence officials at which the secrets of the Enigma machine were shared.
Major Maksymilian Ciezki	Poland	He led a team of Polish mathematicians that cracked the German Enigma machine code in the 1930s.
Marian Rejewski	Poland	He created a machine called the *bomba*, which could read German messages sent by Enigma
Hans-Thilo Schmidt (1888–1943)	Germany	The spy who handed Enigma secrets to the Polish code-breaking division, he was arrested by the Gestapo and executed in July 1943.
Commander Alastair G. Denniston	Great Britain	As head of the British Government Code and Cypher School at Bletchley Park, he supervised the British attempt to crack Italian codes as well as the massive effort to unravel the secrets of Enigma. In 1939 he met with Polish code-breakers, who shared their work on Enigma with Denniston and delivered a duplicate machine to the officer. Denniston later worked with the United States on joint intelligence efforts.

MAJOR SPIES

World War II had more than its share of intrigue and drama. Behind the front lines, women and men worked in the shadows to obtain information or spread disinformation. Their amazing stories have been the subjects of many books and movies. Below is information about the major individuals involved.

Name of Spy	Nation Served	Contributions
Elyesa Bazna (1904–71)	Germany	Working under the code name Cicero, he sent Germany information from a British diplomat's residence in Turkey. He photographed secret British documents and turned them over to the Nazis.

Name of Spy	Nation Served	Contributions
Anthony Blunt (1907–83)	Soviet Union	As part of the Cambridge Spy Ring, he helped infiltrate British intelligence.
Guy Burgess (1911–63)	Soviet Union	A member of the Cambridge Spy Ring, he worked for the Soviet Union to infiltrate British intelligence.
John Cairncross (1913–1995)	Soviet Union	A member of the Cambridge Spy Ring, he worked as a spy for the Soviet Union while at Bletchley Park.
Klaus Fuchs (1911–88)	Soviet Union	A nuclear scientist who left Germany in 1933 for England, as a member of the Communist Party, Fuchs sent information to Moscow on the progress of the Allied atomic bomb program. He became especially valuable after receiving a security clearance with England and traveling to the United States, where he worked with atomic scientists at Los Alamos, New Mexico. Fuchs is credited with stealing the blueprints for manufacturing the atomic bomb.
Juan Pujol Garcia	Great Britain	A Spanish citizen who operated under the code name Garbo, Garcia sent a steady stream of disinformation to Germany.
David Greenglass (b.1922)	Soviet Union	An American army technician, he stole atomic bomb secrets for the Soviet Union.
Fritz Kauder (1903–?)	Soviet Union	He was a Viennese spy who acted as a double agent to send false information to the Abwehr. Operating under the code name of Max, Kauder started directing material to Germany after the June 1941 invasion of the Soviet Union. Top German officials were impressed with the accuracy of his reports, especially a November 4, 1942, message disclosing decisions made by Stalin and his key military advisers that same day. He continued the deception until shortly before the war's end.
Karl-Heinz Kramer (b.1914)	Germany	Kramer worked out of Stockholm under the code name Josephine. His sources provided Germany with valuable reports on British operations such as the Allied decision to postpone the cross-channel invasion from 1943 to 1944.
Donald Maclean (1913–83)	Soviet Union	A member of the Cambridge Spy Ring, he successfully infiltrated British intelligence on behalf of the Soviet Union.
Harold "Kim" Philby (1912–88)	Soviet Union	A British citizen recruited by the Soviet Union in 1929 to infiltrate British intelligence, Philby worked so efficiently that his British superiors, never suspecting that he was sending vast amounts of information to Moscow, considered promoting him. In 1944, British intelligence embarked on a more vigorous investigation of Soviet activity in Great Britain, and the man they put in charge was none other than Philby. Philby was never caught during the war and defected to the Soviet Union in 1963.

Name of Spy	Nation Served	Contributions
Dusko Popov (1912–82)	Great Britain	A Yugoslav businessman, Popov worked as a double agent for Great Britain under the code name Tricycle. Recruited and sent to spy in England by the Abwehr, Popov quickly agreed to work on behalf of the British and sent numerous false reports to Berlin. In 1941, the Abwehr sent him to the United States, where he continued to work as a double agent.
William Sebold (b. 1902)	United States	A German-born American citizen, he became one of the most successful American double agents of the war. Recruited by the Abwehr during a visit to Germany, Sebold agreed to spy out of fear of reprisals against family members who remained in Germany. Upon his return to the United States, Sebold immediately contacted U.S. officials and offered to work in their behalf. Sebold arranged meetings in a New York apartment with German operatives working in the United States, each meeting filmed by an FBI surveillance unit from behind a one-way mirror. Sebold's work resulted in the arrest of 33 German spies.
Richard Sorge (1895–1944)	Soviet Union	One of World War II's most effective spies, Sorge worked for Soviet intelligence in Tokyo, sending an astonishing amount of accurate information on Japan and Germany. He futilely warned of Hitler's decision to attack the Soviet Union in the summer of 1941, since Stalin refused to accept that Hitler would turn on his nation. However, Sorge triumphed later in the year by informing the Soviet leader that Japan intended to strike to the south against British and American-owned possessions rather than against Stalin's forces in Manchuria. This allowed Stalin to transfer a million soldiers to the Moscow area for the climactic battle against the German military.
Leopold Trepper (1904–82)	Soviet Union	Known as the "Grand Chef," Leopold Trepper served as a main conductor in the "Red Orchestra," providing information to the Soviet Union from France. He directed several spy networks in France, which gathered material from German businessmen and military contacts. Trepper hosted posh dinner parties, replete with the finest foods and wines, during which he cleverly unearthed secret information on German troop movements and other operations.
Takeo Yoshikawa (1914–93)	Japan	Acting as a Japanese vice consul in Hawaii, Yoshikawa relayed invaluable information to Tokyo about the American fleet based in Pearl Harbor in the weeks before the December 1941 attack. He observed American ships entering and leaving the harbor and reported on ships' berths. Yoshikawa frequently traveled the area posing as a tourist and spent time at night in popular restaurants or other establishments where he was likely to overhear information. Following the Japanese attack, American authorities interned Yoshikawa along with every other Japanese citizen residing in the islands, but they never concluded that he had been a spy.

Propaganda: The Power of Persuasion

Propaganda, which is the spread of ideas or points of view that promote one's side or damage that of the enemy, came into its own in World War II. Every major combatant nation participated in propaganda, following the dictate of Great Britain's Alfred Harmsworth, a newspaperman who in an earlier war said, "The bombardment of the enemy mind is almost as important as his bombardment by guns." World War II nations added another element—that propaganda also had to be directed at civilians on the home front.

Propaganda is divided into white and black propaganda. White propaganda, based on truth, entails trumpeting one's victories and the enemies' defeats. Black propaganda uses false information to undermine enemy morale or to hamper military operations.

Propaganda in all nations appeared in a variety of media. Posters promoted conservation of resources, unity, and the evil nature of the enemy. Radio, especially the Voice of America and Great Britain's British Broadcasting Corporation (BBC), beamed military instructions to Resistance forces and information programs to

These examples of Axis propaganda were displayed for the media by the U.S. Office of War Information on March 6, 1943. The items include magazines published in Germany, Italy, and Japan.

foreign lands. Newspapers, at least in the dictatorships, spouted party lines. Films exhorted patriotism and valor. Aircraft dropped millions of leaflets on enemy soldiers or in enemy homelands, and songs touted democratic values or flouted Fascist doctrine.

The Axis dictatorships, which were closed societies in which newspapers and broadcasting were controlled by the government, had an easier time creating a unified propaganda message. Bombarded with the glories of Nazism, fascism, or militarism, the people in those lands were more susceptible to whatever the governments told them. In the open societies of Great Britain and the United States, however, the government could stretch the truth only so far. In light of these limitations, it is amazing that the democracies performed so well in the dissemination of propaganda, easily surpassing the Italians and Japanese and keeping pace with Germany. The following is a list of propaganda campaigns led by each country.

GERMANY

ENTERTAINMENT IN THE THIRD REICH
Nazi propaganda minister Joseph Goebbels realized the immense value that lay in using the two major forms of entertainment—radio and the movies—for propaganda purposes. Goebbels not only targeted a German audience but beamed programs to other parts of Europe and to the Americas to promote Nazi war aims. To ensure a huge domestic audience and unite the nation behind Hitler, Germany distributed millions of inexpensive radio receivers to German households. Although movies had to include anti-Jewish and other messages hailing the Nazi point of view, Goebbels recognized that people also had to be entertained. He thus allowed romances and comedies to be broadcast and filmed. Hundreds of films, including Leni Riefenstahl's *Triumph of the Will,* bearing military themes and deemphasizing the role of the individual in a totalitarian state, were also specially made for use in schools.

GERMAN-AMERICAN BUND This pro-Nazi organization operated in the United States in the 1930s. Although it never enrolled significant numbers—the Bund, at its peak, had about 8,000 members—the group struck fear into democracy-loving Americans with its Nazi-style marches, rabid demonstrations, and vicious anti-Semitism. It garnered such attention that Hollywood produced *Confessions of a Nazi Spy* in 1939 to alert the nation to its danger. It was the first anti-Nazi movie to hit American theaters. The leader of the Bund was interned in 1942 and was deported to Germany after the end of the war.

HITLER YOUTH Hitler Youth (Hitler Jugend) was headed by Baldur von Schirach and was intended to indoctrinate the nation's youth in Nazism and produce for Hitler a mass of fervent soldiers. Parents were forced to enroll their children at age six in youth groups or face severe prison sentences. Boys embarked on an apprenticeship of physical and military training that culminated in membership in the Hitler Youth at 14. The most promising of the Hitler Youth then entered one of three institutions designed to produce fanatical Nazis—the Adolf Hitler Schools, the Political Institutes of Education, or the Order Castles. Girls entered programs that promoted physical fitness and stressed the importance of bearing children for the Reich.

MINISTRY OF PUBLIC ENLIGHTENMENT AND PROPAGANDA (MPEP) This German propaganda agency was headed by Joseph Goebbels, who exercised complete control over every aspect of news dissemination with the belief that "propaganda has nothing to do with truth." Formed on March 13, 1933, a few weeks after Hitler came to power, the MPEP cast Hitler as both a superhero who would restore Germany to greatness and a man of the people to whom everyone could relate. Goebbels loved orchestrating mass nighttime demonstrations, lit by thousands of torches and beacons of light, which he believed were more dramatic and influential.

As the war progressed, Goebbels and the MPEP masterfully changed their tactics to fit each situation. In the war's first two years they had to do little more than state the truth because of the heady string of German battlefield triumphs. When disaster unfolded in the Soviet Union in the harsh winter of 1941–42, Goebbels organized clothing drives at home for the freezing German soldiers in order to divert the nation's attention from the ineptness of the campaign. He touted losses not as defeats but as glorious delaying actions. When Soviet armies threatened the homeland, Goebbels exhorted the masses by labeling Germany as the defender of

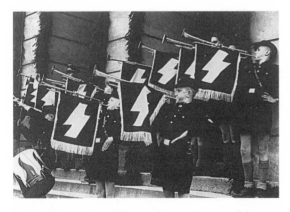

Hitler Youth trumpeters blare a salute on the steps of the town hall in Tomaszow, Poland. Baldur von Schirach, the leader of the Hitler Youth, was sentenced to 20 years in prison during the Nuremberg trials.

Western civilization against the barbaric hordes from the East. Near war's end, he kept hope flickering by hinting of secret weapons that would miraculously save Germany.

> [People] will more easily fall victims to a big lie than to a small one.
> —Adolf Hitler

MINISTRY OF SCIENCE, EDUCATION, AND POPULAR CULTURE The German agency that controlled the educational system was headed by Bernhard Rust and emphasized physical fitness over intellectual pursuits. Thus military training and the promotion of Nazi doctrine rather than debate and discussion were central. Hitler asserted that "knowledge is ruin to my young men. A violently active, dominating, brutal youth—that is what I am after!" To that end, teachers were forced to alter their curricula to reflect Nazi beliefs. Biology teachers explained the supposed differences between

---

EXCERPTS FROM *THE GOEBBELS DIARIES*

Joseph Goebbels, Hitler's minister in charge of propaganda, meticulously kept a diary during the war years. Although portions were lost, many of his writings remain, and they were published after the war. The book provides an illuminating glimpse into the mind of one of Hitler's staunchest supporters.

On Hitler: November 1925, "Wit, irony, humor, sarcasm, earnestness, passion, white heat—all this is contained in his speech. This man has everything it takes to be king. . . . I want Hitler to be my friend. His picture is standing on my table. I simply could not bear it if I ever had to despair of this man."

On Jewish influence: March 12, 1942, "It is surprising how much Jewish influence there is among the English people, especially the upper crust, which is hardly English in character any longer. The chief reason is no doubt the fact that these Upper Ten Thousand have become so infested with the Jewish virus by Jewish marriages that they can hardly think in English."

On domination in Europe: May 8, 1943, "The Germans alone can really organize Europe. There is practically no other leading power left. . . . Even though the Italians today give us many a headache and create many a difficulty, we must nevertheless consider ourselves lucky that they cannot be serious competitors in the future organization of Europe. If the Japanese were settled on the European continent the situation would be quite different. Today we are practically the only power on the European mainland with a capacity for leadership. The Führer sometimes asks himself in a worried sort of way whether the white man is going to be able in the long run to maintain his supremacy over the tremendous reservoir of human beings in the East."

On propaganda: January 29, 1942, "Again I learned a lot; especially that the rank and file are usually much more primitive than we imagine. Propaganda must therefore always be essentially simple and repetitious. In the long run only he will achieve basic results in influencing public opinion who has the courage to keep forever repeating them in this simplified form despite the objections of the intellectuals."

On restricting access to foreign radio broadcasts: February 20, 1942, "It is really amusing to see how all ministers now approach the Führer, asking his permission to listen to foreign radio stations. The reason they assign is nothing short of grotesque. For example, the Minister of Education declared he must know what our enemies are supplying in the way of anti-German news in order that he may indoctrinate youth against such reports! The Führer rejects all such requests brusquely and encourages my efforts to keep news distribution as restricted and limited as possible."

From Louis P. Lochner, ed., *The Goebbels Diaries, 1942–1943* (Garden City, N.Y.: Doubleday, 1948).

Aryan and non-Aryan people, while history teachers harped on the evils of the Versailles Treaty and boasted of the glories of ancient German empires. Anti-Semitism permeated all aspects of German education under Hitler. To ensure loyalty, teachers were required to join the National Socialist Teachers' League, to teach Nazi doctrine, and to take an oath of loyalty to Hitler. Ironically, this rigid approach to education hampered Germany when top intellectuals fled the country. Among the scientists who fled Germany after the rise of Hitler and the Nazis was the physicist Albert Einstein, who lent his considerable talents to the U.S. atomic bomb program.

REICH CHAMBER OF CULTURE This German organization, established on September 22, 1933, promoted the Nazi definition of "German culture" and eliminated foreign influences. Headed by Joseph Goebbels, the chamber estab-

lished seven departments (chambers of fine arts, music, theater, literature, press, radio, and films). Workers in those fields had to register with their respective chamber, and only fervent supporters of Nazism continued to work in their professions. Book manuscripts had to be submitted for approval before publication, and works by Jewish artists or writers were banned. Modern art, which Hitler considered degenerate, was also outlawed.

REICH PRESS LAW This October 4, 1933, law placed German newspapers under Nazi control. Editors were required to be German citizens of Aryan descent and could not be married to a Jew. Each day they met with Goebbels or other top Nazi officials to learn what they could print and what they had to suppress (anything that made Germany appear weak or disunited). Under these harsh rules the number of newspapers in circulation plunged from 4,500 in 1933 to 1,000 six years later, all promoting Nazi doctrine.

> Any man with the slightest spark of honor left in him will take good care in the future not to become a journalist.
> —Joseph Goebbels on his complete control of the press

GREAT BRITAIN

BRITISH BROADCASTING CORPORATION (BBC) The BBC is a renowned government-supported radio network in Britain, and during World War II, it broadcast information about the war to Europeans living under Nazi rule. BBC broadcasts were listened to surreptitiously throughout Nazi-occupied Europe and were often the only source of information from the outside world. Thousands of people listened to the daily broadcasts that countered Hitler's propaganda with a mixture of truths and half-truths, speeches, and music. Military strategists in England sent secret messages over the BBC to Resistance fighters in France to prepare them for the Normandy invasion of June 6, 1944. The BBC also broadcast directly to German citizens, pointing out the failed boasts made by Hitler earlier in the war about defeating England.

DEPARTMENT OF PROPAGANDA TO ENEMY COUNTRIES Just like the title suggests, this British department organized propaganda aimed at enemy nations. Headed by Dr. Hugh Dalton and Sir Robert Bruce-Lockhart, the agency relied on radio transmissions to convey information to Europeans under Nazi rule and to German citizens. The department also used numerous aircraft to drop leaflets over German-occupied territories.

MINISTRY OF INFORMATION (MOI) The MOI was the British agency in charge of domestic propaganda. Led by Duff Cooper and Brendan Bracken, the MOI organized the massive effort to educate British citizens about the war, persuade them to cooperate with ration drives and other drastic measures, and paint the enemy in a poor light. The MOI used all methods to achieve its purposes, including film, radio programs, newspapers, books, and posters.

ITALY

ITALIAN PROPAGANDA The Italian dictator Benito Mussolini evoked the glories of ancient Rome in his attempt to unify the nation behind him. He named his party the Fascists after the revered Roman *fasces,* a bundle of elm or birch rods surrounding an ax that symbolized power, and he proclaimed that "Caesar has come to life again in the Duce!" One frequently appearing image of Mussolini was that of his profile, which mimicked the visages of Roman emperors. Postage stamps bore visages of ancient heroes, and the nation celebrated the birthdays of Julius Caesar and Caesar Augustus. Mussolini hoped that memories of past glory would produce greater loyalty in and effort from his people, and he controlled the media to that end. Newspapers had to receive permission to publish their material, while films carrying Fascist themes played in every theater. To supervise the propaganda efforts, Mussolini established the Undersecretariat for Press and Propaganda in 1933 and the Ministry of Popular Culture in 1937.

Recognizing that future success depended on enlisting the avid support of the youth, Mussolini revised the educational system. From age four through college years, Italian boys and girls were bombarded with Fascist doctrine, wore military uniforms, and trained to be physically and militarily fit. Teachers had to take an oath of loyalty to Mussolini, and textbooks glorified Italy's past. Italian propaganda, however, failed to mirror the successes achieved in Germany or the United States, where the efforts were vastly more organized and better managed.

JAPAN

GREATER EAST ASIA CO-PROSPERITY SPHERE Appealing to the theme that Asians had a common interest against the occupation of Western nations, the Greater East Asia Co-Prosperity Sphere was little more than a Japanese effort to control Asia and the southwestern Pacific for its own purposes. Of special import were the precious natural resources that Japan needed for its military—including iron ore, oil, and rubber—and land for its citizens. Instead of promoting a unified stance based on a common Asian opposition to Westerners, the Japanese treated native people harshly and thus created enmity toward Japanese rule. As a result, Japan found itself governing a string of rebellious nations, which tied up occupation troops and caused military problems throughout the war.

JAPANESE PROPAGANDA Japanese propaganda concentrated on three themes: the joy of militarism, the necessity for sacrifice on the home front, and the duty of women to bear children. The first proved easiest because of the long Japanese military tradition stretching back to the days of the ancient samurai warriors. Proclaiming "Extravagance Is the Enemy," the Japanese government instituted austerity programs to produce money and materiel for its military. People on the home front were exhorted to sacrifice food and other items because their men on the battlefields were sacrificing their lives. Young men were required to volunteer for work details in addition to performing their regular jobs, and young women were urged to produce numerous offspring for the expanding empire.

Press censorship stamped out bad news and exaggerated good news. In the war's first six months, when Japan's army and navy recorded victory after victory over the United States and Great Britain in the Pacific, newspapers and radio could report the truth. But as momentum built in favor of the Allies, the government tightly controlled the media. When the navy suffered its catastrophic defeat at Midway in June 1942, survivors were kept in isolation so news of the loss would not become public. From that point on, the Japanese government turned to Emperor Hirohito to play a larger role in exhorting his countrymen to greater effort.

Government regulations clamped tight controls on the arts. Censors banned jazz as American decadence and collected British and American records. American movies were prohibited in favor of Japanese films, which glorified the military. Even the ballet turned to war—a 1944 performance was titled the "Decisive Aerial Warfare Ballet." As a result of the banning of negative news between 1942 and 1945, the Japanese people were staggered when they were informed by the emperor in August 1945 that Japan had surrendered.

TONARIGUMI The Japanese formed neighborhood groups of 10 to 12 households designed to unite people behind the military effort and to provide a form of domestic surveillance. The groups, known as *tonarigumi*, promoted seven precepts—rise early, be thankful for what you have, cooperate with the government, contribute to public service, be punctual for everything, waste nothing, and be physically and spiritually strong. Each one million *tonarigumi* throughout the nation had a leader who received orders from Tokyo and who reported offenders. In that manner the government enjoyed widespread surveillance of dissidents and control of its citizens.

FRANK CAPRA'S *WHY WE FIGHT*

Few people better epitomized the proficient use of helpful propaganda than the Hollywood director Frank Capra, remembered for his heartwarming films such as *It's a Wonderful Life*. In the first year of war, President Franklin D. Roosevelt turned to Capra to explain the nation's war goals and to graphically portray the evils posed by the totalitarian states. Capra supervised such a stirring string of documentaries that British Prime Minister Winston Churchill ordered the entire series shown in British theaters.

Working with other top-caliber directors, writers, and producers, including John Huston, Capra produced seven U.S. Army documentaries in a series called *Why We Fight*. The initial film, 1942's *Prelude to War,* depicted the rise of the totalitarian states in Italy, Germany, and Japan in the 1930s. Capra used powerful images to convey his message, such as a map of Europe being slowly engulfed by Nazi symbols.

Capra produced four features in 1943: *The Nazis Strike* explained to the American public Hitler's lust for land, which led to the absorption of Austria and the conquest of Poland; *Divide and Conquer* covered the German invasion of Scandinavia, northern Europe, and France; *The Battle of Britain* depicted heroic British citizens and the Royal Air Force defending Great Britain during the Blitz; and *The Battle of Russia* featured Hitler's invasion of his former ally.

Capra's final two films appeared in 1944. In *The Battle of China,* Capra attempted to enlighten audiences about the war in the Far East, and with *War Comes to America,* he turned his talents to events that led the United States to enter the war, including Japan's surprise attack on Pearl Harbor.

UNITED STATES

BUREAU OF MOTION PICTURES (BMP)

This U.S. agency advised Hollywood film producers on their films and how they should portray the war in order to influence the thinking of American citizens. The main question they wanted producers to ask themselves was, "How will this picture help win the war?" The BMP published a manual for Hollywood producers that asked them to insert positive war messages in their films. Thus films showed, for example, people walking around town instead of driving a car, which used up gasoline and wore out rubber tires. Early in the war, the BMP even asked that movies include wounded soldiers to prepare the nation for the sacrifices to come.

HOLLYWOOD'S CONTRIBUTION TO PROPAGANDA

One of the most effective U.S. propaganda methods was the production of movies carrying prodemocracy themes. The Office of Censorship ensured that no films portrayed the nation in a negative light and therefore rejected scripts that discussed some of

A patriotic theme encourages Americans to work for victory in a poster produced by the Office of War Information.

society's ills, especially racial bias toward blacks and Japanese Americans. In 1942 and 1943, a spate of so-called Last Stand movies attempted to put a positive spin on the war's early Pacific defeats at the hands of the Japanese. These films, such as *Wake Island* and *Bataan,* depicted U.S. soldiers heroically fighting to the last man, usually proclaiming a wartime message to the audience moments before death. Other films cast British citizens as stoically enduring Hitler's attacks in the London Blitz. Even cartoons pitched in. Both Bugs Bunny and Donald Duck took their turns mocking—often in racial terms—Hitler, Tojo, and Mussolini.

OFFICE OF WAR INFORMATION (OWI)

The U.S. agency in charge of wartime propaganda, the OWI was headed by the former newsman Elmer Davis. The OWI relied on a variety of methods to disseminate war information, explain U.S. war aims, and develop a feeling of sacrifice and contribution among American citizens. Among its many efforts were dropping propaganda leaflets on enemy soldiers and civilians, creating radio programs, broadcasting surrender appeals by loudspeaker to enemy soldiers, commissioning wartime posters by artists such as Norman Rockwell, sending magazines and newspapers to U.S. soldiers fighting overseas, supervising the Voice of America radio program, and producing 52 propaganda films about the war in the *America Speaks* and the *Victory Films* series.

PSYCHOLOGICAL WARFARE DIVISION

(PWD)   This division was created by the U.S. Office of War Information (OWI) to bombard Germany and Japan with propaganda. Workers in the PWD included some of the top media people in the United States, such as the prominent Columbia Broadcasting System president William S. Paley. Among the fruitful work carried on by the PWD was the dropping of millions of leaflets (see U.S. Leaflets and Office of War Information) over enemy lines and on

A Nazi book burning illustrates an American poster. A quotation from President Franklin D. Roosevelt, "Books cannot be killed by fire . . ." drives the message home.

enemy civilian populations and the use of loudspeakers to entice German or Japanese soldiers to surrender.

U.S. LEAFLETS

The United States excelled at using propaganda leaflets in both the European and Pacific theaters. Bombers dropped leaflets that instructed enemy soldiers how to surrender or informed the enemy's civilian sector about the progress of the war. A special bomb that held as many as 80,000 leaflets automatically opened when it reached 1,000 feet, from where it rained leaflets over the intended target. The United States dropped more than eight billion leaflets over Europe, including 27 million on D-Day alone. Results more than justified the effort. A survey of German prisoners showed that of the Germans who deserted in a

Japanese radio propagandist Tokyo Rose, whose real name was Iva Toguri, is interviewed by the media in 1945. An American citizen, Tokyo Rose was convicted of treason and sentenced to 10 years in prison. Released from prison in 1956, she was granted a full pardon in 1977 by President Gerald Ford.

two-month period in 1944, 90 percent had a leaflet in their possession. When the Japanese government balked at surrendering immediately after the atomic bombings of Hiroshima and Nagasaki, U.S. pilots dropped three million leaflets on Tokyo residents in an effort to prod the Japanese toward peace.

VOICE OF AMERICA The U.S. Office of War Information broadcast this successful propaganda radio show to Europe. The programs tried to counter Nazi propaganda by explaining the war's progress and by referring to the tyrannical aspects of Hitler's rule. The threat of concentration camp sentences, however, failed to deter a significant portion of the German population from listening to the program. The Nazis so detested the influence of the Voice of America that the Gestapo spread a rumor that it had a device that could pinpoint the locations of receivers that were picking up the program.

LEADING PROPAGANDISTS

Both the Allies and the Axis used effective propagandists to project their messages to the world. The three major Axis powers even hired U.S. and British citizens to broadcast propaganda appeals to Allied servicemen in Europe and in the Pacific. The radio programs, containing a mixture of songs, idle chatter, and propaganda, failed to sway Allied soldiers to the Axis cause, despite their often heavy-handed and disingenuous attempts to create a sense of "home" for the soldiers. Other leading propagandists included film directors and broadcasters who, while not employed by their governments, were able to propagandize, usually unofficially, for the cause of their countries.

Name	Nation	Contributions and Fate
Sergei Eisenstein (1898–1948)	Soviet Union	The famous director whose *Alexander Nevsky* became one of the greatest propaganda movies of all time, Eisenstein directed the film in the 1930s, when Germany loomed as the biggest threat to the Soviet Union. To arouse the nation, he portrayed famed Russian hero Alexander Nevsky, who led the Russians to victory over the German Teutonic knights in the 13th century. When Hitler and Stalin signed the nonaggression pact in 1939, the film disappeared from theaters, but two years later, after Hitler's invasion, the movie once again received wide release.

Name	Nation	Contributions and Fate
Mildred E. Gillars, aka Axis Sally (1900–1988)	Germany	An American who broadcast propaganda messages for the Germans, Gillars was born in Maine. She traveled to Germany in the 1920s to work as a singer and teacher. When war began in 1939, she agreed to work for a Berlin radio station, where she assembled a program containing entertainment and Nazi propaganda aimed at American soldiers in Europe. Her work did not seriously affect troop morale. In fact, many soldiers listened to her because of the music she played. After the war, she was tried and spent twelve years in prison.
William Joyce, aka Lord Haw-Haw (1906–46)	Germany	Joyce was a British citizen who collaborated with the Germans by broadcasting anti-Allied propaganda to Great Britain. Born in Brooklyn, New York, to an English mother, Joyce lived in Great Britain from 1921 to 1939. A supporter of fascism, Joyce headed to Germany in 1939, where he started his propaganda programs. British listeners labeled him Lord Haw-Haw because of the aristocratic accent he adopted for his broadcasts, and they generally looked with skepticism at his information. He was hanged for treason on January 3, 1946.
Edward R. Murrow (1908–65)	United States	One of the most revered radio broadcasters of all time, Murrow came to fame with his gripping accounts of the 1940–41 bombings of London by Hitler's Luftwaffe. Murrow opened each broadcast with his familiar, "This . . . is London," then described for his American audiences the pain and hardships endured by average British citizens. The subjects of Murrow's programs were not British officers; but London housewives, firemen, and air raid wardens took top billing. His work helped solidify support for Great Britain in the United States, which was not then in the war. Murrow continued in broadcasting after the war, hosting numerous award-winning television documentaries.
Ezra Pound (1885–1972)	Italy	An American poet living in Italy, Pound broadcast propaganda messages from Rome on behalf of Benito Mussolini and the Fascists. Twice each week, Pound, who had left the United States in 1907 and become an admirer of the Italian dictator, beamed a radio program to the United States, which included a mixture of poetry readings, Fascist doctrine, and attacks on President Franklin Roosevelt. Pound also wrote a series of newspaper articles supporting the Fascist point of view. Pound remained in Rome until Allied soldiers entered, at which time he was arrested and put on trial for treason. Found not guilty by reason of insanity, Pound remained in a Washington, D.C., mental institution until 1958.

(continued)

Name	Nation	Contributions and Fate
Leni Riefenstahl (1902–2003)	Germany	A talented German film director and actress who made propaganda films for the Third Reich, she was born Helena Bertha Amalie in Berlin in 1902. Her *Triumph of the Will*, about the 1934 Nuremberg Nazi Party rally, is considered the classic propaganda film. Its portrayal of throngs of marching soldiers, military banners, and audiences watching Hitler in ecstasy conveyed the image of order and strength. Two years later, Riefenstahl produced *Olympia*, a two-part documentary about the 1936 Berlin Summer Olympics. The Allies handed Riefenstahl a short prison sentence after the war, after which she returned to her film career and has continued to deny that she was a Nazi.
Iva Toguri, aka Tokyo Rose (b. 1916)	Japan	Tokyo Rose was the name given by American soldiers and sailors fighting in the Pacific to American citizen Iva Toguri, who broadcast English-language propaganda programs to American military personnel. She became a favorite because interspersed between her propaganda appeals, reports of supposed attacks, and seductive stories of infidelity by American women back home Toguri played popular American music. In reality, several English-speaking women served as Tokyo Rose. Toguri, a Japanese American born in Los Angeles, California, was the only American citizen associated with the broadcasts. In Japan visiting relatives when the war broke out, Toguri agreed to make the 15-minute broadcasts under what she later claimed was coercion. After the war, American authorities arrested her and she was convicted of undermining the morale of American troops. She received a 10-year prison sentence and a $10,000 fine. Upon her release, Toguri labored to prove her innocence. In 1977, President Gerald R. Ford granted her a pardon.

CHAPTER 11

The Home Front

Away from the battle lines, citizens of warring nations faced stresses, strains, and hardships no matter which side they were on. The term "home front" was accurate: ordinary citizens at home were on a "front" of their own, and in some cases, a front that was every bit as dangerous as the clash of armies in the field. Countries called upon their people to produce military materiel, fuel, food, and supplies and to make sacrifices small and large in order to aid the war effort.

In Great Britain, there was no escaping the war, for reminders were everywhere. Indeed, the British endured four years of bombing that killed 60,000 civilians. Wartime protective measures abounded. Each citizen had a government-issued gas mask, sandbags surrounded public buildings, and every neighborhood had an air raid warden. And then there was the rationing—of food, gasoline, rubber, and numerous other items—a constant reminder of how hardships extended into every corner of one's life.

The German home front was devastated most by the relentless bombing, which built in intensity between 1942 and 1945 and which devastated all of Germany's large and medium-sized cities. Carpet bombing by the Allies was designed to sow terror in the hearts of German civilians. Although rationing was introduced early, the German government was slow to implement certain wartime measures in civilian life. For example, they were reluctant at first to use women in noncombatant labor largely because Nazi ideology proclaimed that a woman's highest calling was to stay at home and bear children. In the end, however, women, old men, and young boys were called up in defense of the Reich, but at an hour when their services could no longer affect the outcome.

To counter the Nazi invasion, the Soviet Union threw the 10 million soldiers of the Red Army at the German army, a strategy that was effective but hideously costly in lives. The Soviet home front fared little better. Almost one million people died during the German siege of Leningrad between 1941 and 1944. Ukrainians destroyed crops and livestock rather than provide sustenance to the advancing Nazis; in addition, the Nazis bled the Ukraine dry, contributing to famine and general hardship. Soviet life during the war was hard and cruel, even for areas not in the direct line of combat. For those portions of the country, especially in the west, where the Nazis penetrated, the years of back-and-forth conflict left millions dead and the survivors living in rubble.

The people of Japan suffered greatly as 70 percent of the Japanese annual budget went to fund the military and their war effort. They also had to deal with tight rations of gas and oil and were required to plant gardens and build home air raid shelters. In the last year of the war, the country was ravaged by incendiary bombing, which reduced all major Japanese cities to ashes. The final assault—the atomic bombing of Hiroshima and Nagasaki—left a deep scar on the Japanese home front unlike any experienced by other combatant nations.

Americans were geographically isolated from the worst effects of war, but they nonetheless found themselves living in a radically changed country during World War II. Fifty million registered for the draft and nearly 16 million served in the armed forces out of a population of about 132 million. The government mandated rationing of essential items from butter and sugar to gasoline and the silk that once went into stockings, for it was needed for parachutes. But of all the changes that affected the U.S. home front, probably none was more profound or long lasting than the mobilization of American women on behalf of the war. They worked the farms, ran the city desks of the nation's newspapers, produced armaments, and held families together, even as they mourned sons, husbands, and brothers who were dying in far-off places.

The War Effort on the Home Front

What was life like for those who stayed behind, whether in the relatively insulated United States, a besieged Great Britain, or those living under dictators in such countries as Germany, Italy, and the Soviet Union? And what was it like in the many countries that were completely—and unwillingly—taken over by

the war? Home front experiences varied widely, from the relative inconveniences of food rationing to the terrors of daily bombings.

GERMANY

The Nazis conceptualized the home front (*Heimatfront*) as a civilian version of the war, with the workplace tantamount to the front lines.

Although they were reluctant to use women in nontraditional work, such as armaments production, or to cut back on certain consumer products, the mobilization for war by German citizens far preceded the actual hostilities. In agriculture, for example, as early as 1933 a fifth of all three million farms in the Third Reich were designated "hereditary farms"; these were permanently owned by the farmer, whose family lineage was first checked to assure racial purity. At the same time the Reich Food Estate was set up to control production, prices, and distribution on the farms and on the 42,000 farm co-ops. These mandatory strictures affected 300,000 laborers in dairies, mills, and processing plants, and another 500,000 in grocery stores. Everything was carefully monitored to expand production, down to the annual quota of 65 eggs laid per hen.

To help with the goals of increased harvests, thousands of members of the Hitler Jugend (Hitler Youth) were sent for six-month stretches of labor service. In their youth camps they were steeped in Nazi ideology, returning home believing, in the words of one youth leader, that "the pattern of our camp was the pattern of the world of the future."

> Farm workers no longer have the right to complain, and thus no complaints will be accepted by any official agency. . . . Visits to theaters, motion pictures or other cultural entertainments are strictly prohibited. . . . Sexual intercourse with women and girls is strictly prohibited. —Heinrich Himmler, 1941

The German home front did not experience any significant hardships during the first two years of the war. But as the war turned against the German army in the field, German civilians, particularly those living in cities, suffered. The center of Nazi industrial war production was the coal-mining and iron-producing Ruhr and Rhine river valleys of western Germany. Cities like Düsseldorf, Cologne, and Essen that made up the "Iron Heart" of Germany because of the aircraft factories and steel plants, as well as scores of other German cities, including Berlin, were the targets of an almost nonstop barrage of Allied bombing throughout 1942–45. In all, 780,000 German civilians died on the home front, most from bombing raids.

THE VOLKSWAGEN: UNFULFILLED PROMISE OF THE HOME FRONT

The Volkswagen, or "people's car," was Hitler's brainchild, inspired by the Model T of Henry Ford. In the 1930s car ownership was rare in Germany. The Volkswagen was designed by Ferdinand Porsche (1875–1951), who had been tinkering with the idea of an affordable small car. He devised the familiar "bug" shape, with an air-cooled engine in the rear, and had the Daimler plant build prototype after prototype, all of which were rigorously tested. Hitler ordered a complex built that would employ 30,000 workers who would do nothing but produce these cars at a rate of 1.5 million per year. He used the 1938 groundbreaking for the Wolfsburg factory as a time to hail the new "Strength-Through-Joy Car." He vowed that the car would be ready by 1939 and that the average German would be able to buy one for 990 reichsmarks ($397). A layaway plan allowed customers to pay five marks (two dollars) per week for an installment stamp; at the end of a designated time they were put on a waiting list for the next available Volkswagen. Before a single car was delivered (but after 280 million marks had been collected), German forces invaded Poland, the war was on, and the plant was converted to war use, as was the vehicle itself. The Volkswagen was not commercially available until 1946, the sole remnant of Nazi war production.

German Industry and the War

In February 1933, soon after being named chancellor, Adolf Hitler convened a meeting with German business leaders. The three business leaders most vital to the war industry and rearmament of the Wehrmacht were present: Baron Gustav Krupp von Bohlen, who made armaments; Karl Bosch and Georg von Schnitzler from I.G. Farben, the chemical maker; and Albert Voegler, head of the United Steel Works. They were predisposed to support the new leader because, in their minds, he stood for order. Business leaders also believed, wrongly, that they could manipulate Hitler. Hitler explained to them that he planned to stay in power indefinitely, even if he did not win future elections. Luftwaffe chief Hermann Göring, also present, explained how certain "financial sacrifices" were necessary and that these "surely would be much easier for industry to bear if it realized that the election of March 5 would surely be the last one for the next ten years, probably even for the next hundred years." Krupp was particularly impressed by the speech. On the spot, the Nazi inner circle was able to get promises of three million marks from the guests. Thus, from the very beginning of his regime, Hitler had enlisted the financial and political support of the major German industrialists.

During the later stages of the war, German industry used slave labor procured from occupied France and Poland, Russian prisoners, and Jewish concentration camp inmates. The living conditions were almost unfathomably harsh: long unpaid hours of work, meager food rations, unheated and inappropriate quarters (for example, dog kennels, stables, bombed work camps), inadequate water, no toilets or sanitation, rampant disease, and no medical attention.

The Krupp munitions plants were the primary recipients of this slave labor force. Krupp even built a fuse factory on the grounds of the Auschwitz extermination camp in Poland, in the same area where I.G. Farben built its synthetic coal-oil and rubber plant. "Resettled" Poles and Jews were forced to build the camp itself at Auschwitz (in 1940) but also to work in these adjoining factories until they collapsed from exhaustion; then they were exterminated.

Although Germany was forbidden by the Treaty of Versailles to make armaments, Krupp had been designing tanks and gun turrets since 1926; by 1933, when his factories went into full war production, the designs were completed and the assembly line ran at top efficiency, nearly a decade ahead of the U.S. plants. Likewise, the treaty forbade Germany to build ships weighing more than 10,000 tons, so the Germans created the "pocket-battleship," the first of which, the *Admiral Graf Spee,* was launched at Wilhelmshaven on January 1, 1934. I.G. Farben stayed at full production in the intervening years too by devising a system of extracting synthetic fuel and rubber (called *buna*) from the rich coal deposits found in the Saar and Ruhr regions of western Germany. By 1934, Farben had the go-ahead to mobilize 240,000 plants for fuel and rubber production, plants that would later be converted to make synthetic nitrates (for explosives) and Zyklon B (the chemical used to create the gas for the gas chambers of the extermination camps).

Other figures instrumental in German war production were the aircraft designers Wilhelm "Willy" Messerschmitt (1898–1978) and Ernst Heinkel (1888–1958). Messerschmitt's forte was fighter planes, of which the Luftwaffe had 1,000 by 1940; his signature plane was the Me-109 fighter, 30,124 of which were manufactured during the war, the most of any single model by any nation. Heinkel's masterwork was the He-111, the twin-engine mainstay of the Luftwaffe's bombing squadrons. More than 7,300 of these were built during the war, as were at least 14 other Heinkel-modeled aircraft. (For more about German equipment, see Chapter 9, "Arms and Equipment.")

GERMAN WAR INDUSTRIAL WORKERS

In 1939, Germany's labor force numbered more than 39 million, a figure that dipped to 29 million by the end of 1944 because men had been inducted into the military. To make up the difference, the Nazi regime pressed able-bodied citizens of those European countries that they had invaded, conquered, and occupied into service as laborers in their war mobilization efforts. In 1939, only 300,000 foreigners were inducted into the labor force; by 1944, the number had risen to 7,130,000, most of them living in harsh circumstances as slave laborers. The table that follows gives the manpower figures (in thousands) in the industrial sector alone.

Group	1939	1940	1941	1942	1943	1944
Germans in industry	10,855	9,745	8,861	8,011	7,948	7,515
Non-Germans in industry	104	236	644	1,001	2,061	2,367

GERMAN WAR PRODUCTION

Item	1939	1940	1941	1942	1943	1944
Coal*	332.8	364.8	402.8	407.8	429	432.8
Steel*	22.5	21.5	31.8	32.1	34.6	28.5
Tanks	2,000	2,200	5,120	9,395	19,885	27,300
Planes	8,296	10,247	12,400	15,409	24,897	37,950
Bombers	2,886	3,952	4,350	6,537	8,589	6,468
Submarines	N.A.	48	195	239	283	234

*millions of tons
Source: Michael Lyons. *World War II: A Short History* (Upper Saddle River, NJ: Prentice Hall, 2003).

GREAT BRITAIN

The British home front was characterized by bombing, shortages, and rationing—and by an incredible sense of unity and purpose. Expecting a blitzkrieg in the wake of the Nazi conquest of Poland in September 1939, British authorities issued gas masks to every citizen. Each neighborhood or village appointed an Air Raid Patrol (ARP) warden who inspected for preparedness, warned of impending attacks, and saw that night-time blackouts were maintained. After traffic fatalities doubled in the last four months of 1939, the government encouraged people to wear white at night so that motorists could see them more easily in the dark streets. Sandbag pyramids surrounded hospitals, churches, museums, and public buildings; plate glass windows were boarded up or taped to keep from shattering during bomb blasts; art treasures were removed to safer locations. As early as November 1939, a government evacuation scheme was in place to send children and young mothers with babies into the countryside of Bath, Devonshire, and Cornwall. Once the Luftwaffe began its regular bombing raids on England, the government's advance precautions proved wise. London burned, citizens slept at night in the Underground (subway), and Churchill rallied his countrymen as they stood alone against the Nazi threat. Some 40,000 British civilians had died in German bombing raids by May 1941; 60,000 were killed in the course of the war.

The British Home Front at War

Because British merchant ships were under constant attack by Nazi submarines and the island itself sustained four years of intermittent bombing—by plane, V-1, and V-2 rockets—England's home front was part of the war zone. The deprivations of food rationing were bad enough, but the nearly constant fear of being obliterated by a bomb or having one's house turned into a smoldering crater by a V-2 rocket took a psychological toll. The initial "bulldog" spirit embodied by Winston Churchill gave way, by 1944, to war weariness, low morale, and fear; hunger, cold, and depression were also constant companions, especially to Londoners.

Because of the timely development of radar, the authorities could tell in advance when a German bombing raid was coming and issue warnings. A sophisticated network of Home Guards and civil defense volunteers had been developed through nearly continuous use. The Home Guard, created by British Foreign Secretary Anthony Eden in May 1940, was a volunteer armed force of men aged 17 to 65 who initially prepared themselves for an expected German invasion but whose duties expanded as the war dragged on.

> No enemy was risking his life up there. It was as impersonal as a plague, as though the city was infested with enormous, venomous insects. —Evelyn Waugh, on the V-1 doodlebugs falling on London, in 1944

London's Underground, a deep and catacomb-like subway system, provided the most ready bomb shelter. By November 1940, although the Luftwaffe had destroyed one out of every five homes in London, it had also lost 2,400 aircraft to Royal Air Force fighter pilots and ground artillery. Later, the Germans deployed their V-1 (Vergeltungswaffe, or Retaliation Weapon), a pilotless plane propelled by a pulse jet engine and stuffed with explosives. Most were aimed at greater London (one passed through an arch of London Bridge without doing damage), and the British people took to calling them buzz bombs, bumble bombs, hellhounds, fire dragons, and, most often, doodlebugs. Although developed by late 1943, the V-1 was not deployed until June 1944. From June 12 until September 5, 1944, the Germans fired 6,725 V-1s at London, the RAF shot down 3,463, and the rest landed randomly, sometimes exploding instantly, sometimes later, which maximized both physical and psychological damage. In all, 2,340 hit London, killing 5,475 people. The rule of thumb was that if you could hear the V-1 engine overhead, you were safe. If it suddenly cut off within earshot, it had begun to dive, and you were well advised to run, duck, and cover.

The V-2 rocket was even worse. It was larger, had longer range and more destructive power, and, unlike the buzz bomb, gave little warning upon arrival. Between September 8, 1944, and March 27, 1945, 1,054 V-2 rockets fell in the London area. Radar operators could get the rockets on their scopes but could do little about warning civilians or shooting the V-2s down. The worst single explosion was just before Christmas 1944, when a V-2 hit a packed Woolworth's in Deptford, killing 168 and wounding 120; the remains of 11 other victims were never found.

The cumulative effect of the V-1 and V-2 rockets, besides destroying 35,000 homes and damaging another 1.25 million, was a mass exodus from London. At first, mothers began to accompany their children to the countryside (more than 100,000 schoolchildren left between June and September 1944), and then, when the

V-2 rockets began falling, nearly everybody tried to leave, heading for East Anglia or Scotland. Exacerbating the misery was that the winter of 1944–45 was the coldest in England in half a century. Still, the British people hung on to achieve victory in May 1945; they and their nation were exhausted psychologically and economically, but their courage and endurance became the stuff of legend.

> The civilians who remain grow more and more haunted and disagreeable; like toads, each sweating and palpitating under his particular stone.
>
> —Cyril Connolly,
> about low morale in London
> in the summer of 1944

The BBC

The British Broadcasting Corporation, the United Kingdom's premier radio station, played a vital role in conveying information to the home front and abroad and to boosting the morale of the British people as well as those under occupation who were able to hear its broadcasts. For British soldiers stationed in combat zones, BBC radio was their primary link to their beloved hearth, and it was the unifying factor in the lives of the English people on the home front. As one Londoner described it, "Promptly at nine o'clock the unnatural quiet ended as in homes throughout the land people switched on for the news—we had become a nation of compulsive listeners, and as the booming of Big Ben died away the rare pedestrian could hear the announcer's familiar voice coming from house after house as he made his way along the street."

Philip Ziegler writes: "The BBC was by far the most potent cultural unifying force in the country, providing in its news bulletins and entertainment a base of shared experience and common reference which linked East Ham and Kensington as effectively as Cornwall and Argyll." The best loved of all BBC radio programs, with a regular audience of 16 million listeners, was *It's That Man Again (ITMA)*, hosted by Tommy Handley, whose surreal misadventures among an odd assortment of characters (including Colonel Chinstrap, a Nazi spy called Funf, Mrs. Mopp, Mona Lott, and the Diver) were vital in buoying national spirits. Other, more elevated BBC programs, like *The Brains Trust* (featuring Professor C. E. M. Joad, Julian Huxley, and Commander A. B. Campbell) and J. B. Priestley's *Postscripts,* were almost as popular.

ITALY

By the time World War II broke out, Mussolini had been the Italian dictator for 17 years, and all political life revolved around this flamboyant, crude peasant from the Romagna hills in northeast Italy. His Fascist movement was, like Hitler's invocation of an earlier racially pure Reich, predicated on a return to the glory days of the Roman Empire. His "Fascisti" wore black shirts, "a symbol of hardihood" and "a virile people," and he was their Caesar, though he preferred the honorific Il Duce, which, like Der Führer, meant "the Leader." He built up a huge though ineffectual army and bankrupted and terrorized the country. Although one of his greatest achievements, it was claimed, was making the trains run on time, the truth is that, as the war dragged on, nothing in Italy worked. While Mussolini spouted lines from Virgil and Dante, his people grew hungry. And his pronouncements grew increasingly absurd. He even suggested that Italian men wear short pants, to save cloth for the war effort. Further, Fascist leaders solicited graft and ate and drank well, while the agricultural laborers were forced into increasingly austere rations. The Italian people were poverty-stricken and endured severe shortages of basic items, such as food, fuel, and medical supplies. A *Herald Tribune* correspondent said of the Italian home front in 1943: "The Italian people have lost faith in Mussolini, faith in their King, and sometimes it seems faith in themselves, except in their capacity to work hard, to breed, and to endure hard standards of living and to survive. . . . Apathy and pessimism grip the people. . . . They pray for some miracle that may bring them peace."

Italy capitulated quickly to Allied assaults, surrendering in September 1943, a month after Mussolini was forced to resign by the Fascist Grand Council. The writer Joseph Heller, who was stationed in Italy at the time, later created a memorable character who embodied the Italian people in his novel *Catch-22*. This 107-year-old man tells an American soldier, "You put so much stock in winning wars. The real trick lies in losing wars. . . . Italy has been losing wars for centuries and see how splendidly we've done nonetheless."

Il Duce was "rescued" from imprisonment by Nazi soldiers and briefly set up in a German-run puppet government in northern Italy. As the war came to an end, he and his mistress were captured by partisans and executed by firing squad in April 1945. From north to the south, the Italian peninsula was left in ruins as a result of Mussolini's folly and his embrace of the German dictator. The wartime hardships of the home front persisted in the immediate postwar years. Although the Italians embraced democracy, material hardships continued, with severe shortages of food and fuel. Because of the devastation of the war, factory and farm production were slow to return to pre-war levels.

JAPAN

Before the war, the Japanese people did not enjoy a high standard of living. The high cost of military expenditures kept a lid on the Japanese economy and diverted the nation's wealth into the army and navy. Beginning as early as 1937, Japan had been on an intense war footing, with more than 70 percent of its total annual budget going to the military. This left little money for domestic needs.

An overcrowded series of islands, Japan needed to expand in order to secure vital resources of fuel and food—or so its military leaders told the people—which was part of the motivation for incursions into China and Southeast Asia and surrounding Pacific islands. But as World War II progressed, Japan's islands were susceptible to blockade and Allied submarine and air attacks, and this reality affected life on the home front. Consequently, supplies of gas and oil (all of which had to be imported) were tightly rationed, as was electricity. Things were so bad that highly fermented apple cider was considered for use as airplane fuel. Every Japanese home had to have an air raid shelter and garden, but they were of only marginal security against the fire bombings by Allied warplanes. Because of the massive call-up of able-bodied men, women and children often staffed the factories.

The Japanese military had promised the people that they would never be bombed. But within four months of the attack on Pearl Harbor, American bombers led by Colonel Jimmy Doolittle were launched from an aircraft carrier and bombed Tokyo. Although the damage was light, the raid stunned the Japanese people. From this point on, they knew they were vulnerable to attacks from the air. And it got only worse. By 1945, the Americans were flying at will over the cities of Japan dropping incendiary bombs that ignited the flimsy wood and paper structures that made up so many sections of Japanese urban areas. Tens of thousands of civilians died in these raids, which occurred largely in the months immediately preceding the atomic bombings of Hiroshima and Nagasaki in August 1945.

The Japanese home front suffered severe hardships and ultimately destruction on the scale of that experienced by Germany and the Soviet Union. In the wake of their defeat, the Japanese people rebounded, adopting a democratic form of government and rising to great heights of economic prosperity.

The Soviet home front suffered the greatest hardship of all the warring nations, in terms of destruction of life and property. Following the invasion by the German military in June 1941, the Red Army, 10 million strong, fought with what Nazis called "stupid Asiatic courage," surviving the greatest offensive onslaught in world history and forcing the Germans into long, bloody assaults on, or sieges of, Leningrad, Odessa, Smolensk, Kiev, Sevastopol, Stalingrad, and Moscow. With German troops on the outskirts of Moscow in October 1941, the Soviet government informed Moscovites: "To retreat one more step is a crime none shall forgive." They held, and winter struck in early December, freezing the Nazis in their tracks.

Within two weeks the tide turned: The Red Army counterattacked, and the United States entered the war against Germany. But the Soviets had suffered losses of 2.5 million by September 1941, and Stalin was seemingly willing to trade the lopsided casualty figures, including civilians, because he had three times the population of Germany. In six months during 1943, the Russians claimed that they had killed 900,000 Nazis and wounded 1.7 million; the Germans claimed that they had killed 1.3 million Russians and wounded 1.6 million.

The Soviet People at War on the Home Front

The entire population of the Soviet Union was involved in the war effort, accepting blackouts, rationing, and scarcity as the price of fighting "a great patriotic war" (as Stalin put it). Office workers regularly helped with foraging for winter fuel. A Moscow ballet performance was even canceled when the premier ballerina was unable to dance because of injuries sustained while chopping wood. The people of Leningrad and Stalingrad put up some of the most tenacious defenses in modern military history. Leningrad was under siege from September 1941 until January 1944, and as many as a third of its three million inhabitants died of starvation or disease. Electricity was cut off, potable water was nonexistent, and the only lifeline was a wintry truck and train route over frozen Lake Ladoga. In addition, the Germans on the outskirts of the city shelled it constantly, adding to the horrific casualty figures. Still, the citizens kept the trolley lines running and built their own fortifications, with the women digging a massive antitank ditch around the city, driving trucks, and operating streetcars. The Nazi assault similarly devastated Stalingrad, although over a shorter period of time. Munitions workers in the city drove the tanks that they had built directly off the assembly line and into battle. When the Nazis retreated, not a single building was left intact in Stalingrad.

The Germans had intended to live off the land during their march across the Soviet Union, and they confiscated the crops of the Ukraine's "bread basket," further depleting domestic supplies. The Nazis thought of the Soviet peasants, as they had the Poles, as *Untermenschen* ("subhumans"); thus brutality was the norm. But rather than terrorizing or softening the civilian population, this strategy fomented stiff resistance and unified the many peoples who had previously chafed under Stalin's Soviet umbrella. Instead of giving up their crops and livestock to Germans, villagers chopped down orchards, smashed beehives, and killed animals before fleeing the advancing Nazi troops. The Cossack spirit resurfaced in isolated skirmishes, when German parachutists or small patrols were overcome by peasants wielding axes, sabers, and fire irons. Ordered to "kill wherever you can and any way you can," they did just that.

Although the Soviets ultimately were victorious, the price was nearly unfathomable: 20 million casualties sustained during what was dubbed the "Great Patriotic War," many of them civilians on the home front, caught in sieges, crossfires, bombings, or simply summary executions by the Nazis.

SOVIET WAR PRODUCTION

In the years before the Nazi invasion, the Soviet government moved some of its factories into the Ural Mountains to safeguard them in the event of a possible invasion. Other factories were moved eastward during the war years. Still, the Nazi incursion in 1940 was devastating, cutting Soviet industrial production in half. The numbers were eventually reversed, following a heroic defensive stand against the Germans that coincided with a massive mobilization of home-front factory workers. The statistics that follow are based on Soviet government figures.

Product	1940	1941	1942	1943	1944	1945
Iron*	14.9	9.1	5	5.5	7.2	8.8
Steel*	18.3	11.4	4.8	8.4	10.8	12.2
War planes	n/a	3,950	25,437	34,900	40,301	26,478
Tanks	2,794	4,742	24,668	24,000	29,000	22,590
Artillery	29,561	130,000	122,000	77,000	N.A.	N.A.

*millions of tons
Source: Michael Lyons, *World War II: A Short History* (Upper Saddle River, NJ: Prentice Hall, 2003).

UNITED STATES

Of all the major World War II combatants, the United States was the most insulated from the fighting. No Axis powers or surrogates had bases in the Western Hemisphere (beyond the outlying Aleutian Islands), and oceans protected the U.S. mainland on two sides. Only once did an enemy plane bomb the mainland, having been launched from a Japanese submarine with the mission of starting forest fires in the Pacific Northwest. The attempt failed. Except for 350 mostly ineffectual balloon bombs that drifted from Japan and some sinkings of merchant ships off the Atlantic and Pacific coasts by Axis submarines, stateside Americans were relatively unscathed (except, of course, for the island bombing of Pearl Harbor). The home front was, however, profoundly touched in many other ways, particularly as the leading producer of military materiel, fuel, food, supplies, and entertainment for the Allied forces.

Labor on the U.S. Home Front

While real war raged in Europe, labor wars rocked the country at home. The steel plants of Pennsylvania, the coal mines of West Virginia and Pennsylvania, and the car manufacturing plants in and around Detroit were periodically paralyzed in 1940 and 1941, threatening U.S. war readiness. The last company to negotiate with the unions was the Ford Motor Company, whose founder, Henry Ford, declared, "Labor union organizers are the worst thing that ever struck the earth."

With union contracts in hand, workers made a swift, remarkably efficient transition to a war manufacturing economy. Auto manufacturing plants, for example, with their assembly-line setup and their ability to swiftly produce large quantities of goods, were converted to war production. General Motors switched from the manufacture of cars to B-25 bombers, Chrysler built B-26 bombers and tanks, and Ford focused on the B-24. Once the assembly-line system was running at top efficiency, Ford was able to build one B-24 every 63 minutes. In all, Ford plants produced 8,685 of these four-motored bombers. After the United States entered the war, labor unions on the whole joined the effort for victory and deferred their wage and other work issues for another day.

U.S. War Production

More than any other combatant nation, the United States had a seemingly limitless capacity to produce war materiel. The following are examples of the vast output of U.S. industry during the war years:

84,027 tanks
631,873 Jeeps
372,431 artillery pieces
47,000,000 tons of ammunition
87,620 warships
54,000 torpedoes
37,701,000 bombs
12,573,000 rifles/carbines

Source: I.C.B. Dear and M.R.D. Foot, *Oxford Companion to World War II* (New York: Oxford University Press, 1995); Robert Goralski, *World War II Almanac: 1931–1945* (New York: G. P. Putnam's Sons, 1981).

Americans in Uniform

In late 1940, Congress passed the Selective Training and Service Act, the first peacetime military draft in U.S. history. All men aged 21 to 35 were required to register by October 16, 1940, at one of 6,175 draft boards. Of the 16,316,908 who registered, each received a draft number from 1 to 9,000. The first drawing, by lottery from capsules placed in a huge fishbowl, was done by the secretary of war in the presence of President Franklin D. Roosevelt and the news cameras. The first number drawn was 158; 6,175

men had it. After filling out a questionnaire and taking a physical examination, each man received one of a dozen different classifications. The most common, 1A, was "available for military service." Conversely, 4F was "physically, mentally or morally unfit for service." Anything from flat feet, a hernia, and venereal disease to lack of height (shorter than five feet) or lack of weight (less than 105 pounds) qualified for a 4F classification. Draft boards gave deferments to men in vital industries and essential occupations, such as farming. At first, eight million fathers received deferments, but by 1944 only 80,000 of the original number still had deferments.

Between 1940 and 1945, 50 million Americans registered for the draft. The army grew from 300,000 in the 1940 draft to 1.5 million by the time of the Pearl Harbor attack. In all, 11.2 million American soldiers and airmen, 4.1 million sailors, and 500,000 marines served during the war. Of these, 38.8 percent were volunteers, and 61.2 percent draftees. Overseas duty made up 73 percent of the assignments, and the average duration of service was 33 months, domestic and overseas combined. On average, enlisted men were paid $71.33 per month, while officers made $203.50. Two hundred thousand women were on active duty in the military by 1945 (see Chapter 6, "Officers and Soldiers").

Leading Figures on the U.S. Home Front

Many people from all walks of life played important roles on the U.S. home front during the war. They were instrumental in harnessing the tremendous industrial capacity of the United States and focusing it on winning the war. Some were better known than others, and many buoyed the morale of the American people. The following are a few of the major home front leaders:

ELMER DAVIS (1890–1958) A renowned CBS radio commentator, Davis was picked by President Franklin D. Roosevelt to be director of the Office of War Information in December 1942

LIBERTY SHIPS

In the early stages of the war, Allied demand for ships far exceeded production capabilities as the war effort accelerated and Axis bombs and torpedoes destroyed vessels. To correct the shortage of cargo vessels, a system was devised by William F. Gibbs, whose New York–based naval architectural firm, Gibbs and Cox, was the largest ship design firm in the United States. In addition to being the nation's main builder of naval vessels, Gibbs added extra watertight compartments in the hold and made the ships safer and more resistant to sinking. He also designed a mass-produced cargo vessel, which became known as the Liberty ship.

The British ordered 60 cargo ships from the United States in September 1940 that were dispatched quickly by being welded rather than riveted together. Gibbs modified the simple British design, and in January 1941 the United States began an emergency ship construction program using Gibbs's standardized plans. Shipbuilders Henry J. Kaiser and Andrew Higgins built about 2,700 of these "workhorses of World War II" at 14 different shipyards. They were put together in sections from prefabricated parts. When the hulls were done, the ships were launched, and the rest of the construction was completed in the harbor. Although they came in varying sizes, the typical Liberty ship weighed 7,126 tons and had a top speed of 11 knots. The first one off the assembly line was the *Patrick Henry,* launched on September 27, 1941 (dubbed "Liberty Fleet Day"). Higgins also perfected the manufacture of versatile and reliable "landing craft, vehicle, personnel" (LCVP) that could carry 36 troops and a three-ton vehicle. These became known as the "Higgins boats."

In addition to his design for Liberty ships, Gibbs helped increase naval vessel production levels by 700 percent. During one eight-month stretch in 1943, U.S. shipyards completed 1,200 seagoing vessels, with an average weight of 10,000 tons. From January 1, 1942, to mid-1945, the shipyards built 6,500 naval vessels, 64,500 landing craft, and 5,400 cargo ships totaling 28 million gross tons (21 million gross tons were lost to Axis action). Behind all this tonnage was a workforce of 700,000 that labored around the clock in U.S. shipyards.

The organizational genius behind the massive output of man- and womanpower for these ships was Kaiser, who rounded up the unemployed and even paid to move entire families to his eight shipyards in Oregon, Washington, and California. Through his efforts, the Allied cause turned a strategic corner. In 1937, the United States produced only 15 naval vessels a year; during the war, U.S. shipyards launched 17 to 30 tankers a month, with one Kaiser-run plant building and launching a single ship in just under 81 hours. After his Oregon plant launched a Liberty ship in 10 days in 1942, his Richmond, California, plant devised 250 time-saving assembly tactics and had a ship in the water, 90 percent complete, in just under five days. In all, 40 times more shipping tonnage was produced than before the war. All shipyards worked full-time, from the West Coast to Wisconsin (where submarines were built) to Maine. So many ships were produced, in fact, that deciding what to do with them became a problem after the war.

Patrick Henry, the first Liberty ship, floats just after launching. Conceived by shipping magnate Henry J. Kaiser, the Liberty ship could be produced rapidly and cheaply. These vessels became the backbone of U.S. cargo transportation overseas. By war's end, 1,490 of the vessels were built.

(see Chapter 10, "Intelligence, Espionage, and Propaganda"). Davis, like the poet Archibald MacLeish—who was librarian of Congress and director of the Office of Facts and Figures—insisted that the Nazi propaganda flooding U.S. shores be fought with counterpropaganda that relied on "aggressive truth." Davis was able to provide information about the war within the strict guidelines of wartime censorship. The American public may not have had all the details, especially about casualties and future operations, but throughout the war they had an accurate ongoing narrative of the progress of the conflict.

DONALD DOUGLAS (1892–1981) The president of Douglas Aviation, the largest aircraft manufacturer in the world, was responsible for one-sixth of all aircraft that the United States made during the war. He ran six major plants and more than 100 smaller ones (including repair stations), employing nearly 200,000 Americans. Douglas was an example of a leading industrialist who ably converted his peacetime industry to wartime production and, in the process, played a crucial (although behind the scenes) role in the Allied victory.

HENRY FORD (1863–1947) The greatest U.S. car manufacturer balked at U.S. entry into the war. As late as February 1941, Ford was a vocal opponent of the Lend-Lease Act. He changed his mind, a bit, after Pearl Harbor (the $4 billion in war contracts helped), converting Detroit's Willow Run plant to the largest manufacturing structure in the world (see Chapter 3, "The Economics of World War II"). Ford was probably the best-known industrialist in the country. His antiunion positions, combined with his earlier pacifism and embarrassing and vocal anti-Semitism, cloud his otherwise significant wartime contribution.

WILLIAM F. GIBBS (1886–1967) His New York–based company, Gibbs and Cox, was the country's largest ship design firm and the main builder of U.S. naval vessels. He developed the use of watertight compartments in his ships, which gave them greater insurance against penetration of the hull. One of his greatest contributions was in the designs that led eventually to the building of the Liberty ships.

ANDREW JACKSON HIGGINS (1886–1952) This New Orleans–based shipbuilder had a friendly rivalry with the industrialist Henry Kaiser to see who could obtain the most government contracts for war materiel. Higgins was best known for turning out the "landing craft, vehicle, personnel" (LCVP) used in every major war theater, as well as 1,200 twin-engine all-plywood troop- and tank-carrying planes (see sidebar, p. 384).

HENRY J. KAISER (1882–1967) The one leader of industry probably as well known as Henry Ford, Kaiser was a larger-than-life figure, a shipbuilding magnate who embodied the can-do spirit of the American home front by spearheading the creation of "Liberty ships" and bending the rules to reach nearly superhuman production goals. He operated eight separate shipyards in Washington, Oregon, and California and was known, by some, as "the Wizard of the West Coast" (see sidebar, p. 384). His irrepressible personality was a familiar sight in wartime newsreels and in the newspapers.

GLENN L. MARTIN (1886–1955) The Baltimore-based engineer designed the B-26, a medium-size bomber with a 1,000-mile range, two-ton bomb capacity, twirling gun-turrets, leakproof fuel tanks, and armored cockpits. The B-26 was a workhorse bomber that was surpassed only with the arrival of the B-29 Superfortress.

PAUL MCNUTT (1891–1955) As head of the War Manpower Commission, McNutt had authority, by presidential executive order, to keep war workers on the job. Among McNutt's powers were conferring with draft boards about quotas, exempting crucial workers from military service, and "freezing" workers in jobs considered essential to the war effort. In December 1942, McNutt ordered 600,000 workers in the Detroit area to stay on their jobs (or give "good and ample" reasons for leaving). He also froze the jobs of 110,000 merchant seamen and nearly two million aircraft workers on the West Coast. By keeping the work front stable, and by having the power to shift and allocate resources, McNutt played a major role in keeping U.S. war production at peak levels.

DONALD M. NELSON (1888–1959) As head of the War Production Board, Nelson had nearly full control of the U.S. economy. It was his job to make sure that industry fulfilled the wartime production goals set by the president and Congress. Nelson was sometimes considered the second most powerful man in the country during the war because of his authority to direct and cajole what was still a privately owned and operated industrial economy. The former Sears Roebuck executive had to walk a fine line between public need and private enterprise, but as a person who came out of private enterprise, he had credibility with the leaders of industry and was able to get them to adjust to the temporary input of government in their operations.

ELEANOR ROOSEVELT (1884–1962) The First Lady was a conspicuous figure on the wartime home front. Her "My Day" column, which was widely syndicated in newspapers across the country, offered advice, encouragement, and hope to a civilian population consumed with worry about soldiers overseas. Her gentle words segued seamlessly from the avuncular "fireside chats" provided by her husband. In addition, Mrs. Roosevelt was an indefatigable traveler— from schools, hospitals, and factories around the country to overseas trips to Great Britain and to visits to the troops throughout the South Pacific. Eleanor Roosevelt served as her husband's "eyes and ears," bringing back detailed reports containing her impressions and recommendations, all of which were highly valued by her husband.

Home-Front Rationing: Four Examples

Perhaps nothing symbolized life on the home front during World War II more than rationing. In the warring nations, production was only part of the government's worries at home; officials also closely scrutinized consumption, instituting rationing for everything from shoes to butter to gasoline, either to prevent or cope with war-related shortages. The following section describes four examples of rationing: in occupied France, Germany, Great Britain, and the United States.

OCCUPIED FRANCE

After France capitulated to the Nazis, the icons of French culinary culture fell under the control of the Germans, who initiated a harsh system of food rationing. The government restricted flour, required a 10 percent reduction in the sweetening in cakes, and forbade the sale of pastries on Mondays, Tuesdays, and Wednesdays. Restaurants could no longer serve butter, and they could not serve fish and cheese with a meat entree. Meat could not be served after 3 P.M., except on Sundays and holidays. Compounding the food shortage was the sudden return of five million demobilized troops and the confiscation of tons of provisions by the occupying German army. The French petitioned the Nazis to return some of the larder, but to no avail.

French rationing and the portions allotted were even more spartan than what the British had (3.5 ounces of butter, fat, or oil per person per week, compared with 8 ounces of the same items in Britain). Consequently, a sophisticated black market developed, and partaking of it was considered a patriotic act, because it meant trading with another French person. Nonetheless, the prices remained steep throughout the war.

GERMANY

Hitler's austere "peacetime" measures extended to ration cards *(Lebensmittelkarten)*, the first of which were printed in 1937, although they were not officially distributed until August 27, 1939. Like the ration coupons in the United States, these cards were color coded for different types of foodstuffs and valid for set lengths of time. Nursing mothers, industrial workers, night workers, and soldiers on leave received special supplemental cards. Jews, alien workers, and civilians in occupied territory received smaller rations. By war's end, all Germans were on short rations. In 1945, an adult's weekly allotment was 125 grams (4.38 ounces) of fat; 250 grams (8.75 ounces) of meat; and 1,700 grams (3.72 pounds) of bread.

The German system was inconsistent with full-scale rationing. Although food rationing was instituted early in the conflict—and became more and more severe as the war turned against the Germans—certain consumer goods (such as perfume) continued to be produced. The Nazis, some people speculated, were reluctant to admit that the war was going as badly as it was and hoped that a facade of normality could be maintained by the retention of consumer items associated with peacetime. By war's end, however, rationing and hardship were the order of the day.

GREAT BRITAIN

While Americans on the home front complained about shortages, the British people made do with much less after strict rationing began in 1939. By January 1940, the Ministry of Food had distributed 48 million ration cards to every man, woman, and child (along with a National Registration card). The consumer would present the ration cards to the grocer, and the availability of the item, price controls, and regulations determined the number of coupons that the grocer clipped from them. Meat, milk, milk powder, eggs, butter, cheese, and sugar were the staples rationed. Average allotments per person were two eggs, four ounces of bacon or ham, eight ounces of fats, two ounces of butter, and two to four ounces of cheese per week. Even with these restrictions, England's food stocks fell at one point to levels not seen since 1917, when the country was within six weeks of running empty.

A telltale sign of deprivation: the fish-and-chips birthright was, by 1941, fish and mashed potatoes (to save the lard from frying). One of the Ministry of Food's suggested recipes was for "oatmeal sausage," which used two ounces of meat per four ounces of oatmeal, some bread crumbs, and fat. Other makeshift items were "macon," bacon made from mutton, and "nutter," a mix of native and imported butter.

To save ration points, those who could afford it ate out often. The government imposed maximum price limits on restaurants in June 1942, to counter the criticism that only the rich could eat out often and thus ignore the spirit of food rationing. Restaurants that exceeded these price limits were fined, but most stayed in business.

Clothing and shoes were also tightly rationed and made to standard wartime specifications. Gasoline was almost completely unavailable for nonemergency vehicles. Many Britons grew some of their own vegetables and swapped the surplus among themselves for ration coupons or such luxuries as fruit, clothing, and soap. Much more so than in the United States, even those items that were not rationed were much harder to find and the deprivations were fairly evenly scattered among the social classes. Rationing in Britain continued for several years after the end of the war, a sign of the devastating effect the war had on the British economy.

UNITED STATES

Even if the American people were not fully aware that war was looming, the government was prepared. Officials were making plans for rationing as early as mid-1941, and with the bombing of Pearl Harbor, rationing began in earnest. The Office of Price Administration (OPA) set up a nationwide network of 5,500 rationing boards by January 5, 1942. The first items rationed were tires, followed by retreads, then the whole car. Police could not get new patrol cars unless their old models were pre-1937 and had more than 100,000 miles on the odometer. Typewriters and bicycles were soon controlled too, as were most household appliances—the government desperately needed metal and rubber for the war effort.

The first food item rationed was sugar, the sale of which was banned altogether during the week of April 24, 1942, and tightly rationed thereafter. War Ration Book No. 1, distributed by the OPA during the week of May 4, 1942, was nicknamed the "Sugar Book." One member of each household was required to report to a designated distribution site (mostly schools) for registration; 122,604,000 people (91 percent of the U.S. population) were registered as participants in the first two weeks! All the ration books came with detachable inch-square stamps, designated as various denominations and in colors. In addition, War Ration Book No. 2 came with the notice: "Persons who violate rationing regula-

An 11-year-old girl from Buffalo, New York, completes the day's shopping from a list left by her widowed mother, who is working as a crane operator. The grocer is seen reaching for the precious ration coupons, which were part of everyday life.

tions are subject to $10,000 fine or imprisonment, or both," a warning that did little to deter a black market from developing. In fact, the black market (affectionately called "Mr. Black") was responsible for nearly one-quarter of all retail business during the war. Thus, War Ration Book No. 4 contained this less ominous message: "Never Buy Rationed Goods Without Ration Stamps. Never Pay More Than the Legal Price." It also contained this notice, in smaller print: "When you have used your ration, salvage the Tin Cans and Waste Fats. They are needed to make munitions for our fighting men. Cooperate with your local Salvage Committee." These sorts of gentle reminders were adopted to counter the anger, frustration, and bitterness that rationing engendered on the American home front.

Other essential items affected by rationing were butter, lard, shortening, margarine, fats, milk, cheese, heating oil, gasoline, canned food, alcohol, cigarettes, tires, meat, shoes, coffee, and razor blades. Each person was given a certain number of points per month: 48 blue points and 64 red points were the average (or 192 points total for a family of four). Blue points covered canned goods, red points meat and butter. The number of points per item fluctuated according to its availability or the quality of meat cuts. Choice cuts like beef sirloin and sliced ham cost the most ration points per pound, while brains, tongue, ears, kidneys, knuckles, jowls, chitterlings, and bellies cost the least. The average meat ration was two pounds per week (28 ounces at the start of the war). Butter rations averaged about 12 pounds per year; coffee, less than a pound per month.

To supply some of their own fresh vegetables, many Americans started "victory gardens," a term coined by Secretary of Agriculture Claude R. Wickard (1893–1967). His department was lukewarm to the idea at first, fearing that the "amateurs" would engage in imprudent gardening, not to mention undercut the profits of the nation's farmers, who were already producing a surplus. As the war dragged on, victory gardens sprang up everywhere—10 million by the end of

1942, and more than 20 million by 1943, producing a third of the vegetables grown in the United States. Farmers produced 10 million tons of food in 1943; victory gardeners produced eight million tons. In addition to providing new items like Swiss chard and kohlrabi, victory gardens improved the nutritional content of the food on the home front. Portions were smaller, but people ate a healthier diet.

Gasoline rationing caused major headaches, not only because some cars got better mileage than others but because some drivers were more privileged than others. In fact, driving had five priority levels, designated A through E. An "A" sticker was for pleasure driving, which was allotted three to five gallons per week (when available) and banned altogether in 1943. "B" was for commuters (who squeezed the maximum number into each vehicle); and on down to "E," which was for emergency vehicles. A speed limit

of 35 mph was imposed, to save fuel and rubber. To reinforce the need to conserve gasoline, the Office of War Information distributed a number of posters with the message "Is Your Trip Necessary?" Another popular saying, which was also inscribed on posters, was "Use it up, wear it out, make it do, or do without."

Home Fronts Under Nazi Occupation

Home fronts that were under Nazi occupation faced unique challenges. They had to contend not only with production and consumption issues and the destruction and loss of life caused by their occupiers, but internal issues such as their country's morale, identity, and pride, if not its very existence, as they fought—or succumbed to—the Nazis. The struggles of collaborators versus the Resistance added another dimension to the hardships of home fronts under the Nazis.

AUSTRIA

After the Anschluss (annexation) of 1938, the Nazis made Austria part of "the Union of Greater Germany." The Nazis installed Baldur von Schirach as Nazi governor and *Gauleiter* (party district leader) of Vienna, and for all intents and purposes, Austria was officially part of Nazi Germany—not an occupied territory. Austria's seven million people were now German subjects. Hitler said, "When we crossed the former frontier into Austria there met me such a stream of love as I have never experienced. Not as tyrants have we come, but as liberators."

As a young man, Hitler had tried to make his name as an artist in Vienna but was a miserable failure. Although he professed to be ecstatic about the unification of all Germanic peoples, Hitler had residual contempt for his own Austrian roots.

Indeed, the initial staged welcome disguised some disillusionment and hid from the world what William Shirer has called "an orgy of

Conserving precious gasoline and tire rubber is the theme of this poster from the Office of War Information, which promotes sharing the ride.

sadism." The Nazis rounded up Jews and humiliated them publicly by forcing them to scrub the streets of Vienna and the latrines of Nazi soldiers. The Viennese stood by and laughed. The Germans also looted homes (including the palace of Baron Louis de Rothschild) of silver and art. The Nazis sent thousands of Austrians to concentration camps in Germany and Poland, and the country became just a series of administrative districts that the Nazi regime exploited for resources. Although Austria had not been invaded by hostile German armies, and was legally part of Germany, many of its citizens were treated in the same way as those of the other occupied countries. By and large, however, the majority of the Austrian population supported the Nazis.

CZECHOSLOVAKIA

When Nazi troops entered Prague in March 1939, Hitler proclaimed, "Czechoslovakia has ceased to exist." It became the protectorates of Bohemia, Moravia, and Slovakia, designations that went back a thousand years in German history. The Nazis took symbolic delight in basing their regime in Hradschin Castle in Prague, the ancient seat of Bohemian kings. While the nine million Czechs were treated somewhat less severely than the Poles—primarily, the Czechs were put to work making munitions—it was still, as William L. Shirer put it, "a long night of German savagery." That long night ended five years later, when the Czechs were liberated in March 1944, by Soviet troops. Another, different sort of darkness was on its way as the country soon fell under the rule of the Communist Party dictatorship.

The symbol of German occupation of Czechoslovakia was the extermination of the peaceful farm village of Lidice in retribution for the assassination of Reinhard Heydrich, deputy chief of the Gestapo in May 1942. Following Heydrich's death, the Germans rounded up and shot 1,331 Czechs. Then, on June 9, 1942, Nazi security forces descended on Lidice, surrounded it, and locked the entire male population in a barn, to be shot in groups of 10 over the next 24 hours. All the women and children were separated and sent to different concentration camps. Only one person survived the Lidice massacre. This act of brutality was indicative of the harshness of Nazi rule.

FRANCE

Despite making extensive preparations for the inevitable hostilities—women, children, and old men had gone out by the thousands to help bring in the 1939 harvest, then into the factories to make explosives, detonators, fuses, and wiring for radios—France fell easily in June 1940. Its national morale fell just as precipitously. The armistice, signed by the French government at Compiègne, allowed the Germans to occupy three-fifths of the country. The unoccupied "free" zone was in the south, its capital a former health spa, Vichy. As a further humiliation, Hitler obtained willing "collaboration" from the former French national hero, 84-year-old Marshal Henri Pétain, the World War I hero who had been the embodiment of French patriotism. Pétain, who headed the puppet Vichy government, dutifully signed into law edicts against French Jews' holding public jobs, in the army, navy, or air force, as teachers, journalists, or filmmakers, a policy that paved the way for later deportations of French Jews to concentration camps in Eastern Europe.

The Germans divided occupied France into four zones: *Greater Paris*, *Northwest*, *Southwest*, and *Northeast*. German ordinances penetrated every facet of French life, from confiscation of guns, ammunition, and broadcasting sets to the banning of unauthorized newspapers and radio programs, and imposed a hated 9 P.M. curfew. German currency became legal tender, alongside the franc. Street signs in German were put up, and German soldiers were everywhere in Paris. In 1942, the Nazis occupied Vichy, France, as well and ended the fiction of an independent French government. They were also aided by

Pierre Laval, the most hated French leader during this ordeal. Laval openly and willingly collaborated with the Germans. Backed by the Gestapo, he organized a labor recruiting service that sent hundreds of thousands of Frenchmen to Germany to work in Nazi munitions plants; the work was mandatory, essentially slave labor, which was a bitter blow to French pride.

The indomitable French spirit and pride, however, resurfaced in other ways, especially in the guerrilla tactics of the French Resistance. Many ad hoc groups formed in the occupied north as well as the slightly more open Vichy south, but the best known were the Forces Françaises de l'Interieur (French Forces of the Interior, FFI), which engaged in carefully planned acts of sabotage and uprising. The leading figure of the Resistance was Jean "Max" Moulin, who succeeded in unifying the various factions in the struggle against Nazi occupation. Despite intense Gestapo retaliation and mass arrests, executions, and exile to concentration camps, the cumulative effect of the French Resistance was profound, hastening the liberation of France and immeasurably helping the Allied cause. Typical of the bravery of these factions was the Immigrant Workers, an offshoot of the banned Communist Party that became a deadly threat to Nazis in France. After nearly three years of targeting Nazi officers and convoys, 22 members of the Immigrant Workers (mostly Armenian and Jewish exiles) were arrested and executed.

General Charles de Gaulle's Free France, headquartered in exile in London, consisted of an army of 40,000, an air force of 1,000, and a navy of 17 battleships. After the armistice with the Nazis, de Gaulle told the French people, via radio from London, "There is no longer on the soil of France an independent government capable of upholding the interests of France and the French overseas." *Time* magazine characterized the spirit of the French people in 1940 as "cold, determined, grim, brave, calm and proud."

The backlash against collaborators after Paris was liberated in August 1944 was intense and tinged with bitterness and guilt. Women who had collaborated with the Nazi occupiers, mostly as prostitutes, had their heads shaved and were marched through the streets of cities throughout France, and 700,000 people were placed on a blacklist. Two of the most famous on the list were Marshal Pétain and Pierre Laval, both of whom were put on trial. Pétain was sentenced to "national dishonor" after his death sentence was commuted. Laval made a mockery of his trial, disrupting it with outbursts and heated exchanges with vengeful, perhaps guilt-ridden, observers. He was eventually shot by firing squad after trying to poison himself.

Even as late as the 1970s, the French remained highly sensitive about their history of collaboration. French television banned Marcel Ophuls's 1971 documentary about the widespread French collaboration, *The Sorrow and the Pity,* as well as Mosco Boucault's *Terrorists in Retirement,* a 1984 documentary about the Immigrant Workers resistance group.

LOW COUNTRIES

The Netherlands and Belgium had declared their neutrality before the war, and this had given them false hope that the Nazi war machine would leave them relatively unscarred. The Belgian and Dutch armies put up some resistance to the Nazi invasion of May 1940, but threats of destruction to Brussels, Amsterdam, The Hague, and Utrecht (to match the rubble made of Rotterdam) unless resistance abated, were enough to effect an unconditional surrender only days after they were invaded. The Dutch and Belgian royal families went into exile, to return another day.

In Denmark, the Netherlands, and Belgium the occupying Germans adhered to a policy of killing 100 hostages for every Nazi killed by partisans. Regardless of these savage reprisals, an underground resistance developed quickly and remained strong. The Dutch were the least accommodating, enduring the Nazi presence with stubborn placidity, trying to lead normal lives despite the circumstances. While the Dutch had little more than a ceremonial military presence (and the royal retinue), they did have Les Gueux (the Beggars), a secret society that had, since the 16th century, stealthily battled its country's various oppressors. Les Gueux was responsible for poisoning Nazi soldiers in restaurants, drowning isolated Nazis in the canals, and other acts of patriotic terrorism. Dutch resistance was stubborn and courageous, and in the end, the Netherlands suffered enormously under the occupation, including thousands who starved during the severe winter of 1944–45 as the Allied invasion of Germany stalled on the Dutch border.

Because of its location between Germany and Belgium, Luxembourg (population 293,000) was quickly occupied by the Nazis on May 10, 1940. Its ruling family escaped to England and formed a government-in-exile. In an October 1941 plebiscite, the Luxembourg people voted overwhelmingly (97 percent) against the German occupation; nevertheless, the Nazis drafted 13,000 Luxembourgers into military service; 2,848 died in German uniform.

NORWAY

After a fierce, month-long struggle, the Nazis occupied Norway in May 1940, and the country's leaders escaped to London, where they set up a government-in-exile. Ninety percent of Norway's fleet relocated to the Shetland Islands rather than return to home port. The solidarity of the Norwegian people (population three million) against the Nazi occupation was epitomized by the nation's schoolteachers, who walked out en masse rather than teach a "Nazified" history of the world. The Nazis mainly exploited Norway for its natural resources and hydroelectric power—with a resultant drop in living standards and some rationing—but conditions on the home front never reached the deprivations experienced in other Nazi-occupied

countries. Although Norwegians conducted little in the way of sustained guerrilla warfare against the Nazis, Norwegian Resistance fighters were responsible for one of the most devastating acts of sabotage of the war—the bombing destruction of Norsk Hydro, a plant that was manufacturing heavy water for the Nazi atomic weapons program.

POLAND

The home front in occupied Poland was a veritable Nazi reign of terror. Polish Jews were herded off to concentration and extermination camps, and the treatment of Poles in general was what might be expected from an occupier who thought of them, at best, as *Untermenschen*. Because Poland was one of the first nations that the Nazis occupied (in 1939), they tested the limits of barbarity on Polish soil. Hallmarks of the Polish home front were massacres; forced labor; murders of Jews, intellectuals, clergy and the nobility; mass deportations of Poles, to be replaced by Germans; freezing; hunger; and misery.

The Nazi governor of Poland, Hans Frank (later hanged as a war criminal at Nuremberg),

His arms loaded with bread made from flour delivered by the American Red Cross, a young Polish refugee smiles in anticipation of a full stomach.

was in charge of the Extraordinary Pacification Action (or AB Action), which meant securing food and supplies from the Poles to give to the Germans, opening forced labor camps, and eliminating the intelligentsia. The Gestapo was in charge of liquidating the Jews. After one year of Nazi occupation, 1.2 million Poles and 300,000 Jews had been expelled from their homes and replaced by 497,000 Germans. Most of this exodus took place under unusually severe winter conditions, and many died en route or later from the effects of the exodus. The newly mobilized Poles were put to work building the camps at Cracow, Treblinka, and Auschwitz.

Jewish ghettos were set up in major cities, and thousands of Jews were crammed into these small areas, where they died of disease. The survivors were ultimately shipped to the death camps in Poland for extermination. The German occupation of Poland eliminated the centuries-old Jewish life from the country forever. Non-Jewish Poles also died by the hundreds of thousands. In terms of harshness, perhaps only the Soviet Union suffered comparable or greater devastation from the German occupation.

Women and Minorities on the U.S. Home Front

During the war, the number of women in the American labor force increased dramatically as men were drafted and sent off to combat. At first, single women answered the call, but the wartime labor pool was too small so the government undertook a massive recruitment campaign. "These jobs will have to be glorified as a patriotic war service if American women are to be persuaded to take them and stick to them," wrote the Office of War Information. Actually, U.S. women did not need that much convincing. Many were eager to get out of the house or, in the case of single women, away from home, and many found the work experience—particularly in the service of their country—liberating.

Despite the most steadfast intentions, however, there were costs. By 1945 the divorce rate was double that of 1940. Not only were the long separations and the resultant infidelities by both genders a factor, but circumstances had forced many married women to become more independent during the war years. In 1945, one of every four wives in the United States was employed, either in a defense plant or a government office. When their war-weary husbands returned, the women found it hard to return to the prescribed subservience of their prewar roles.

The wartime experience of other disenfranchised groups was also mixed. Although the war served as a catalyst in helping blacks gain more rights, it was also a time of race riots, and many Japanese Americans found themselves uprooted, deprived of property, deported to internment camps, and even physically harmed.

DAY TO DAY FOR WOMEN IN WARTIME

American women achieved an unprecedented degree of independence during World War II. Many joined the military, and many others found themselves working outside the home for the first time in their lives. For those who entered the labor force and accepted employment in nontraditional jobs, the civilian day often began earlier and ended later. They were working a 48-hour week and still had a household to maintain (see Chapter 3, "The Economics of World War II").

Everything from breakfast to bedtime seemed to have changed. Rationing and shortages affected the preparation of every meal, and the useful life of a piece of clothing was extended far beyond what it once had been. Working women adapted to the use of mass transportation, crowding into buses or streetcars rather than driving their own automobiles. Household items as mundane as metal bobby pins were prized because they were scarce. Working mothers had to provide for the well-being of their school-age children. Because day care was virtually nonexistent, grandparents or neighbors often helped. The phenomenon of the latchkey child began to grow.

Because of the demands of wartime, juggling work schedules and maintaining the home, two or three generations of family members often lived under one roof, pooling their resources and sharing responsibilities. They planted victory gardens to supplement rationed staples, recycled whatever they could, and banked much of their income because there was little to buy. These nest eggs would play a part in the U.S. postwar economic boom as pent-up demand for consumer goods was satisfied.

Although most husbands and boyfriends did return from overseas—some having been absent for more than three years—the definition of "normal" home life had been forever changed, and aspects of the changed lives of American women in World War II endure today.

THE INTERNMENT OF JAPANESE AMERICANS

At the outbreak of war, there were 900,000 Americans of Japanese, German, or Italian origin. Of these, 127,000 were Japanese Americans, two-thirds of whom were born in the United States, either as Nisei (children of immigrants) or Sansei (grandchildren of immigrants). But because of the Japanese attack on Pearl Harbor, Japanese Americans were singled out for suspicion and, in many cases, physical violence. This discrimination received the imprimatur of the federal government with President Franklin D. Roosevelt's Executive Order 9066, signed February 19, 1942, which sent 114,490 Japanese Americans to 10 "relocation centers" in six western states and Arkansas. Many had just 48 hours to set their personal affairs in order and make arrangements concerning their property (including shops, homes, and cars).

Although the same thing had happened to German Americans during World War I and to some extent during World War II (when 5,000 German Americans and Italian Americans were relocated to Ellis Island for less than a year), the experience of the Nisei, Sansei, and the Isei (Japanese Americans born elsewhere) was quite different. These law-abiding, well-educated, and bicultural Americans were interned in camps for more than three years, and the U.S. government compensated them for only a fraction of their property that was stolen or vandalized. Some Japanese Americans were put to work on "government projects" that paid them $50 to $94 a month, with $15 deducted for living expenses. The only way that most of these citizens could leave their camp was to enlist in the U.S. military, which 8,000 Japanese Americans did. Many died in combat, defending freedom for a nation that had locked up their families.

Of the 10 relocation centers, Manzanar was the most thoroughly photographed, because the celebrated American photographer Ansel Adams was a friend of the camp director, Ralph Merritt, who in 1943 invited Adams to photograph Manzanar. Within six weeks in 1942, this inhospitable desert located in the Owen Valley 200 miles northeast of Los Angeles was turned into a city inhabited by 10,271 Japanese Americans from California, Oregon, Washington, and Hawaii. Surrounded by barbed wire and gun towers, they were required to grow their own food. Summer temperatures often topped 110 degrees and fell below freezing during the winter. Nonetheless, the internees adapted. As Adams wrote in his subsequent book *Born Free and Equal* (1944): "Out of the jostling, dusty confusion of the first bleak days in raw barracks they have modulated to a democratic internal society and a praiseworthy personal adjustment to conditions beyond their control." When copies of his book were burned in protest, Adams gave his entire Manzanar project files (negatives, prints, field notes) to the Library of Congress as a public record.

Mine Okubo, a young Nisei artist, documented in drawings her two-and-a-half-year internment at Topaz Center in Utah. These drawings, and her commentary on them, appeared in her book *Citizen 13660,* published in 1946. Decades later, many Japanese Americans were compensated financially for their internment ordeal.

Japanese Americans board a bus bound for the Manzanar Relocation Center in California. Interned by the Roosevelt Administration at the beginning of the war for security reasons, American citizens of Japanese descent were forced to leave their homes and businesses for the duration.

JAPANESE RELOCATION CENTERS

The U.S. government operated 10 so-called relocation centers. Information on the relocation centers is given in the following table:

Location	Opened	Closed	Residents
Gila River, Arizona	8/42	11/45	13,400
Granada, Colorado	9/42	10/45	7,600
Heart Mountain, Wyoming	9/42	11/45	11,100
Jerome, Arkansas	11/42	6/44	8,600
Manzanar, California	6/41	11/45	10,200

Location	Opened	Closed	Residents
Minidoka, California	9/42	10/45	9,990
Poston, Arizona	6/42	11/45	18,000
Rohwer, Arkansas	10/42	11/45	8,500
Topaz, Utah	10/42	10/45	8,300
Tule Lake, California	6/42	3/46	18,800

Source: War Relocation Authority figures, 1942–45.

HILDA RUBLI, HIGGINS INDUSTRIES EMPLOYEE

Working for Higgins

Well, my husband was in the navy, and he was on leave, and he went back to California to Port Hueneme, and I decided I couldn't go back right away. I decided that I wanted to go to work for Higgins because my father worked for Higgins on City Park Avenue [in New Orleans] and he liked his job so much, and I said, well, that would be a good place for me to go to work.

So I went over to Elk's Place and got my card to refer me to Higgins' office, where they were hiring people. . . . They gave me a typing test, which I passed. I wanted to type and file. They brought me out there the next morning, and I was hired.

Mister Schwartz was my boss, and Missus Lucille Swift was his secretary. I did typing. My desk was right by the doors. I could look right out into the Industrial Canal, and I could see the boats and the tugs and everything going up and down. The horn would blow, and the bridge would go up. Sometimes Higgins boats would land there. They would come right up. People would pass my desk.

Andrew Higgins Junior had his office right near mine, and Mister Higgins had his office—big office—in the back. There was a man who was a porter—his name was Joe—and he took care of Mister Higgins with his lunch and different things. We had one great big office up there and desks all over. Some people had small offices. I would type letters. I would make stencils. It was just one happy family up there.

—Eisenhower Center for American Studies Archives

ROSIE THE RIVETER

Rosie the Riveter was the invention of Lockheed Aircraft, which used the image of a determined woman in coveralls in a motivational poster. In its various renderings, it became an iconic image, a symbol of the contribution of women on the home front to the victory over the enemies of freedom.

As a tribute to the unprecedented phenomenon of women in the U.S. workplace, especially those doing what was previously perceived to be "men's work," Norman Rockwell created his version of Rosie the Riveter for the cover of the May 29, 1943, issue of the *Saturday Evening Post*. He took Rosie's pose from Michelangelo's Sistine Chapel depiction of Isaiah. By placing the American flag behind her and a copy of *Mein Kampf* under her foot, he created a nice bit of propaganda in the bargain.

Later that same year, Rockwell expanded his theme in the September 4, 1943 (Labor Day), issue of the *Saturday Evening Post*, a tribute to "Women War Workers." His central image was of a woman in red, white, and blue work uniform who carried, in her hands, draped over her shoulders, or attached to her work belt, items intended to depict 31 different occupations that women were undertaking in support of the war effort. Among the professions that Rockwell included were house manager, household worker, superintendent, switchboard operator, milk deliverer, electrician, plumber, garage mechanic, seamstress, typewriter repairer, editor/reporter, baggage clerk, bus driver, railroad/bus conductor, taxi driver, railroad maintenance worker, section hand, bookkeeper, farmer, teacher, and nurse.

A popular song, "Rosie the Riveter," was recorded in 1942, and the name Rosie the Riveter entered American legend, alongside Paul Bunyan and Babe the Blue Ox.

WOMEN IN THE WORKFORCE

Between 1940 and 1945 the number of working women increased by 50 percent and the percentage of women in the U.S. workforce increased from 27.6 percent to nearly 37 percent. In the aviation industry, the increase was even more dramatic, from 1 percent to 65 percent by 1943. *Time* reported that in 1943: "Many a factory manager has found that when women are good they are better than men. They are more painstaking as inspectors, are nimbler with their fingers, don't fret or get bored with repetitious work, are generally quicker, and particularly good at assembling small parts."

Nonetheless, the disparity in pay for women and men was even greater during the war years as shown in this table:

Item	1940	1941	1942	1943	1944	1945
Percentage of workforce made up of women	27.9	28.5	31.0	35.8	36.5	35.9
Women's wages as a percentage of men's	55.6	53.5	50.8	50.4	51.8	52.7

Source: Ian Dear and M.R.D. Foot, *Oxford Companion to World War II* (Oxford: Oxford University Press, 2001).

RACE RELATIONS ON THE U.S. HOME FRONT

Relations between black and white Americans were strained prior to World War II. In World War I, 380,000 black soldiers (10 percent of the U.S. forces) served with distinction in Europe. Little progress had been made to provide greater socio-economic opportunities for black Americans during the interwar years and they were unenthusiastic about enlisting in the service or answering draft board notices. Harry Carpenter, a black draftee from Philadelphia who was tried for treason, spoke for many in 1942 when he said, "This is a white man's war, and it's no damn good."

Indeed, black soldiers made up only 8 percent of the troops, or nearly 300,000, and they balked at the unequal treatment accorded them even when they did enlist. The navy, for example, forbade black sailors to serve as anything but messmen. The marines did not take black recruits at all until June 1, 1942, and the army relegated 40 percent of its black soldiers to either the Engineers or the Quartermaster Corps, otherwise known as pick-and-shovel brigades. Racial incidents regularly rocked military training camps, sometimes leading to violence. (See the sidebar on Port Chicago in Chapter 6, "Officers and Soldiers," p.186)

On the home front, the hiring rate for black workers increased tenfold, but defense industries still discriminated in hiring, and skilled black workers earned less than their white counterparts. A. Philip Randolph, head of the Brotherhood of Sleeping Car Porters, began organizing a massive black demonstration, set for July 1941, in Washington, D.C. He called for a "thundering march" to "shake up white America." Fearing violence and divisiveness when the country was on the brink of war, President Franklin D. Roosevelt signed Executive Order No. 8802, which forbade discrimination in job hiring for all manufacturers with federal defense contracts, and the march was canceled. Citing similar patterns of discrimination, the Congress of Racial Equality (CORE) was formed in 1942, emphasizing nonviolent resistance to racial injustice. Already well established in the black community were the Urban League and the National Association for the Advancement of Colored People (NAACP).

Notwithstanding these attempts to ameliorate racial tension, the country was rocked by race riots throughout the war—riots precipitated by both whites and blacks. In January 1942 a group of black soldiers on leave in Alexandria, Virginia, were involved in a brawl with police and other (white) troops. White workers rioted in a Mobile, Alabama, shipyard in 1944, when blacks were given job promotions, and whites rioted again at a Baltimore defense plant that integrated its locker rooms.

But the worst race riot during the war occurred in June 1943 in Detroit, a center of the defense industry. The violence was precipitated by the circulation of various rumors concerning rape, murder, and reprisal by both whites and blacks. But unrest had been brewing since 1940, when a mass migration of southern black families and workers had begun (thousands of blacks had moved to Detroit by 1943), causing a housing crisis and exacerbating tensions among other ethnic groups in the city. By the summer of 1943, the "race war" that ensued left 34 people dead (25 of whom were black) and 700 injured and ultimately required the intercession of 6,000 federal troops. Other riots followed in that summer—in Springfield, Massachusetts; El Paso and Port Arthur, Texas; Hubbard, Ohio; and in New York's Harlem, where an August 1943 riot left six dead and 500 injured.

Mexican Americans were also involved in racial unrest during the war. The most visible of this minority were the "Pachucos," gangs of young men who sported zoot suits, broad-rimmed felt hats, flared trousers, and "Argentine ducktail" haircuts and who were regularly involved in confrontations with servicemen. The most widely reported incident, the so-called zoot suit riots, occurred in Los Angeles in une 1943, when, over four days, sailors from the Chavez Ravine Naval Base went into the Mexican American neighborhoods and assaulted, disrobed, and cut the hair of any Pachuco in a zoot suit.

The racial unrest that occurred on the home front during the war years was a sign of the turmoil that would lead to advances in civil rights during the 1950s and 1960s. The wartime experience—with blacks serving their nation in a segregated military, and home front workers employed in war industries across the nation— was one of the factors that helped awaken the nation to the issues of discrimination.

Josie Lucille Owens works as a welder on the Liberty ship SS *George Washington Carver.* More than 1,000 black women worked in various trades at the Kaiser Shipyards in Richmond, California.

CHAPTER 12

Man's Inhumanity

W orld War II produced wanton cruelty on a grand scale never equaled in modern times, before or since. In addition to the millions of battlefield casualties, civilians by the millions died in ways never before seen in the history of warfare. Horrific air raids blasted cities across Europe and Japan. Civilians died in the crossfire of battle; and, unique to the annals of war, the Nazis sought to systematically exterminate the Jews of Europe using a variety of technologies, including gas chambers constructed solely for the purpose of killing innocent men, women, and children.

Sometimes the inhumanity was manifested in crimes of omission. Hitler wanted a Europe without Jews, yet his regime made it all but impossible for Jews to flee. Few countries in the West were willing to accept Jews who were able to flee the Nazi clutches. The refusal of the U.S. government to help large numbers of Jews—by giving them refuge in America or by facilitating their placement somewhere in the world—is a dark stain on America's otherwise heroic efforts to rid the world of Nazism and militarism. Once the war had begun, the Jews of Europe were doomed. Nearly six million died in the Holocaust, wiping out cultures that had existed in Western and Eastern Europe for centuries. Homosexuals, Gypsies, Jehovah's Witnesses, and the disabled were among the other groups who had no place in the new Nazi order, and they, too, were swept into the gas chambers by the thousands.

The bodies of hundreds of Nazi victims are lined up awaiting burial in mass graves at Nordhausen concentration camp, April 12, 1945.

But the cruelties were not limited to Europe. The Japanese military participated in some of the most inhumane acts ever committed during warfare. Even before the conflict with the United States broke out in 1941, the Japanese military, on its march through China, killed more than 250,000 civilians in the city of Nanking during an unbelievable orgy of murder and rape. After the outbreak of hostilities, the Japanese marched thousands of American and Filipino prisoners of war to prison camps. Many of the 600 Americans and 5,000 Filipinos who died during the Bataan Death March in 1942 were shot, beheaded, and bayoneted by the Japanese as the prisoners fell by the wayside from exhaustion and malnutrition. Over the course of the next four years, military prisoners as well as civilians caught in the Japanese net were brutalized in prison camps. Thousands died of starvation, disease, and beatings.

> You are the remnants of a decadent white race and fragments of a rabble army. This railway will go through even if your bodies are to be used as sleepers.
> —Greeting to prisoners sent to work
> on the Burma-Siam railway, 1942

The Allies were also guilty of carrying out unnecessary brutalities. In the Katyn Forest in 1940, the Soviet secret police murdered 4,000 Polish officers and shoved them into a mass grave. German POWs in Soviet camps were brutalized and murdered by the thousands. The Americans and British were severely criticized for the bombing of the German city of Dresden in February 1945. The war was almost over and Dresden had no military value, but the bombers came and leveled the beautiful Baroque city, leaving some 40,000 civilians dead.

In sum, World War II witnessed the worst examples of man's inhumanity to man, as millions, combatants as well as hapless civilians, were destroyed by the relentless forces of war and murder.

The Holocaust

The genesis of the Nazi campaign against the Jews was the dark writings and speeches of Adolf Hitler, who from his earliest days inveighed against them. On the assumption that he could nurture political power by identifying and persecuting a common enemy, Hitler named the Jews the archcriminals, the source of every misery in defeated, hungry, depression-ridden Germany. The 1935 Nuremberg Laws restricted Jews in virtually all areas of life in Germany, and in the 1930s violence against Jews steadily grew. Extermination of them and other "useless mouths," such as Gypsies and the mentally retarded, would purify the homeland. The Slavs to the east would perish or be reduced to slavery, providing the German master race with *Lebensraum,* room to expand, a new thousand-year empire in the rich black earth of Russia.

Of the more than half-million German Jews, about half had emigrated by 1938. Of these, about 250,000 traveled to the United States, Britain, or elsewhere in the British Empire or the Americas. Others, like the 25,000 or so who moved to Poland, chose lands that would fall to the Nazis after 1939. For them, like young diarist Anne Frank, whose family fled to the Netherlands, the agony was only delayed.

About 250,000 foreign Jews fell into German hands after the 1938 annexation of Austria (the Anschluss) and the annexation of Bohemia and Moravia in March 1939. When Poland was invaded that same year, 1.5 million more Jews became captives. The Germans systematically tore Jews from their homes and confined them on miserable rations in overcrowded Polish ghettos, half a million in Warsaw alone. All over Europe, Jews were forced to wear a yellow Star of David on their clothing and were deprived of property and jobs, harassed, and humiliated. No Jewish child could go to school or to a movie, play on a playground, or run on the green grass of a park.

When Operation Barbarossa—the German invasion of the Soviet Union—began in June 1941, the combat formations were quickly followed by the Einsatzgruppen, the mobile death squads. These killers, fresh from exterminating Poles, now systematically butchered Soviet Jews, as many as 600,000 by late 1941. At Kiev, in the Ukraine, they murdered about 33,000 in just three days, most machine-gunned into the infamous ravine of Babi Yar outside the city.

The weapons of choice were bullets and carbon monoxide gas. But these methods were too slow and inefficient to achieve the "final solution," the *Endlösung*: mass extermination by means of gas chambers in camps far from the public gaze. The Nazis referred to movement of the doomed to the east as "resettlement," the destination "somewhere in the east."

By late 1941, the Germans were experimenting on captive Jews and Soviet POWs, seeking a lethal gas that would give the victims little or no warning. The favorite was a rat poison called Zyklon B, a cyanide compound tried on mental patients and handicapped children as early as 1939.

> We are fighting for three lines in history. For this our youth has fought and not gone like sheep to the slaughter. For this it is worthwhile even to die.
> —Dolek Liebeskind,
> fighting organization leader
> in the ghetto of Krakow, June 1942

The Nazis first established four major death camps in Poland: Chelmno, Treblinka, Belzec, and Sobibor. At Treblinka alone, it is estimated that some 900,000 people died. Some estimates place the count of murdered Jewish children as high as 1.2 million. Most victims came from the East, but the dead included deportees from Germany and the Netherlands. More Jews died in the gas vans of Riga, in Latvia, and at Maly Trostenets, near Minsk. Only a few prisoners at the Eastern camps were kept alive for a little while to work as laborers who sorted the victims' clothing, harvested women's hair, and dragged bodies to the ovens.

> So, there are still some there? I thought we had knocked off all of them. Somebody slipped up again.
> —Hermann Göring,
> on hearing that some Hungarian Jews
> had escaped liquidation, 1944

In 1942 another camp opened in Poland at Auschwitz-Birkenau. Here more than two million Jews died: gassed, worked to death as slave labor, or dead of untreated illness or starvation. Nazi officials sorted out those strong enough to work. The rest—including most women and children—were herded to the buildings marked "showers," sometimes to the music of a prison band. They would find no water, only a cloud of

The exhumed bodies of Poles who had been summarily executed by the Germans bear witness to the horrors of occupation.

lethal gas. The total number of Jews killed by the Nazis in Europe is estimated to be between 5.8 and 6.0 million. It was a staggering, unbelievable event, all the more incomprehensible for having emerged from one of the most "civilized" nations in Europe, a nation that had given the world great literature, art, and music. While rumors of the death camps persisted during the war, the Allies could actually do very little short of physically occupying German territory and liberating the camps. When Allied troops discovered such German atrocities on a grand scale in 1945, civilians who lived in villages near the camps were forced to view the scenes of unspeakable horror which they claimed to know nothing about. Evidence gathered at the death camps was used in the prosecution of Nazi war criminals at Nuremberg.

TIME LINE OF THE HOLOCAUST

Hitler's anti-Jewish campaign began with loud talk and jeers, jostling on the street, and his brown-shirted storm troopers, the SA (Sturmabteilung), holding signs warning shoppers not to patronize Jewish shops. Then came window breaking, beatings, firings of Jewish employees, and obscene graffiti on buildings inhabited by Jewish businesses. When Hitler came to power in 1933, systematic persecution began, and in 1935 the Nazi government promulgated the repressive Nuremberg Laws, which revoked Jews' citizenship and stripped them of most of their civil rights. Many smaller towns were declared *Judenfrei,* "Jew-free," forcing their longtime Jewish citizens to abandon their businesses and homes. The time line that follows details the development of the Holocaust from beginning to end.

1933
JANUARY: Hitler becomes chancellor of Germany. Acts of anti-Semitism increase in daily life following the Nazi accession to power.

MARCH: The first major concentration camp opens at Dachau, north of Munich. Most of its internees are political prisoners.

APRIL: The Nazis organize a one-day boycott of Jewish business. New laws limit Jewish participation in the law, medicine, civil service, and education.

MAY: Public burning of books begins. The works of Jewish authors are singled out.

1935
MAY: Jews are excluded from service in the German army, another step in the elimination of Jews from participation in German life. Further restrictions on Jews are enacted throughout 1935.

JUNE: The Sterilization Law permits abortions of the "eugenically unfit." Although not directed at Jews, the law becomes another step in the legalization of racial "purification" policies.

SEPTEMBER: The Racial Laws outlaw marriage between "Aryans" (non-Jewish Germans) and Jews in Germany.

DECEMBER: Jews in civil service are discharged.

1936
JUNE: The Office to Combat the Gypsy Menace opens in Munich, the beginning of Nazi persecution of other minorities. Because of the presence of athletes from all over the world, overt signs of anti-Semitism are toned down during the Olympic Games in Berlin in the summer of 1936.

1937
JULY: The Buchenwald concentration camp opens in Germany. It will become a major camp holding Jews and political prisoners.

DECEMBER: Heinrich Himmler, head of the SS (Schutzstaffel), decrees that "asocial" persons may be detained, even if they are not guilty of criminal violations. This category includes Jews and is another tool used in their persecution.

1938
MARCH: Anschluss; Austria and Germany are united following the invasion of German troops. Jews in Austria are immediately persecuted and subject to the same anti-Semitic laws enacted in Germany between 1933 and 1938.

APRIL: Germany requires Jews to register their assets, the first step in the Nazi theft of Jewish wealth in Germany.

JUNE: The Germans begin deporting Gypsies to Dachau and other camps.

AUGUST: Adolf Eichmann opens the Office for Jewish Emigration, a bureau ostensibly designed to assist in the overseas migration of Jews from Germany.

SEPTEMBER: Jews are restricted from practicing law or medicine in Germany.

NOVEMBER: In the wake of Kristallnacht, Jews are fined a billion marks to force them to pay for the aftereffects and cleanup following the pogrom.

1939
JANUARY: By law, Jewish businesses are forced to close.

MARCH: Germany occupies Bohemia and Moravia. Arrests of Jews and Czech leaders follow.

MAY: Ravensbrück women's concentration camp opens. It holds Jews and political prisoners.

SEPTEMBER: Germany invades Poland and the Nazis begin the program to exterminate the mentally and physically handicapped. The Soviets enter eastern Poland. Polish Jews are concentrated in ghettos.

1940

JANUARY: State-sanctioned gassing of disabled patients begins in Germany. The program is an early testing ground for the techniques used eventually to exterminate the Jews.

APRIL: Germany invades Denmark and Norway. Heinrich Himmler orders the establishment of the Auschwitz death camp.

MAY: Germans begin their offensive against France and the Low Countries.

JUNE: The first prisoners arrive at Auschwitz.

OCTOBER: The Germans establish the Warsaw ghetto and herd in the city's Jews.

NOVEMBER: The Germans seal the Warsaw ghetto, preventing Jews from leaving.

1941

MARCH: Himmler orders the expansion of Auschwitz. Hitler orders *Vernichtungskrieg*— "extermination war"—in the Soviet Union.

APRIL: Germany invades Yugoslavia and Greece.

MAY: Germans stop emigration from France and Belgium.

JUNE: Einsatzgruppen are ordered to exterminate Russian Jews. Germany invades the Soviet Union.

JULY: In Romania, 150,000 Jews are murdered by the end of August. Göring orders Reinhard Heydrich, head of the RSHA, to prepare the "final solution"—the extermination of all Jews in Europe.

AUGUST: The Nazi government forbids all Jewish emigration from Germany.

SEPTEMBER: German Jews must wear the Star of David. Ninety thousand Jews are murdered on removal from Romanian provinces. Nazis murder 33,000 at Babi Yar in the Ukraine.

ANNE FRANK

The author of one of the most famous—and tragic—diaries ever written, Anne Frank was a German Jew born in 1929. She and her family fled Nazi Germany in 1933, the year that Adolf Hitler came to power. Sadly, the family settled in the Netherlands, only to face renewed persecution after that nation fell to Hitler in 1940. Anne wrote her poignant tale during two years of hiding in constant fear, until the family's betrayal and arrest in 1944. Anne and other members of the group that had hidden from the Nazis disappeared forever in the pit of darkness that was Bergen-Belsen, a concentration camp near Hannover in north-central Germany. Only Anne's father, Otto, liberated from the notorious death camp at Auschwitz, and Anne's diary survived. Published in 1947, *The Diary of a Young Girl* became and remains an international bestseller. Anne Frank has become a symbol of poignant courage against overwhelming odds, of the tender banalities of a teenage girl facing certain death at the hands of a ruthless and heartless regime of murderers.

OCTOBER: The German army adopts a policy of killing 100 hostages for the death of one German at the hands of partisans.

NOVEMBER: Construction begins at Belzec. The Nazis gas 5,000 Gypsies at Chelmno and murder 53,000 Ukrainian Jews.

1942

JANUARY: The Wannsee Conference, in Berlin, meets to discuss and implement the "final solution."

MARCH: Construction begins at Sobibor concentration camp in Poland; Jews are murdered in Minsk; mass gassings at Auschwitz-Birkenau begin; deportation of Jews begins from Slovakia; first deportations from France to Auschwitz.

APRIL: Dutch Jews must wear the yellow badge signifying they are Jews.

MAY: Heydrich is assassinated in Bohemia. French Jews are ordered to wear the yellow badge.

JUNE: Germans murder most of the citizens of Lidice in retaliation for Heydrich's murder. The transport of Austrian Jews to Theresienstadt, a holding camp in Bohemia, begins.

JULY: Himmler orders extermination of all Jews in German-occupied Poland. German and Austrian Jews are murdered in Minsk, Treblinka concentration camp is completed and murders there begin.

OCTOBER: Germans routed by British at El Alamein; murder of most of Pinsk Jews.

NOVEMBER: The Allies invade North Africa; Germans occupy Vichy France; first deportations of Jews from Norway to Auschwitz.

DECEMBER: Sterilization experiments begin at Auschwitz-Birkenau.

1943

JANUARY: Facing deportations to death camps, Jews in the Warsaw ghetto revolt against German occupation forces. They are eventually overwhelmed (April), and the survivors are sent to Treblinka and murdered.

FEBRUARY: The German Sixth Army surrenders to Soviets at Stalingrad, the military turning point on the Eastern Front.

MARCH: The Germans announce discovery of graves in Katyn Forest, scene of Soviet killings of Polish officers in 1940.

MAY: The Allies control all of North Africa. Dr. Josef Mengele, Nazi doctor at Auschwitz, orders gassing of Gypsies.

AUGUST: More liquidations of Eastern ghettos occurs. Prisoners rebel at Treblinka.

SEPTEMBER: The last Belgian Jews are deported. Italy surrenders, and Germans occupy it. SS liquidates more ghettos.

OCTOBER: Almost all Danish Jews, a small community of a few thousand, escape to Sweden with the help of the Danish population.

NOVEMBER: As the Soviet forces close in on Germany, liquidations of Eastern Jews continue; Sobibor, Treblinka, and Belzec close; the Soviets retake Kiev; Germans begin moving Italian Jews to camps.

1944

APRIL: Hungarian Jews are forced into ghettos; deportations to Auschwitz begin.

JUNE: The Allies reach Rome. The Normandy invasion begins.

JULY: A bomb plot to kill Hitler fails. Hungarian leader Horthy halts deportation of Hungarian Jews.

AUGUST: The Allies land in southern France. The last transport of Jews from Lodz ghetto to Auschwitz is made.

SEPTEMBER: Last shipment of Jews from Holland to Auschwitz.

OCTOBER: The Warsaw population rises up against Germans, hoping to be aided by nearby Soviet forces, but the Soviets sit by as Germans crush the rebellion.

NOVEMBER: Last transport to Auschwitz; Eichmann deports Hungarian Jews on foot in death marches.

DECEMBER: Battle of the Bulge, the last major German offensive in the West.

1945

JANUARY: The last roll call at Auschwitz was followed by the movement of prisoners to the West in a death march. The Soviets enter Auschwitz.

MARCH: American troops cross the Rhine River at Remagen.

APRIL: The Americans reach Buchenwald. The British enter the concentration camp of Bergen-Belsen; Soviets reach Berlin; Himmler agrees to release 15,000 women from Ravensbrück; the Americans reach Dachau; Soviets enter Ravensbrück; Hitler commits suicide.

MAY: Germany surrenders.

AUGUST: Japan surrenders.

NOVEMBER: The International Military Tribunal convenes in Nuremberg. Among the charges are crimes against humanity for the murder of Europe's Jews.

KRISTALLNACHT

For those Jews who did not or could not leave Germany after the Nazis came to power, persecution reached a climax in a nationwide, government-sponsored pogrom called Kristallnacht, the "Night of Broken Glass." Its ostensible cause—or, more accurately, its excuse—was the shooting of a German diplomat in Paris. His assassin was Herschel Grynszpan, a teenage refugee who was incensed because his parents, Polish Jews, had been expelled from Germany but refused admittance to Poland.

HAROLD KENNEDY, 104TH DIVISION

Liberating Germany

Starting out across Germany, we went right down the highways. . . . There was fighting going on one way or another all the way across Germany. . . . On one particular day we went sixty miles; so you could see how fast we were going across Germany . . . Hitler had killed himself in April . . . the war was over. The civilians adapted very rapidly to the American occupation. . . . One of the places that we overran as we came eastward was Nordhausen; the military installation and concentration camp. I was not part of the operation; I was there several hours after they had overrun it. There were 6,000 dead inmates lying about on the ground. It was a ghastly sight. Worse than that, it smelled to high heaven. The American military made the people of Nordhausen come over and see what was going on right next to them. I talked to German civilians and they always said, "Well, we didn't know." I'd say, "You could smell it, couldn't you?"

—Fort Collins Public Library Local History Archive, http://library.ci.fort-collins.co.us/local_history/topics/wwii/hist3b27.htm

Hermann Göring, head of the Gestapo and one of Hitler's most powerful henchmen, seized the chance to strike at German Jews and their livelihood and orchestrated a series of riots, beginning on the night of November 9, 1938. Nazi thugs struck at Jews in a coordinated orgy of window smashing, arson, and assault and murder as police, under orders, stood idly by. The rioters destroyed about 500 synagogues and ravaged hundreds of Jewish businesses, offices, and homes; the streets were strewn with broken glass as rioters smashed show windows and looted stores. About 100 Jews were murdered, many Jewish women were raped, and more than 20,000 men were arrested and confined at Dachau, Buchenwald, and other concentration camps within Germany. The stage was set for additional horrors to come.

On November 12, as the rioting died away, Göring announced that Jews could no longer own retail businesses or be independent craftsmen; they could not attend any sort of public entertainment, drive automobiles, or work for Aryans. Göring also released German insurance companies from the obligation to pay claims on Kristallnacht damages and ordered that the Jewish community bear the entire cost of the pogrom, their losses, and the cleanup afterward. It was a death blow to Jewish financial resources. In the wake of Kristallnacht, as many as 150,000 Jews fled Nazi Germany in less than a year.

ZYKLON B

A trade name for the gas used to murder hundreds of thousands in Nazi death camps, Zyklon—the word means "cyclone"—was a commercial pesticide based on prussic acid (hydrocyanic gas), one of several substances tried out as a murder agent. The substance was first used on mental patients and handicapped children as early as 1939. By late

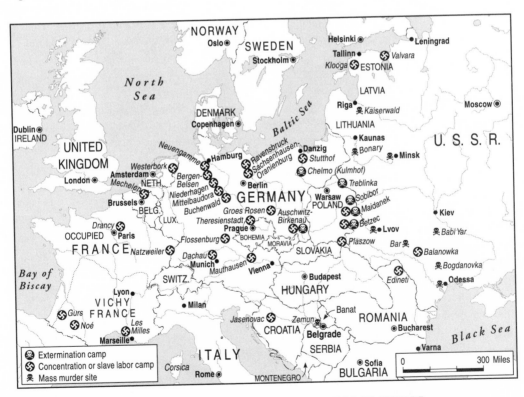

CONCENTRATION CAMPS AND ATROCITIES IN EUROPE

1941, the Nazis were experimenting on captive Jews and Soviet POWs, seeking some lethal gas that would give the victims little or no warning. By that summer, after the Nazis had murdered about 90,000 "useless mouths" in Germany, the domestic extermination program lost momentum in the face of public disapproval. But they had learned much about the effect of various gases on human bodies.

Zyklon B came in pellet form and released its deadly fumes when the can was opened to the air. The Nazis used Zyklon B extensively at Auschwitz, where they took elaborate pains not to alert the victims about their fate. They directed the Jews to "showers," which held as many as 2,000 people at a time, and told them to hang their clothing on a numbered hook and remember the number. Once the victims were inside, the Nazis locked the airtight doors and dropped the deadly pellets through the ventilating system. Zyklon B worked quickly on its victims, but in the packed gas chambers of Auschwitz, the gas did not reach all its victims at one time, leading to panic as the people sought to escape. As the Auschwitz commandant reported, the people nearest the gas began to fall at once. Those farther away "staggered about and began to scream and struggle for air. The screaming, however, soon changed to the death rattle and in a few minutes all lay still." When the chamber was opened, a pyramid of bloody victims, their limbs entwined, met those who had to remove the bodies.

None of the camps controlled by Operation Reinhard, the murder apparatus named for Reinhard Heydrich, the SS lieutenant general shot down by Czech patriots in 1942, used Zyklon B. Many of those murders took place before the poison was introduced. The Reinhard camps—Treblinka, Belzec and Sobibor, all in Poland—used carbon monoxide. Nor did the Germans use Zyklon B in the murders in the Soviet Union and the Baltic States, where much of the slaughter was by gunfire, as at Babi Yar near Minsk.

> I pray you to believe what I have said about Buchenwald. I have reported what I saw and heard, but only part of it. For most of it I have no words.
>
> —U.S. reporter Edward R. Murrow

HOLOCAUST DENIERS

Inevitably people have emerged who deny that the murders of Jews, Gypsies, homosexuals, and others ever took place. The deniers are not German alone, but American, Canadian, British, and French. A great number of revisionist books and articles have either rejected the Holocaust altogether or attempted some justification of the murders. They have appeared both in the United States and overseas, and they bear titles such as *Six Million Swindle; Debunking the Genocide Myth; Auschwitz Lüge (Auschwitz Lie);* and *Hoax of the Twentieth Century.*

Much opposition to Holocaust history comes from something called the Institute for Historical Review and its publications. In 1981, after a camp survivor sued, the institute paid the $50,000 that it had offered for proof that Jews were gassed at Auschwitz. One denial was based on a chemical test of scrapings from the brick walls of the Auschwitz gas chambers. The absence of cyanide residue in the scrapings was offered as proof that no gassings took place, at least with Zyklon B. However, the chemist who did the tests stated that gas could not have penetrated more than 10 microns—one-tenth the thickness of a human hair—into the brick. In the samples, which came to the chemist as large pieces of brick and concrete, any Zyklon traces would have "been diluted by a factor of hundreds of thousands." The brick had, moreover, been exposed to the elements for almost 50 years when the scrapings were taken.

One who applauded this "test" was the British historian and prolific writer David Irving, who persistently announced that he was a "hard-core disbeliever" in the Holocaust. He has, however, acknowledged that enormous numbers of people died in the camps. Irving sued the historian Deborah Lipstadt, the author of a book on the Holocaust, for libel in the United Kingdom, claiming that he was defamed by her assertions that, among other things, he was a Holocaust denier. The verdict went against Irving, refuting his position that Hitler knew nothing of the final solution and that the Holocaust was a Jewish invention designed to extort reparations from Germany. It was a severe setback for Irving's reputation and for the cause of Holocaust denial.

JEWISH DEATHS DURING THE HOLOCAUST

The Germans systematically persecuted, hunted, and exterminated the Jews of Europe during the Nazi era. Once the war had started, they rounded up Jews from virtually every nation on the continent and summarily executed them, murdered them in gas chambers, or worked them to death in slave labor camps. This table reflects the Jewish populations of major European nations and the approximate number of those killed (numbers rounded off to nearest hundred).

Country	Pre-Holocaust Jewish Population	Approximate Number of Deaths
Austria	185,000	50,000
Belgium	65,700	28,900
Bulgaria	50,000	0
Czechoslovakia*	207,200	149,200
Denmark	7,800	Fewer than 100
Estonia	4,500	2,000

Country	Pre-Holocaust Jewish Population	Approximate Number of Deaths
Finland	2,000	Fewer than 100
France	350,000	77,300
Germany	566,000	135,000–140,000
Greece	77,400	60,000–67,000
Hungary	825,000	550,000–569,000
Italy	44,500	7,700
Latvia	91,500	70,000–71,000
Lithuania	168,000	140,000–143,000
Luxembourg	4,000	700
The Netherlands	140,000	100,000
Norway	1,700	800
Poland	3,300,000	2,900,000–3,000,000
Romania	609,000	271,000–287,000
Soviet Union	3,020,000	1,000,000–1,100,000
Yugoslavia	78,000	56,200–63,300

*Bohemia, Moravia, and Slovakia
Engel, David, *The Holocaust* (Harlow, England: Longman, 2000).
Fischel, Jack R., *The Holocaust* (Westport, CT: Greenwood Press, 1998).
Gilbert, Martin, *The Holocaust* (New York: Holt, Rinehart and Winston, 1985).

I have gotten rid of the Jews.   —Adolf Hitler, 1944

MURDERS IN MAJOR NAZI DEATH CAMPS

Large Nazi concentration camps were located in Germany, Poland, and Austria. This table lists the largest camps, along with their locations and the approximate number of people who perished in each.

Camp	Location*	Approximate Number of Deaths
Auschwitz-Birkenau	West of Cracow, Poland	1,600,000
Belzec	South of Lublin, Poland	600,000
Bergen-Belsen	North Germany	35,000–50,000
Buchenwald	Weimar, Germany	43,000
Chelmno	Lodz, Poland	320,000
Dachau	Munich, Germany	31,500
Gross-Rosen	Southwest Poland	40,000
Majdanek	Lublin, Poland	360,000
Mauthausen	Linz, Austria	71,000
Ravensbrück	North of Berlin	92,700
Sachsenhausen	Berlin, Germany	30,000
Sobibor	Lublin, Poland	250,000
Stutthof	Danzig, Poland	65,000
Treblinka	Northeast Poland	870,000

*Locations are generally in the vicinity of nearby major cities.

NUREMBERG TRIALS AGAINST TOP LEADERS OF THE THIRD REICH

The defendants at the Nuremberg trials received sentences ranging from 10 years in prison to death by hanging. Three former high-ranking members of the Nazi regime were acquitted.

Defendant	Position in the Nazi Regime	Sentence*
Hermann Göring	Luftwaffe Chief	Death (committed suicide before execution)
Rudolf Hess	Deputy Führer	Life
Joachim von Ribbentrop	Foreign Minister	Death
Wilhelm Keitel	High Command Chief	Death
Ernst Kaltenbrunner	RSHA Chief**	Death
Alfred Rosenberg	Nazi racial philosopher	Death
Hans Frank	Governor of Poland	Death
Wilhelm Frick	Interior Minister	Death
Julius Streicher	Jew-baiting newspaper editor	Death
Walther Funk	Minister of Economic Affairs	Life
Hjalmar Schacht	Reichsbank president	Acquitted
Karl Dönitz	Admiral, navy	10 years
Erich Raeder	Navy Commander in Chief	Life
Baldur von Schirach	Hitler Youth leader	20 years
Fritz Sauckel	Plenipotentiary for Labor	Death

(continued)

Defendant	Position in the Nazi Regime	Sentence*
Alfred Jodl	High Command operations chief	Death
Martin Bormann	Party Secretary	Death***
Franz von Papen	Chancellor, 1932; diplomat	Acquitted
Artur Seyss-Inquart	Netherlands Governor	Death
Albert Speer	Minister of Armaments	20 years
Konstantin von Neurath	Diplomat	Acquitted

*All death sentences were carried out by hanging.
**RSHA: (Reichssicherheitshauptamt), Reich Main Security Office, which controlled, among other things, the Gestapo.
***Convicted and sentenced in absentia, he had fled from the party chancellery in Berlin in the last days of the war. Killed in Berlin, his remains finally were found in 1972.

In the defendant's dock at Nuremberg, leaders of the Nazi regime are brought to justice. Front row (top to bottom) are Luftwaffe chief Hermann Göring, former Deputy Führer Rudolf Hess, Foreign Minister Joachim von Ribbentrop, and General Wilhelm Keitel.

The Nuremberg Trials

The most famous postwar trial of Nazi war criminals was the Nuremberg proceeding against the top leaders of the Third Reich (see table, pp. 411-12). However, Nuremberg was the site of 12 other major prosecutions:

- The Doctors' Case: prosecuted physicians who experimented on prisoners
- The Milch Case: for forced labor and medical experiments at Dachau
- The Justice Case: for abuses of the legal process in Nazi Germany
- The Oswald Pohl Case: prosecuted SS prison-camp administrators
- The Flick Case: for industrialist use of slave labor and theft of Jewish property
- The I.G. Farben Case: prosecuted the huge chemical combine for use of slave labor
- The Hostage Case: for maltreatment of civilians in Southeast Europe
- The RSHA Case: against officials of the Reich Main Security Office implicated in genocide
- The Einsaztgruppen Case: trial of members of the SS murder squads
- The Krupp Case: for industrial use of slave labor and theft of property
- The Ministries Case: prosecuted officials from the German foreign and other ministries responsible for constructing the Nazi regime
- The High Command Case: trial of senior officers for crimes against POWs and civilians in conquered areas.

These trials produced 24 death sentences, 20 life terms, and 87 shorter prison sentences.

THREE NAZIS WHO ESCAPED

A few of the worst war criminals escaped before they could be found and tried. Among the most notorious were Klaus Barbie, Adolf Eichmann, and Josef Mengele. Barbie and Eichmann were apprehended years after the war and brought to trial.

Klaus Barbie

This SS captain was a notorious torturer and murderer of Jews and other civilians in Lyons, France, from late 1942 to August 1944. Perhaps his worst crime was the abduction of 44 Jewish children, mostly orphans, from the French village of Izieu. All were shipped to either Estonia or Dachau. None survived. U.S. intelligence sources are said to have helped Barbie to escape Europe. In 1944–45, Barbie was employed under the watchful eye of British and American agents who used him for counterintelligence work. He fled to Bolivia in 1955. Extradited to France, he was sentenced to life imprisonment in 1987. Barbie died of cancer while in prison in 1991, unrepentant to the end.

Adolf Eichmann

This SS lieutenant colonel became head of RSHA's "Race and Resettlement Office" and was one of the main architects of the final solution. In January 1942, a planning group of high-level officials convened in the Berlin suburb of Wannsee. Eichmann participated in the conference, where Reinhard Heydrich, head of RSHA, bluntly briefed the state secretaries of several government ministries on the "final solution." Eichmann said later that "they minced no words about it at all. . . . They spoke about methods of killing, about liquidation, about extermination." To these people Eichmann recited the terrible numbers of Jews who were to be transported to the East, never to return. He was quite meticulous: he had figures for all of Europe, even for defiant Great Britain and neutral Ireland.

Eichmann and his staff efficiently oversaw every detail, from camp construction to railroad timetables to gassing techniques. Eichmann visited Auschwitz in 1941, familiarizing himself with the details of camp operation, and after Wannsee became the recognized "Jewish specialist" of RSHA. Eichmann was industrious and tireless, impatient with German allies who were slow or reluctant in giving up their Jewish citizens.

He fled to Argentina in 1946 but eventually was tracked down by Israeli agents, who kidnapped him in May 1960 and brought him to Israel for trial. After a lengthy public trial, during which he was confronted by some of his victims who survived the Holocaust, he was convicted and sentenced to death by hanging. Eichmann was executed in May 1962.

Josef Mengele

Josef Mengele was the chief medical officer at Auschwitz. Obsessed with notions of developing "racially perfect" people, he performed hideous medical experiments on inmates, including many children, and killed thousands with lethal injections. Mengele selected who in the new prisoner shipments would live and be saved temporarily for medical experiments or labor and who would die immediately in the gas chambers. Dressed always in an immaculate white coat, he was called "the angel of death."

Mengele escaped to Argentina at war's end. He was nearly apprehended by Israeli agents in 1960 but escaped to Paraguay. Unlike Eichmann and Barbie, he was able to elude his captors and died without having to stand trial for his crimes. In 1985 remains found in a Brazilian grave were positively identified as his.

The Rescuers

More easily forgotten than the perpetrators of the Holocaust are the rescuers, the handful of courageous men and women who saved people from the Nazis. Their numbers appear small when compared with the armies of perpetrators, but their deeds are a beacon of hope for humanity against the death-laden landscape of Nazi persecution. They are what postwar Jews would come to call "Righteous Gentiles."

Many rescuers remain unknown. Of the known, some come readily to mind:

RAOUL WALLENBERG A Swedish diplomat in Budapest, Hungary, in 1944 he saved more than

30,000 Jews by issuing them Swedish passports and negotiating with German security officials, before he was forced to go underground. For reasons that remain unclear, he was arrested by the Soviets at the end of the war and imprisoned; he died in captivity.

CARL LUTZ   The Swiss consul in Budapest, he worked with Wallenberg and established 76 safe houses, saving an estimated 60,000 Jews from transportation to the crematoria.

SEMPO SUGIHARA   The Japanese consul in Kovno, Lithuania, he issued thousands of visas for Jews to travel eastward, through Moscow and Siberia, to Japan and beyond.

OSCAR SCHINDLER   A German Catholic, he was a member of the Nazi Party and managed a factory near Plaszow, Poland. He used his outwardly cordial relations with the Nazis to protect the Jews who worked in his factory—more than 500, by the summer of 1944. In all, Schindler and his wife, Emilia, saved more than 1,500 Jews between 1943 and 1945. He was the subject of an acclaimed film, Steven Spielberg's *Schindler's List.*

HIRAM BINGHAM   The American vice consul, he converted his residence in Marseilles, France, into a safe house and saved more than 2,000 Jews, including the artists Marc Chagall and Max Ernst. Bingham was one of about 85 humanitarian diplomats from 22 countries who issued passports and transit visas—many of them unauthorized by their own governments—to thousands of desperate European refugees, enabling them to flee to safety. The legacy of these men lives on—in the descendants of those they rescued—even if their names are, by and large, obscure. Collectively, the diplomats who participated in the rescue of Jews issued more than 200,000 visas and passports to refugees during World War II.

ARISTIDES DE SOUSA MENDES   One of the most courageous "Righteous Gentiles" and least known of the war's diplomat-humanitarians, Sousa Mendes was the Portuguese consul general in Bordeaux, France in 1940. From the outbreak of the war in September 1939, he deemed it a moral imperative to assist all who sought to flee from Europe through Portugal. The war was barely two months old when he was first taken to task by his government, because he had issued a transit visa to an Austrian Jew. He was formally warned, and the Portuguese border patrol was instructed to look out for, and report, his transgressions, by keeping track of the visas issued in Bordeaux and presented by people seeking admission to the country.

Then came May 1940 and the German invasion of the Low Countries and France. Hundreds of thousands of refugees trudged to Bordeaux with vague hopes of leaving the continent. First, though, they needed to leave France—before the advancing Germans occupied the southwest.

Spain's Generalissimo Franco closed his country's borders to those fleeing the advancing Germans, although those with a Portuguese visa could enter. Thus a refugee needed a Portuguese visa to cross from France into Spain. But the Portuguese premier, António de Oliveira Salazar, was alive to the need for Iberian solidarity in the face of German aggression. He likewise declared his country's borders closed to refugees of the conflict and suspended absolutely the authority of his consuls to grant visas unless such visas were preapproved by Lisbon.

Sousa Mendes had only to do what was officially required of him in order to keep his status as an able and honorable diplomat. Instead, overcoming all personal and professional considerations, he did the diplomatically unthinkable: he used his office to overturn his government's policy, on behalf of humanity. First in Bordeaux, and then in the city of Bayonne and on the streets of Hendaye at the Franco-Spanish border, Aristides de Sousa Mendes indiscriminately issued transit visas for entry into Portugal to an astounding 30,000 refugees, saving them from the Nazis. By sheer magnitude of daring and weight of numbers, he effectively opened up a refugee escape route where none had existed. It would remain through the war and be used by an estimated one million refugees.

The name of Aristides de Sousa Mendes was removed from all official documents and government publications, and he spent the remaining 14 years of his life as an outcast. In his willingness to pay any price to fight evil, Aristides de Sousa Mendes stands alongside the other World

JAPANESE ATROCITIES IN THE PACIFIC AND ASIA

War II heroes of conscience, most of whose names will always remain outside the history books.

Atrocities in the Pacific Theater

From the outset of their conquests, the Japanese military treated both the civilian population of conquered lands and surrendered Allied soldiers with contempt and gratuitous cruelty. Because surrender was so shameful to the Japanese, they had no sympathy for civilians or soldiers who surrendered. Murder, rape, torture, neglect, starvation, and bizarre medical experiments were endemic in areas controlled by the Japanese.

Killings in the Far East are not as fully documented as those in Europe, and the actual numbers of deaths are uncertain and disputed, but Chinese civilian casualties alone may have been as high as 30 million between 1937 and 1945. Thousands more, POWs and civilians, died elsewhere in the East. How many of these deaths were from sickness, starvation, and other results of neglect is unknown; many victims were murdered outright. Documentation of atrocities has been hindered by official Japanese attitudes, which to this day tend to minimize or deny the problem of wartime atrocities on the part of the Japanese military.

JAPANESE ATROCITIES

The list that follows, arranged alphabetically, details the worst atrocities in the Pacific theater.

AMBON ISLAND (FEBRUARY 1943) The Japanese beheaded more than 200 Australian and Dutch prisoners after taking control of this small island in the Dutch East Indies.

BALLALAE ISLAND, SOLOMONS (1942–45) Of 516 British POWs shipped from Singapore to New Britain Island to build an airstrip for the Japanese, not one survived the war.

BATAAN (APRIL 1942) After the fall of the Philippines, U.S. and Filipino military prisoners were marched 65 miles over land to prison camps. Exhausted and undernourished, about 600 Americans and perhaps as many as 5,000 Filipinos died on the way, many bayoneted, shot, or beheaded when they could not continue. Others died after they were crammed into boxcars for the last stage of their trip, baking in the tropical sun. Thousands more POWs of both nations died after arriving at Camp O'Donnell.

CHERIBON, JAVA (JULY 1945) The Japanese loaded 90 civilian prisoners onto the outside

---

THE GENEVA CONVENTION OF 1929

This international agreement extended the Geneva Conventions of 1864 and 1906 and replaced the convention of 1907 on treatment of prisoners of war. Its 97 articles set out the duties and rights of the International Red Cross and required that the sick and wounded of belligerents be respected and cared for, regardless of nationality. It established that medical personnel, transport, buildings, and other facilities marked with the red cross were immune from attack.

When war broke out in 1939, most nations had ratified the convention, but Japan and the Soviet Union had not done so. In Geneva in 1925, 29 countries had signed an additional protocol, dealing with both biological and chemical warfare.

The Geneva Convention has remained the standard against which the treatment of prisoners of war is measured. Atrocities were committed on both sides. However, in many instances the Japanese did not consider themselves bound by the convention since their country was not a signatory. In the European theater, ruthless Nazi ideology influenced many of the atrocities committed by German troops.

of a Japanese submarine, which took them to sea. The submarine then submerged, leaving the civilians—men, women, and children—foundering in shark-filled waters. One mutilated survivor lived long enough to tell the story.

KALAGON, BURMA (JUNE 1945) Japanese troops hunting for British-led Burmese guerrillas surrounded this village, then bayoneted or shot more than 600 villagers.

KINSU AND CHEKIANG PROVINCES, CHINA (APRIL–MAY 1942) After the Doolittle raid on Tokyo shocked Japan in April 1942, Japanese troops launched a massive search for the raiders, most of whom had had to crash-land in China (see Chapter 8, "Campaigns and Battles: Asia and the Pacific"). Three captured raiders were executed; during their hunt for the

Their hands bound behind them, gaunt American prisoners pause during the grueling Death March from the Bataan Peninsula to a POW camp at Cabanatuan, Philippines.

LESTER TENNEY, U.S. ARMY, FORMER POW

Surviving as Prisoner of War

Within seconds, dozens of Japanese soldiers came into our area, some asking politely for cigarettes while others pounded our heads with bamboo sticks whose ends were loaded with sand. These rough soldiers did not ask for a thing; they just took whatever they wanted. They ransacked our bodies and our sleeping area. They were belligerent, loud, and determined to act like the winners of a tough battle (which they were). Once again we were frightened by what was happening and fearful that our future treatment was going to be worse.

The first Japanese soldier I came into contact with used sign language to ask if I had a cigarette. Fingers together, he moved his arm to his mouth, and inhaled, making it easy to see what he meant. I had to tell him I did not have any cigarettes. He smiled and then a second later hit me in the face with the butt of his gun. Blood spurted from my nose and from a deep gash on my cheekbone. He laughed and said something that made all of his buddies laugh, too. He walked away from me and went to the GI on my right. He used the same sign language, and this time my buddy had cigarettes and offered him one. The Japanese soldier took the whole pack, and then he and his friends began beating my friend with rifle butts and cane-length pieces of bamboo until he could not stand. Then they left, laughing, laughing at the defeated and weak Americans.

My God, what was next? I wondered how I would stand up to this type of punishment for a prolonged period. If we had known earlier just how we would be treated and for how long, I think [we] would have fought on Bataan to the last man, taking as many of the enemy with us as possible, rather than endure the torture, hunger, beatings, and inhumane atrocities we were to undergo during the next three and a half years.

—*My Hitch in Hell* (London: Brassey's, 2000), p. 43

Americans the Japanese killed thousands of Chinese civilians and destroyed entire villages.

LOA KULU, BORNEO (JULY 1945) Japanese troops murdered more than 140 native men and many of their wives and hurled the children down a mine shaft.

NANKING, CHINA (DECEMBER 1937) In the worst single massacre of the war, Japanese troops murdered as many as 250,000 Chinese in and around the city.

PRISON SHIPS The Japanese shipped thousands of Allied POWs to Japan from the occupied territory during the war by cramming them into the holds of dilapidated, overcrowded freighters with insufficient water and food. Many died, and some were murdered by sadistic crew or guards. Thousands more perished when Allied forces sank some of the unmarked ships (see table, p. 429).

SANDAKAN, NORTH BORNEO (JUNE 1945) Of approximately 2,400 British and Australian POWs taken here for labor, more than 2,000 died: murdered, marched to death, starved, dead of untreated disease. Of about 4,000 Javanese civilian slave-laborers, almost none survived. The Japanese camp commandant at Sandakan was tried and hanged after the war.

TOL PLANTATION, RABAUL (FEBRUARY 1942) Japanese troops shot or bayoneted more than 100 Australian soldiers who had surrendered when their defense of the island of New Britain in the Solomons collapsed.

WAKE ISLAND (JANUARY 1943) The Japanese machine-gunned 98 American civilians after capturing them on the island. A small detachment of U.S. Marines and civilian construction workers had put up a spirited defense of Wake Island in December 1941.

THE RAPE OF NANKING

Japan invaded China in 1937, after fighting in both Shanghai and North China. Ten million to 30 million Chinese died during that war, most of them civilians. They died of disease, starvation, and simple murder, as well as in combat with the Japanese, which included the use of biological agents.

The city of Nanking fell to the Japanese in December 1937, and the butchery that followed was the worst example of Japanese cruelty in the war. The death toll was probably around 250,000 (but may have been as high as 300,000) in the city and surrounding region, although many sources regard that figure as far too high, saying that it exceeds the entire population of Nanking. Some Japanese sources say the death toll was minimal, but others acknowledge that many innocent civilians were murdered.

First the Japanese searched out and killed Nationalist soldiers in or out of uniform and other males who might have been soldiers. Then marauding bands of Japanese soldiers also turned on the civilian populace; raping and killing many women and butchering children. The Japanese shot, tortured, beheaded, burned, and buried people alive, despite heroic efforts by members of the international community—including a Nazi official—to protect the helpless.

The "Rape of Nanking" remains to this day a point of contention between Japan and China and other former occupied countries. The Japanese have refused to fully embrace responsibility for the event, insisting that the death tolls claimed by the Chinese are an exaggeration. The Chinese have long demanded that Japan accept responsibility for its actions and apologize without reservations, while the Japanese have offered only conditional apologies (often in the form of "regrets").

When the alarm was sounded for an impending Japanese air raid against the city of Chungking, China, on June 5, 1941, panic ensued. Four thousand people were crushed or trampled to death in the rush for shelter.

WAR CRIMES TRIALS

American, British, Australian, French, Filipino, Canadian, Soviet, New Zealand, and Dutch military courts all across the Far East held war crimes trials. The trials of major criminals, including Premier Hideki Tojo, who was hanged, were held in Tokyo. Altogether, about 5,600 defendants were tried, leading to roughly 4,000 convictions, 1,000 executions, and approximately 1,000 acquittals.

JAPANESE OFFICERS AND OFFICIALS TRIED FOR WAR CRIMES IN THE FAR EAST

Name	Title	Verdict	Sentence
Kenji Doihara	Commander, Kwantung Army and numerous POW camps	Guilty	Death
Koki Hirota	Foreign Minister, Premier in 1930s	Guilty	Death
Seishiro Itagaki	War Minister; Chief of General Staff	Guilty	Death

JAPANESE OFFICERS AND OFFICIALS TRIED FOR WAR CRIMES IN THE FAR EAST

Name	Title	Verdict	Sentence
Hyotaro Kimura	Vice War Minister; Burma Army Commander	Guilty	Death
Iwane Matsui	Rape of Nanking Army Commander	Guilty	Death
Akira Muto	Sumatra and Philippines Commander	Guilty	Death
Hideki Tojo	War Minister and later Premier	Guilty	Death
Sadao Araki	War Minister in 1930s	Guilty	Life
Kingoro Hashimoto	High-ranking officer advocating war	Guilty	Life
Shunroku Hata	Commander in China; War Minister	Guilty	Life
Kiichiro Hiranuma	Premier in 1939	Guilty	Life
Naoki Hoshino	Chief Cabinet Secretary	Guilty	Life
Okinori Kaya	Finance Minister	Guilty	Life
Koichi Kido	Emperor's Advisor	Guilty	Life
Kuniaki Koiso	Governor of Korea; Premier	Guilty	Life
Jiro Minami	Kwantung Army Commander; Governor of Korea	Guilty	Life
Takasumi Oka	Naval Affairs Chief; Deputy Navy Minister	Guilty	Life
Hiroshi Oshima	Ambassador to Germany	Guilty	Life
Kenryo Sato	Military Affairs Chief	Guilty	Life
Shigetaro Shimada	Navy Minister	Guilty	Life
Toshio Shiratori	Career Diplomat	Guilty	Life
Teiichi Suzuki	Cabinet Minister	Guilty	Life
Yoshijiro Umezu	Kwantung Army Commander; Army Chief of Staff	Guilty	Life
Yosuke Matsuoka	Foreign Minister	Died During Trial	
Osami Nagano	Navy Chief of Staff	Died During Trial	

Name	Title	Verdict	Sentence
Shumei Okawa	Prominent War Advocate	Released	
Mamoru Shigemitsu	Foreign Minister	Guilty	7 Years
Shigenori Togo	Foreign Minister	Guilty	20 Years

Atrocities in the European Theater

German and Italian troops usually accepted the surrender of American, French, and British enemies, although sometimes unarmed or injured surrendering men were murdered, especially by SS units. In late 1942, responding to British raids on the continent, Hitler issued his Commando Order, which directed troops to turn their captured raiders over to the Sicherheitsdienst, implying that they were to be shot. As a result, the Germans murdered a number of surrendered soldiers in full uniform.

On the Soviet front, both sides often indulged in acts of cruelty, ranging from simple neglect to torture and murder. The Nazi contempt for the "subhuman" Slav set the stage for atrocities unparalleled on other fronts. The Soviets responded in kind. Hundreds of thousands of prisoners on both sides died of sheer neglect or were brutally murdered.

The German handling of military prisoners reflected a conflict between the old officer corps of the German army, which predated Hitler and which was steeped in the tradition of honorable treatment of prisoners, and hard-core Nazis, who were more than willing to execute prisoners without second thought. In the Soviet Union, the extreme suffering caused by the German invasion helped spur harsh retaliation against members of the German military. Many German prisoners were kept in Soviet camps under severe conditions into the mid-1950s, when the survivors were released following the establishment of diplomatic relations between the Soviet Union and West Germany.

> No one, whether Nazi or not, should be led summarily before a firing squad without legal trial and consideration of the relevant facts and proofs. Rather would I here and now be led out into the garden and shot than that my honor and that of my country should be smirched by such baseness. —Winston Churchill at Teheran, answering Stalin's demand for summary execution of German officials, 1943

MAJOR BATTLEFIELD ATROCITIES

The alphabetical list that follows provides examples of atrocities by military units in combat in the European theater.

BRONIKI, UKRAINE, SOVIET UNION (JULY 1941) Soviet troops captured about 180 German soldiers, many of whom had been wounded, herded them naked into a field, and shot them. A few men ran into nearby woods and survived.

FEODOSIA, CRIMEA, SOVIET UNION (DECEMBER 1941) German troops recaptured the city after withdrawing from it and found that occupying Red Army troops had murdered about 160 wounded German soldiers.

GERMAN ATROCITIES IN THE SOVIET UNION The war in the East was marked by ferocity on both sides, with infinitely more brutality than either the Allies or the Wehrmacht demonstrated on other fronts. During the first summer of the Eastern war, 1941, the Germans marched vast masses of Soviet military prisoners hundreds of miles to shelterless camps, where rations were at or below starvation level. Many who could not keep up along the road were shot. The death toll among Soviet POWs may have been as high as 3.3 million of the 5.7 million captured during the war.

GRISCHINO, UKRAINE, SOVIET UNION (FEBRUARY 1943) This area, near the present city of Donetsk, changed hands in fighting between German troops and Soviet forces. On retaking the area, German troops found the corpses of almost 600 Germans, Italians, Romanians, and Hungarians who had been murdered by the Soviets. Among the dead were German nurses who had been both raped and mutilated.

KATYN FOREST, NEAR SMOLENSK, RUSSIA (APRIL 1940) NKVD men murdered 4,400 Polish officers. The Soviets murdered other Polish officers in separate mass executions near Kharkov and a site near Kalinin. Altogether, the Soviets murdered about 26,000 Polish officers.

KOS, GREECE (OCTOBER 1943) After the Germans captured the island of Kos in the Aegean, German troops responded to a Hitler order by murdering 102 Italian officers, who were fighting on the side of the Western Allies.

LEPARADIS, FRANCE (MAY 1940) British soldiers of the Royal Norfolk Regiment, out of ammunition, surrendered to elements of the SS Totenkopf (Death's Head) Division. The SS lined up 99 prisoners near a group of farm buildings and machine-gunned them; 97 soldiers died. Fritz Knoechlein, commander of the German unit involved, was hanged for this crime in January 1949.

MALMEDY MASSACRE (DECEMBER 1944) German soldiers in the 1st Panzer Division captured and killed 83 U.S. prisoners of war during the second day of the Battle of the Bulge.

NORMANDY (JUNE 1944) The 12th SS Panzer Division ("Hitler Jugend") captured several groups of Canadian soldiers near the villages

MURDER IN THE KATYN FOREST

During the Nuremberg trials of the leading Nazis, the Soviet prosecutors insisted on bringing up the 1940 massacre of Polish officers, supposedly by German forces in the forest of Katyn. Hermann Göring's defense counsel, Dr. Otto Stahmer, was the chief author of the intense embarrassment of the Soviets that followed. He attacked a parade of puppet witnesses who damned the Germans as murderers, and Stahmer tore apart the flimsy fabric of the Soviet case.

Among other things, Stahmer showed that a doctor of international status believed that the corpses at Katyn could not have been shot earlier than the last quarter of 1941—therefore, the deaths could not have occurred in 1940, as the Soviets alleged. The Soviets, bogged ever deeper in a morass of lies, dropped the Katyn allegation altogether.

The truth was grim. After the Soviet Union carved out its share of Poland in 1939, the NKVD, the secret police, segregated captured Polish officers in its camps. After Germany invaded the Soviet Union in June 1941, the Soviets announced that they had released all Polish officers. Then, in 1943, the Germans announced that they had found buried in the Katyn Forest, near Smolensk, thousands of corpses believed to be Polish officers. All had been murdered. A team of international experts visited the site and found no documents on the bodies dated later than April 1940, predating the invasion of the Soviet Union by Germany. Therefore, the murders must reasonably have taken place while the area was under Soviet control. This laid the guilt squarely on the Soviet Union despite its belligerent denials. At last, in 1990 the Russian government admitted that the officers had been murdered on Stalin's orders, and two more mass graves were revealed. The total of Polish officers murdered by the Soviets is estimated at 26,000.

of Le Mesnil-Patty, Authie, and Buron, the Abbaye Ardenne, and the Château d'Audrieu. Various units shot more than 130 Canadian prisoners, individually or in groups.

SAGAN, GERMANY (MARCH 1944) Seventy-nine Royal Air Force officers staged a spectacular escape after digging a 360-foot tunnel out of a prison camp at Sagan, in Silesia. All were recaptured save three, who ultimately reached Great Britain. Infuriated, Hitler directed that 50 of the Sagan escapees be shot as soon as they were captured. This was done at various places in Germany, near the points of recapture. The official excuse was that they were shot while trying to escape. Twenty-one Germans involved in the crime were hanged after the war, and 17 more were sent to prison.

WORMHOUDT, FRANCE (MAY 1940) The SS regiment Leibstandarte Adolf Hitler captured 80 soldiers, men from several British units, and herded them into a barn. The SS men threw grenades in among them, then let loose with automatic weapons. Although 15 British soldiers survived to bear witness to the killings, no one was ever able to identify the SS soldiers involved.

GERMAN RETALIATION AGAINST CIVILIANS AND HOSTAGES

Of all combatants in the European theater, the Germans were most prone to retaliate against civilians and hostages. In many cases, retaliatory actions occurred directly on the orders of Hitler and were often in response to an attack on German forces by resistance fighters or by ordinary civilians. German police, local paramilitary units, the SS, and occasionally the Wehrmacht murdered hostages in occupied territory, often killing 100 local people for every German killed by local partisans. Some examples:

ASCQ, FRANCE (APRIL 1944) When troops of the 12th SS Panzer Division ("Hitler Jugend"), traveling by rail, reached this village on their way into Normandy, an explosion destroyed part of the tracks. The commander ordered the arrest of all men living in houses near the track. The SS shot more than 90.

BANDE, BELGIUM (DECEMBER 1944) When partisans killed three German soldiers, a German Security Service unit murdered 34 local men in retaliation.

DE WOESTE HOEVE, HOLLAND (MARCH 1945) After the Dutch underground ambushed and badly wounded a German general, SS men arrested and shot 116 civilians. The revenge killings totaled 263 after German security forces murdered other prisoners already in Gestapo custody. The British army tried the SS officer responsible—Dr. Eberhardt Schongarth—and hanged him in 1946.

KALAVRYTA, GREECE (DECEMBER 1943) In retaliation for Greek partisan activity in the area, German troops herded the entire adult male population of Kalavryta—696—into a hollow near the village and shot them all. Approximately 600 more men from neighboring villages were also murdered that day.

KORTELISY, UKRAINE, SOVIET UNION (SEPTEMBER 1942) Responding to Ukrainian guerrilla activity, SS men and Ukrainian police exterminated the entire village population, about 2,900 men, women, and children. This was only one of hundreds of villages ravaged by the Germans and collaborationist local police.

LIDICE, CZECHOSLOVAKIA (JUNE 1942) After Czech patriots assassinated Reinhard Heydrich, the SS leader and Nazi ruler of Bohemia and Moravia, SS men arrested thousands of Czechs, murdering more than 2,000. The SS destroyed the village of Lidice (the population was about 450), killed its men, sent the women to Ravensbrück concentration camp, and gassed the children—81 of them—in a concentration camp.

MONTE SOLE, ITALY After Italian partisans attacked German units, SS elements struck a series of villages on Monte Sole, rounding up the inhabitants and killing them, some by burning them to death in locked barns. The death toll exceeded 1,800.

ORADOUR-SUR-GLANE, FRANCE (JUNE 1944) After attacks by local partisans, troops of the second SS Division ("Das Reich") separated the men of the village from the women and children and shot the men. The SS locked the women and children in the local church, which they set afire by throwing live grenades in the windows. In all, the SS murdered 642 civilians, more than two-thirds of whom were women and children.

PUTTEN, HOLLAND (SEPTEMBER 1944) The Dutch resistance took a German lieutenant hostage near Putten village. Although the group released him, the local German commander transported 589 men to work as slave labor in Germany. Forty-nine survived the war.

ROME, ITALY (MARCH 1944) On a Roman street, a bomb killed or wounded almost 90 SS police, prompting Hitler to order revenge killings. The Germans trucked more than 300 civilians to the Ardeantine Caves and killed them all.

SAULX VALLEY, FRANCE (AUGUST 1944) After local partisans, led by British members of the Special Air Service, ambushed a German staff car, SS units rounded up civilians in four Saulx Valley towns, murdered 36 local men, burned most houses, and forced the women to watch the destruction.

Allegations of Allied Atrocities

Although Axis atrocities are well documented, the Western Allies also are accused of deliberate mass murder. In *Other Losses: An Investigation into the Mass Deaths of German Prisoners at the Hands of the French and Americans After World War II*, the Canadian author James Bacque accuses General Dwight Eisenhower of complicity in the starvation deaths of about a million German prisoners just after the end of the European war. Bacque's thesis is that Eisenhower deliberately withheld food from POWs, even though food was available.

The respected historian Stephen E. Ambrose has roundly rejected Bacque's allegations, con-

---

CHARLES STOCKELL, U.S. ARMY

Taking Revenge

We had a young private, a sweet-natured nineteen-year-old kid. However, he had had two brothers killed in Normandy, and it had turned the kid into a fiend where Germans were concerned; he killed every one he could, including any prisoner. It had become a court-martial offense to send a prisoner back with Junior.

The battalion CO [commanding officer] and I were standing on the step in front of the headquarters in Odenwald when Junior was given a note to deliver to one of the companies. Junior trotted off down the street. A German who had been hiding in one of the houses for seventy-two hours appeared at the front gate, bowing, smiling, hands on his head. "Kamerad! Kamerad!" Junior never broke his stride but pulled his pistol and shot the man in the face as he jogged past. The battalion commanding officer swore and dashed his helmet to the ground; Junior had struck again.

—Eisenhower Center for American Studies Archives

cluding that "when scholars do the necessary research, they will find Mr. Bacque's work to be worse than worthless. . . . He reaches conclusions and makes charges that are demonstrably absurd." Ambrose concluded that Eisenhower made the conscious decision to feed the POWs at the same level as the German civilian population, about 1,550 calories a day. To do so, on orders from the Joint Chiefs of Staff, he changed the classification of the prisoners from POW to "DEF"—"disarmed enemy forces"—because according to the Geneva Convention, POWs must be fed the same ration as the victorious forces.

The British took the same necessary step. In fact, at war's end, Europe was desperately short of food, and the amount of food that German prisoners received approximated the daily ration in civilian Germany and in Paris. It was only slightly lower than British rations at the time

and substantially higher than those in contemporary Vienna or in the Soviet Union generally. At the same time, occupation forces in Germany were trying to feed not only the civilian population but also millions of displaced people, as well as to stockpile food against the coming winter. As Eisenhower told the Combined Chiefs of Staff in April, 1945: "Unless immediate steps are taken to develop to the fullest extent possible the food resources in order to provide the minimum wants of the German population, widespread chaos, starvation and disease is inevitable during the coming winter."

While the Allies' treatment of POWs might not have been entirely clean, the overall death rate among German POWs, as estimated by the Army Center for Military History, was about 1 percent, and a German army historian has estimated that prisoner deaths from all causes could

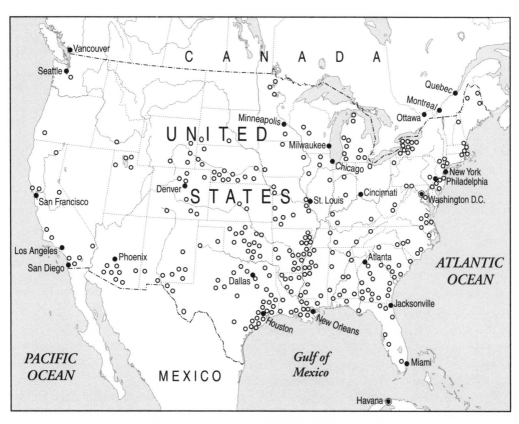

POW CAMPS IN THE UNITED STATES, 1944

POW CAMPS IN GERMANY, 1939–45

not have exceeded 56,000, nothing even approaching the figures of 800,000 to a million that Bacque claims. Even in the worst of the overcrowded transient camps, the Rheinwiesen-lager, the death rate—as estimated by another German historian—was between 0.6 percent and 0.8 percent.

Ambrose suggests that the "losses" that Bacque attributes to death from starvation were nothing more sinister than transfers to other zones and releases of Volkssturm militia, men as old as 80—many of them veterans of World War I—and boys 16 or younger. These people were simply sent home and removed from the camp rolls as "other losses."

Prisoners of War

Whether a prisoner would survive the war depended largely upon where he fought and by whom he was captured. The death rate for

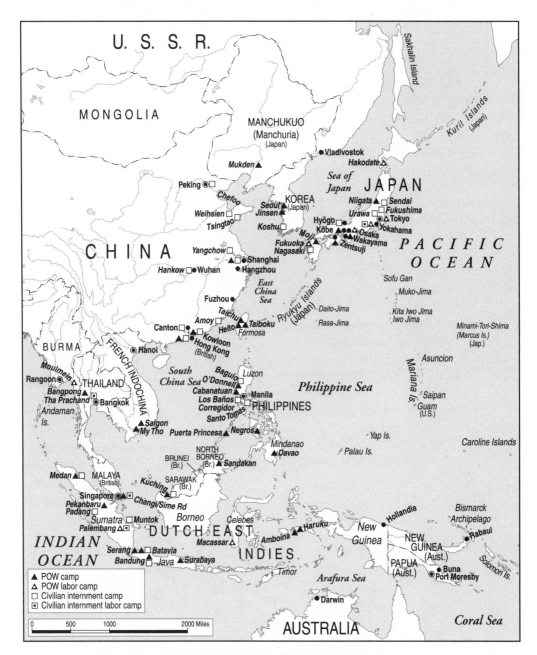

POW CAMPS IN THE PACIFIC, 1941–45

Allied prisoners in Japanese hands was approximately 27 percent. In sharp contrast, only about 4 percent of POWs held by the Germans or Italians died in captivity. However, all POWs found that hunger, isolation, boredom, and disease were common companions. The thousands of soldiers, sailors, and airmen who endured the harsh prisoner-of-war camps in both Europe and Asia were forever changed by the experience. Japanese military personnel often chose to fight to the death or commit suicide rather than be captured. Many German prisoners of the Soviet Union died in captivity. Thousands were held for several years after the end of hostilities and were repatriated to Germany in the 1950s. However, thousands of German and Italian soldiers that had been taken prisoner during the war and were held in prison camps in Europe, as well as throughout the United States and Canada, received humane treatment and were allowed to work and exercise regularly. After the war, some of these Axis POWs became citizens of the nations that had once imprisoned them.

JAPANESE PRISON CAMP FATALITIES

Most likely the worst offender, Japan was responsible for the deaths of approximately 12,000 POWs during the construction of the Burma-Siam railway (an ordeal that was depicted in the celebrated film *Bridge on the River Kwai*). Overwork, disease, and exhaustion killed many, but there and elsewhere deliberate murder and torture took thousands of other lives. Sadistic Japanese and Korean guards beat and tormented prisoners for little or no reason: they would bind prisoners with barbed wire and pump them full of water, for example,

then jump on their distended bellies. They suspended other prisoners by their thumbs or wrists in the sun for hours or days or forced them to kneel on sharp-edged bamboo while holding heavy stones. Prisoners—including women—were burned with cigarettes or candles, hot oil, or water; guards jerked out their fingernails or subjected them to electric shocks.

The following table shows the numbers of prisoners and the death rates by country of those held in Japanese POW camps.

	Western Prisoners of War	Number Deceased	Death Rate (%)
United States	21,500	7,100	33
Great Britain	50,000	12,400	25
Australia	21,700	7,400	34
Holland	37,000	8,500	23
Canada	1,700	270	16

(Numbers are rounded off)

Heinrich Himmler, leader of the ruthless Nazi SS, inspects a POW camp in the Soviet Union during the early days of the war on the Eastern Front. Himmler was captured by the British in 1945 but committed suicide before he could be tried for war crimes.

Allied forces torpedoed or bombed a number of Japanese prison ships that were carrying Allied prisoners to the home islands of Japan. The Allies had no way of knowing that the cargoes of these vessels were their captive countrymen. The table below lists the details of these tragedies.

Ship Name	Date Sunk	POWs on Board	POW Deaths*
Montevideo Maru	July 1, 1942	1,000	1,000
Asaka Maru	August 13, 1942	700	50
Lisbon Maru	October 2, 1942	1,800	840
Suez Maru	November 29, 1943	1,100	500
Tango Maru	February 25, 1944	3,500	3,000
Tomohoku Maru	June 24, 1944	750	550
Harukiku Maru	June 26, 1944	Unknown	180
Kachidoki Maru	September 5, 1944	900	400
Rokyo Maru	September 5, 1944	1,300	1,200
Shinyo Maru	September 7, 1944	750	700
Junyo Maru	September 18, 1944	6,500	5,600
Fuku Maru	September 21, 1944	1,300	1,200
Unknown	September 22, 1944	1,000	900
Arisan Maru	October 24, 1944	1,800	1,800
Unknown	October 25, 1944	1,800	1,800
Oryoko Maru	December 15, 1944	1,600	1,100

*Numbers of fatalities are rounded off to nearest 50 and do not include POWs murdered or dead from other causes while at sea.

CHAPTER 13

Aftermath

W orld War II was the most cataclysmic event in human history. Previous wars, even the
somewhat misnamed World War I (which was fought in Europe), were confined to specific regions. But the period from September 1939 to August 1945 saw war encompass
the globe—from Europe, to North Africa, to Asia, and to the Pacific. The human suffering and lost
lives reached astronomical proportions. The Soviet Union paid the highest cost—about 16 million
civilians and 12 million military personnel died during the conflict. Other nations on both sides suffered extremely high losses, particularly Germany, China, and Japan.

The war also cost many nations their prewar eminence. Before 1939, Great Britain, France, Germany, and Italy were the most influential nations in the world, but when the war ended, Germany,
Italy, and France were in shambles, and Great Britain was nearly bankrupt and its colonies were pressing for independence. The only nation that emerged more powerful from the war was the United
States, which became the preeminent world power in possession of the most destructive weapons ever
seen—or even imagined.

The Soviet Union, although devastated by the war, remained a powerful nation. Within four
years of the end of the conflict, it too, like the United States, was producing nuclear weapons and
was in a position to challenge the Americans for postwar dominance. The Soviets maneuvered into a

position of influence—or of outright control—over a number of countries in both Eastern Europe and Asia, precipitating a philosophical struggle for world domination—the cold war—that would continue into the final decade of the 20th century, when the Soviet system collapsed.

Allied prisoners of war cheer their liberators in August 1945. The captives had been held at a former convent in Saitama Prefecture, 30 miles north of Tokyo.

World War II created millions of refugees. An estimated 5.9 million Jews had been murdered by the Nazis and millions of others were uprooted, and at the end of the war, surviving European Jews, many of whom had previously been lukewarm to the Zionist movement, set their sights on the establishment of a national homeland in Palestine, a dream that came to fruition with the creation of the state of Israel in 1948. The establishment of a Jewish state also ushered in a seemingly interminable conflict between Israel and its Arab neighbors. Another great movement of refugees occurred when millions of Germans fled

JAMES PEMBERTON, 103RD INFANTRY DIVISION

At the End of the War

The night of May 8, 1945, I was looking down from our cabin on the mountain at the valley. It was black. And then the lights in Innsbruck went on. If you have not lived in darkness for months, shielding even a match light deep in a foxhole, you can't imagine the feeling. I said to myself, "The war is really over." I hadn't really grasped it till the city lit up.

We goofed around, relaxing in Innsbruck. Then, toward the end of June, they broke up the 103rd into other divisions. I was sent to the 9th Infantry Division. We were in the hills of Austria. Once in a while we'd be rousted out in the middle of the night to surround a village and then search it. For what, I never knew, but I guess SS men and weapons. There were a few incidents, but all in all [it was] pretty peaceful. Boredom was our enemy. No training, no balls, no bats, no basketballs, and a hell of a lot to eat. Someone really screwed things up. Most of the time we slept. It's very hard, believe it or not, to do nothing.

Rumors flew! Back to the States, thirty-day furlough, and the South Pacific. No, we weren't going home but were being shipped by rail directly across Russia to China and then to invade Japan.

The bomb was dropped in early August, and we were in heaven. Now the war was really over, and we started figuring how soon we'd be home. I was in good shape, but I knew it would probably be after the first of the year. So I wasn't unhappy to be sent with another guy to escort Polish displaced persons back to Krakow, Poland. We had two box cars—one for us and the other for about forty DPs. They were a happy, confident lot, going back after four to five years as German slave labor.

—Eisenhower Center for American Studies Archives

from Eastern Europe as the Red Army swept to victory. These Germans settled largely in West Germany.

A major legacy of World War II was political upheaval and revolution. Often led by Marxists and influenced and supported by the Soviet Union, Communists began struggles to gain control of their national governments. In Eastern Europe, countries fell into the Soviet sphere of influence and became one-party states. In Asia, a titanic struggle was waged between the Chinese Nationalist government of Chiang Kai-shek and the Communists under Mao Tse-tung. With the Japanese defeated, the Communists rose against the Nationalists and resumed a civil war that the Communists would ultimately win. The victory of the Chinese Communists represented a huge geopolitical shift in the politics of Asia, one that is still felt to this day.

The political aftermath of World War II changed the face of Europe and the shape of international relations, giving rise to the influence of NATO, the United Nations, and the Warsaw Pact. While the United Nations was created to prevent future wars, NATO and the Warsaw Pact were essentially military alliances brought about by conflicting Western and Soviet-style Communist philosophies.

The Wages of War

The wages of war were counted in the overwhelming loss of human life, but also in the physical destruction wrought on property across the continent; by the untold millions of refugees and displaced persons who wandered the roads of Europe either seeking their way home or looking for a new home; and by the political and economic turmoil that was the legacy of a conflict that would last for decades to come.

DEATH TOLL

The actual numbers of deaths, both military and civilian, can only be estimated. Nevertheless, World War II was the most terrible war in human history—and it was the first war in which the death toll among civilians exceeded military losses.

MILITARY DEATHS   The military forces of the Soviet Union suffered the greatest losses, in part because of the military tactics used by the Soviet generals but also because of the special ferocity of

Seated in the back of a staff car (left to right), President Harry S Truman, Secretary of State James Byrnes, and Fleet Admiral William Leahy drive past the ruins of Hitler's chancellery in Berlin prior to the beginning of the Potsdam Conference.

the war on the Eastern Front. About 12 million Soviet troops died in the war, 7.5 million in combat. Germany lost an estimated 3.25 million military personnel, with the greatest losses suffered on the Eastern Front. In Asia, the greatest losses were suffered by Japan, which lost 1.6 million military personnel, and China, whose military losses were estimated at 1.3 million. The United States, by comparison, lost 293,000 military personnel to combat and another 106,000 to other causes in all

COMBAT DEATHS

The table that follows shows the number of combat deaths suffered by the major warring nations compared to the populations of each country in 1940. While the statistics for some countries are precise, others are estimates. Some include noncombat deaths from illness and accident, whereas others do not. The U.S. figures are for combat losses only; 115,185 more American men and women died of other causes.

Country	Combat Deaths	Deaths per Million (based on 1940 population)	Percentage of Population Killed (1940 population)
Australia	27,073 =	2,143.5	0.21
Canada	42,042 =	1,973.8	0.2
China	1,319,958 =	3,880.5	0.39
France	210,000 (estimated)	5,122	0.51
Germany	1,810,061 + 1,902,704 MIA* and presumed dead = 3,712,865	60,866	6.09
India	24,338	76	.01
Italy	300,000 + (estimated)	6,865	0.69
Japan	1.6 million (estimated)	21,877.8	2.19
New Zealand	11,671	7,294.4	2.19
Poland	123,000 (estimated)	3,773	0.38
Soviet Union	8.7 million (some estimates go as high as 12 million)	44,574.8	4.46
United Kingdom	264,443	4747.6	0.47
United States	293,131	2218.9	0.22

*MIA = missing in action.
Dear, I.C.B., and Foot, M.R.D. (eds) *Oxford Companion to World War II* (Oxford: Oxford University Press, 1995).

In a captured German photograph, dead American soldiers lie stripped of shoes and equipment at a Belgian crossroads in December 1944. Hitler's last, desperate gamble for victory in the West, the Battle of the Bulge ended in catastrophic losses for Germany.

deaths. Roughly 3.6 million German civilians died in the war, but their country—along with the Soviet Union—caused the deaths of an estimated 6 million Poles and 1.4 million Yugoslavs. In addition, approximately 5.9 million European Jews were murdered by the Nazis in camps and by firing squads. In Japan, as many as 200,000 people were killed in the atomic bomb attacks.

CIVILIAN CASUALTIES

Exact numbers of wounded of both military and civilian are extremely difficult to determine for several reasons—lack of adequate record keeping, loss of records, and specific circumstances on the battlefield or in the countries as territory rapidly changed hands.

theaters. British combat losses—including troops from Australia and Canada—were 326,000. Although the majority of military deaths were the direct result of combat, substantial numbers died from other causes, including accident, illness, and starvation, particularly in POW camps.

CIVILIAN DEATHS The civilian death toll in World War II exceeded that among military personnel. Previous wars had seen conflict confined to literal battle "fields," but World War II saw much of the world as one huge battlefield on which millions found themselves unwilling participants. The use of aerial and artillery attack dramatically increased civilian casualties, as the architects of air raids on both sides turned their attention toward the destruction of enemy cities. Soviet civilians suffered the most: about 16 million died in the war. China was second, with about 10 million civilian

Country	Civilians Killed
Australia	Included in UK
Canada	Included in UK
China	13 million +
France	470,000
Germany	3,600,000
Italy	100,000
Japan	400,000
New Zealand	Included in UK
Poland	6 million
United Kingdom	62,000
United States	Unknown
USSR	16 million

Dear, I.C.B., and Foot, M.R.D. (eds.), *Oxford Companion to World War II* (Oxford: Oxford University Press, 1995).

WARTIME POPULATION

The table that follows shows in millions the populations of the principal nations involved in the war, beginning in 1939 and continuing through the war years. These figures can be considered only as estimates, as the sources do not agree. Statistics for Germany after 1944 are not available.

Nation	1939	1940	1941	1942	1943	1944	1945
Australia		7.0		7.1			7.58
Canada			11.5	11.8			12.5
China		537					542
France	40.0	39.0	37.8	37.7	37.08	36.5	38.0
Germany	80.6					89.9	
Greece		8.8					
India		329	318.7				343.8
Italy		43.78					
Japan		71.93					71.98
Netherlands	8.7	8.8	8.9	9.0	9.07	9.1	9.2
Poland	34.7	24.88					24.85
United Kingdom	47						
United States	130.8	131.9	133.4	134.67	134.69	134.0	133.3
USSR		170.5					

DESTRUCTION

With the deployment of the most powerful weapons yet developed, it was inevitable that cities, towns, and villages would suffer major damage; some were obliterated. The Soviet city of Stalingrad (now Volgograd) was turned into rubble during the fierce fighting that raged there in the winter of 1942–43. The city of Leningrad, under German siege for more than two years, was pounded by artillery shells for much of that time. Berlin, the capital city of Germany, was reduced to ruins as it became the scene of bitter house-to-house fighting in the war's final days. Although Berlin had been subjected to a massive Allied bombing campaign for more than a year, the city continued to function until it fell under attack by Soviet ground forces. Other cities in Germany were also decimated. Cities across

Britain were pounded by German bombers, which inflicted heavy damage to centuries-old buildings. Priceless artifacts and historic buildings all over Europe suffered major damage, and some were destroyed.

No ground fighting took place in Japan, but Tokyo, the capital, was the target of a massive firebombing campaign that destroyed more than 60 percent of the city. Other Japanese industrial cities suffered major damage from firebombing attacks in the final months of the war. In Hiroshima and Nagasaki, targets for the only nuclear weapons ever used in combat, destruction was widespread. Hiroshima had more than 60 percent of the city's structures destroyed. Nagasaki was less affected by the weapon's power because of the topography, which dispersed the bomb's force and reduced the destruction and loss of life, but its city also lay in rubble and thousands of people were killed.

DISPLACED PERSONS

An accurate accounting of people displaced by the war will never be possible. The best estimates place the number well into the millions. Some authorities have said that as many as 30 million were displaced. While the encroachment of the battlefield drove hundreds of thousands from their homes, deliberate actions by individual nations, particularly Germany and the Soviet Union, created the vast majority of refugees. Many refugees moved willingly in order to escape the Germans or, in the last months of the war, to avoid the advancing Soviet forces in Eastern Europe. Hundreds of thousands of people, brought to Germany from other countries to work in fields and factories as slave laborers, also became refugees and walked the roads of Europe trying to find their way home.

At the end of the war, the newly created United Nations set up the UN Relief and Rehabilitation Administration to resettle refugees in areas outside the Soviet Union. The Soviets kept as laborers the refugees in areas under their control and refused to allow them to leave. Eventu-

ally, many refugees were reunited with their families, while some found citizenship in other countries. Many former Nazis left Europe and migrated to areas that housed their sympathizers, particularly in South America. Other European refugees also chose to resettle in South American countries. Many refugees from Eastern Europe, especially Germans from East Prussia and those portions of Germany given to Poland in 1945, were expelled by the Soviets and ended up in West Germany.

Millions of refugees were victims of the deportation policies of occupying countries, especially in the East. The deportation of Jews to ghettos and death camps had been a policy of the Nazis immediately before and during the early years of the war. In November 1938, about 30,000 German Jews with Polish passports were dumped in the no-man's-land along the German-Polish border. Thousands of Poles and Polish Jews were deported from territory that was annexed by Germany; most were imprisoned and executed. Even as the Nazis were staging mass deportations (and importing slave laborers), the Soviets were conducting their own policies of mass upheaval in territories they occupied, often trying people considered

With troops of the American 101st Airborne Division holding their town during the Battle of the Bulge, residents of Bastogne, Belgium, evacuate with a few of their possessions.

PILLAGE, RAPE, AND REPRISALS

Japanese troops fighting in China were notorious for their ill treatment of civilians, particularly during the occupation of the city of Nanking, where some 250,000 civilians were murdered and rape was widespread. Young women in captured countries (Korea, for example) were placed in brothels to service Japanese soldiers. Americans and Western Europeans considered themselves to be civilized, yet many Allied soldiers felt that they had a right to help themselves to cameras, weapons, clocks, artwork, and other valuables they found as they made their way across Germany. They looted millions of dollars' worth of family treasures and heirlooms from German homes (while occupying German forces had looted millions more from French, Belgian, Polish, Norwegian, and other European homes at the beginning of the war).

Although some British and American troops did commit rape, attitudes, combined with strict military discipline, kept the number of incidents far lower than it could have been in Western Europe. Not so with Soviet troops. Years of Communist purges had stripped the Soviet military of its leadership, and the Soviet forces were filled with men with few scruples and whose hatred was spurred by what the Germans had done in Russia. Soviet soldiers repeatedly raped hundreds of thousands of German women and girls, then tossed many aside and left them to die. As often as not, the Soviets would slit the woman's throat or shoot her. Rape was a problem while the invading army entered and conquered enemy territory. Once the enemy was under occupation, the incidents of rape declined.

Reprisals against those who had collaborated with the Germans were common in the weeks following the war. Concentration camp guards were often murdered by their former victims, even though the policy of the American military

was opposed to vigilante justice. In France—where a significant percentage of the population had collaborated with the Nazis and even assisted in the deportation of French Jews to the death camps—reprisals were brutal and often humiliating. Young women who had dated or had relationships with German troops in France were dragged into public squares, where they were beaten and had their hair shaved off their heads. Others were not so lucky, being beaten to death or shot by enraged mobs.

Eventually, these kinds of reprisals ceased, and punishment shifted into a judicial mode. All over Europe, military tribunals meted out justice to Nazis and collaborators. These trials went on for years. The Nuremberg proceedings, the most famous of which occurred in 1945–46 with the trial of the top Nazi leaders, continued for years as Nazis from all walks of life were tried and punished (see Chapter 12, "Man's Inhumanity").

POLITICAL TURMOIL

The political turmoil unleashed at the end of World War II shaped international relations for the remainder of the 20th century. In Europe, the continent became divided by the "Iron Curtain," which separated the countries of the East, under Soviet domination, from those in the West, under the influence of the United States. The former Axis countries of Italy and the newly formed West Germany, while under Allied occupation, were placed on a path toward democratic government. They soon recovered economically as well, and by the 1950s, Italy and West Germany were well on their way to becoming stable, representative democracies. Democratic impulses in the East, however, were stifled by the one-party governments of all pro-Soviet countries. Turmoil continued for years against the backdrop of U.S.-Soviet rivalry, in Europe as well as elsewhere in the world.

In Asia, Japan was placed under the tight control of U.S. military occupation, during which time the United States wrote a constitution for Japan and encouraged the beginnings of genuine democratic reform. Korea remained divided, however, and was a flashpoint of conflict that erupted into war (the Korean War) in 1950. Indochina, however, much of which was under French colonial occupation, broke out almost immediately into civil conflict and war that went on for another 30 years and ultimately involved the United States. The political turmoil of the postwar years was not limited to Europe and Asia. Throughout Africa, peoples under colonial occupation pressed for independence, and the decades of the 1950s and 1960s saw an unprecedented number of countries gain their independence from their Belgian, French, and British colonial rulers. The political legacy of World War II was accelerated change, on all continents, as peoples struggled to achieve national independence, and for those in areas destroyed by the conflict, to achieve a return of prosperity and civic stability.

War Crimes Trials

At the Moscow Conference in 1943, U.S. President Franklin Roosevelt, British Prime Minister Winston Churchill, and Soviet Premier Josef Stalin made clear their determination to punish the principal leaders of the German Nazi Party. When the war ended and these Nazi leaders fell into Allied hands, the United States led an effort pressing for full-scale legal proceedings against them. The British cabinet was largely opposed to the idea, adopting the view of the Lord Chancellor of England, Lord Simon, that the fate of the German leadership should be a "political, not a judicial" question. Not until May 1945 did the American position finally prevail, and war crimes trials were scheduled to be held in Nuremberg, Germany.

Indictments were handed up in October 1945 against 24 former Nazi officials (the whereabouts of one—Martin Bormann, Hitler's private secretary—was unknown; he was tried and convicted in absentia). Each of the accused was tried under at least two of four types of crimes that had been devised. Count 1 covered "a common plan or conspiracy," count 2 was for "crimes against peace," count 3 was for "war crimes," and count 4 was for "crimes against humanity." These are crimes committed against the human race. As the trials progressed, it became apparent that convicting anyone under the first two counts would be difficult, particularly because some allegations involved actions that the Allies had themselves used against the German population. Some of the

---

KINGSBURY SMITH, AMERICAN PRESS REPRESENTATIVE

Witnessing the Execution of Ernst Kaltenbrunner

He entered the execution chamber at 1:36 A.M., wearing a sweater beneath his blue double-breasted coat. With his lean haggard face furrowed by old dueling scars, this terrible successor to Reinhard Heydrich had a frightening look as he glanced around the room.

He wet his lips apparently in nervousness as he turned to mount the gallows, but he walked steadily. He answered his name in a calm, low voice. When he turned around on the gallows platform he first faced a United States Army Roman Catholic chaplain wearing a Franciscan habit. When Kaltenbrunner was invited to make a last statement, he said, "I have loved my German people and my fatherland with a warm heart. I have done my duty by the laws of my people and I am sorry my people were led this time by men who were not soldiers and that crimes were committed of which I had no knowledge."

—From *It Happened in 1946*, 1947, as published in *A Mammoth Book of Eyewitness World War II*, ed. Jon E. Lewis, (New York: Carroll & Graf, 2002).

first atrocities attributed to the Germans turned out to have been committed by Soviet troops in areas of Poland under Soviet control before Germany and the Soviet Union went to war.

Twelve of the accused were sentenced to death by hanging, three received life imprisonment, four received prison terms ranging from 10 to 20 years, and three were acquitted. Hermann Göring, the commander of the German Luftwaffe and the senior Nazi to fall into Allied hands, committed suicide a few hours before his scheduled execution. Ten others were hanged in October 1946. (See Chapter 12, "Man's Inhumanity.")

War crimes trials were also held in Tokyo and other locations in the East. As was the case with the Nuremberg trials, the validity of the charges came under question, and some critics believed that General Douglas MacArthur, the U.S. military governor of Japan, was carrying out a personal vendetta against certain Japanese generals. Definite irregularities occurred that might have led to overturned verdicts in a U.S. court of law. The Soviet judge who sat on the court could not speak or understand English or Japanese, and one American judge was a survivor of the Bataan Death March and could hardly be impartial. The main charge was "conspiracy to commit war," with seven specific charges involving "waging war" against specific nations. Counts 54 and 55 were "ordering, authorizing or permitting atrocities" and "disregard of duty to secure observance of and prevent breaches of Laws of War." The emperor was exempted from indictment even though Japan had gone to war in his name and with his approval. Seven Japanese military and civilian leaders—including General and former Prime Minister Hideki Tojo, who had approved the attack on Pearl Harbor—were hanged, 16 were sentenced to life in prison, and two were given the lesser sentences of seven and 20 years.

The war crimes trials in Germany and Japan have been criticized by some as having no legal, judicial basis. Many critics making this argument have stated that the Allies would have been better off simply executing the top German and Japanese leaders under military law instead of engaging in an elaborate legal charade. Those who supported the trials, however, believe that they were an important step in the establishment of internationally accepted standards of behavior, and that all future political leaders needed to know that they could be held accountable in an international forum for wartime behavior. Whatever their legality, narrowly defined, the trials were an unprecedented public airing of German and Japanese policies and conduct. In addition, the Axis leaders tried and punished were given a kind of due process their victims never enjoyed.

The Emotional Toll

Unlike other emotionally draining human experiences, which often happen in an instant, war exposes participants to hours, days, weeks, months, and even years of one highly emotional and often terrorizing moment after another. Combat soldiers, sailors, and airmen may live in constant fear for their lives for days on end, and they are often exposed to the trauma of the death of a buddy as well as witnessing others being killed. It is little wonder that 37 percent of all U.S. ground combat troops were discharged from the service for psychiatric reasons. "Battle fatigue" was the World War II term for what had been known in World War I as "shell shock" and what Civil War soldiers referred to as "nostalgia." The symptoms in each case included a general lethargy from prolonged exposure to combat as well as fatigue, shortness of breath, palpitations, headache, excessive sweating, dizziness, insomnia, fainting, and an inability to concentrate. In the 1980s psychiatrists came up with a term for the condition—posttraumatic stress disorder (PTSD).

Men discharged from the service for psychological reasons were not the only veterans who experienced the symptoms later diagnosed as

Each of the major participants used millions of dollars from its national treasury, taxes imposed upon its citizenry, and money borrowed from worldwide financial institutions to finance the war. In the case of the United States, "cost" is probably a misnomer because a large share of the spending by other nations went to the United States to pay for war materiel purchased before the war or through the Lend-Lease program. Although European nations never repaid much of their war debts, the U.S. industry received payment from the U.S. government for its products, payments that kept factories running and put money in the pockets of wartime workers. This table shows the approximate costs of the war for each of the major nations involved:

Nation	Cost in Millions of 1945 U.S. Dollars
Australia	$ 10,036
Belgium	$ 6,324
Canada	$ 20,104
China	$ 49,072
France	$111,272
Germany	$212,336
India	$ 4,804
Italy	$ 21,072
Japan	$ 41,272

Nation	Cost in Millions of 1945 U.S. Dollars
Netherlands	$ 9,624
New Zealand	$ 2,560
Norway	$ 992
South Africa	$ 2,152
United Kingdom	Unknown
United States	$288,000
USSR	$ 93,012

Source: The American War Library,
http://members.aol.com/veterans/index.htm.

PROMINENT ÉMIGRÉS

As the power of the Nazis grew in Germany and nearby countries, many of the region's more prominent citizens emigrated to the United States or other countries. Some men and women were already famous, whereas others were parents of young children who would make their mark on the postwar world.

Name	Contribution and History
Albright, Madeline Korbel	Her family fled Czechoslovakia in 1937 and moved to the U.S. in 1949. She served on the U.S. National Security Council under President Jimmy Carter, and as secretary of state under President Bill Clinton.
Bettelheim, Bruno	An Austrian psychoanalyst, arrested by the Nazis and imprisoned at Buchenwald and Dachau, he emigrated to the United States upon release in 1939, and became an American citizen in 1944; taught psychology at the University of Chicago and authored several books.

Name	Contribution and History
Brzezinski, Zbigniew	His family fled Poland in 1938. He was U.S. national security adviser in the Carter administration in the 1970s.
Dietrich, Marlene	A famous German actress, she denounced the nationalism of post–World War I Germany and came to America before Hitler was in power, becoming an American citizen in 1939.
Einstein, Albert	A prominent physicist and active Zionist, he left Germany immediately after Hitler came to power, then emigrated to the United States.
Freud, Sigmund and Anna	Sigmund Freud, the father of psychoanalysis, fled Austria for Great Britain in 1938 and died the following year. His daughter, Anna, became a leader in the study of child psychology.
Kissinger, Henry Alfred	Born in Fürth, Germany, in 1923, he came to the United States with his family in 1938. He served in the U.S. Army, 1943–46, was a professor at Harvard, and served as foreign policy adviser to Presidents Kennedy, Johnson, and Nixon, and as secretary of state in the Nixon and Ford administrations.
Koppel, Ted	Koppel was born in England in 1940 after his parents fled Germany. He moved to the United States in 1953 and became a prominent TV newsman and commentator.
Lorre, Peter	A German actor, he moved to England when the Nazis came to power, then to Hollywood. Lorre returned to West Germany in 1951.
Mann, Thomas	A German writer who opposed Hitler, he was forced into exile in the early 1930s, then moved to the United States in 1938. In 1951, he moved to Switzerland.
Straus, Oscar	A Viennese composer, he fled Austria and emigrated to the United States to escape the Nazis in 1940, and became a U.S. citizen in 1948. He returned to Austria in 1949.
Toller, Ernst	Toller, a German playwright, fled the Nazis and moved to the United States. He committed suicide in 1939.
Werfel, Franz	The Austrian author, poet, dramatist, and playwright fled Austria for France in 1938, then moved to the United States in 1940.
Weyl, Hermann	A German mathematician and associate of Albert Einstein, he left Germany in 1933 and moved to the United States, where he became a faculty member at Princeton University.

PTSD. The Congressional Medal of Honor winner Audie Murphy (see Chapter 6, "Officers and Soldiers"), who fought from Sicily into the heart of Germany before he was felled by wounds, complained of insomnia for seven years—and could not sleep without a weapon beside his bed. But while many men had trouble coping with their wartime experiences, others—including men who had experienced heavy combat and who knew they had killed untold numbers of enemy troops and civilians—claimed no such problems. Retired U.S. Air Force Brigadier General Paul Tibbets, the man whose unit dropped the first atomic bombs, and who dropped the first one himself, told the author Bob Greene, "I have never lost a moment's sleep" over the experience.

In 1955, the National Academy of Sciences concluded that one-third of U.S. combat veterans suffered some emotional disorder. Most veterans kept their problems to themselves, if they experienced them at all. After the Vietnam War and the attention paid to veterans of that conflict, some World War II veterans began seeking treatment for their problems; by 1994 about 210,000 cases of posttraumatic stress disorder had been reported among their ranks.

Devastation

World War II was the most devastating event in human history, yet while much of Europe and parts of Asia were left in ruins, the postwar economic recovery of the participating nations showed that the damage was not nearly as extensive as had been feared. Even as the war continued, the United States commissioned the Strategic Bombing Survey to determine the extent of the damage done to German industry by the Allied bombing campaign; a similar study was conducted in Japan. The survey found that although the German economy had suffered major damage, it was far from totally destroyed—although it might have been had the war continued.

While buildings housing an industrial complex may have been damaged, the heavy machinery and machine tools often suffered only superficial damage and were easily repaired. Despite incessant bombing from January 1, 1943, until the end of the war, production in Germany actually continued to increase right up to the closing weeks of the war in Europe. Once the Allies had defeated Germany, the victorious

nations collected machine tools, precision equipment, and other production materials—as well as German engineers and scientists—for use in their own national industries. This was particularly true in the areas under Soviet domination.

But the damage to civilian property was significant. Although Allied airpower advocates had maintained that U.S. bomber crews were capable of "pickle barrel accuracy," the realities of combat meant that both the British and U.S. bomber commands carried out what was essentially area bombing. The U.S. Army Air Forces established a policy that all bombs falling within a 2,000-foot circle around the designated target were considered on target, yet the U.S. Strategic Bombing Survey determined that only 20 percent of all bombs dropped by U.S. bombers fell within the target area. The 80 percent that fell wide often destroyed civilian homes, schools, hospitals, and other nonmilitary structures. After suffering heavy losses during daylight attacks early in the war (the Germans intentionally dumped their bombs over cities and did not aim for specific targets), the British turned to night bombing of cities, causing wider destruction than the American daylight bombers did.

According to the Strategic Bombing Survey, Allied air attacks destroyed about 485,000 dwellings in Germany, leaving more than 7.5 million people homeless. The survey estimated that 305,000 civilians were killed, which was more than the official German figure of 250,253 civilians killed by air attack.

Destruction in Japan was massive as the U.S. Army Air Forces adopted the British tactic of night area bombing of Japanese cities. Using incendiary bombs designed to start massive firestorms among the flimsily constructed (wood and paper) Japanese buildings, the B-29 bombing campaign was aimed at destroying cottage industries all over Japan. The first firebombing attack on Tokyo burned 15 square miles of the city to the ground. Similar attacks on Nagoya, Osaka, and Kobe, as well as a second attack on Tokyo, did similar damage. An estimated 40 percent of Japan's built-up cities were destroyed by the air attacks, and 330,000 Japanese civilians were killed. The atomic bomb attacks on Hiroshima and Nagasaki destroyed 50 percent of the two cities and killed some 100,000 people (included in the previous figure).

The war devastated some parts of other countries, particularly in areas that saw bitter fighting. Heavy artillery attacks by both sides killed more than 100,000 Filipino civilians during the battle for Manila (1945) as the Allies were liberating the Philippines. The most severe destruction from ground fighting undoubtedly occurred on the Eastern Front, although information from that theater is limited. The Russian cities of Leningrad, Stalingrad, and Kursk all saw major battles that caused massive destruction and severe loss of life. Small towns and villages in Italy and Western Europe were often caught between the armies and received major damage from shelling and bombs.

> What is Europe now? A rubble heap, a charnel house, a breeding ground of pestilence and hate.
> —Winston Churchill, 1947

An obliterated oil refinery in the Tokyo area illustrates the degree of destruction wrought by American B-29 bombers on major Japanese cities in the final months of World War II.

The Postwar World

The war brought devastation and suffering to much of the European continent and led to the loss of colonies by the previously powerful Great Britain and France. Political and philosophical differences caused a major rift in the precarious alliance between the Western nations on the one hand and the Soviet Union on the other. No sooner had the "hot" war ended than the cold war began. Civil war threatened some countries in Europe, where local Communist parties attempted to achieve power and align their nations on the side of the Soviet Union. In Asia, civil conflicts and wars of liberation erupted, threatening old colonial governments and, as in Europe, injecting the influence of communism into the struggles.

In the United States returning veterans found themselves in a nation that was turning its industrial might from war to peacetime production. And the returning veterans and their new wives turned out babies—the generation that would be called the "baby boomers"—almost as if they were being put together on a wartime assembly line.

THE NEW WORLD ORDER

After 1945 the world was totally different from what it had been in 1939; mid-century saw the balance of power shift westward across the Atlantic Ocean to a newly internationalist United States. Europe found itself divided along lines that were drawn up at wartime conferences in which most of the affected nations did not participate. Political division also took place in Asia, although not immediately after the war. Another consequence of the war was the decline of European colonialism. Empires were just too costly to maintain, and even though political leaders in Great Britain and France tried to hold on to their colonial possessions, the move toward independence in Africa and Asia was inevitable and irreversible.

The postwar world also brought changes and a new world order. Some of the most significant changes are described below.

Africa

Africa had been heavily colonized in the 19th century, with most of the major European powers taking a piece of the "Dark Continent." As the war changed the shape of Europe, it also affected the European colonies in Africa. British forces gained ground against the Italians early in the war, then liberated Ethiopia—which Italy had invaded in 1936—and drove Italian troops out of Libya.

When the war ended, local inhabitants of European colonies began pressing for independence. France granted independence to Morocco in 1956, and Belgium freed its colony in the Congo in 1960. Two years later, France granted independence to Algeria after a bitter war against Algerian guerrillas. Other European countries gave up their claims to African colonies. Independence did not necessarily bring peace and democracy to every country in Africa. In fact, much of Africa remained in political turmoil through the end of the 20th century. But the war did serve as a catalyst that brought to an end colonialism across the continent.

Balkans

With the exception of Greece, the Balkans region of southeastern Europe was occupied by Soviet troops at the end of the war and fell under Soviet domination. The Balkans were a patchwork of different ethnic groups; and during the conflict, various groups had supported different sides. The Germans set up a puppet regime in Croatia, while the Serbs formed guerrilla groups to fight the Germans. One of these groups was also aligned with the Soviets. General Draza Mihajlovic, a Serb, commanded an anti-German group called the Chetniks, and Josip Broz Tito, a Croatian Communist, led an anti-German group aligned with the USSR. The Yugoslav government-in-exile recognized Mihajlovic as the national commander of the Resistance. In 1942, Tito's partisans won control of much of Bosnia, established a provisional government known as the Council for National Liberation, and organized a partisan army of more than 100,000 troops. In 1943, British and U.S. military missions joined with Tito's partisans. Tito refused to accept the authority of the national Yugoslavian government and established his own parliament.

British negotiators engineered a settlement between the two factions that placed Tito in charge of the Yugoslavian military—he became Marshal Tito—replacing General Mihajlovic. In the final months of the war, conferences in Moscow involving the British, the Soviets, and the two Yugoslavian factions led to a merger of the competing governments. In March 1945, a new government was formed with Marshal Tito as premier. In August the monarchy was abolished, and the Yugoslavian King Peter remained in exile.

Marshal Tito began a campaign to take complete control of Yugoslavia as he nationalized the economy, restricted the churches, especially the Roman Catholic Church, which in his view had collaborated with the Nazis in Croatia, censored newspapers, and liquidated his political enemies. Tito ordered the capture and arrest of Mihajlovic. Along with eight other Chetnik leaders, Mihajlovic was tried for collaboration and treason and executed. Although a Communist, Tito refused to be subordinate to Moscow and showed independence as he joined with the United Nations in supporting an arms embargo against North Korea and China in the early 1950s. Yugoslavia also engaged in trade with the West. Before Tito's death in 1980, political factions reemerged in the region as the Communist Party attempted to purge Croats from leadership roles. With Tito's death, however, the federation he had presided over disintegrated and the region was plunged into genocidal civil war. From Tito's Yugoslavia the independent nations of Slovenia, Croatia, Serbia and Montenegro, Bosnia and Herzegovina, and Macedonia emerged, but not before fratricidal wars took more than a million lives across the Balkans throughout the 1990s.

Bamboo Curtain

A term sometimes applied to the borders of the Asian Communist nations—China, North Vietnam, North Korea—and non-Communist Asia; it is the Asian version of Europe's Iron Curtain.

China

At the Yalta Conference in February 1945, U.S. President Franklin Roosevelt, British Prime Minister Winston Churchill, and Soviet Premier Josef Stalin made decisions that would determine the future of China. Chiang Kai-shek, the Nationalist Chinese president, was not present, nor had he been informed of the meeting. In a secret move designed to encourage Stalin to declare war against Japan, Roosevelt promised the Soviets that they could reoccupy Manchuria and other territories in the Far East that had been under Russian control before the Russo-Japanese War of 1904–5.

Civil war was already brewing in China, although the Communist leader Mao Tse-tung had agreed to join with the Kuomintang (Nationalists) under Chiang Kai-shek to fight the Japanese. As soon as it became clear that the Allies would win, the Communists resumed their revolutionary war against the Nationalist government. In early August 1945, the Soviets invaded Manchuria and captured an entire Japanese army and its equipment virtually intact, then promptly turned it over to Mao's Chinese Communist forces. The civil war continued in China until 1949, when the Nationalists retreated across the Formosa Strait to the island of Formosa (now Taiwan) and Mao's Communists took control of the mainland.

In 1950, China invaded Tibet, then assisted the North Koreans in their war against United Nations forces. China was a major supporter of the Viet Minh revolution against the French in Indochina and assisted the North Vietnamese in their war against the United States. With the collapse of the Soviet Union in 1991, China became the only remaining major Communist power in the world, although with the end of U.S. involvement in the Vietnam War and the rapprochement policies of the Nixon administration and its successors, U.S.-Chinese relations entered a new and more constructive phase.

French Indochina

In 1940, France, which had established a presence in Indochina in the latter half of the 19th century, controlled the region consisting of Cambodia, Laos, and Vietnam. After France fell to the Germans, the Japanese moved into Indochina and took control of the region but left the French as a puppet government.

With Allied aircraft flying combat missions over Indochina, the U.S. Office of Strategic Services (OSS) began looking for a group to train as a resistance movement within the country. They found a Vietnamese expatriate in China, a man of many aliases whom the world would come to know as Ho Chi Minh. Although he had apparently not set foot in his native country since early in the 20th century, Ho Chi Minh had been sending pamphlets into the country and was the leader of an anti-French guerrilla group led by fellow expatriates who called themselves the Viet Minh. The OSS elected to develop a resistance with Ho's followers inside Indochina.

In the spring of 1945, an OSS team led by U.S. Army Major Archimedes Patti parachuted into northern Vietnam and began arming and organizing a resistance made up of Ho's followers. Ho Chi Minh himself elected to walk into Vietnam. When he arrived, he quickly established himself as a leader and began working toward the overthrow of the French and the Vietnamese government.

During the war, U.S. President Franklin Roosevelt had made clear his intentions of refusing to allow France to maintain its colonies in Indochina. In the closing months of the war, the Japanese pressed the Vietnamese and other Indochinese leaders to declare themselves independent. Emperor Bao Dai, who controlled two of Vietnam's three provinces, declared them independent on March 11, 1945. The Japanese retained control of Cochin China, the southern portion of the former Vietnam, until May 16, when they turned it over to Bao Dai. On August 13, 1945, Ho Chi Minh read a proclamation of independence in Hanoi that he had modeled on the U.S. Declaration of Independence. Ironically, a flight of U.S. fighters flew low over the city as he was making the proclamation.

But the French opposed independence for Vietnam, and the Viet Minh took up arms against the French. The French Indochina War ended on May 7, 1954, with the disastrous defeat of the French at Dienbienphu.

After Dienbienphu, France pulled its troops out of Indochina. Vietnam was divided along the 16th parallel, with the northern half of the country under Viet Minh control and the southern half under a Vietnamese government supported by the United States. The Geneva Accords (1955) that settled the French Indochina War provided for national elections to reunify the country, but neither the Vietnamese government nor the United States, which had supported France during the war, signed the accords, which were signed by France, the Soviet Union, and the Viet Minh. The elections were never held, and Vietnam remained divided north and south, with Hanoi and Saigon the respective capitals.

In the late 1950s, the Hanoi government turned to military means to overthrow the South Vietnamese and began building a network of trails over which to send cadre, arms, and ammunition to form Communist cells in South Vietnam and promote an armed revolution. Political problems also boiled in Laos, where civil war broke out in 1960, and where the Hanoi government began establishing a large military presence.

The Laotian Civil War officially ended in 1962, although fighting continued in the country for more than a decade. Meanwhile, the Hanoi-sponsored rebellion in South Vietnam gathered speed, and the United States began increasing its military assistance to South Vietnam, including sending military advisers. By 1965 it had become apparent to the administration of U.S. President Lyndon Johnson that the South Vietnamese would lose the war without massive U.S. intervention, and he sent in U.S. ground combat troops. The Johnson administration also mounted a massive bombing campaign against North Vietnam.

The Vietnam War ended in 1975 in a military defeat of the South Vietnamese and a political defeat for the United States. Vietnam was reunited under a Communist government. Laos and Cambodia also became Communist.

Germany

At the Yalta Conference in February 1945, the leaders of the Big Three powers (Great Britain, the Soviet Union, and the United States) agreed on a plan for the division of Germany after the country surrendered unconditionally. The plan called for each power to have a slice of the country, although the Americans and British insisted that France be included. Even though Berlin was located more than 100 miles inside the territory allocated to the Soviets, it too would be divided into four zones. Each of the powers stripped the local industry of materiel and technology that would be beneficial to their own economies, then set about establishing a form of government based on their own political philosophies. They removed former Nazis from all positions of leadership, and many Nazis were identified and then brought to trial as war criminals.

At first, the Allies treated the German people with animosity, but as Communist governments took control in more and more European countries, the United States and Britain adopted a more benevolent stance designed to promote the development of democracy in their zones of occupation. West Germany was one of the four leading recipients of economic aid offered under the U.S.-funded European Economic Recovery Program (the so-called Marshall Plan). Simultaneously, the Soviets established a Communist dictatorship in the division under their control.

As the Soviets drew further away from their former allies, they began to press for a withdrawal of Western troops from Berlin. After numerous threats, in June 1948 the Soviets imposed a blockade on all road and rail routes leading into the city. Only the air routes into

Berlin from the West remained open. The U.S. forces in Europe proposed to supply the city by air and mounted an airlift that lasted for nearly a year. Fearful of the U.S. atomic capability, the Soviets failed to follow through on threats to attack U.S., British, and French transports that had fashioned a literal "aerial bridge" over Soviet territory to bring supplies into the city.

After the Soviets failed to block access to Berlin, the city became a symbol to the German people of the benevolence of their former enemies from the West. The Berlin Airlift was considered to be the first great U.S. victory in the cold war. Throughout the 1950s and into the 1960s, the Soviets sponsored frequent attempts to disrupt the democratic-ruled western sections in Berlin, and dozens of Germans were shot and hundreds imprisoned for attempting to flee the Eastern Zone. In 1961, the Soviets and East Germans erected a wall dividing the eastern and western sections of the city. Political stress and the threat of war between East and West continued in Germany into the 1980s. Finally, an unprecedented and unexpected change occurred with the collapse of Communist regimes in Eastern Europe in 1989. The Berlin Wall was torn down and East and West Germany were reunified as a democratic nation with a market economy.

Greece

The Germans occupied Greece in 1941. Following the German occupation, several British-sponsored guerrilla organizations came to life within the country. Motivated by different political ideologies, the groups were at odds with each other to the point of civil war. The German army withdrew from Greece in October 1944, and the Greek prime minister, Georgios Papandreou, ordered the resistance movements to disband. The Communist Ethnikos Laikos Apoleftherotikos Stratos (ELAS), or National Popular Liberation Army, refused. In anticipation of civil war, the British reinforced their troops in the country. Fighting broke out in December 1944 between the ELAS and Greek government forces. Two months later a truce temporarily ended the fighting.

In the immediate postwar years, civil war continued as Communist guerrillas operating in mountainous northern Greece threatened the government. Until 1947, Britain provided economic aid to the Greek government and maintained troops in the country. When Britain became financially strained, the United States assumed the role of aiding the Greek government and provided U.S. military advisers. With U.S. assistance the Greek government went on the offensive against the guerrillas and captured many of their strongholds in the summer of 1949. The guerrillas finally capitulated and Greece was spared from falling into the Soviet orbit. The U.S. program of aid to Greece and nearby Turkey, under what was known as the Truman Doctrine, was intended to keep those countries from falling under the influence of the USSR.

> I believe that it must be the policy of the United States to support free peoples who are resisting attempted subversion by armed minorities or by outside pressures.
> —President Harry S Truman

India

As a British colony, India was drawn into World War II by proxy when the British Parliament declared war on Germany on India's behalf. Some leading political leaders in India were opposed to entering the war, the principal one being Mahatma Gandhi. Political strife continued in India throughout the war years, and the British jailed Gandhi for organizing the "Quit India" movement, an attempt to force Britain to withdraw all troops from the country in 1942. He remained in jail until 1944.

After the war ended, violence erupted within India, both among factions divided along religious lines and against the British, who had decided to grant independence to India by 1948. The two dominant religious groups—Hindu and Muslim—argued for a partition of the country, whereas Gandhi sought a unified country with joint rule. The British plan for independence partitioned the country, with the predominately Muslim areas becoming Pakistan, which was further split geographically. The Hindu regions remained in India. Religious differences between the two new countries continued after the division, and border disputes arose between India and China. In 1963, China invaded the Assam Valley, provoking a limited military response from the United States. In 1971, East Pakistan, which was remote from Pakistan, declared itself independent. India supported the rebellion, which ended with East Pakistan becoming the new country of Bangladesh.

Indian-Pakistani hostility continued unabated throughout the remainder of the 20th century and assumed an ominous turn when both countries developed nuclear weapons.

Iron Curtain

In a speech in Missouri on March 5, 1946, the former British Prime Minister Winston Churchill described the division of Europe: "From Stettin in the Baltic to Trieste in the Adriatic, an iron curtain has descended across the continent." He was referring to the system of armed guards, barbed wire fences, minefields, and other measures that the Soviets were erecting along the frontiers of the Soviet-dominated countries. The term was quickly adopted to describe the dividing line between the democratic West and communist, totalitarian East.

The Iron Curtain indeed proved to be a barrier, not to keep foreigners out but to keep the inhabitants of the Warsaw Pact nations in. When Sir Winston uttered his famous remarks, the struggle for dominance in many European countries was still under way. By the end of the 1940s, Communist governments were in place in Czechoslovakia, Hungary, Romania, Bulgaria, and Poland—in addition to Albania and Yugoslavia, which had become Communist before the end of the war. The Balkan countries, which adjoined the Soviet Union on its western border, had fallen under Moscow's influence at the beginning of World War II. The Iron Curtain became an anachronism in 1989, when the Communist regimes of Eastern Europe collapsed and were replaced by democratic governments. In 1991, the Soviet Union collapsed, and the Iron Curtain era in European history ended.

Japan

As World War II in the Pacific turned in the Allies' favor, U.S. forces began moving toward Japan, while Australian troops liberated the islands of the southwestern Pacific and British forces fought the Japanese in Burma. The United States, however, was the sole occupier of Japan. Although U.S. President Franklin Roosevelt had stressed a policy of unconditional surrender, the Americans acquiesced to the one request of the Japanese—that the emperor remain on his throne and not be treated as a war criminal. The emperor was a much-loved figure; by not deposing and prosecuting him, the Americans offered a gesture of peace to the people of Japan.

President Harry Truman ordered General Douglas MacArthur to Tokyo to assume the role of military governor; he had led the Allied forces north from Australia to the Philippines and was preparing to command the invasion of the Japanese home islands. MacArthur became a benevolent ruler who set out to establish democracy in what had been a nearly feudal society. He insisted on a constitutional form of government with a clause that forbade war and endeared himself to Japanese women by giving them the vote. MacArthur also insisted on land reform policies and encouraged the development of new Japanese industry. To this day, MacArthur remains a revered figure in Japan.

Before the 1960s, many Americans regarded the stamp "Made in Japan" as a sign of inferior goods, but during the Vietnam War GIs in the Pacific purchased millions of dollars' worth of Japanese cameras and electronics equipment, which helped lead to a growing acceptance of Japanese-manufactured materials. An embargo on Middle Eastern oil caused gasoline prices to rise dramatically in the United States and throughout the world in the 1970s—and led to a sudden demand for fuel-efficient Japanese automobiles. With a worldwide demand for its cars and electronic equipment, Japan was once again a major world economic power.

Korea

Ruled by Japan since 1910, Korea was part of the Japanese empire during the war. In August 1945, the United States agreed with the Soviets to divide the country along the 38th parallel. Soviet troops who had moved into the area accepted the surrender of Japanese forces north of the line, while U.S. troops disarmed those to the south.

Both sides then took steps to bring the divisions under their control into their sphere of influence. The Soviets eradicated non-Communists in the northern half of the country, and the United States brought Syngman Rhee, a Korean living in the United States, back to Korea to govern the southern portion. In 1947 the country was formally divided, and the following year U.S.-sponsored elections led to the establishment of the Republic of Korea. North Korea became the People's Republic of Korea, firmly allied with Communist China and the Soviet Union.

In June 1950, North Korean forces attacked South Korea, beginning the Korean War, which ended in a stalemate in 1953. Since 1953, the two countries have remained divided, with the southern half prospering as a democracy and the north remaining a militarized dictatorship. With the death of the North Korean dictator Kim Il Sung in 1994, prospects for reunification of the country began to brighten. In 2002 and 2003, however, the North Koreans announced that they would resume producing nuclear weapons, a program they agreed to give up in 1994 in an agreement with the Clinton administration. Their threatening gestures once again thrust the Korean peninsula into the limelight as tensions over the North Korean nuclear program grew.

Marshall Plan

This great postwar U.S. aid program for Europe was named after U.S. Secretary of State George C. Marshall, who had been the senior officer of the U.S. Army during the war, although the program was developed in 1947 within the Truman administration, including the president himself. Marshall announced the plan in an address at Harvard University. Officially called the European Economic Recovery Program, it was designed to provide massive infusions of U.S. aid to European countries to help them stabilize politically while recovering economically from the war. The "Marshall Plan," as it soon came to be known, was offered to the Soviet Union and its satellite countries in Eastern Europe, but the Soviets declined and developed an aid program of their own, which was in fact a public relations move and not a serious attempt to rebuild the nations under their control.

> It was a life line to sinking men. We grabbed the life line with both hands.
> —British Foreign Minister Ernest Bevin on the Marshall Plan

The U.S. Congress appropriated more than $13 billion for the plan, more than 70 percent of which was spent in the United States for manufactured goods, including military equipment. Britain, France, Italy, and West Germany were the primary beneficiaries and in that order. Aid under the Marshall Plan ended in 1952. The Marshall Plan is considered a major step in the reconstruction of Europe and in the binding of the nations of Western Europe to the United States.

THE MARSHALL PLAN

In 1947, President Harry Truman and Secretary of State General George C. Marshall asked Congress to fund the European Economic Recovery Program, with a special fund providing assistance to European nations in recovering from the effects of World War II. In a three-year period, the United States disbursed more than $13 billion, mostly in the form of credits for the purchase of U.S.-produced goods.

Nation	Amount Received (in millions of dollars)
United Kingdom	3,189.8
France	2,713.6
West Germany	1,390.6
Netherlands	1,083.5
Greece	708.7
Austria	677.8
Belgium/Luxembourg	559.3
Denmark	273
Norway	255.3
Turkey	225.1
Ireland	147.5
Sweden	107.3
Portugal	51.2
Iceland	29.3

North Atlantic Treaty Organization (NATO)

On April 4, 1949, 11 European countries, along with Canada and the United States, signed the North Atlantic Treaty in response to Soviet-sponsored aggression in Europe, particularly the blockade of Berlin. The Korean War led to the formation of a military command organization known as the North Atlantic Treaty Organization, more commonly known as NATO. NATO member nations pledged to defend each other and to join in a common effort against Soviet aggression in Western Europe.

After the collapse of the Soviet Union in 1991, NATO expanded significantly, with the addition of a number of former Soviet-dominated countries of Eastern Europe to the alliance. NATO played a major role in the conflict in the Balkans when its air forces bombed Yugoslavia in a successful effort to stop that country from pursuing ethnic cleansing of Albanians from its province of Kosovo. NATO forces also deployed under treaty obligations to assist the United States after the terrorist attacks of September 11, 2001.

Occupation Forces

As World War II in Europe drew to a close, President Franklin Roosevelt promised that U.S. troops would remain overseas as an occupation force for no more than two years. But more than half a century has passed since V-E Day, and U.S. troops remain at bases in Germany, England, Italy, and elsewhere. As hostilities ceased in Europe, combat units were scheduled to move to the Far East to take part in the invasion of Japan, but the war ended before they were needed. Troops were required in the newly occupied areas to keep order. As it became apparent that the presence of U.S. troops would be required overseas to counter the threat from the Soviets, U.S. troops were permanently assigned to bases in both Europe and the Far East.

Palestine/Israel

During World War I, British troops captured Palestine from the Turks, and after the war the new League of Nations granted Britain a mandate to govern it. In 1917, Britain issued the Balfour Declaration, a proclamation that promised the Jews of the world a national homeland in the region that had, according to Jewish tradition, been promised to their ancestors by the god Jehovah. Late in the 19th century, in part to escape the persecution that plagued Jews in Europe, a movement known as Zionism arose to establish a Jewish homeland in Palestine. Encouraged by the British mandate, many European Jews emigrated to Palestine between 1920 and 1938, increasing the number of Jews in the region from 50,000 to 600,000, with the majority of immigrants fleeing Nazi persecution.

But Britain had also made promises to the Arab population of Palestine, and after an Arab revolt in 1939, Britain established rigid immigration policies for Jews and promised the creation of a Palestinian state within 10 years. With hundreds of thousands of Jews among the millions of displaced persons in Europe after the war, Palestine became a destination for many, so many that the British military began turning away boatloads of refugees.

Because Britain had changed its position regarding the Zionist movement in 1939, many Zionist leaders came to look upon England as a major obstacle to the founding of a Jewish homeland. To combat Britain, Zionist leaders, some of whom would become noted statesmen in later years, engaged in guerrilla tactics and terrorism. Even as British troops were defeating the Nazi movement responsible for the death of nearly six million European Jews, Zionist guerrillas in Palestine were beginning a war of terrorism against the British government. Led by Menachem Begin, a future prime minister of Israel, Zionist guerrillas attacked British military and government installations in Palestine, culminating in an attack on British offices in Jerusalem's King David Hotel in 1946. As its mandate drew to an end, Britain proposed the establishment of two states in Palestine, one for Jews and one for Arabs.

On May 14, 1948, the day the British mandate ended, Jews in Palestine declared Israel to be an independent state and were immediately attacked by most of their Arab neighbors, including Egypt, Syria, and Jordan. During that war the new nation of Israel captured a significant amount of territory that the British had originally allotted to the Palestinian state. The war ended in 1949 with a truce negotiated by the United Nations that gave Israel territory that had not been within the original borders of the Jewish state. After the

Israelis captured and occupied the West Bank of Jordan following the Arab-Israeli war of 1967, the territorial problem was exacerbated. Since this time the region has remained a center of controversy, strife, and war between Israel, its Arab neighbors, and the Palestinian people.

Poland

Poland suffered hideous losses during World War II, and the end of the war brought no relief as the country fell under Soviet control. An agreement between the Polish government and the Soviet Union placed the eastern border much farther west than it had been in 1939. To compensate for these losses of its eastern territory, Poland was given territory in the west that had belonged to Germany. Postwar Poland had moved significantly westward.

In the immediate postwar years, a coalition government ruled Poland, but elections in 1947 saw a joint Communist-Socialist victory, with the two parties gaining more than 85 percent of the vote in a rigged election. The United States denounced the election as undemocratic, but that did not stop the Stalinists, who set out to further purge the government. At the end of 1948, the Communist and Socialist parties merged to become the Polish United Workers Party, a pro-Stalinist organization. Poland then officially became a satellite state of the Soviet Union, although it had been under Soviet military occupation since 1944–45.

Throughout the 1950s political strife continued as various elements of Polish society pressed for more freedom. Some reforms took place, though most were reversed in 1957, when the Communists tightened their hold. Calls for reform resumed in 1968, when Polish students began protesting against the government. In retaliation the Polish Communist Party launched an attack on Jews. In 1972, Poland and West Germany signed a treaty that gave Poles of German descent the right to emigrate to Germany and gave Poland claim to land that Germany had annexed before the war. Relations between Poland and the West continued to improve through the 1970s. In 1980, a Polish labor movement known as Solidarity, which was led by Lech Walesa and supported by the Polish Catholic Church, gained political power in Poland. With the collapse of communism in Poland in 1989, the country adopted a democratic form of government and a market economy. Walesa was ultimately elected president of Poland. Much of the pressure on the Polish Communist regime in its last years came from an unexpected source: the Vatican, which was led by a Polish-born pope, John Paul II, who was elected to the papacy in 1978 after serving as archbishop of Krakow.

United Nations

Although the League of Nations continued to exist through World War II, the organization had not been able to prevent war, in part because the United States was not a member. In August 1941, British Prime Minister Winston Churchill and U.S. President Franklin Roosevelt worked out and signed the Atlantic Charter, in which the two nations agreed to work together to create a system to promote world peace and cooperation among nations. Less than a year later, Britain and the United States led the formation of a 26-nation alliance to defeat the Axis, with each nation signing the Declaration of the United Nations, adopting a term suggested by Roosevelt.

In 1944, representatives of Britain, China, the United States, and the Soviet Union met in Washington, D.C., and drafted a charter for a new organization that would be called the United Nations. The issue came up again at the Yalta Conference in early 1945, and a meeting was held in San Francisco in April to create the new organization. Delegates from 50 nations worked for two months to develop a charter, and the United Nations officially came into being on October 24, 1945.

Universal Declaration of Human Rights

In 1948, the United Nations adopted the Universal Declaration of Human Rights, a statement regarding rights that members of a special commission, chaired by the former first lady Eleanor Roosevelt, felt citizens of member nations should have. The principal author was René Cassin, a prominent French attorney. Based on principles found in the UN charter, the three-part declaration addresses basic human rights—freedom of religion, freedom of speech, the right to marry and raise a family, the right to work, and so forth. Member nations are required to report to the council every three years on progress within their country.

Warsaw Pact

In 1955, to counter the rearming of West Germany and its admission to the North Atlantic Treaty Organization, seven Communist countries met in Warsaw and signed a pact, agreeing to come to each other's aid in the event of war. Ironically, the only action taken under the Warsaw Pact was against a member nation when troops were sent to Prague to put down the Czech rebellion in 1968.

Cold War

Throughout World War II, Britain, the United States, and the Soviet Union maintained a fragile alliance. British Prime Minister Winston Churchill especially distrusted the Soviets and their ambitions for postwar Europe. As the conclusion to the war in Europe became obvious, the possibility of a continuing conflict between the democratic West and totalitarian East became more and more of a threat.

The U.S. journalist Walter Lippmann coined the term "cold war" in a 1947 book about the relations between the United States and the Soviet Union, which had so deteriorated that the two countries were near war but without actual military confrontation. However, there were some occasions when the forces of the two countries met in combat: Since the collapse of the Soviet empire and the opening of formerly classified Soviet files, Russia has acknowledged that Soviet pilots flew combat missions against Americans during the Korean War.

Although the United States and Soviet Union never were involved in direct overt military action against each other during the cold war, both countries devoted a large portion of their gross national product to arms and armament. The cold war began with the United States as the only nuclear power, but Communist spies had obtained its nuclear secrets, and before 1950 the Soviet Union had become a nuclear power; the two countries thus engaged in a race to develop more powerful weapons, along with more advanced and accurate methods of delivering them.

The climax of the arms race came with the development of the intercontinental ballistic missile (ICBM) by both sides. By the 1960s, major cities in the United States and the Soviet Union, along with military and other key installations, were targets for nuclear missiles that could be launched at a moment's notice. The United States adopted a policy known as MAD, the acronym for mutually assured destruction, as its main deterrent to nuclear war. The closest the two nations ever came to actual war was during the Cuban Missile Crisis in 1962, when the Soviets installed long-range and tactical nuclear weapons in Cuba, a mere 90 miles from American soil. The United States responded with an embargo of Cuba—an act of war—and the Soviets eventually pulled back and removed the missiles. The two countries came perilously close to nuclear conflict, but war was avoided when President John F. Kennedy refused the advice of some of his advisers for an immediate invasion, thus allowing Nikita Khrushchev, the Soviet leader, the time to arrive at the decision to remove the missiles.

Throughout the cold war, the United States and the Soviet Union fought each other by proxy, first in Korea, then in Vietnam and Afghanistan, then in other smaller conflicts that many Americans are not even aware of. Political unrest in many former European colonies provided fertile ground for Marxist rebellion. In many instances, Warsaw Pact nations, as well as China and Cuba, provided aid and advisers to rebel forces.

The cold war ended with the collapse of the Soviet Union, which came about largely because of their economic crisis and because the United States had been able to outspend the Soviets in the arms race. In the 1980s, the Soviet Union found itself involved in its own version of the Vietnam quagmire when Islamic rebels in Afghanistan took up arms against the Soviet occupation. The extent of the role played by the United States in supporting the Afghan rebels has not yet been fully revealed, but the war ended with the Soviet Union bankrupt and in a state of political turmoil brought on by military defeat. The end of the cold war brought the end of the political and military turmoil that had started with World War I and continued through World War II until the 1980s.

GI Bill

One of the greatest legacies of World War II in the United States was the Servicemen's Readjustment Act of 1944, which provided returning servicemen with government assistance for education and for the purchase of homes and farms. The act was a reflection of the gratitude of the nation to the millions of men who had sacrificed years of their young lives to protect their country.

In 1944, prompted by veterans groups such as the American Legion, Congress passed what came to be known as the "GI Bill" in anticipation of the return to civilian life of millions of young men. The bill was designed to allow the veterans to reenter civilian life with certain benefits, including government aid for college and technical training; low-cost loans for the purchase of homes, businesses, and farms; and medical benefits. It also provided for unemployment benefits as the former servicemen made the transition from military to civilian life.

Millions of young Americans took advantage of the benefits and were able to obtain an education that would have otherwise been beyond their reach. Veterans accounted for nearly half the enrollment in U.S. colleges in 1947, and by 1955, 7.8 million veterans, almost half the total, had used GI Bill educational benefits. Many people who went on to become national leaders in the latter half of the 20th century got their start by attending college under the GI Bill. They also were able to purchase homes, precipitating a postwar building boom, especially of prefabricated housing, which led to the sprawl of the American suburbs. The GI Bill was also a contributing factor to the economic boom of the 1950s.

"Me? Naw—I'm prewar," reads the caption to Bill Mauldin's cartoon commentary on the postwar baby boom. From war's end through the early 1960s, millions of babies were born to families of former GIs as the U.S. experienced an unprecedented era of economic prosperity.

The benefits of the GI Bill helped the young veterans to settle down and start families. The population increased 1.5 to 2 percent from 1947 to 1961 as a result of births, compared with 0.5 percent at the end of the 20th century. The increasing numbers of young children led to an unprecedented demand for new schools, medical facilities, and government services. The baby boom also spawned the development of new industries centered on babies and children—clothing, baby food, and toys, for example. The baby boom also led to new theories about how to raise children. The pediatrician Benjamin Spock advocated a style of childrearing that centered on a greater degree of permissiveness and attention, a stark contrast to the attitudes in the prewar United States.

The table that follows shows the number of births and the birthrates for the years 1946 to 1964, the years known as the baby boom, when the U.S. birthrate rose to and remained at more than 20 births per 1,000 women. The rates did not decline until 1965, perhaps largely as a result of increasing acceptance of birth control. Statistics for 1940, 1945, 1965, and 1970 are also shown for comparison:

Year	Number of Births (millions)	Births Per 1,000 Population	Births Per 1,000 Women Ages 18–44
1940	2,360	17.9	73.5
1945	2,735	19.5	82.5
1946	3,289	23.3	98.3
1947	3,699	25.8	110.0
1948	3,535	24.2	104.8
1949	3,559	24.0	105.2
1950	3,554	23.6	106.2
1951	3,751	24.5	111.3
1952	3,847	24.7	113.5
1953	4,017	24.6	114.7
1954	4,017	24.9	117.6
1955	4,047	24.6	118.0
1956	4,163	24.9	120.8
1957	4,255	25.0	122.7
1958	4,204	24.3	120.1

Year	Number of Births (millions)	Births Per 1,000 Population	Births Per 1,000 Women Ages 18–44
1959	4,245	24.0	120.1
1960	4,258	23.7	118.0
1961	4,268	23.3	117.2
1962	4,167	22.4	112.1
1963	4,081	21.6	108.5
1964	4,027	21.0	105.0
1965	3,760	19.4	96.6
1970	3,731	18.4	87.9

Transition to Suburbia

World War II increased the rate of urbanization in the United States, a trend that began at the beginning of the 20th century as people left farms and moved to large cities in search of work in manufacturing industries. The war changed the face of America as communities sprang up around military bases and special installations, including the nuclear research facilities at Alamogordo, New Mexico, and Oak Ridge, Tennessee.

When the war ended, real estate developers saw opportunity in the GI Bill home-buying benefits of the returning veterans and set about establishing communities in the suburban areas on the outskirts of cities. Although hundreds of firms across the United States specialized in building low-cost homes for veterans using prefabrication methods, Levitt and Sons of New York City is perhaps the best known. The company built three separate communities, one on Long Island (Levittown), another in the Philadelphia area, and a third in New Jersey. Beginning with the New York development, immediately after the end of the war, Levitt and Sons constructed more than 17,000 new homes using prefabrication and assembly-line techniques that they had used in fulfilling wartime military contracts.

Builders nationwide adopted the Levitts' construction methods, purchasing tracts of farmland near metropolitan areas and erecting small homes on tiny lots, leading to the term *tract housing*; communities of prefabricated homes began appearing in the suburbs of smaller cities and towns across the United States.

The homes of Levittown all looked the same. They were small, and each was made with the same interior design. In the early years, there were few trees on the streets of Levittown. But for a returning GI, a low-cost home in Levittown was a castle. For thousands of former servicemen, it represented a new start in life after years of sacrifice and danger. Home ownership was a symbol of success. Levittown was an example of the transition to suburbia. Workers in postwar America now had the opportunity, if they chose, to own their own homes in neat, middle-class communities that were within commuting distance to the large cities where the jobs were.

CHAPTER 14

World War II and the Arts

World War II touched every aspect of life in the United States, including the arts. The issues of the war, the nature of the enemy, the United Nations, work and production, the home front, and the fighting forces—all these themes appeared in literature, film, radio, posters, painting, photography, and journalism. In the movies, for example, films with war themes began to appear, their pro-Allied messages presented in a clear and unambiguous fashion. Noted Hollywood stars such as James Stewart and Clark Gable went into uniform, while others traveled the country promoting the purchase of war bonds. The war affected the arts in other Allied countries and in the Axis nations as well. In Great Britain, where the war exacted a heavy toll, artists had almost no choice but to turn their talents toward the war effort. Soviet artists, musicians, writers, and filmmakers felt a sacred duty to defend "the motherland," and Soviet leaders encouraged the most virulent anti-Nazi propaganda, relaxing stringent censorship rules to get it. The united front of Soviet artists was epitomized by V. I. Lebedev's poem "Holy War," published two days after the Germans invaded. Quickly set to music, it became the battle hymn of the Soviet Union.

The totalitarian governments of the Axis powers strictly controlled all creative expression. In Germany, five separate Reichskulturkammern (Reich Chambers of Culture) controlled art, theater, publishing, filmmaking, and broadcasting. Among the fine arts, the Nazi Party's prewar move to banish "degenerate art" and "purify" painting and sculpture along Aryan racial lines backfired. Although the 1937 showings of "degenerate art" were intended to turn people away from the "decadent expressionism" of the Weimar regime, they were the most popular shows that the Reich ever mounted. At the same time, most of Germany's (and eventually occupied France's) greatest artists and intellectuals went into exile. Approximately 5,000 artists, scholars, and writers fled Nazi Germany. Those who stayed remained silent or turned their hand to propaganda. (See Propaganda in Chapter 10, "Intelligence, Espionage, and Propaganda.")

While controls were not this well organized in Japan, they did not need to be, because most writers, filmmakers, artists, and journalists spontaneously supported the government action. The attack on Pearl Harbor, for example, was not just a great military victory but an epic cultural event in the eyes of Japan's creative elite. Many in the Japanese media and the arts believed that support of the government and the war were their patriotic duty.

The War in Literature

Although geographically removed from the combat zone, not all U.S. book buyers turned to escapist literature to cushion themselves from the carnage. The hard-boiled novels of James M. Cain and inspirational literature of A. J. Cronin and Lloyd Douglas did find receptive audiences, but so did a number of bestsellers from 1941 to 1945 that addressed the war either directly (Richard Tregaskis's *Guadalcanal Diary,* William L. Shirer's *Berlin Diary,* and even Henry DeWolf Smyth's *Atomic Energy for Military Purposes*) or indirectly, through the themes of totalitarianism and fascism (John Steinbeck's *The Moon Is Down,* Arthur Koestler's *Darkness at Noon,* Antoine de Saint-Exupéry's *Flight to Arras,* and John Hersey's *A Bell for Adano).* Many writers in uniform (Norman Mailer, James Michener, Irwin Shaw, William Styron, Kurt Vonnegut, Joseph Heller, Gore Vidal) and correspondents (John Hersey, Edward R. Murrow, William Shirer, Joseph Alsop Jr., Martha Gellhorn) would turn their war experiences into popular, acclaimed works in the ensuing years.

In Great Britain, where the war was impossible to escape, writers like J. B. Priestley, Evelyn Waugh, John Lehmann, Stephen Spender, Vera Brittain, the Sitwells, and George Orwell waged it with their typewriters. Cyril Connolly, editor of *Horizon* magazine, coordinated much of the literary activity, as writers and artists experienced the same camaraderie exhibited by the British people. British Prime Minister Winston Churchill dubbed this collective national spirit "their finest hour," using that phrase as the title of a volume of his history of the war. Orwell's regular dispatches to the *New York Tribune* and *Partisan Review* kept Americans informed of the mental state of the British, as did Mollie Panter-Downes's letters from London to the *New Yorker.*

It is difficult to find literary merit in what was published for public consumption in Germany or Italy, as publishing was strictly controlled by the Nazi and Fascist governments and virtually no underground literature existed. Germany required that all books adhere to National Socialist ideology. Hitler regularly featured campaigns like "Week of the German Book," which championed officially sanctioned writers and burned the works of those deemed decadent (Sigmund Freud, Karl Marx, Marcel Proust, H. G. Wells, Margaret Sanger). The only fiction allowed was *Heimatromane* ("homeland novels"), peasant tales set in a gloriously nostalgic past. The most popular of these novelists were Ludwig Bartel, Walter Bloem, Karl May (Hitler's favorite), and Hermann Stehr, all of whom were popular before World War I. Also widely read were the colonial novels of Hans Grimm and heroic war tales set in World War I.

During World War II the "new guard" of writers was limited to those like Heinrich Anacker, Hans Baumann, Herbert Bohme, and Kurt Eggers, who wrote patriotic lyrics for Nazi cultural festivals. Hitler himself profited greatly from sales of his autobiographical work, *Mein Kampf:* he mandated that his publisher give him a generous royalty rate; all married couples were required to buy a copy; and he paid no taxes.

MAJOR LITERARY WORKS DEALING WITH WORLD WAR II

Below is a listing of major literary works dealing with the war. Within the subsections, works are arranged alphabetically by author. Although this list includes both works written during World War II and those written years after, it is not intended to be comprehensive or to endorse the various titles; rather, it is meant to highlight landmark works.

Fiction

Elizabeth Bowen, *The Heat of the Day* (1948): This is a doomed love story set in war-ravaged London by a novelist who lived through the Blitz.

Günter Grass, *Die Blechtrommel* (*The Tin Drum,* 1959): The first part of the Nobel Prize–winning novelist's Danzig trilogy, it chronicles the Nazi years through the eyes of a mute drummer boy.

Henry Green (pen name for Henry Yorke), *Caught* (1943): This is one of several novels that Green wrote about his World War II experiences in the National Fire Service in London.

Joseph Heller, *Catch-22* (1961): This is Heller's darkly satirical novel about war-weary U.S. bomber pilots and the illogic of military bureaucracy during the campaign to retake Italy.

James Jones, *From Here to Eternity* (1951) and *The Thin Red Line* (1962): The personal dramas of servicemen are set against the backdrop of the novelist's war experiences.

Anatoly Petrovich Kuznetsov, *Babi Yar* (1967): In this Russian's "documentary novel," the Nazis' brutal occupation of Kiev in 1941 is seen through the eyes of a Ukrainian boy.

Norman Mailer, *The Naked and the Dead* (1948): This monumental novel, based on Mailer's war experience, is about an American reconnaissance patrol's advance mission on Japanese-held Anapopei.

Thomas Pynchon, *Gravity's Rainbow* (1973): A U.S. lieutenant is assigned to England in 1944 to ascertain a pattern to German V-2 missiles aimed at London.

Ignazio Silone, *Bread and Wine* (1955): This is a fictional document of Italy in 1938 and after, as described by Pietro Spina, who is fighting the Mussolini dictatorship.

Kurt Vonnegut, *Slaughterhouse Five* (1969): This satiric novel depicts the exploits and fantastical coping mechanisms of Billy Pilgrim, a GI lost behind enemy lines just before the 1945 fire-bombing of Dresden.

Rex Warner, *The Aerodome* (1941): One of the widest-selling books in England during the war, this is a futuristic account of British village life in the shadows of an enormous air base during a time of impending war.

Herman Wouk, *The Caine Mutiny* (1951): Set on a navy minesweeper, the captain is driven mad by war experiences. This novel and Wouk's later *The Winds of War* (1971) and *War and Remembrance* (1978) are historically accurate and offer a compelling human portrait of World War II.

Nonfiction (General)

Sir Winston Churchill, *The Second World War,* six volumes (1948–54): The British prime minister wrote this monumental history of the war from his unique insider's perspective; an essential document for understanding the conflict.

Roger Freeman, *The Mighty Eighth* (1970): Freeman provides a history of the U.S. Eighth Army Air Force, which played a vital role in the air war against Germany.

John Keegan, *The Second World War* (1989): This is the noted British historian's comprehensive one-volume synopsis of the war.

Samuel Eliot Morison, *History of the United States Naval Operations in World War II,* 15 volumes (1947–62). Morison, a distinguished American historian, produced this definitive history of the U.S. Navy during World War II, a 15-volume masterpiece unsurpassed in its detail.

Ernie Pyle, *Brave Men* (1944) and *Here Is Your War* (1945): The famed World War II correspondent wrote a weekly column that reflected the feelings and beliefs of the average soldier. Much beloved, he was killed during the battle for Okinawa, in the Pacific, in April 1945.

Studs Terkel, *The Good War* (1984): Terkel's book, a collection of interviews with Americans from all walks of life who lived through World War II, reveals what average men and women experienced and felt in the war years.

The United States Army in World War II, 78 volumes (1948–77): This is also known as "The Green Book Series." This multivolume reference work contains the complete history of the U.S. Army in the war years.

Nonfiction (Europe)

Stephen E. Ambrose, *Pegasus Bridge* (1984), *D-Day June 6, 1944: The Climactic Battle of World*

WINSTON CHURCHILL—AUTHOR, WAR HERO

Winston Churchill was a writer and maker of history. Before he entered politics in 1900 as a member of Parliament, he was an acclaimed war correspondent and military historian. Before he became Adolf Hitler's nemesis and two-time British prime minister (1940–45 and 1951–55), he was a renowned biographer, memoirist, and commentator.

He was born at Blenheim Palace, the son of Lord and Lady Randolph Churchill. His father was a direct descendant of the first duke of Marlborough, England's greatest soldier, whose six-volume biography was written by the young Winston. Lord Randolph was a great statesman in his own right; his son also wrote a two-volume biography of him.

After graduating with honors from Sandhurst (as England's Royal Military College is commonly called), Winston joined the Fourth Hussars in 1895, serving with distinction in Cuba, India, Tirah, and Egypt. As a war correspondent, he covered South Africa during the Boer War. It has been widely reported that, during one bloody skirmish in Egypt, he cried out to the troops, "Keep cool, men. This will make excellent copy for my paper."

His greatest literary works were his monumental *History of the English-Speaking People* and the six-volume *The Second World War*. The great U.S. historian Henry Steele Commager summed up Sir Winston's startling career: "Churchill wrote history in order to mold it and, so we sometimes suspect, he made history in order to write it."

War II (1994), and *Citizen Soldiers* (1998): The popular American historian produced many books on World War II that focused on the experiences of the American citizen-soldier who, in Ambrose's view, is the real hero of the war.

Martin Blumenson, ed., *The Patton Papers*, two volumes (1974): The papers of the famous general, a tank commander, show his unforgettable style.

Vera Brittain, *England's Hour* (1941): Brittain, a noted English writer, feminist, and pacifist, wrote a book about life in Britain during the German onslaught of 1941.

Alan Bullock, *Hitler: A Study in Tyranny,* rev. ed. (1962): This is one of the earliest full-length biographies of Hitler in English. Bullock's work is still considered one of the best.

Angus Calder, *The People's War: Britain, 1939–1945* (1969): A noted Scottish writer and poet, Calder wrote a social history of Great Britain during World War II.

William Craig, *Enemy at the Gates: The Battle for Stalingrad* (1973): This is a recounting of the horrendous battle for the city of Stalingrad, which resulted in the destruction of the German Sixth Army and the turning of the war against Germany.

Dwight D. Eisenhower, *Crusade in Europe* (1948): The supreme Allied commander and future president of the United States wrote this memoir of his service as head of the Allied forces that defeated Germany.

Joachim Fest, *Adolf Hitler,* rev. ed. (1995): Fest, a German historian, wrote this best-selling biography of Hitler in German; it was later translated into English and became an international best-seller.

Anne Frank, *Diary of a Young Girl* (1952): This poignant diary was written by a teenage German girl whose family had fled to Holland to avoid the Nazis. Anne Frank's work was written during the years in Amsterdam when they hid from the Nazis in the attic of a sympathetic Dutch family. After their betrayal by neighbors, the family was sent to a concentration camp, where Anne died in 1945. Her diary was saved by her father, the only member of the family to survive.

Charles de Gaulle, *Memoires de Guerre,* three volumes (1954–59): The memoirs of the towering French leader, de Gaulle's work is an important document by one of the key players in the war—one who also enjoyed a long political career in the postwar years as president of France.

Major General Heinz Guderian, *Achtung— Panzer!* (1937): Guderian was one of the strategists of the panzer tank blitzkrieg strategy used to overwhelm France in the spring of 1940. This highly influential tactical guide described the development and tactics of armored forces.

Ken Hechler, *The Bridge at Remagen* (1957): A book about the bridge at the German town of Remagen, which the Germans failed to demolish before the Allies were able to seize it and cross the Rhine River.

Richard Hillary, *The Last Enemy* (1942): This Spitfire pilot's firsthand account of the Battle of Britain was wartime England's best-selling work of nonfiction.

Adolf Hitler, *Mein Kampf* (1925; 1939, English translation): Hitler wrote this autobiographical work in 1925 while in prison for the failed 1923 Beer Hall Putsch in Munich. It describes in great detail everything he said he would do—and did do—including his anti-Semitic policies and his expansionism.

Horizon (1940–45): This London magazine, edited by Cyril Connolly, contained the best firsthand accounts of the war, provocative and censor-free commentary, and war poetry by Alun Lewis ("All Day It Has Rained"), Stephen Spender, Dylan Thomas ("A Refusal to Mourn the Death, by Fire, of a Child in London"), Keith Douglas, and Roy Fuller.

Ludovic Kennedy, *Pursuit* (1974): This is the tale of the sinking of the German battleship *Bismarck,* the pride of Hitler's surface fleet.

Ian Kershaw, *Hitler: Nemesis, 1936–1945* (2000): The second volume of a recent English-language biography of Hitler is praised for its scholarship and attention to detail.

Charles B. MacDonald, *A Time for Trumpets* (1985): The story is of the last German offensive in the West, the Battle of the Bulge, which occurred in December 1944 and which set back the Allied timetable for the conquest of Germany.

Cornelius Ryan, *The Longest Day: June 6, 1944* (1959), *The Last Battle* (1966), and *A Bridge Too Far* (1974): Ryan was a popular historian who wrote about specific battles, in this case, D-Day, the battle for Berlin, and Operation Market-Garden.

William L. Shirer, *Berlin Diary* (1941), *The Rise and Fall of the Third Reich* (1960), and *The Nightmare Years, 1930–1940* (1984): A correspondent in Germany in the 1930s, Shirer witnessed firsthand the rise of the Nazi regime and its march toward war. His *Rise and Fall of the Third Reich* was an international bestseller when it appeared in 1960.

Konstantin Simonov, *No Quarter: On Russia's Fighting Lines* (1943) and *Days and Nights* (1943; 1945, English translation): This account of the battle and siege of Stalingrad is one of the most widely read books of the war.

Albert Speer, *Inside the Third Reich* (1970): Speer, Hitler's architect and last minister of armaments, served 20 years in prison after his conviction for war crimes at Nuremberg in 1946. Supremely intelligent, he carved out a position for himself as the "good Nazi" by confessing to some of his crimes, a stark contrast to other Nazis who frequently denied any role in atrocities or in the creation and implementation of Nazi policies.

Erich von Manstein, *Lost Victories* (1958): This is the memoir of "Hitler's most brilliant general."

THE ARMED SERVICES EDITIONS

In 1942, Ray L. Trautman, of the U.S. Army's Library Section, and H. Stahley Thompson, a graphics specialist, conceived these squat, pocket editions for service personnel. To underwrite expenses, they recruited the Council on Books in Wartime, a private group of librarians, publishers, and booksellers. They used an inventive printing method, sold paper and printing to the army at cost, and distributed the books only overseas, so as not to compete with domestic sales.

Between 1943 and 1947 the council distributed nearly 123 million copies of 1,322 titles to U.S. troops. These Armed Services Editions were often the only books available to service personnel. Most books were bestsellers, mysteries, and other non-war-related titles, but some were contemporary, for example, Sergeant George Baker's *The Sad Sack, The Best from Yank,* Harry Brown's *Artie Greengroin, Pfc.,* Captain Harry C. Butcher's *My Three Years with Eisenhower,* and Bill Mauldin's *Up Front.* Armed Services Editions proved to be popular and a welcome relief to the soldiers.

Penguin Books in England adopted this bargain format too, publishing millions of inexpensive paperbound editions that British soldiers and civilians read voraciously. The "paperbacks" that the project produced broadened public tastes in both countries and revolutionized the publishing industry after the war.

Nonfiction (Pacific)

James Bradley, *Flags of Our Fathers* (2000): This is the story of the six men who raised the flag at Iwo Jima in 1945 and were captured in a photograph that is perhaps the most famous one of the war. It is told by the son of a survivor of the battle.

Mitsuo Fuchida and Masatake Okumiya, *Midway* (1955): Fuchida, the lead Japanese pilot of the attack on Pearl Harbor, wrote this history of the Battle of Midway, describing from the inside what the Japanese defeat was like.

Donald Knox, *Death March: The Survivors of Bataan* (1981): Knox's book is an account of the horrific Bataan Death March told through the eyes of the survivors.

Captain Ted W. Lawson, *Thirty Seconds over Tokyo* (1943): Lawson, one of the pilots who took part in the Doolittle raid on Tokyo in 1942, wrote this best-selling account of his experiences the following year.

Gordon W. Prange, with Donald M. Goldstein and Katherine V. Dillon, *At Dawn We Slept: The Untold Story of Pearl Harbor* (1991) and *Miracle at Midway* (1982): Prange's exhaustive works recount the early days of the war, from Pearl Harbor to Midway. He all but implies that President Franklin D. Roosevelt goaded the Japanese into attacking the United States.

Eugene B. Sledge, *With the Old Breed at Peleliu and Okinawa* (1981): Sledge, a U.S. Marine private at the Battle of Peleliu, wrote this memoir of his wartime experiences more than 25 years after the conflict.

Ronald H. Spector, *Eagle Against the Sun: The American War with Japan* (1985): Spector's book is a one-volume synopsis of the Pacific war, focusing on the major land, air, and sea battles.

Richard Tregaskis, *Guadalcanal Diary* (1943): Tregaskis, a war correspondent, went ashore with the first wave of marines on Guadalcanal in August 1942. This book, published the following year, recounts his experiences.

WRITERS WHO SERVED

The armed services drew from all walks of life, including many writers whose wartime experiences would inspire and shape their works.

Writer	Branch of Service	Dates of Service	Area of Activity
Paul Fussell	U.S. Army	1943–46	Served in France, Germany
Joseph Heller	U.S. Air Force	1943–45	Bombardier in Italy
James Jones	U.S. Army	1939–44	Wounded at Guadalcanal
Norman Mailer	U.S. Army	1944–46	The Philippine Campaign
William Styron	U.S. Marines	1944–45	Okinawa
Gore Vidal	U.S. Army	1944–46	The Aleutians
Kurt Vonnegut	U.S. Army	1944–45	Infantry scout taken prisoner at Dresden

The War in Film, Theater, Television, and Music

When World War II broke out, Hollywood's film industry was a $2-billion-a-year international business. Because films had been, since the mid-1930s, subject to fascist censorship or outright banning in Germany, Italy, Spain, and elsewhere, Hollywood was acutely aware of the Nazi menace and the specter of world war long before the rest of the country. Antifascist themes appeared in *Blockade* (1938), set during the Spanish Civil War, and, even more controversially, in Warner Brothers' anti-isolationist drama *Confessions of a Nazi Spy* (1939). So outspoken was Hollywood before the United States entered the war that the Senate formed a subcommittee to investigate whether the film industry was guilty of "warmongering."

Two months after the bombing of Pearl Harbor, the Selective Service declared Hollywood film production an "essential industry," which legally exempted most moviemaking people from serving. The Screen Actors' Guild, however, feared public backlash and declared that its 10,000 union members would accept the same draft requirements as anyone else. By 1944 more than 1,500 guild members had joined the service, an influx of talent and vision that shored up the military's combat photography and film crew units.

In April 1942, the Army Signal Corps took over a Paramount Pictures facility in Long Island City, New York. There the Army Pictorial Service made 1,300 films by 1945. These films had patriotic themes or were practical guides to subjects of interest to wartime audiences. The army hired some of the top directors in Hollywood (John Huston, Frank Capra, William Wyler, William Wegman, George Cukor, John Ford, among others) to work on these short films (sample titles: *Kill or Be Killed, Baking in the Field, Sex Hygiene,* and *Hasty Sign Making),* and by 1943 the government had budgeted $1,226,000 to produce these films. The government cut the budget to $50,000 in 1944, and Hollywood took over, at no cost to the taxpayers.

Joseph Goebbels, minister of enlightenment and propaganda, orchestrated Germany's film industry. When the Nazis ascended to power in 1933, he formed the Film Office and put the state in charge of the industry. Of the 1,100 films produced by 1945, about 15 percent were pure propaganda, intended to demonize the Jews and deify Adolf Hitler. The rest were officially sanctioned dramas that Goebbels said were "to keep our people happy." The most talented filmmaker in Germany was, without doubt, Leni Riefenstahl, whose *Triumph of the Will* (1934), a film about the Nazi Party congress in Nuremberg in 1934, was so influential worldwide that even Frank Capra, an ardent antifascist, cited it as an inspiration.

PETER MASLOWSKI

The extensive World War II photographic record has permitted Americans to relive this unique war again and again, repeatedly reinforcing the collective historical memory. Television and VCR technologies have been especially influential in expanding the use of wartime motion pictures by making them readily available and familiar at all levels of society. And because motion pictures mate sight and sound, they can have a more intense impact than still photos. Sitting in their darkened dens and family rooms, people watch the same newsreels and documentaries that appeared on the home front during "the" war. For fifty years World War II has remained frozen in time, devoid of those fresh and searching historical perspectives that the passing decades ordinarily bring to events, even such momentous ones as "the Good War."

—From *Armed with Cameras: The American Military Photographers of World War II* (New York: Free Press, 1993).

The medium of television, meanwhile, was just being developed. As early as 1929, the BBC had successfully experimented with a prototype of television, but war put an end to its television broadcasting efforts. Instead, the British used television technology in the 1940 development of radio detection and ranging (RADAR), an invaluable defense against Luftwaffe bombers. Actual programming remained in its infancy until January 2, 1947, with the live broadcast of the opening session of the U.S. Congress. Only two networks, CBS and NBC, had programs in the first years, and they avoided the war as subject matter. One trusted wartime icon, Edward R. Murrow, made the transition in 1951 from his popular *Hear It Now* CBS radio program to television's *See It Now*. Murrow's presence perhaps softened the medium toward war coverage; in 1952, NBC produced a popular series called *Victory at Sea*. Compiled from combat footage provided by the military, the series was written by the historian Samuel Eliot Morison as a chronology of World War II naval warfare. The show's half-hour installments ran for 26 weeks, striking a patriotic chord with anxious cold war audiences. A stirring score by the famous theater composer Richard Rodgers contributed to *Victory at Sea*'s success. Many other war-themed programs would follow.

PATRIOTISM IS PROFITABLE: THE HOLLYWOOD STORY

During the war, Hollywood found itself in the enviable position of increasing its revenues (and profits) while decreasing the number of films it made. From 1937 to 1941, Hollywood's "Big Eight" studios released 1,833 features. From 1942 to 1946 they released 1,395. According to figures from *Box Office Digest,* despite the 25 percent decline, profits climbed from $34 million in 1941 to $50 million in 1942 and $60 million in each of the next three years. Despite the hardships of war on the home front, Americans continued to attend the movies for entertainment

and information. The increase in revenues despite the drop in production may be partly explained by the viewing public's continued support and the savings realized by producing fewer films. *Hollywood Quarterly* estimates that three out of every 10 feature films made in the United States from 1942 to 1944 (or 374 of 1,313) were "directly concerned with some aspect of the war."

> On the Anzio beachhead in Italy, there was a comedy on the screen when a stray German shell exploded nearby. A moment later—to the delight of the shell-conscious audience—a film character spoke the line, "What was that?"   —*Movie Lot to Beachhead*

The top U.S. box office draws during the war were (in order of their popularity):

1942: Abbott and Costello, Clark Gable, Gary Cooper, Mickey Rooney
1943: Betty Grable, Bob Hope, Abbott and Costello, Bing Crosby, Gary Cooper
1944: Bing Crosby, Gary Cooper, Bob Hope, Betty Grable, Spencer Tracy
1945: Bing Crosby, Van Johnson, Greer Garson, Clark Gable, Spencer Tracy

Source: *Motion Picture Herald.*

NOTEWORTHY FILMS ABOUT WORLD WAR II

World War II has been a compelling subject for filmmakers from wartime to the present. A list of major films about World War II follows; it is not intended to be comprehensive or to endorse specific works. Listed here are movies made both during the war and after.

1940–45

GERMANY

BAPTISM OF FIRE (1940) This documentary is about the blitzkrieg campaign in Poland.

JUD SÜSS (JEW SUSS) (1940) This anti-Semitic propaganda is set in the Middle Ages. A grotesque Jew rapes a woman played by Kristina Soderbaum, the Nazis' most popular actress. Soderbaum's character commits suicide rather than be polluted by bearing the child.

OLYMPIA (1936) Documentary. Leni Riefenstahl, director, producer. It celebrates Aryan racial superiority at the 1936 Olympic Games in Berlin.

SIEG IM WESTEN (VICTORY IN THE WEST) (1940–41) This documentary celebrates the German army's victories in Norway, the Low Countries, and France.

TRIUMPH OF THE WILL (1934) Documentary. Leni Riefenstahl, director, producer. This movie, about the 1934 Nuremberg rally, is a template for all future Nazi films.

GREAT BRITAIN

DESERT VICTORY (1943) This British army–produced documentary is about the defeat of Rommel's troops at El Alamein.

IMMORTAL BATTALION (1944) Carol Reed, director. Written by Eric Ambler and Peter Ustinov, this movie is based on their war experiences in the British army.

IN WHICH WE SERVE (1943) This movie was directed by David Lean and Nöel Coward, who wrote the screenplay based on the experiences of Lord Mountbatten (uncle of the future Queen Elizabeth II) aboard HMS *Kelly*.

LIFEBOAT (1944) Director Alfred Hitchcock's only war-era film is about survivors of a ship sunk by a German U-boat and stars Tallulah Bankhead and Hume Cronyn.

MRS. MINIVER (1942) Made by American director William Wyler, this is a tribute to British courage during the Blitz. It stars Greer Garson and Walter Pidgeon as the Minivers.

JAPAN

FIVE SCOUTS (1939) More subtle than most Japanese feature films, this was the story of Japanese soldiers in northern China.

THE NEW EARTH (1942) Intended as a Japanese-German collaboration, each Axis power ended up distributing its own version. This one, Manasaka Itami's, was the best, about a Japanese war hero's conversion away from democracy.

VICTORY SONG OF THE ORIENT (1942) The racism of the West and its co-opting of Asian culture, a common theme of the War Ministry, is set against the conquest of the Philippines.

SOVIET UNION

THE CITY THAT STOPPED HITLER— HEROIC STALINGRAD (1942) This documentary is about the siege of Stalingrad; 13 Soviet photographers were killed while making this film.

MOSCOW STRIKES BACK (1942) An American remake, with an original soundtrack, is based on a Soviet documentary of resistance called *Defeat of the German Armies near Moscow*.

RADUGA (1944) This narrative is about the Soviet resistance to Nazi occupation, based on the novel by V. L. Vasilevskaya.

UNITED STATES

ACTION IN THE NORTH ATLANTIC (1943) Starring Humphrey Bogart and Raymond Massey, it's a story of merchant mariners dodging Nazi U-boats.

AIR FORCE (1943) Howard Hawks, director. John Garfield plays an Army Air Forces B-17 crewman called into action after the bombing of Pearl Harbor. The screenplay was cowritten by William Faulkner. It won an Oscar and was nominated for two others.

BATAAN (1943) This movie stars Robert Walker as a navy crewman stuck with an army outfit whose job is to delay the Japanese in the jungle long enough for General Douglas MacArthur and his troops to evacuate the Philippines.

BATTLE OF THE MARIANAS (1944) Made by combat cameramen on Saipan and Guam, six Marine Corps photographers died during filming of this documentary.

BATTLE OF MIDWAY (1942) John Ford, director. This documentary was made by Ford, a navy commander who was on Midway when the Japanese attacked it. It won an Oscar.

THE BATTLE OF SAN PIETRO (1944) This documentary, directed and narrated by John Huston, is about the bloody Nazi retreat through Italy's Liri Valley.

THE BLITZ WOLF (1942) Created by Tex Avery. It's an animated retelling of "Three Little Pigs," with Hitler as the Big Bad Wolf.

CASABLANCA (1943) Michael Curtiz, director. Set in Free French Casablanca, the film's war takes place in the conscience of cynical American nightclub owner Rick Blaine (Humphrey Bogart). Also starring Ingrid Bergman, *Casablanca* has remained one of the most popular films of all time.

DER FÜHRER'S FACE (1942) Created by Walt Disney. This anti-Nazi animated film features Donald Duck having a nightmare that he works in a German munitions factory.

THE FIGHTING SULLIVANS (1944) Based on the true story of five brothers who died when the U.S. cruiser *Juneau* was sunk at Guadalcanal, it's also the inspiration for *Saving Private Ryan* (see p. 470).

GUADALCANAL DIARY (1943) This fictional adaptation of Richard Tregaskis's frontline reporting, stars William Bendix, Anthony Quinn, and Lloyd Nolan.

LET THERE BE LIGHT (1944) This John Huston–directed documentary is about battle fatigue, the stress-related combat disorder that afflicted many American GIs.

MEMPHIS BELLE (1944) This documentary produced by the War Department and directed by William Wyler is about bombing runs over Europe. Two Army Air Forces photographers were killed while making this film.

THE NEGRO SOLDIER IN WORLD WAR II (1943) Frank Capra, director. Capra argues in this documentary that blacks should be integrated into the military.

OBJECTIVE, BURMA! (1945) Raoul Walsh, director. Starring Errol Flynn; he leads a commando raid behind Japanese lines as U.S. troops aim to retake Burma.

REPORT FROM THE ALEUTIANS (1943) Documentary. John Huston, director, narrator. This film is about the U.S. military in the Aleutian Islands, an isolated area of Alaska that was partially occupied by the Japanese.

SHORES OF TRIPOLI (1942) This was the top box office hit of the year for Twentieth Century Fox.

SO PROUDLY WE HAIL (1943) This movie starred Claudette Colbert, Paulette Goddard, and Veronica Lake as U.S. nurses who escaped the Japanese after the fall of Corregidor.

THE STORY OF G.I. JOE (1945) William Wellman, director. Starring Burgess Meredith and Robert Mitchum, it's based on the writings of Ernie Pyle and made with Pyle's assistance before his death in combat the same year.

THIRTY SECONDS OVER TOKYO (1944) Mervyn LeRoy, director. Starring Spencer Tracy as Colonel James Doolittle, it's about the crew of a B-25 Mitchell bomber that took part in the raid on Tokyo in 1942. It won one Oscar.

THUNDERBOLT (1945) Documentary. William Wyler, John Sturgis, directors. Narrated by Lloyd Bridges, the film describes the exploits of the 57th Fighter Group as it attacks German supply lines.

TUNISIAN VICTORY (1944) Documentary. Frank Capra, Ray Boulting, directors. It describes the U.S. effort in North Africa, from 1942 until the German defeat and expulsion from Africa in 1943.

TWO DOWN, ONE TO GO (1945) Documentary. Frank Capra, director. It offers a detailed description, battle by battle, of the U.S. involvement in the war.

WAKE ISLAND (1942) John Farrow, director. Starring William Bendix and Robert Preston as members of a marine outfit ordered to defend this Pacific island, it won five Academy Award nominations.

A WALK IN THE SUN (1945) Lewis Milestone, director. This drama is about U.S. troops fighting Germans in Italy in 1943.

WHY WE FIGHT (1942–43) These seven 50-minute documentaries (*Prelude to War, The Nazis Strike, Divide and Conquer, Battle of Britain, Battle of Russia, Battle of China, War Comes to America*) were directed by Frank Capra and Anatole Litvak and produced by the U.S. War Department.

1946–Present

FRANCE

UN CONDAMNÉ À MORT S'EST ÉCHAPPÉ (A CONDEMNED MAN HAS ESCAPED) (1957) Robert Bresson, director. It's based on the real-life experiences of Andre Devigny in a German POW camp in Lyon, France, in 1943.

LE DERNIER METRO (THE LAST METRO) (1980) François Truffaut, director. It's about the Nazi occupation of Paris and the attempts to circumvent it in the theater district.

PARIS BRULE-T-IL? (IS PARIS BURNING?) (1966) An unusual collaboration between French and American filmmakers, it has a script by Gore Vidal and Francis Ford Coppola and stars Jean-Paul Belmondo and Alain Delon, with Kirk Douglas as General George Patton.

AU REVOIR LES ENFANTS (GOODBYE, CHILDREN) (1987) Louis Malle, director. The story is set in a boarding school in occupied France.

LE TRAIN (THE TRAIN) (1965) This Franco-American collaboration, with John Frankenheimer directing and Burt Lancaster starring, is a tense tale about intercepting a train full of priceless stolen art headed to Germany with the Nazis.

GERMANY

DAS BOOT (THE BOAT) (1981) Wolfgang Petersen, director. Set on the doomed German submarine U-96 during the last days of the war, this is arguably the greatest film ever made about submarine warfare.

***DIE BRÜCKE (THE BRIDGE)* (1959)** Based on Erwin Dietrich's autobiographical novel, it's about a pointless German military mission near the end of the war.

***DAS EISERNE KREUZ (THE IRON CROSS)* (1976)** This film was directed by Sam Peckinpah but made through the German film industry. It's about Nazi soldiers retreating from the Eastern Front.

***DIE WEISSE ROSE (THE WHITE ROSE)* (1983)** The story is of a brave few Germans who resisted Nazi rule and were brutally executed after being apprehended by the Gestapo.

GREAT BRITAIN

***THE BATTLE OF BRITAIN* (1969)** Starring Michael Caine, Laurence Olivier, Robert Shaw, and Edward Fox as Spitfire and Messerschmitt pilots dogfighting in the skies over England.

***THE BRIDGE ON THE RIVER KWAI* (1963)** David Lean, director. Set in a Japanese POW camp in the Burmese jungle, the film pits the rigid career officer Colonel Nicholson against the camp leader, Colonel Saito. It won seven Academy Awards.

***A BRIDGE TOO FAR* (1977)** Richard Attenborough, director. With an all-star cast, the film is about Operation Market-Garden, an unsuccessful Allied airborne and ground assault in 1944 to capture bridges in Holland.

***THE GUNS OF NAVARONE* (1961)** American actors Gregory Peck and James Darren share the sets with a mostly English crew, as British commandos plot to take out a German gun emplacement on a Greek island.

***HOPE AND GLORY* (1987)** John Boorman, director. This partly autobiographical film shows the war on the British home front through the eyes of a London boy.

***SINK THE BISMARCK* (1960)** This is based on C. S. Forester's account of the search-and-destroy mission to sink the large German battleship.

JAPAN

***FIRES ON THE PLAIN* (1959)** Kon Ichikawa, director. A horrific tale set in the Philippines in 1945, it shows Japanese troops in retreat.

***THE HUMAN CONDITION* (1959–61)** Masaki Kobayashi, director. The story of Kaji, a soldier of the Japanese army, is related in three parts.

***TORA! TORA! TORA!* (1970)** Toshio Masuda and Kinji Fukasaku directed the Japanese sequences; Richard Fleischer directed the U.S. sequences. This epic movie tells the story of the attack on Pearl Harbor from both the Japanese and American perspectives.

SOVIET UNION

***IDI I SMOTRI (COME AND SEE)* (1985)** A film about the Nazi genocide in Byelorussia in 1943.

UNITED STATES

***BATTLE CRY* (1955)** Raoul Walsh, director. Based on Leon Uris's novel. Starring Van Heflin, Aldo Ray, and James Whitmore (who also narrates), it follows a group of marines from boot camp to South Pacific jungles.

***THE BATTLE OF THE BULGE* (1965)** Starring Henry Fonda, Dana Andrews, and Robert Ryan, this is Hollywood's depiction of Hitler's final, desperate offensive on the Western Front.

BATTLEGROUND (1949) William Wellman, director. Starring Van Johnson, John Hodiak, and James Whitmore, it's about men returning to the front in time for the Battle of the Bulge.

THE BIG RED ONE (1980) Sam Fuller, director. It's about members of the First Infantry Division led by "the Sergeant" (Lee Marvin) from North Africa in 1942 to Normandy in 1944.

THE DIRTY DOZEN (1967) Robert Aldrich, director. Lee Marvin stars as a major assigned to mold a group of convicts into a tight-knit commando unit just before D-Day.

FROM HERE TO ETERNITY (1953) Fred Zinneman, director. Starring Burt Lancaster, Deborah Kerr, Frank Sinatra, and Montgomery Clift, it chronicles the lives of U.S. servicemen in Hawaii on the eve of U.S. entry into World War II. It won eight Academy Awards.

HELL IS FOR HEROES (1962) Don Siegel, director. James Coburn, Steve McQueen, and Bobby Darin star as an infantry detail up against a large German force in the last days of the war in France.

KING RAT (1965) Set in the notorious Changi, a Japanese prisoner-of-war camp, it is based on the experiences of the novelist James Clavell. George Segal stars as the entrepreneurial Corporal King.

THE LONGEST DAY (1962) (**FIVE DIRECTORS**) John Wayne, Henry Fonda, Robert Mitchum, and Richard Burton depict the 24 hours of D-Day.

MERRILL'S MARAUDERS (1962) Sam Fuller, director. Stars Jeff Chandler, who leads his men through the jungles of Burma after the Japanese have run out General Joseph Stillwell's forces.

A MIDNIGHT CLEAR (1992) Six members of a reconnaissance team are caught behind Nazi lines during the Battle of the Bulge; it is based on a novel by William Wharton.

PATTON (1970) Franklin J. Schaffner, director. George C. Scott inhabits the role of General George S. Patton, for which Scott won an Oscar (the film won seven in all). Francis Ford Coppola cowrote the screenplay. General Omar Bradley was a technical adviser.

SAVING PRIVATE RYAN (1998) Steven Spielberg, director. Starring Tom Hanks. This unusually accurate re-creation of the Omaha Beach landing follows a mission to find, and save, the remaining son of a family who has lost its other sons to the war. It won the best director Oscar for Spielberg.

SCHINDLER'S LIST (1993) Steven Spielberg, director. This is the story of Oscar Schindler, a businessman and member of the Nazi Party who saved Polish Jews from deportation to the death camps by putting them to work in his factory in Poland. It won Oscars for best picture and best director.

TO HELL AND BACK (1955) Jesse Hibbs, director. Audie Murphy plays himself in this autobiographical film about his war experiences in North Africa, Anzio, and France.

TWELVE O'CLOCK HIGH (1949) Henry King, director. Gregory Peck and Dean Jagger (who won an Oscar) star in a taut psychological drama about daylight precision bombing of German industrial sites by B-17s based in England.

TELEVISION PROGRAMMING WITH WORLD WAR II THEMES

After Edward R. Murrow's 1951 *See It Now* and NBC's 1952 series *Victory at Sea*, numerous U.S. television shows carried a World War II theme. Most were produced in the 1960s and 1970s; aside from an occasional miniseries on World

War II subjects, the war has largely disappeared from regular network television programming and is now largely covered on cable TV channels such as the History Channel.

Great Britain

DANGER UXB A BBC series about the 97th Bomb Disposal Company, Royal Engineers, it ran in England in 1978–79 and the following year in the United States on Public Broadcasting.

United States

BAA BAA BLACK SHEEP (SEPTEMBER 21, 1976–SEPTEMBER 1, 1978) This program covered the lives and trials of Marine fliers in the South Pacific.

COMBAT (OCTOBER 2, 1962–AUGUST 29, 1967) This show detailed the lives of U.S. troops in Europe after D-Day.

COMBAT SERGEANT (JUNE 29–SEPTEMBER 27, 1956) This program focused on the adventures of Allied troops in North Africa.

HOGAN'S HEROES (SEPTEMBER 17, 1965–JULY 4, 1971) This popular satirical show was about Allied POWs in a German camp in which the Germans are portrayed as harmless buffoons.

RAT PATROL (SEPTEMBER 12, 1966–SEPTEMBER 16, 1968) This show detailed the lives of Allied commandos in North Africa.

12 O'CLOCK HIGH (SEPTEMBER 18, 1964–JANUARY 13, 1967) This show was about the 918th Bombardment Group of the U.S. Eighth Air Force flying B-17 missions over Germany.

WAR AND REMEMBRANCE (NOVEMBER 18–23, 1988; MAY 7–14, 1989) This 30-hour miniseries, based on the novel by Herman Wouk, covered the entirety of the war. It was one of the docudramas that began to appear in the 1970s and 1980s and often relied on historical themes and backgrounds.

WHEN TRUMPETS FADE (1998) This was an HBO remake of Don Siegel's 1962 *Hell Is for Heroes* (see p. 470).

THE WINDS OF WAR (FEBRUARY 6–13, 1983) This docudrama aired for seven nights, depicting the early years of the war, from the Nazi blitzkrieg attack on Poland to Pearl Harbor. It is based on the novel by Herman Wouk.

CELEBRITIES WHO SERVED

The actors listed in the table that follows were among those who served despite Hollywood's status as an "essential industry." They followed the lead of the Screen Actors' Guild, which had its union members meet the same draft requirements as anyone else.

Celebrity	Service
Eddie Albert	U.S. Navy
Gene Autry	Air Transport Command
Jackie Coogan	Air Force pilot
Douglas Fairbanks Jr.	Won the Silver Star for action at Salerno and capture of Elba
Henry Fonda	Naval Air Combat
Clark Gable	Air Force
Sterling Hayden	Marines
Lee Marvin	Marines
Victor Mature	Chief boatswain's mate, Coast Guard
Robert Montgomery	Navy

Celebrity	Service
Wayne Morris	Navy pilot
David Niven	British army
Tyrone Power	Marines
James Stewart	Army, led bombing missions over Germany

MUSIC, MUSICAL THEATER, AND DANCE

Like other forms of artistic expression, music, musical theater, and dance served the purposes of war. In Germany, Great Britain, and the United States, these forms of art raised morale and provided a welcome means of escape. In Germany, the arts also managed to serve the interests of the Nazi state.

Germany

According to the historian William Shirer, music fared the best of all the arts under Nazi rule, mainly "because Germans had such a rich store of it from Bach through Beethoven and Mozart to Brahms." The Nazis banned Paul Hindemith's music for being modern, Mendelssohn's for being Jewish (likewise, the Nazis dismissed all Jewish musicians from orchestras). The great opera composer Richard Strauss remained in Germany and was even named president of the Reich Music Chamber. Although he never left Germany, he eventually fell out with the Nazis and spent the remainder of the war at his home in Garmisch.

The Berlin Philharmonic Orchestra and Berlin State Opera continued to perform throughout the war years. In fact, the Berlin Philharmonic gave concerts until the week before the Soviets entered Berlin in 1945. The orchestra was then spirited out of Berlin to safety in the West, partly as a result of a plan put together by Albert Speer, Hitler's minister of armaments. Recordings of the Dresden Staatskapelle were made as late as 1944, even as the Allied bombers were flying overhead.

The Germans also continued to celebrate the Bayreuth Festival, which (to this day) celebrates the work of Richard Wagner (1813–83), Hitler's favorite composer. On Hitler's birthday, Wagner's *Meistersinger Overture* was always played, and on the national Heroes Day, Hitler's speech was signaled by Beethoven's Third Symphony, the "Eroica." Wherever Hitler was scheduled to appear, his arrival was heralded by the playing of his favorite march, the *Badenweiler*. The most widely heard piece of music in Nazi Germany, however, was the "Horst Wessel Lied," the anthem of the party, which was named in honor of a Nazi street fighter who was killed in a brawl in the 1920s.

Great Britain

London was the center of the arts, but bars and dance halls were filled to capacity all over England. "Jitterbug marathons," among other frantic activities, were regular events. To enhance the dancing, wartime hit singles included "We're Going to Hang Out Our Washing on the Siegfried Line," "The White Cliffs of Dover," "I'm Going to Get Lit Up When the Lights Go On in London," and "Shine On, Harvest Moon." Dance hall and bar life was greatly changed by the influx of American GIs, who flooded into England by the millions between 1942 and 1944 in preparation for the D-Day invasion of France. GIs spent money on alcohol and women, and they injected a new, at times unwelcome, life into the British pub.

Because trustees of the National Gallery feared it would be destroyed by Luftwaffe bombs, the museum stored most of its art in North Wales, and the gallery director Kenneth Clark opened the space as an ad hoc concert venue. War-weary Londoners flocked to gallery concerts by the classical pianist Myra Hess. The crowning achievement in classical music was the 1942 Albert Hall debut of Vaughan Williams's

Fifth Symphony. Despite the Blitz, concert life continued, if at times in unconventional venues. Perhaps the most popular singer during the war years was Vera Lynn, whose "We'll Meet Again" became an anthem for homesick soldiers and their wives and lovers. Lynn also visited the troops overseas, traveling as far as the remote corners of Burma.

United States

As far back as 1934, the playwright Elmer Davis—who later headed the Office of War Information—was warning about the Nazis in his play *Judgment Day,* which depicted them as gangsters. The novelist Sinclair Lewis picked up on that theme in 1935 with his grimly ominous *It Can't Happen Here,* about a fascist takeover of the United States. Nonetheless, by the outbreak of war only two popular musicals even touched on the military, and the war played little part in either. These were *This Is the Army,* written by Irving Berlin in 1942, and *On the Town,* music by Leonard Bernstein, words and book by Betty Comden and Adolph Green, in 1944. The latter, about three sailors on shore leave for 24 hours, was developed from a ballet, *Fancy Free.* The most popular musical in the United States during the war was *Oklahoma!* (1943), by Richard Rodgers and Oscar Hammerstein II, which nearly single-handedly revived musical theater. Rodgers and Hammerstein's great musical set during the war, *South Pacific* did not appear until 1949. The story of U.S. Navy men, romance, and danger on a Pacific island during World War II, it was one of the most popular musicals in the history of the theater.

To boost morale in the military, swing orchestras like Kay Kyser's and Teddy Powell's recorded such upbeat songs as "Good-bye Mama (I'm Off to Yokohama)," "Praise the Lord and Pass the Ammunition!," "(There'll Be Bluebirds Over) The White Cliffs of Dover," and "There'll Always Be an England." One of the saddest moments of the war, and a great loss to the world of music, was the death of Glenn Miller, whose plane went down on a flight from London to Paris (see Chapter 6, "Officers and Soldiers"). His meteoric rise, before his October 1942 enlistment in the military, was the result of his thrice-weekly CBS radio concert series *Glenn Miller's Moonlight Serenade,* where he showcased signature songs like "In the Mood," "Little Brown Jug," "Pavanne," "Runnin' Wild," and "Sunrise Serenade." Other popular bandleaders were Duke Ellington, Benny Goodman, Harry James, Tommy Dorsey, Kyser, and Powell.

Music and the theater, like the movies, were a crucial means of escape during the war. Musicians and theater people, like their Hollywood counterparts, played a vital role in keeping home-front morale high during the dark years of the war.

MOST POPULAR SINGLES

Popular music was indispensable for boosting morale at home and overseas. Many tunes that were huge hits on the home front (e.g., "Mairzy Doats") did not have crossover appeal to the combat zone. The songs that follow were the most popular among U.S. troops. While many artists have recorded these songs, the versions cited here were the most popular during the war.

"As Time Goes By," sung by Dooley Wilson (used in *Casablanca*)

"Boogie Woogie Bugle Boy," "Don't Sit Under the Apple Tree," Andrews Sisters

"Chattanooga Choo Choo," Glenn Miller Orchestra

"Comin' in on a Wing and a Prayer," Eddie Cantor

"Der Führer's Face," from a 1942 Walt Disney cartoon starring Donald Duck

"I'll Be Home for Christmas," sung by Bing Crosby

"I'll Be Seeing You," recorded by both Frank Sinatra and Bing Crosby

"I'll Walk Alone," sung by Dinah Shore

"My Shining Hour," sung by Fred Astaire

"Praise the Lord and Pass the Ammunition!"
Kay Kyser Orchestra

"There Are Such Things," Tommy Dorsey
Orchestra, with Frank Sinatra

"There's a Star-Spangled Banner Waving
Somewhere," by Elton Britt

"White Christmas," written by Irving Berlin,
sung by Bing Crosby

Source: *Variety,* "Fifty Year Hit Parade"

MOST POPULAR U.S. SINGERS

Popular singers on the home front included Nelson Eddy, Lily Pons, Gene Autry, the Mills Brothers, and Frank Sinatra. On the battlefront, Sergeant Johnny Desmond, who sang with Glenn Miller's Air Force Band and had hits with "I'll Be Seeing You" and "Long Ago and Far Away," earned the nicknames "The G.I. Sinatra" and "The Creamer." The country musician Roy Acuff was also popular.

Source: *Time*

The War in Visual Art

Visual art continued to exist during World War II and was often used to further the war effort. Artists painted battle scenes, illustrated training and field manuals, designed propaganda posters, and created cartoons as war commentary. Whether propaganda, social satire, or pure escapism, art remained a part of life during World War II. Even under the strict living conditions of the war and a shortage of time and supplies, both Axis- and Allied-aligned artists created art in the name of the war effort.

GERMANY AND OTHER AXIS POWERS

In Nazi Germany, artists made propaganda. The best known signed his work Mjolnir (real name: Hans Schweitzer). His storm trooper–bedecked recruitment posters, leaflets, murals, and postage stamps were omnipresent in Germany, as were the anti-Semitic cartoons of "Fips," whose work set the tone for the weekly *Der Stürmer.* War artists were assigned to the Wehrmacht and Luftwaffe, and they managed to depict the raw realities of battle. These included Luitpold Adam (commander of the war artists), Josef Arens, Heinz Hendorf, and Franz Eichhorst. Two German artists who had an ability to tread fine lines were Erich Schilling and Karl Arnold. Both were satirists whose work predated Hitler's rise—and who, in fact, were originally anti-Nazi—but whose talents were enlisted for the German war effort. Germany lost its greatest artists to exile, including Max Beckman, George Grosz, Jacob Epstein, John Heartfield, Hans Jelinek, Henry Koerner, and Arthur Szyk, who became the Allied forces' greatest anti-Axis artist. One who bravely stayed, Hannah Hoch, continued to make her satiric montages throughout the war.

Each July the Nazis put on the German Art Congress in Munich's Haus der Deutschen Kunst (House of German Art). In 1942, 745 artists exhibited 1,347 works, all carefully screened to adhere to the National Socialist identity of "race, blood and Volk." Among the works were several by the sculptor Arno Brecker, who recast Greek classical art in contemporary Aryan themes *(Amazon* and *In Readiness)* and by Adolf Ziegler, Hitler's favorite contemporary artist, who was dubbed "master of German pubic hair." The historical-allegorical work of Hitler's favorite "old school" painter, Hans Makart (1840–84), experienced a rebirth during the Third Reich. The Nazi government, led by Alfred Rosenberg and Hermann Göring, also confiscated an estimated 22,000 works of fine art from all over Europe, to augment the work of its own 32,000 officially sanctioned painters, sculptors, and architects. The ultimate aim was to create a great museum in Linz after the "final victory."

In Italy, Barbara Buriko and Giovanni Guareschi were renowned for their incendiary pro-fascist posters. In Japan, Hideo Kondo created his cartoon magazine, *Manga,* which served

UNITED SERVICE ORGANIZATIONS

A group of nonprofit organizations formed the United Service Organizations (USO) in February 1941 to set up safe, relaxing havens for off-duty servicemen. These groups were staffed by nonmilitary volunteers offering "wholesome social contact." In October 1941 the nonprofits established USO Camp Shows as a separate branch. Stage, radio, and film stars contributed their talents to variety shows at military bases. The first show was put on at Fort Bragg, North Carolina, in late 1941. After Pearl Harbor, the shows expanded dramatically. From 1942 until war's end, USO Camp Shows, Inc., was the largest theatrical circuit in the world, enlisting 3,500 performers who made more than 35,000 appearances worldwide.

The camp shows had four circuits. The Victory Circuit covered the 600 army posts and navy stations in the United States with adequate concert halls. The Blue Circuit was a scaled-down version of the Victory Circuit, playing at 1,150 military installations without theaters. The Hospital Circuit visited wards and hospital auditoriums. The most famous was the massive Foxhole Circuit, which visited overseas bases in combat zones or out-of-the-way locations.

The USO Camp Shows' vast audience did not pay admission, so the National War Fund paid the tab; big-name performers played without compensation, defraying a great expense. The military did not dictate the content of the shows—the Broadway producer Eddie Dowling headed USO Camp Shows. The regular stable of entertainers—including Laurel and Hardy, Jack Benny, George Raft, Gary Cooper, Ann Sheridan, Ingrid Bergman, Marjorie Reynolds, Martha Raye, Marlene Dietrich, Ella Logan, Paulette Goddard (the first woman civilian to fly the Himalayan Hump in an army plane), Dinah Shore, the Andrews Sisters, Bing Crosby, John Garfield, Al Jolson, Ray Milland, Fred Astaire, Ray Bolger, Humphrey Bogart, and Joe E. Brown and Bob Hope (the two most tireless)—settled on a winning formula for the Foxhole Circuit. They carefully rehearsed the skits and musical numbers and planned the overseas tour months in advance. By the end of 1944, Hope and his regular troupe of Jerry Colonna, Tony Romano, Frances Langford, and Patty Thomas had logged 150,000 miles and given shows to more than two million military personnel overseas.

When the USO was not available, the army's Overseas Motion Picture Service made first-run Hollywood movies available to service personnel of all branches at post theaters, on ships, or at shore installations. In February 1942, Hollywood agreed to make 16mm prints of all its new films (which were usually 35mm), to be distributed free of charge to the military. By the end of 1944, Hollywood had distributed 25,000 military prints of feature films and newsreels. According to one estimate, more than one million service personnel in 3,000 venues saw a film each day during the war.

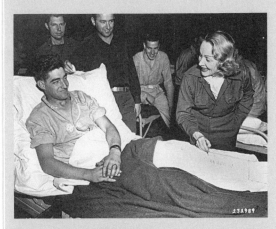

Actress Marlene Dietrich signs the cast of an injured American soldier after entertaining troops at a hospital in Belgium in November 1944.

USO performers reveled in the enthusiastic responses of their audiences overseas. The best-known USO entertainer was Bob Hope, who traveled thousands of miles to raise the spirits of Allied troops, often relatively close to the front lines.

To help underwrite these programs for service personnel, entertainers staged benefits. In March 1942, for example, a show at Madison Square Garden starring Kate Smith and Martha Raye, with Walter Winchell as master of ceremonies, raised $142,000. In August 1942, Babe Ruth and Walter Johnson came out of retirement to play in a benefit game that raised $85,000. On April 6, 1942, Sergeant Joe Louis stationed at Fort Dix, New Jersey, defended his heavyweight boxing championship at Madison Square Garden. He donated $3,000 worth of tickets to his fellow soldiers and his $45,000 purse to the Army Emergency Relief Fund.

as an officially sanctioned vehicle of satire and propaganda throughout the war. Among the war artists, Arai Shori, Hoshun Yamaguchi, Suzuki Tsuguo, and Katsuda Totsu created stunningly realistic and lasting battle images.

GREAT BRITAIN AND OTHER ALLIES

Among the Allies, few artists on either side wielded the power of British editorial cartoonists like David Low, Osbert Lancaster, and Sidney Strube, or war artists like David Langdon, "Raff," and Ronald Searle, to shape opinion and capture the tenor of battle. Renowned fine artists like Dame Laura Knight, Sir Stanley Spencer, Sir Muirhead Bone, his son Stephen Bone, Norman Wilkinson, Graham Sutherland, and Paul Nash celebrated the heroic resilience of British civilians and soldiers. Even the sculptor Henry Moore, who created a unique chalk-and-wax-crayon style for a series of "shelter paintings," joined the massive mobilization effort known as the War Artists Scheme.

Another important artist for the Allies was Adolf Hoffmeister, in Nazi-held Czechoslovakia, said to be the inspiration for the character "Victor Lazlo" in the movie *Casablanca.* Fellow Czech "Bert" was one of the greatest draftsmen in World War II. In the Soviet Union, artists were subject to the grueling war duties and deprivations suffered by the rest of the population. Some of the best war art was produced near the end of the war, when time and supplies permitted. Nonetheless, Aleksandr Deineka and Piotr Krivionogov rendered early heroic stands in *The Defense of Sebastopol, 1942,* and *The Defenders of the Brest Fortress,* respectively. The most famous piece of

Soviet art, *Glory to the Fallen Heroes,* was not completed until 1945, but Fyodor Bogorodsky's work is now an icon of patriotic art. The Soviet artist Boris Efimov, who created stunning posters as well as satiric editorial cartoons, may have been the most brutally frank artist of the war years.

Canada and Australia also enlisted artists for the Allied war effort, and their work has steadily grown in stature since the end of the war as it has been more widely exhibited. Among the great Canadian war artists were Lawren P. Harris, George Pepper, Anthony Law, Alfred Leete, and Alex Colville. Australians of note were Ivor Hele, Alan Moore, Geoffrey Mainwaring, and William Dargie.

Setting the anti-Fascist tone for artists among the Allies was Pablo Picasso and his 1937 painting *Guernica,* which depicts the obliteration of the Spanish town in a bombing raid by the Luftwaffe's Condor Legion during the Spanish Civil War. The event, and Picasso's painting, served as a warning to the world about Nazi brutality, which would resurface in Ben Shahn's 1942 depiction *This Is Nazi Brutality,* about a similar obliteration of the Czech village of Lidice.

UNITED STATES

Less than two weeks after Pearl Harbor, the Office of Emergency Management announced an art competition for defense and war pictures. The Graphics Division of the Office of Facts and Figures, directed by Librarian of Congress Archibald MacLeish, sponsored its own competition, as did the Works Progress Administration (WPA) and the U.S. Treasury Department's Section of Painting and Sculpture. Commercial artists like Walt Disney, Theodore Geisel, and Norman Rockwell also joined the war effort, and Arthur Szyk, an émigré from Nazi terror, became the most ardent anti-Fascist artist in the world. The Office of War Information enlisted the services of a number of fine artists, including Rockwell Kent, who called on artists to be "spokesmen of the nation's will to victory."

Artists helped the war effort by illustrating training and field manuals, designing recruitment and morale-boosting posters, and painting murals in mess halls and USO centers. In the line of fire they painted camouflage and made a visual record of battle. Among the best of the latter group are David Fredenthal, Donald L. Dickson, and Kerr Eby, as well as those sent by *Life, Colliers,* and *Saturday Evening Post,* like Aaron Bohrod, Fletcher Martin, George Biddle, Tom Lea, Grant Wood, and Bernard Perlin.

Even before the United States officially entered the war, groups like the National Defense Committee formed, as did ad hoc contingents of radical artists who banded to fight "the threat of Fascism" in the arts. The two biggest nongovernment groups were the National Art Council for Defense and the Artists Societies for Defense, both formed in 1941. They merged after Pearl Harbor to become Artists for Victory, Inc., with a membership of more than 10,000 painters, sculptors, designers, and printmakers. After President Franklin Roosevelt's State of the Union Address on January 6, 1942, Artists for Victory pledged five million hours to the war effort. Among the renowned artists who took part were Moses and Raphael Soyer, Louis Lozowick, Will Barnet, Robert Gwathmey, and Harry Sternberg. Other Americans who contributed their unique slant on the war were Saul Steinberg, Thomas Hart Benton, and Alexander Samuel MacLeod.

Artists played direct roles in the actual events in battle, too. Among the most popular cartoonists were serviceman Bill Mauldin ("Willie and Joe"), Sergeant George Baker ("The Sad Sack"), and Sergeant Dave Breger ("G.I. Joe").

MAJOR ARTISTS

Here are brief descriptions of major wartime artists and their works.

Axis Artists

ARNOLD, KARL (1883–1953) An accomplished graphic artist, Arnold was the driving force behind the Munich-based *Simplicissimus,* a satiric weekly that predated Hitler's rise to power. His attacks on the "master race," depicted as bloated and sinister, are remarkable in hindsight. More remarkable is that he kept his magazine afloat until 1944.

HOHLWEIN, LUDWIG (1874–1949) The grand old man of German poster design, Hohlwein offered his patented formula of brilliant colors and strong lines—popularized on his prewar travel, film, and advertising posters—for the Nazi Party's use.

KONDO, HIDEO (B. 1908) Kondo created *Manga,* which became the official wartime cartoon magazine of the Japanese military regime. Although the magazine was almost completely propaganda, Kondo's superior graphic skills were widely recognized and imitated.

SCHWEITZER, HANS (1901–80) His work, signed "Mjolnir," had the Nazi Party's official stamp of approval, and was featured on posters, stamps, pamphlets, and book jackets. He was given the official title of "Reich Plenipotentiary for Artistic Formulation."

SPEER, ALBERT (1905–81) As Hitler's personal architect, Speer was commissioned in 1933 to redesign Berlin along National Socialism's neoclassical lines. Much of his work remained on the drawing board when he became Reich minister of armament and production in 1942. He was convicted at Nuremberg of using slave labor and sentenced to 20 years in prison.

TROOST, PAUL LUDWIG (1878–1934)
Before Speer, Troost was Hitler's favorite architect; he developed the heroic neoclassicism that the Reich demanded. His last project was the design of the Haus der Deutschen Kunst in Munich.

Great Britain and Other Allies

COLE, LESLIE (1910–76) One of the most prolific members of the British War Artists Scheme, Cole was on the front lines in Sicily, Italy, North Africa, Burma, Borneo, and Germany. His paintings are among the most gripping and fully document the actual fighting. Most are now at the Imperial War Museum in London.

GAMES, ABRAM (1914–96) Games was the British War Office's only full-time poster designer, a master of graphic art who wielded great influence on other poster makers. His motto was "maximum meaning, minimum means." The gently surrealistic look of his designs dictated the tone of everything from personal hygiene campaigns to warnings about "careless talk" in more than 100 posters.

LOW, DAVID (1891–1963) The greatest World War II editorial cartoonist, Low worked for the *Evening Standard* from 1927 to 1950. He was among the first to warn of fascism's rise and the dangers of appeasement. His biting caricatures were so influential that Hitler banned them in Germany as early as 1933. He also turned his unmistakable graphic wit on the British—partly because he was born in New Zealand and trained in Australia—and his best-known, enduring character was the blustering reactionary Colonel Blimp.

MARENGO, KIMON (1904–88) An Egyptian artist who drew under the pen name Kem, his brilliantly drawn and wholly original anti-Axis posters and cartoons did much to sway the Middle East against fascism.

SEARLE, RONALD (B. 1920) Searle was an art student when he joined the British army in September 1939. In late 1941 his company (the 53rd Brigade) was sent to Singapore. It engaged the Japanese in January 1942, was defeated in battle, and the survivors imprisoned. Searle spent most of the rest of the war in the notorious POW camp at Changi, which was liberated by the Royal Navy on September 3, 1945. Searle's furtive ink sketches from this captivity provide one of the best visual records of the brutal treatment of prisoners of war by the Japanese and the camaraderie of soldiers under the worst conditions. Almost all of Searle's war drawings are now at London's Imperial War Museum.

United States

BAKER, GEORGE (1915–75) An army staff sergeant who was a professional animator before the war, Baker called his famous "Sad Sack" character "a bewildered civilian trying to be a soldier." "Sad Sack" first ran in *Yank* in May 1942 and continued after the war.

BIDDLE, GEORGE (1885–1973) A friend of Franklin Roosevelt's and the driving force behind the New Deal's Federal Art Project, Biddle organized the War Department's Art Advisory Committee and then joined the Allied forces in the field.

BREGER, SERGEANT DAVE (1908–70) Breger started the "G.I. Joe" comic strip for the Mediterranean edition of *Stars and Stripes,* and *Yank*. The character originated in the *Saturday Evening Post* on August 30, 1941, as "Private Breger." When the war started, the renamed strip moved to *Yank,* but the character remained the same: a freckled, bespectacled naïf.

DICKSON, CAPTAIN DONALD L. (?–1974) An accomplished artist in watercolors, oils, and sculpture before the war, Dickson was a columnist, cartoonist ("Sgt. Stony Craig"), and illustrator for the Marine Corps magazine, *Leatherneck*. He was called up from his marine reserve unit and saw combat at Guadalcanal and in the Solomon Islands.

HIRSCH, JOSEPH (1910–81) An acclaimed Federal Arts Project muralist and top prize winner at the 1939 World's Fair, Hirsch created war bond posters and then became a war artist and correspondent in the South Pacific, Italy, and North Africa in 1943–44. His sensitive renderings from hospital units are some of the most moving of the war.

KOERNER, HENRY (1915–94) After fleeing Austria in 1938, Koerner came to the United States and was drafted in 1943. The Office of Strategic Services sent him to Germany in 1945 to document the Third Reich's fall and the Nuremberg trials.

LEA, TOM (1907–2001) A staff artist for *Life,* Lea traveled with navy convoys through U-boat-infested waters, lived aboard the aircraft carrier *Hornet* (later sunk), and witnessed firsthand the bloody invasion of Peleliu (1944), the subject of many of his, and the war's, most memorable paintings. Much of his work is at the El Paso (Texas) Museum of Art.

MAULDIN, BILL (1921–2003) Mauldin was best known for his field sketches and cartoon commentaries on army life in wartime. From 1941 until 1943, he worked part time for the *45th (Infantry) Division News,* then was hired full-time by *Stars and Stripes* in early 1944, after the famed Ernie Pyle wrote a column about him. Mauldin's cartoons were so popular that they were syndicated in hundreds of U.S. newspapers. They helped humanize the rigors of the frontline troops through his most enduring characters, Willie and Joe, two sardonic, battle-weary infantrymen slogging through the European theater.

SZYK, ARTHUR (1894–1951) A Polish Jew who left Poland for Paris, London, and, finally, New York in 1940, Szyk created some of the most brutally frank and graphically brilliant anti-

Axis images. His gruesome depictions of Hitler, Goebbels, Yamamoto, Tojo, and Mussolini appeared on the covers of *Time, Colliers,* and the *Saturday Evening Post.*

AIRCRAFT NOSE ART

Every outfit, squadron, or fighting unit, it seemed, had a distinctive insignia, which its members dutifully replicated on jeeps, helmets, shoulder patches, and the noses of airplanes. The demand for insignia art became so great, in fact, that by 1943, Disney Studios had five artists working full-time making designs for the soldiers. Among the favorite places to display an artistic identity were the sides and noses of combat aircraft, the shapes of which seemed to lend themselves to artistic renderings.

The artists would incorporate popular slogans in the design of the insignia. The most popular was "SNAFU," an acronym for "situation normal, all fouled up." Private Snafu was, in fact, a popular cartoon character that service personnel followed regularly in newsreels, on the radio (voice by Mel Blanc), and in film shorts.

POSTER ART

Poster art was an effective way to reach the masses. TASS, the Soviet news agency, mobi-

Artist George "Randy" McCraw decorates the fuselage of a Lockheed Ventura bomber as it rolls off the assembly line. Many Allied aircraft were also decorated with colorful nose art.

LET ME DO THE
TALKING !

SERVE IN SILENCE
ISSUED BY THE SAN FRANCISCO JUNIOR CHAMBER OF COMMERCE

Produced by the Works Progress Administration art program, this poster reminds citizens to avoid discussing potentially sensitive information and allow the military to deal with the Axis threat.

with unsolicited information about the Allied war effort. On the home front the most effective weapon in this campaign was Homer Ansley's gently reproachful poster, *Let Me Do the Talking! (Serve in Silence),* featuring a sad-eyed cocker spaniel with its head on a sailor's uniform and the slogan "... because somebody talked!" Overseas and on all military installations and factory floors, foreign and domestic, the posters were considerably less subtle in their reminders that "Loose lips sink ships" and admonishments not to discuss "troop movements, ship sailings, war equipment."

In Germany, Mjolnir's work, although not nearly as accomplished or seamless as that of Ludwig Hohlwein, nonetheless perfectly captured the Aryan ideal and the grim, iron-jawed

lized citizens to fight the Nazis in any way possible after Hitler invaded the Soviet Union in June 1941. The Nazis made one of the largest, most sustained assaults in human history, only to fall short (see Chapter 2, "Causes of War," and Chapter 7, "Campaigns and Battles: Europe and the Atlantic"). The resistance of the Soviet people is unmatched for bravery (and misery) in World War II. To sustain the Soviets' morale, TASS each week printed posters filled with patriotic fervor and anti-Nazi fever. Some hand-stenciled posters, such as *The Result of Fascist Culture* by P. Sokolov-Skalia, decried the crimes that Nazis committed against Soviet culture.

The U.S. Office of War Information conducted a campaign against providing the enemy

Civilian and military personnel stand shoulder to shoulder, looking resolutely toward the future in this poster designed to boost the morale of the German people.

determination of Nazi storm troopers and foot soldiers. Because it was featured on posters, stamps, pamphlets, and book jackets, his work permeated every layer of German society and aspect of German life.

Japanese artist Hideo Kondo created *Manga,* the official wartime cartoon magazine of the Japanese military regime. His most famous and widely distributed poster image was one of Franklin Delano Roosevelt as a green-skinned, fanged monster that was lurching—not unlike Godzilla—toward Tokyo.

PINUP ART

Often overlooked for their vital role in the war effort are the countless pinup photographs and drawings of scantily clad women. *Yank,* the servicemen's weekly, ran a "Pinup Girl" in each issue; the term *pinup* derives from this feature.

The smoke-shrouded atoll of Tarawa forms a strange backdrop for a marine's photo of a pinup girl. As his landing craft churns toward the beach, he takes a moment for one more look.

The most famous World War II–era photograph may be the one of Betty Grable's "million-dollar legs," which first appeared in *Time* in 1942 and was reproduced in *Yank;* the second most popular was of Rita Hayworth.

The titles of other publications containing pinups that were passed around the foxholes, barracks, and field tents suggest a wholesome "girl next door" eroticism: *Wink, Cutie, Flirt, Eyeful, Nifty, Grin,* and *Titter.* The pinups, many of which were drawings rather than photos, had titles like "Girl We'd Like to Fly With in Plane with Automatic Pilot" and "Girl We'd Like to Submerge With." The most famous artist of women was Alberto Vargas, whose sleek airbrushed Valkyries first appeared in *Esquire* in 1940 and later became the staple of the postwar publishing sensation, *Playboy.*

The "sweetheart of the British troops" was "Jane," which ran from 1932 until 1959 in the *Daily Mirror;* during the war British Prime Minister Winston Churchill cited her as "Britain's secret weapon." Drawn by Norman Pett, who used a chorus girl named Christabel Leighton-Porter as his model, Jane was a blonde secret agent who was forever outsmarting the Nazis. Her likeness appeared on the sides of bombers, and her strip was even picked up by *Round-Up,* a weekly distributed to U.S. troops in the Far East.

Journalism and the War

Although the job of the Office of War Information was to control the flow of information to the press, the director of OWI was a former CBS radio newsman, Elmer Davis, who was sympathetic to the needs of journalists. He and Librarian of Congress Archibald MacLeish, who headed the Office of Facts and Figures, believed that truth was the best propaganda. In contrast, the Axis powers screened all dispatches before they went to print and shut down all opposition newspapers. Even so, Germany alone had 12,000 members of the war press, including artists and photographers.

Among the already-well-known U.S. writers who had press credentials were Ernest Hemingway, A. J. Liebling, Robert St. John, Clare Boothe Luce, and Janet Flanner. While mostly male reporters went overseas to cover the war at first, women began filling job vacancies on the home front; they also moved out of the journalistic ghetto of the "women's pages" (as newspaper feature sections then were known) to run city desks everywhere. By 1945, 127 women were accredited as war correspondents. Among the most noteworthy were Sigrid Schultz, who covered Europe for the *Chicago Tribune* from 1919 on, Luce, Dorothy Thompson, Martha Gellhorn, Therese Bonney, Peggy Hull Deuell, Helen Kirpatrick, and May Craig. Flanner (1892–1978) is best known for her *New Yorker* "letters," but during the final days of the war she made weekly radio broadcasts from concentration camps and from liberated European towns.

War journalism was a dangerous occupation. The Geneva Convention stipulated that members of the press could not carry guns; they were considered "civilians in uniform." Even so, 37 U.S. journalists were killed in action, and 112 wounded, not nearly as dire as the toll of Soviet journalists, who sustained more than 400 deaths (the best Soviet journalists, like Ilya Ehrenberg and Konstanin Simonov, were among the country's best writers). Among the journalists killed in action was Ernie Pyle (1900–1945), the most widely read U.S. war correspondent. His foxhole-level dispatches for Scripps Howard were syndicated in 700 U.S. dailies and weeklies. His first assignment was North Africa. Then he followed the troops to Sicily, Italy, Normandy, and across France toward Germany. At every station he offered what he called a "worm's eye view of the war," and he was as beloved by fighting men as by readers. After the European theater, Pyle went

to the Pacific, where he was killed by Japanese fire on the island of Ie Shima on April 18, 1945, during the Okinawa campaign.

> The first one came early in the morning. They slid him down from the mule, and stood him on his feet for a moment. In the half light he might have been merely a sick man standing there leaning on the other. Then they laid him on the ground in the shadow of the stone wall alongside the road. I don't know who the first one was. You feel small in the presence of dead men, and you don't ask silly questions.
> —Ernie Pyle, January 10, 1944

RADIO IN THE WAR

A lifeline for U.S. troops in combat zones all over the world was Armed Services Radio, which broadcast from Los Angeles. All the programming was recorded onto "V-disks," so that the far-flung military bases could hear it over their airwaves as if it were being broadcast live. In this manner, troops were made to feel, in the words of regular guest Dorothy Lamour, "almost as if they were home." Although its promotional material described the regular guests of Armed Services Radio as "Benny and Hope and Toscanini," they more often included stars from nearby Hollywood, like Lamour, Cass Daley, Abbott and Costello, the Andrews Sisters, and Marlene Dietrich, with music by Kay Kyser and his swing orchestra. Mel Blanc, who created the voice and animation for the Warner Brothers staples Bugs Bunny and Porky Pig, regularly broadcast on Armed Services Radio, providing the voices of Private Snafu and Sad Sack.

Among the most popular of the 106 programs regularly aired on Armed Services Radio were *Mail Call,* in which stars would dedicate songs to servicemen who had written in with requests, and *Jubilee,* a groundbreaking show featuring African American performers like Ernie Whitman, Timmy Rogers, Eddie "Rochester" Robinson, and Lena Horne.

The greatest figure in radio broadcasting during the war was Edward R. Murrow (1908–65), who was director of European programming for CBS Radio from 1938 to 1945. His regular dispatches from London were indispensable to Americans who were following the progress of the war. His assistant, William L. Shirer (1904–93), was also one of the great CBS news correspondents from Europe; his biggest coups were reporting firsthand on the annexation of Austria in March 1938 (see Chapter 2, "Causes of War") and the surrender of France in June 1940. He resigned in December 1940, fearing he would be arrested by the Nazis as an undercover agent.

Also on the staff of CBS Radio were Eric Sevareid and Walter Cronkite, as well as Marvin Breckenridge Patterson, the first woman to broadcast from Europe. Sevareid, who was renowned for his erudite reportage, may have braved the most combat, offering firsthand dispatches from the fall of Paris, the battle for North Africa, and the London Blitz. He had a particularly harrowing stint in China and Southeast Asia, where he survived an air crash in Burma that killed the copilot. The best known of NBC Radio's journalists was Robert St. John, who reported on the war from London. St. John was the first radio journalist to report the surrender of Japan; he duplicated the feat on television an hour later.

In Great Britain, the BBC reached out to British soldiers in combat zones as well as the home front with popular programs such as *It's That Man Again* (see Chapter 11, "The Home Front"), *The Brains Trust,* and *Postscripts.* The BBC also used the talents of a number of renowned writers in its Overseas Service, which was intended to defuse and compete with the propagandistic radio programs broadcast by Axis powers in the Far East and Europe, such as those by Lord Haw-Haw, Axis Sally, Tokyo Rose, Ezra Pound, Free India Radio, Radio Himalaya (see Chapter 10, "Intelligence, Espionage, and Propaganda"). Among those tapped by the BBC were T. S. Eliot, Herbert Read, William Empson, E. M. Forster, and Louis MacNiece. George Orwell was put in charge of creating and broadcasting programming for the Indian Section of the BBC's Eastern Service, an experience in the propaganda mills that he later used when writing his masterpiece, *1984.*

Here are excerpts from two of the war's most famous radio broadcasts:

I have reported what I saw and heard, but only part of it. For the most of it I have no words. Dead men are plentiful in war, but the living dead, more than twenty thousand of them in one camp. . . . And the country round about was pleasing to the eye, and the Germans were well fed and well dressed. American trucks were rolling toward the rear filled with prisoners. Soon they would be eating American rations, as much for a meal as the men at Buchenwald received in four days. If I've offended you by this rather mild account of Buchenwald, I'm not in the least sorry.

—Edward R. Murrow,
radio broadcast from Buchenwald,
April 15, 1945

Now we get our picture through the dusty windows of the historic old wagon-lit car. Hitler and the other German leaders rise from their seats as the French enter the drawing room. Hitler, we see, gives the Nazi salute, the arm raised. The German officers give the military salute; the French do the same. . . . Hitler, so far as we can see through the windows just in front of here, does not say anything. He nods to General Keitel, adjusting his papers, and then he starts to read. He is reading the preamble of the German armistice terms. The French sit there with marble-like face.

—William L. Shirer,
CBS Radio broadcast from Compiègne,
France, June 21, 1940

Unlike in previous wars, World War II photographers were on the battlefields taking photographs and risking their lives in action. So many photographers died in uniform that they are too numerous to list. In some cases, the cameras that they carried documented posthumously the scenes that they witnessed in their last moments. The army and navy both had their own staffs of still photographers; the army's Signal Photographic Company had 10,000 staffers, and the navy's Combat Photography Section numbered 3,000. Most of these talented, brave photographers worked in anonymity, their work never signed or credited,

even after the war. Some, like David Douglas Duncan and Gordon Frye, went on to greater fame after the war.

> The wonder of the Pearl Harbor pictures never abates. In one of the darkest hours we have ever known, we photographed ourselves as we had never done before. The Pearl Harbor pictures must certainly be one of the highlights of our entire history.
> —Tom Maloney, war photographer

The quality and unique perspective of their photographs—shot through submarine periscopes, bomber bays, and cockpits; from unprotected high-level reconnaissance jets or low-flying

This photograph of the hulk of the battleship USS *Arizona* after the attack on Pearl Harbor was not released to the American people until the first anniversary of the attack. Enlistments soared in the weeks that followed the release of this photo and others.

Piper Cubs, parachutes, blimps, aircraft carrier decks, machine-gun posts; on beachheads, and in foxholes—were every bit the equal of those produced by the better-known magazine and wire-service photographers. Nonetheless, the copious work of military photographers was filed away in military regimental archives or public information offices, and only a fraction appeared in print; many reconnaissance photographs were published in classified publications, like the army's *Handbook on German Military Forces,* or the *U.S. Army-Navy Journal of Recognition,* or the monthly *Impact,* distributed to crews of Army Air Forces missions. Some were picked up from the still-picture pool and used by wire services, without credit or, worse, credited to someone else.

When their photographs did appear in *Stars and Stripes* or *Yank* (the daily newspaper and the weekly magazine, respectively, of the armed services), they carried U.S. Navy, U.S. Army Signal Corps, U.S. Army Air Corps, U.S. Army Air Forces, or U.S. Marine Corps photo credits. The most often used shots in these more open forums were, frustratingly, "grip and grin" or heroic poses by publicity-seeking commanding officers. All this—while photographers in the Office of War Information and the Coast Guard received credit lines—engendered some bitterness. The military photographers nonetheless recognized the courage under fire shown by professional photographers—Robert Capa, Joe Rosenthal, Carl Mydans, W. Eugene Smith, Margaret Bourke-White, and Toni Frissell—whose work appeared in publications around the world. Of the 21 photographers that *Life* sent into combat, five were wounded and 12 contracted malaria.

The main venue for U.S. freelance and spot news photographers was *Life* magazine, begun in 1936 by *Time* publisher Henry Luce. *Life* thrived during World War II; Luce claimed that two of every three U.S. servicemen read *Life*. Although U.S. censors forbade any photographs of American dead in the first two years of the war—so as not to demoralize other troops or the home front—*Life*'s stellar group of staffers and freelancers brought the war home in other ways. As the war turned in the Allies' favor in 1944, the magazine often obscured faces but regularly showed dead Americans in order to guard against complacency.

> You cannot say to a tank "Please move to the left as I want to get those men running in the background." . . . You must, by your own mobility and enterprise, be in the right position to photograph. —Eliot Elisofon, war photographer, 1943

Other venues for combat photojournalists were *Newsweek, National Geographic,* the *Saturday Evening Post, Collier's,* and the wire services: the Press Association, Acme Photos, International News Photos, and Wide World for American service photographers, as well as the Office of War Information. The main venues for British photojournalists, in addition to the wire services, were the *London Illustrated News, Horizon,* and, as freelancers, U.S. newspapers and magazines.

Although the work of German combat photojournalists was put to good use by propaganda minister Joseph Goebbels, the primary mode of propaganda was the poster and the newsreel. Photography also appeared regularly in the multieditioned *Signal* magazine, founded as a biweekly supplement to Germany's largest daily, the *Berliner Illustrierte Zeitung*. Posing as a newsmagazine, *Signal* was published in 20 languages, primarily as a propaganda organ to trumpet exaggerated victories of the German armed forces and the superiority of German culture. The total circulation was said to be 2.5 million, and English-language editions were distributed in the United States and Ireland. The quality of photography in *Signal* was superior to that found in Germany's own domestic venues, which the Press Section of Goebbels's propaganda ministry strictly monitored. Photographs almost never carried credit lines. The lone exception was for Heinrich Hoffmann, Hitler's personal photographer and business partner.

War Photographers

Below is a list of famous war photographers, with details of their wartime work. A representative selection of military combat photography can be found in a series of books published by *U.S. Camera,* edited by Tom Maloney and Edward Steichen. Large collections of combat photography are held at the Air Force Historical Research Agency (Maxwell Air Force Base, Alabama); Combined Arms Research Library (Fort Leavenworth, Kansas); the Marine Corps Historical Center; and the National Archives (Washington, D.C.).

GERMANY

HOFFMANN, HEINRICH (1885–1957) Hoffmann was Hitler's personal photographer and as such carried the title of Reich photo reporter. By 1940, he had published more than 30 folios of his photographs of Hitler and other high-ranking Nazis, most of which sold as many as 100,000 copies. To make even more money, he and Hitler started a publishing house (publishing coffee-table books about Hitler) and shared the lucrative income. Hoffmann's assistant, Eva Braun, became Hitler's mistress and committed suicide with him in Berlin in 1945. After the war, Hoffmann was sentenced to a labor camp for war profiteering. After his release, he lived on the profits from his archive of 2.5 million Nazi-related photographs.

GREAT BRITAIN

BEATON, CECIL (1904–80) Before the war, Beaton was known for his portraits of high society and the British royal family. From 1939 to 1945, however, he was England's best-known war photographer. His peerlessly composed, almost elegant images of combat and rubble appeared in *Horizon* and *Life* and were syndicated worldwide.

JAPAN

YOSUKE YAMAHATA (1917–66) Assigned to the navy division of the Japanese News and Information Bureau, Yamahata filmed combat zones throughout Southeast Asia. He was in Hiroshima the day before the first "New Style Bomb" was dropped, and three days later he was assigned to go to Nagasaki to "photograph the situation so as to be as useful as possible for military propaganda." What resulted was the most extensive photographic record of the aftermath of both atomic bombs.

UNITED STATES

BOURKE-WHITE, MARGARET (1904–71) She began as a staff photographer for *Fortune* in 1929, moved to *Life* in 1936, and was sent to the Soviet Union (the only foreign photojournalist there) only weeks before the Nazis invaded. Overcoming strict censorship by the Soviet government, she chronicled the Nazi invasion, then moved to the North Africa campaign, where on January 22, 1943, she became the first woman to fly on an American combat bombing mission. She photographed nighttime air raids in Italy, England, and France, and, at war's end, the suicides of German citizens and liberation of the concentration camps. Her photographs and manuscripts are in the Special Collections Department at Syracuse University Library.

BUSHEMI, SERGEANT JOHN (1920–44) Bushemi was *Yank*'s ace combat photographer. In addition to his military assignments, he sold photographs to the *New York Times* and *Saturday Evening Post.* After setting up *Yank*'s Central Pacific bureau in Honolulu, Bushemi joined army infantry units in action on Guadalcanal, New Georgia, Tarawa, and the Marshalls, and in the invasion of Eniwetok, where he was killed by a Japanese mortar shell.

CAPA, ROBERT (1913–54) Before he arrived in England in April 1941, Capa had established himself as one of the most talented and fearless of frontline photographers during the Spanish Civil War (1936–38). His work appeared in *Time, Picture Post, Illustrated London News,* and, most notably, *Life.* He was in the pool of still photographers, which included Frank Scherschel and David Scherman, who took part in the D-Day invasion. Capa's beach-level combat photographs of D-Day are among the most stunning of the war.

ELISOFON, ELIOT (1911–73) Elisofon traveled with the navy and army as a war photographer, landing with troops at Casablanca in November 1942 and covering the North African campaign through May 1943.

> I always try to do pictures of our wounded, too, so that people back home can see the cost of war. I don't know if the picture has been released by the censors but I had one shot of a cyclist being treated in the field by the doctors. He insisted on smiling for the camera. He had been shot through the leg and stomach by a strafing enemy aircraft.
>
> —Eliot Elisofon, war photographer, 1943

MILLER, LEE (1907–77) Miller learned photography from the master surrealist Man Ray, who used her as a model. She was on the London staff of *Vogue* and managed to convince her editors to open the pages to pictures from the war in Europe, including bomb-devastated London (her pictures became the book *Grim Glory*); combat field hospitals; the liberation of France

and Belgium; the final days of Cologne, Frankfurt, and Munich under the Nazis; and the human toll of recently liberated Dachau and Buchenwald.

MYDANS, CARL (B. 1907) Mydans covered the war from beginning to end for *Life,* first from England in 1939, then Finland in 1940 and Italy in 1941. He documented the antics of Mussolini and the fall of France and went to the Philippines just as the islands were taken by Japan. He and his wife, Shelley, a *Life* reporter, were held as prisoners of war until December 1943. He resumed his photography, covering the Pacific and European theaters and participating in the liberation of the same Filipino prison camp where he had been held. His final war assignment was photographing the Japanese surrender aboard the battleship USS *Missouri,* on September 2, 1945.

ROSENTHAL, JOE (B. 1911) Best known for his photograph of six marines raising a flag on Mount Suribachi on the island of Iwo Jima—perhaps the most enduring image of the war—Rosenthal had weathered four days of intense combat, and numerous close calls, before taking that shot for the Associated Press.

SMITH, W. EUGENE (1918–78) His application to Edward Steichen's naval unit was denied because of bad eyesight, so he freelanced for magazines, mostly *Flying* and *Life,* and wire services, photographing the Pacific theater for three years before being wounded by Japanese artillery fire on Okinawa in the spring of 1945 while he was taking a photograph. He was working on a story, "24 Hours with Infantryman Terry Moore," and finished the writing from his hospital bed. It took him a year to recover from his wounds.

STEICHEN, EDWARD (1879–75) During World War I, Steichen headed the Air Service's

Photographic Section and flew reconnaissance missions with General Billy Mitchell. When World War II started, the navy gave Steichen an age waiver. He put together the Naval Aviation Photographic Unit that filmed naval air combat in the Pacific. Steichen made two tours of duty aboard the aircraft carrier USS *Lexington,* which sustained heavy damage. He exhibited his war photographs in a show called "Power in the Pacific" at the Museum of Modern Art in early 1945.

Associated Press photographer Joe Rosenthal took what is probably the most famous photograph of World War II as five U.S. Marines and a Navy Corpsman raised the U.S. flag on the summit of Iwo Jima's Mount Suribachi, February 23, 1945.

CHAPTER 15

Documents, Organizations, and Monuments

The documents, organizations, and monuments of World War II are the tangible record of the momentous military and political events that shook the world in the middle of the 20th century. They are the lasting link to the past, the evidence, and the reminder for future generations of the sacrifices of those who have gone before.

The documents presented include some of the most stirring words ever uttered by humans in crisis, as well as some of the most vile. The writings in the archives contain both ringing statements of hope for a better world, as well as those containing the grave miscalculations, leading to the deaths of thousands, the blueprints for conquest, and the framework for peaceful resolution of disagreements among nations, and the basis for international justice.

The organizations represent the collective voices of those who served, suffered, and survived the terror and privations of total war. Although today the ranks of World War II veterans are rapidly thinning, the thoughts, opinions, and recollections of those who were there have taken on a greater significance.

The monuments, constructed primarily of stone and steel, are lasting tributes. They tell the stories of historic events and will do so long after the last living reminders are gone. Commemorating triumph and tragedy, heroism and heartache, in all regions they stand exposed to all kinds of weather, year in and year out. From the rows and rows of white marble crosses and headstones comprising cemeteries across the globe, to the relics of war machinery that sit in town squares throughout Europe, the monuments are permanent reminders that something of great significance took place. Most poignant of all the memorials are the cemeteries. While war graves, marked and unmarked, exist worldwide, the cemeteries are well known for their beauty and quiet dignity.

Although it presents a great deal of information, this chapter, by definition, has its limitations. For example, the World Wide Web grows larger every day; therefore, the Web sites listed here are but a fraction of those available. Every monument and memorial is a symbol of the great struggle, but cataloging each and every one would require a volume all its own. Our hope is that the user of this chapter will at least find a starting place in the quest for knowledge.

Documents

The documentation of World War II, whether on the page, on the artist's canvas, or through the camera lens, brings immediacy to events that may otherwise seem distant. Through words, British Prime Minister Winston Churchill aroused the courage and determination of an embattled people, and these spoken words have endured in written form as a testament to succeeding generations. In contrast, Adolf Hitler's spoken and written words sowed the seeds of hatred and destruction.

Some documents were official government publications, yet they continue to express values that persist to this day. From sinister schemes to terms of surrender, the documents convey different points of view. They describe the prosecution of the war and provide a glimpse of the world to come.

ATLANTIC CHARTER

Issued jointly by U.S. President Franklin D. Roosevelt and British Prime Minister Winston Churchill on August 12, 1941, the Atlantic Charter was the primary result of a historic meeting between the two heads of state at Placentia Bay, Newfoundland. Roosevelt secretly traveled to the rendezvous aboard the cruiser USS *Augusta,* while Churchill arrived aboard the battleship HMS *Prince of Wales.*

Although the United States was not yet at war, the document put forth eight principles shared by the U.S. and British peoples: neither nation sought territorial gains; neither sought territorial changes that conflicted with the will of the people concerned; they respected the right of the peoples of the world to choose their form of government; nations were entitled to trade freely; the United States and Great Britain agreed to foster cooperation among nations to bring about greater economic prosperity; with the defeat of Nazism all people should be able to live in freedom within the boundaries of their nations; the high seas should be open to all; and all nations should abandon the use of armed force as means of resolving the conflict.

AUTHORIZATION TO PREPARE FOR USE OF THE ATOMIC BOMB

On July 25, 1945, General Carl Spaatz, commander of the U.S. Army Strategic Air Forces, received a directive ordering him to prepare for the dropping of the first atomic bomb. The order, signed by General Thomas T. Handy, acting Army chief of staff, reads as follows:

1. The 509 Composite Group, 20th Air Force will deliver its first special bomb as soon as weather will permit visual bombing after about 3 August 1945 on one of the targets:

Hiroshima, Kokura, Niigata and Nagasaki. To carry military and civilian scientific personnel from the War Department to observe and record the effects of the explosion of the bomb, additional aircraft will accompany the airplane carrying the bomb. The observing planes will stay several miles distant from the point of impact of the bomb.

2. Additional bombs will be delivered on the above targets as soon as made ready by the project staff. Further instructions will be issued concerning targets other than those listed above.

3. Dissemination of any and all information concerning the use of the weapon against Japan is reserved to the Secretary of War and the President of the United States. No communiques on the subject or releases of information will be issued by Commanders in the field without specific prior authority. Any news stories will be sent to the War Department for special clearance.

4. The foregoing directive is issued to you by direction and with the approval of the Secretary of War and of the Chief of Staff, USA. It is desired that you personally deliver one copy of this directive to General MacArthur and one copy to Admiral Nimitz for their information.

BRITISH PRIME MINISTER NEVILLE CHAMBERLAIN'S ADDRESS OF APRIL 5, 1940

Scarcely a month before the German blitzkrieg rolled into France and the Low Countries, British Prime Minister Neville Chamberlain addressed the Central Council of the National Union of Conservative and Unionist Associations. Referring to a seven-month lull in the fighting in Western Europe, Chamberlain declared that Britain had initially postponed an arms buildup but had used the time to strengthen its military. He spoke confidently of victory and, in a profound misstatement, proclaimed that Germany had lost its initiative:

The result was that when war did break out, German preparations were far ahead of our own, and it was natural then to expect that the enemy would take advantage of his initial superiority to make an endeavor to overwhelm us and France before we had time to make good our deficiencies. Is it not a very extraordinary thing that no such attempt was made? Whatever may be the reason—whether it was that Hitler thought he might get away with what he had got without fighting for it, or whether it was that after all the preparations were not sufficiently complete—however, one thing is certain: he missed the bus.

BRITISH PRIME MINISTER WINSTON CHURCHILL'S ORATIONS

British Prime Minister Winston Churchill, the symbol of his embattled nation's resolute stand against the Nazis, used his oratorical skills to the fullest during the war, particularly during the Battle of Britain. His speeches before Parliament were also broadcast to the British people and served to buoy the nation's morale during dark times.

May 13, 1940

I have nothing to offer but blood, toil, tears and sweat. . . . You ask what is our policy? I can say: It is to wage war, by sea, land and air, with all the might and with all the strength that God can give us; to wage war against a monstrous tyranny never surpassed in the dark, lamentable catalogue of human crime. That is our policy. You ask, what is our aim? I can answer in one word: It is victory, victory at all costs, victory in spite of all the terror, victory, however long and hard the road may be; for without victory there is no survival.

June 4, 1940

We shall go on to the end, we shall fight in France, we shall fight on the seas and oceans, we shall fight with growing confidence and strength in the air, we shall defend our island, whatever the cost may be, we shall fight on the beaches, we shall fight on the landing grounds, we shall fight in the fields and in the streets, we shall fight in the hills; we shall never surrender.

June 18, 1940

Hitler knows that he will have to break us in this Island or lose the war. If we can stand up to him, all Europe may be free and the life of the world may move forward into broad, sunlit uplands. But if we fail, then the whole world, including the United States, including all that we have known or cared for, will sink into the abyss of a new Dark Age made more sinister, and perhaps more protracted, by the lights of perverted science. Let us therefore brace ourselves to our duties and so bear ourselves that if the British Empire and its Commonwealth last for a thousand years men will still say, "This was their finest hour."

August 20, 1940

Never in the field of human conflict was so much owed by so many to so few.

March 5, 1946 (at Westminster College in Fulton, Missouri)

A shadow has fallen upon the scenes so lately lighted by the Allied victory. Nobody knows what Soviet Russia and its Communist international organization intend to do in the immediate future, or what are the limits, if any, to their expansive and proselytizing tendencies. From Stettin in the Baltic to Trieste in the Adriatic, an iron curtain has descended across the Continent. Behind that line lie all the capitals of the ancient states of Central and Eastern Europe. Warsaw, Berlin, Prague, Vienna, Budapest, Belgrade, Bucharest and Sofia—all these famous cities and the populations around them lie in what I must call the Soviet sphere, and all are sub-

Supreme Allied Commander Dwight D. Eisenhower visits 101st Airborne Division paratroopers before their jump into Normandy, D-Day, June 6, 1944. Eisenhower had agonized over postponing the invasion of Europe due to bad weather and had written a statement accepting blame if Operation Overlord had failed.

ject in one form or another not only to Soviet influence but to a very high and, in many cases, increasing measure of control from Moscow.

U.S. GENERAL DWIGHT D. EISENHOWER'S D-DAY MESSAGE

As Allied forces launched the invasion of Western Europe on June 6, 1944, Supreme Allied Commander Dwight D. Eisenhower released an address to those who would eventually carry the fight to the German homeland:

Soldiers, sailors and airmen of the Allied Expeditionary Force: You are about to embark upon a great crusade toward which we have striven these many months. The eyes of the world are upon you. The hopes and prayers of liberty-loving people everywhere march with you. . . . I have full confidence in your courage, devotion to duty and skill in battle. We will accept nothing less than full victory!

Good luck! And let us all beseech the blessing of Almighty God upon this great and noble undertaking.

U.S. GENERAL DWIGHT D. EISENHOWER'S VICTORY MESSAGE

Upon the cessation of hostilities in the European theater on May 8, 1945, Supreme Allied Commander Dwight D. Eisenhower issued the following message to the U.S. troops who contributed to the final victory over Nazi tyranny:

The route you have traveled through hundreds of miles is marked by the graves of former comrades. Each of the fallen died as a member of the team to which you belong, bound together by a common love of liberty and a refusal to submit to enslavement. Our common problems of the immediate and distant future can be best solved in the same conceptions of cooperation and devotion to the cause of human freedom as have made this Expeditionary Force such a mighty engine of righteous destruction.

Let us have no part in the profitless quarrels in which other men will inevitably engage as to what country, what service, won the European war. Every man, every woman, of every nation here represented has served according to his or her ability, and the efforts of each have contributed to the outcome. This we shall remember—and in doing so we shall be revering each honored grave and be sending comfort to the loved ones of comrades who could not live to see this day.

GERMANY'S DECLARATION OF WAR WITH THE UNITED STATES

On December 11, 1941, four days after Pearl Harbor, the German government formally declared war on the United States. The declaration was delivered both to the State Department in Washington and to the U.S. embassy in Berlin.

The Government of the United States having violated in the most flagrant manner and in ever increasing measure all rules of neutrality in favor of the adversaries of Germany and having continually been guilty of the most severe provocations toward Germany ever since the outbreak of the European war, provoked by the British declaration of war against Germany on September 3, 1939, has finally resorted to open military acts of aggression.

On September 11, 1941, the President of the United States publicly declared that he had ordered the American Navy and Air Force to shoot on sight at any German war vessel. In his speech of October 27, 1941, he once more expressly affirmed that this order was in force. Acting under this order, vessels of the American Navy, since early September 1941, have systematically attacked German naval forces. Thus, American destroyers, as for instance the Greer, the Kearney and the Reuben James, have opened fire on German submarines according to plan. The Secretary of the American Navy, Mr. Knox, himself confirmed that American destroyers attacked German submarines.

Furthermore, the naval forces of the United States, under order of their government and contrary to international law, have treated and seized German merchant vessels on the high seas as enemy ships.

The German government therefore establishes the following facts:

Although Germany on her part has strictly adhered to the rules of international law in her relations with the United States during every period of the present war, the Government of the United States from initial violations of neutrality has finally proceeded to open acts of war against Germany. The Government of the United States has thereby virtually created a state of war.

The German Government, consequently, discontinues diplomatic relations with the United States of America and declares that under these circumstances brought about by President Roosevelt Germany too, as from today, considers herself as being in a state of war with the United States of America.

GERMANY'S FORMAL SURRENDER

In the spring of 1945, Allied troops were victorious on all fronts in the European theater. The Red Army captured Vienna in April and took Berlin, the Nazi capital, on May 2. In the West, the 21st Army Group of British Field Marshal Bernard Law Montgomery was in control in northern Germany, southern Denmark, and the Netherlands. On May 7, in a schoolhouse in the French town of Rheims, German forces unconditionally surrendered to the Allies under General Dwight D. Eisenhower. Colonel General Alfred Jodl, army chief of staff, represented Germany. The document reads as follows:

1. We the undersigned, acting by authority of the German High Command, hereby surrender unconditionally to the Supreme Commander, Allied Expeditionary Force and simultaneously to the Soviet High Command all forces on land, sea, and in the air who are at this date under German control.

2. The German High Command will at once issue orders to all German military, naval and air authorities and to all forces under German control to cease active operations at 2301 hours Central European time on 8 May and to remain in the positions occupied at that time. No ship, vessel, or aircraft is to be scuttled, or any damage done to their hull, machinery or equipment.

3. The German High Command will at once issue to the appropriate commanders, and ensure the carrying out of any further orders issued by the Supreme Commander, Allied

Colonel General Alfred Jodl signs the surrender documents ending the war in Europe at Reims, France, on May 7, 1945. Following the surrender, Supreme Allied Commander Dwight D. Eisenhower and his chief of staff, General Walter Bedell Smith, pose with other Allied officers.

Expeditionary Force and by the Soviet High Command.

4. This act of military surrender is without prejudice to, and will be superseded by any general instrument of surrender imposed by, or on behalf of the United Nations and applicable to GERMANY and the German armed forces as a whole.

5. In the event of the German High Command or any of the forces under their control failing to act in accordance with this Act of surrender, the Supreme Commander, Allied Expeditionary Force and the Soviet High Command will take such punitive or other action as they deem appropriate.

Signed at Rheims, France, at 0241 hours on the 7th day of May, 1945.

EMPEROR HIROHITO'S STATEMENT TO THE JAPANESE PEOPLE

On August 15, 1945, Emperor Hirohito announced to his people that the war was at an end. It was the first time that he had addressed them directly.

We, the Emperor, have ordered the Imperial Government to notify the four countries, the United States, Great Britain, China and the Soviet Union, that We accept their Joint Declaration. To ensure the tranquillity of the subjects of the Empire and share with all the countries of the world the joys of co-prosperity, such is the rule that was left to Us by the Founder of the Empire of Our Illustrious Ancestors, which We have endeavoured to follow. Today, however, the military situation can no longer take a favourable turn, and the general tendencies of the world are not to our advantage either.

What is worse, the enemy, who has recently made use of an inhuman bomb, is incessantly subjecting innocent people to grievous wounds and massacre. The devastation is taking on incalculable proportions. To continue the war under these conditions would not only lead to the annihilation of Our Nation, but to the destruction of human civilization as well.

GERMAN CHANCELLOR ADOLF HITLER'S ORATIONS

German Chancellor Adolf Hitler was a captivating speaker. His booming voice and theatrical displays raised audiences of thousands to frenzy on many occasions. Lies and propaganda were instruments of the Nazi regime, and Hitler dispensed them with regularity in his addresses to both the German people and the Reichstag.

March 16, 1935

In this hour the German government renews before the German people and before the entire world its assurance . . . that it does not intend in rearming Germany to create an instrument for military aggression but, on the contrary, exclusively for defense and thereby for the maintenance of peace.

After hearing Emperor Hirohito announce their country's unconditional surrender, Japanese POWs on Guam bow reverently. The announcement came on August 14, 1945, and the formal surrender documents were signed two weeks later in Tokyo Bay.

May 21, 1935

National Socialist Germany wants peace because of its fundamental convictions. And it wants peace also owing to the realization of the simple primitive fact that no war would be likely to alter the distress in Europe. . . . Without taking the past into account, Germany has concluded a non-aggression pact with Poland. . . . We shall adhere to it unconditionally. . . . We recognize Poland as the home of a great and nationally conscious people.

April 28, 1939

The reply in all cases was negative. . . . Apart from this fact, however, all states bordering on Germany have received much more binding assurances . . . than Mr. Roosevelt asked from me in his curious telegram.

GERMAN CHANCELLOR ADOLF HITLER'S POLITICAL TESTAMENT

In his bunker beneath the smoking ruins of the German capital, Adolf Hitler dictated his political testament on April 29, 1945, the day before he committed suicide. Hitler refused to accept responsibility for plunging the world into war. He continued to persecute the Jews until the end.

More than thirty years have passed since I contributed my modest strength in 1914 as a volunteer in the First World War, which was forced upon the Reich.

In these three decades only love and loyalty to my people have guided me in my thinking, my actions and my life. They gave me the strength to make the difficult decisions, such as have never before confronted mortal man. I have used up my time, my working strength and my health in these three decades.

It is untrue that I or anybody else in Germany wanted war in 1939. . . .

But nor have I left any doubt that if the nations of Europe are once more to be treated only as collections of stocks and shares of these international conspirators in money and finance, then those who carry the real guilt for the murderous struggle, this people will also be held responsible: the Jews! I have further left no one in doubt that this time it will not be only millions of children of Europeans of the Aryan peoples who will starve to death, not only millions of grown men who will suffer death, and not only hundreds of thousands of women and children who will be burned and bombed to death in the cities, without those who are really responsible also having to atone for their crime, even if by more humane means. . . .

But before everything else I call upon the leadership of the nation and those who follow it to observe the racial laws most carefully, to fight mercilessly against the poisoners of all the peoples of the world, international Jewry.

Set down in Berlin, April 29, 1945, 4:00 o'clock.

JAPAN'S FOURTEEN-PART MESSAGE

On December 7, 1941, Japanese emissaries in Washington, D.C., entered the office of U.S. Secretary of State Cordell Hull and handed to him a response to a document that the United States had delivered to the Japanese government on November 26 that sought a peaceful solution to the growing political crisis in the Pacific. As the Japanese delivered their reply, bombs were already falling on Pearl Harbor. Known as the Fourteen-Part Message, the document concluded:

The Japanese Government regrets to have to notify hereby the American Government that in view of the attitude of the American Government it cannot but consider that it is impossible to reach an agreement through further negotiations. December 7, 1941.

JAPAN'S INSTRUMENT OF SURRENDER

On September 2, 1945, aboard the battleship USS *Missouri* anchored in Tokyo Bay, representatives of the Japanese empire signed the document of unconditional surrender to the Allied forces, officially ending World War II. Delegates from the United States, Great Britain, China, the Soviet Union, Australia, Canada, France, the Netherlands, and New Zealand signed for the Allies. The document reads in part:

> We, acting by command of and in behalf of the Emperor of Japan, the Japanese Government and the Japanese Imperial General Headquarters, hereby accept the provisions set forth in the declaration issued by the heads of the Governments of the United States, China, and Great Britain on 26 July 1945 at Potsdam and subsequently adhered to by the Union of Soviet Socialist Republics, which four powers are hereafter referred to as the Allied Powers.
>
> We hereby proclaim the unconditional surrender to the Allied Powers of the Japanese Imperial General Headquarters and of all Japanese armed forces and all armed forces under Japanese control wherever situated.
>
> We hereby command all Japanese forces wherever situated and the Japanese people to cease hostilities forthwith, to preserve and save from damage all ships, aircraft, and military and civil property and to comply with all requirements which may be imposed by the Supreme Commander for the Allied Powers or by agencies of the Japanese Government at his direction.

THE LEND-LEASE AGREEMENT

On March 11, 1941, the U.S. Congress authorized Lend-Lease, which provided for the transfer of war materiel from the United States to Great Britain in its battle against the Nazis. Although the United States was not yet at war, it was clearly in the nation's best interest to keep Britain fighting. Because the British government was financially strapped, Lend-Lease delayed payment for supplies and further allowed for other forms of compensation. On February 23,

1942, the governments of the United States and Great Britain formalized the terms of the Lend-Lease program in an agreement. Lend-Lease aid was also authorized for and extended to the Soviet Union.

CHARLES LINDBERGH'S ISOLATIONIST SPEECH

A national hero since his historic transatlantic flight in 1927, Charles A. Lindbergh was a leading figure in the isolationist movement in the United States. As a leader of the America First Committee, Lindbergh spoke on April 23, 1941, of his concern for the consequences should the United States enter the war in Europe:

> It is not only our right, but is our obligation as American citizens to look at this war objectively and to weigh our chances for success if we should enter it. I have attempted to do this, especially from the standpoint of aviation; and I have been forced to the conclusion that we cannot win this war for England, regardless of how much assistance we extend. . . .
>
> If you believe in an independent destiny for America, if you believe that this country should not enter the war in Europe, we ask you to join the America First Committee in its stand. We ask you to share our faith in the ability of this nation to defend itself, to develop its own civilization, and to contribute to the progress of mankind in a more constructive and intelligent way than has yet been found by the warring nations of Europe. We need your support, and we need it now. The time to act is here.

U.S. GENERAL DOUGLAS MACARTHUR'S ADDRESS OF OCTOBER 20, 1944

As his troops fought inland on the island of Leyte, General Douglas MacArthur made good on his promise to return to the Philippines. After wading ashore, he announced that the liberation of the islands was at hand:

People of the Philippines, I have returned. By the grace of Almighty God our forces stand again on Philippine soil. The hour of your redemption is here. Your patriots have demonstrated an unswerving and resolute devotion to the principles of freedom. . . . Rally to me. Let the indomitable spirit of Bataan and Corregidor lead on. As the lines of battle roll forward to bring you within the zone of operations, rise and strike. . . . For future generations of your sons and daughters, strike! In the name of your sacred dead, strike! Let no heart be faint. Let every arm be steeled.

U.S. GENERAL DOUGLAS MACARTHUR'S SPEECH UPON JAPAN'S SURRENDER

Presiding at the ceremonies in which representatives of the Japanese and Allied governments signed the instrument of surrender formally ending World War II, General Douglas MacArthur spoke briefly. His address of September 2, 1945, reads in part:

We are gathered here, representatives of the major warring powers, to conclude a solemn agreement whereby peace may be restored. The issues involving divergent ideals and ideologies, have been determined on the battlefields of the world and hence are not for our discussion or debate. Nor is it for us here to meet, representing as we do a majority of the people of the earth, in a spirit of distrust, malice, or hatred. But rather it is for us, both victors and vanquished, to serve, committing all peoples unreservedly to faithful compliance with the understandings they are here formally to assume. It is my earnest hope, indeed the hope of all mankind, that from this solemn occasion a better world shall emerge out of the blood and carnage of the past . . . a world dedicated to the dignity of man. . . . Let us pray that peace be restored to the world, and that God will preserve it always. These proceedings are closed.

U.S. GENERAL DOUGLAS MACARTHUR'S STATEMENT OF MARCH 12, 1942

Ordered by President Franklin D. Roosevelt to leave the embattled Bataan Peninsula in the Philippines, General Douglas MacArthur, along with his wife and three-year-old son, boarded a PT boat and arrived safely in Australia hours later. Upon arrival, he spoke briefly to the media:

The President of the United States ordered me to break through the Japanese lines and proceed from Corregidor to Australia for the purpose, as I understand it, of organizing the American offensive against Japan, a primary object of which is the relief of the Philippines. I came through and I shall return.

THE MARSHALL PLAN

At the June 1947 commencement exercises of Harvard University, U.S. Secretary of State George C. Marshall, formerly General of the Army and Army Chief of Staff during World War II, described the far-reaching aid program that hastened the economic recovery of postwar Europe, buttressed the West against the spread

Left to right, President Harry S Truman, Secretary of State George C. Marshall, and diplomats Paul Hoffman and Averell Harriman discuss the Marshall Plan to aid the economic recovery of war-ravaged Europe.

of communism, and saved thousands from the horrors of starvation and disease. For his efforts, Marshall was awarded the Nobel Prize for Peace in 1953. His statement reads in part:

The truth of the matter is that Europe's requirements for the next three or four years of foreign food and other essential products—principally from America—are so much greater than her present ability to pay that she must have substantial additional help or face economic, social and political deterioration of a very grave character. The remedy lies in breaking the vicious circle and restoring the confidence of the European people in the economic future of their own countries and of Europe as a whole. The manufacturer and the farmer throughout wide areas must be able and willing to exchange their product for currencies, the continuing value of which is not open to question. Aside from the demoralizing effect on the world at large and the possibilities of disturbances arising as a result of the desperation of the people concerned, the consequences to the economy of the United States should be apparent to all. It is logical that the United States should do whatever it is able to do to assist in the return of normal economic health in the world, without which there can be no political stability and no assured peace.

SOVIET FOREIGN MINISTER VYACHESLAV MOLOTOV'S ADDRESS TO THE RUSSIAN PEOPLE AFTER THE NAZI INVASION

After the Nazis invaded the Soviet Union on June 22, 1941, Soviet Foreign Minister Vyacheslav Molotov addressed his people in an attempt to rally them to resistance. His statement reads in part:

Citizens of the Soviet Union:
The Soviet Government and its head, Comrade Stalin, have authorized me to make the following statement:

Today at 4 o'clock a.m., without any claims having been presented to the Soviet Union, without a declaration of war, German troops attacked our country, attacked our borders at many points and bombed from their airplanes our cities; Zhitomir, Kiev, Sevastopol, Kaunas and some others, killing and wounding over two hundred persons.

There were also enemy air raids and artillery shelling from Rumanian and Finnish territory. This unheard of attack upon our country is perfidy unparalleled in the history of civilized nations. The attack upon our country was perpetrated despite the fact that a treaty of non-aggression had been signed between the U.S.S.R. and Germany and that the Soviet Government most faithfully abided by all provisions of this treaty. . . .

The government calls upon you, citizens of the Soviet Union, to rally still more closely around our glorious Bolshevist party, around our Soviet Government, around our great leader and comrade, Stalin. Ours is a righteous cause. The enemy shall be defeated. Victory will be ours.

THE MUNICH LETTER OF 1938

In addition to the Munich Pact, which served as the death warrant for the nation of Czechoslovakia, Adolf Hitler and British Prime Minister Neville Chamberlain signed a letter at Munich on September 30, 1938. This was the meaningless piece of paper that Chamberlain triumphantly waved, proclaiming, "Peace in our time," when he returned from his final meeting with the Nazi chancellor. It reads:

We, the German Führer and Chancellor and the British Prime Minister, have had a further meeting today and are agreed in recognising that the question of Anglo-German relations is of the first importance for the two countries and for Europe.

We regard the agreement signed last night and the Anglo-German Naval Agreement as symbolic of the desire of our two peoples never to go to war with one another again.

We are resolved that the method of consultation shall be the method adopted to deal with any other questions that may concern our two countries, and we are determined to continue our efforts to remove possible sources of difference and thus to contribute to assure the peace of Europe.

THE POTSDAM DECLARATION, 1945

Issued on July 26, 1945, during the Potsdam Conference held in a suburb of Berlin, the capital of a defeated Germany, the Potsdam Declaration demanded the unconditional surrender of Japan. The document warned that Allied forces were positioned for the final assault against imperial Japan and that devastation would be wrought against the Japanese homeland if the ultimatum was not accepted. It included provisions that would eliminate the militaristic government of Japan and its influence and stated that Allied troops would occupy the home islands.

THE RAINBOW WAR PLANS

Developed by the United States in the event of war with more than one country and even involving alliances, the Rainbow plans included several different scenarios. Rainbow 5 was finished only months before Pearl Harbor and envisioned an alliance of the United States, Great Britain, and France against the combined forces of Germany, Italy, and Japan.

U.S. PRESIDENT FRANKLIN D. ROOSEVELT'S FOUR FREEDOMS SPEECH

On January 6, 1941, U.S. President Franklin D. Roosevelt addressed the 77th Congress. In what has become known as his Four Freedoms Speech, Roosevelt eloquently enunciated the high moral purpose behind his nation's support of Great Britain against the aggression of Nazi Germany and the totalitarian nations aligning themselves with it:

In the future days, which we seek to make secure, we look forward to a world founded upon four essential human freedoms. The first is freedom of speech and expression—everywhere in the world. The second is freedom of every person to worship God in his own way—everywhere in the world. The third is freedom from want—which, translated into world terms, means economic understandings which will secure to every nation a healthy peacetime life for its inhabitants—everywhere in the world. The fourth is freedom from fear—which, translated into world terms, means a world-wide reduction of armaments to such a point and in such a thorough fashion that no nation will be in a position to commit an act of physical aggression against any neighbor—anywhere in the world.

U.S. PRESIDENT FRANKLIN D. ROOSEVELT'S PROCLAMATION OF UNLIMITED NATIONAL EMERGENCY

After he announced that a limited national emergency existed in the United States following the outbreak of war in Europe in 1939, President Franklin D. Roosevelt issued the Proclamation of Unlimited National Emergency on May 27, 1941. Roosevelt stated that the threat to the country "requires that its military, naval, air and civilian defenses be put on the basis of readiness to repel any and all acts or threats of aggression directed toward any part of the Western Hemisphere."

U.S. PRESIDENT FRANKLIN D. ROOSEVELT'S TELEGRAM TO SOVIET PREMIER JOSEF STALIN

On August 18, 1942, U.S. President Franklin D. Roosevelt cabled Soviet Premier Josef Stalin on the progress of the war in the Pacific and his understanding of the urgency of the fight against Nazi Germany:

I am sorry that I could not have joined with you and the prime minister [Churchill] in the

Moscow conferences. I am well aware of the urgent necessities of the military situation, particularly as it relates to the situation on the Russian Front.

I believe that we have a toehold in the Southwest Pacific from which it will be very difficult for the Japanese to dislodge us. Our naval losses there were substantial but it was worth it to gain the advantage we have. We are going to press them hard.

On the other hand, I know very well that our real enemy is Germany and that our force and power must be brought against Hitler at the earliest possible moment. You can be sure that this will be done, just as soon as it is humanly possible to put together the transportation. In the mean time, over 1000 tanks will leave the United States in August for Russia, and other critical supplies, including airplanes, are going forward.

The United States understands that Russia is bearing the brunt of the fighting and losses this year. We are filled with admiration of your magnificent assistance. Believe me when I tell you that we are coming as strongly and as quickly as we possibly can. Roosevelt.

U.S. PRESIDENT HARRY S TRUMAN'S COMMENTS AFTER JAPAN'S SURRENDER

At 7 P.M. on August 15, 1945, U.S. President Harry S Truman issued a short statement after being informed that Japanese Emperor Hirohito had addressed his people, stating that resistance to the Allies was to end. Truman told the press:

I have just received a note from the Japanese government in reply to the message forwarded to that government by the Secretary of State on August 11. I deem this reply a full acceptance of the Potsdam Declaration, which specifies the unconditional surrender of Japan.

U.S. PRESIDENT HARRY S TRUMAN'S STATEMENT ON USING THE ATOMIC BOMB

On August 9, 1945, the day that the United States dropped the second atomic bomb on the Japanese city of Nagasaki, President Harry S Truman made the following statement regarding his decision to use the weapon:

Having found the bomb we have used it. . . . We have used it against those who attacked us without warning at Pearl Harbor, against those who have starved and beaten and executed American prisoners of war, against those who have abandoned all pretense of obeying international laws of warfare. We have used it in order to shorten the agony of war, in order to save the lives of thousands and thousands of young Americans. We will continue to use it until we completely destroy Japan's power to make war. Only a Japanese surrender will stop us.

U.S. PRESIDENT HARRY S TRUMAN'S V-E DAY PROCLAMATION

On May 8, 1945, U.S. President Harry S Truman issued a proclamation of victory over Germany and designated Sunday, May 13, 1945, as a national day of prayer. It reads in part:

The Allied armies, through sacrifice and devotion and with God's help, have wrung from Germany a final and unconditional surrender. The western world has been freed of the evil forces which for five years and longer have imprisoned the bodies and broken the lives of millions upon millions of free-born men. They have violated their churches, destroyed their homes, corrupted their children, and murdered their loved ones. Our Armies of Liberation have restored freedom to these suffering peoples, whose spirit and will the oppressors could never enslave.

Much remains to be done. The victory won in the West must now be won in the

East. The whole world must be cleansed of the evil from which half the world has been freed. United, the peace-loving nations have demonstrated in the West that their arms are stronger by far than the might of dictators or the tyranny of military cliques that once called us soft and weak. The power of our peoples to defend themselves against all enemies will be proved in the Pacific as it has been proved in Europe.

THE UNITED NATIONS CHARTER

Issued at San Francisco on June 6, 1945, the United Nations Charter announced the formation of the international organization formed to maintain world peace and security, develop friendly relations among nations, achieve international cooperation in solving international problems, and guarantee the respect for human rights around the world. The preamble to the charter reads as follows:

WE THE PEOPLES OF THE UNITED NATIONS DETERMINED to save succeeding generations from the scourge of war, which twice in our lifetime has brought untold sorrow to mankind, and to reaffirm faith in the fundamental human rights, in the dignity and worth of the human person, in the equal rights of men and women and of nations large and small, and to establish conditions under which justice and respect for the obligations arising from treaties and other sources of international law can be maintained, and to promote social progress and better standards of life in larger freedom, AND FOR THESE ENDS to practice tolerance and live together in peace with one another as good neighbours, and to unite our strength to maintain international peace and security, and to ensure, by the acceptance of principles and the institution of methods, that armed force shall not be used, save in the common interest, and to employ international machinery for the promotion of the economic and social advancement of all peoples, HAVE RESOLVED TO COMBINE OUR EFFORTS TO ACCOMPLISH THESE AIMS. Accordingly, our respective Governments, through representatives assembled in the city of San Francisco, who have exhibited their full powers found to be in good and due form, have agreed to the present Charter of the United Nations and do hereby establish an international organization to be known as the United Nations.

U.S. DECLARATION OF WAR WITH JAPAN

On December 8, 1941, the day after the Japanese attack on Pearl Harbor, President Franklin D. Roosevelt addressed a joint session of the U.S. Congress, asking for a formal declaration of war against Japan.

Yesterday, December 7, 1941, a date which will live in infamy, the United States of America was suddenly and deliberately attacked by naval and air forces of the Empire of Japan. The United States was at peace with that nation and, at the solicitation of Japan, was still in conversation with its government and its emperor looking toward the maintenance of peace in the Pacific. . . .

No matter how long it may take us to overcome this premeditated invasion, the American people, in their righteous might, will win through to absolute victory. . . .

Hostilities exist. There is no blinking at the fact that our people, our territory, and our interests are in grave danger. With confidence in our armed forces—with the unbounded determination of our people—we will gain the inevitable triumph, so help us God. I ask that Congress declare that since the unprovoked and dastardly attack by Japan on Sunday, December 7, 1941, a state of war has existed between the United States and the Japanese Empire.

Major Archives and Collections

A wealth of information about World War II is available through archives and collections of documents in repositories around the world. The following is a selected listing of some of the best known:

Air Force Historical Foundation
1535 Command Drive
Suite A122
Andrews AFB, MD 20762-7002
Tel: (301) 736-1959
Fax: (301) 981-3574
www.afhistoricalfoundation.com
This organization is dedicated to preserving and understanding the history of U.S. airpower.

Army Historical Foundation, Inc.
2425 Wilson Boulevard
Arlington, VA 22201
Tel: (703) 522-7901
Fax: (703) 522-7929
www.armyhistoryfnd.org
Dedicated to preserving the heritage of the U.S. Army and educating future generations, this organization provides extensive online research information.

Australian War Memorial
G.P.O. Box 345
Canberra ACT 2601
Australia
Tel: (61) 2 62 43 42 11
Fax: (61) 2 62 43 43 25
www.awm.gov.au
This memorial provides archival information about Australia's participation in the war.

Bildarchiv Preussischer Kulturbesitz
Unter den Linden 8
10117 Berlin
Germany
Tel: (49) 30 26 60
sbb.spk-berlin.de
This is a source of German archival information.

Bundesarchiv
Finckensteinallee 63
12205 Berlin
Germany
Tel: (49) 1 88 87 77 00
Fax: (49) 1 88 87 77 01 11
www.bundesarchiv.de
This is another source of German archival information.

Dwight D. Eisenhower Library and Museum
200 SE Fourth Street
Abilene, KS 67410
Tel: (785) 263-4751
Fax: (785) 263-4218
www.eisenhower.utexas.edu
This is a place to access papers, memorabilia, and other documents relating to the famous general and president.

Eisenhower Center for American Studies
923 Magazine Street
New Orleans, LA 70130
Tel: (504) 539-9560
Fax: (504) 539-9563
www.uno.edu/~eice/
This research institute is dedicated to the study and preservation of U.S. history and leadership from a variety of perspectives, including foreign policy, social history, literature, and popular culture.

Franklin D. Roosevelt Library, Museum and Digital Archives
4079 Albany Post Road
Hyde Park, NY 12538
Tel: (845) 229-8114
Fax: (845) 229-0872
www.fdrlibrary.marist.edu
This extensive archive and documentary source is focused on President Franklin D. Roosevelt.

George C. Marshall Center Library
Gernackerstrasse 2
82467 Garmisch-Partenkirchen
Germany
Tel: (49) 88 21 75 01 13
www.marshallcenter.org
This is a good source for information concerning the career of the great soldier and statesman, as well as issues of international relations.

Harry S Truman Library
500 W. US Highway 24
Independence, MO 64050-1798
Tel: (816) 833-1400
Fax: (816) 833-4368
www.trumanlibrary.org
The papers and other documents related to the presidency of Harry S Truman are archived here.

History Place
P.O. Box 692740
Quincy, MA 02269-2740
www.historyplace.com
This contains a collection of numerous documents related to the war, including transcripts of great speeches.

Hoover Institution on War, Revolution and Peace
Stanford University
Stanford, CA 94305-6010
Tel: (650) 723-1754
Fax: (650) 723-1687
www.hoover.org
A major collection of documents on economics and politics is on display here.

Imperial War Museum
Lambeth Road
London SE1 6HZ
United Kingdom
Tel: (44) 20 74 16 53 20
Fax: (44) 20 74 16 53 74
www.iwm.org.uk
This famed British repository contains artifacts, documents, and art of World War II and other conflicts.

Library of Congress
101 Independence Avenue SE
Washington, DC 20540
Tel: (202) 707-5000
Fax: (202) 707-1389
www.loc.gov
With an accessible location for researchers, the collection here includes writings, posters, and more.

National Archives and Records Administration
8601 Adelphi Road
College Park, MD 20740-6001
Tel: (866) 272-6272
Fax: (301) 837-0483
www.nara.gov
This is the location of the major documents concerning World War II, including many captured from enemy sources at the end of the war.

Smithsonian Institution
P.O. Box 37012
SI Building, Room 153, MRC 010
Washington, DC 20013-7012
Tel: (202) 357-2700
www.si.edu
This collection holds artifacts and art related to the war.

Superintendent of Documents
U.S. Government Printing Office
732 North Capital Street NW
Washington, DC 20401
Tel: (202) 512-1800
Fax: (202) 512-2250
www.access.gpo.gov
This is the U.S. government publisher of books related to World War II.

U.S. Air Force Historical Research Agency
600 Chennault Circle
Building 1405
Maxwell AFB, AL 36112-6424
Tel: (334) 953-2395
Fax: (334) 953-4096
www.au.af.mil/au/afhra
This is the source for various types of information relating to the U.S. Air Force.

U.S. Air Force History Support Office
3 Brookley Avenue
Box 94
Bolling AFB, DC 20332-5000
Tel: (202) 404-2264
Fax: (202) 404-2271
www.afhso.general.inquiries@pentagon.af.mil
A research-friendly organization, those interested in the history of the U.S. Air Force can find information here.

U.S. Army Center of Military History
103 Third Avenue
Fort McNair, DC 20319-5058
www.army.mil/cmh-pg
A well-known source for information about the history of the U.S. Army, this collection has extensive holdings relating to World War II.

U.S. Army Military History Institute
U.S. Army War College
22 Ashburn Drive, Carlisle Barracks
Carlisle, PA 17013-5008
Tel: (717) 245-3971
Fax: (717) 245-3711
www.carlisle.army.mil
This institute has archival information about the history of the U.S. Army.

U.S. Commission on Military History
Loyola College
Vice President Joseph P. Hanrahan
P.O. Box 2786
Springfield, VA 22152
Tel: (703) 569-9684
Fax: (703) 767-4450
www.uscmh.org
This is a source of information on research topics; it encourages the submission and publication of historical papers.

U.S. Marine Corps Research Center
2040 Broadway Street
MCCDC
Quantico, VA 22134
Tel: (703) 784-4685
Fax: (703) 784-4306
www.mcu.usmc.mil
This is a good source of information for researchers interested in the U.S. Marine Corps.

U.S. Merchant Marine Academy
300 Steamboat Road
Kings Point, NY 11024
Tel: (516) 773-5000
Fax: (516) 773-5774
www.usmma.edu
This collection holds historical materials relating to the merchant marine during World War II.

U.S. Naval Academy Archives
Nimitz Library
589 McNair Road
Annapolis, MD 21402-5029
Tel: (410) 293-6922
Fax: (410) 293-4926
www.usna.edu/library
A repository of documents in U.S. naval history is held here.

U.S. Naval Historical Center
Washington Navy Yard
805 Kidder Breese Street, SE
Washington, DC 20374-5060
Tel: (202) 433-4882
Fax: (202) 433-8200
www.history.navy.mil
This research location is devoted entirely to U.S. naval history.

U.S. Naval Institute
291 Wood Road
Annapolis, MD 21402
Tel: (410) 268-6110
Fax: (410) 269-7940
www.usni.org
This institute is a publisher of books and periodicals related to the history of the U.S. Navy.

U.S. Navy Memorial Foundation
701 Pennsylvania Avenue NW
Suite 123
Washington, DC 20004-2608
Tel: (202) 737-2300
Fax: (202) 737-2308
www.lonesailor.org
This contains listings of active duty and former service personnel, as well as related information.

U.S. Navy Office of Information
805 Third Avenue
9th Floor
New York, NY 10022-7513
Tel: (212) 784-0131
Fax: (212) 784-0139
www.chinfo.navy.mil
This office contains general information about the U.S. Navy.

U.S. Navy War College
686 Cushing Road
Newport, RI 02841
Tel: (401) 841-2220
Fax: (401) 841-1071
www.nwc.navy.mil
U.S. Navy–related archival information is stored here, including a database of ships and transcripts of speeches and documents.

Yad Vashem
P.O. Box 3477
Jerusalem 91034
Israel
Tel: (972) 26 44 34 00
Fax: (972) 26 44 34 43
www.yadvashem.org
This valuable archive and memorial is of the Holocaust, including artifacts, photographs, and artwork.

Yale University Law School
The Avalon Project
127 Wall Street
New Haven, CT 06520
Tel: (203) 432-4992
Fax: (203) 432-2112
www.yale.edu/lawweb/avalon/avalon.htm
This ambitious project has placed transcripts of World War II documents online.

Photo and Film Footage

World War II is perhaps the most highly photographed and filmed conflict in human history. During the war, professional and amateur photographers took thousands upon thousands of photographs, sometimes risking their lives to capture images of war's brutality. The evidence that they compiled is undeniable. Some images have become well known, while others remain obscure. Film, both black-and-white and color, was used extensively to record events during the war era. Film footage of the war brought the savagery of battle and the dimensions of human suffering home like no other medium. The following is a partial listing of major sources for the photographic record of World War II:

Time Warner
75 Rockefeller Plaza
New York, NY 10019
Tel: (212) 484-8000
Fax: (212) 333-3987
www.timewarner.com
This is a collection of a large number of film and print resources available through its Time-Life subsidiary.

Associated Press/Wide World
International Headquarters
50 Rockefeller Plaza
New York, NY 10020
Tel: (212) 621-1930
Fax: (212) 621-1567
www.ap.org
This is the primary news service that recorded much of the photographic history of the war.

Bildarchiv Preussischer Kulturbesitz
see p. 503

Bundesarchiv
see p. 503

Corbis
15395 SE 30th Place
Suite 300
Bellevue, WA 98007
Tel: (425) 641-4505
Fax: (425) 643-9740
www.corbis.com
Corbis is a major holder of photographs and other images from the war.

Imperial War Museum
see p. 504

ITAR-TASS
10 Tverskoy Blvd.
Moscow 103009
Russia
Tel: (7) 9 52 92 3614
Fax: (7) 9 52 91 83 72
www.itar-tass.com
This is a valuable source of photographs from the former Soviet Union.

Library of Congress
see p. 504

Mainichi Shimbun
1-1-1 Hitotsubashi
Chiyoda-Ku
Tokyo 100-8051
Japan
Tel: (81) 3 32 12 03 21
Fax: (81) 3 32 11 25 09
mdn.mainichi.co.jp
Japanese war photos can be found in this collection.

National Archives and Records Administration
see p. 504

Roger-Viollet
6 Rue de Seine
75006 Paris
France
Tel. (33) 1 55 42 89 00
Fax (33) 1 43 29 72 88
www.roger-viollet.fr
This is a good French source of photographic information on the war.

TRH Pictures
Bradley's Close
74-77 White Lion Street
London N1 9PF
United Kingdom
Tel: (44) 20 75 20 76 47
Fax: (44) 20 75 20 76 06
www.trhpictures.co.uk
This British source has a collection of war photos.

United Press International
1510 H Street NW
Washington, DC 20005
Tel: (202) 898-8000
Fax: (202) 898-8057
www.upi.com
This is a good source of news photos from the war.

Wilson Library
University of North Carolina at Chapel Hill
Chapel Hill, NC 27514-8890
Tel: (919) 962-0114
Fax: (919) 962-4452
www.lib.unc.edu
The Wilson Library has an excellent listing of World War II–related film.

Yad Vashem
see p. 506

Document Preservation

The preservation of historic documents relating to World War II is a continual effort that uses the latest in technological advances and procedures. Now more than half a century old, World War II–era documents require extreme care and monitoring so that future generations may retain this important component of history.

Many official documents related to World War II, including the Atlantic Charter, Lend-Lease Agreement, and formal surrender documents, are located in the National Archives and Records Administration's Archives II facility in College Park, Maryland. Completed in the summer of 1993, Archives II is a 1.8-million-square-foot building capable of housing nearly 2 million cubic feet of federal records. Complex systems in the facility maintain rigid environmental standards for the storage of records, monitoring temperature and humidity levels while also filtering harmful gases and airborne materials from the air circulating through the building. Archives II is located at 8601 Adelphi Road, College Park, MD 20740-6001.

Organizations

The thousands of organizations relating to World War II include government agencies, veterans groups, associations, auxiliaries, foundations, efforts dedicated to the preservation and maintenance of battlefields, cemeteries, memorials, and monuments, and more. In addition, the World Wide Web has provided a seemingly inexhaustible resource for research and the exchange of information. Museums around the world display artifacts of the war, ranging from equipment and machinery to uniforms, photographs, and artwork.

GOVERNMENT AGENCIES, VETERANS GROUPS, FOUNDATIONS

Air Force Historical Foundation
see p. 503

American Battle Monuments Commission
Courthouse Plaza II
Suite 501
2300 Clarendon Boulevard
Arlington, VA 22201
Tel: (703) 696-6780
Fax: (703) 696-6667
www.usabmc.com
This organization of the executive branch of the U.S. government administers 24 military cemeteries and 27 memorials in 15 countries.

American Legion
P.O. Box 1055
Indianapolis, IN 46206
Tel: (317) 630-1200
Fax: (317) 630-1223
www.legion.org
This is the major U.S. veterans group.

AMVETS
4647 Forbes Boulevard
Lanham, MD 20706-4380
Tel: (301) 459-9600
Fax: (301) 459-7924
www.amvets.org
This U.S. veterans group was organized in 1943.

Army Historical Foundation, Inc.
see p. 503

Disabled American Veterans
P.O. Box 14301
Cincinnati, OH 45250-0301
Tel: (859) 441-7300
Fax: (859) 442-2088
www.dav.org
An organization of veterans disabled while serving the United States, it was formed after World War I.

Library of Congress
see p. 504

Military Order of the Purple Heart
5413-B Backlick Road
Springfield, VA 22151-3960
Tel: (703) 642-5360
Fax: (703) 642-2054
www.purpleheart.org
Those who have received this U.S. military decoration can join.

National Archives and Records Administration
see p. 504

Paralyzed Veterans of America
801 18th Street, NW
Washington, DC 20006-3517
Tel: (202) 416-7659
Fax: (202) 416-7641
www.pva.org
This is a veterans organization for those who have experienced spinal cord or related injuries.

U.S. Department of Veterans Affairs
Office of Public Affairs
Washington, DC 20420
Tel: (800) 827-1000
www.va.gov
This U.S. government agency is responsible for coordinating programs and benefits for veterans.

U.S. Navy Memorial Foundation
see p. 506

Veterans of Foreign Wars
National Headquarters
406 W. 34th Street
Kansas City, MO 64111
Tel: (816) 756-3390
Fax: (816) 968-1149
www.vfw.org
This is a major U.S. veterans organization.

MUSEUMS AND COLLECTIONS

Airwar Museum Fort Veldhuis
Geniegweg 1
Heemskerk
The Netherlands
Tel: 31 251 230670
(no e-mail address)
This Dutch museum has numerous aircraft on display.

American Air Power Heritage Museum
Confederate Air Force Headquarters
Midland International Airport
9600 Wright Drive
Midland, TX 79711
Tel: (915) 567-3009
Fax: (915) 567-3047
www.airpowermuseum.org
This collection includes many flyable examples of World War II aircraft.

Auschwitz-Birkenau Memorial and Museum
ul. Wiezniow Oswiecimia 20
32-603 Oswiecim
Poland
Tel: (48) 3 38 43 20 22
Fax: (48) 3 38 43 19 34
www.auschwitz-muzeum.oswiecim.pl
This museum is at the site of the infamous concentration camp.

Australian War Memorial
see p. 503

Bastogne Historical Center
Colline du Mardasson
B-6600 Bastogne
Belgium
Tel: (32) 61 21 14 13
Fax: (32) 61 21 73 73
www.bastognehistoricalcenter.be
Displays related to the fight for the crossroads town during the Battle of the Bulge are shown here.

Bavarian Army Museum
Neues Schloss
Postfach 210255
85017 Ingolstadt
Germany
Tel: (49) 84 19 37 70
Fax: (49) 84 19 37 72 00
www.bayerisches-armeemuseum.de
This German museum has some information about World War II.

Bayerische Staatsbibliothek
Ludwig Route 16
80328 Munich
Germany
Tel: (49) 89 28 63 80
Fax: (49) 89 28 63 82 200
www.bsb.badw-muenchen.de
This library includes a collection of World War II artwork.

Canadian War Museum
General Motors Court
330 Sussex Drive
Ottawa, Ontario
K1A OM8 Canada
Tel: (819) 776-8600
Fax: (819) 776-8623
www.civilization.ca/cwm
This is a museum of the Canadian war experience.

Diekirch Historical Museum
10, Bamertal
9209 Diekirch
Luxembourg
Tel: (352) 80 89 08
Fax: (352) 80 47 19
www.nat-military-museum.lu
This museum includes artifacts and displays of the Battle of the Bulge.

Fleet Air Arm Museum
Royal Naval Air Station
Box D6, RNAS Yeovilton
Somerset BA22 8HT
United Kingdom
Tel: (44) 19 35 84 05 65
Fax: (44) 19 35 84 26 30
www.fleetairarm.com
This museum is dedicated to aviation in the British Royal Navy.

Imperial War Museum
see p. 504

Luftwaffenmuseum Flugplatz
Gatow/Kladower-Damm 182-188
14089 Berlin
Germany
Tel: (49) 30 36 87 26 00
Fax: (49) 30 36 87 26 10
www.luftwaffenmuseum.de
Displays of German aviation and aircraft are shown here.

Marine Corps Air-Ground Museum
2014 Anderson Avenue
Quantico, VA 22134-5002
Tel: (703) 640-2606
Fax: (703) 784-5856
Hqineto01.hqmc.usmc.mil/HD/
This museum holds documentation of U.S. Marine Corps aviation.

Musée d'Histoire Contemporaine
Hôtel National des Invalides
75007 Paris
France
Tel: (33) 44 42 54 91
Fax: (33) 44 18 93 84
www.paris.org/musees/histoire.contemp/info.html
This is one of several Paris museums containing information on World War II.

Museo Nazionale della Scienza e della Tecnologia
Via S. Vittore 21-20123
Milan, Italy
Tel: (39) 2 48 55 51
Fax: (39) 2 48 01 00 16
www.museoscienza.org
This museum includes Italian aircraft and artwork of World War II.

Museum of Flying
2772 Donald Douglas Loop North
Santa Monica, CA 90405
Tel: (310) 392-8822
Fax: (310) 450-6956
www.museumofflying.com
There is a large collection of aircraft on display here.

Museum of London
London Wall
London EC2Y 5HN
United Kingdom
Tel: (44) 20 76 00 36 99
Fax: (44) 20 76 00 10 58
www.museum-london.org.uk
This is a museum of the history of London, including the war years.

National Archives of New Zealand
10 Mulgrave Street, Thorndon
Wellington, New Zealand
Tel: (64) 44 99 55 95
Fax: (64) 44 95 62 10
www.archives.govt.nz

These archives hold documentation of the experiences of New Zealanders during the war.

National Atomic Museum
1905 Mountain Road NW
Albuquerque, NM 87104
Tel: (505) 284-3243
www.atomicmuseum.com
Exhibits on the history and technical aspects of the nuclear age are displayed.

National D-Day Museum
945 Magazine Street
New Orleans, LA 70130
Tel: (504) 527-6012
Fax: (504) 527-6088
www.ddaymuseum.org
The D-Day museum holds excellent displays, including video, artifacts, and audio, of the D-Day invasion.

National Maritime Museum
Greenwich, London
SE10 9NF
United Kingdom
Tel: (44) 20 88 58 44 22
Fax: (44) 20 83 12 66 32
www.nmm.ac.uk
This is a naval history museum, including World War II.

National Museum of Naval Aviation
1750 Radford Boulevard
Suite C
Naval Air Station
Pensacola, FL 32508
Tel: (850) 452-3604
Fax: (850) 452-3296
This museum commemorates achievements in naval aviation.

National Museum of Modern Art
3 Kitanomaru Koen
Chiyoda-ku Tokyo
Japan
102-8322
Tel: (81) 3 32 14 25 61
Fax: (81) 3 32 14 25 77
www.momat.go.jp
This holds some artwork related to World War II.

Royal Air Force Museums
Grahame Park Way
Hendon, London
United Kingdom
Tel: (44) 18 12 05 22 66
Fax: (44) 18 12 00 17 51
www.rafmuseum.org.uk
(Other locations at Duxford, Hawkings, Kent, and Bedfordshire)
These museums commemorate the history of the Royal Air Force, including vintage aircraft on display.

Royal Australian Air Force Museum
RAAF Base Williams
Point Cook, Victoria 3027
Australia
Tel: (61) 3 92 56 12 36
Fax: (61) 3 92 56 16 92
www.raafmuseum.com.au
This museum relates the history of the Australian Air Force.

Smithsonian Institution
see p. 504

Sotamuseo (Military Museum of Finland)
Maurinkatu 1
P.O. Box 266
00170 Helsinki
Finland
Markku.mekko@mpkk.fi
www.mil.fi
This is a Finnish museum that includes a collection of World War II art.

State Russian Museum
Inzhenernaya ul. 4
St. Petersburg
Russia
Tel: (7) 81 22 19 16 12
Fax: (7) 81 23 14 41 53
www.rusmuseum.ru
This is an extensive museum that includes a collection of art from World War II.

U.S. Air Force Museum
1100 Spaatz Street
Wright-Patterson Air Force Base, OH 45433
Tel: (937) 255-3286
Fax: (937) 255-3910
www.wpafb.af.mil/museum
The history of the U.S. Air Force is on display here.

U.S. Army Aviation Museum
U.S. Army Aviation Center
P.O. Box 620610-0610
Fort Rucker, AL 36362
Tel: (334) 598-2508
Fax: (334) 598-3054
The history of U.S. Army aviation is the concern of this museum.

U.S. Army Center of Military History
see p. 505

U.S. Army Transportation Museum
300 Washington Boulevard
Bessen Hall
Fort Eustis, VA 23604-5260
Tel: (757) 878-1115
Fax: (757) 878-5656
www.eustis.army.mil
U.S. Army vehicles of the World War II era are on display.

U.S. Coast Guard Academy Museum and Library
15 Monhegan Avenue
New London, CT 06320-4195
Tel: (860) 444-8511
Fax: (860) 701-6700
www.uscg.mil
The history of the U.S. Coast Guard's participation in World War II is shown.

U.S. Holocaust Memorial Museum
100 Raoul Wallenberg Place SW
Washington, DC 20024-2126
Tel: (202) 488-0400
Fax: (202) 488-2613
www.ushmm.org
This museum holds stirring documentation of the Holocaust in film, photographs, and exhibits.

U.S. Marine Corps Research Center
see p. 505

U.S. Naval Academy Archives
see p. 505

U.S. Naval Historical Center
see p. 506

Vojenské Muzeum
Kbely, Prague
Czech Republic
Tel: (42) 2 27 29 65
www.militarymuseum.cz
This museum includes a collection of World War II art.

Yad Vashem
see p. 506

Selected Web sites

Aerial combat: www.tailside.firelight.dynip.com
Airborne operations: www.thedropzone.org
American Memory Library of Congress: rs6.loc.gov/amhome.html
Cyberlibrary of the Holocaust: www.remember.org

AMERICAN LEGION AND VFW PROMOTE U.S. PATRIOTISM

Between them, the American Legion and the Veterans of Foreign Wars (VFW) have nearly five million members. The two organizations are major advocates for the rights of veterans and support various programs that engender patriotism in the United States. They also administer scholarships, athletic programs, educational assistance, and funds designated for disaster relief.

The VFW was founded in 1899 by a group of U.S. veterans returning from the Spanish-American War. The organization played a key role in the designation of Veterans Day as a national holiday, the selection of the *Star-Spangled Banner* as the national anthem in 1931, and the formulation of the GI Bill. During World War II, the VFW provided 15 training aircraft and qualified 100,000 servicemen for the military.

The American Legion received its charter from Congress in 1919 and consists of 15,000 posts in the United States, France, Mexico, and the Philippines. The American Legion has supported a popular baseball program in the United States since 1925; provided support for the Boy Scouts of America; sponsored oratorical contests, awards, and programs on civics and government for high school students; and advocated respect for the American flag. The legion also has established a national emergency fund for disaster relief. Since its inception, the group has remained active in veterans affairs.

Perhaps the American Legion's greatest contribution to postwar prosperity in the United States was its support for what has come to be known as the GI Bill. The legislation was drafted by the legion's former national commander, Harry W. Colmery, on December 15, 1943. President Franklin D. Roosevelt signed it on June 22, 1944.

D-Day: geocities.com/paddyjoe_m/index.html

General history: www.historychannel.com or www.thehistorynet.com

General index: angelfire.com/ct/ww2europe/index.html

Hiroshima: history1900s.about.com/library/weekly/aa080300a.htm

Japanese Imperial Navy: www.combinedfleet.com

Japanese Maritime Self-Defense Force homepage: www.jda.go.jp

Normandy D-Day links: gofrance.about.com

Original documents: www.ibiblio.org/pha

Social history: www.lib.ox.ac.uk

Statistics: gi.grolier.com/wwii/wwii_16.html or www.warmemorial.com

U-boats: uboat.net

Weaponry: angelfire.com/ab/worldwar2weapons

World War II sites in Belgium: www.visitbelgium.com/worldwar.htm

Monuments

The monuments of World War II serve as a constant reminder to future generations, bearing testimony to the sacrifices, triumphs, and tragedies that took place around the world. A lasting tribute to the fighting spirit of those who liberated vast areas of Europe, Asia, and the Pacific, and to those who suffered unspeakable horrors, the monuments also serve as a warning that freedom comes with a price.

The memorials and cemeteries, where millions, civilian and military, have found their final rest, are generally places of quiet dignity. Many World War II dead lie where they fell, in designated war graves beneath the oceans, or in deep jungles, barren deserts, the vastness of the steppes, or deserted beaches. From beautifully manicured grass and hedges with rows of crosses, chapels, and pylons recounting the campaigns in which they gave their lives, to mass graves marked by a single stone inscribed with the year of interment, the memorials and cemeteries seem to whisper the words "Lest we forget."

The following monuments, memorials, and cemeteries are representative of countless others that may be found worldwide. They are located in town squares across the United States, in villages and along routes of march throughout Europe, on Pacific islands, and on the many battlefields. Some are grand and of imposing size, while others are simple and small yet nevertheless moving.

ALEUTIAN NATIONAL HISTORIC AREA Located on Amaknak Island in the Aleutian island chain of Alaska, this monument commemorates the defensive efforts to protect U.S. territory in the North Pacific. Congress designated the site a national historic area in 1996.

ANNE FRANK HOUSE Known worldwide for her famous diary, Anne Frank was a young German-born Jewish girl who perished in the horror of the concentration camp at Bergen-Belsen. Opened to the public on May 3, 1960, the house, which includes the secret annex where Anne, her family, and others hid from the Nazis, is located at 265 Prinsengracht in Amsterdam, the Netherlands. A 150-year-old chestnut tree, about which Anne wrote, is still standing.

ARIZONA MEMORIAL Dedicated on Memorial Day 1962, the USS *Arizona* Memorial spans the sunken hull of the battleship that was destroyed during the Pearl Harbor attack on December 7, 1941. A total of 2,403 Americans died in the attack, 1,177 of them aboard the *Arizona*. Many remain entombed in the hull. The memorial is constructed with a depressed center, rising to its highest point on either end, symbolic of the ultimate victory. Designed by the architect Alfred Preis, the memorial, located near Honolulu, Hawaii, was placed under the administration of the National Park Service in 1980.

AUSCHWITZ-BIRKENAU MEMORIAL AND MUSEUM Dedicated in 1947, the Auschwitz-Birkenau Memorial and Museum is located near the city of Oswiecim, Poland, on the site of the largest and most notorious Nazi concentration camp. Estimates of the number put to death at Auschwitz range from 1.1 million to 1.5 million. Memorials have also been erected and buildings preserved at other concentration camp sites throughout the former Nazi-occupied Europe.

BLETCHLEY PARK Located outside London, Bletchley Park was the center of Allied efforts to decrypt German messages, particularly those encoded by the sophisticated Enigma machine (see Chapter 10, "Intelligence, Espionage, and Propaganda"). Colossus, the world's first computer, operated at Bletchley Park. Known as Ultra, the information gleaned from the decoded German messages provided a decided edge to the Allies and proved to be one of the most important developments of World War II. Bletchley Park was opened to visitors in 1993 after a group of concerned citizens saved the site from the wrecking ball.

BRANAU, AUSTRIA In the town of Hitler's birth, a large stone sits in front of the house where the Nazi dictator was born. Its simple inscription reads: "For peace, freedom and democracy. Never again fascism. Millions of dead remind you."

CANADIAN NATIONAL MEMORIAL Rising slightly more than 69 feet in downtown Ottawa, the National War Memorial of Canada pays tribute to Canadians who have fought in all their country's wars.

CASSINO MEMORIAL The names of more than 4,000 soldiers of the British Commonwealth who gave their lives during the Italian campaign are inscribed on the walls of a memorial adjacent to Cassino War Cemetery, near the site of some of the most bitter fighting in Italy.

CORENO AUSONIO In this Italian town, a rough column dedicated in 1994 memorializes all the victims of World War II.

D-DAY MEMORIAL (U.S.) Dedicated on June 6, 2001, the U.S. National D-Day Memorial is located in Bedford, Virginia, a town that suffered great loss on the day of the Normandy invasion. Of 35 young men from Bedford, 19 were killed in the opening moments of the invasion on Omaha Beach, and two more were killed later in the day. All were members of Company A, 116th Infantry Regiment, 29th Division.

D-DAY MEMORIALS (U.K.) In Great Britain, memorials to the men who invaded Normandy on D-Day include a modest marker in Hythe, Hampshire; a stained glass window in the cathedral at Portsmouth; and a memorial obelisk near Rowlands Castle on the site where King George VI reviewed troops before their departure.

D-DAY MONUMENTS (NORMANDY) Normandy is dotted with monuments to the Allied soldiers who brought liberation from Nazi oppression with them on June 6, 1944. A simple slab at Pointe du Hoc pays homage to the U.S. Army Rangers who scaled the adjacent cliffs in search of German guns. Its inscription reads: "To the heroic ranger commandoes D2RN E2RN F2RN of the 116th Inf who under the command of Colonel James E. Rudder of the First American Division attacked and took possession of the Pointe du Hoc." Other D-Day monuments are located on the invasion beaches and in the coastal towns. A memorial window is located in the cathedral in the town of Bayeux.

ERNIE PYLE MEMORIAL Located on the island of Ie Shima near Okinawa in the Pacific, a simple marker commemorates the death of the beloved journalist Ernie Pyle, who was killed there on April 18, 1945. The inscription reads: "In this spot the 77th Infantry Division lost a buddy, Ernie Pyle, 18 April 1945."

FRANKLIN DELANO ROOSEVELT MEMORIAL The memorial to President Franklin D. Roosevelt, the only U.S. president to serve more than two terms in office, is located in Washington, D.C., near the Tidal Basin. Excerpts from Roosevelt's most famous speeches adorn the walls. A 10-foot-high statue of the president in his wheelchair is also located there. The memorial was dedicated on May 2, 1997.

GUADALCANAL On a hill overlooking the town of Honaira, a monument remembers Americans who lost their lives in their nation's first offensive land campaign of the Pacific war. Pylons bear the names of U.S. and Allied ships lost in the fighting and descriptions of the battle for the island. An inscription on a 24-foot central pylon reads: "This memorial has been erected by the United States of America in humble tribute to its sons and its allies who paid the ultimate sacrifice for the liberation of the Solomon Islands 1942–1943."

HALL OF VALOUR Located in Stalingrad (now Volgograd), Russia, the Hall of Valor is built in the shape of a cylinder 40 meters in diameter. Its floors are of polished black granite. Seven thousand names, a fraction of those who died in defense of Stalingrad, are carved into the walls. A hand rises from the center of the sunken floor; it holds an eternal flame. The monument was dedicated in 1967.

HIROSHIMA PEACE PARK The first atomic bomb to be used in war was dropped on the Japanese city of Hiroshima on August 6, 1945. The Peace Park, dedicated in 1949, consists of gardens, statues, and memorials, including the famous A-Bomb Dome, the ruined shell of a

building directly above the epicenter of the blast. Other monuments include the Children's Peace Monument, Hypocenter, and the Atomic Bomb Memorial Mound.

IWO JIMA A monument marks the position of the historic flag-raising by U.S. Marines atop Mount Suribachi on this Pacific island on February 23, 1945. Nearly 7,000 U.S. service personnel were killed in the monthlong battle.

JAPANESE AMERICAN INTERNMENT MEMORIAL Located in San Jose, California, this memorial was dedicated on March 5, 1994, to the approximately 110,000 Japanese Americans who were interned by the U.S. government during World War II.

MEMORIAL HALL OF THE VICTIMS OF THE NANKING MASSACRE In a six-week period during late 1937 and early 1938, the Japanese army murdered hundreds of thousands of Chinese civilians in the city of Nanking. This memorial preserves the memory of the atrocities and those who lost their lives in Nanking (Chapter 12, "Man's Inhumanity").

MOTHER RUSSIA STATUE Standing 171.6 feet high, the statue crowns Mamayev Kurgan, a hill that was the scene of heavy fighting during the Battle of Stalingrad (now Volgograd), Russia. Its sword alone weighs 14 tons. Dedicated in 1967, the statue is the focal point of a large museum complex.

NAGASAKI Nagasaki was the second Japanese city to be destroyed by an atomic bomb (August 9, 1945). Today, it is the home to the memorial monolith in Hypocenter Park, which marks the location directly beneath the bomb's detonation point. The Atomic Bomb Museum is located in the Nagasaki International Culture Hall, and the 33-foot bronze Peace Statue, sculpted by Seibo Kitamura, is the site of a ceremony on every anniversary of the bombing.

NATIONAL WORLD WAR II MEMORIAL Years of discussion and dissension have marked the evolution of the National World War II Memorial. Both its design and location on the Mall near the Washington Monument in Washington, D.C., have stirred debate, with many groups opposed to its location arguing that it would disrupt the architectural beauty of the Mall. In 2001, Congress gave the project its final approval, the last step before construction. The memorial's design features two semicircular colonnades, 56 pillars, one for each state and territory of the nation during the war, and a reflecting pool. The site was dedicated on November 11, 1995. Friedrich St. Florian designed the memorial.

OKINAWA This Pacific island, scene of the climactic ground engagement of the war, has numerous shrines to both Japanese and American dead. The cornerstones for Peace Memorial Park contain tablets listing the names of the dead from both sides.

PORT CHICAGO NAVAL MAGAZINE Located at Concord Naval Weapons Station, California, this memorial is dedicated to 320 U.S. service personnel who died in a catastrophic munitions explosion at the site in 1944 (see Chapter 6, "Officers and Soldiers").

SAIPAN A carillon and modest memorial honor Americans who died in the fighting to capture this strategically important island in the Marianas archipelago and throughout the Pacific. The monument was dedicated in 1987, and the carillon in 1995, on the 50th anniversary of the end of the war.

TOBRUK This Libyan port city was the scene of heavy fighting during the North African campaign. World War II sites located there include several cemeteries; the American B-24 Liberator bomber *Lady Be Good,* which was lost for years in the Sahara Desert; a museum; and the underground operations room of German Field Marshal Erwin Rommel, "the Desert Fox."

TRINITY SITE The first detonation of an atomic bomb in human history occurred in the desert of New Mexico on July 16, 1945, at a site designated Trinity. After witnessing the test, the scientist J. Robert Oppenheimer, who led the group that developed the atomic bomb, quoted from a sacred Hindu text: "I am become death, the shatterer of worlds." Today, a monument to the test is located on what is now the White Sands Missile Range.

U.S. MARINE CORPS MEMORIAL Dedicated on November 10, 1954, the U.S. Marine Corps Memorial depicts the raising of the U.S. flag atop Mount Suribachi on the Pacific island of Iwo Jima during World War II. Cast in bronze, the figures stand 32 feet high and raise a 60-foot flagpole. The overall height of the memorial is 78 feet. It is located just north of the Ord-Weitzel gate of Arlington National Cemetery.

VICTORY MEMORIAL AND MONUMENT Rising nearly 469 feet, the Victory Monument towers above the Victory Memorial located on Poklonnaya Hill in Moscow, Russia. Dedicated on May 9, 1995, the memorial includes a victory park, museum, memorial mosque, and memorial synagogue, as well as outdoor exhibits commemorating the victory in the Great Patriotic War, as World War II is known in Russia.

WAR DOG MEMORIAL This handsomely sculpted Doberman pinscher commemorates the bravery of the war dogs that died in service to the U.S. Marine Corps on the island of Guam in the Marianas. Its inscription reads in part: "25 marine war dogs gave their lives liberating Guam in 1944. They served as sentries, messengers, scouts. They explored caves, detected mines and booby traps. Semper fidelis."

WARSAW Numerous memorials and statues pay tribute to the suffering of the citizens of the Polish capital, the virtual annihilation of its Jewish population and the heroic uprising of its ghetto in 1943. More than 350,000 people perished in the city's general uprising the following year.

WEST COAST MEMORIAL U.S. servicemen who died in the waters off the U.S. Pacific Coast are remembered at this memorial located in the Presidio in San Francisco. The names of 412 missing personnel are inscribed on the monument wall.

WOMEN IN MILITARY SERVICE FOR AMERICA MEMORIAL Dedicated on October 18, 1997, the Women in Military Service for America Memorial is located on about four acres at the ceremonial entrance to Arlington National Cemetery near Washington, D.C. It is the first major memorial to commemorate the courage and sacrifice of women in the armed forces of the United States, including those of World War II.

YAD VASHEM The largest museum in the world documenting the story of the Holocaust, Yad Vashem, the Holocaust Martyrs' and Heroes' Remembrance Authority, was established in 1953. Located in Jerusalem, the archives of Yad Vashem contain 55 million pages of documents and nearly 100,000 photos. Its memorials include the Hall of Remembrance, the Memorial to Deportees, the Children's Memorial, and the Valley of the Communities.

WARSHIP MEMORIALS

A number of World War II–era warships, of various classes and types, are on display around the world as floating museums and memorials to those who fought on or flew from their decks. This listing includes many of these.

Warship	Classification	Location
USS *Intrepid*	Aircraft Carrier	New York, NY
USS *Yorktown*	Aircraft Carrier	Charleston, SC
USS *Alabama*	Battleship	Mobile, AL
USS *Massachusetts*	Battleship	Fall River, MA
USS *Missouri*	Battleship	Pearl Harbor, HI
USS *North Carolina*	Battleship	Wilmington, NC
USS *Texas*	Battleship	La Porte, TX
HMS *Belfast*	Cruiser	London, U.K.
USS *Des Moines*	Cruiser	Philadelphia, PA
USS *Little Rock*	Cruiser	Buffalo, NY
USS *Salem*	Cruiser	Quincy, MA
USS *Cassin Young*	Destroyer	Boston, MA
USS *J. P. Kennedy, Jr.*	Destroyer	Fall River, MA
USS *Kidd*	Destroyer	Baton Rouge, LA
USS *Laffey*	Destroyer	Charleston, SC
USS *The Sullivans*	Destroyer	Buffalo, NY
USS *Stewart*	Destroyer Escort	Galveston, TX
USS *Batfish*	Submarine	Muskogee, OK
USS *Becuna*	Submarine	Philadelphia, PA

Warship	Classification	Location
USS *Bowfin*	Submarine	Pearl Harbor, HI
USS *Cavalla*	Submarine	Galveston, TX
USS *Clamagore*	Submarine	Charleston, SC
USS *Cobia*	Submarine	Manitowoc, WI
USS *Cod*	Submarine	Cleveland, OH
USS *Croaker*	Submarine	Buffalo, NY
USS *Drum*	Submarine	Mobile, AL
USS *Lionfish*	Submarine	Fall River, MA
USS *Pampanito*	Submarine	San Francisco, CA
USS *Requin*	Submarine	Tampa, FL
USS *Silversides*	Submarine	Chicago, IL
USS *Torsk*	Submarine	Baltimore, MD
K-21	Submarine	Severomorsk, Russia
S-56	Submarine	Vladivostok, Russia
U-505	Submarine	Chicago, IL
U-995	Submarine	Laboe, Germany
U-2540	Submarine	Bremerhaven, Germany
USS *Hazard*	Minesweeper	Omaha, NE
USS *Inaugural*	Minesweeper	St. Louis, MO
PT *619*	Patrol Torpedo	Memphis, TN
PT *796*	Patrol Torpedo	Fall River, MA
SS *Jeremiah O'Brien*	Liberty	San Francisco, CA

Continuing Efforts to Memorialize World War II

Succeeding generations continue their efforts to remember the heroism and sacrifices of World War II. As evidenced by the decade-long effort to begin construction on the National World War II Memorial in Washington, D.C., opinions and directions may vary. In 2001, the U.S. National D-Day Monument was dedicated in Bedford, Virginia, 57 years after the event it commemorates.

During the 1990s, controversy surrounded the plans of the Japanese government to build a World War II museum. Memorials to individuals, battles, campaigns, and the victims of atrocities continue to be built around the world as interest in the war and appreciation of its historical significance grow.

CEMETERIES

The dead of World War II rest in large cemeteries; some are for a single nationality, others are multinational. They also lie in small plots far from their homelands, in family burial grounds, in mass graves, and in unknown locations where they fell.

The American Battle Monuments Commission is responsible for the administration of 18 cemeteries and memorials, 16 of them abroad. Arlington National Cemetery, under the jurisdiction of the U.S. Army, contains the graves of many World War II dead. Other national cemeteries in the United States are under the administration of the Department of Veterans Affairs; the best known probably is the National Memorial Cemetery of the Pacific in Honolulu. More than 38,000 graves and the inscribed names of more than 26,000 missing U.S. service personnel, many from World War II, are located at this cemetery, commonly referred to as the Punch Bowl.

The Commonwealth War Graves Commission maintains cemeteries in 148 countries, many of which include burial sites of soldiers of the British Commonwealth who died in World War II, including cemeteries at Singapore; Cassino,

Italy; Rabaul in the South Pacific; Sangro River, Italy; Kohima, India; Sfax, Tunisia; Port Moresby, Papua New Guinea; Normandy; and Arnhem, Netherlands.

A small cemetery at Urville-Langannerrie in Normandy holds 650 graves of Polish soldiers who died fighting to liberate France.

The German War Graves Commission has responsibility for the maintenance of 366 cemeteries in 80 countries. Five German World War II cemeteries are located in Normandy. More than 22,000 German dead are buried in Sologubovka Cemetery in Russia. In recent years more than a quarter of a million German war dead in Eastern Europe have been removed from isolated, unmarked graves and reburied in cemeteries opened in the Polish city of Gdansk; in Bratislava, the capital of Slovakia; and elsewhere. More than 75,000 German graves are located in the area of the Hurtgen Forest on their home soil and in the Netherlands. Nearly 3,000 German casualties of World War II are buried at Cannock Chase Cemetery in England.

In 1985, President Ronald Reagan made a controversial visit to a German military cemetery in the city of Bitburg. The visit aroused controversy because the Bitburg cemetery contained graves of the Waffen SS, the military arm of the notorious SS organization responsible for the murder of Jews throughout Europe.

A staggering half-million Russian dead from the 900-day siege of Leningrad (now St. Petersburg), most of them civilians, are buried in 186 mass graves in Piskariovskoye Memorial Cemetery near the city.

Here is a list of the sites of 18 cemeteries and monuments under the administration of the American Battle Monuments Commission:

CEMETERIES AND MONUMENTS

Name	City/State	Burials	Missing
Ardennes	Neupre, Belgium	5,328	428
Brittany	St. James, France	4,410	498
Cambridge	England	3,812	5,126
East Coast	New York City, New York	——	4,609
Épinal	France	5,255	424
Florence	Italy	4,402	1,409
Henri-Chapelle	Belgium	7,989	450
Honolulu	Hawaii	——	18,096
Lorraine	St. Avold, France	10,489	444
Luxembourg City	Luxembourg	5,076	371

Name	City/State	Burials	Missing
Manila	Philippines	17,206	36,282
Netherlands	Margraten, Netherlands	8,302	1,723
Normandy	Colleville, France	9,387	1,557
North Africa	Carthage, Tunisia	2,841	3,724
Rhône	Draguignan, France	861	294
Sicily-Rome	Nettuno, Italy	7,861	3,095
Suresnes	Paris, France	24	——
West Coast	San Francisco, California	——	412
Totals		**93,243**	**78,976**

Glossary of World War II Terms

During World War II, military terminology became familiar to both the soldier and the civilian. The war engendered the increased use of military language and gave rise to new words and phrases. The reader of World War II history will find this glossary helpful in understanding reference material and informational texts. It includes military terms as well as proper nouns that were part of the wartime lexicon.

ABDA Cooperative command organizational structure established in December 1941 for the military forces of the United States, Great Britain, the Netherlands, and Australia. It derived its name from the words *American, British, Dutch,* and *Australian.*

ACE Title given to a pilot who claimed at least five aerial victories against enemy planes. The term was first used in World War I and first coined by the media.

ACK-ACK A primarily British term for antiaircraft fire, which evolved from the use of the word *Ack* for the letter *A* in the British phonetic alphabet.

AIRBORNE Troops transported to combat areas by air, parachuting into action or arriving in gliders.

ALAMOGORDO Site of the test detonation of the atomic bomb in the New Mexico desert.

ALLIES Term describing the cooperative military and political alliance that opposed the Axis in World War II and was headed principally by the United States and Great Britain, and later the Soviet Union as well.

ARMISTICE OF CASSIBILE Agreement signed September 3, 1943, ending hostilities between the Allies and Italy.

ARP Air Raid Precaution, a British air defense organization.

ASDIC Antisubmarine Detection Investigation Committee. Similar to American SONAR, this British submarine detection equipment was carried aboard ships to detect German U-boats.

ATABRINE Drug used to combat malaria and given to U.S. military personnel during the war.

ATLANTIC WALL Term used to describe Hitler's string of fortifications along the coast of Western Europe, primarily in France.

AVG More popularly known as the Flying Tigers, the American Volunteer Group included U.S. pilots who flew Curtiss P-40 fighters against the Japanese in China early in the war. The group was incorporated into the U.S. Army Air Forces as the 14th Air Force in July 1942.

AXIS In 1936, Benito Mussolini used the term to describe Germany, Italy, and their allies as a bloc around which the events of the world would turn.

BANDIT U.S. Navy designation for enemy aircraft.

BANZAI Japanese battle cry that literally translated means "May you live 1,000 years."

BAR The Browning automatic rifle.

BEACHHEAD A foothold on the shore of an enemy-held area.

BEF The British Expeditionary Force, which landed on the continent of Europe in 1939.

BERCHTESGADEN Town located in the Bavarian Alps that was the site of Hitler's mountaintop retreat.

BERGHOF Hitler's name for his mountain retreat in the Bavarian Alps.

BERLIN Capital city of Germany.

BIGOT Designation for the highest level of top-secret clearance concerning the D-Day invasion of June 6, 1944.

BLACK CODE U.S. State Department code that was compromised and provided valuable intelligence to the Germans in North Africa.

BLACK SHEEP Nickname given to U.S. Marine fighter squadron VMF-214, commanded by Major Gregory "Pappy" Boyington.

BLACKSHIRTS Fascist supporters who helped sweep Italian dictator Benito Mussolini into power.

BLITZ British term for the period from September to November 1940 during which the Luftwaffe bombed London regularly.

BLITZKRIEG Literally translated as "lightning war," this word describes the coordinated German offensive use of tactical airpower and concentrated armored thrusts supported by quickly moving infantry.

BLONDI The name of Hitler's pet German shepherd.

BOCK'S CAR The U.S. Boeing B-29 Superfortress bomber that dropped the atomic bomb on Nagasaki on August 9, 1945.

BOEING Large U.S. aircraft manufacturer.

BOGEY An unidentified aircraft.

BRAINS TRUST A group of close personal advisers to President Franklin D. Roosevelt.

BRIDGEHEAD A foothold on the enemy side of a contested span, usually over water.

BROWNSHIRTS Nazi Party members who belonged to the SA; refers to the color of their uniforms.

BUG RIVER Demarcation line between German and Soviet forces during their invasion of Poland in 1939.

BÜRGERBRÄU KELLER Munich beer hall that was the site of the abortive Nazi putsch of 1923.

BURMA ROAD The 700-mile land supply line between Lashio, Burma, and Kunming, China.

CACTUS American code name for Guadalcanal.

CAM SHIP An Allied merchant ship equipped with a catapult and a single Hawker Hurricane fighter to provide defense against attacking German aircraft.

CAN DO The motto of the U.S. Navy's construction battalions, popularly known as Seabees.

CARGO SHIP DESIGNATIONS:

AK   Cargo ship
AKA   Attack cargo ship
AKD   Deep-hold cargo ship
AKS   General stores issue ship
AKV   Cargo ship and aircraft ferry

CASE BLUE Germany's campaign to conquer the oil-rich Caucasus in 1942.

CASE GREEN The occupation of Czechoslovakia by Nazi troops in 1938.

CASE RED The June 1940 German assault on France, crossing the Seine and Somme Rivers.

CASE WHITE The German invasion of Poland on September 1, 1939.

CASE YELLOW The German invasion of France and Western Europe on May 10, 1940.

CASUALTY DESIGNATIONS The U.S. armed forces used several abbreviated designations to describe the condition of its personnel, such as:

AI   Accidental injuries
DAI   Death from accidental injuries
DD   Died from disease
DOW   Death from wounds received in action
KIA   Killed in action
M   Missing
MIA   Missing in action
PWOP   Pregnant without permission
SIW   Self-inflicted wounds
SK   Sick
WIA   Wounded in action

CHANNEL ISLANDS The only parts of Britain occupied by the Germans in World War II, the four small islands of Jersey, Guernsey, Alderney, and Sark, situated in the English Channel off the coast of France, were under Nazi control from 1940 until the end of the war.

CHEQUERS The personal residence of British Prime Minister Winston Churchill near London.

CHERBOURG Major French seaport on the English Channel liberated by U.S. forces on June 26, 1944.

CHETNIKS Promonarchist Yugoslav partisans under Draja Mihajlovic who were opposed to the Communist partisans led by Josip Broz (Tito). Although they originally fought the Germans, the Chetniks later operated in uneasy coexistence with them.

CHINDITS British military unit operating in the China-Burma-India theater under Brigadier Orde Wingate.

CICERO Code name of the immensely successful German spy, born Elyesa Bazna.

CINCUS Commander in Chief of the U.S. Fleet until 1941, when the designation was changed to COMINCH.

COLOSSUS The world's first operational, modern computer, used at Bletchley Park to assist in deciphering intercepted German communications.

COMBAT COMMAND Generally a U.S. Army term describing a unit assembled from several elements for a specific mission.

COMPIÈGNE French forest site where Germany had surrendered to the Allies to end World War I; Hitler chose it as the site for the French surrender to Germany on June 22, 1940. Hitler brought the railroad car in which the first surrender took place back to the site for the second.

CONCENTRATION CAMPS Those areas where enemies of the Nazi state were imprisoned, and many put to death, before and during the war.

CONDOR LEGION Powerful detachment of the Luftwaffe that was sent to Spain to assist the Nationalist forces of Generalissimo Francisco Franco during the Spanish Civil War.

CONVOY DESIGNATIONS Used to describe the origination and termination points of Allied convoys. These included

HX	Fast convoys from Halifax, Nova Scotia, to England
JW	Convoys from England to the Soviet Union after December 1942
KN	U.S. convoys northbound along the East Coast
KS	U.S. convoys southbound along the East Coast
ON	Fast convoys from England to Canada
ONS	Slow convoys from England to Canada
PQ	Convoys from England to the Soviet Union before December 1942
QP	Convoys from the Soviet Union to England
SC	Convoys from New York or Sydney to England

CONVOY SYSTEM The grouping of Allied merchant ships for voyages across the Atlantic rather than allowing vessels to travel alone. The system provided for easier protection by screening vessels and for mutual support.

COSSAC Chief of Staff Supreme Allied Command.

DACHAU Built outside Munich in 1933, this was the first of the Nazi concentration camps.

DESERT FOX Nickname of German Field Marshal Erwin Rommel.

DESERT RATS The British Seventh Armored Division, which distinguished itself in combat in North Africa.

DEVIL'S BRIGADE Popular name of the First Special Service Force, which was made up of U.S. and Canadian troops and fought in the Aleutians and Italy.

DIEPPE French coastal town that was the site of an abortive commando raid by Canadian troops accompanied by a small contingent of U.S. Rangers, on August 19, 1942.

DOPPEL   The German designation for radar.

DRESDEN   German city ravaged by Allied bombing in February 1945. Estimates of the casualties from the raid and the resulting firestorm number 135,000.

DUCE   Italian term translated as "leader," the title of dictator Benito Mussolini.

DUKW   Designation for the amphibious craft used by the U.S. Army. It was popularly known as the "Duck."

E-BOAT German motor torpedo boat.

EAGLE'S NEST Hitler's tearoom at Berchtesgaden.

EAGLE SQUADRON One of three squadrons of the British Royal Air Force that was made up of American pilots and flew combat missions against the Germans during the Battle of Britain.

EINSATZGRUPPEN German death squads that followed the Nazi army into occupied territory in the East and systematically massacred perceived enemies of the state.

ENIGMA   A German encoding machine that resembled a typewriter and used a system of rotors; it was capable of millions of combinations.

ENOLA GAY   The name of the B-29 bomber piloted by Colonel Paul Tibbets that dropped the atomic bomb on Hiroshima, Japan, on August 6, 1945.

ETA JIMA   The site of the Japanese Naval Academy, located on an island in Hiroshima Bay.

FAHNENEID   Members of the German military swore this oath of allegiance to Adolf Hitler.

FAT MAN   The plutonium-based atomic bomb dropped on the Japanese city of Nagasaki on August 9, 1945.

FFI   French Forces of the Interior, an organization of the French Resistance.

FIFTH COLUMN   Term for a secret, subversive organization working within a country to assist an invading country's efforts.

FIGHTER-BOMBER A tactical combat aircraft capable of supporting ground forces or being used in aerial action.

FIRESIDE CHAT   A periodic radio address delivered by President Franklin D. Roosevelt to the American people discussing domestic and world events.

FLAGSHIP   The ship carrying the commander of a naval task force.

FLAK   Antiaircraft fire, derived from the German term Flieger Abwehr Kanone, meaning antiaircraft cannon.

FLYING TIGERS   See AVG.

FOGGIA   Italian city that served as the base of operations for the U.S. 15th Air Force.

FOO FIGHTER   Term for lights and other visual phenomena of unexplained origin that Allied airmen saw during the war.

FORCE H   Unit of the British Royal Navy based at Gibraltar that participated in several major operations in the Atlantic.

FORCE Z   The British battleship *Prince of Wales* and the battle cruiser *Repulse,* which were sunk by Japanese aircraft off Malaya on December 10, 1941.

FOXHOLE   Hole dug by an infantryman for protection.

FREYA   A type of German mobile radar.

FUBAR   Acronym for F——ed Up Beyond All Recognition.

FUGO   The Japanese attempt to attack the United States with balloon bombs.

FÜHRER   German word for "leader," the title of Adolf Hitler.

FUSAG   First U.S. Army Group, a fictional unit meant to deceive the Germans before D-Day.

GAULEITER   District governor under the Nazi regime.

GENEVA CONVENTION   One of several meetings held in the Swiss city to establish rules for the humane treatment of prisoners of war. The last one held before World War II was in 1929.

GERMAN-AMERICAN BUND   Pro-Nazi organization in the United States.

GERMANIA   The name Hitler planned to give to a new, modern Berlin.

GESTAPO   The German secret state police.

GHETTO   A section or quarter of a European city in which a minority, particularly Jews, were restricted.

GI   Standing for Government Issue, this was the nickname of the American foot soldier.

GOLD BEACH   D-Day invasion beach that was the landing point of the British 50th Division.

GRAN SASSO   The highest peak in the Italian Apennine Mountains, this was the location from which Mussolini was rescued by German commandos after the surrender of Italy in 1943.

GREAT ARTISTE   A B-29 bomber that participated in both U.S. atomic bomb missions, August 6 and 9, 1945.

GREATER EAST ASIA CO-PROSPERITY SPHERE   Term used by the Japanese to describe their area of influence from the Pacific Rim to mainland Asia.

GREAT PATRIOTIC WAR   The name given by the Soviets to their war with Germany between 1941 and 1945.

GUNG HO   A Chinese phrase that means "work together," this was the motto of the Marine Raiders of General Evans Carlson. It has since become widely used.

H2S   A type of British radar used aboard aircraft.

H2X   An American-built version of the British H2S radar.

HARA-KIRI   Japanese ritual suicide.

HEAVY WATER   Common term for several types of water, including deuterium oxide, that have been used to control the rate of a nuclear reaction.

HEDGEHOG   Nickname given to an effective Allied antisubmarine weapon that used a number of bomblets.

HEDGEROWS   The bocage country of France, featuring ancient earthen embankments with tangled masses of trees and vegetation that separated fields in Normandy and presented a significant challenge to the Allied ground advance after D-Day.

HOME GUARD   An armed force of British citizens mobilized as a final defense against a German invasion in 1940.

HUFF DUFF   High Frequency Direction Finding, a system used by the Allies to locate German U-boats during the Battle of the Atlantic.

HUMP, THE   The Himalaya Mountains, over which Allied pilots were required to fly on a long supply route from India to China.

HYPO   Station HYPO was the name of the U.S. Navy's cryptanalysis unit located at Pearl Harbor.

IE SHIMA   Small island near Okinawa where the famed war correspondent Ernie Pyle was killed by Japanese fire.

IMPHAL   Town in northeastern India that was the site of a major battle in which the British turned back an attempted invasion of India from China in 1944.

INTERNATIONAL MILITARY TRIBUNALS   Judicial panels made up of Allied judges that convened to try war criminals at Nuremberg and Tokyo after the war.

IRONBOTTOM SOUND   The area between the islands of Guadalcanal and Florida in the Solomons, so named because of the great number of ships lost there during the Guadalcanal campaign.

ISSEI   A Japanese American born in Japan.

IWO JIMA   Island in the Bonins that saw heavy fighting in February–March 1945, when U.S. Marines took the island from the Japanese.

JEEP   Term originally applied to anything of little value, it came to be synonymous with the four-wheel-drive vehicles produced in great numbers for the U.S. armed forces.

JERRY   British slang term for a German.

JERRY CAN   German-made container for gasoline or water.

JOINT CHIEFS OF STAFF   Group that includes the commanders of all branches of the U.S. military forces.

JUNO BEACH   D-Day invasion beach assigned to Canadian forces, including the Third Infantry Division, Second Armored Division, and the Fourth Special Service Brigade Commando.

KAITEN   Manned suicide torpedoes used by the Japanese against Allied ships late in the Pacific war.

KAMIKAZE   Japanese suicide aircraft that attacked U.S. ships late in the Pacific war.

KARINHALL   Hermann Göring built this opulent wooded retreat and named it for his deceased first wife.

KATYN FOREST   Near Smolensk, Russia, this was the site of a massacre of thousands of Polish officers and soldiers. Long thought to have been committed by the Nazis, the atrocity was actually the work of the Soviet NKVD.

KEMPEITAI   The Japanese army's secret police.

KIEV   Capital city of the Ukraine.

KILROY   Elusive character whose name was scrawled around the world by U.S. military personnel with the phrase "Kilroy was here."

KOHIMA   City in eastern India that was the site of a siege during a Japanese offensive in 1944.

KOKODA TRAIL   The route from Port Moresby to Buna across the Owen Stanley Mountains of New Guinea.

KRAGUJEVAC More than 7,000 civilians were massacred by the Germans in this Yugoslavian town in October 1941.

KRIEGSMARINE The German navy of World War II.

KUOMINTANG The National People's Party of China, which was the party of Chiang Kai-shek.

KURSK Russian city that was the site of the largest tank battle in history.

LANDING CRAFT Vehicles designed to deliver military personnel and equipment to beaches and to provide logistical and fire support. Their designations included:

LCA	Landing Craft, Assault
LCC	Landing Craft, Control
LCF	Landing Craft, Flak
LC (FF)	Landing Craft, Flotilla Flagship
LCI	Landing Craft, Infantry
LCI (L)	Landing Craft, Infantry Large
LCM	Landing Craft, Mechanized
LCP	Landing Craft, Personnel
LCR	Landing Craft, Rubber
LCS	Landing Craft, Support
LCS (S)	Landing Craft, Support Small
LCT	Landing Craft, Tank
LCT (R)	Landing Craft, Tank Rocket
LCV	Landing Craft, Vehicle
LCVP	Landing Craft, Vehicle, Personnel
LSD	Landing Ship, Dock
LSM	Landing Ship, Medium
LSM (R)	Landing Ship, Medium Rocket
LST	Landing Ship, Tank
LST (H)	Landing Ship, Tank Hospital
LSV	Landing Ship, Vehicle
LVT	Landing Vehicle, Tracked

LASHIO Burmese town that was at the western end of the Burma Road.

LEDO ROAD Land supply route from Ledo in the Assam Province of India to a junction with the Burma Road in China.

LEND-LEASE U.S. program of supplying Great Britain and later the Soviet Union with war materiel from 1941 to 1945.

LENINGRAD (now St. Petersburg)—The second largest city of the Soviet Union, it was besieged by the Germans for nearly 900 days, sustaining as many as 800,000 casualties.

LIDICE Czech village destroyed by the Nazis in reprisal for the assassination of Reinhard Heydrich in 1942.

LITTLE BOY Uranium-based atomic bomb dropped on Hiroshima, Japan, on August 6, 1945.

LODZ Polish city where a large Jewish ghetto was established.

LORIENT A French port city on the Atlantic that was the site of a major German U-boat base.

LOS ALAMOS City in the desert of New Mexico where the atomic bomb was designed and constructed.

LUDENDORFF BRIDGE Popularly known as the bridge at Remagen, the Ludendorff railroad bridge across the Rhine River was captured intact by U.S. troops on March 7, 1945.

LUFTWAFFE The German air force in World War II.

MAGIC The intelligence gleaned from Japanese messages, primarily in the Purple diplomatic code, deciphered by cryptanalysts of the U.S. Navy.

MAGINOT LINE Series of fixed fortifications built by the French along their frontier with Germany during the 1930s.

MALINTA TUNNEL Headquarters of the embattled U.S. forces on the island of Corregidor before its fall in 1942.

MALTA Mediterranean island that withstood massive German air attacks for more than two years.

MANCHUKUO The puppet state established by the Japanese in mainland China after their military occupation of Manchuria.

MANCHURIA Province in northwestern China that was under increasing Japanese domination and economic exploitation in the 1920s and that the Japanese later named Manchukuo.

MANDALAY Burma's second-largest city, which fell to the Japanese in 1942 and was liberated in 1945.

MANILA Capital city of the Philippines.

MAQUIS French Resistance forces.

MARETH LINE Defensive line built by the French and stretching more than 20 miles from the coast into southeast Tunisia.

MAUTHAUSEN Nazi concentration camp located in Austria near the town of Linz.

MEIN KAMPF The title of Adolf Hitler's book (My Struggle), primarily written while he was imprisoned in the 1920s; it describes his views on Germany's expansion and his anti-Semitism.

MESSINA Port on the northeastern coast of Sicily, the primary geographic objective of the Allied campaign on the island in 1943.

MILK COW Nickname given to long-range German supply submarines.

MINE An explosive device used on land or in water, usually detonated by direct contact or proximity.

MOSCOW Capital city of the Soviet Union.

MULBERRIES Code name for artificial harbors constructed by the Allies to facilitate landing supplies in Normandy.

MUNICH Capital city of Bavaria, located in southern Germany.

MYITKYINA Small town in northern Burma located on the Ledo Road that fell to the Japanese in 1942 and was liberated in 1944.

NAGASAKI Japanese city that was the target of the second atomic bomb, dropped by the Americans on August 9, 1945.

NANKING Chinese city occupied by the Japanese in 1937 and subjected to atrocities on a large scale, which came to be known as the Rape of Nanking.

NATO The North Atlantic Treaty Organization, a Western alliance formed during the cold war for purposes of mutual defense and opposition to Communist expansion.

NAZI A member of the National Socialist German Workers Party, or the shortened name of the party itself—originally a term of derision.

NCO A noncommissioned officer in the U.S. Army or Marine Corps.

NEW DEAL President Franklin D. Roosevelt's program for economic recovery in the United States during the Great Depression.

NISEI A Japanese American born in the United States.

NKVD Narodnyi Komissariat Vnutrennykh Del, the Soviet secret police.

NORMANDY Region of northern France that was the scene of the D-Day invasion by the Allies.

NSDAP Nationalsozialistische Deutsche Arbeiterpartei, translated from the German into the National Socialist German Workers Party, the Nazis.

NUREMBERG German city that was the scene of massive Nazi Party rallies during the 1930s and of the war crimes tribunal that tried major Nazi figures after the war.

OAK RIDGE City in Tennessee that was the site of much research for the U.S. atomic bomb program.

OBOE British-developed system that used two intersecting radio beacons to guide bombers to their targets on night missions.

OKH Oberkommando des Heeres, the German army high command, later responsible only for operations on the Eastern Front.

OKINAWA Island in the Ryukyus (off Japan), which was the scene of heavy fighting in the spring of 1945, and the last of the major U.S. amphibious operations against the Japanese during the war.

OKW Oberkommando der Wehrmacht, the German army high command after 1938, when Hitler assumed personal command.

OMAHA BEACH Beach assigned to U.S. troops during the D-Day invasion and the scene of heaviest Allied casualties.

ORADOUR-SUR-GLANE Village in southwestern France destroyed by the Second SS Division Das Reich in reprisal for Resistance operations. Approximately 1,000 men, women, and children were murdered.

OSS U.S. Office of Strategic Services, the forerunner of the Central Intelligence Agency (CIA).

OWI U.S. Office of War Information, responsible for dispensing war-related information to the public.

PALERMO Port city in northwest Sicily occupied by U.S. troops in 1943.

PANZER German term for a tank or armored vehicle.

PARTISAN A Resistance fighter.

PEARL HARBOR U.S. naval installation on the Hawaiian island of Oahu, where the Pacific Fleet was attacked by the Japanese on December 7, 1941, plunging the United States into World War II.

PEENEMÜNDE German research site on the Baltic Sea where development of the jet engine was conducted.

PENTAGON The five-sided building in Washington, D.C., where the U.S. military is headquartered. It was completed in 1943.

PHONY WAR The lull in combat on the Western Front between the declaration of war and the invasion of France in May 1940.

PILAR Yacht owned by the author Ernest Hemingway, in which he searched for German U-boats in the Caribbean.

PLUTO Pipeline Under the Ocean, which delivered fuel from Great Britain to Allied forces from beneath the English Channel.

POTUS President of the United States, used to identify President Franklin D. Roosevelt during World War II.

POW A prisoner of war.

PROPAGANDA The systematic dissemination of information supporting a certain point of view, intended to persuade the masses to support that point of view.

PSP Pierced steel planking—the material used to construct aircraft runways quickly.

PT BOAT Patrol torpedo boats used by the U.S. Navy.

PURPLE The Japanese diplomatic code, broken by U.S. cryptanalysts.

QLA A short-range mine-detecting sonar used on U.S. submarines.

Q SHIP Used in both world wars, these were armed merchant ships with their weaponry concealed and used to lure enemy submarines into surfacing for an attack.

QUISLING A reference to the Norwegian Nazi Vidkun Quisling, the term became generic for traitor.

QUONSET HUT Manufactured in the town of Quonset, Rhode Island, these were structures made of prefabricated metal recognizable by their curved construction.

RABAUL Site of a large Japanese air and naval base in the Solomons on the island of New Georgia.

RADAR The acronym for Radio Detection and Ranging, a system that allows a wide area to be swept by radio waves in order to detect aircraft and ships that reflect these waves.

RAF British Royal Air Force.

RAINBOW 5 U.S. contingency plan in the event of war with Germany and Japan.

RANGERS Elite troops of the U.S. Army.

RANGOON Capital city of Burma.

RATIONING The restricted availability and use of certain commodities because of the demands of a wartime economy.

RAVENSBRÜCK Nazi concentration camp north of Berlin, primarily occupied by women.

RDF Radio Detection Finding, an early name for radar.

RED AIR FORCE The air force of the Soviet Union.

RED ARMY The army of the Soviet Union.

RED NAVY The navy of the Soviet Union.

REGIA AERONAUTICA The Italian Air Force.

REICH The territory of Nazi Germany, translated as "empire."

REICHSTAG German parliament.

REMAGEN German city where units of the U.S. First Army captured the Ludendorff railroad bridge intact across the Rhine River.

RLB The Reichsluftshutzbund, a German civil defense organization that dealt with air raid preparedness.

ROME Capital city of Italy, and the first Axis capital to fall to the Allies (June 1944).

RHINE RIVER   A European river that was a major natural barrier to the Allied advance into the German homeland.

ROA   The Russian Liberation Army, consisting of anti-Communist Russians who fought with the Germans.

RUHR   The industrial heart of Germany.

SA   Sturmabteilung, a Nazi paramilitary organization popularly known as the Brownshirts.

SACHSENHAUSEN   Nazi concentration camp in the Berlin area.

SALERNO   Port city in western Italy where the U.S. Fifth Army landed in September 1943.

SAMURAI   A member of the Japanese warrior class.

SAPPER   A military engineer.

SCHNORKEL   A device used by German submarines to cruise underwater for extended periods (snorkel).

SD   Sicherheitsdienst, the intelligence and security section of the Nazi Party.

SD   A form of radar used early in the war by U.S. submarines.

SHAEF   Supreme Headquarters Allied Expeditionary Force, the Allied command structure headed by General Dwight D. Eisenhower.

SHIP CLASSIFICATIONS (U.S. NAVY)

BB	Battleship
CA	Heavy cruiser
CC	Battle cruiser
CL	Light cruiser
CL (AA)	Light antiaircraft cruiser
CV	Aircraft carrier
CVA	Attack aircraft carrier
CVB	Large aircraft carrier
CVE	Escort aircraft carrier
CVL	Light aircraft carrier
DD	Destroyer
DE	Destroyer escort
SS	Submarine

SINGAPORE   Capital city of Malaya, which fell to the Japanese on February 15, 1942, in one of the worst defeats in British military history.

SJ   Updated radar system deployed on U.S. submarines.

SN-2   Also known as Lichtenstein, an airborne radar system used by German nightfighters.

SNAFU   U.S. acronym for "situation normal, all fouled up."

SOE   Special Operations Executive, a clandestine British organization established in 1940 that promoted guerrilla operations in occupied territories.

SONAR   Sound Navigation and Ranging, a U.S. version of submarine detection gear similar to the British ASDIC.

SOS   International distress signal.

SPANDAU   Prison located in Berlin where several Nazi war criminals convicted at Nuremberg served their time.

SS   Schutzstaffel, originally founded as the personal bodyguard of Hitler; this organization grew into an elite military and political organization within the Nazi state.

STARS AND STRIPES U.S. Army newspaper.

STAVKA   The high command of the Soviet Red Army.

STRAIGHT FLUSH A B-29 bomber that flew on both atomic bomb missions against Hiroshima and Nagasaki in 1945.

SWASTIKA Ancient symbol adopted by the Nazis.

SWORD BEACH Easternmost of the D-Day invasion beaches, assaulted by the British Third Division, 27th Armored Brigade and First Special Service Brigade Commando.

TARANTO Port and home base of Italy's Mediterranean fleet, this was the site of a surprise attack by British torpedo planes on November 11, 1940.

TARAWA Atoll in the Gilbert Islands that was the site of a fierce four-day battle between the Japanese and U.S. Marines in November 1943.

TASK FORCE Term most often used to describe a naval squadron.

THERESIENSTADT Nazi concentration camp located in Czechoslovakia.

THIRD REICH The regime of Nazi rule in Germany, from 1933 to 1945.

TOBRUK Libyan port city on the Mediterranean Sea that changed hands several times during the fighting in North Africa.

TOKYO Capital city of Japan.

TOKYO EXPRESS Nickname given to Japanese resupply runs, under cover of darkness, from their great base at Rabaul to Guadalcanal in the Solomons.

TORA! TORA! TORA! Tiger! Tiger! Tiger! was the message sent by Captain Mitsuo Fuchida while he was over Pearl Harbor, signaling that the December 7, 1941, attack was a surprise.

TREASON The betrayal of one's country to a foreign power.

TREBLINKA Nazi concentration camp near Warsaw, Poland.

TRINITY Name given to the site of the first nuclear bomb explosion in the desert of New Mexico.

TRIPOLI Libyan port city used to disembark supplies during the fighting in North Africa.

TRUK Major Japanese base in the Caroline Islands that was subjected to heavy U.S. air attacks in early 1944.

U-BOAT A German submarine.

ULITHI Major U.S. base southwest of Guam.

ULTRA Code name for the intelligence gathered from decrypted German messages, particularly that derived from the compromised Enigma encoding machine.

USO United Service Organizations, formed to provide entertainment and comfort to U.S. soldiers.

USTASHI Italian-supported Yugoslav guerrillas opposed to the Communists under Tito.

UTAH BEACH Westernmost of the D-Day invasion beaches, assaulted by U.S troops.

V-E DAY May 8, 1945, the day victory in the war in Europe was proclaimed.

VICHY A town in central France, previously best known for its healthful waters, that became the seat of the puppet government of France after the nation fell to the Nazis.

V-J DAY September 2, 1945, the day victory in the war against Japan was proclaimed.

VICTORY GARDEN Vegetable garden planted by many Americans to supplement the vegetable supply grown on farms during the war.

VICTORY SHIP Cargo ships produced in U.S. shipyards on a large scale, improving on the original Liberty ship design.

VOLKSSTURM Translated as "People's Guard," these were German army units consisting primarily of old men and boys who defended their homeland late in the war.

VOLKSWAGEN Translated as "People's Car," this was an inexpensive auto first produced in the 1930s for civilian use.

WAAC Women's Army Auxiliary Corps, a U.S. organization founded in 1942.

WAC Women's Army Corps, successor to WAAC after September 30, 1943.

WAFFEN SS The military arm of the Nazi SS.

WAKE ISLAND Atoll 1,000 miles west of Hawaii that fell late in December 1942, after a heroic stand by U.S. forces.

WAR BONDS Bonds sold by the U.S. government to finance the war effort.

WAR CRIMINAL One who commits or orders an act contrary to international law or military convention during wartime.

WASPS Women's Airforce Service Pilots, a unit of female pilots engaged primarily in ferrying aircraft for the U.S. Army Air Forces.

WAVES Women Accepted for Voluntary Emergency Service, this was the women's organization within the U.S. Navy.

WEHRMACHT The German armed forces, but particularly used to refer to the army.

WEST POINT The U.S. Military Academy, located on the Hudson River in New York State.

WEST WALL Also known as the Siegfried Line, this was a network of German fortifications along the nation's border with France.

WINDOW An Allied attempt to jam German radar by using strips of aluminum dropped from aircraft.

WOLFPACK A group of several German U-boats that attacked Allied convoys in the Atlantic in force.

WOLF'S LAIR Site of the July 20, 1944, attempt on Hitler's life, this was the German dictator's military headquarters in East Prussia.

WRENS Women's Royal Naval Service, the women's section of the British Royal Navy.

WURZBURG German shortwave radar used against attacking Allied aircraft formations.

XCRAFT A British midget submarine.

YANK British slang for an American.

YANK A U.S. Army magazine.

ZIPPO Brand of cigarette lighter carried by many U.S. service personnel during the war.

Comprehensive Bibliography

Adams, Henry H. *Italy at War.* New York: Time-Life Books, 1982.

Adelman, Robert H., and Colonel George Walton. *The Champagne Campaign.* Boston: Little, Brown, 1969.

Alsop, Joseph. *FDR, 1882–1945: A Centenary Remembrance.* New York: Viking, 1982.

Ambrose, Stephen. *D-Day: The Climactic Battle of World War II.* New York: Touchstone, 1994.

Ambrose, Stephen E. "Ike and the Disappearing Atrocities." *New York Times Book Review,* February 24, 1991.

———. *The Victors.* New York: Simon and Schuster, 1998.

Anderson, Benjamin M. *Economics and the Public Welfare.* Indianapolis, Ind.: Liberty Fund, 1979.

Anderson, William L. "Risk and the National Industrial Recovery Act: An Empirical Evaluation." *Public Choice,* Vol. 103, June 2000.

Anderson, William L., and Derek Tittle. "All's Fair: War and Divorce from a Beckarian Perspective." *American Journal of Economics and Sociology,* October 1999.

Armor, John, and Peter Wright. *Manzanar.* Photographs by Ansel Adams. Commentary by John Hersey. New York: Times Books, 1988.

Arnold-Forster, Mark. *The World at War.* New York: Stein and Day, 1973.

Astor, Gerald. *The Greatest War.* Novato, Calif.: Presidio Press, 1999.

Bacque, James. *Other Losses.* Toronto: Stoddart Publishing Co., 1989.

Bailey, Major Alfred D. *Alligators, Buffaloes, and Bushmasters.* History and Museums Division: USMC Headquarters, Washington, D.C., 1986.

Bailey, Ronald H. *The Home Front: U.S.A.* Alexandria, Va.: Time-Life Books, 1978.

Baldwin, Hanson W. *Battles Lost and Won, Great Campaigns of World War II.* Konecky and Konecky, 1966.

Bard, Mitchell G. *Forgotten Victims.* Boulder, Colo.: Westview Press, 1994.

Baruch, Bernard M. *The Making of the Reparation and Economic Sections of the Treaty.* New York: Harper, 1920.

Basinger, Jeanine. *The World War II Combat Film: Anatomy of a Genre.* New York: Columbia University Press, 1986.

Benford, Timothy B. *The World War II Quiz and Fact Book. Vol. 2.* New York: Harper and Row, 1984.

Bird, William L., Jr., and Harry R. Rubenstein. *Design for Victory: World War II Posters on the American Home Front.* New York: Princeton Architectural Press, 1998.

Bischof, Guenter, and Stephen E. Ambrose. *Eisenhower and the German POWs.* Baton Rouge, La.: Louisiana State University Press, 1992.

Bishop, Chris, ed. *Encyclopedia of Weapons of World War II.* London: Orbis Publishing, 1998.

Blum, John Morton. *V Was for Victory: Politics and American Culture During World War II.* New York: Harcourt Brace Jovanovich, 1976.

Boatner III, Mark M.*The Biographical Dictionary of World War II.* Novato, Calif.: Presidio Press, 1996.

Bourke-White, Margaret. *"Dear Fatherland, Rest Quietly"* New York: Simon and Schuster, 1946.

Bowman, Martin W. *USAAF Handbook 1939–1945.* Mechanicsburg, Pa.: Stackpole Books, 1997.

Bradley, John H., and Jack W. Dice. *The Second World War: Asia and the Pacific.* Wayne, N.J.: Avery Publishing Group, 1984.

Bredhoff, Stacey. *Powers of Persuasion: Poster Art from World War II.* Washington, D.C.: National Archives, 1994.

Breuer, William B. *Retaking the Philippines.* New York: St. Martin's Press, 1986.

Brinkley, Alan. *The End of Reform: New Deal Liberalism in Recession and War.* New York: Alfred A. Knopf, 1995.

Bryant, Mark. *World War II in Cartoons.* New York: Gallery, 1989.

Buhite, Russell D., and David W. Levy, eds. *FDR's Fireside Chats.* Norman: University of Oklahoma Press, 1992.

Bull, Stephen. *Twentieth Century Arms and Armor.* New York: Facts on File, 1996.

Burgess, Anthony. *Ninety-nine Novels: The Best in English since 1939.* New York: Summit, 1984.

Calder, Angus. *The People's War: Britain 1939–1945.* New York: Pantheon, 1969.

Capra, Frank. *The Name Above the Title.* New York: Macmillan, 1971.

Carnes, Mark C., ed. *Past Imperfect: History According to the Movies.* A Society of American Historians Book. New York: Henry Holt, 1995.

Chamberlain, Peter, and Hilary L. Doyle. *Encyclopedia of German Tanks of World War Two.* London: Arms and Armour Press, 1978.

Chambers II, John Whiteclay. *The Oxford Companion to American Military History.* New York: Oxford University Press, 1999.

Chandler, David. *Oxford Illustrated History of the British Army.* New York: Oxford University Press, 1994.

Chang, Iris. *The Rape of Nanking.* New York: Basic Books, 1997.

Churchill, Winston S. *The Gathering Storm,* Boston: Houghton Mifflin, 1948.

———. *Their Finest Hour.* Boston: Houghton Mifflin, 1949.

———. *The Grand Alliance.* Boston: Houghton Mifflin, 1950.

———. *The Hinge of Fate.* Boston: Houghton Mifflin, 1950.

———. *Closing the Ring.* Boston: Houghton Mifflin, 1951.

———. *Triumph and Tragedy.* Boston: Houghton Mifflin, 1953.

Cirurgiao, M. Julia, and Michael D. Hull. "Aristides de Sousa Mendes: Angel Against the Blitzkrieg." *Lay Witness,* a monthly publication of C.U.F., Steubenville, Ohio. October 1998.

Cole, John Y., ed. *Books in Action: The Armed Services Editions*. Washington, D.C.: Library of Congress, 1984.

Colley, David P. *The Road to Victory*. Washington, D.C.: Brasseys Inc., 2000.

Commager, Henry Steele. *The Story of the Second World War*. 1945 Reprint, Washington, D.C.: Brasseys Inc., 1991.

Connaughton, Richard. *Celebration of Victory*. London: Brasseys Ltd., 1995.

Conot, Robert E. *Justice at Nuremberg*. New York: Harper and Row, 1983.

Cooper, Matthew. *The German Air Force 1933–1945: An Anatomy of Failure*. London: Jane's Publishing, 1981.

Costello, John. *The Pacific War, 1941–1945*. New York: Quill Books, 1982.

Cotterrell, Arthur. *East Asia: From Chinese Predominance to the Rise of the Pacific Rim*. Oxford, U.K.: Oxford University Press, 1993.

Couch, Jim F., and William F. Shughart II. *The Political Economy of the New Deal*. Northampton, Mass.: Edward Elgar, 1998.

Cowley, Robert, and Geoffrey Parker. *The Reader's Companion to Military History*. Boston: Houghton Mifflin, 1996.

Craven, Wesley Frank, and James Lea Cate, eds. *The Army Air Forces in World War II*. Vol. 2, *Europe: Torch to Pointblank, August 1942 to December 1943*. Chicago: University of Chicago Press, 1949.

———. *The Army Air Forces in World War II*. Vol. 3, *Europe: Argument to V.E. Day, January 1944 to May 1945*. Chicago: University of Chicago Press, 1951.

———. *The United States Army Air Forces in World War II*. 1948. Reprint, Washington, D.C.: Office of Air Force History, United States Air Force, 1995.

Cressman, Robert J. *Official Chronology of the U.S. Navy in World War II*. Annapolis, Md.: Naval Institute Press, 2000.

Darman, Peter. *Surprise Attack*. London: Brown Books, 1993.

Dear, I. C. B., and M. R. D. Foot, eds. *The Oxford Companion to World War II*. Oxford: Oxford University Press, 1995.

D'Este, Carlo. *Decision in Normandy*. New York: HarperCollins, 1983.

Divine, Robert A. *Roosevelt and World War II*. New York: Penguin Books, 1969.

Dudley, William, ed. *World War I: Opposing Viewpoints*. San Diego: Greenhaven, 1998.

Dunnigan, James F., and Albert A. Nofi. *The Pacific War Encyclopedia*. New York: Checkmark Books, 1998.

———. *Dirty Little Secrets of the Vietnam War*. New York: Thomas Dunn Books, 1999.

Editors of Reader's Digest. *Illustrated Story of World War II*. Pleasantville, N.Y.: The Reader's Digest Association, 1969.

Ellis, John. *World War II, A Statistical Survey*. New York: Facts on File, 1993.

Elson, Robert T. *Prelude to War*. New York: Time-Life Books, 1976.

Encyclopedia Britannica. *Encyclopedia Britannica CD: 1998 Standard Edition*. Chicago: Encyclopedia Britannica, 1998.

Engel, David. *The Holocaust*. Harlow, U.K.: Longman, 2000.

Farquhar, Samuel T., et al., eds. *Hollywood Quarterly*, Vol. I, 1945–1946. Berkeley: University of California Press.

Fischel, Jack R. *The Holocaust*. Westport, Conn.: Greenwood Press, 1998.

Fischer, Klaus P. *Nazi Germany: A New History*. New York: Continuum Publishing, 1995.

Flapan, Simha. *The Birth of Israel Myths and Realities*. New York: Pantheon Books, 1987.

Fox, Annette Baker. *The Power of Small States (Diplomacy in World War II)*. Chicago: University of Chicago Press, 1959.

Frank, Anne. *Diary of a Young Girl*. New York: Modern Library, 1994.

Friedman, Milton, and Rose Friedman. *Free to Choose: A Personal Statement*. New York: Avon Books, 1980.

Fussell, Paul. *Wartime: Understanding and*

Behavior in the Second World War. New York: Oxford University Press, 1989.

Gailey, Harry A. *The War in the Pacific.* Novato, Calif.: Presidio Press, 1995.

Garraty, John A., and Peter Gay, eds. *The Columbia History of the World.* New York: Harper and Row, 1972.

Gilbert, Martin, *The Holocaust.* New York: Holt, Rinehart and Winston, 1985.

———. *The Second World War: A Complete History.* New York: Henry Holt, 1989.

Golomstock, Igor. *Totalitarian Art.* New York: HarperCollins, 1990.

Goodenough, Simon. *War Maps.* New York: St. Martin's Press, 1982.

Goodwin, Doris K. *No Ordinary Time.* New York: Touchstone/Simon and Schuster, 1995.

Goralski, Robert. *World War II Almanac: 1931–1945.* New York: G.P. Putnam's, 1981.

Gow, Ian. *Okinawa 1945: Gateway to Japan.* Garden City, N.Y.: Doubleday, 1985.

Greene, Bob. *Duty, A Father, His Son and the Man Who Won the War.* New York: William Morrow, 2000.

Hamburg Institute for Social Research. *The German Army and Genocide.* New York: The New Press, 1999.

Harries, Meirion, and Susie Harries. *Soldiers of the Sun: The Rise and Fall of the Imperial Japanese Army.* New York: Random House, 1991.

Harris, Whitney R. *Tyranny on Trial.* Dallas: SMU Press, 1954.

Hart, B. H. Liddell. *History of the Second World War.* New York: Putnam, 1971.

Havens, Thomas R. *Valley of Darkness: The Japanese People and World War II.* New York: W.W. Norton, 1978.

Herzstein, Robert Edwin. *The Nazis.* Alexandria, Va.: Time-Life Books, 1980.

Hewison, Robert. *Under Siege: Literary Life in London, 1939–45.* New York: Oxford University Press, 1977.

Heydecker, Joe Jules, and Johannes Leeb. *The Nuremberg Trial.* Westport, Conn.: Greenwood Press, 1975.

Higgs, Robert. "Wartime Prosperity? A Reassessment of the U.S. Economy in the 1940s." *The Independent Review,* vol. 52, no. 1 (March 1992).

———. "Regime Uncertainty: Why the Great Depression Lasted So Long and Why Prosperity Resumed after the War." *The Independent Review,* vol. 1, no. 4 (Spring 1997).

Hogg, Ian. *Twentieth-Century Artillery.* New York: Barnes and Noble, 2000.

Homze, Edward L. *Foreign Labor in Nazi Germany.* Princeton, N.J.: Princeton University Press, 1967.

Hoover, Robert A. "Bob." *Forever Flying.* New York: Pocket Books, 1996.

Horsnell, Michael. "False Witness." *The London Times,* 12 April 2000.

Hough, Richard, and Denis Richards. *The Battle of Britain: The Greatest Air Battle of World War II.* New York: W.W. Norton, 1989.

House, Edward M., and Charles Seymour, eds. *What Really Happened at Paris: The Story of the Peace Conference, 1918–1919.* New York: Scribner, 1921.

Howard, Michael, and Louis William Roger, eds. *The Oxford History of the Twentieth Century.* New York: Oxford University Press, 1998.

Hoyt, Edwin P. *Japan's War.* New York: Da Capo Press, 1986.

Jane's Fighting Aircraft of World War II. New York: Crescent Books, 1998. (Originally published by Jane's in 1945.)

Jane's Fighting Ships of World War II. New York: Random House, 2001. (Originally published by Jane's in 1945.)

Johnsen, Frederick. *B-24 Liberator: Rugged but Right.* New York: McGraw-Hill, 1999.

Kahn, David. *The Codebreakers: The Story of Secret Writing.* New York: Macmillan, 1967.

Keegan, John. *Encyclopedia of World War II.* New York: Rand McNally, 1977.

———, ed. *The Time Atlas of the Second World War.* New York: Harper and Row, 1989.

———, ed. *World War II: A Visual Encyclopedia.* London: PRC Publishing, 1999.

Kennett, Lee. *For the Duration: The United States Goes to War.* New York: Scribner's, 1985.

Kerr, E. Bartlett. *Surrender and Survival.* New York: William Morrow, 1985.

Knightley, Phillip. *The First Casualty.* New York: Harcourt Brace Jovanovich, 1975.

Kraemer, Arnold. *Nazi Prisoners of War in America.* Briarcliff Manor, N.Y.: Stein and Day, 1979.

Kukral, L. C. "The Navajo Code Talkers." Navy and Marine Corps World War II Commemorative Committee. DSN 225-3161, no date. www.chinfonavy.mil/navpalib/wwII/facts/navajos.txt (July 23, 2002).

Lael, Richard L. *The Yamashita Precedent: War Crimes and Command Responsibility.* Wilmington, Del.: Scholarly Resources, 1982.

Landau, Ellen G. *Artists for Victory.* Washington, D.C.: Library of Congress, 1983.

Layton, Rear Admiral Edwin T., USN (Ret.), Captain Roger Pineau, USNR (Ret.), and John Costello. *And I Was There: Pearl Harbor and Midway—A Breaking the Secrets.* New York: William Morrow, 1985.

Leckie, Robert. *Delivered from Evil: The Saga of World War II.* New York: Harper and Row, 1987.

Lewin, Ronald. *The American Magic: Codes, Ciphers and the Defeat of Japan.* New York: Farrar Straus Giroux, 1982.

Lewy, Guenter. *The Nazi Persecution of the Gypsies.* Oxford, U.K.: Oxford University Press, 2000.

Lindbergh, Charles A. *The Wartime Journal of Charles A. Lindbergh.* New York: Harcourt, Brace and World, 1970.

Lingeman, Richard R. *Don't You Know There's a War On? The American Home Front 1941–1945.* New York: G.P. Putnam's Sons, 1970.

Lochner, Louis P., ed. *The Goebbels Diaries, 1942–1943.* Garden City, N.Y., Doubleday: 1948.

Look Magazine Editors. *Movie Lot to Beachhead: The Motion Picture Goes to War.* New York: Doubleday, Doran, 1945.

MacLear, Michael. *The Ten Thousand Day War, Vietnam 1945–1975.* New York: St. Martin's Press, 1981.

Maloney, T. J., ed. *U.S. Camera 1943, U.S. Camera 1944, U.S. Camera 1945, U.S. Camera 1946.* Photographs selected by Captain Edward Steichen, USNR. New York: Duell, Sloan and Pierce, 1942–45.

Manchester, William. *American Caesar.* New York: Little, Brown, 1978.

Martel, Gordon, ed. *The Origins of the Second World War Reconsidered: The A.J.P. Taylor Debate After Twenty-five Years.* Boston: Allen and Unwin, 1986.

Maslowski, Peter. *Armed with Cameras: The American Military Photographers of World War II.* New York: Free Press, 1980.

Mauldin, Bill. *Up Front.* New York: Henry Holt, 1945.

———. *The Brass Ring: A Sort of Memoir.* New York: W.W. Norton, 1971.

Mayo, Mike. *War Movies.* Detroit: Visible Ink, 1999.

McCormick, Ken, and Hamilton Darby Perry, eds. *Image of War: The Artist's Vision of World War II.* New York: Orion, 1990.

Merriam-Webster. *Webster's American Military Biographies.* Springfield, Mass.: G. and C. Merriam Co., 1978.

Messenger, Charles. *The Second World War in the West.* London: Cassell, 1999.

Meyer, Susan E. *Norman Rockwell's World War II: Impressions from the Homefront.* Baltimore: Norman Rockwell Museum Press, 1991.

Michel, Henri. *World War II: A Short History.* Translated from French by Gilles Cremonesi. Farnborough, Hampshire, U.K.: Saxon House, 1973.

Miller, David. *Great Battles of World War II.* New York: Crescent Books, 1998.

Miller, Nathan. *War at Sea: A Naval History of World War II.* New York: Charles Scribner's Sons, 1995.

Milsom, John, and Peter Chamberlain. *German Armoured Cars of World War Two.* New York: Charles Scribner's Sons, 1974.

Milward, Alan S. *The German Economy at War.* London: Athlone Press, 1965.

Morison, Samuel Eliot. *The Two-Ocean War.* Boston: Little, Brown, 1963.

Morison, Samuel Eliot, and Henry Steele Commager. *The Growth of the American Republic.* Vol. 2. New York: Oxford University Press, 1968.

Morris, Richard B. *Encyclopedia of American History.* New York: Harper and Row, 1976.

Morris, Richard B., and Graham W. Irwin, eds. *Harper Encyclopedia of the Modern World.* New York: Harper and Row, 1970.

Moskin, J. Robert. *The U.S. Marine Corps Story.* New York: McGraw-Hill, 1977.

Muggenthaler, August Karl. *German Raiders of World War II.* Prentice Hall Press, 1977.

Murphy, Edward F. *Heroes of World War II.* Novato, Calif.: Presidio Press, 1990.

Murray, Williamson, and Allan R. Millett. *A War to Be Won.* Cambridge, Mass.: Belknap Press/Harvard University, 2000.

Myatt, Major Frederick C. *Modern Small Arms: An Illustrated Encyclopedia of Famous Military Firearms from 1873 to the Present Day.* New York: Crescent Books, 1978.

Nelson, Donald. *Arsenal of Democracy: The Story of American War Production.* New York: Harcourt, Brace, 1946.

Niewyk, Donald, and Francis Nicosia. *The Holocaust.* New York: Columbia University Press, 2000.

Nye, Roger H. *The Patton Mind.* New York: Avery Publishing Group, 1993.

Overby, R. J. *War and Economy in the Third Reich.* Oxford, U.K.: Clarendon Press, 1994.

Overy, R. J. *The Air War: 1939–1945.* London: Europa Publications, 1980.

Overy, Richard, and Andrew Wheatcroft. *The Road to War: The Origins of World War II.* New York: Random House, 1989.

Packard, Jerrold M. *Neither Friend Nor Foe (The European Neutrals in World War II).* New York: Charles Scribner's Sons, 1992.

Parker, R. A. C. *The Second World War.* New York: Oxford University Press, 1997.

Parrish, Thomas, and Brigadier General S. L. A. Marshall. *The Simon And Schuster Encyclopedia of World War II.* New York: Simon and Schuster, 1978.

Pelling, Henry. *Winston Churchill.* New York: E.P. Dutton, 1974.

Perret, Geoffrey. *There's a War to Be Won.* New York: Random House, 1991.

Perrett, Bryan. *Allied Tank Destroyers.* London: Osprey Publishing, 1979.

Perrett, Bryan, and Ian Hogg. *Encyclopedia of the Second World War.* Novato, Calif.: Presidio Press, 1989.

Persico, Joseph. *Nuremberg, Infamy on Trial.* New York: Viking, 1994.

Peters, James Edward. *Arlington National Cemetery, Shrine to America's Heroes.* Kensington, Md.: Woodbine House, 1986.

Piccigallo, Phillip. *The Japanese on Trial: Allied War Crimes Operations in the East, 1945–1951.* Austin: University of Texas Press, 1979.

Pimlott, John. *The Historical Atlas of World War II.* New York: Henry Holt, 1995.

Pohl, Frances K. *In the Eye of the Storm: An Art of Conscience, 1930–1970.* San Francisco: Pomegranate, 1995.

Polenberg, Richard. *War and Society: The United States, 1941–1945.* Philadelphia: Lippincott, 1972.

Polmar, Norman, and Thomas B. Allen. *World War II, America at War 1941–1945,* New York: Random House, 1991.

———. *World War II: The Encyclopedia of the War Years, 1941–1945.* New York: Random House, 1996.

———. *Spy Book: The Encyclopedia of Espionage.* New York: Random House, 1998.

Pope, Stephen, Elizabeth Anne Wheal, and James Taylor. *Encyclopedia of the Second World War.* New York: Castle Books, 1989.

Prange, Gordon W. *At Dawn We Slept: The Untold Story of Pearl Harbor.* New York: Penguin, 1981.

Ready, J. Lee. *World War Two: Nation by Nation.* London: Arms and Armour Press, 1995.

Reynolds, Michael. *Steel Inferno.* New York: Sarpedon Publishers, 1997.

Rhodes, Anthony. *Propaganda, The Art of Persuasion: World War II*. Broomall, Pa.: Chelsea House Publishers, 1993.

Richelson, Jeffrey T. *A Century of Spies: Intelligence in the Twentieth Century*. New York: Oxford University Press, 1995.

Roeder, George H., Jr. *The Censored War: American Visual Experience During World War Two*. New Haven: Yale University Press, 1993.

Rohrbach, Peter T. *The Largest Event: A Library of Congress Resource Guide for the Study of World War II*. Washington, D.C.: Library of Congress, 1994.

Rooney, Andy. *My War*. New York: Adams Media Corporation, 1995.

Rose, Norman. *Churchill: The Unruly Giant*. New York: The Free Press, 1994.

Ross, Stewart. *Causes and Consequences of World War II*. Austin, Tex.: Raintree/Steck-Vaughn, 1996.

Rothbard, Murray N. *America's Great Depression*. Kansas City, Mo.: Sheed and Ward, 1975.

Rowe, Vivian. *The Great Wall of France: The Triumph of the Maginot Line*. New York: Putnam, 1961.

Russell, Francis. *The Secret War*. Alexandria, Va.: Time-Life Books, 1981.

Searle, Ronald. *To the Kwai—and Back: War Drawings, 1939–1945*. Boston: Atlantic Monthly Press, 1986.

Sennholz, Hans F. *Age of Inflation*. Belmont, Mass.: Western Islands, 1979.

Shermer, Michael, and Alex Grobman. *Denying History*. Berkeley, University of California Press, 2000.

Shirer, William L. *Berlin Diary*. New York: Alfred A. Knopf, 1941.

———. *The Rise and Fall of the Third Reich*. Greenwich, Conn.: Fawcett (Crest reprint), 1960.

———. *The Collapse of the Third Republic: An Inquiry into the Fall of France in 1940*. New York: Simon and Schuster, 1969.

Shukman, Harold. *Stalin's Generals*. New York: Grove Press, 1993.

Skarmeas, Nancy J. *Victory*. Nashville: Ideals Publications, 1995.

Smith, Bradley F. *The Road to Nuremberg*. New York: Basic Books, 1981.

Snyder, Louis L. *Encyclopedia of the Third Reich*. New York: Paragon House, 1989.

Soames, Mary, ed. *Winston and Clementine, The Personal Letters of the Churchills*. Boston: Houghton Mifflin, 1999.

Southworth, Samuel A. *Great Raids in History: From Drake to Desert One*. New York: Sarpedon, 1997.

Spector, Ronald H. *Eagle Against the Sun: The American War with Japan*. New York: The Free Press, 1985.

Speer, Albert. *Inside the Third Reich*. New York: Avon Books, 1970.

Stillwell, Paul. *Air Raid: Pearl Harbor!* Annapolis, Md.: Naval Institute Press, 1981.

Stokesbury, James L. *A Short History of World War II*. New York: William Morrow, 1980.

Strachan, Hew, ed. *World War I: A History*. Oxford, U.K.: Oxford University Press, 1998.

Strawson, John. *The Battle for Berlin*. New York: Charles Scribner's Sons, 1974.

Sulzberger, C. L. *American Heritage Picture History of World War II*. New York: American History–Bonanza Books, 1966.

———. *New History of World War II*. Rev. and updated by Stephen E. Ambrose. New York: Viking-Penguin 1966, 1997.

Swearingen, Ben. *The Mystery of Hermann Goering's Suicide*. San Diego: Harcourt Brace Jovanovich, 1985.

Takaki, Ronald. *Double Victory*. Boston: Little, Brown, 2000.

Tanaka, Chester. *Go for Broke*. Novato, Calif.: Presidio Press, 1982.

Tanaka, Yuki. *Hidden Horrors*. Boulder, Colo.: Westview Press, 1996.

Taylor, Telford. *The Nuremberg Trials*. New York: Carnegie Endowment for International Peace, 1949.

———. *The Anatomy of the Nuremberg Trials*. New York: William Morrow, 1987.

Thomas, Dorothy Swaine, and Richard Nishimoto. *The Spoilage: Japanese-American Evacuation and Resettlement During World War II.* Berkeley: University California Press, 1969.

Thompson, H. K., and Henry Strutz. *Doenitz at Nuremberg: A Reappraisal.* New York: Amber Publishing, 1976.

Thum, Gladys, and Marcella Thum. *The Persuaders: Propaganda in War and Peace.* New York: Atheneum, 1972.

Time Capsule: History of the War Years, 1939–1945. New York: Bonanza, 1972.

Time-Life Books. *Japan at War.* Alexandria, Va.: 1980.

———. *The SS.* Alexandria, Va.: 1988.

Toland, John. *Adolf Hitler.* Garden City, N.Y.: Doubleday, 1976.

Toliver, Colonel Raymond, and Trevor Constable. *Fighter Aces of the Luftwaffe.* Fallbrook, Calif.: Aero Publishers, 1977.

Tomita, Mary Kimoto. *Dear Miye: Letters Home from Japan, 1939–1946.* Stanford, Calif.: Stanford University Press, 1995.

Tusa, Ann, and John Tusa. *The Nuremberg Trial.* New York: Atheneum, 1984.

United States Strategic Bombing Survey. *Summary Report: European War.* Washington, D.C., 30 September 1945.

Van der Vat, Dan. *The Pacific Campaign.* New York: Simon and Schuster, 1991.

Voss, Frederick S. *Reporting the War: The Journalistic Coverage of World War II.* Washington, D.C.: Smithsonian Institution Press, 1994.

Waterford, Van (Willem F. Wanrooy). *Prisoners of the Japanese in World War II.* Jefferson, N.C.: McFarland and Company, 1994.

Watt, Donald C. *How War Came: The Immediate Origins of the Second World War.* New York: Pantheon, 1989.

Weinberg, Gerhard L. *A World at Arms: A Global History of World War II.* New York: Cambridge University Press, 1994.

West, Rebecca. *A Train of Powder.* New York: Viking Press, 1955.

Wheal, Elizabeth-Anne, and Stephen Pope. *The MacMillan Dictionary of the Second World War.* 2nd ed. London: MacMillan, 1997.

Wheeler, Richard. *A Special Valor: The U.S. Marines and the Pacific War.* New York: New American Library, 1983.

Whiting, Charles. *The Home Front: Germany.* Alexandria, Va.: Time-Life Books, 1982.

Winton, John. *Ultra in the Pacific.* Annapolis, Md.: Naval Institute Press, 1993.

Wistrich, Robert. *Who's Who in Nazi Germany.* New York: Macmillan, 1982.

Yamamoto, Masahiro. *Nanking: Anatomy of an Atrocity.* Westport, Conn.: Praeger, 2000.

Yenne, William P., and Keith W. Dills. *German War Art: 1939–1945.* New York: Crescent, 1983.

Zabecki, David T., ed. *World War II in Europe: An Encyclopedia.* London: Garland, 1999.

Zeman, Zbynek. *Selling the War: Art and Propaganda in World War II.* London: Orbis, 1978.

Ziegler, Philip. *London at War.* New York: Alfred A. Knopf, 1995.

Index

Heflin, Van, 469
Hegemony, 27
Heimatromane (homeland novels), 459
Heinck, Heinrich, 348
Heinkel, Ernst, 376
Hein ter Poorten, 259
Hele, Ivor, 476
Helferinnen, 185
Heller, Joseph, 380, 458, 459, 463
Hell Is for Heroes (film), 470
Hemingway, Ernest, 482
Hendorf, Heinz, 474
Here Is Your War (Pyle), 460
Hermes (British aircraft carrier), 280
Hersey, John, 458
Herzegovina, emergence of post World
   War II, 445
Hess, Myra, 472
Hess, Rudolf, 8, 119, 120, 122, 134, 138, 411
Hewitt, H. Kent, 162–163
Heydrich, Reinhard, 182, 346, 350, 351,
   356, 390, 405, 413, 438
   assassination of, 406
Hibbs, Jesse, 470
Hiei (Japanese battleship), 293
Higgins, Andrew Jackson, 384, 385, 397
Higgins Industries, 397
Hillary, Richard, 461
Himalayan Hump, 311
Himmler, Heinrich, 115, 120–121, 127,
   404, 405, 428
   suicide of, 15, 120
Hindemith, Paul, 472
Hindenburg, Paul von, 2, 75, 122, 123,
   132, 154
   death of, 3
Hipper (German cruiser), 240
Hiranuma, Kiichiro, 420
Hirohito (Emperor of Japan), 16, 115,
   121, 142, 144, 145, 153, 298, 367
   statement to Japanese people, 495
Hiroshima, dropping of atomic bomb
   on, xiv, 16, 56–58, 81, 145, 153,
   258, 267, 295, 297–298, 310, 341,
   343, 370, 374, 380, 436, 443
Hiroshima Peace Park, 516
Hirota, Koki, 419
Hirsch, Joseph, 479
Hiryu (Japanese carrier), 284, 292
History of the English-Speaking People
   (Churchill), 460
*History of the United States Naval
   Operations in World War II*
   (Morison), 460
History Place, 504

Hitler, Adolf, 114–115, 172
   Anchluss and, 21
   assassination attempts on, 5, 13, 135
   attack on Soviet Union, 345
   Austria and, 74
   as author of *Mein Kampf,* 31, 32, 120,
      123, 365, 459, 461
   as chancellor of Germany, 2–3
   financing of war and, 49–50
   hatred of Jews by, 21, 27, 29, 31, 402,
      404
   home front and, 375 (*See also*
      Germany)
   Munich Beer Hall Putsch and, 31–32,
      120, 122, 123, 132
   Munich Pact and, 105, 499
   Mussolini and, 3, 141–142
   orations of, 490, 495–496
   parachute operations and, 173
   political testament, 496
   as president, 3
   prewar aggressive actions of, 19–20,
      25–26
   rise to power, 2–3, 18–19, 24, 75,
      121–123, 127, 132–135, 154
   Spanish Civil War and, 38
   suicide of, 15, 75, 115, 120, 135
   vision of, xv, 19
   Volkssturm and, 181
Hitler, Adolph, Schools, 363
Hitler: A Study in Tyranny (Bullock), 461
Hitler: Nemesis, 1936–1945 (Kershaw),
   462
Hitler Youth, 22, 32, 181, 363, 375
Hiyo (Japanese carrier), 292
Hoax of the Twentieth Century, 409
Hoch, Hannah, 474
Ho Chi Minh, 446
Hodges, Courtney H., 163
Hodiak, John, 470
Hoffmann, Heinrich, 486
Hoffmeister, Adolf, 476
Hogan's Heroes (TV), 471
Hohlwein, Ludwig, 477, 480
Holland. *See* Netherlands
Hollandia, 347
Holloway, Penny Gooch, 394
Hollywood, contribution to propaganda,
   368–369
Holocaust, xvi, 75, 402–411
   deniers, 410
   Jewish deaths during, 410
   murders in major Nazi death camps,
      411
   time line of, 403–407

Holy War (Lebedev), 457
Home front, 54–60, 373–399
   in Austria, 389–390
   in Belgium, 391–392
   in Czechoslovakia, 390
   in Denmark, 391–392
   in France, 390–391
   in Germany, 373–374
   in Great Britain, 373, 376–379
   in Italy, 379–380
   in Japan, 374, 380
   in the Netherlands, 391–392
   in Norway, 392
   in Poland, 392–393
   in Soviet Union, 374, 381–382
   in United States, 374, 382–386, 393–399
Home Guard, 180–181, 378
Homma, Masaharu, 157, 170, 259, 262,
   272
Homosexuals, treatment of, in World
   War II, 400
Honda, Masaki, 170
Hong Kong, Japanese attack on, 9, 81,
   257, 259, 265
Hood (British ship), 240, 243
   sinking of, 8
Hoover, Herbert Clark, 46, 130
   administration of, xi
Hoover, J. Edjar, 357
Hoover Institution on War, Revolution
   and Peace, 504
Hope, Bob, 475
Hope and Glory (film), 469
Hopkins (U.S. Liberty ship), 242
Hopkins, Harry, x, 123–124
Horbaczewski, Eugeniusz, 245
Horii, Tomitaro, 259, 267
Horizon (Connolly), 461–462
Horizon (newspaper), 485
Horne, Lena, 483
Hornet (U.S. aircraft carrier), 190, 288,
   302
Horthy, 406
Hoshino, 420
Hosho (Japanese carrier), 292
Hradschin Castle, 390
Hughes, Pat, 245
Hugh W. Hadley (U.S. destroyer), 286
Hull, Cordell, 124, 144, 150, 496
The Human Condition (film), 469
Hungary
   as axis nation, 75–76
   cession of Transylvania to, 81
Hurtgen Forest, 157
Huston, John, 368, 369, 464, 467

St.-Nazaire, France, 166, 217

St.-Lambert-sur-Dives, 193

Saipan, 167, 171, 258, 264, 517
    U.S. troops landing on, 12

Sakai, Saburo, 302

Sakai, Takashi, 259

Sakawa (Japanese cruiser), 294

Sakhalin Island, 80

Salazar, António de Oliveira, 99,
    128–129, 414

Salerno, Allied invasion of, 11, 161, 165,
    168, 213

Samar, 282

Sanananda, 267

San Bernardino Strait, 162

Sandakan, North Bornea, Japanese
    atrocities in, 418

San Francisco Conference (1945), 112,
    148, 152, 452

Sanger, Margaret, 458

San Jacinto (U.S. aircraft carrier), 289

Sansei, 394–395

Santa Cruz Islands, Battle of (1942), 164,
    279, 288, 334

Saratoga (U.S. aircraft carrier), 289

Sasai, Jun-ichi, 302

Sato, Kenryo, 420

Sauckel, Fritz, 411

Saulx Valley, France, atrocities at, 424

Saving Private Ryan (film), ix, 470

Savo Island, 279

Scerbius, Arthur, 352

Schacht, Hjalmar, 50, 411

Schaffhausen, Allied bombing of, 101

Schaffner, Franklin J., 470

Scharnhorst (German battle cruiser), 162,
    234, 236, 238, 239, 240, 241

Schellenberg, Walter, 356

Scherbius, Arthur, 359

Scherf, C. C., 245

Scherman, David, 487

Scherschel, Frank, 487

Schilling, Erich, 474

Schindler, Emilia, 414

Schindler, Oscar, 414, 470

Schindler's List (film), 414, 470

Schirach, Baldur von, 363, 389, 411

Schleicher, Kurt von, 2, 127

Schleswig, 107

Schleswig-Holstein (German training
    ship), 35

Schmidt, Hans-Thilo, 359

Schmidt, Harry, 260

Schnitzler, Georg von, 375

Schongarth, Eberhardt, 423

Schultz, Sigrid, 482

Schuschnigg, Kurt von, 74

Schweinfurt, 244

Schweitzer, Hans, 474, 477

Scientist (British freighter), 239

Scorched-earth policy, 135

Scott, George C., 470

Scott, Norman, 279

SD (Sicherheitsdienst), 346, 350, 351,
    356, 419

Searle, Ronald, 476, 478

Sebold, William, 361

The Second World War (Churchill), 460

The Second World War (Keegan), 460

Sedlackek, Karl, 352

See It Now (TV), 465, 470

Segal, George, 470

Selassie, Haile, 129, 141

Selective Training and Service Act (U.S.,
    1940), 149–150, 177, 383

Self-propelled artillery and tank
    destroyers
    in Germany, 319
    in Italy, 321
    in Japan, 322
    in Soviet Union, 323
    in United States, 325

Sendai (Japanese cruiser), 294

Senger und Etterlin, Fridolin Von, 172

Seravezza, Italy, 190

Serbia, emergence of post World War II,
    445

Sevareid, Eric, 483

Sevastopol, German siege of, 381

Sex Hygiene (film), 464

Sextant Conference. *See* Cairo
    Conference

Seyss-Inquart, Artur, 74, 412

Shahn, Ben, 476

Shanghai, Japanese capture of, 4

Shangri-La (U.S. aircraft carrier), 289

Shaw, Irwin, 458

Shaw, Robert, 469

Sherbrooke, Robert St. V., 193

Sheridan, Ann, 475

Sherwood, Robert, x–xi

Shetland Islands, 392

Shibasaki, Keiji, 259

Shigemitsu, Mamoru, 145, 421

Shima, Kihohide, 277, 280

Shimada, Shigetaro, 420

Shinano (Japanese carrier), 293

Shinyo (Japanese carrier), 293

Shinyo Maru (Japanese prison ship), 429

Shipping, air assaults on, 243

Ships, 327–336. *See also* Aircraft carriers;
    Battleships; *by name;* Cruisers;
    Destroyers; Submarines

Shiratori, Toshio, 420

Shirer, William L., 389–390, 458, 462,
    472, 483

SHO-₁, 280

Shoho (Japanese carrier), 279, 293

Shokaku (Japanese carrier), 191, 279, 285,
    293

Shore, Dinah, 475

Shores of Tripoli (film), 467

Shori, Arai, 476

Short, Walter C., 163, 167

Sicily, Allied invasion of, 10, 11, 79, 160,
    161, 164, 165, 166, 167, 198, 213,
    313
    casualties of, 215

Sidi Bu Baker, Tunisia, 217

Sieg im Westen (Victory in the West)
    (film), 466

Siegred Line, 36

Signal Intelligence Service (SIS), 351, 357

Signal magazine, 485–486

Sikorski, Wladyslaw, 93, 167

Silone, Ignazio, 459

Simon, John, 137, 438

Simonov, Konstantin, 462

Simpson, Wallis, 136

Simpson, William H., 167

Sinatra, Frank, 470, 474

Singapore
    Japanese attack on, 9, 81, 257, 266
    surrender of, 173, 175

Sink the Bismarck (film), 469

Sinn Fein rebellion, 135

Sino-Japanese War, 4

Sitwells, 458

Sitzkrieg ("Phony War"), 36

Six Million Swindle, 409

Skalski, Stanislaw, 245

Skorzeny, Otto, 125, 142

Slaughterhouse Five (Vonnegut), 459

Slave labor, use of, during World War
    II, 54–55

Slavs, Hitler's racial hatred of, 27

Sledge, Eugene B., 463

Slim, William, 167, 263

Slovakia, German takeover of, 4, 23

Slovenia, emergence of post World War
    II, 445

Smart, Jacob, 255

Smith, Holland, 167, 259, 260

Smith, Kate, 476

Smith, Maynard H. "Snuffy," 192